Rediscover the Bible

Or Discover It for the First Time

Michael Pickard

KITSAP PUBLISHING

KITSAP PUBLISHING

Rediscover the Bible – Or Discover It for the First Time
First edition, published 2017

By Michael Pickard
Cover design: Kitsap Publishing
Editor: Beth Cockrel

Published by Kitsap Publishing
Poulsbo, WA 98370
www.KitsapPublishing.com

50-10 9 8 7 6 5 4 3 2 1

TABLE OF CONTENTS

A Word from the Author

It has been my joy, for over 40 years, to serve as the pastor of four congregations, two of which have been long term. A pastor's work is like that of an ancient shepherd—leading, feeding, protecting and enjoying the flock. I have relished all these, but "feeding the flock" by preaching and teaching is what has energized me most.

Pastors occupy the ground between the world of biblical scholarship and the world of the local congregation. A pastor's task is to translate the Bible's teaching and wisdom into the language of ordinary people who, like me, need to make sense of this world and be equipped to face manifold challenges at all stages of life. My belief, and personal experience, is that we are best equipped for this journey by the unique message of the Bible.

I have believed in God for as long as I can remember, even before I had any formal instruction about Christianity or had read the Bible for myself. My family rarely attended church, but individuals appeared in my life, at just the right times, to nudge me towards Jesus. One notable time was sixth grade, when a neighborhood boy invited me to a small local church with a youth ministry led by adult volunteers. From these kind adults who took an interest in me, I learned about Jesus for the first time. I gradually understood the Gospel, and a desire to read the Bible stirred within me.

I remember taking an old King James Bible into a storage room at my house and attempting to read it for the first time by myself, starting with the first chapter of Genesis. It wasn't long before I got bogged down in Elizabethan English, and in a strange world of people and ideas that I could barely comprehend.

Nevertheless, over the years, I listened faithfully to teaching and preaching, trying to wrap my young mind around the compelling story of a God who loved me, sent his Son to die for my sins, overcame death in his resurrection, and offered me forgiveness and everlasting life. I gradually understood that the Bible was more about relationship than religion.

Having discovered the Bible's "Big Story," I never looked back. God's Word has been for me, *"a lamp to guide my feet and a light for my path"* (Psalm 119:105). Many men and women of faith have shaped and refined my understanding of the Bible along the way, mentoring me in the life of faith. In college, I began to feel a calling to ministry, away from a career in illustration which I had expected to pursue. This led to studies at Fuller Theological Seminary and Gordon-Conwell Theological Seminary.

I have been surprised to discover, over all these years, that the Bible never gets stale. It remains relevant and life-giving to me. No matter how much I learn, there is always more. How could there not be, given the fact that it reveals the infinite, personal God, our Creator. When do you run out of new things to discover about the infinite? I hope that this book adequately conveys the wonder and joy of God's presence, which continues to transform my thinking and living.

Writing it has been a labor of love. I likely would not have persevered without the continuing support, encouragement and prayers of my wife, Joy. She has put up with countless late nights of writing. She smiled while I hauled my laptop with us everywhere, even on vacation in Germany. She has listened patiently to my occasional fretting about the project. I dedicate this book to her, with love and appreciation.

I thank Darla Muya, and Alane Basco-Yu, co-workers at my church who were generous with their time and expertise in helping me give birth to the book in its first form as a daily blog: "Blogging through the Bible."

Publisher Ingemar Anderson encouraged me to turn the blog into a book and has patiently guided me through the weeds of publishing. Many friends, colleagues in ministry, and acquaintances have graciously read sections and given helpful feedback. I especially thank: Dr. Iain Provan, the Marshall Sheppard Professor of Biblical Studies at Regent College; Dr. Jeanine Tweedie who offered many encouraging comments on my writing; Dr. Jonathan Wells, scientist and Research Fellow at the Discovery Institute in Seattle, on matters of Science and the Bible.

My editor and longtime friend, Beth Cockrel, has given important feedback on content, and carefully combed through the 700+ pages to make it readable, and by her suggestions it became a better book. Most recently, Alane Basco-Yu has become my director of social media to help promote the book. What a great team!

Above all, I thank the Lord who opened my eyes to his presence when I was young, and then led me to a local church where his Word was faithfully taught. By his Word, understanding was added to faith, faith was expressed in baptism and later in a call to teach and preach—and now to write—about his Word.

Michael Pickard
Poulsbo, Washington 2017

Introduction

The Bible is the most influential book ever written. More than three thousand years have passed since the events described in the Old and New Testaments, yet the Bible is still the best-selling book in the world by far. Today, approximately one third of the earth's population identifies as Christian, looking to the Bible, in various ways, as God's Word to them. It is estimated that over twenty-five million copies are sold each year in the United States, and two hundred million more, in whole and in part, around the world.

However, research indicates that in many cases the Bible sits on our shelves unread. Kenneth Briggs' fine book, *The Invisible Bestseller: Searching for the Bible in America,* surveys the practice of Bible reading among American Christians of various traditions and finds that reading the Bible, like reading books in general, is in decline. He concludes: *"For more and more Americans, the Bible has become a museum exhibit, hallowed as a treasure but enigmatic and untouched."*

While lamenting that the stories and teachings of the Bible are becoming lost to our culture, Briggs is hopeful they can be rediscovered. I share this hope; it has energized me to write this book.

Many Christians read parts of the Bible only—a verse here or there connected to an inspirational thought—or they listen to occasional sermons. For them, the grandeur of the Bible's Big Story remains an undiscovered country. It is like a tourist traveling randomly about, visiting America's little towns and quaint places, without ever seeing the Grand Canyon.

My reason for writing this book is to help readers discover, rediscover, or deepen their understanding of the Bible's Big Story—its Grand Canyon. The Big Story comes into view within the diverse characters, events and instruction of its 66 books.

The truth is, the Bible is difficult to understand. The Old and New Testaments are written by 40 authors, from ancient cultures, over the course of 1,500 years. Therefore, readers will benefit from having a guide to explain—or attempt to explain—its original meaning and then demonstrate its continuing relevance to our lives.

This is not an academic book, but it engages the mind and heart, nudging the reader to devotion. I believe that God speaks to us when we read the text of the Bible. Its various books bear witness to the God who lovingly created us and then graciously pursued us when we rebelled against him. He did this, at great personal cost, because he wants to be in relationship with us.

The biblical account of God reconciling us to himself unfolds slowly and progressively within the ambiguities and contradictions of human experience in the world. We learn that God reveals himself, not by a secret code known only to enlightened ones, but by engaging ordinary people, struggling with the brutal realities of life and the exasperating challenges of faith. Ironically, the clearest revelation of himself occurs on an instrument of suffering and death—a Roman cross—where his Son hangs in agony, bearing the sins of the world.

Here we are confronted with the astonishing fact of a deity who humbles himself and suffers for the world he loves, atoning for its sin and then defeating death through resurrection. This Big Story, called "gospel" (meaning good news), has been preserved for all generations because God directed certain writers to faithfully record its events and comment upon their meaning. Therefore, its authority comes from God the Story-Teller himself, especially when he enters his own story through the incarnation of Jesus in order to speak clearly and directly to us.

In the daily readings of the book, I seek to connect the diversity of the biblical narratives with the four main themes of the Big Story: Creation, Fall, Redemption and New Creation. I make observations and offer commentary, pointing forward or backward in the story, to explain how the pieces of the narrative puzzle begin to come together.

The Bible's most important achievement is revealing Jesus to us. Therefore, he is the interpretive key to making sense of both the Old and New Testaments. Through Jesus, God fulfills his ancient Promise to Abraham to make things right in the world.

Jesus' victory over death launches a new era in human history, opening the door to resurrection life to all who believe in him. At Pentecost, God's Spirit is poured out into the hearts of those who believe, giving them spiritual life, calling them into a new community, and empowering them to announce the Good News of salvation to the world. What was broken by our rebellion against God is now being restored by Jesus. He is the head of a new humanity, reconciled to God, spiritually reborn and destined for resurrection life in a New Heavens and Earth.

The ancient story has become our story.

I have formatted the book into 366 daily readings of about fifteen minutes each (or longer if the full biblical text is read). This takes the reader through the whole Bible, Genesis to Revelation, in one year. The daily readings follow the format of the *Daily Walk Bible* in the New Living Translation, published by Tyndale. You will benefit most by reading the designated chapters, but the daily readings stand on their own.

Each day begins with a key text taken from the chapters covered. A summary of the text follows, with commentary. The commentary is meant to move the story along and connect the dots between the daily reading, the Big Story, and your life. Sometimes I insert myself into the commentary, reacting as you might react to what is going on in the story.

Following each commentary, I include a short section called "Focus," where I drill a little deeper on something from that day's reading. Finally, there is a brief prayer you may use for devotional purposes.

One more feature: Every seven days, there is a break in the commentary, and the reading of the day is an elaboration on an important subject or a common question about the Bible's story. This is entitled, "Reflection."

I am hopeful that this book will encourage readers everywhere to rediscover the Bible, discover it for the first time, or enrich their present understanding. There is a reason why the Bible continues to be the best-selling book in the world: It is indeed the greatest story ever told. There is nothing like it. We read it and then discover that it reads us. It describes life as we know it. It speaks to our minds and hearts in a self-authenticating way. Its great themes of Creation, Fall, Redemption and New Creation resonate with us. It calls us to faith and moves us to worship and thanksgiving. It inspires us to acts of love, goodness, beauty, truth, justice and compassion. Above all, it reveals how passionately our Creator loves us and desires to be in relationship with us, forever!

If the reader gains a broader vision of God's amazing grace, and is drawn to him in faith and devotion, then the purpose of this book will be realized.

January 1

> Key Text: In the beginning, God created the heavens and the earth. (Genesis 1:1)

The story of the Bible begins with the momentous declaration: *"In the beginning, God created the heavens and the earth."* These ten words speak to the questions everyone asks—*where did I come from* and *what is the meaning of life*—by joyfully announcing that God exists, and that all things come from him and exist for his pleasure. The universe is not a product of unguided, impersonal forces, but of loving purpose.

As the story of creation unfolds in Genesis 1 and 2, God speaks the universe into existence. What he wills to do, he accomplishes with divine power, like an artist painting on canvas the masterpiece in his heart and mind.

Significantly, human beings are the centerpiece of his creation. We are created in God's image and given a unique status and calling within the creation. Unlike the other animals, we are granted free will by which we can have a relationship with our Creator. This essential relationship informs our relationships with one another, with the animals, and with nature *(Genesis 1:26–2:25)*.

Consequently, men and women experience marriage and family, create culture, and manage the earth on God's behalf. To this end, God gives us the gifts of reason, curiosity, imagination, and love.

Keep in mind, Genesis was written to ancient people, within their frame of reference. We should not expect it to provide a modern, scientific account of creation. At the same time, Genesis presents a universe in which the empirical sciences are inevitable. Because the universe is a product of divine thought, it is intelligible. The earth, our home, can be understood, measured, harnessed, celebrated, and shaped for human flourishing.

Science, in turn, encourages faith by describing a universe of astonishing diversity and complexity, exquisitely fine-tuned for human life. With so many factors of the universe needing to be exactly as they are—not a little less or more—biological life seems improbable. Yet, here we are! It has been suggested that the universe must have seen us coming! Better to say that God had us in mind from the beginning.

Genesis 1 uses the metaphor of a human week to tell the story of creation. Over the course of the first six days, God speaks the material universe into existence out of his imagination and will. The details of the story speak first to the issues and questions of ancient people, but its message about God, the world and human beings is unique, incredibly hopeful, and timeless.

For ancient pagans, and modern secularists, it is a paradigm shift of epic proportions. It declares that nothing exists outside of God's creative thought and loving purpose. His goodness and wisdom are embodied in his creation, defining, shaping, and sustaining all living and non-living things. The universe is his handiwork, and a perfect habitat for humanity. Above all, it gives him pleasure and brings him glory.

On the sixth day, human beings are created in God's image as gendered creatures, male and female *(Genesis 1:27–28)*. They are the reason for which everything else exists and therefore the highlight of the creation week. They are blessed and called to fill the earth with human life.

Unlike lesser animals, the man and woman are capable of intimate fellowship and covenant love. This is experienced most completely in one-flesh marriage. Marriage is introduced in chapter 2. Before Eve is created, Adam becomes aware that there is no one like him among the animals. God responds to Adam's recognition by declaring that it is not good for him to be alone. It is God's design that Adam is completed by another, who is like him but not him.

So, God creates Eve from Adam's side and brings her to him as an equal partner in life. Adam's response is a joyful recognition that she is a fellow human being—equal to, yet different from him. *"At last!"* Adam exclaims. *"This one is bone from my bone, and flesh from my flesh!"* (Genesis 2:18–23). The writer of Genesis then comments to readers: *"This explains why a man leaves his father and mother and is joined to his wife, and the two are united into one. Now the man and his wife were both naked, but they felt no shame"* (Genesis 2:24–25).

Together, Adam and Eve experience the joy of creaturely love and fellowship, and out of their loving union comes new life. Thus, human beings in the image of God become creators themselves, and covenant marriage is established as the foundation of human society and culture.

On the seventh day of creation, God calls it all "very good" and he "rests" from his work. This doesn't mean he is tired or disinterested.

Quite the opposite. He has created it for his own pleasure and participation, so his rest is "mission accomplished!" Now he intends to enjoy it—to enjoy us!

God's desire to be present with us will be a continuing theme in the story of the Old and New Testaments. This will be dramatically revealed to the world when God becomes a human to live among us through the incarnation of Christ *(John 1:14)*.

> **Focus:** Each of us has at one time stared at the stars in the vast night sky and been overwhelmed with the enormity of the universe, and of our own smallness by comparison. *Where did it come from?* we wondered. *Is there a Creator? What is my life about?* The Bible begins with the good news of a loving Creator who brought us into existence for his pleasure. And what pleases him most is having a relationship with us!
>
> **Prayer:** *God, we thank you for the gift of existence. Wow! Even more, we praise you for the amazing calling we have been given to know and serve you in the world. Help us to see your glory and point it out to others. Amen.*

Day 2   Genesis 3–5

January 2

> Key Text: The serpent was the shrewdest of all the wild animals the Lord God had made. One day he asked the woman, "Did God really say you must not eat the fruit from any of the trees in the garden?" (Genesis 3:1)

If loving purpose moved God to create everything that exists, and if it pleased him above all to have a relationship with us, why is life so messed up? Why am *I* so messed up? Let's be honest. You've wondered about it, and so have I. Perhaps "messed up" is not strong enough—the world is broken; it's Humpty-Dumpty broken. Human effort on all fronts has not been able to put it together again. Genesis 3 through 5 explains why the world is broken, by giving us an account of the human "Fall" and its immediate consequences.

When the creation is complete, and the first man and woman appear, everything is perfect. There is a harmonious and deeply fulfilling relationship between Adam, Eve and God. And since the humans are made from the earth, and for the earth, they are at peace with nature as well.

Everything is permitted for the couple, except one thing. God says that they must not eat the fruit from one tree—the tree of *"the knowledge of good and evil."* There are prerogatives which belong to God alone. It is our place to trust him and accept the life he has given us. He has drawn the boundaries within which Adam and Eve—and all subsequent humanity—will flourish if they trust their Creator.

So it begins. Then it all unravels.

The account of the fall of humanity might be easier to take if it turned out that we humans were attacked by demon hordes in the Garden of Eden, tortured and forced to deny allegiance to God our Maker by eating the forbidden fruit from the tree of *"the knowledge of good and evil."* But all it took was a clever little reptile raising a doubt: *"Did God really say?"* This was followed by an intoxicating prospect: *"...your eyes will be opened as soon as you eat it, and you will be like God, knowing both good and evil"* (Genesis 3:5).

The appeal of the temptation was this: Being a creature dependent on God, and following *his* rules, is not enough, is it? Wouldn't you rather be god of your own life, controlling everything and determining what is right and wrong for you?

Sounds very contemporary.

Well, Adam and Eve bit. But the serpent's promise, *"You won't die!"* turns out to be a demonic lie. Adam and Eve's eyes are opened all right, but opened to experiences that distort and dehumanize their life. The joy of life in fellowship with God, and one another, gives way to a tsunami of shame, blame, family strife, violence, spiritual alienation and biological death. Having broken the connection with their Creator, they lose track of what it means to be human.

The doubting, resisting and forsaking of God is what the Bible calls "sin." Sin means falling short, in this case falling short of what it means to be human in the image of God. Sin is an act, but also a condition that is passed on like a virus. Everyone is born with the propensity to sin, and the sickness is passed on to the next generation. Sinning becomes our nature. Like the law of gravity, our sinful nature pulls us down to selfishness, pride and rebellion. God's image in us is dimmed. We sense that we're better than this—or should be—but are slaves to sin's power. Falling short becomes the new normal.

We want to blame God for it, and I suppose he could be blamed for giving us free will. But who of us would choose to be a hand puppet without freedom to act of our own volition? Not me, and probably not you either. Yet when we choose badly and act violently, we blame God.

Welcome to life in a fallen world!

To hold fallen humanity in check, God establishes consequences for the choice Adam and Eve have made. Life will be difficult now. The human calling to fill the earth with life will be marked by conflict in marriage and pain in childbirth. The ground, which easily yielded food, is cursed because of them. Just staying alive will be wearisome work. In short, life will be tough…and then we die. *"For you were made from dust, and to dust you will return"* (Genesis 3:19).

Adam and Eve are then banished from Eden. Scholar Iain Provan suggests that Eden is not so much a place as it is the experience of being in a right relationship with God. Being banished "east of Eden" means, therefore, that human life will be diminished by the weariness, disharmony and hopelessness of a fallen world. There are clues in the story, however, that inspire hope for a return to Eden.

In the meantime, life in the fallen world progresses as God had warned for those who would be gods. Cain kills his brother Abel out of resentment and is banished to be a wanderer on earth. Sin spreads as the banished Cain becomes the father of ungodly descendants who build fortified cities and go to war against one another.

Chapter 5 seems to be an interruption of the story. It is a genealogy, accounting for the descendants of Adam and Eve. Early humans appear to live extraordinarily long lives, although the numbers could be symbolic or representative of several generations. Still, what is chilling about the genealogy is the repetition, like a melancholy drumbeat, of the birth, life and death of each generation. When unplugged from God, everything dies.

But, this is not the end of the story. There are already hints of redemption. God is more gracious than we could imagine, and so there is good news ahead!

Focus: The Bible posits that alienation from God is the root of the world's brokenness. This is not surprising, given the assumption that all reality is grounded in divine love and purpose. Genesis reveals that the whole creation, including nature, is diminished by sin, and death is the end. The crowning achievement of creation is humanity in the image of God; its greatest tragedy is the fall of humanity. The story of the Bible is concerned with what God is going to do about it.

Day 3　　　　　Genesis 6–9

January 3

> Key Text: The Lord observed the extent of human wickedness on the earth, and he saw that everything they thought or imagined was consistently and totally evil. (Genesis 6:5)

Genesis 6 reports that the rapid growth of evil on earth moves God to announce that in the future he will shorten the human life span, thereby limiting human opportunity for doing evil. In the meantime, things have come to a head. The Lord sadly observes that *"everything [humans] thought or imagined was consistently and totally evil. So the Lord was sorry he had ever made them and put them on the earth. It broke his heart"* (Genesis 6:5–6). The brilliant, burning image of God in humanity has been reduced to a mere smoking ember.

However, human rebellion reveals something significant about God: He feels intense sorrow over what humans have become. He is not a God far removed and indifferent.

What will God do? As he considers his options, one of which would be eliminating humans from the earth, we get further insight into his heart. God will not let things stay as they are, but he will not destroy what he loves. However, he must remain faithful to his holy character, meaning that his justice and love must both be satisfied. So God will act on both fronts—*for* his creation because of love and *against* evil because of justice.

Humans will learn, by an epic act of divine judgment, that sin has consequences and God is the Judge of all the earth. He will wash the earth with a great, cleansing flood that is terrifying in scope. At the same time, he will demonstrate that he has not given up on the human race.

Contemporary people hate the idea of *"divine judgment,"* but in truth it is a gift from God. Sin erases the boundaries God has established for human well-being, but God acting as Judge redraws the boundaries, making human well-being possible again.

6

Were it not for God's judgment, the human race would be a failed, forgotten experiment. When God judges, he acts in accordance with his character, which is justice and love. Thankfully, his justice is established by his love. God knows what he will ultimately do—he will take the judgment of human sin upon himself when Jesus dies on the cross. But even here at the beginning, God acts graciously towards humans, even if they don't recognize it.

Here is how it comes about:

God looks and finds a man on earth named Noah who is different from other people. He stands apart from his generation as a *"righteous man,"* walking *"in close fellowship with God."* He is the only man on earth that still has a spiritual pulse and is open to God. So God makes a covenant with Noah, which is the first of several covenants he will make with the human race. He will not destroy all human life, but restart it through a gracious act of deliverance through an ark. This is the first of many steps God will take to make things right and prepare the world for the coming of Jesus, our true Ark of deliverance.

Chapters 6 through 9 describe what happens to Noah and his family. Noah is told by God to build a boat according to a specific blueprint: *"Make the boat 450 feet long, 75 feet wide, and 45 feet high. Leave an 18-inch opening below the roof all the way around the boat. Put the door on the side, and build three decks inside the boat—lower, middle, and upper"* (Genesis 6:15–16).

Noah obeys God. When the ark is built, he and his extended family, along with a pair of *"every kind of animal,"* board the boat that will keep them alive during the coming flood and make a new beginning possible. When aboard, the group waits for a week, presumably to the great amusement and mockery of their neighbors.

Then it begins. *"All the underground waters erupted from the earth, and the rain fell in mighty torrents from the sky. The rain continued to fall for forty days and forty nights"* (Genesis 7:11–12). The waters cover the visible region and the ark floats away to safety. Only those who listened to the Lord, and came with Noah, survive the flood judgment.

When the waters finally recede, Noah and his family restart the human race. Their first act upon leaving the ark is to build an altar to the Lord and offer sacrifices to him. The Lord is pleased with Noah. He says to himself, *"I will never again curse the ground because of the human race,* even though everything they think or imagine is bent toward evil from childhood. I will never again destroy all living things" (Genesis 8:21).

God blesses Noah in chapter 9 and repeats his mandate for humans to fill the earth with life. Noah and his descendants, like Adam and Eve before, are given stewardship over the earth and all living things. To formalize his promise, God establishes a covenant with Noah.

Human beings now know that God is Almighty and can do whatever he pleases, but they will learn over time that what pleases God most is to be in fellowship with human beings. The rainbow in the sky will remind them.

> **Focus:** Many ancient Near Eastern cultures independently wrote stories about a great flood judgment. Though the details differ, there are several similar themes. This suggests a widespread memory of an actual event. God's revelation of this story to Moses gives Israel (and us) a true account of its meaning, presenting a God who is both Judge and Savior. The New Testament sees the ark as a foreshadowing of God's rescue of sinners in Christ. See, for example, Matthew 24:37–41 and 1 Peter 3:18–21.

> **Prayer:** *Father, we are grateful that your grace and mercy stop the judgment we all deserve. Thanks for giving us a second chance. Thanks for throwing a life preserver our way when we are drowning in confusion, rebellion and bad choices. Thanks for Jesus! Oh, and thanks for rainbows to remind us of your promises. Amen!*

Day 4   Genesis 10–11

January 4

> Key Text: Then they said, "Come, let's build a great city for ourselves with a tower that reaches into the sky. This will make us famous and keep us from being scattered all over the world." (Genesis 11:4)

Following the flood judgment, Noah and his family show a glimmer of hope for humanity by beginning their post-flood life with worship. They build an altar to the Lord and offer the sacrifices God requires *(Genesis 8:20)*. After the trauma of the flood judgment, they are humbled, aware of God as Judge, and grateful for a second chance for the human race. Given the long history of human sinfulness since the Fall, this new beginning is possible only because the Lord has balanced his justice with love.

Nevertheless, there is a new normal. Things are not as they were in the

Garden of Eden. Men and women's relationship with God has been structurally damaged by sin. There is a loss of innocence, and human nature is bent toward sin. Consequently, our relationship with God now needs to be mediated by a covenant.

The covenant God makes with Noah is contingent upon keeping the conditions of the mutual agreement *(Genesis 9:1–17)*. God promises to forgive our sins and bless us if we honor him with our worship and seek to order our community life around simple justice.

It is a provisional relationship sustained by God's grace and not our merit, but it is a beginning. And it is realistic. God knows that despite all he has done to create, sustain, correct and renew the earth, we will continue to sin.

Sure enough, after Genesis 10 gives an account of Noah's sons and their descendants, we find the human race back to its old tricks in chapter 11. After an unspecified period of time, *"all the people of the world spoke the same language and used the same words"* (Genesis 11:1). Anthropologists know that language is the foundation of culture. So we can deduce that a powerful and unified fallen human culture has arisen. With the growth of cultural power comes a grandiose vision of building a great city as a tribute to human power and glory: *"Come, let's build a great city for ourselves with a tower that reaches into the sky. This will make us famous and keep us from being scattered all over the world"* (Genesis 11:4).

The human city, as the center of population, wealth, power, technology and culture, becomes the breeding ground of rebellion against God.

To control the damage, God intervenes. He confuses the people with different languages and scatters them all over the earth, so that they cannot achieve the evil and self-defeating goals they had set for themselves. It is just for God to oppose human rebellion; it is loving to keep humans from doing what will damage them. The further they drift from basing their lives and culture on loving God, their Creator, the further they will drift from their true humanity.

This is the second time God acts to minimize the growth of evil on earth. First, he limits human life expectancy *(Genesis 6:3)*, and now he scatters humanity into various cultures and languages. Just as the two-party system of American democracy guards against tyranny—and guarantees that not much gets done!—so the scattering of people into various nations limits the growth of evil by creating competing cultures.

The prospects for humanity don't look promising, but fear not. God has a plan for the next step of Redemption—when the time is right.

Focus: The Tower of Babel alerts us to the dangers of concentrated wealth and power. In the beginning, God created Adam and Eve to multiply and fill the earth with life and culture. Now that same calling becomes, in a fallen world, the occasion for great evil. We must always remember the adage that sin is the hidden factor in every equation of life.

Prayer: Lord, thank you for your wise parenting of the human race. We are like children asserting ourselves against your authority, conspiring together against you one day and then fighting one another the next. But you watch over our lives by your loving discipline. Thank you for allowing us to call you "Father." Amen.

Day 5   Genesis 12–14

January 5

> Key Text: "I will make you into a great nation. I will bless you and make you famous, and you will be a blessing to others." (Genesis 12:2)

As we come to Genesis 12, we learn that God's long-term plan to redeem humanity and restore the creation is coming into focus. Since the rebirth of the human race through Noah, human memory of the one true God has dimmed and our imagination has retreated into idolatry and myth. So, God will engage his creation in a new way now. He calls a man named Abram to believe in him and then gives him an amazing promise. The Promise is a key moment in the Bible:

"The Lord had said to Abram, 'Leave your native country, your relatives, and your father's family, and go to the land that I will show you. I will make you into a great nation. I will bless you and make you famous, and you will be a blessing to others. I will bless those who bless you and curse those who treat you with contempt. All the families on earth will be blessed through you'" (Genesis 12:1–3).

Christians reading these verses believe that God's promise to bless the families of the earth will ultimately be fulfilled in Christ. But that is getting ahead of the story. The first phase of God's Promise to Abram is to make his descendants into the First Family of faith. God's calling is for them to become *"a great nation"* and take the knowledge of him to the other nations.

This will be the focus of the rest of the Old Testament story.

Along the way, we will meet fascinating, flawed people with complex personalities and mixed motives, who strive to understand who this God is, who has made himself known to them. Despite their many failures and setbacks, they will progressively come to know him as a God who will not let them go, nor give up on his plan to make things right in the world. No matter how much the First Family of faith exasperates him!

Those we meet will be people whose lives are shaped by the culture and sensibilities of the ancient Near East, so we will find ourselves often puzzled and even offended by how they think and act. In order to hear God's voice in their stories, we will need to do the hard work of understanding them from within their frame of reference.

Remember, God always speaks to people of any generation in terms they can understand, given their limited frame of reference. It was true of Abram and it is true of us today.

Abram is a flawed man, but he is also a man of faith—sometimes spectacularly so. Therefore, God shows him abundant mercy. On one occasion, early in his life of faith, Abram begins a slow journey towards the land of Canaan, which God had promised to give him in the future—the Promised Land! Chapter 12 says that during this journey a severe famine strikes the land of Canaan, and Abram is forced to go down to Egypt, where he lives as a foreigner. This means he has few rights and is very vulnerable.

Knowing the practices of the area, Abram coaches his wife Sarai—a very beautiful woman for her age—about the following: If approached by Egyptians who find her beautiful, the Egyptians will kill him, Abram, and take her. So she must tell them that he is her sister. She'll still get taken, but Abram will be spared!

I know, not a great moment.

Sure enough it all happens just as Abram predicted. The Egyptians give Abram many gifts as a bride price for his "sister," and they take her away to Pharaoh. But God intervenes by sending sickness upon Pharaoh, and Pharaoh assumes that Abram knows why. There is an awkward, angry conversation between them about the deceit, but Pharaoh is smart enough not to anger Abram's God. In the end, Abram gets Sarai back, keeps the gifts, and is given a free escort out of the country!

We learn, by this unflattering incident, that God is gracious to Abram even when Abram is selfish and unloving. Starting with Adam and Eve, we are learning that God treats us better than we deserve.

Later, however, Abram redeems himself somewhat by treating his ambitious nephew, Lot, with generosity. Abram allows Lot to occupy the better land around the city of Sodom, to pasture his growing herds. However, Lot gets drawn into local disputes, and he and all his wealth are captured in battle. Abram courageously risks everything to attack the army that has taken Lot captive. God honors Abram's loyalty and gives him victory.

It will be generations before Abram's family grows to the point where they can occupy the Promised Land, but right away Abram is beginning to learn about the God who has blessed him and called him to an amazing future.

Focus: The calling of Abram (later Abraham) demonstrates that God has decisively acted to make things right in the world he loves. He will continue to do so through the long story of Israel, the nation of Abram's descendants, to whom he will uniquely reveal himself, and through whom he will reveal himself to the wider world.

Prayer: *Father, we thank you for your patience and flexibility in revealing yourself to us. You know our minds and hearts and draw us into your presence in ways, grand and subtle, that we recognize and respond to. You even speak our language! Now, help us today to listen carefully! Amen.*

Day 6 — Genesis 15–17

January 6

> **Key Text: And Abram believed the Lord, and the Lord counted him as righteous because of his faith. (Genesis 15:6)**

God's promise to bless the world has gotten off to an unpromising start. We saw Abram protect his own hide by pawning off his wife as his sister. Then, we met his nephew, Lot the opportunist. As they moved their livestock, Abram graciously negotiated with Lot about where to graze their respective herds. Lot was given first choice and chose the best grazing land. Thanks a lot, Lot!

Clearly, if God's great Promise has any chance to move forward, it will not be through human merit, but only divine grace.

In chapter 15, God reassures Abram: *"Do not be afraid, Abram, for I will protect you, and your reward will be great"* (Genesis 15:1). But Abram expresses concern that his wife Sarai has not given him a son. This, of course, is a threat to the Promise that Abram will be the father of a great nation. God has Abram look up into the night sky and count the stars, saying, *"That's how many descendants you will have!"*

In response to this object lesson, Abram has one of his best moments—a moment that resonates throughout the Old and New Testaments as a clear statement of the Gospel: *"And Abram believed the Lord, and the Lord counted him as righteous because of his faith"* (Genesis 15:6).

This verse helps us understand how God can use an imperfect man like Abram to bring about his good purposes. Abram is counted as *"righteous"* not because he is worthy; he clearly is not. But he trusts in God who declares him worthy. Little does Abram know, as he stares into the night sky counting stars, that one day in the distant future God's Promise will be fulfilled when a descendant with his DNA will die on a cross to make atonement for our sins.

Abram's faith, therefore, is more than merely believing that God exists. He believes that God has spoken to him, revealing his purpose to make things right in the world. To that end he has promised to make Abram's descendants into a great nation with its own land. Abram also believes that God is able to bring about his purpose despite human weakness, so he lives his life as if the Promise is "in the bank." By faith, he has left his father's family and his native country to go to the land that God has promised.

Nevertheless, his faith will waver along the way. God will need to reassure him many times when circumstances don't seem to support the Promise. To make his intentions crystal clear, God formalizes his covenant with Abram by a covenant ceremony. In chapter 15, the ceremony is described—animals are offered and cut in half (making a covenant in Abram's time was described as "cutting" a covenant). While Abram sleeps that night, the Lord speaks to him in a dream with more information about the distant future. His descendants will be enslaved for 400 years and then delivered—a reference to the Exodus. After that, the people will occupy the Promised Land.

Time drags on. Abram's next test of faith comes when Sarai gets anxious about her inability to conceive a child in her old age. She persuades Abram to follow the cultural practice of having a child through a proxy wife—in this case Hagar, her Egyptian servant. Now, God has told Abram repeatedly that his heir would be born to Sarai, but it now seems unlikely to happen. So they take matters into their own hands.

Their lack of faith, while understandable, creates a problem when a son, Ishmael, is born to Hagar. Sarai becomes jealous of Hagar, and Hagar in turn treats Sarai with contempt. Abram is forced to send Hagar and Ishmael away to live elsewhere.

Later, when Abram is ninety-nine years old, God appears to remind him of the covenant once again. Since Abram will be *"the father of a multitude of nations,"* God changes his name to Abraham, meaning "father of many." Sarai's name is also changed to Sarah, meaning "princess." God insists that she will become the mother of many nations—a prediction that seems laughable to this old "princess."

Abraham also laughs. With his faith weakening, he negotiates with God: *"'May Ishmael live under your special blessing!' But God replied, 'No— Sarah, your wife, will give birth to a son for you. You will name him Isaac* [meaning "he laughs"], *and I will confirm my covenant with him and his descendants as an everlasting covenant'"* (Genesis 17:18–19).

God will not punish Ishmael because of Abraham's lack of faith. Ishmael will be blessed with many descendants who become a great nation—just not the family line of the Promise. To make things clear, the children of Abraham shall now be distinguished by the covenant mark of circumcision.

Focus: As Tim Keller explains the Gospel: *"We are more sinful and flawed in ourselves than we ever dared believe, yet at the very same time we are more loved and accepted in Jesus Christ than we ever dared hope."* This wonderful news about grace is revealed by God in the Old Testament first. Some misunderstand the Old Testament, thinking that people then were made righteous by keeping the Law. But the Law was given much later, during the time of Moses, and as we shall see, it could not make anyone righteous anyway. We are saved by faith alone, through grace alone, all the way!

Prayer: *Lord, it is as if the weight of the world is lifted off our shoulders! How wonderful to know that we are loved and accepted by you because of Christ, despite our sinfulness. We will rejoice in this Good News, and seek to share it with others. Amen!*

Day 7   Reflection

After many years of waiting for the Promise of God to be fulfilled, Abraham still has no son by his wife Sarah. How can he possibly be the father of a great nation? Surrendering to anxiety, he goes to Plan B, Ishmael, thinking that God must help those who help themselves.

Abraham has failed the test of faith, but we can be sympathetic. Time and disappointment can grind down even the most faithful believer. Presumably, Abraham reasoned that he wasn't so much disobeying God as giving him a hand. After all, Abraham was almost one hundred years old, and Sarah was in her nineties. Maybe God had overreached in his Promise.

So Abraham reaches for Hagar and, predictably, bad things follow *(Genesis 16).*

In response, God reveals himself to Abraham once again, this time as *El-Shaddai*—God Almighty. By this self-revelation, God reminds Abraham that he hasn't forgotten his Promise. If he is mighty enough to create the universe, he is certainly mighty enough to make Sarah pregnant. But Abraham laughs at the ridiculous mental picture of a pregnant ninety-year-old. Awkward!

Obviously, he still isn't convinced. Instead, he pressures God to let Ishmael be the child of the Promise *(Genesis 17:18–19).* But God grabs Abraham by his shoulders (anthropomorphically speaking), looks him in the eye and says, *"No—Sarah, your wife, will give birth to a son for you. You will name him Isaac, and I will confirm my covenant with him and his descendants as an everlasting covenant"* (Genesis 17:19).

So God persists with Abraham. His persistence is grounded in the key insight of the book of Genesis—everything that exists comes from God the Creator, and exists for his glory.

We human beings, created in his image, have a special place in God's heart. Together, as male and female, we are designed to live out God's calling. From within the covenant union of marriage, husbands and wives will love one another, establish families, fill the earth with human life, create culture and serve as stewards of the earth.

This is so central to God's purpose that, even when we turn against him and break his heart, he passionately pursues us with a promise to make things right again, no matter what it takes. He demonstrated this first through Noah and then through Abraham. It means that much to him.

Prayer: Father, we rejoice in the comforting truth that you are the Creator, Redeemer and present Lord of history. You are with us and keep us going as we journey through our brief time on earth. More than anything, in this preseason of everlasting life, we want to learn to love you, and one another. Thanks for moving us along, as you did Abraham. Help us to be patient. Amen!

Day 8   Genesis 18–20

January 8

> Key Text: Then the Lord said to Abraham, "Why did Sarah laugh? Why did she say, 'Can an old woman like me have a baby?' Is anything too hard for the Lord?" (Genesis 18:13–14)

In chapter 18, three visitors come to Abraham and Sarah. They are recognized by Abraham as being angels from God—perhaps even God himself. They have come with three messages for Abraham: *First,* Sarah will bear a child by him next year. *Second,* God's promise that Abraham will become a mighty nation will certainly come to pass. And *third,* Sodom and Gomorrah, where Abraham's nephew Lot and family are now living, will be destroyed.

The first announcement is met with a chuckle from Sarah: *"She laughed silently to herself and said, 'How could a worn-out woman like me enjoy such pleasure, especially when my master—my husband—is also so old?'"* (Genesis 18:12).

Circumstances seem to make God's first promise impossible. But, let's be honest, aren't we all laughing with Sarah? It's ridiculous. It simply isn't going to happen!

Once again, we are asked to decide whether God is able to keep his promise, no matter how unlikely it seems. The angel asks: *"Is anything too hard for the Lord?"* (Genesis 18:14).

The second announcement is yet another affirmation of God's Promise to Abraham. It is the seventh given to Abraham since chapter 12: *"Abraham will certainly become a great and mighty nation, and all the nations of the earth will be blessed through him. I have singled him out so that he will direct his sons and their families to keep the way of the Lord by doing what is right and just"* (Genesis 18:18–19).

Clearly, Abraham and Sarah are being tested—tested until they giggle! But isn't that the nature of faith? Until faith is tested, it really isn't faith at all. Faith occurs in the moment when we are willing to trust God and keep moving forward in the absence of clear evidence—or even in the presence of evidence to the contrary.

Meanwhile, Abraham's nephew, Lot, has taken a different path. He has been seduced by the moral depravity of Sodom. Depravity often seems "sexier" than goodness. Old Uncle Abraham's life of faith must have seemed boring and ridiculous to Lot. Lot is a mover and a shaker. He would rather be unhinged than buttoned down, so he has made his move. He's moved from the surrounding hills into the city of Sodom, jumping into its social life and seemingly determined to become a citizen. But the Lord tells Abraham, *"I have heard a great outcry from Sodom and Gomorrah, because their sin is so flagrant"* (Genesis 18:20).

We learn here that God's patience has limits. He hears the tears of victims. When an individual, group, city or nation crosses a certain line, they invite God's judgment. But before we roll our eyes again about God's "judgment," consider that even we sinful humans have moral lines, such as child abuse, terrorism or sexual trafficking. When these boundaries are crossed, we are moved to moral outrage and demand justice. If we who are sinners feel this way, how much more must Holy God?

After an investigation, it turns out that the "great outcry" from Sodom and Gomorrah is legitimate. God will move ahead with judgment. Lot and his family will be spared because of Abraham's intercession, but with great difficulty because Lot doesn't want to leave. He and his family are grabbed by God's angels and rushed to safety outside the city, dragging their heels.

They are warned not to look back because God is going to destroy the cities by raining down fire and burning sulfur. But tragically, Lot's wife is even more attached to city life than he is. She lags behind and looks back (perhaps considering going back?) and is killed by burning sulfur: *"She turned into a pillar of salt"* (Genesis 19:26).

Lot's life subsequently continues its tragic moral decline, which includes alcohol abuse and incest. The influence of the cities have had its effect. Meanwhile, Abraham falls back to an old selfish deception when he perceives his life could be threatened by a king named Abimelech.

Focus: God reveals himself in the drama of human life. As the author of life, he inserts himself into the story, and then interacts with us based on choices we freely make. He variously encourages, reminds, disciplines, and rewards—but always motivated by love. What he wants more than anything is for us to trust in him.

Prayer: Lord, keep our minds and hearts focused on you lest we, like Lot, find ourselves pulled away by our sinful desires. Help us to be patient in our present circumstances and continue trusting you because, despite the obstacles in the way, nothing shall be impossible with you. Help us to laugh with joy, and not cynicism. Amen!

Day 9   Genesis 21–24

January 9

Key Text: "Because you have obeyed me and have not withheld even your son, your only son, I swear by my own name that I will certainly bless you. I will multiply your descendants beyond number, like the stars in the sky and the sand on the seashore." (Genesis 22:16–17)

At long last, Abraham's faith is rewarded and the tension is lifted. Chapter 21 begins, *"The Lord kept his word and did for Sarah exactly what he had promised. She became pregnant, and she gave birth to a son for Abraham in his old age. This happened at just the time God had said it would. And Abraham named their son Isaac. ... And Sarah declared, 'God has brought me laughter. All who hear about this will laugh with me.'"*

This time Sarah's laughter is not the restrained laughter of cynicism, but the full-throated laughter of amazement and joy. The angel was right. Is anything too hard for God?

God's Promise is given momentum by the birth of Isaac. The story of God giving Abraham and Sarah a child in their old age is so wonderful that it will enhance the reputation of God and sustain the faith of generations to come. He is the God for whom nothing is impossible!

With Isaac, the second generation of the Promise officially begins. It closes the story arc of the birth of Ishmael. Isaac is the child of God's Promise to Abraham, while Ishmael is the child of Abraham's impatience and disobedience. Hagar and Ishmael are formally sent away. According to ancient Near Eastern custom, this means that Ishmael has no legal claim of inheritance. God will bless Ishmael *(Genesis 21:11–21),* but the Promise will continue through Isaac.

Isaac's miraculous birth is a great moment in the story thus far, but God isn't finished with testing Abraham's faith. The greatest test remains: *"Take your son, your only son—yes Isaac, whom you love so much—and go to the land of Moriah. Go and sacrifice him as a burnt offering on one of the mountains, which I will show you"* (Genesis 22:2). Will Abraham now obey when God asks him to return what he loves most?

Amazingly, Abraham obeys God, believing that the God who creates life can also bring the dead back to life. He takes Isaac up the mountain and then listens with great pain when his son asks him about the sheep to be offered as a burnt offering. Abraham simply says that God will provide.

When they arrive at the place where God had told him to go, Abraham builds the altar and arranges the wood. Then, with great distress, he ties Isaac and lays him on the altar. With Isaac lying there, wide-eyed and shaking with fear, Abraham raises his knife.

Just then, the angel of the Lord calls to him, *"Abraham! … Don't lay a hand on the boy! Do not hurt him in any way, for now I know that you truly fear God. You have not withheld from me even your son, your only son"* (Genesis 22:11–12). Abraham looks up and sees a ram caught in a thicket! God has provided a substitute for Isaac!

It seems inconceivable that Abraham would agree to offer his son as a sacrifice—or that God would ask. But it was common among the pagan religions of the ancient world that the gods would require the death of the firstborn son as an offering. God wants Abraham to know that he is not like those gods. He is the God who provides what we need and gives what we do not deserve. Worship is not appeasement of an angry god; it is joyous fellowship with the one true God.

From the vantage point of the New Testament, we understand that Abraham's test and God's provision are pointers to Christ who is *"the Lamb of God!"* The God who refuses to ask us to sacrifice our sons will one day sacrifice his Son for us.

Chapters 23 and 24 begin to wind down the story of Abraham. He is truly the iconic man of faith in the Bible. But now his life has been spent.

Sarah dies in chapter 23, and a wife is found for Isaac in chapter 24, thus highlighting the fact that God keeps his promises, and does so according to his own timetable.

> **Focus:** The wonderful story of Isaac, the child of the Promise, is filled with unexpected twists and turns, anguishing delays and a hilarious outcome. Faith grows in the drama of life. What Abraham, Isaac, and others learn from their experiences, good and bad, will be passed on to the next generation as a heritage of faith and growing knowledge of the one true God. From a biblical perspective, history is His-story.

> **Prayer:** *Father, we thank you for the grace you give to meet every test of faith you send. Help us not to complain or be afraid of what you permit. Instead, give us the faith we need to see you at work in all things—good and bad—for the sake of our spiritual development, and for your purpose to make things right in the world. Amen!*

Day 10   Genesis 25–26

January 10

> Key Text: Then Jacob gave Esau some bread and lentil stew. Esau ate the meal, then got up and left. He showed contempt for his rights as the firstborn. (Genesis 25:34)

In chapter 25, the first generation of the Promise comes to an end: *"Abraham lived for 175 years, and he died at a ripe old age, having lived a long and satisfying life. He breathed his last and joined his ancestors in death"* (Genesis 25:7).

We may ask why God chose Abraham in the first place. We can't really say, other than that God chose Abraham in the same way he determined to create the heavens and earth—out of the sheer freedom that comes with being Almighty God. It simply pleased him to do so! Whatever God does is always motivated by love and joy.

There is a note written in my Bible beside Genesis 25:7. It says, "One of the great people of the Bible!" Abraham, with all his faults—and they were many—becomes the iconic man of faith in the Bible: *"And Abram believed the Lord, and the Lord counted him as righteous because of his faith"* (Genesis 15:6).

The apostle Paul will point to Abraham as justification for his ministry to the Gentiles, saying that anyone who has the faith of Abraham can become a child of God *(Galatians 3)*. So we pay our respects to Abraham, and move on to the story of Isaac and his wife Rebekah.

The account of Isaac and Rebekah covers only a few chapters. The most significant event is the birth of twins, Jacob and Esau. But as he has done before, God does what is unexpected. God has already notified Rebekah, *"your older son will serve your younger son"* (Genesis 25:23). This goes against the prevailing tradition which says that the firstborn son will be the son of inheritance. Again, we don't know why God chooses Jacob over Esau. Perhaps he is exercising his authority over human culture and tradition. Or, perhaps he regards Jacob to be congenitally better suited to lead the third generation.

As the boys grow up, Esau becomes his father's favorite because he is a hairy, earthy outdoorsman. By contrast, Jacob has a quiet temperament, preferring to stay at home. It turns out that Jacob is also a clever and deceitful son. Plus, he is his mother's favorite. With Rebekah's complicity, Jacob tricks his brother out of his birthright, and then later, the blessing of the firstborn.

Jacob lacks Abraham and Isaac's moral fiber, but once again God shows that he will bring about his purposes even through sinful people. Thankfully!

In time, a severe famine strikes and Isaac moves to Gerar, where Abimelech, king of the Philistines, lives. Abimelech kindly allows him to stay in his land. While there, the Lord appears to Isaac to confirm the Promise that he had given to his father Abraham: *"I will cause your descendants to become as numerous as the stars of the sky, and I will give them all these lands. And through your descendants all the nations of the earth will be blessed. I will do this because Abraham listened to me and obeyed all my requirements, commands, decrees, and instructions"* (Genesis 26:4–5).

This is another special moment in Isaac's life. But before we get too excited, we discover that that the sin of his father Abraham is passed on to Isaac. Isaac grows worried that the local boys in Gerar will be attracted to his lovely wife Rebekah, and kill him to get her, so guess what? That's right, he says that she is his sister! He is found out by King Abimelech, who is not happy. He chews Isaac out, telling him that because of his deceit, one of his men could have taken Rebekah as a wife and thereby sinned against the Lord, albeit ignorantly. So Isaac wears out his welcome and is asked to leave the country.

God blesses Isaac nevertheless. In fact, his household has become so large and wealthy that Abimelech begins to worry that Isaac may hold a grudge against him. So Abimelech visits Isaac to propose a formal treaty guaranteeing that Isaac will never harm him. Isaac has the grace to sign it. But chapter 26 ends on a quick but ominous note: Whereas Isaac will be careful to match Jacob with a Jewish wife, he is careless with Esau, who marries two Hittite wives who are worshipers of pagan gods. Polygamy and paganism! They make life miserable for Isaac and Rebekah.

Focus: The Bible shows again and again that God's grace is greater than our sin. He takes up the slack in our lives, and always pays the bill. For that reason alone, God's people are called saints—saints who sin. Our repentance and faith draw against the account of Grace, and God's checks never bounce.

Prayer: Father, thank you for the life of Abraham, who demonstrated the meaning of faith for all subsequent generations. Help us to live by faith as well, and to accept the things we don't understand about your sovereign way in the world and in our lives. Amen!

Day 11   Genesis 27–31

January 11

Key Text: "What's more, I am with you, and I will protect you wherever you go. One day I will bring you back to this land. I will not leave you until I have finished giving you everything I have promised you." (Genesis 28:15)

Having tricked his brother into giving him his birthright, Jacob now tricks his father into giving him the blessing of the firstborn son. Isaac is near death and, according to custom, he should call all his sons together before him and give them their respective blessings. But Isaac favors Esau and calls him alone to prepare a favorite meal for him, after which he will be given the blessing of the firstborn.

Rebekah overhears Isaac's plan and summons Jacob. While Esau is out hunting for wild game to make his father's favorite dish, Jacob and Rebekah conspire. She sends him to the flocks to get lamb and quickly makes Isaac's favorite dish. Jacob is afraid that his father will not be fooled, even though he is mostly blind, because Esau is a hairy outdoorsman with a wild smell. So they take some of Esau's clothing. Mom retrofits Jacobs arms and neck with the skin of young goats. The treachery is prepared—the tasty food, the smelly clothes, and the hairy arms!

There are tense moments during the scam, but after Isaac smells the clothes, feels the hair and eats the tasty dish, Jacob gets the blessing of the firstborn. Just then, Esau returns from the hunt and prepares his father's favorite dish.

Well, you can imagine what happens next. Jacob gets what he wants, fulfilling the Lord's prophecy to Rebekah when she conceived twins: *"The sons in your womb will become two nations. From the very beginning, the two nations will be rivals. One nation will be stronger than the other; and your older son will serve your younger son"* (Genesis 25:23). But Jacob also earns the hatred of his twin brother Esau, who now plans to kill him. Tipped off by his co-conspiring mother, Jacob flees to Uncle Laban's until everything cools down.

Clearly, Jacob has a long way to go before he becomes a man of faith and moral character. God begins working on him through both revelation and a renewal of the Promise. God reveals himself to Jacob in a dream *"of a stairway that reached from the earth up to heaven. And he saw the angels of God going up and down the stairway"* (Genesis 28:12).

In the dream, Jacob sees God at the top of the stairway. He identifies himself as *"the Lord, the God of your grandfather Abraham, and the God of your father, Isaac."* The third generation of the Promise has begun, and so God renews his covenant promise with Jacob. Jacob learns by this unusual stairway dream, and the covenant renewal, that God is always working on earth to bring about his promise to bless the nations.

Chapters 29 to 31 give the detailed account of Jacob's time at his uncle Laban's, where he has gone to find a wife. He quickly discovers that Laban is just as tricky as he is. Laban fools Jacob into marrying his daughter Leah when he thinks he's marrying Rachel, whom he loves. He ends up with both, working fourteen years for Laban to pay the dowries.

But despite Laban's treachery, God blesses Jacob and he becomes wealthy during his years with Laban. Between Leah and Rachel, Jacob has twelve sons who will become the twelve tribes of Israel. The rest of chapters 30 and 31 recount the maneuverings of Jacob and Laban to outwit one another, but eventually Jacob is able to leave.

What strikes me so far about the story of Abraham and his son and grandson is the messiness of it. These are not superheroes, but real people. They have character flaws, make bad choices, display questionable character, and occasionally fall flat on their faces. And yet, God in his sovereignty chooses them just like he chooses us to serve him in the world.

Focus: Though we are deeply flawed now, God sees what we will become one day when his grace has finished its work in us. In the meantime, God will build character in us, teaching us especially how to love one another.

Prayer: *Father, help us not to grow anxious by thinking that your love for us is dependent upon our performance. Teach us what it means to live by faith through grace. Amen!*

Day 12   Genesis 32–36

January 12

> Key Text: "Your name will no longer be Jacob," the man told him. "From now on you will be called Israel, because you have fought with God and with men and have won." (Genesis 32:28)

Free at last from his deceitful uncle/father-in-law Laban, Jacob now faces the prospect of returning home to Canaan and facing his brother Esau, who hates him because of his earlier treachery. Esau may not be smart, but he is scary and he is still mad. His plan for revenge—possibly killing Jacob—raises a threat to God's Promise to Abraham.

So Jacob prays for God's protection, reminding him of his promise to treat him kindly and multiply his descendants *(Genesis 32:9–12)*. Two things occur next to assuage Jacob's fear.

First, Jacob lays the groundwork for an elaborate plan to appease Esau. He divides up a large portion of his herds into several smaller herds and sends them, wave after wave, as gifts for Esau. The hope is that by the time Jacob and his family arrive, Esau will be pacified.

Second, after sending his family to a safe place, Jacob remains alone at the camp where something strange occurs. A man appears and begins wrestling with him throughout the night. Jacob is tenacious, so it is a standoff. But then the man merely touches Jacob's hip and wrenches it out of its socket! This is no ordinary man; it is an angel of the Lord. He changes Jacob's name to Israel, meaning "he strives with God," and says to him, *"you have fought with God and with men and have won"* (Genesis

32:28).

We learn here that God is willing to struggle with us, like a parent does with a child, in order to shape us into mature people of faith. As Proverbs 3:11–12 teaches: *"My child, don't reject the Lord's discipline, and don't be upset when he corrects you. For the Lord corrects those he loves, just as a father corrects a child in whom he delights."*

Jacob's clever plan to approach his brother with humility and lots of gifts pays off, at least for now. Esau's anger and pride is satisfied, and he leaves his brother alone. Jacob moves his flocks and family to Shechem, in the land of Canaan, where he sets up camp.

But trouble seems to follow Jacob. In chapter 34, his daughter Dinah is raped by a local Canaanite prince, and Jacob's sons take horrific revenge for their sister through a devious plot to kill every man from that city. They then seize all the flocks and herds and donkeys—everything they can lay their hands on. They loot all the men's wealth, plunder their houses, and take all their little children and wives as captives.

The rape was terrible, but the revenge taken by Jacob's sons was horrific and disproportionate. He angrily confronts his sons: *"You have ruined me! You've made me stink among all the people of this land—among all the Canaanites and Perizzites. We are so few that they will join forces and crush us. I will be ruined, and my entire household will be wiped out!"* (Genesis 34:30).

Fearing retaliation, Jacob moves his household to Bethel. There he builds an altar. God hears his prayers and reassures him: *"I am El-Shaddai—'God Almighty.' Be fruitful and multiply. You will become a great nation, even many nations. Kings will be among your descendants! And I will give you the land I once gave to Abraham and Isaac. Yes, I will give it to you and your descendants after you"* (Genesis 35:11–12).

Chapter 35 ends with the death of Jacob's beloved wife Rachel during childbirth, and then the death of his father Isaac.

Jacob's story reminds us that the life of faith is difficult. We face our own shortcomings as well as the struggles and losses that are common to all human beings. Sometimes we have to deal with the sudden occurrence of evil. Moments of clarity are followed by long periods of uncertainty. In these times, Jacob must remember God's covenant Promise for assurance.

Day 13   Genesis 37–40

January 13

Key Text: The Lord was with Joseph, so he succeeded in everything he did as he served in the home of his Egyptian master. (Genesis 39:2)

The continuing story of God's Promise now shifts from Jacob to his sons—the twelve who head up the families that will one day become twelve tribes and then the nation of Israel. The launching of Israel as a nation will occur in Egypt. But how do the twelve tribes get to Egypt? This is the question that frames the rest of Genesis.

It is an amazing story. Someone should make it into a Broadway musical and name it something like...*Joseph and the Amazing Technicolor Dreamcoat.* Oh wait, they have!

In Genesis 37, we find out that Jacob has a son, Joseph, who is a half-brother to the other sons, and is his father's favorite: *"Jacob loved Joseph more than any of his other children because Joseph had been born to him in his old age. ... But his brothers hated Joseph because their father loved him more than the rest of them. They couldn't say a kind word to him"* (Genesis 37:3–4).

To make matters worse, Joseph is a dreamer, and God has given him the gift of interpreting dreams. One day he tells his family about a series of his dreams which strongly suggest that one day the whole family will bow low before him! Imagine their indignation! Their annoying little half-brother will rule over them?!

Jacob appears oblivious to the sibling rivalries among his sons. One day, he sends Joseph out to the fields to check on his brothers and their flocks. When the brothers see him coming, they conspire to kill him out of jealousy. But clearer heads prevail. One of the brothers, Reuben, has a slight quiver of conscience about the plan. He persuades them not to kill him but to sell him to some slave traders who happen along. It's a win-win situation—they get a little money and also get rid of their annoying little brother!

But what will they tell their father?

They decide to take Joseph's colorful coat, which was a gift from their father, tear it up and smear it with animal blood. Then, they report to Jacob that Joseph has been killed by a wild animal. So their father weeps bitterly, unaware of their deception.

Crossing moral boundaries damages our heart, so chapter 38 shows how Judah, one of the conspiring brothers, spirals into a moral mess. It is an ugly story, showing how crossing one ethical boundary makes it easier to cross the next, sending a person on a downward spiral into further depravity.

Meanwhile, God is with Joseph. Having been sold by his brothers to slave traders, the slave traders then sell Joseph to Potiphar, an Egyptian officer and captain of Pharaoh's guard. One can only imagine the dehumanizing horrors of the slave-trading world. Nevertheless, Genesis 39:2 says, *"The Lord was with Joseph, so he succeeded in everything he did as he served in the home of his Egyptian master."* He is given more trust and responsibility in Potiphar's service, but Potiphar's wife takes notice of him and tries to seduce him. Joseph repeatedly refuses, until one day she angrily gives up and falsely accuses him of attempted rape.

He is thrown into prison, but even there, *"the Lord was with Joseph... and showed him his faithful love"* (Genesis 39:21). While there, God enables him to interpret the dreams of two other prisoners—Pharaoh's cup-bearer and his chief baker, who had both managed to offend him. They are impressed with Joseph's ability. Unexpectedly, they are freed to serve at Pharaoh's birthday celebration. The baker has a gruesome death, as Joseph had interpreted from the man's dream. Similarly, the cup-bearer's dream comes true: he lives to serve again. But he totally forgets about Joseph.

So, chapter 40 ends with Joseph still in jail for doing what was right.

So far, the story of Joseph and his brothers shows that the power of sin is still at work in the lives of the covenant people. But so is the power of God. While it makes us cringe to see what believers sometimes do, we are inspired by the courage and character of Joseph. God has chosen him for an important task—to get his family to Egypt.

> **Focus:** Most of us have life stories that are shaped by events both good and evil. We are familiar with family dysfunction, with evil practices like slave trading, with false accusations and wrongful imprisonment. But we are amazed to discover that God is also at work in these things to bring about his purpose for us, as he did for Joseph. Faith is sometimes required to trust God in the dark.

> **Prayer:** *Father, it encourages us to see how a mistreated young man can thrive even in the midst of injustice and ill treatment. It is evidence of your grace. You have said that your strength is made perfect in our weakness, so would you perfect it in me? Amen!*

Day 14   Reflection

January 14

It is helpful to think about the Bible as one great story with four themes: Creation, Fall, Redemption and New Creation. Genesis introduces three of the themes right away.

The first theme is Creation. We learn that there is one God who created the heavens and earth—from the vastness of the cosmos, to the smallness of the sub-atomic realm. Occupying this vast outer and inner space—on one planet that we know of—are living creatures, large and small. Among those creatures are a privileged species—human beings created in the image and likeness of God. As God's image bearers, human beings exist to know, enjoy, represent and glorify God on earth.

In particular, we are stewards of the earth on God's behalf. To this end, we are given unique gifts of self-awareness, rational thought, morality and free will. By means of these gifts, human beings are enabled to thrive and create diverse cultures which glorify God.

Tragically, this was forfeited by the Fall, which is the second theme of the Bible. The Fall was a catastrophe brought about by a simple doubting question, *"Did God really say...?"* followed by a daring claim: *"You will be like God, knowing good and evil."* The doubt and dare were a challenge to the authority of God the Creator, and a temptation directed to beings created in God's image. Only creatures with a privileged access to God could be tempted by the thought of overthrowing him as king.

Importantly, the doubt and dare came from within the created world. It was a serpent, animated and voiced like a hand puppet by the devil. The devil—a fallen angel—is a created being as well, not a rival deity. Perhaps the fallen angels were angry at God, and jealous of humans, because God gave humans the unique gift of his image. All the devil can do is influence human free will by means of temptation, deceit and fear.

The greatest effect of the Fall was to separate us from God, like a deep sea diver being cut off from his oxygen. Spiritual death followed, along with a loss of our identity and moral vision as humans. The image of God in us was dimmed. Life on earth became confused, conflicted and chaotic, ending in physical death.

It turns out that being the god of one's own life is no easy matter.

At this point in the story, God could very well have abandoned us, or even reconsidered and taken away our free will. But he did not create us as pets to amuse himself. He created us as his children to share his life by our free choice to love him.

I don't believe that the Fall took God by surprise. He knew that it was possible, perhaps inevitable, that we would rebel. But he was willing to risk it, like any parent today who decides to have children. He would bear the pain of our rejection, and then pay the cost to make things right.

This brings us to the third theme: Redemption. Starting right away with Adam and Eve, God makes a cryptic promise that the serpent would be crushed by an offspring of woman. In other words, the work of the devil—sin and death—would one day be defeated by a human being. Exactly what this meant and how it would come about was unclear at the beginning. As we know from our vantage point, the Promise will slowly come into focus over thousands of years. The light brightens considerably with the story Abraham and his children. It will brighten further with the story of the nation of Israel under Moses and Joshua, and then the judges and kings. All the while, the story is moving forward to its ultimate fulfillment in the bright light of Christ.

So we see that the themes of Creation and Fall are introduced within the first three chapters of the first book of the Bible, but the story of Redemption, to prepare us for the New Creation, will be the focus for the rest of the Bible—Old and New Testaments.

But where is it all going? Is there an end in view? There is, only the end is better described as a "new beginning." The Promise of God is to rescue us from sin and death so that we can be reconciled to him. It is a return to Eden, but much more. Our destiny is resurrection life in a New Heaven and Earth where God will once again rule as King over the whole creation. We will be free at last to experience our full humanity as God intended when he created us in his image. It will be life beyond our imagination! What a story! And we've only just begun.

> *Prayer: Lord, we feel the tension of living as creatures that were made for greatness but fell into sin and death. We are so grateful that you didn't leave us there. We were lost but now have been found, and we rejoice in the amazing future that awaits us! May we live today as you intended—knowing, enjoying and glorifying you. Amen!*

Day 15   Genesis 41–44

January 15

> **Key Text:** Pharaoh said to Joseph, "I hereby put you in charge of the entire land of Egypt." (Genesis 41:41)

God wants the twelve sons of Jacob to move their households to Egypt for protection because there is a severe famine coming to the whole region. In a few years, Egypt will be the only place where they can live long and prosper. How will God do it? He's already started by leveraging the treachery of Joseph's brothers, who out of jealousy sold him to slave traders, who then sold him to Potiphar, an official of the Egyptian Pharaoh. So what looked to be a tragic story is actually a further step in the fulfillment of God's Promise. Here's how.

Joseph shows himself to be a capable and wise manager, and so his "career" as Potiphar's slave begins to advance—until Potiphar's wife makes an advance toward Joseph! He refuses her and she has him thrown in jail.

Two years later, Pharaoh has some disturbing dreams and wants them interpreted. Joseph is summoned from jail because Pharaoh's cup-bearer remembers that he interprets dreams. Joseph first gives glory to God for this ability, and then tells Pharaoh that seven years of prosperity are to be followed by seven years of severe famine. So God is giving a heads-up to Pharaoh through his dreams.

Isn't it interesting that God uses family treachery, a lonely housewife, climate change and the dreams of a pagan ruler to set everything in place for what he is about to do?

Here it comes: *"Pharaoh said to Joseph, 'I hereby put you in charge of the entire land of Egypt'"* (Genesis 41:41). Unbelievable!

Joseph creates a brilliant plan to warehouse huge amounts of grain during the seven years of abundance, so that when the famine arrives, Pharaoh will be able to thrive by selling grain to refugees looking for food. Meanwhile, back home in Canaan, Joseph's father Jacob (who thinks he is dead), is oblivious to what God has been preparing all these years. He says to his sons, *"Why are you standing around looking at one another? I have heard there is grain in Egypt. Go down there, and buy enough grain to keep us alive. Otherwise we'll die"* (Genesis 42:1–2).

When Joseph's brothers arrive in Egypt, they don't recognize him and, of course, he speaks Egyptian now. He plays with them a bit, accusing them of being spies and then having them put in prison. But God is in this little ruse. The brothers conclude that they are being punished because of what they did to their brother. Little do they know that they are being blessed, despite what they did to their brother!

Joseph overhears their regrets about what they had done to him, so he sends them home with grain, but requires one of them to stay behind as collateral. In addition, when they return they must bring with them their father's youngest son, Benjamin. Nice moral symmetry—they will be forced, as chapter 44 recounts, to revisit their treachery with Joseph by putting their youngest brother in potential danger.

We learn here that God does not sit idly by while life happens among his people. Even when we are not aware of it, God inserts himself into our story through people, circumstances, dreams, and even the weather, to finally bring about his plans for us.

Focus: Life often doesn't make sense when we are in the middle of it. In this story, the treachery of Joseph's brothers, together with Joseph's enslavement in Egypt, are used by God to bring about a bigger purpose—to protect his covenant people by moving them to Egypt. But these insights are gained only after the fact. Understanding comes by looking in the rear-view mirror.

Prayer: Father, we thank you that you are behind us and beside us, above us and before us. Through all the big and little events of our lives, you work to bring about your good purposes for us. This gives us great confidence to not be afraid or discouraged when we don't understand what is going on right now. Amen!

31

Day 16 — Genesis 45–47

> Key Text: "I am Joseph, your brother, whom you sold into slavery in Egypt. But don't be upset, and don't be angry with yourselves for selling me to this place. It was God who sent me here ahead of you to preserve your lives." (Genesis 45:4–5)

Chapter 45 begins, *"Joseph could stand it no longer."* After all these months of keeping his brothers in the dark and on edge, while at the same time secretly maneuvering to have his family moved to Egypt, Joseph finally reveals himself to them. There is weeping, rejoicing and reconciliation.

In the ancient Near East, when someone was shamed—as was Joseph by the treatment of his brothers—that shame could only be lifted in the eyes of others by taking revenge. So we might expect Joseph to have his brothers killed, especially after the satisfaction of revealing himself to them with power to harm them. This is what his brothers are expecting.

Instead, we see grace. *"I am Joseph, your brother, whom you sold into slavery in Egypt. But don't be upset, and don't be angry with yourselves for selling me to this place. It was God who sent me here ahead of you to preserve your lives"* (Genesis 45:4–5). Joseph acknowledges that God had been the one acting, not his brothers.

Pharaoh tells Joseph that his brothers can move to Egypt and settle in the very best land. So his brothers return to Canaan, loaded with gifts, and tell their father all that has happened. You can imagine his joy to learn that Joseph is alive, and that because of him all of them will be spared from the terrible famine.

As they leave for Egypt, God speaks to Jacob, saying, *"I am God, the God of your father.... Do not be afraid to go down to Egypt, for there I will make your family into a great nation. I will go with you down to Egypt, and I will bring you back again. You will die in Egypt, but Joseph will be with you to close your eyes"* (Genesis 46:2–4).

Chapter 47 recounts how Pharaoh prospers under the wise management of Joseph during the years of the famine. People throughout the region who lost everything are treated kindly by the policies of Joseph— especially his brothers: *"Meanwhile, the people of Israel settled in the re-*

gion of Goshen in Egypt. There they acquired property, and they were fruit-ful, and their population grew rapidly" (Genesis 47:27).

There is a little more left to the story of Joseph, but already we see God's hand at work in all these events, keeping his people safe and his Promise moving forward. What really stands out is the character of Joseph. If Abraham is the iconic man of faith, Joseph is the iconic man of grace and mercy who gives his brothers what they don't deserve.

Does this sound like anyone else in the Bible we know? (Hint: It's Jesus.)

Focus: One of the distinctives of Judeo-Christianity is the practice of grace—unmerited favor. Grace is a huge moral and spiritual leap forward in human society from societies based on honor and shame. A stigma of shame comes from the community because of something the individual or a member of his family has done. The shame is only relieved, and honor restored, when revenge has been taken. In some cases, the revenge (including death) is taken out on a dishonored family member. When families and societies operate this way, the cycle of revenge never ceases. The only thing that breaks the cycle, and restores peace, is forgiveness, freely given. Our motivation as Christians for showing grace towards others is the amazing grace that we have received from God.

Prayer: Dear Lord, thank you for this amazing story of forgiveness and reconciliation. It reminds us of how Jesus has taken our shame upon himself, bearing its consequences, so that we may be forgiven. Help us to pass it on to those who have sinned against us. Amen!

Day 17   Genesis 48–50

January 17

> Key Text: But Joseph replied, "Don't be afraid of me. Am I God, that I can punish you? You intended to harm me, but God intended it all for good. He brought me to this position so I could save the lives of many people." (Genesis 50:19–20)

The story of Genesis concludes by recounting the last days of Jacob and Joseph, who are now settled in the land of Goshen in Egypt. As God told Abraham long ago *(Genesis 15:13)*, his descendants would live as foreigners in Egypt for 400 years and eventually become slaves. But for now, they are spared from the devastation of a terrible famine and will live in

Goshen, an area perfectly suited to their rapid growth as a people.

As Jacob is dying, Joseph comes to see him. Once again, a generation is passing away. So Jacob reminds Joseph of God's Promise: *"God Almighty appeared to me at Luz in the land of Canaan and blessed me. He said to me, 'I will make you fruitful, and I will multiply your descendants. I will make you a multitude of nations. And I will give this land of Canaan to your descendants after you as an everlasting possession'"* (Genesis 48:3–4).

Jacob blesses Joseph's two sons, Ephraim and Manasseh. But just as his father Isaac did with him and his brother Esau, Jacob blesses his grandchildren in the wrong order, saying that the younger brother Ephraim will be a greater nation than Manasseh. Once again, we see events moving contrary to culture and convention. But God's divine election in matters great and small ensure that his purpose to redeem the world will come about despite challenge after challenge.

In chapter 49, Jacob blesses his other twelve sons and then *"breathed his last, and joined his ancestors in death."* He is taken back to Canaan for burial as he requested. But now that their father is dead, Joseph's brothers fear Joseph will show his anger and pay them back for all the wrong they did to him.

But suffering has made Joseph wise, not angry: *"Don't be afraid of me. Am I God, that I can punish you? You intended to harm me, but God intended it all for good. He brought me to this position so I could save the lives of many people"* (Genesis 50:19–20). And then he assures them: *"Soon I will die...but God will surely come to help you and lead you out of this land of Egypt. He will bring you back to the land he solemnly promised to give to Abraham, to Isaac, and to Jacob"* (Genesis 50:24).

Much has occurred in the book of Genesis. It has introduced the one true God, Creator of the heavens and earth. It has revealed that human beings are unique because they are created in his image. It has explained why human life has become chaotic, broken and sinful, and ends in death. It has introduced God's plan to redeem the world, beginning with a promise to Abraham and his descendants, that they will become a great nation with their own land.

Before they can take possession of the Promised Land, they must grow into a nation, and that will take several generations. There are amazing adventures awaiting them, as well as sobering lessons to learn about who God is and what he expects of them.

But Genesis has laid the groundwork for the rest of the story. God has revealed his plan of redemption to make things right in the world through the story of Abraham and his children and grandchildren. The first phase of the Promise, to make them into a great nation, living in their own land, is taking shape.

God has shown himself to be faithful to his Promise. He has demonstrated his power to overcome the most daunting obstacles—like Sarah becoming pregnant in her old age. He has protected Abraham from his own lapses of faith, as when he passed off Sarah as his sister. He has reassured Isaac and then Jacob that the Promise is still in effect. He has protected Abraham's family from dangers within and without.

And now he has brought the twelve tribes to Egypt so that, over the next 400 years, they can grow into a nation, ready for the next phase of the journey!

Focus: God has determined to bring about his plan of redemption for the world through the long story of his "chosen people," beginning about 4,000 years ago in the Middle-Bronze Age. In comparison with the great ancient civilizations around her, like Mesopotamia and Egypt, Israel was a tiny nation, barely worthy of a footnote in ancient history. Yet it was through Israel's story that God made himself known to the world. It is characteristic of God, as the apostle Paul explains, to choose things that are foolish, weak, and despised by the world to bring about his purposes. *(See 1 Corinthians 1:26–29.)*

Prayer: *Lord, you are awesome in knowledge and power—beyond human reason and imagination. You are also loving and gracious, pursuing us when we rebel against you. For reasons we cannot understand, it pleases you to share life with us forever. What more can we say, except we praise your holy name! Amen.*

Day 18 — Exodus 1–2

January 18

> Key Text: Then Pharaoh gave this order to all his people: "Throw every newborn Hebrew boy into the Nile River. But you may let the girls live." (Exodus 1:22)

It is a perfect storm. The Israelites have multiplied greatly in Egypt and now are extremely powerful. After Joseph and his brothers die, the memory of Joseph's service for Pharaoh dies also. Now a new king comes to power *"who knew nothing about Joseph or what he had done"* (Exodus 1:8).

The new Pharaoh is afraid of the numbers and strength of the Israelites, so he enslaves them, hoping to wear them down with ruthless, crushing labor. In addition, he directs the Hebrew midwives to kill the baby boys, which they refuse to do, deviously claiming that the Hebrew women deliver their babies too quickly, before they can get there. Frustrated, Pharaoh orders every Egyptian to drown newborn Hebrew boys in the Nile River.

Anti-Semitism is born.

In the midst of this horrible edict, we see the providence of God at work through a courageous Hebrew woman. She has a child whom she recognizes as "special." She hides him as long as she can, then creates a little papyrus boat and places him among the reeds in the Nile River. Amazingly, the boy is found by Pharaoh's daughter, who recognizes him as a Hebrew child. For reasons unknown, and in defiance of her father's edict, she wants to keep the child.

Seeing what is happening, the baby's sister approaches the princess and offers to find a Hebrew woman to nurse the baby for her. What good fortune! Of course, she takes the baby home and gives him to her mother to nurse! Later, when the boy is older, his mother brings him back to Pharaoh's daughter, who adopts him as her own son.

She names him Moses.

Fast-forward many years, and an adult Moses, who has grown up with royal privilege and education, begins to feel a sense of calling. Perhaps he was saved from the Nile and set apart to one day help his fellow Israelites. He goes out to visit his people and witnesses their brutal servitude. He is angered by what he sees, especially when he witnesses an Egyptian slave master beating one of the Hebrews. Looking around to make sure he is not being watched, he kills the Egyptian and hides his body.

The Hebrews are nervous about the murder, and about Moses. When Moses returns to visit his people again, he intervenes in a fight between two of them, demanding to know: *"'Why are you beating up your friend?' ...The man replied, 'Who appointed you to be our prince and judge? Are you going to kill me as you killed that Egyptian yesterday?'"* (Exodus 2:13–14).

So the word has gotten out! Moses is anxious for good reason, because

Pharaoh has already heard about what Moses did and now seeks to kill him. So Moses flees and goes to the land of Midian to hide.

Eventually, Pharaoh dies. God has delayed acting, but not forgotten the Israelites' suffering: *"They cried out for help, and their cry rose up to God. God heard their groaning, and he remembered his covenant promise to Abraham, Isaac, and Jacob. He looked down on the people of Israel and knew it was time to act"* (Exodus 2:23–25).

We see how people and events repeatedly threaten to disrupt God's Promise, but his plan is unstoppable. What comes next is one of the defining events in the Old Testament.

Focus: God's purposes are always worked out in the messiness of history, and not outside of it. So the Gospel is not esoteric or hidden knowledge revealed only to the initiated, and with little relevance to life as we know it. The Gospel is Good News for real life and ordinary people. It finds us in our brokenness and ignorance, giving us hope and new life.

Prayer: *Lord, we are amazed to watch you work in and through events and people, and across generations. It encourages our confidence of your work in our personal lives. We trust you to guide us, and we resolve not to grow discouraged. Amen!*

Day 19   Exodus 3–6

January 19

> Key Text: **"Now go, for I am sending you to Pharaoh. You must lead my people Israel out of Egypt."** (Exodus 3:10)

Moses has gone from being an Egyptian insider to a Hebrew outsider hiding from Pharaoh. Time passes in Midian as Moses herds sheep for his father-in-law Jethro, and he remains confused about his future. Then one day, confusion turns to clarity when God appears to Moses as a blazing fire from the middle of a bush.

As Moses draws near the fire, he hears the voice of God: *"I have certainly seen the oppression of my people in Egypt. I have heard their cries of distress because of their harsh slave drivers. Yes, I am aware of their suffering. So I have come down to rescue them from the power of the Egyptians and lead them out of Egypt into their own fertile and spacious land. It is a land flowing with milk and honey..."* (Exodus 3:7–8).

And by the way, Moses, *"Go, for I am sending you to Pharaoh. You must lead my people Israel out of Egypt."* Moses vigorously protests that he is not the right man, but God promises to be with him. He says to tell the Israelites that his name is "I AM"—the God of their ancestors Abraham, Isaac and Jacob. "I AM" is a way of saying that he is timeless—he is Eternal God. No one can define him. He defines himself and will reveal himself to Moses, Israel and the whole world by the mighty things he does.

It's important to note that Jesus claims this same title for himself in John 8:57–58. He makes the outrageous claim that Abraham rejoiced as he looked forward to his coming: *"The people said, 'You aren't even fifty years old. How can you say you have seen Abraham?' Jesus answered, 'I tell you the truth, before Abraham was even born, I AM!'"* Jesus uses the "I AM" statement several times in the Gospel of John*: "I AM the bread of life"; "I AM the light of the world"; "I AM the way, the truth and the life,"* etc. In this, and other ways, Jesus connects his story with the story of God in the Old Testament, and claims that he is the final revelation of God.

But we are getting ahead of ourselves.

With Aaron's help, Moses goes to the people of Israel with God's plan to deliver them, but also with a warning that Pharaoh will not let them go unless a mighty hand forces him. *"So I will raise my hand and strike the Egyptians, performing all kinds of miracles among them"* (Exodus 3:20).

In chapter 4, God prepares Moses and the people for his confrontation with Pharaoh. God instructs him in what to say, and gives him authority to perform miracles in front of Pharaoh. Moses insists, however, that he needs help: *"I'm not very good with words. I never have been, and I'm not now, even though you have spoken to me. I get tongue-tied, and my words get tangled"* (Exodus 4:10). God reassures Moses that he will give him words to speak and give understanding to the hearers. Nevertheless, Moses pleads for God to give him an assistant. God relents and appoints his brother Aaron to go with him and be his spokesman. But Moses must perform the miracles.

Carrying his shepherd's staff—an instrument God will use to show his miraculous power—Moses heads back to Egypt. God tells him ahead of time that when he demands that Pharaoh let the people go, and then performs the miracles in front of him, Pharaoh will refuse to let them go. He will harden his heart against God, and in return God will harden his heart against Pharaoh.

In chapter 5 Moses and Aaron demand for the first time, *"Let my people go!"* As predicted, Pharaoh responds with mockery, then orders that the Israelite slaves be abused even more, making their work impossible.

The people understandably protest to Moses, but God forcefully reaffirms his Covenant Promise and his intention to deliver them: *"I will free you from your oppression and will rescue you from your slavery in Egypt. I will redeem you with a powerful arm and great acts of judgment. I will claim you as my own people, and I will be your God. Then you will know that I am the Lord your God who has freed you from your oppression in Egypt"* (Exodus 6:6–7).

As we shall see, this is not just to be a conflict between Israel and the Egyptians—it is a contest between Israel's God and the pagan gods of Egypt.

And it's going to get crazy!

> **Focus:** The idea that Moses and Aaron would stand before the most powerful king of the time and demand that he allow the people of Israel to leave is ridiculous. Yet God is with them, and through them he is going to take on the pagan gods of Egypt and defeat them. The God of the Bible is a God who rules over the nations of the world by his power and authority.

> *Prayer: Lord, it is comforting to know that you are our powerful redeemer. You go before us as our protector and defeat our enemies. Nothing can separate us from you. Nothing can stop you from bringing about your good purposes in our lives. Thanks for your protection. Amen!*

Day 20   Exodus 7–10

January 20

> Key Text: **"When I raise my powerful hand and bring out the Israelites, the Egyptians will know that I am the Lord."** (Exodus 7:5)

The battle begins! It is the God of Abraham, Isaac and Jacob versus the Egyptian gods and the mighty Pharaoh. Paganism is so deeply rooted in the minds and hearts of the people that only a divine "power encounter" can break through their false worldview.

God tells Moses that he is going to leverage Pharaoh's stubborn heart in order to multiply his miraculous signs and wonders: *"Then I will rescue my forces—my people, the Israelites—from the land of Egypt with great acts of judgment. When I raise my powerful hand and bring out the Israelites, the Egyptians will know that I am the Lord"* (Exodus 7:4–5).

In Exodus 7 through 10, there is a struggle back and forth. Each time God sends a plague, Pharaoh agrees to the let the people leave, then hardens his heart and changes his mind. But with each new plague, the misery of the Egyptians increases. First, God turns the water of the Nile River into blood; then he sends a plague of frogs across the land, followed by gnats, flies, dead livestock, boils, hail, locusts and darkness.

Time after time, God appeals to Pharaoh to give up and recognize him as the one true God. On the surface this may seem unfair. To modern ears, a religious claim to universal truth is offensive. But Pharaoh is learning that there is indeed one true God—the God of the Hebrews. Knowing this has increased his accountability. Egypt's continued worship of false gods is putting Pharaoh's soul and his nation at risk.

Pharaoh seems at times to concede defeat. Following the plague of locusts, which devour every plant in the fields, and all the fruit on the trees that had survived the hailstorm, he quickly summons Moses and Aaron: *"'I have sinned against the Lord your God and against you,' he confessed. 'Forgive my sin, just this once, and plead with the Lord your God to take away this death from me'"* (Exodus 10:16–17).

Moses asks the Lord to stop the plague, but Pharaoh eventually hardens his heart again. His confession seems more like a maneuver than a change of heart. To truly acknowledge the Hebrews' God as the one true God would mean for Pharaoh to humble himself. So far, despite all the suffering he has brought upon himself and his nation, that is something he will not do, or perhaps cannot do.

Then God sends the ninth plague, a deep darkness covering the entire land of Egypt for three days. During all that time the people cannot see each other, and no one moves. Yet where Israel lives, there is light as usual.

Again, Pharaoh maneuvers by bargaining with Moses. He will let the people go and worship their God, but they must leave a deposit—their flocks and herds. Moses insists that the animals must also come. Pharaoh shouts at Moses: *"'Get out of here! I'm warning you. Never come back to see me again! The day you see my face, you will die.' 'Very well,' Moses replied. 'I will never see your face again'"* (Exodus 10:28–29).

The apostle Paul warns in Romans, chapter 1, that when people and nations suppress the knowledge of God that is apparent in nature to all rational people with humble hearts, it causes their minds to become *"dark and confused."* They become fools, worshiping the things God has made instead of worshiping him, and thereby giving themselves over to moral depravity and all manner of antisocial behavior.

Pharaoh has seen more than the evidence of nature and reason; he has seen the power of God firsthand, a power greater than all the false gods of his religion. But even pain and fear cannot soften his heart, so God sees that Pharaoh is beyond repentance. He will not extend further grace to him. Pharaoh has been given nine opportunities to humble himself and recognize the Lord as God, but he refuses. So one more plague is coming, the terrible tenth plague that will finally break Pharaoh.

Focus: Despite God's amazing grace and bountiful patience, it seems that there are those who will refuse these gifts to the very end, like Pharaoh. In Milton's *Paradise Lost,* Satan boasts that he would rather "reign in hell than serve in heaven." This is an astonishing insight into the malignant pride and love of power that can enslave the human mind and heart.

Prayer: *Lord, we praise you for giving us many opportunities to humble ourselves and recognize you alone as God. Forgive us for our idolatry—not for worshiping gods of wood and stone, but for making the good things of life the ultimate things that we run to for comfort and happiness. You alone are worthy of our worship. Only you can fill the hole in our soul. Amen!*

Day 21   Reflection

January 21

When reading the Bible, we encounter a book unlike any other book. It's actually a library of sixty-six books, written by over forty authors in various literary forms, and in three languages—Hebrew, Aramaic and Greek—over a period of 1,400 years. But there is a unity in its astonishing diversity. The Bible is one story about a loving God committed to redeeming his creation.

It is commonly understood that the Bible deals with "holy history." This means that it views history through the specific lens of the story of God's people in the world. In secular history the story of Israel is a short chapter or a footnote, but in the Bible it is front and center. Great ancient nations appear, such as Sumer, Mesopotamia, Egypt, Babylonia, Assyria, Greece and Rome, but only as they impact the story of God's people. In fact, the great cities and nations of the world are almost background noise—ever-present manifestations of human rebellion, arrogance and the lust for power—like mighty Egypt who enslaved the Israelites.

But as the story of Moses and Pharaoh illustrates, the Kingdom of God and the kingdoms of this world are in conflict with one another.

Since the Fall *(Genesis chapter 3),* humans have presumed to usurp the power of God. Mighty empires have come and gone; their ruins are the artifacts of this grasping. From the moment that humans were cast out of Eden, they planted the seeds of their own destruction. Men began to build "fortified cities," meaning cities that are ready for war. Cities became centers where fallen human culture metastasized.

Perhaps the most iconic example is the Tower of Babel. In Genesis 11:4, humans boast: *"Come, let's build a great city for ourselves with a tower that reaches into the sky. This will make us famous and keep us from being scattered all over the world."*

This doesn't mean that God doesn't love cities. In fact, he desires the diversity of human cultures. As we shall see along the way, the vision of Israel's prophets is of redeemed humanity creating redeemed cultures. Cities and nations will no longer be the centers of rebellion, but centers of worship where everything is done for the glory of God.

In Revelation 7:9, we are given a picture of the future when the redeemed peoples of the world are standing before God and Christ, who is the Lamb of God: *"After this I saw a vast crowd, too great to count, from every nation and tribe and people and language, standing in front of the throne and before the Lamb. They were clothed in white robes and held palm branches in their hands."*

Indeed, the New Creation will be like a great city, a New Jerusalem, where God is the center of human life and culture once again. Accordingly, *"He will wipe every tear from their eyes, and there will be no more death or sorrow or crying or pain. All these things are gone forever"* (Revelation 21:4).

In the meantime, which is our time, God continues to work out his plan for our salvation!

Prayer: Lord, it is fascinating to follow the story of your people Israel amidst the great and powerful nations of the world. We know that what you do for them will one day benefit all the people of the world. We long for that great day when you make all things new, and when cities are centers of enterprise that glorify you! Amen.

Day 22   Exodus 11-12

January 22

> Key Text: That night the people of Israel left Rameses and started for Succoth. There were about 600,000 men, plus all the women and children. A rabble of non-Israelites went with them, along with great flocks and herds of livestock. (Exodus 12:37–38)

After an arrogant, stubborn Pharaoh refuses for the ninth time to relieve the suffering of his own people by letting God's people go, the terrible tenth plague is announced: *"I will strike Pharaoh and the land of Egypt with one more blow. After that, Pharaoh will let you leave this country. In fact, he will be so eager to get rid of you that he will force you all to leave"* (Exodus 11:1).

This is an epic conflict, and a revelation to both Israelites and Egyptians of God's awesome power. He is able to protect his people and keep his promises. No earthly power can resist his will. As we read further in the Old Testament, the Exodus will be celebrated by Israel as a defining moment in their relationship with God. It will also be talked about in hushed voices among the local nations.

So what is the final blow to Pharaoh? God says to Moses, *"On that night I will pass through the land of Egypt and strike down every firstborn son and firstborn male animal in the land of Egypt. I will execute judgment against all the gods of Egypt, for I am the Lord! But the blood on your doorposts will serve as a sign, marking the houses where you are staying. When I see the blood, I will pass over you. This plague of death will not touch you when I strike the land of Egypt"* (Exodus 12:12–13).

Even before it happens, God tells Moses how to celebrate his deliverance of Israel for generations to come. It will be called the Passover, and it will stand as "Exhibit A" that God loves his people and is at work in the world on their behalf.

At midnight, God passes over His people and brings judgment upon Egypt: *"Pharaoh and all his officials and all the people of Egypt woke up during the night, and loud wailing was heard throughout the land of*

Egypt. There was not a single house where someone had not died" (Exodus 12:30). It is the wailing of sorrow and anger for the judgment Pharaoh has brought upon them by his persistent, willful defiance of the one true God.

So, on the last day of the 430th year, Israel leaves Egypt. The Lord causes the Egyptian people to look favorably on the Israelites and give them whatever they ask. Think of it as severance pay for generations of slavery. Many Egyptians have come to respect and fear the God of the Hebrews.

The Exodus from slavery in Egypt is a defining moment for Israel. It is also a pointer to a greater Exodus to come. One day, through Jesus, God will deliver us all from a greater slavery—slavery to sin and death. The lambs' blood put on the doorposts of the Hebrew homes, which caused God to "pass over" their homes and save them from judgment, will be fulfilled in the blood of Jesus, by which all people are forgiven and saved from judgment.

Focus: The deliverance of Israel from slavery in Egypt reveals God to be sovereign and all-powerful—a God to be feared. But the greatest manifestation of his power is yet to come: his power over death through the resurrection of Jesus. This is a power that is fueled by love. When the apostle Paul writes to the Christians in Ephesus, he says, *"I also pray that you will understand the incredible greatness of God's power for us who believe him. This is the same mighty power that raised Christ from the dead and seated him in the place of honor at God's right hand in the heavenly realms. Now he is far above any ruler or authority or power or leader or anything else—not only in this world but also in the world to come"* (Ephesians 1:19–21).

Prayer: Lord, we praise you for your mighty power to save us from our sins, just as you delivered your ancient people from slavery in Egypt. As Lord over all earthly and heavenly powers, you are able to watch over your people and bring us safely home to the Promised Land—to the New Heavens and Earth. Amen.

Day 23   Exodus 13-15

> Key Text: "Who is like you among the gods, O Lord—glorious in holiness, awesome in splendor, performing great wonders? You raised your right hand, and the earth swallowed our enemies." (Exodus 15:11–12)

As Moses prepares the people to leave Egypt, Pharaoh broods and seethes with rage over his defeat.

Three million strong, Israel takes an indirect route around Philistine territory to avoid freaking them out and provoking a battle. God is their navigation system on this journey: *"The Lord went ahead of them. He guided them during the day with a pillar of cloud, and he provided light at night with a pillar of fire. This allowed them to travel by day or night"* (Exodus 13:21).

Their erratic route prompts Pharaoh to think that the Israelites are confused and trapped in the wilderness. But, of course, it is Pharaoh who is confused. Enraged by pride, he harnesses his chariot and takes his best fighters and 600 other chariots to chase the Israelites.

Even after all that has happened, Pharaoh persists. I suppose that it is hard to maintain sanity when you think you are a god!

When his chariots catch up to the Israelite camp, it creates the first crisis of faith for the Israelites. They are panicked and turn on Moses: *"Why did you bring us out here to die in the wilderness? ... What have you done to us? Why did you make us leave Egypt? Didn't we tell you this would happen while we were still in Egypt? We said, 'Leave us alone! Let us be slaves to the Egyptians. It's better to be a slave in Egypt than a corpse in the wilderness!'"* (Exodus 14:11–12).

We can be sympathetic with their fear. After all, they have suffered from dehumanizing slavery with its mental and emotional damage—not to mention the trauma of the plagues and the threats of the mighty Pharaoh. The best they can do is to rely on Moses' faith and courage: *"But Moses told the people, 'Don't be afraid. Just stand still and watch the Lord rescue you today. The Egyptians you see today will never be seen again. The Lord himself will fight for you. Just stay calm'"* (Exodus 14:13–14).

Moses does what great leaders do—he gives the people hope and shows the way forward. Turning toward the Red Sea, Moses raises his hand and the Lord opens up a dry path through the water, with a strong east wind blowing all night that turns the seabed into dry land: *"So the people of Israel walked through the middle of the sea on dry ground, with walls of water on each side!"* (Exodus 14:22).

When Pharaoh's chariots follow, Moses raises his hand over the Red Sea again and the waters rush back, drowning the Egyptian army and sweeping them and their chariots out to sea: *"When the people of Israel saw the mighty power that the Lord had unleashed against the Egyptians, they were filled with awe before him. They put their faith in the Lord and in his servant Moses"* (Exodus 14:31).

Then they sing a song to the Lord—three million voices strong—about God's amazing triumph and their faith in him: *"Who is like you among the gods, O Lord—glorious in holiness, awesome in splendor, performing great wonders? You raised your right hand, and the earth swallowed our enemies"* (Exodus 15:11–12).

Can you imagine the volume of that song, thundering across the land and heard by the nearby Canaanites as they shuddered in fear, wondering, "Who is this God of the Israelites?"

Focus: In the ancient Near East, it was believed that each nation, tribe or region had its own god to be placated (henotheism). Moving from one region to another meant coming under the jurisdiction of another god. The measure of a god was his power to defend his region and provide for his people when properly placated. Granting fertility was particularly important since this meant abundant crops and many children. It is not surprising, therefore, that God would reveal himself to Moses, the Israelites and the surrounding nations as a powerful God who defeats his enemies and provides for his people. The defeat of Egypt's gods, and the nature miracle of parting the Red Sea, would have sent a chill throughout the wider region.

Prayer: *Father, who is like you, indeed! Parting the Red Sea is nothing for you who created the whole universe with a word. You are frightening to those who oppose you, but a protector and loving provider to those who love you. What a privilege it is to know and love you! Amen.*

January 24

> Key Text: Then Moses cried out to the Lord, "What should I do with these people? They are ready to stone me!" (Exodus 17:4)

After the Israelites celebrate their deliverance from slavery in Egypt, they begin their semi-nomadic life of *"wandering in the wilderness."* Their wandering will continue for forty years, during which time they will be tutored by God regarding who he is and what he requires of them. Think of it as a School of Discipleship, although sometimes it will seem more like Reform School!

Not surprisingly, as the people adjust to their new circumstances, Moses faces challenges from within and without. The first challenge is complaints about food: *"'If only the Lord had killed us back in Egypt,' they moaned. 'There we sat around pots filled with meat and ate all the bread we wanted. But now you have brought us into this wilderness to starve us all to death'"* (Exodus 16:3).

The second challenge is complaints about water. In both cases, God listens to their complaining and then responds in an extraordinary manner to make it clear that he is able to provide for his people. He gives them water from a rock, along with manna for bread and quail for meat. In each case, he gives only what is needed for one day—their *"daily bread"*—teaching the people to trust him for the next day, and then the next.

There is one exception: On the sixth day, the people are instructed to collect two days' worth of food because the seventh day is to be *"a day of complete rest, a holy Sabbath day set apart for the Lord"* (Exodus 16:23). The Sabbath rest will become a distinctive feature of Israelite life and faith, setting them apart from their neighbors.

The third challenge to Moses comes from without—angry relatives. While the people are encamped at Rephidim, they are attacked by the *"warriors of Amalek."* The Amalekites were a nomadic tribe that had descended from Jacob's brother, Esau. Remember him? He was tricked long ago by his brother out of his birthright and inheritance. But Amalekites never forget!

The attack proves to be a bad move. Joshua leads the Israelites into battle against their attackers and defeats the Amalekite army convincingly. God will condemn the Amalekites for this act of treachery against their brothers, but that is a story for later.

In addition to dealing with complainers and attackers, Moses has another problem. He has undertaken the impossible task of settling the disputes that arise between quarreling parties of Israelites. With all these people, it is like having one "Judge Judy" to service all the disputes in a group the size of a major American city!

He's wearing himself out, so Jethro, his father-in-law, gives him some organizational wisdom in chapter 18. Moses should continue to intercede in prayer for the people and teach them God's decrees so that they know how to conduct their lives. But he should appoint and train a large group of capable, honest and God-fearing men to resolve the people's disputes. Fortunately, Moses listens to his father-in-law and spares himself an emotional breakdown.

In these chapters, we learn that the exhilaration of God's miraculous deliverance is no substitute for the ongoing difficult lessons of faith and discipleship. We sense here that there are plenty more lessons coming!

Focus: Every leader has to deal with complaints and opposition, especially a transformational leader of a great movement, like Moses. The Israelites are overwhelmed and afraid by what has happened to them, and wonder what is next. They are literally and metaphorically entering new territory. They must learn to trust Moses by trusting God who called Moses to lead them out of Egypt into an unknown future. Moses wisely listens to advice about delegating responsibility and then devoting himself to the most important things he must do. God calls us, respectively, to be good leaders and good followers.

Prayer: *Lord, thanks for your incredible patience with our complaining about the circumstances of our life. The truth is, we complain because we are afraid, and we are afraid because we lack faith. Teach us to trust you for our daily bread. Amen.*

January 25

> Key Text: Then God gave the people all these instructions: "I am the Lord your God, who rescued you from the land of Egypt, the place of your slavery. You must not have any other god but me." (Exodus 20:1–2)

Two months after the Israelites leave Egypt, they arrive at the wilderness of Sinai and set up camp at the base of Mount Sinai. There, Moses climbs the mountain to appear before God.

Moses has been performing a priestly function for Israel, meaning that he goes before Holy God on behalf of the sinful people, and then back to the sinful people on behalf of Holy God. This is an arrangement that God initiates and makes possible, since Moses is just as much a sinner as the people themselves. Later on, God will establish a full-blown priesthood to facilitate the worship of the people, but Moses will remain in his privileged position as God's spokesman until he dies.

On Mount Sinai, God tells Moses to give these instructions to the people: *"You have seen what I did to the Egyptians. You know how I carried you on eagles' wings and brought you to myself. Now if you will obey me and keep my covenant, you will be my own special treasure from among all the peoples on earth; for all the earth belongs to me. And you will be my kingdom of priests, my holy nation"* (Exodus 19:4–6).

Moses takes these instructions to the people and calls for their affirmation: *"All the people responded together, 'We will do everything the Lord has commanded.' So Moses brought the people's answer back to the Lord"* (Exodus 19:8).

What God has proposed, and the people have accepted, is a covenant relationship. To be more precise, it is a further development of the covenant relationship God began with Abraham back in Genesis 12. This covenant will be called the "Mosaic Covenant" because Moses mediates it. We know it as the Old Testament.

A covenant is a mutual commitment to be in a relationship under the terms specified, not unlike a marriage covenant. It's important to understand that such an idea was unheard of in the ancient Near East. No god or gods of the people's imagination had ever loved people or wanted to be in relationship with them. So Israel's covenant with God—along with the idea of monotheism—is a revelation. It is a paradigm shift of epic proportions in human understanding, and will profoundly shape the development of human history.

God's covenant proposal to Israel is a relationship motivated by love, and established by his act of redeeming the people from slavery in Egypt. Israel was indeed God's "chosen people," but not because they were better than other people or somehow more worthy. They were chosen simply because it pleased God to do so.

Israel's part is to trust God and demonstrate their faith by keeping his commandments. We should understand that Israel becomes God's people by grace through faith.

In chapter 20, Moses presents the Ten Commandments, which outline the stipulations of the covenant relationship. The first four commandments describe the people's responsibilities to God, and the final six, their responsibilities to one another. They express the character of God and his will for human life—a way of life that makes a just and loving community possible.

Though they are generally stated in the negative—don't do this or that—they imply a positive action. For example: don't steal, but respect your neighbor's property; don't commit adultery, but respect the holy bond of marriage, etc. Think of the commandments as boundaries, outside of which lie conflict, injustice, and antisocial behavior, but within which lies immense opportunity to do good and show love.

The effect of the commandments is to set Israel apart from the religious practices and moral behavior of the surrounding nations. They demonstrate a new way of being human in a fallen world.

In summary, the Ten Commandments function as a moral constitution that informs and shapes Israel's life and witness.

> **Focus:** By keeping the Ten Commandments, Israel will worship God properly, and also be able to live in community with one another. The commandments are an elaboration of the general call for all Israelites to love God with all their heart, soul, mind and strength, and also to love their neighbors as themselves. They are not meant to stifle human life, but to allow it to flourish.

> **Prayer:** *Lord, how amazing it is that you, the eternal, infinite God—Creator of the universe—deeply desire to have a relationship with us! Help us to get to know you more, that we may worship you with understanding and gratefulness. Amen!*

January 26

> **Key Text:** "You must not worship the gods of these nations or
> serve them in any way or imitate their evil practices. Instead,
> you must utterly destroy them and smash their sacred pillars."
> (Exodus 23:24)

The pagan gods of the ancient world were understood to be indifferent and even hostile towards humans. In this context, Israel's belief that God loved them, and wanted to dwell among them by means of a mutual covenant, was astonishing. It was a shift of epic proportions away from paganism!

As such, the Covenant is God's initiative; it arises out of his own nature. The Old Testament hints at, and the New Testament more clearly reveals, that the Lord God is one God, yet he exists as three distinct persons—Father, Son and Holy Spirit. This means that God exists in community within himself, and not in isolation. He is not a unit, but a unity of persons.

Therefore, his desire to enter into relationship with his creation is an extension of his way of being. Or to put it another way, it is an invitation for Israel to share his own life—a life of love and unity.

By this covenant relationship, God promises to bless Israel, and in turn Israel promises to keep his commandments, which outline her responsibilities to God and one another.

The first three commandments forbid worshiping other gods, forbid the use of idols in worship, and forbid the misuse of God's name. *"Misusing his name"* means to claim his authority or approval for something contrary to his nature or will. The nature and dangers of idolatry will be further developed theologically as we move along in the Old Testament. For now, it is enough to know that a false understanding of God not only dishonors God, it also undermines human flourishing.

The Fourth Commandment about keeping the Sabbath reminds us that we were created for fellowship with God, not just for work. Moses grounds this Sabbath theology in the story of creation. In Genesis 1 and 2, God creates for six days and then rests on the seventh to enjoy his creation.

So the Sabbath commandment reminds us why we were created, and that our lives will be blessed when God is kept at the center.

Commandments 5 through 10 identify our moral responsibilities to our neighbors. As we have already noted, they are stated in the negative to serve as moral boundaries. Crossing the boundaries is self-defeating because it undermines the life God has intended for us. In particular, it disrupts community.

However, within the boundaries of honoring family and respecting human life, the sanctity of marriage, personal possessions, truth-telling, and happiness for others' success, there is plenty of room to enjoy life and maintain community.

Moses will apply the moral standard of the Ten Commandments to specific laws that will bring moral clarity to specific situations, resolve conflicts, provide for justice and generally guide the lives of the people.

Chapters 21 through 23 contain many examples of these laws. Although some of the specific laws are strange and even offensive to us, they did reflect the thinking of the ancient world which Israel occupied, and therefore made perfect sense to them.

The laws reflect the principles of proportionate justice and restitution when the rights of others have been violated. The principle *"an eye for an eye, a tooth for a tooth"* (Exodus 21:24) has been criticized by some, but the idea of proportionate justice was a huge moral step forward from the mindless revenge commonly practiced in that time.

In chapter 24, the covenant relationship is embraced by the people: *"Then [Moses] took the Book of the Covenant and read it aloud to the people. Again they all responded, 'We will do everything the Lord has commanded. We will obey'"* (Exodus 24:7).

It is important to understand that Israel considered the Covenant and commandments to be expressions of God's love for them. The moral and spiritual life expressed in the commandments outlined what it meant to be God's people. It was a different and more difficult way, compared with the wildly immoral way of the Canaanites. But when followed, it enabled Israel to flourish as a people, demonstrating a way of life and an understanding of God that has transformed human civilizations for thousands of years.

Focus: The moral law of Israel reflects insights into human life and behavior that many cultures have intuitively discerned, in some form, through reason and life

52

experience. The Golden Rule of *"do unto others as you would have them do unto you"* resonates with people of all times and places, even if it has not been consistently practiced. This should not surprise us; we are all created in God's image, even if fallen. The apostle Paul writes that *"even Gentiles, who do not have God's written law, show that they know his law when they instinctively obey it, even without having heard it. They demonstrate that God's law is written in their hearts..."* (Romans 2:14–15).

Prayer: *Lord, it is amazing that you, Almighty God, desire to have a relationship with us! We thank you for this honor. Thank you also for your commandments, because they show us how to live successfully and experience your blessing. Amen.*

Day 27   Exodus 25-27

January 27

> Key Text: **"When the Ark is finished, place inside it the stone tablets inscribed with the terms of the covenant, which I will give to you."** (Exodus 25:16)

Having established his relationship with Israel by means of covenant and commandments, God now directs the people to build a portable worship space, called a tabernacle or tent, whereby he may be personally present to them: *"Have the people of Israel build me a holy sanctuary so I can live among them. You must build this Tabernacle and its furnishings exactly according to the pattern I will show you"* (Exodus 25:8–9).

The Tabernacle is to be funded by the *"sacred offerings"* of the people whose hearts are moved to offer them. No one is forced to participate; it is to be a love offering. And why not give? Who would not be utterly amazed and honored to learn that God wants to move into their neighborhood?!

Chapters 25 through 27 contain the detailed specifications for the dimensions, design and materials for the Tabernacle. To be honest, it is pretty mind-numbing to read unless you are a general contractor and love to read architectural drawings!

But if you think of it as God moving "into the neighborhood" and designing the house he wants to live in, then it gets a lot more interesting. It reveals, first of all, the way that God will live among his people. Since his people are semi-nomadic for the moment, his house will need to be easily assembled, disassembled and transported from place to place—

like a mobile home!

For Israel, this means that God will go with them anywhere they move. He's already hinted at this by being their travel agent, guiding them by a pillar of clouds by day, and a pillar of fire by night *(Exodus 13:20–22)*.

This may seem a mundane point to us, but in the context of the ancient Near Eastern belief in territorial gods, it is significant. It was believed that each territory had its own god who exercised power within its borders. Move outside the borders and you lose your cell phone coverage, so to speak. So, God is saying to Israel, by means of the portable Tabernacle, that he gives coverage anywhere they go! He is the Creator of everything, so the whole world belongs to him!

A further point of interest is God's insistence that they build the Tabernacle and its furnishings exactly according to the pattern he gave them. This suggests that the specifications for the dimensions, design and materials for the Tabernacle—as well as the instructions for moving it—are a message in themselves about who God is and how he wants to be worshiped.

It is a unique insight of Judeo-Christian thought that God can be understood and experienced within the material world, without himself being part of the material world. The world is not God, but is his handiwork. It reflects God in the way that a painting reflects an artist, but is not the artist him- or herself. One can gain insight into the mind of Michelangelo, for example, by studying his art. This idea is expressed in many ways in the Bible. For example, Psalm 19 begins: *"The heavens proclaim the glory of God. The skies display his craftsmanship. Day after day they continue to speak; night after night they make him known. They speak without a sound or word; their voice is never heard. Yet their message has gone throughout the earth, and their words to all the world."*

Moses is fully aware, of course, that God cannot be contained within any human construction. Indeed, the whole world cannot contain him. But the Tabernacle is the place where infinite God humbles himself to come close to his people. It is the place where heaven and earth meet. And of course—you've probably already thought of this—it points forward to the time when God will go "all in" to be with us, by becoming human in Jesus Christ.

Focus: Contrary to the Indiana Jones movies, the legendary "Ark of the Covenant" is not a magic box giving eternal life. Instead, it contains the terms of the

Covenant which makes a relationship with God possible—and, in that sense, brings eternal life. The Lord told Moses to put the Ark of the Covenant in the Tabernacle, and from there he would meet with Moses. God's gracious initiative in committing himself to us, is what makes a relationship possible. It is all his doing; it is all of grace and not human merit.

Prayer: Lord, we rejoice that you want to live among us! You are not a God who is far away, unconcerned and uninvolved. This means that when we ask, you give; when we seek, we find; when we knock, you open the door. We don't deserve the honor of your presence, but we do give thanks for your always being there for us! Amen.

Day 28   Reflection

January 28

Our thoughts thus far on the Ten Commandments, and on the civil and ceremonial laws that arise from them, bring to mind one of the common misunderstandings of the Bible. Some claim that in the Old Testament people are made right with God by keeping the Law, but in the New Testament they are made right with God by grace through faith.

This is a faulty reading of both the Old and New Testaments. There is law and grace in both the Old and New Testaments, and each has a role in our lives.

Regarding grace, the people of God have always been made right with God by grace through faith alone. Long before the Ten Commandments were given, Abraham was made right with God by his faith: *"And Abram believed the Lord, and the Lord counted him as righteous because of his faith"* (Genesis 15:6).

This is the clear teaching of the New Testament as well. Ephesians 2:8–10, for example, says: *"God saved you by his grace when you believed. And you can't take credit for this; it is a gift from God. Salvation is not a reward for the good things we have done, so none of us can boast about it. For we are God's masterpiece. He has created us anew in Christ Jesus, so we can do the good things he planned for us long ago."*

When Adam and Eve sinned against God, they unleashed sin and death like a virus into the human race. From that time forward, everyone was born with a nature bent toward sin, incapable of attaining the righteousness God requires. Spiritually speaking, the human race barely has a pulse. And, of course, everyone physically dies.

Thankfully, God's righteous judgment of the human race was satisfied by his gracious act of taking the debt of our sin upon himself through Christ. It's important to understand that the benefits of Christ's atoning death apply backwards as well as forwards. This means that God had Christ in mind from the very moment he moved to redeem his fallen creation after the Fall. In fact, Ephesians 1:4 suggests that God had Christ in mind before he even made the world.

This means that everyone, everywhere, and at all times, is made right with God in the same way—by Christ's death on the cross. This is the grace of God!

So then, what about the Law and commandments? It's clear that God didn't give them as a means to attain righteousness. He knew that Israel couldn't keep them perfectly, because along with the Law and commandments, he instructed Israel to establish a priesthood and sacrificial system to provisionally remove human guilt when the Law was violated.

But even if the Law cannot make us righteous, it serves an important diagnostic purpose. It names sin for what it is and thereby shows us that we are sinners in need of grace. In fact, the demands of the Law actually stir up resistance in us, just like a sign saying "Don't walk on the grass" makes us want to walk on the grass!

In the New Testament, the apostle Paul reveals, from his own efforts as a zealous Jew, that the Law could not save him. Instead, it has revealed his moral powerlessness. In a moment of remarkable transparency, he confesses: "*I know that nothing good lives in me, that is, in my sinful nature. I want to do what is right, but I can't. I want to do what is good, but I don't. I don't want to do what is wrong, but I do it anyway*" (Romans 7:18–19).

So what about the present-day relevance of the civil and ceremonial laws of Moses? These were applications of the Ten Commandments specifically for the national life of Israel. They were therefore provisional. So don't worry about cooking a young goat in its mother's milk! *(Exodus 23:19)*

However, the Ten Commandments continue as the moral vision and boundary for the New Testament believer. Their wise instruction still outlines our responsibility to God and our neighbor. And though we need to apply careful moral reasoning, seasoned by grace, they continue to show the way to human flourishing in the complexities of the contemporary world.

The disheartening recognition that we can't perfectly keep the Law has a good purpose, however. It pushes us to grace, where we find the forgiveness that we don't deserve, and receive the righteousness that we could never attain for ourselves!

As Martin Luther said, we need to hear from the Law the bad news about our sin, before we are able to hear the Good News about God's grace.

> *Prayer: Lord, thank you for your commandments, which reveal your will for our lives and force us to admit that we cannot consistently do your will. But in our powerlessness and hopelessness, you offer us your grace! May we accept it with humility and gratefulness. Amen!*

Day 29   Exodus 18-31

January 29

> Key Text: "Make sacred garments for Aaron that are glorious and beautiful. Instruct all the skilled craftsmen whom I have filled with the spirit of wisdom. Have them make garments for Aaron that will distinguish him as a priest set apart for my service." (Exodus 28:2–3)

After providing instructions for building the Tabernacle as a place of worship, God now instructs Moses about the priests who will serve the people as leaders of worship. Moses' brother Aaron and his descendants are chosen by God to serve as priests.

In chapter 28, detailed instructions for priestly garments are given. The garments express skill, beauty and spiritual symbolism. Interestingly, Aaron is given two flat stones, called the Urim and the Thummim *(Exodus 28:30).* Apparently, these are used to determine the will of God when things aren't clear, like the toss of a coin or the throw of dice. Each stone, it is theorized, had a "yes" and "no" side. This meant that three outcomes were possible when both stones were tossed: yes, no, and a "no decision" (when a yes and no both came up). Perhaps the Urim and Thummim served the same purpose as a vote of the House when there is no consensus on a matter.

This suggests that God can make his will known through actions of chance, or through a majority vote.

Chapter 29 outlines the ceremony of consecration and ordination of the priests, concluding with a fresh promise by God to be present to Israel by means of the Tabernacle and priests: *"I will meet the people of Israel there, in the place made holy by my glorious presence. Yes, I will consecrate the Tabernacle and the altar, and I will consecrate Aaron and his sons to serve me as priests. Then I will live among the people of Israel and be their God, and they will know that I am the Lord their God. I am the one who brought them out of the land of Egypt so that I could live among them. I am the Lord their God"* (Exodus 29:43–46).

Chapter 30 lists a number of responsibilities for the priests, emphasizing that these actions and tasks express, in their symbolism, the principle of holiness.

Chapter 31 gives instructions for the craftsmen God has chosen to build the Tabernacle and its utensils and furnishings. It is fascinating to learn that the craftsmen serve God through their skills, by the power of the Spirit of God: *"Then the Lord said to Moses, 'Look, I have specifically chosen Bezalel son of Uri, grandson of Hur, of the tribe of Judah. I have filled him with the Spirit of God, giving him great wisdom, ability, and expertise in all kinds of crafts'"* (Exodus 31:1–3).

These instructions make clear what is implied in the larger theology of creation, that artistry is a gift of God and a means to worshiping him. All forms of art, including music, drama, literature, dance—and modern television and filmmaking—are legitimate means by which to create beauty for the glory of God, and also to comment on the human condition.

Finally, God tells Moses to remind the people of their Sabbath responsibilities: *"Tell the people of Israel: 'Be careful to keep my Sabbath day, for the Sabbath is a sign of the covenant between me and you from generation to generation. It is given so you may know that I am the Lord, who makes you holy. You must keep the Sabbath day, for it is a holy day for you'"* (Exodus 31:12–14).

What strikes me about these chapters is the way God employs art, craftsmanship, beauty and symbolism—including the symbolism of the Sabbath day rest—to reveal his holy nature, his covenant love for Israel, and through Israel, his love for the whole world.

Focus: The detailed building plans for the Tabernacle and its prescribed furnishings, together with the dress of the priesthood and the elaborate rituals they must perform, give testimony to the importance of artistic creation in the Judeo-Christian faith. There are some realities that are grasped through narrative and explanation, but others that are grasped through illustration, symbol and liturgy. These gifts give us an immediate experience of transcendence, which explanation is incapable of.

Prayer: Lord, we thank you for the way we experience you in material ways. The beauty and symbolism of art, music and liturgy speak to us in ways that ordinary words cannot. Indeed, the whole of nature declares your glory. Teach us to look and listen! Amen.

Day 30 — Exodus 32-34

January 30

> **Key Text: The Lord told Moses, "Quick! Go down the mountain! Your people whom you brought from the land of Egypt have corrupted themselves. How quickly they have turned away from the way I commanded them to live!"** (Exodus 32:7–8)

God's Covenant with Israel has been established. The people have given their vow of fidelity to God. The terms of the Covenant have been inscribed on two stone tablets and given to Moses while he is on Mount Sinai.

All is well—*or is it?*

Apparently, the people have grown anxious because Moses has been on the mountain for a long time. They conclude that he must be dead, so they quickly lose faith and regress back to old pagan habits from their days in Egypt: *"'Come on,' they said* [to Aaron]*, 'make us some gods who can lead us. We don't know what happened to this fellow Moses, who brought us here from the land of Egypt'"* (Exodus 32:1).

"This fellow Moses"? They are already distancing themselves from their great leader? It's not hard to dislike these people. But there is an opportunity here for Aaron to step up and boldly bring the people back to their senses as God's Covenant people! But Aaron does NOT "boldly go where no man has gone before." Instead, he goes back to where he came from. He creates an Egyptian idol in the shape of a calf! When the people see it, they exclaim: *"O Israel, these are the gods who brought you out of*

the land of Egypt!"

It's breathtaking how quickly the people violate the First and Second Commandments that they have just vowed to obey—no other gods and no worshiping idols. But old ways of thinking and behaving are hard to change, so the people *"celebrated with feasting and drinking, and they indulged in pagan revelry"* (Exodus 32:6).

God sees their revelry and is really angry. After all he has done to prove himself to them, who can blame him? He tells Moses: *"Quick! Go down the mountain because the people are corrupting themselves."* He threatens to start over again with a new chosen people, but Moses begs God to remember his Covenant and not give the Egyptians the opportunity to mock him, saying that he rescued the Israelites from Egypt only to slaughter them in the mountains.

At least Moses fears God, so God changes his mind in response to Moses' prayer.

When Moses goes down the mountain, he hears the wild carousing of God's people worshiping idols, much to the amusement of their neighboring enemies. Moses confronts Aaron, but Aaron weakly blames the people, claiming that the golden calf they are worshiping just magically appeared: *"So I told them, 'Whoever has gold jewelry, take it off.' When they brought it to me, I simply threw it into the fire—and out came this calf!"* (Exodus 32:24).

Nice try, Aaron.

Moses is understandably shaken by this incident. He fears that the people's lack of faith and their betrayal of the Covenant will cause God to remove his presence from among them. But God hears his prayer and reassures Moses that he will continue with them. He then reveals his glory to Moses, and Moses sees that God is indeed merciful and compassionate.

God is not a vengeful warrior, but neither is he a sentimental old fool. His love is fierce and dangerous to those who trifle with him.

Those who are responsible for inciting the people to idolatry are given capital punishment, and the Lord sends sickness among the rest. So the people experience God's judgment for their sins, but they also receive his forgiveness, meaning that he will not abandon them. The New Testament book of Hebrews will look back on this incident as an expression of God's tough love: *"My child, don't make light of the Lord's discipline, and don't give up when he corrects you. For the Lord disciplines those he loves, and he punishes each one he accepts as his child"* (Hebrews 12:5–6).

So we learn that this forty-year journey in the wilderness is not going to be a walk in the park. It's going to be more like a Special Forces boot camp!

Focus: People who treat God as nothing more than an idea—an object of study—have a hard time imagining him to be a person who would get angry, let alone jealous. But even allowing for some anthropomorphism in the Bible's descriptions of God, it is still clear that the God of the Bible is a Person of passion. He has intense feelings for his people, and reacts with fierce jealousy when his people worship other gods!

Prayer: Lord, you have made us in your image to represent you on earth now, with a view to ruling with you in the New Creation. Yet, we often behave as if we don't take our calling seriously. We easily choose the Golden Calf. Forgive us for this serious sin, and reveal your fierce love so that we may see you for who you are. Amen.

Day 31   Exodus 35-40

January 31

Key Text: Then the Lord said to Moses, "Set up the Tabernacle on the first day of the new year. Place the Ark of the Covenant inside, and install the inner curtain to enclose the Ark within the Most Holy Place." (Exodus 40:1–3)

The book of Exodus closes with a detailed account of the construction of the Tabernacle—the place where God will be present to his people and meet them in worship.

Before construction begins, Moses reminds the people of the Sabbath commandment. Worshiping God is not about a building, *but a relationship*, and the Sabbath day reminds Israel that the covenant relationship is at the heart of their identity and calling.

How serious is this to God? Violation of the Sabbath is considered a capital offense. As treason is the ultimate betrayal of one's country, so Sabbath-breaking is the ultimate betrayal of Israel's Covenant with God. We have already seen that the people are weak in faith, stubborn, and complaining, easily sliding back into idol worship. The stakes are high, so the punishment is severe.

It is hard for modern sensibility to accept this, but there are values more important than individual rights. When an individual threatens the wider community by encouraging cynicism and unbelief among others—thereby putting them at spiritual risk—the individual forfeits their rights. Secular states don't believe this, of course, and there should not be misguided attempts to associate secular government with the Kingdom of God.

Nevertheless, for Israel and for the Church, God judges by a higher standard.

In chapters 35 through 39, skilled craftsmen and artisans are put to work after a fundraiser is held to secure the Tabernacle materials—precious metals, stones, and cloth for the priestly clothing. It is a great success: *"So the people of Israel followed all of the Lord's instructions to Moses. Then Moses inspected all their work. When he found it had been done just as the Lord had commanded him, he blessed them"* (Exodus 39:42–43).

Then in chapter 40, God tells Moses to assemble everything and place the Ark of the Covenant, which contains the stone tablets inscribed with the terms of the Covenant, inside the innermost curtained area, the Most Holy Place. The furnishings are set in their proper places and everything is anointed with oil to consecrate them to the Lord's service, thereby making them holy *(Exodus 40:4–9).*

Finally, Aaron and his sons are dressed with the sacred garments and consecrated to serve God as priests: *"With their anointing, Aaron's descendants are set apart for the priesthood forever, from generation to generation"* (Exodus 40:15).

Moses then makes a burnt offering and a grain offering, just as the Lord had commanded him. Everything has been done exactly as specified by God. Now, everyone waits: *"Then the cloud covered the Tabernacle, and the glory of the Lord filled the Tabernacle. Moses could no longer enter the Tabernacle because the cloud had settled down over it, and the glory of the Lord filled the Tabernacle"* (Exodus 40:34–35).

It is an overwhelming sight and fearful moment. The physical manifestation of God's holy presence by means of a glowing fire inside a cloud is too much for even Moses to see. The glorious "cloud" of God's presence will serve as a mechanism of his guidance, as well as a revelation of his presence: *"Now whenever the cloud lifted from the Tabernacle, the people of Israel would set out on their journey, following it. But if the cloud did not rise, they remained where they were until it lifted"* (Exodus 40:36–37).

The presence of God among the people in his Tabernacle points forward to the time when the glory of God will be revealed face-to-face in the person of Jesus. John 1:14 says of Jesus: *"So the Word became human and made his home* [literally 'tabernacled'] *among us. He was full of unfailing love and faithfulness."*

> **Focus:** The glorious presence of God filling the Tabernacle is one of the great moments of the Old Testament. His tangible presence is a manifestation of his greatness—his glory. With respect to God, the word "glory" is not only a noun, but also a verb (glorify) and an adjective (glorious). To see God's glory is glorious, and our intuitive response is to glorify him! His glorious presence on earth is evidence that God not only wants a relationship with us, but also wants to live among us in the material realm he has created. The greatest manifestation of God's glory will come in the Incarnation: *"And we have seen his glory, the glory of the Father's one and only Son"* (John 1:14).

> **Prayer:** *Father, in our skeptical, casual world, we easily forget that you are an awesome and glorious God—and were we to see you as you truly are, we would not survive. Thank you for sending Jesus as a human being so that we can truly see you through his words and deeds. Amen.*

Day 32   Leviticus 1–3

February 1

> Key Text: The Lord called to Moses from the Tabernacle and said to him, "Give the following instructions to the people of Israel." (Leviticus 1:1–2)

The book of Leviticus gets its name from the Hebrew tribe of Levi, to whom God entrusted the ceremonies of worship and the physical care of the Tabernacle.

It is a ponderous book by any account, because it is mostly instruction about offerings, the functions of priests and the regulations required for the people to be a "holy nation." So there is little narrative action, unlike the book of Exodus. However, there is plenty of theology.

The main focus of Leviticus is how a holy God reconciles himself to sinful people and a broken world. This question is at the heart of God's ancient Promise to Abraham to make things right in the world. To this end, Leviticus covers in some detail how Holy God defines sin, forgives sin and helps people avoid sinning. It discusses how God's will is revealed, and how God's presence can be assured.

Leviticus also describes how God's people may be declared holy. Holiness has to do with the nature and character of God. For a believer to be holy means to be conformed to God's character. Ultimately (as we will see in the New Testament), it means to be like Christ, who is the perfect expression of humanity as God intended.

As we have already seen, the Israelites are not holy in all their behavior. Far from it. But they are first *declared to be holy* by God, meaning that he makes them so in principle first, so that they can progressively become so in fact as they keep his moral and ritual commandments as outlined and agreed to in the Covenant.

Leviticus begins, in chapters 1–3, with instructions concerning the various burnt offerings to be given to God. The instructions for the animal sacrifices are revealing. First, the animal offered must be without defect, symbolizing perfection or innocence. Second, the person making the offering must lay his hands upon the animal's head, symbolizing substitution—the innocent animal for the guilty human. Then, the animal is put to death, taking the judgment for sin upon itself. In this way, Leviticus says to the people, *"the Lord will accept its death in your place to purify you, making you right with him"* (Leviticus 1:4).

By means of the burnt offerings, Israel learns the seriousness of sin and the moral debt it incurs. Because God is holy, he cannot ignore sin or say that it doesn't matter. Justice must be satisfied. Most people understand this. When a great injustice has been done to us or to someone we love, we want justice to be restored. Though some deny it, we inhabit a moral universe that echoes God's own character. For human life to be bearable, there needs to be justice.

But thankfully, God is not only just, he is also loving and gracious. As noted above, he provides a way for his people to be forgiven for their sins by means of the offerings. The priestly ministry, together with the sacrificial system, will burn into Israel's corporate memory the principle of substitution and atonement.

This will prepare Israel for that future day when a man named John the Baptist will reveal what all this is leading up to. He will point to Jesus and say to Israel: *"Look! The Lamb of God who takes away the sin of the world!"* (John 1:29). And a few years after that, the apostle Peter will write: *"Christ suffered for our sins once for all time. He never sinned, but he died for sinners to bring you safely home to God"* (1 Peter 3:18).

One day, the priesthood, sacrifices and Tabernacle will go away because they will have served their purpose of preparing us for Christ.

Focus: Levitical laws about the Tabernacle, priesthood, sacrifices, liturgies, moral scruples and ceremonial cleanness may seem far removed from our ways, but they address the same issues we struggle with as modern people: Is there forgiveness for sin? What is righteousness? How do we worship God? How shall we live?

Prayer: Lord, thank you for the greatest gift we could imagine—your Son dying in our place on the cross, to pay the debt of our sin. Your gracious forgiveness lifts the burden of guilt and hopelessness from our hearts. It sets us free to live life with gratefulness and hope. We praise your holy name! Amen.

Day 33   Leviticus 4–7

February 2

> Key Text: The Lord gave these instructions to Moses on Mount Sinai when he commanded the Israelites to present their offerings to the Lord in the wilderness of Sinai. (Leviticus 7:38)

To put the complicated book of Leviticus in perspective, let's review where we've come so far:

Genesis is about beginnings: the beginning of the heavens and earth; the beginning of sin and death; the beginning of Israel through whom God plans to make things right in the world.

Exodus is about God rescuing Abraham's descendants from slavery in Egypt, showing himself to be Almighty God—the God who redeems his people.

Leviticus is about God telling Israel what kind of people he expects them to be. They must be holy because he is holy. He is preparing them to live in the land he will give them as his holy people.

To that end, they are first given instruction in how to worship God properly. The offerings, elaborate rituals and symbolism remind the people that access to God is on his terms only and not according to their own whims. Later in Leviticus, the people are shown how to worship God in their sexual behavior and social practices.

Chapters 1 through 3 outline three kinds of offerings: the burnt offering—*for giving thanks or praying*; the grain offering—*for praying or praising*; and the peace offering—*for fellowshipping with the Lord.* Now chapters 4 through 7 add the sin offering—*for repairing one's relationship with the Lord*; and the guilt offering—*for repairing one's relationship with God in more serious matters.*

God's holiness is an impossibly high standard for sinful people, of course. But it is implied that Israel can make progress in holiness in this life because God is with them, teaching them what is required and giving them his blessing as they seek to honor him. When they do fall short, the specified offerings make it possible for them to be reconciled with God.

We should not be put off by these practices. Many are provisional and time-bound for Israel as a nation. While confusing—and sometimes offensive—to us, they are culturally relevant to the Israelites. The requirements of the Ten Commandments, however, are timeless. They express what it means to love God and then to love one's neighbor. The goal of biblical interpretation is to bridge the gap between then and now. This includes determining what is provisional or culturally contained, and what is universal and perpetually applicable.

So what does Leviticus teach us about holiness? It teaches us that holiness means, above all, that we belong to God and are therefore set apart for his use.

This is what the apostle Paul means when he writes, *"And so, dear brothers and sisters, I plead with you to give your bodies to God because of all he has done for you. Let them be a living and holy sacrifice—the kind he will find acceptable. This is truly the way to worship him. Don't copy the behavior and customs of this world, but let God transform you into a new person by changing the way you think"* (Romans 12:1–2).

And so, by moral purity, spiritual faithfulness, and dedication to doing God's will, we are to be different from the fallen culture around us.

Focus: To be holy—set apart for God—is to experience the joy of fellowship with God. It also means that we experience resistance. We are different. We swim upstream against a world in rebellion against God. The world calls us to live for ourselves, whereas God calls us to live for him. This creates unavoidable tension, even danger. Therefore, one of the things Jesus prayed for on our behalf was safety. He acknowledged to the Father that the world would hate us because we don't belong to the world *(John 17:13–15).*

Prayer: *Lord, we are completely over our heads in trying to be holy. We cannot do it in our own strength. Our sinful nature is like the force of gravity, pulling us* *toward selfishness and pride. Teach us to listen to, and lean on, your Holy Spirit in us, for it is he who causes us to desire and do your will. Amen.*

Day 34 Leviticus 8–10

February 3

> Key Text: Fire blazed forth from the Lord's presence and consumed the burnt offering and the fat on the altar. When the people saw this, they shouted with joy and fell face down on the ground. (Leviticus 9:24)

Leviticus now moves from instruction about sacrifices to instruction about the consecration of priests, the ministry of priests, and finally the behaviors that will disqualify priests from ministry.

In chapter 8, Aaron and his sons are consecrated to their ministry as priests. The ceremony is rich with symbolism: *"Then he poured some of the anointing oil on Aaron's head, anointing him and making him holy for his work"* (Leviticus 8:12). Anointing with oil symbolizes consecration, or the setting aside for special service to the Lord. This priestly symbolism will one day reach its final expression in Jesus, the "anointed one" of God, who is our great High Priest.

After Aaron and his sons are thus consecrated in chapter 8, the inaugural service in the Tabernacle is held. Guided by Moses, *"Aaron presented the offerings of the people. He slaughtered the people's goat and presented it as an offering for their sin, just as he had first done with the offering for his own sin"* (Leviticus 9:15).

Notice that the priest, who intercedes for the people before God, is himself a sinner needing forgiveness. This is an important principle of spiritual leadership. Leaders who see themselves as different from or better than the people they lead are in grave danger of pride and even the abuse of power.

But leaders who humbly and obediently serve for the sake of others are a conduit of blessing, helping believers experience God's powerful presence with joyous worship.

After Aaron completes his offering in the Tabernacle on behalf of the people, he and Moses bless the people. Then *"the glory of the Lord appeared to the whole community. Fire blazed forth from the Lord's presence and consumed the burnt offering and the fat on the altar. When the people saw this, they shouted with joy and fell face down on the ground"* (Leviticus 9:23–24).

The visual and auditory impact of the blazing fire, along with the strong smell of animals cooking on the altar, gives the strong impression of God's presence and his pleasure with what they have done. In response, the people are overcome with joy.

Sadly, in chapter 10, Aaron's sons Nadab and Abihu violate their position as priests by acting disrespectfully, willfully disregarding the careful instructions for worship given by God. It shows that they do not take God seriously. So another fire blazes at the altar, but this time a fire of judgment. By playing with fire, they are themselves burned up and die near the altar, before the Lord. Their sin, and God's judgment upon them, serve as a warning that leaders will be held to a high standard of accountability, lest they dishonor God and mislead the people.

Aaron, the father of Nadab and Abihu, is horrified by the event, and remains silent. He and his other sons are warned by Moses not to take the Lord's instructions lightly. Moses then reminds them: *"You must distinguish between what is sacred and what is common, between what is ceremonially unclean and what is clean"* (Leviticus 10:10).

We may find it hard to understand why ceremonial purity laws were taken so seriously. Their seriousness lay in the fact that they were given to affirm that Israel belonged to God. When Israel followed the ceremonies, she was set apart from other nations. They also call attention and pay respect to the holiness of God. Ceremonial purity by itself wasn't enough, of course, but the outward ritual helped establish and maintain the inward reality of a life fully devoted to God.

Focus: It is a curious fact that people who show great respect for worldly dangers, such as wild animals or precipices or riptides at the beach, show such disrespect for the commandments of God. It is foolish not to fear God. As C.S. Lewis expresses it in his Narnia stories, Aslan, the lion who represents God, is *"not a tame lion."*

Prayer: Lord, thanks for this reminder of the sacred trust that spiritual leaders must strive to keep with you and with those they serve. We pray for our leaders, that they would be faithful to you so that they can be a blessing to others. Keep them from the temptations that are unique to leadership. Amen.

Day 35   Leviticus 11–15

February 4

> Key Text: "For I, the Lord, am the one who brought you up from the land of Egypt, that I might be your God. Therefore, you must be holy because I am holy." (Leviticus 11:45)

As we have noted, to be holy is to be "set apart" by God for his special use. For Israel, it means that they as a society will be *different* from other societies that do not worship God. Inwardly, holiness refers to love and loyalty to God. Outwardly, it is expressed by the symbolism and example of a defined way of life.

In this section of Leviticus, God directs Moses to give the people laws regarding cleanliness and uncleanness. On one level, these laws regarding personal diet, hygiene and medical treatment might be regarded as Hebrew Health Department standards. Disease control is certainly a by-product.

We can appreciate this. Our culture is obsessed with health and fitness. But the laws in Leviticus point beyond mere health, to holiness. The key interpretive verse is Leviticus 11:45: *"For I, the Lord, am the one who brought you up from the land of Egypt, that I might be your God. Therefore, you must be holy because I am holy."*

We should understand the personal, social and ceremonial cleanliness required here to be a symbol of holiness.

As we all know, cleanliness is next to godliness, right? Well, actually that is not in the Bible, but cleanliness does preserve social unity and wholeness. To put it bluntly, there is a reason why we practice personal hygiene and change babies' dirty diapers—it's for our sake and everyone else's as well!

Old Testament scholars believe that the purity laws helped Israel grasp the unity and perfection of God's creation, which in turn led to a shared worldview and a common sense of purpose that set Israel apart from her neighbors.

So the rules benefit Israel in many ways, but the chief benefit is God's presence among them. Observing these laws protects Israel from falling into the practices of the polytheistic religions around them. In this way, God creates a people who will pursue the Promise made to Abraham by standing against the sin and personal dissolution that mark a sinful world, and by modeling reverence for the one true God.

As you read through the laws, you'll be fascinated, puzzled, creeped out and amused. I was relieved to discover, for example, that *"if a man loses his hair and his head becomes bald, he is still ceremonially clean"* (Leviticus 13:40)!

Perhaps you are offended by the number, specificity and seriousness of these—at least to our thinking—odd rules. But in their cultural context they expressed a personal and corporate discipline worthy of Marines at boot camp. They created identity, unity and a sense of purpose, which set Israel apart from her neighbors. And being "set apart" is the meaning of holiness.

> **Focus:** Although God takes his laws and rules seriously, they are secondary to the attitude of the heart. It is possible to keep the "rules" but not love God in our heart. As we shall see, all the commandments of God can be summarized by two great commandments: to love God with all our heart, mind, soul and strength; and to love our neighbor as ourselves. If what we do (or don't do) is not motivated by love, it does not honor God. People may adopt an outward religiosity for many reasons, including tradition, pride, or peer pressure to conform, but God looks for a grateful, generous and loving heart.

> **Prayer:** *Lord, help us keep the disciplines of faith which, today, under the New Covenant and guided by the Holy Spirit, keep us close to you, undefiled by the world, and in alignment with your will. More than anything, we want to enjoy your presence in our lives and serve you faithfully in the world. Amen.*

Day 36   Leviticus 16–17

February 5

> Key Text: Then the Lord said to Moses, "Give the following instructions to Aaron and his sons and all the people of Israel. This is what the Lord has commanded." (Leviticus 17:1–2)

Chapter 16 begins with God speaking to Moses about the death of two of Aaron's sons, Nadab and Abihu, which occurred in Leviticus 10, because of their disobedience to God's clear command about how he must be worshiped.

We may wonder: What's the big deal? Boys will be boys. Why was God so angry about Nadab and Abihu ignoring a detail about how to worship him? Wasn't their punishment excessive?

Ironically, our offense to God's "offense" may illustrate the issue at hand. We presume to tell God what is important; we disobey because we don't agree with his commandment, or at least don't take it seriously. The petulant, presumptuous disobedience of Nadab and Abihu reveals the rebellion in their hearts, and in our own.

The secular man of our own day boldly enters God's space and defies him. He judges God according to his enlightened sensibility—challenging God's authority and even his existence, correcting him when he thinks he is wrong, and ignoring him when his commandments get in the way of disordered desires.

The "heroic" picture of human defiance is just as ridiculous now as it was then. As one wag has put it: *"Your arms are too short to box with God."*

The warning to Moses is a preamble to instructions about the most important day of the year in ancient Israel, the Day of Atonement. Two special things happen on the Day of Atonement: First, the high priest enters into the Most Holy Place of the Tabernacle to make atonement for the nation's sins. Second, a goat called the "scapegoat" is presented to God as a sin offering, but then let go. It symbolically carries off Israel's sins into the wilderness *(Leviticus 16:8–10).*

The forgiveness God extends to Israel on the Day of Atonement is a promissory note deferred from year to year, until Jesus offers his own life for the sins of the world and the debt is paid in full. Psalm 103:12 anticipates this day by saying: *"[God] has removed our sins as far from us as the east is from the west."*

One of the themes of chapters 16 and 17 is blood of atonement. Animal blood is given a sacramental meaning. Consequently, Israelites are forbidden to drink blood or eat raw meat: *"I have given you the blood on the altar to purify you, making you right with the Lord. It is the blood, given in exchange for a life, that makes purification possible"* (Leviticus 17:11).

It is in this context that the shed blood of Christ and the sacrament of the Lord's Supper is to be understood in the New Testament: *"After supper he took another cup of wine and said, 'This cup is the new covenant between God and his people—an agreement, confirmed with my blood, which is poured out as a sacrifice for you'"* (Luke 22:20).

Day 37   Leviticus 18–20

February 6

Key Text: Then the Lord said to Moses, "Give the following instructions to the people of Israel. I am the Lord your God. So do not act like the people in Egypt, where you used to live, or like the people of Canaan, where I am taking you. You must not imitate their way of life." (Leviticus 18:1–3)

We have noted that the central theme of Leviticus is holiness. The Lord says to Israel, *"you must be holy because I am holy"* (Leviticus 11:45). To be holy means to be "set apart" for God in accordance with his will for us.

As our Creator, God has the absolute right to define what it means to be human in his image, and this includes human identity and sexual morality. Of course, this idea is furiously resisted by secularists.

Secularism ordinarily denies the existence of God and, consequently, the existence of moral absolutes. Instead, each individual is given autonomy to decide what is right and wrong for themselves. Sound familiar? It is the same lie by which the serpent seduced and deceived Adam and Eve in the Garden of Eden *(Genesis 3:1–7)*.

Not surprisingly, secularists have a real problem with Leviticus 18 through 20, because here the Lord defines what is permitted and forbidden for human beings created in his image. God knows that for human life and culture to thrive, we must respect the moral boundaries he has established.

In Leviticus 18, the boundaries are established for human sexual behavior. Incest is forbidden, along with sexual relations within the extended family. Prostitution, bestiality and homosexuality are also forbidden. To pursue such passions involves using our bodies in ways that dishonor God's natural order: *"Do not defile yourselves in any of these ways, for the people I am driving out before you* [the Canaanites] *have defiled themselves in all these ways. Because the entire land has become defiled, I am punishing the people who live there. I will cause the land to vomit them out"* (Leviticus 18:24–25).

It is important to remember that the Gospel offers forgiveness for all the sexual sins mentioned in Leviticus 18. In addition, the Holy Spirit is given to help us hold all our disordered impulses in check *(Galatians 5:16–23).*

While sexual sins are never identified as worse than other sins, the fact remains that the emotional and physical consequences of sexual sin can be severe.

There is no getting around the fact that some of us are called to a more difficult life of discipleship in these matters than others, but God knows our hearts, our stories and our struggles. There is no one more compassionate, willing to forgive and able to help. Our lives as believers are permeated with grace and empowered by hope. None of us need to be enslaved by our passions, nor feel condemned by our failures.

Chapter 19 reviews, applies and comments on the social meaning of the Ten Commandments, and chapter 20 establishes God's judgment in these matters. It needs to be remembered that, however severe or offensive to modern ears that God's judgments may seem, they were all borne by Christ on the cross. . . .

> **Focus:** We should not be surprised that the Bible's teaching on sexual ethics raises angry denunciations, along with accusations of hate and fear. We might pause to ask *why?* We know, by God's design, that sexual feelings are among the strongest of human drives. They promise (and point to) an experience of transcendence, intimacy and joyful release. But as we also know, they can lead to deep disappointment, hurt and even abuse. Experience shows that God's boundaries for a fallen world are a wise provision, protecting us physically, emotionally and spiritually. G
> claim on us includes our bodies, and we are to worship him with our bodi
> gift of sex is meant to be enjoyed within covenant marriage, where it r

full beauty. At the same time, God is sympathetic to our weaknesses and is always willing to forgive and heal.

Prayer: Lord, it is disheartening to read the long list of ways that we trespass your boundaries—if not in act, then in thought and imagination. But you are the one who lifts our heads when they hang in shame, to reassure us that you love us and have joined yourself with us for eternity, in Christ. Thank you that there is no condemnation for those who belong to Christ Jesus! Amen.

Day 38   Reflection

February 7

Since God's deliverance of Israel from slavery in Egypt, there have been several significant developments, intended to shape the Israelites into God's holy people. Chief among them are the Ten Commandments and the Law, the building of the Tabernacle, and the function of the Aaronic priesthood. Holding this all together was the Covenant by which God's relationship with Israel was made explicit and then formalized.

God's Covenant, along with the institutions to support it, served to reveal his nature and to separate his people from the practices of the nations around them. As the Lord told the people through Moses: *"I am the Lord your God. So do not act like the people in Egypt, where you used to live, or like the people of Canaan, where I am taking you. You must not imitate their way of life. You must...obey my decrees, for I am the Lord your God. If you obey my decrees and my regulations, you will find life through them. I am the Lord"* (Leviticus 18:1–5).

But against these great developments, we see an ominous stubbornness growing among the people. They have continually complained to Moses, wanting to return to Egypt every time they faced a challenge along the way. The incident of the golden calf idolatry, in Exodus 32, was particularly troubling.

These events portend more trouble ahead. It will prove to be, as has often been said, "easier to get Israel out of Egypt than to get Egypt out of Israel."

However, God is determined to do whatever is necessary to shape his strong-willed people into the holy people he called them to be when he delivered them from slavery in Egypt.

Marriage— relationship for a fallen world

74

Matt 22:29-30

e.g. "10 commandments like the constitution" guidelines on how to live, love God

Holiness is a gift from God that we must grow into, through the development of faith and character over the course of our lives. This is not easy, of course, but God loves us too much to leave us the way we were in our slavery to sin. He has big plans for us. As the apostle Paul wrote to the Philippians: *"And I am certain that God, who began the good work within you, will continue his work until it is finally finished on the day when Christ Jesus returns"* (Philippians 1:6).

journey to learn about God / his character

> **Prayer:** *Lord, we confess that we are a stubborn, willful people, easily squeezed and shaped by the world around us. Help us to become in practice what you have declared us to be in principle, by faith—holy and pleasing in your sight. Amen.*

Day 39   Leviticus 21–23

February 8   God's Boundaries - show where the danger is

> **Key Text:** The Lord said to Moses, "Give the following instructions to the priests, the descendants of Aaron."
> (Leviticus 21:1)

Leviticus continues in chapters 21 and 22 with instructions about the qualifications and duties of priests. The instructions reflect a rigorous attention to the symbolism of God's holiness—particularly, cleanness and perfection.

As we noted earlier regarding Leviticus, we shouldn't get bogged down in the peculiar details, but keep their function in mind. The rituals and the symbolism, with their exacting details, are intended to help the people grasp the nature of God as holy and perfect, completely unlike the gods which they have previously worshiped. When Israel is faithful to keep the commandments and instructions, she not only comes to know God, but also makes him known to the surrounding nations.

commitment / character / love

As the Lord said to Moses: *"You must faithfully keep all my commands by putting them into practice, for I am the Lord. Do not bring shame on my holy name, for I will display my holiness among the people of Israel. I am the Lord who makes you holy. It was I who rescued you from the land of Egypt, that I might be your God. I am the Lord"* (Leviticus 22:31–33).

Learning to love / working out of love

As an attribute of God, holiness speaks of his "otherness." He is not like us. He is infinite in his perfection. As sinful people, we cannot see his face and live *(Exodus 33:19–23)*. So his holiness must be seen indirectly, through the peculiar requirements and symbolism of the priestly work.

Trinity = community — like marriage instead of homosexuality where two are the same ("narcissism")

75

In Leviticus 23, the Lord establishes the feasts of Israel—joyous times of celebration and reflection on God's goodness in dealing with his people.

In addition to the weekly Sabbath, Israel must celebrate the following feasts: Passover, to celebrate their redemption; Firstfruits, to celebrate the harvest; Weeks, to celebrate the Lord as provider (called the Feast of Pentecost in the New Testament); Trumpets—Rosh Hashanah—to celebrate the New Year; and Atonement and Booths, to commemorate the release from Egypt.

The feasts are celebrations and reminders that God blesses his people with all they need for life when they remember him and keep his Covenant. By keeping God's Sabbath and his seasonal feasts, Israel acknowledges that people matter to God.

Old Testament scholar Paul House observes: *"As Israel adopts this notion, the people gain rest, freedom from self-enslavement to success, release from greed and an appreciation for community. In other words, they become holy as their God is holy when they recognize that God orders time, directs events, and guides his people through a history they themselves cannot control."*

Focus: Rituals, routines and symbolism have a teaching purpose to reinforce and act out the great truths of our faith. The Old Covenant practices of Israel were provisional, and later gave way to the New Covenant towards which they pointed—the advent of Jesus our Savior to redeem us once and for all, and make us his holy people. Early Jewish Christianity continued initially in the traditions of the Old Covenant, but with the growth of Christianity among the Gentiles, the Jewish traditions were eventually left behind. The Sabbath day of rest and worship was changed to "The Lord's Day" on Sunday, the day of Jesus' resurrection. The sacraments of the Lord's Supper and baptism as established by Jesus will continue until the Lord returns.

Prayer: God, you are holy "other," and yet you are also close to us. Out of the sheer joy of your existence, you created us in your image and entered into a relationship with us so that we might share your holy life. What a mystery! Everything comes from you, is sustained by your power, and exists for your pleasure. We celebrate with you! Thank you for the sacraments you gave to teach us, and by which we experience your continuing presence with us. Amen.

February 9

> Key Text: "Show your fear of God by not taking advantage of
> each other. I am the Lord your God." (Leviticus 25:17)

The book of Leviticus closes with various instructions—about breaking the Third Commandment by blasphemy; about the way the land must be treated; about the canceling of debts every 50 years (the year of Jubilee); about the effects on the land of keeping or breaking covenant with God; and about vows and freewill offerings being carried out as promised.

A few matters stand out in these chapters:

First, in Leviticus 24:10–16, we are reminded of the seriousness of breaking the Third Commandment against misusing the name of God *(Exodus 20:7).* Blasphemy, in effect, slanders God by misrepresenting him. Whenever we use his name to give sanction to something unworthy of him, we drag his name in the mud. In this way, the true nature of God is hidden from people. This creates a huge obstacle to the very thing God is seeking to do in the world—to make himself known so that people can have a relationship with him.

Second, in Leviticus 25, we are given insight into stewardship of the earth by means of the instructions given to Israel regarding the Promised Land she will soon inhabit. We learn that the land must not be abused by overwork. The Sabbath rest is for the whole creation. All creation, including the land, exists to glorify God; it is not to be misused as an instrument of human greed and ambition.

We learn also that the land is not "owned" but is given to Israel by God. Although the land may be bought and sold for various reasons during a generation, after 50 years all debts are canceled and the land is returned to the original families to whom it was gifted by God. In this way, wealth and power are not accumulated by the few.

Third, in Leviticus 26, God makes it clear that he will bless or withhold his blessing from the land, based upon Israel's faithfulness to the Covenant. When Israel is hostile toward God and refuses to obey him, he will curse the land by withholding his protection and blessing. If the people do not repent, the curse intensifies—bringing to mind the intensifying of the plagues in Egypt when Pharaoh kept hardening his heart.

By the end of the chapter, the potential scenario has become horrifying. If Israel utterly refuses to repent but returns to the paganism from which she was delivered, the nation will become desolate, dehumanized, conquered and scattered as exiles among the nations. Tragically, it becomes a chilling prophesy of what does actually occur in the future.

Even so—even when Israel utterly forsakes God, he will not utterly forsake her: *"But despite all this, I will not utterly reject or despise them while they are in exile in the land of their enemies. I will not cancel my covenant with them by wiping them out, for I am the Lord their God. For their sakes I will remember my ancient covenant with their ancestors, whom I brought out of the land of Egypt in the sight of all the nations, that I might be their God. I am the Lord"* (Leviticus 26:44–45).

There will be much more to say later about God's amazing faithfulness in the face of Israel's serial hard-hearted rebellion, but even now we can conclude that the story of the Bible is all about God's irresistible grace. Aren't you glad?

Leviticus ends in chapter 27 with detailed instructions concerning vows to dedicate various things to the Lord. A key idea here is to think carefully before pledging something to the Lord. Do it thoughtfully and sincerely. Once you give something, you must not take it back: *"Anything specially set apart for the Lord—whether a person, an animal, or family property—must never be sold or bought back. Anything devoted in this way has been set apart as holy, and it belongs to the Lord"* (Leviticus 27:28).

Vows and pledges are serious matters of the heart, given in response to God's giving of himself to us. We must take them seriously and make them wholeheartedly, as he does.

Focus: The instructions regarding the right use of God's name, the proper management of the land which belongs to him, and finally the vows and pledges we make to him, all reflect the seriousness and sincerity of our commitments to God. For Israel, and for us, everything we do must be done for the glory of God and the honoring of his name.

Prayer: Father, we are mystified by your willingness to face and absorb the worst that the human race is capable of doing in its depravity. We abuse one another and even the earth as we blaspheme your name in our rebellion. Forgive our sins. Humble us. Transform us. Amen!

February 10

> Key Text: So the people of Israel did everything as the Lord had commanded Moses. Each clan and family set up camp and marched under their banners exactly as the Lord had instructed them. (Numbers 2:34)

The book of Numbers narrates events starting one year after Israel's departure from Egypt. The time has come to prepare for occupying Canaan, the Promised Land, so the raising of an army begins.

Remember, the promise of land was given by God to Abram in Genesis, chapter 12: *"The Lord had said to Abram, 'Leave your native country, your relatives, and your father's family, and go to the land that I will show you. I will make you into a great nation. I will bless you and make you famous, and you will be a blessing to others. I will bless those who bless you and curse those who treat you with contempt. All the families on earth will be blessed through you'"* (Genesis 12:1–3).

Those who presently occupy the land of Canaan are so depraved that they are described as a sickness in the land. In warning Israel about her own behavior, God says, *"So do not defile the land and give it a reason to vomit you out, as it will vomit out the people who live there now"* (Leviticus 18:28).

This is a disturbing metaphor of spiritual and moral sickness. Think of the barbaric behavior of ISIS in the Middle East today to put the moral depravity of the Canaanites in perspective. We learned early in Genesis that God, out of mercy, was giving them 400 more years to cease from their wickedness. But to no avail. So the agent of God's judgment against the Canaanites will be the Israelite army.

In chapter 1, the Lord instructs Moses to take a census of eligible men who are able to go to war. The tribe of Levi is exempt from serving so that they can take responsibility for the setup and takedown of the Tabernacle when Israel is on the move.

In chapter 2, a detailed template is drawn up for the marching order and the physical location of each tribe when they move and set up camp elsewhere. As you can imagine, it is a logistical and organizational challenge to facilitate the movement of a nation!

Curses / judgement - consequences (natural)
God withholding his protection

Lev. 26:14 Word w/o God when men refuse him.

79

In chapter 3, we learn that the Levites stand in for the firstborn sons of all the other tribes because the firstborn of each family belongs to the Lord's service. The exemption costs each family five pieces of silver, to be given in support of the Levites' Tabernacle ministry.

Finally, in chapter 4, the clans and families of the Kohathite division of the tribe of Levi (that's a mouthful!) are given the serious responsibility of caring for the most sacred objects of the Tabernacle—notably, the Ark of the Covenant, which contains the stone tablets on which the Ten Commandments were written. (By the way, forget everything you learned about the Ark of the Covenant from the Indiana Jones movies!)

As we are beginning to see, the preparation for entering the Promised Land is extensive, and the logistics and organization complex. Each tribe and family has a particular calling and responsibility, including the sending of their sons to war—a heartache familiar to many of us today.

God's ancient Promise to make things right in the world will be furiously resisted by the Canaanites, even as it is today. Think of it as spiritual warfare. It will be a constant theme in the story of Israel.

> **Focus:** One of the implications of monotheism for Israelite faith is accepting the fact that the whole world belongs to God. We are merely stewards of God's resources. In particular, he can give or take land according to his will. Land is being taken from the Canaanites because of their persistent idolatry and moral evil. So much so that the land is said to be vomiting them out. God is giving Canaan to the Israelites, but he can just as easily take it away if they fail to keep his Covenant. We need to rethink our concepts of ownership.
>
> **Prayer:** *Lord, it is sobering to think of the depravity that would cause a land to vomit up its inhabitants, and the great cost for you to reclaim the land. Help us to rethink the meaning of owning things so that we increasingly think of ourselves as stewards of those things, on your behalf, because the whole world belongs to you! Amen.*

Day 42   Numbers 5–8

February 11

> Key Text: "Whenever Aaron and his sons bless the people of Israel in my name, I myself will bless them." (Numbers 6:27)

With the huge task of occupying Canaan looming ahead, the people of Israel are challenged to address their moral and spiritual behavior. The challenge of war is significant, but so is the challenge of spiritual warfare—to remain obedient to God in the midst of pervasive pagan influence.

In chapter 6, the opportunity is given for men and women to voluntarily take a public vow of special dedication and personal discipline, called the Nazirite vow. The Nazirites would serve as role models, challenging the rest of the people to commit themselves to holiness as well.

Chapter 6 ends with what is known as the "Aaronic Blessing," which is frequently quoted today as the benediction to a worship service. The blessing is to be given by Aaron, the high priest, to the people: *"May the Lord bless you and protect you. May the Lord smile on you and be gracious to you. May the Lord show you his favor and give you his peace"* (Numbers 6:24–26).

And then God tells Moses in verse 27: *"Whenever Aaron and his sons bless the people of Israel in my name, I myself will bless them."* This wonderful verse suggests that the blessing of God is mediated to people we love and serve when we pray for God's protection, grace, favor and peace upon them!

Chapter 7 reports on the offerings of the people for the support of the Tabernacle ministry. The leader of each of the twelve tribes presents the offerings, which are listed and inventoried, and then totaled at the end. The effect of this accounting is to demonstrate the generosity of the twelve tribes in supporting the ministry.

Then chapter 8 gives instruction for dedicating the Levites to their service of maintaining and transporting the Tabernacle when God calls Israel to move. (Interestingly, the Levites can only work for 25 years before enjoying their retirement. Wouldn't it be nice!)

Focus: Serving God in the manner he desires requires discipline and dedication from us. However, we are never left in the dark to guess what God wants from us, because he always lets us know by his instructions and commandments, such as with Israel. Although the elaborate rituals and symbolism of Israelite Temple worship are foreign to us, the principle of holiness remains. We must see ourselves as "set apart" for the service of God. The Lord blesses those who seek to serve him with seriousness!

Prayer: Lord, we are reminded today that the need for vigilance and discipline in our spiritual devotion and moral behavior never goes away. Thank you for

Day 43   Numbers 9–12

February 12

> Key Text: And Moses said to the Lord, "Why are you treating me, your servant, so harshly? Have mercy on me! What did I do to deserve the burden of all these people?" (Numbers 11:11)

In the wilderness of Sinai, Israel celebrates a special Passover feast and then packs up to move on. As they go, the Lord leads them with a visual display of his presence: *"On the day the Tabernacle was set up, the cloud covered it. But from evening until morning the cloud over the Tabernacle looked like a pillar of fire. This was the regular pattern.... Whenever the cloud lifted from over the sacred tent, the people of Israel would break camp and follow it. And whenever the cloud settled, the people of Israel would set up camp"* (Numbers 9:15–17).

Chapter 10 describes the logistics of moving. In response to the blowing of a silver trumpet, the Ark of the Lord's Covenant moves to the head, with each tribe following in an orderly and prescribed fashion, one after the other. Imagine the difficulty of coordinating the movement of a large body of people, including the disassembling of the Tabernacle and breaking camp!

The trumpet sound was a clever and effective communication device. Its blast indicated that God was on the move and Israel was to follow. Each move took them a step closer to the end of their nomadic life and the beginning of their occupation of the Promised Land. The trumpet blast was also a reminder that God was their protector. As they moved, he would keep them safe from potential enemies: *"And whenever the Ark set out, Moses would shout, 'Arise, O Lord, and let your enemies be scattered! Let them flee before you!' And when the Ark was set down, he would say, 'Return, O Lord, to the countless thousands of Israel!'"* (Numbers 10:35–36).

Despite the impressive spectacle of a nation marching in order, behind the Ark of the Covenant and under tribal banners, following a divine cloud compass, it doesn't take long for the people to begin complaining again.

Actually, "whining" is more accurate.

They whine about the hardship of moving and about the limited menu of manna and water: "'*Oh, for some meat!' they exclaimed. 'We remember the fish we used to eat for free in Egypt. And we had all the cucumbers, melons, leeks, onions, and garlic we wanted. But now our appetites are gone. All we ever see is this manna!'*" (Numbers 11:4–6).

God hears their complaining and sends them quail—lots of quail! It is a protein extravaganza! But they eat like gluttons, like there is no tomorrow. Their lack of faith makes them sick, literally. And it makes God angry: "*While they were gorging themselves on the meat—while it was still in their mouths—the anger of the Lord blazed against the people, and he struck them with a severe plague. So that place was called Kibroth-hattaavah (which means 'graves of gluttony') because there they buried the people who had craved meat from Egypt*" (Numbers 11:33–34).

The people's whining about food turns to whining about Moses' leadership. Even Miriam and Aaron whine about him: "*Has the Lord spoken only through Moses? Hasn't he spoken through us, too?*" (Numbers 12:2).

Apparently, they have concluded that God didn't know what he was doing when he chose Moses to lead them. So God intervenes. He says, "*Of all my house, [Moses] is the one I trust. I speak to him face to face, clearly, and not in riddles! He sees the Lord as he is. So why were you not afraid to criticize my servant Moses?*" (Numbers 12:7–8).

Why not, indeed!

Miriam's skin becomes white as snow from leprosy. The leprosy makes her unclean and she is put outside the camp. Seeing what happened to her, Aaron rightly becomes afraid for himself. He quickly humbles himself before Moses, begging Moses to pray that God would heal Miriam. His humility and repentance are noted, and God heals her. Within a week, she is brought back into the community.

The whole community sees that even Aaron, Moses' brother, and Miriam, Moses' sister, are held accountable by God for rebellion and ungratefulness. But they also see God's mercy. His love moves him to forgive and restore. Having quieted the whining, God now addresses Moses. Moses needs help with the burden of caring for the people's needs. So God tells him to select seventy recognized leaders and elders from among the people. They are given God's Spirit, like Moses, and they assist Moses in the burden of leadership.

Focus: One of the marks of leadership is the ability to live with complaining and criticism without taking it personally, or trying to bear it alone. Moses was able to do this in the end by listening to God's wisdom and sharing the responsibility with others. At the same time, the people needed to learn how to trust God by following the Moses and the elders he chose. Leaders and followers need to be responsible to one another for the well-being of the whole.

Prayer: Lord, for some reason we continually fall back into fear—even when you have proved yourself faithful and powerful on our behalf. Forgive us for our lack of faith. Give us courage to trust you, and those you have appointed to lead us. Help us not to waste our time and your patience by complaining. Amen!

Day 44 Numbers 13–16

February 13

> Key Text: "Please Lord, prove that your power is as great as you have claimed. For you said, 'The Lord is slow to anger and filled with unfailing love, forgiving every kind of sin and rebellion.'" (Numbers 14:17–18)

Israel is now camping at the edge of Canaan and the Promised Land, preparing to move in and occupy. But first, Moses sends spies into the land to check it out: *"See what the land is like, and find out whether the people living there are strong or weak, few or many. See what kind of land they live in. Is it good or bad? Do their towns have walls, or are they unprotected like open camps? Is the soil fertile or poor? Are there many trees? Do your best to bring back samples of the crops you see"* (Numbers 13:18–20).

First, the good news: They report that indeed the land is bountiful—a land flowing with milk and honey! Now the bad news: *"The people living there are powerful, and their towns are large and fortified. We even saw giants there, the descendants of Anak!"* (Numbers 13:28).

Giants! Yikes! A vote is taken among the spies and a strong majority decides: *"We can't go up against them!"* The minority report by Joshua and Caleb—*"We can certainly conquer it!"*—is ignored. The fear of Canaan quickly spreads among the people. They plot among themselves: *"Let's choose a new leader and go back to Egypt!"*

Here we go again.

As the people began threatening to stone Joshua and Caleb, and to abandon Moses, *"the glorious presence of the Lord appeared to all the Is-*

raelites at the Tabernacle. And the Lord said to Moses, 'How long will these people treat me with contempt? Will they never believe me, even after all the miraculous signs I have done among them? I will disown them and destroy them with a plague'" (Numbers 14:10–12).

Once again, Moses intercedes with God on behalf of the people *(Numbers 14:13–19)*. It is a magnificent prayer, expressing concern for God's reputation among the surrounding nations. The nations have heard of his deliverance of Israel from Egypt, and of his leading them in the pillar of cloud by day and the pillar of fire by night. What will they think if God now destroys his own people? Moses then reminds God that he has promised to be *"slow to anger and filled with unfailing love, forgiving every kind of sin and rebellion"* (Numbers 14:18).

God is glad that Moses acknowledges his mercy. In response to Moses' prayer, God relents, but the people will be punished for their persistent unbelief and rebellion. God will delay occupation of the Promised Land until this generation has died. In the meantime, their children will pay the consequences. God says, *"And your children will be like shepherds, wandering in the wilderness for forty years. In this way, they will pay for your faithlessness, until the last of you lies dead in the wilderness"* (Numbers 14:33).

Now we know why Israel "wandered in the wilderness" for forty years!

It may seem that God is being petulant with his people, but he is not. He knows that they cannot survive if they will not trust him to lead and protect them. To let them enter the land, unprepared, would be irresponsible and unloving. The ungodly, brutal nations that presently inhabit the land are watching Israel's movements carefully, preparing to pounce.

So the nation must wait. They can't occupy the land on their own because the Lord is not with the present generation and they would be slaughtered. But—not surprisingly—the people defiantly ignore God's warning and attack the Amalekites anyway. They lose.

The narrative now pauses while God directs Moses, in chapter 15, to do a review of what is expected of the people. He is like a coach calling the team together after a series of failures on the field, in order to review the basics about what it means to be the people of God in the land they will eventually enter.

By this review, God impresses upon the Israelites the significance of their calling: *"But those who brazenly violate the Lord's will, whether na-*

tive-born Israelites or foreigners, have blasphemed the Lord, and they must be cut off from the community" (Numbers 15:30). Why cut off? Because they have treated the Lord's word with contempt and deliberately disobeyed his command. Israel's calling to be the people of God is not just about them. Their calling is serious business. Through Israel, God is going to change the world.

But, as we are seeing, it will be a struggle of wills.

Chapter 16 recounts yet another rebellion against Moses' leadership, this time led by Korah and 250 of his followers. They presume to do an intervention, demanding to meet with Moses and Aaron before the Tabernacle, and to let God decide who is right! He does. Korah and his followers are swallowed up by the ground, perhaps by an earthquake. A plague follows and thousands more die.

We see that the events following the spies' report have shaken Israel, postponed the occupation of the Promised Land, and brought the judgment of God upon them. Without Moses' longsuffering and intercession, the judgment of God would have fallen on the whole nation. In this way, Moses is like Christ, whose intervention spares the world from the wrath of God against our sin.

Focus: The Children of Israel are, indeed, rebellious *children.* They cannot quite grasp the significance of their role in what God is doing to make things right in the world. We shouldn't judge them too severely. We have the considerable advantage of knowing where all this is leading, and yet we often don't behave much better ourselves. Nevertheless, the Israelites still struggle with what they *do* know, and with what is right in front of them. Lessons about trusting God are hard for all of us.

Prayer: *Lord, when will we ever get it into our heads that you are serious about what you say? We need to be serious about our faith and obedience. Thank you that, time and again, your mercy and forgiveness mitigate your judgment. Thank you above all for Jesus. Amen.*

Day 45   Reflection

February 14

In Leviticus and Numbers, the subject of God's holiness has been front and center. We see it in the moral and spiritual imperatives of the Ten Commandments, and in the justice of the civil law. We see it also in the careful design of the Tabernacle and the priestly garbs, in the ceremonial and symbolic rituals about cleanness and perfection, in the carefully specified way in which worship is done, and in the divine judgment which follows willful rebellion against God's instructions.

All of this seems a bit over the top to modern sensibilities. Perhaps we children of the Enlightenment have become more secular in our thinking than we realize. Many of us have denied the very existence of God, let alone his blazing holiness. Our rebellion against God is equal to anything that the Israelites did while wandering in the wilderness. We, too, rebel against authority, resist discipline, and long for the distracting comforts of "Egypt."

At the same time, we worry about the brokenness of the world, and of our own lives. Every once in a while we drop our guard and let cynicism and unbelief give way to a deep longing for perfect love, goodness, beauty and truth. Though we may not recognize it, that longing is for holiness. God put it in our hearts. Though it is often ignored or redirected, we can't evade it forever.

Saint Augustine famously prayed: *"Thou hast made us for thyself, O Lord, and our hearts are restless until they find their rest in thee."*

The good news is that God won't leave us alone. He loves us as he loved Israel. He loved Israel enough to get angry with her and to discipline her as a parent disciplines a strong-willed child.

God's plan of redemption is a difficult and messy business!

> **Prayer:** *Lord, open our eyes to your holiness, lest we inadvertently treat you with contempt or apathy. Fortify our hearts so that we may take you seriously. Keep us in your word. Amen.*

Day 46   Numbers 17–20

February 15

> Key Text: But the Lord said to Moses and Aaron, "Because you did not trust me enough to demonstrate my holiness to the people of Israel, you will not lead them into the land I am giving them!" (Numbers 20:12)

Israel's rebellion against Moses and Aaron has had terrible consequences, both immediate and long-term. Most importantly, the present generation, which experienced the Exodus out of Egypt, will not be allowed to enter the Promised Land. Israel is on probation. The people will wander in the wilderness until the next generation is in place.

In chapter 17, God puts a dramatic end to the *"people's murmuring and complaining"* against Moses. Despite Aaron's sinfulness, God reaffirms him, among all the others, as the priestly leader of the people. He does this by the miraculous budding of Aaron's wooden staff *(Numbers 17:1– 11).*

Aaron's relatives from the tribe of Levi will continue in their sacred duties in the Tabernacle as further outlined in chapters 18 and 19. And as a warning to any group or individual who wants to seize control through mutiny, God makes his command clear: *"Any unauthorized person who comes too near the sanctuary will be put to death"* (Numbers 18:7).

As we move along in Israel's story, we must keep in mind that there will be constant attempts from within and without to disrupt God's will and redirect his people. The pull of the sinful human heart is always to take control and go back to "Egypt."

In chapter 20, we are disheartened to discover that spiritual leaders are also capable of rebellion against God—even Moses. No doubt he is depressed by the death of his sister Miriam *(Numbers 20:1).* And on top of his grief, he is assaulted (once again) by the angry complaints of the people—this time because there is no water to drink.

Moses and Aaron intercede (once again) before God and God gives Moses specific instruction about another demonstration of his power. God says, *"As the people watch, speak to the rock over there, and it will pour out its water. You will provide enough water from the rock to satisfy the whole community and their livestock"* (Numbers 20:8).

But Moses is angry. Who can blame him? After all these years of trying to be a faithful leader to the people, nothing much has changed. He is burned out. As the people watch, Moses disobeys God's instruction. Instead of speaking to the rock, he angrily strikes it twice with his staff. The people get the water all right, but Moses and Aaron are disciplined by God: *"Because you did not trust me enough to demonstrate my holiness to the people of Israel, you will not lead them into the land I am giving them!"* (Numbers 20:12).

We shouldn't be surprised by this, because leaders are human also. They are subject to emotional burnout like everyone else. But still, it does disappoint. The very nature of spiritual leadership is to lead by example and build trust in those you lead, so that they are willing to follow. When this trust is broken, it saddens us and makes us cynical. When leaders fail, lots of others are affected. Trust can be regained, of course, but it takes time. In the meantime, precious time and momentum is lost.

And so, for example, Numbers 20 ends with the frustrating encounter of Israel with the king of Edom while the Israelites are camped nearby at Kadesh. (Edomites are descendants of Esau, and therefore no friends to Israel).

Moses requests permission to pass through their land because it is a more favorable route. The king of Edom refuses and makes a show of force, so Israel is forced to tuck tail and turn around to retrace their steps. To make matters worse, Aaron dies a short time later and Israel mourns him.

It's one thing after another!

It is hard to maintain hope when disappointment, loss and setbacks come in waves. But Israel is learning that faith grows in times of adversity. To use a sports analogy, God sometimes calls us "to play through the pain."

Focus: It is startling to learn that after all he has gone through in response to the calling of God, Moses will not be permitted to enter the Promised Land. Yes, it seems unfair at the very least. But it highlights both the privilege and accountability of leadership. The more powerful the leader, the greater the rewards and punishments. Perhaps when Israel sees that the "rules" apply to the great Moses and Aaron also, they may be more inclined to take those rules seriously themselves. As the apostle Paul will later write, it is in our weakness that the power of God is made known.

Prayer: *Lord, when we are emotionally run down and our faith is weak, strengthen us by your Holy Spirit. Give us grace for perseverance so that we do not give up and simply return to Egypt. Take us to the Promised Land! Amen.*

Day 47   Numbers 21–25

February 16

> Key Text: "Look, a vast horde of people has arrived from Egypt. They cover the face of the earth and are threatening me. Please come and curse these people for me because they are too powerful for me." (Numbers 22:5–6)

As the Israelites wander around the land of Canaan, the local nations get nervous. In chapter 21, the Canaanite king of Arad, who has heard that Israel is approaching his area, attacks the Israelites and takes some of them as prisoners. This provocation starts a series of wars between Israel and the Canaanites, Amorites and Bashanites. Israel wins some impressive early victories and begins to occupy Canaanite towns.

However, the initial victories are tainted by the continual complaining and unbelief of the older generation who experienced the Exodus from Egypt.

There are now two Israels traveling through the desert. One Israel is the older generation that will die in the wilderness, never fully possessing the land because of their unbelief. The other Israel is the second generation that is growing, maturing and preparing to possess Canaan.

The tension between the "two Israels" must be palpable.

In chapters 22 through 24, there is a long and interesting narrative about a Moabite king named Balak. He has heard about Israel's recent victories in battle and is terrified about their size. So instead of engaging Israel in battle, he seeks the help of a local pagan prophet named Balaam. He offers Balaam a lot of money to curse the Israelites through magic: *"Please come and curse these people for me because they are too powerful for me. Then perhaps I will be able to conquer them and drive them from the land. I know that blessings fall on any people you bless, and curses fall on people you curse"* (Numbers 22:6).

But something quite unexpected happens. When Balaam seeks to place a curse upon Israel, God suddenly speaks to him and warns him not to curse the Israelites because they have been blessed. Balaam reports this to King Balak, who of course is outraged and tells him to try again.

But Balaam's second attempt results in a hilarious encounter with an invisible angel of the Lord, who is blocking the road. Balaam's donkey senses the angel and balks. Balaam, in turn, beats his faithful old donkey. But again, the donkey refuses to move forward. So in a fit of rage, Balaam beats the animal again and again with his staff.

In a scene worthy of Monty Python, the donkey is given the ability to speak: *"What have I done to you that deserves your beating me three times?"* And Balaam, apparently not realizing that his donkey is actually *talking to him*...talks back to his donkey! *"You have made me look like a fool! If I had a sword with me, I would kill you!"* They continue back and forth.

Finally, the angel of the Lord (whom I imagine to be smiling) reveals himself to Balaam and commands him to tell King Balak what the Lord has said, and only this. So ironically, the pagan prophet Balaam is compelled once again to speak the truth about the God of Israel. His messages are powerful revelations about who God is and what he is doing through Israel. Balaam reveals that Israel is blessed of God. They are a people who live by themselves, set apart from other nations. He impresses upon Balak that *"God is not a man, so he does not lie. He is not human, so he does not change his mind. Has he ever spoken and failed to act? ...the Lord their God is with them; he has been proclaimed their king. ... No curse can touch Jacob; no magic has any power against Israel"* (Numbers 23:19–23). Balaam soon realizes that God *"devours all the nations that oppose him."* His attempt to curse Israel is futile: *"Blessed is everyone who blesses you, O Israel, and cursed is everyone who curses you"* (Numbers 24:9).

So having failed to defeat Israel through a curse, King Balak now tries a more successful strategy: seduction of the young Israelite men. In chapter 25, some of the Israelite men have sex with Moabite women, and then participate with them in offering sacrifices to the gods of Moab—including the vile worship of Baal—*"causing the Lord's anger to blaze against his people."*

Unfortunately, this is a strategy that will prove successful many times in the future. Canaanite worship was very sensual, incorporating temple prostitution of all varieties, and wild ceremonies. You get the picture.

Again, we see challenges within Israel and attacks from without. The people waver in faith, but God keeps his promises nevertheless.

Focus: The story of the pagan prophet Balaam reveals that God is able to speak truth through anyone's mouth—even, in this case, the mouth of a donkey! It reinforces what we have noted since the book of Genesis: that the God of the Bible is a God who speaks, and who wants to be known. For he is not just the God of Israel, but the God of all nations. Indeed, the God of all creation.

Prayer: Lord, your promise to bless the world through a descendent of Israel is rock solid, even if Israel was not. We see ourselves in Israel, for we too are weak, rebellious and prone to wander. Thank you for being faithful to us even when we fail you. Our hope, and the hope of the world, is in your gracious Promise and nothing else. Amen!

February 17

> Key Text: One day the Lord said to Moses, "Climb one of the mountains east of the river, and look out over the land I have given the people of Israel. After you have seen it, you will die like your brother, Aaron, for you both rebelled against my instructions in the wilderness of Zin." (Numbers 27:12–14)

Forty years have passed since the Exodus. The first generation has passed away without occupying the Promised Land because of their perpetual complaining and rebellion against the Lord and his servant Moses. The next generation now comes forward to take their place.

In chapter 26, the Lord tells Moses and Eleazar, the son of Aaron the priest, that the census of Israel must be retaken: *"List all the men twenty years old or older who are able to go to war."* In addition, the land of Canaan is platted out and assigned to the various tribes of Israel to occupy.

In chapter 27, the Lord prepares Moses for a change of national leadership. God tells him to climb a particular mountain with an aerial view of the land he is giving to the people of Israel. This gives Moses reassurance that God will fulfill his Promise. But it also reminds him that he will not be around when it is occupied because of his personal failure as a leader, when anger at the people caused him to disobey God at Kadesh.

Despite his lapse, Moses is a good man and a good leader. He doesn't complain but accepts his discipline from God, and then expresses concern for the transition of leadership: *"O Lord, you are the God who gives breath to all creatures. Please appoint a new man as leader for the community. Give them someone who will guide them wherever they go and will lead them into battle, so the community of the Lord will not be like sheep without a shepherd"* (Numbers 27:16–17).

Great leaders like Moses understand that leadership means servanthood, and a servant cares first about the well-being of those that he or she is leading. Most leaders will never be remembered like Moses because their sphere of influence is limited. Yet, leadership may be understood as influencing others—however few the "others" may be.

For example, parents influence their children; students influence their classmates; workers influence coworkers; friends influence friends, and so on. In this understanding of leadership, all Christians are called to be leaders.

What distinguishes leaders like Moses is not talent or charisma, but passion, perseverance, humility and love. Remember, Moses protested to God that he was not qualified to appear before Pharaoh and lead the people of Israel out of Egypt *(Exodus 3:7–15)*. But look what God did with what Moses offered him.

I must confess that it is sad to imagine Moses staring at the land of Canaan from high on a mountain, knowing that God's ancient Promise is about to be fulfilled, but that he will not be the one to lead the people in. He was a great leader, but now he must step aside.

Generations come and go, each with their own part to play in the Grand Story of Redemption. Our challenge is to know our time and our role, and then fulfill it like Moses—with humility and faithfulness.

The next generation of Israel steps forth, prepared for battle *(Numbers 26)*, with new leadership *(Numbers 27)*, instructed in the ways of personal integrity *(Numbers 28–30)*, and standing at the borders of the Promised Land. Here we go!

Focus: One essential quality for life and leadership is humility. Think of great athletes who wouldn't retire and ended up becoming a mockery of themselves. Accepting change, admitting failure, and recognizing when the time has come to move on are all marks of humble people. Humility in this sense is not self-reproach; it is self-knowledge. Humble people know that God is in control. Like Moses, they are merely God's servants who have the great privilege to serve him, and the people around them, until their time on stage is finished.

Prayer: Lord, as we follow the story of your chosen people in their calling to become a great nation that serves you in the midst of a world of spiritual darkness, we see the importance of spiritual leaders who faithfully pour out their lives for the sakes of those they serve. Bless and strengthen our spiritual leaders, we pray, as they lead us in faithful service to our generation. Amen!

February 18

> Key Text: "When you cross the Jordan River into the land of
> Canaan, you must drive out all the people living there. You must
> destroy all their carved and molten images and demolish all
> their pagan shrines. Take possession of the land and settle in it,
> because I have given it to you to occupy." (Numbers 33:51–53)

As a leader, Moses finishes well. His final act of leadership is to prepare the people for what is next. In chapters 31–36, he addresses the people about issues related to their occupation of the land of Canaan. Notably, the Lord says through Moses: *"When you cross the Jordan River into the land of Canaan, you must drive out all the people living there. You must destroy all their carved and molten images and demolish all their pagan shrines. Take possession of the land and settle in it, because I have given it to you to occupy"* (Numbers 33:51–53).

Here is where God's story gets offensive for modern people. Since the Enlightenment, when human reason was exalted over divine revelation, God has been put on trial and accused of being an angry, violent God. People who believed themselves to be more intelligent and moral than God judged him to be evil, and/or declared that they must refuse to worship such a God.

Without commenting on the laughable idea of putting God on trial, and making moral judgments about him, we must remember that we have no existence outside of him. As sovereign Creator, he has the right to give life or take it for his own purposes.

The fact is, it doesn't matter what we think about him. God is not increased if we like him, nor diminished if we don't—although *we* surely are. Common sense tells us that our part is to fear him and obey his commandments. To refuse is the height of irrationality.

Having gotten that out of my system, I must say how fortunate we are that God is good and just and very, very patient with our foolishness. He loves us in spite of our ourselves. But he makes moral judgments to accomplish his purposes, and now he is going to judge the Canaanites and give their land to Israel. It is his right to do so, for the whole earth belongs to him, and all the nations are accountable to him.

The Canaanites must leave with their idols and shrines. Despite God's persistent warnings over the course of 400 years, they have forfeited their right to the land by unrepentant idolatry and moral evil. They are a sickness and the land is vomiting them out *(Leviticus 18)*. God is giving occupancy now to Israel.

Israel will live in Canaan in order to bear national witness to the love and holiness of God, and to show the nations what it means to be fully human in the image of God. ···

Idolatry is dehumanizing as well as dishonoring to God. It produces depraved culture. Therefore, idolaters must be displaced and idols destroyed. There can be no compromise. As Moses warns: *"If you fail to drive out the people who live in the land, those who remain will be like splinters in your eyes and thorns in your sides. They will harass you in the land where you live. And I will do to you what I had planned to do to them"* (Numbers 33:55–56).

Israel is set apart for God. There can be no mixing of Covenant life with pagan life, lest Israel misrepresent God and thereby mislead others.

But this will prove to be as difficult for Israel as it is for us. Jesus tells us: *"You can enter God's Kingdom only through the narrow gate. The highway to hell is broad, and its gate is wide for the many who choose that way. But the gateway to life is very narrow and the road is difficult, and only a few ever find it"* (Matthew 7:13–14).

Few find the "gateway to life," not because it is hidden, but because it is hard. We must leave behind the idols we cling to for comfort and commit ourselves to the hard work of loving God and one another. When we do, we are blessed and begin to experience the life that is really life—life in the Promised Land!

Focus: The moral relativism of the modern, secular world cannot tolerate such a view of God as we have described. Excessive pride, with a sprinkling of moral superiority, gets in the way. Such foolishness comes from rebellion against God.

The apostle Paul explains to the believers in Rome that people who act this way are nevertheless capable of knowing God's eternal nature and divine power, through simple observation and logical reasoning. But pride gets in the way: *"Yes, they knew God, but they wouldn't worship him as God or even give him thanks. And they began to think up foolish ideas of what God was like. As a result, their minds became dark and confused. Claiming to be wise, they instead became utter fools"* (Romans 1:21–22).

95

Day 50　　　Numbers 34–36

February 19

> Key Text: These are the commands and regulations that the Lord gave to the people of Israel through Moses while they were camped on the plains of Moab beside the Jordan River across from Jericho. (Numbers 36:13)

In the final three chapters of the book of Numbers, Moses is concerned with assigning the land of Canaan to the various tribes, even before it is occupied by Israel. Some tribal concerns are resolved and the special needs of the Levites, who maintain the Tabernacle, are provided for.

In addition, some practical legal matters are addressed. For example, provision is made for an accidental killing through cities of refuge. Each tribe is directed to provide cities of refuge within the land allocated to them: *"When you cross the Jordan into the land of Canaan, designate cities of refuge to which people can flee if they have killed someone accidently. These cities will be places of protection from a dead person's relatives who want to avenge the death"* (Numbers 35:9–12).

In this humane way, justice is maintained for the slayer and time is given for relatives to accept what has happened and forgive. This stops a potential cycle of retaliation and provides peace for the community. It also reflects the wisdom of God.

Theologically, there is something quite interesting in these chapters. The giving of the land occurs before the actual occupation through military conquest. On the surface, we may shrug and say, *so what?* But this act of God illustrates an important pattern that is followed in all of God's dealings with us. By his sovereign will, God declares something to be true for us before we actually experience it.

In the case of Israel, God, who owns the whole earth, had declared hundreds of years before that Canaan would belong to the Israelites *(Genesis 12:1–5)*. Now, as they camp on the shore of the Jordan River, the land is surveyed and assigned to each tribe, before any actual possession has taken place. It is as if each tribe already has the deed and title to the section of Canaan they will inhabit. What remains is to live land that already belonged to them before they arrived.

If we think about this moment in time—the in-between time of what Israel has been given by God, and their actual possession of it—we see a pattern of the Christian life. Some call it the "already" and "not yet" of our faith.

"Already," God has declared us to be forgiven, but we are "not yet" perfect. "Already," we have received a heavenly inheritance from God, who has blessed us with every spiritual blessing in the heavenly realms, but we have "not yet" taken possession of that inheritance *(Ephesians 1:3–4, 11)*.

God has "already" raised us from the dead along with Christ, and seated us with him in the heavenly realms because we are united with Christ Jesus, but we have "not yet" fully experienced resurrection glory *(Ephesians 2:6)*.

This is heady stuff, and we can't comprehend all that it means yet, but one day we will. However, it is by God's decree a done deal. We have the deed and title to the "Promised Land" in hand.

Like Israel, we must also in these "in-between" days begin to occupy the place that God has already given us. We do this by living faithfully as God's children in the world.

Focus: Living in the "in-between" days requires wisdom and perseverance. We feel the tension between what we are, and what we want to be, as individuals and as a nation. The space between our ideal self and our real self is the place where God works in our lives, edging us forward even as we await the Day when we shall be all that he made us to be. It is the same in our understanding: *"Now we see things imperfectly, like puzzling reflections in a mirror, but then we will see everything with perfect clarity. All that I know now is partial and incomplete, but then I will know everything completely, just as God now knows me completely"* (1 Corinthians 13:12).

Prayer: *Lord, we are amazed and humbled to be called your children and inheritors of all the blessings of everlasting life. While we cannot conceive of all that this means, we have experienced enough of your blessings already to know that what lies ahead must truly be magnificent. Thank you for this great gift of new life, both now and forever! Amen.*

Day 51   Deuteronomy 1–4

February 20

> Key Text: "And now, Israel, listen carefully to these decrees and regulations that I am about to teach you. Obey them so that you may live, so you may enter and occupy the land that the Lord, the God of your ancestors, is giving you." (Deuteronomy 4:1)

Deuteronomy is considered to be one of the most theologically influential books of the Old Testament. The New Testament quotes it directly in seventeen of its twenty-seven books, and alludes to it more than eighty times. It doesn't contain any new action, but instead reflects on what has already happened in Genesis, Exodus, Leviticus and Numbers—and on what is coming ahead in the conquest and settlement of the land as told in the book of Joshua.

One important feature of Deuteronomy is its structure. It is widely believed that God's Covenant with Israel, as described in Exodus and Leviticus, is patterned after legal treaties known in the ancient world between kings and their vassals in a feudal system. Simply put, a king would enter into a legal agreement whereby he offered land and other privileges in exchange for soldiering, if necessary, to help protect the kingdom.

God's willingness to bind himself to Israel by means of a covenant, like a good earthly king to his subjects, would have made a deep impression on the surrounding pagan nations. *What god would do such a thing?* But Israel's God did! He entered into a relationship with his people, committing himself to bless, protect and provide for them. The people, in turn, promised to honor God by keeping the terms of the Covenant.

Ancient treaties began with preambles, which reviewed the kings' past relationships with their people. Accordingly, Deuteronomy begins with a preamble reminding the Israelites of God's dealing with them in the events following their escape through the Red Sea from Egypt. Moses notes that, when the people had long ago arrived at Mt. Sinai where the Ten Commandments were given and the Covenant established, they had only been a short distance away from where they are now. But forty years have passed! Why haven't they gotten very far? Because of Israel's constant bickering and unbelief *(Deuteronomy 1:2–4).*

When we don't trust God, we don't get anywhere!

Moses goes on to review in a single narrative, with commentary, everything that has happened since their arrival at Sinai after crossing the Red Sea. In short, he reminds them of what whiners they have been!

Moses is not just rubbing it in; he is drawing lessons from it. By summarizing the past 40 years, he hopes that the next generation at least will have a change of heart and prepare themselves for the challenge ahead. Above all, they must understand how blessed they are that God has been faithful to them despite their incredible lack of faith, bad behavior, and ungratefulness.

In chapter 4, Moses delivers a stirring sermon to remind the people of God's favor, of his call upon their lives, and of their privilege in belonging to him. He then challenges them to be faithful: *"Has any other god dared to take a nation for himself out of another nation by means of trials, miraculous signs, wonders, war, a strong hand, a powerful arm, and terrifying acts? Yet that is what the Lord your God did for you in Egypt, right before your eyes. ... So remember this and keep it firmly in mind: The Lord is God both in heaven and on earth, and there is no other. If you obey all the decrees and commands I am giving you today, all will be well with you and your children. I am giving you these instructions so that you will enjoy a long life in the land the Lord your God is giving you for all time"* (Deuteronomy 4:34, 39–40).

Focus: It may seem like Israel's 40 years of wandering in the wilderness are lost years, filled with nothing but complaining and rebellion. But keep in mind that Israel, as a nation, is a spiritual child at this point. The first generation of Israelites, delivered from Egypt, are essentially pagan in their thinking. Paganism defines reality in all the nations around them. It's going to take a while to get it into their DNA that there is one God, the maker of heaven and earth, who loves them and wants to dwell among them, and to make them his holy people. It's a tough journey. God's disciplining them along the way is for their instruction, and it will just take time. A lot of time.

Prayer: *Lord, we praise you for wanting to be with us. We thank you for staying faithful to us even in the times and places that we have been unfaithful to you. Above all, thank you for being patient with us. Along with Moses we say, "Has anything as great as this ever been seen or heard before?" Amen!*

99

Day 52   Reflection

Deuteronomy 4 contains one of the great theological narratives of the Old Testament. Moses reviews the Covenant responsibilities with the second generation of Israelites. His concern is that they understand who God is, what he has done on their behalf, and what their obligations to him involve. And, of course, he warns them not to do what their parents did, which resulted in forty years of wandering in the wilderness.

We can read this chapter as Old Testament *Gospel*.

Israel's very existence as the *chosen people* points to God's gracious decision to make things right in the world. Presently, things are wrong because the human race made a wrong-headed decision to live *east of Eden*, outside a relationship with God. But life is difficult east of Eden. Darkness is everywhere. Sin and death reign.

So Moses reminds the people that human life flourishes only in relationship with God, and in the land where he places them to live: *"And now, Israel, listen carefully to these decrees and regulations that I am about to teach you. Obey them so that you may live, so you may enter and occupy the land that the Lord, the God of your ancestors, is giving you"* (Deuteronomy 4:1).

As we have noted several times, Israel must listen to God's *"decrees and regulations"* because they express truth and reality by means of precept, symbol and ceremony. They reveal God's nature and character. They also define the boundaries of human moral behavior, pointing the way to genuine community grounded in justice and love. All of this is freely given by God. It is not human wisdom or achievement. It can only be received by faith and personally experienced by obedience.

But this is not just theological truth. It is a better way to live with tangible benefits: *"Obey them* [the decrees and regulations] *completely, and you will display your wisdom and intelligence among the surrounding nations. When they hear all these decrees, they will exclaim, 'How wise and prudent are the people of this great nation!' For what great nation has a god as near to them as the Lord our God is near to us whenever we call on him? And what great nation has decrees and regulations as righteous and fair as this body of instructions that I am giving you today?"* (Deuteronomy 4:6–8).

All of this is great, but the lure of paganism is significant. So Moses warns the people of the consequences of breaking the Covenant and returning to idol worship. To do so will corrupt them *(Deuteronomy 4:16)* and place them under God's judgment—meaning that the Covenant blessings and protections will unravel if they harden their hearts and rebel against him.

But even if they sin against the Lord and suffer all the consequences that they were warned about *(Deuteronomy 4:26–28)*, God will not forget them. There will always be a way back home: *"...if you search for [the Lord] with all your heart and soul, you will find him. ... For the Lord your God is a merciful God; he will not abandon you or destroy you or forget the solemn covenant he made with your ancestors"* (Deuteronomy 4:29,31).

This is almost too good to be true, but it *is* true—it is "gospel"! And it is a motivation for continuing wonder and praise: *"Has anything as great as this ever been seen or heard before? Has any nation ever heard the voice of God speaking from fire—as you did—and survived? Has any other god dared to take a nation for himself out of another nation by means of trials, miraculous signs, wonders, war, a strong hand, a powerful arm, and terrifying acts? Yet that is what the Lord your God did for you in Egypt, right before your eyes. He showed you these things so you would know that the Lord is God and there is no other"* (Deuteronomy 4:32–35).

> *Prayer: Lord, all we can say is, "Hallelujah!" You are a God who consistently gives us what we do not deserve! Amen.*

Day 53   Deuteronomy 5–7

February 22

> Key Text: "And you must love the Lord your God with all your heart, all your soul, and all your strength." (Deuteronomy 6:5)

Moses continues in these chapters with his brilliant and theologically rich recounting of Israel's history with God. It is repetitious, but don't skim over it, because Moses adds commentary that helps bring all that we've read so far into clearer focus. In fact, if you were to master one Old Testament book, this might be the one.

Chapter 5 begins with a challenge to study the Law and commandments of God by intentional listening, learning and obeying. They express the will of God and therefore the contours of truth and reality. When followed, they enable human life to flourish.

Of course, the Israelites never kept the commandments faithfully. So Jesus, representing the true Israelite, came to do what neither Israel nor anyone else could do—to perfectly keep the commandments. *(See Matthew 5:17–20.)* The Law is fulfilled and embodied by Jesus. Therefore, he is able to become for us, *"the way, the truth and the life."*

In Deuteronomy 6, the motivation for keeping the commandments is given: *"Listen, O Israel! The Lord is our God, the Lord alone. And you must love the Lord your God with all your heart, all your soul, and all your strength. And you must commit yourselves wholeheartedly to these commands that I am giving you today. Repeat them again and again to your children"* (Deuteronomy 6:4–7).

We learn by this distillation of the Law and commandments that the core imperative is love—loving God with our whole selves, inwardly and outwardly. Of necessity, loving God means loving what God loves, and God loves our neighbor also. So loving God also means loving our neighbor as ourselves.

God himself is the example for what he calls us to do. We love him (and each other) because he first loved us. In chapter 7, he tells Israel that love and faithfulness moved him to choose them as his special people—nothing else: *"The Lord did not set his heart on you and choose you because you were more numerous than other nations, for you were the smallest of all nations! Rather, it was simply that the Lord loves you, and he was keeping the oath he had sworn to your ancestors. ... Understand, therefore, that the Lord your God is indeed God. He is the faithful God who keeps his covenant for a thousand generations and lavishes his unfailing love on those who love him and obey his commands"* (Deuteronomy 7:7–9).

Moses then challenges the people not to be afraid. With assurance of God's love and powerful presence, they will be able to drive out the nations whose moral and spiritual corruption has become a cancer, and must be removed: *"No, do not be afraid of those nations, for the Lord your God is among you, and he is a great and awesome God"* (Deuteronomy 7:21).

Moses understands that truth and love are powerful forces in the world, capable of defeating any lie or hatred that arises in the fallen creation. But we need to fortify ourselves accordingly—loving God and one another, by listening, learning and living his commandments.

> **Focus:** One of the Bible's great assertions is that God is love. Love moved God to create and then redeem the world. Human life is blessed when men and women reflect God's own nature by loving one another. That is why it is important to understand the nature of God. A.W. Tozer famously wrote: *"The history of mankind will probably show that no people has ever risen above its religion, and man's spiritual history will positively demonstrate that no religion has ever been greater than its idea of God."*

> **Prayer:** *Lord, we want to be people who love, because by loving one another ,we reflect your image and realize the purpose for which you created us. Use us to change the world as we love our neighbor. Despite resistance from the powers of evil, we will not be afraid, but we will love. Amen!*

Day 54   Deuteronomy 8–11

February 23

> Key Text: "And now, Israel, what does the Lord your God require of you? He requires only that you fear the Lord your God, and live in a way that pleases him, and love him and serve him with all your heart and soul." (Deuteronomy 10:12)

I love Moses' honesty. As he continues preparing the second generation of Israelites to occupy the land, he reminds them of hard lessons learned by their parents.

Their parents learned humility, for example, when they complained about the lack of food—at least the good food they enjoyed in Egypt. So God gave them *"manna,"* which literally means "*what is it?*" Manna was about as appealing as a slice of white bread every morning. Nevertheless, it was food, even if it wasn't filet mignon with sautéed mushrooms and baked potato. Moses said that God did it *"to teach…that people do not live by bread alone; rather, we live by every word that comes from the mouth of the Lord"* (Deuteronomy 8:3).

Yes, Jesus later quoted this in the desert when tempted by the devil *(Luke 4:3–4).*

Living only to satisfy one's bodily appetites is diminishing to human life. We are spiritual beings as well as physical, and our spirits are nourished when we consume the calories of wisdom and goodness from God's Word: *"The laws of the Lord are true; each one is fair. They are more desirable than gold, even the finest gold. They are sweeter than honey, even honey dripping from the comb"* (Psalm 19:9–10).

This is true in times of abundance as well as in times of want, so Moses warns the people about the dangers of abundance when they occupy the land of Canaan, a land flowing with milk and honey: *"When you have eaten your fill, be sure to praise the Lord your God for the good land he has given you. But that is the time to be careful! Beware that in your plenty you do not forget the Lord your God and disobey his commands, regulations, and decrees that I am giving you today. For when you have become full and prosperous and have built fine homes to live in, and when your flocks and herds have become very large and your silver and gold have multiplied along with everything else, be careful! Do not become proud at that time and forget the Lord your God, who rescued you from slavery in the land of Egypt"* (Deuteronomy 8:10–14).

Moses warns them next about fear and pride—fear, when they see how much greater and more powerful are the nations they will dispossess, and then pride when the Lord, who is like *"a devouring fire,"* gives them victory and they are then tempted to boast that they have been given the land because *"we are such good people."*

The truth is, as chapter 9 recounts, the Lord has nearly destroyed them several times because of their sinfulness. Moses tells them bluntly that they deserved it: *"Yes, you have been rebelling against the Lord as long as I have known you"* (Deuteronomy 9:24).

Finally, Moses asks the people, *"What does the Lord your God require of you? He requires only that you fear the Lord your God, and live in a way that pleases him, and love him and serve him with all your heart and soul"* (Deuteronomy 10:12).

Chapter 11 encourages the people over and over again to do what God requires and to teach their children the same. They must remember that their children never experienced the discipline of the Lord, nor did they see his greatness, his strong hand and powerful arm. They didn't see the miraculous signs and wonders he performed in Egypt against Pharaoh when he delivered their parents from slavery.

There is a lot at stake. Moses says: *"Look, today I am giving you the choice between a blessing and a curse! You will be blessed if you obey the commands of the Lord your God that I am giving you today. But you will be cursed if you reject the commands of the Lord your God and turn away from him and worship gods you have not known before"* (Deuteronomy 11:26–28).

> **Focus:** It is said that Christianity is always one generation away from extinction. The ministry of teaching and mentoring the young is critical. Discerning truth and moral behavior is not automatic, or even instinctual in a fallen world. We need to learn these things from our parents and then pass them on to our children. History is full of the stories of families and nations who have forgotten this. There is nothing sadder than a generation of belief giving rise to a generation of unbelief.

> **Prayer:** *Lord, you are the Bread of Life, and so you are our Daily Bread. May we find our sustenance in your Word as we listen to it, reflect upon it and apply it to our lives. Remind us also to teach it to our children. Amen.*

Day 55   Deuteronomy 12–16

February 24

> Key Text: "Do not worship the Lord your God in the way these pagan peoples worship their gods." (Deuteronomy 12:4)

Having emphasized the importance of loving God from the heart, Moses now outlines how love expresses itself in the outward forms and institutions of the Covenant, which the people must follow in the land of Canaan.

Remember, Israel is entering a land that is spiritually and morally sick, and about to "vomit" the inhabitants out. Canaanite worship is "detestable," and shocking by modern sensibilities. We would be horrified to find a culture today that worshiped in these ways. So, chapter 12 begins with instructions about proper worship. It is a commentary on the First and Second Commandments, which God gave Moses in Exodus 20.

Moses' instruction gives some chilling insights into the nature of Canaanite worship: *"...do not fall into the trap of following their customs and worshiping their gods. ... You must not worship the Lord your God the way the other nations worship their gods, for they perform for their gods every detestable act that the Lord hates. They even burn their sons and daughters as sacrifices to their gods"* (Deuteronomy 12:30–31).

Chapter 13 gives detailed instructions about actively avoiding false gods. The people must not listen to anyone who encourages them to worship false gods, whether a prophet who demonstrates spiritual power, or a spouse, family member or close friend who whispers in their ear. Any who tempt others to idolatry must face capital punishment, for idolatry is a great a betrayal of God.

Chapter 14 sets the menu for Israelite dining. It is interesting that even food choices have theological meaning. This is not unlike those today who have moral objections to eating certain kinds of food, or of eating animals that have been raised in cages, etc. Moses identifies which animals, fish, birds and insects may be eaten and which must be avoided. The dietary restrictions probably served several purposes, including health considerations and the practices of the Canaanites around them.

Moses devotes the rest of chapter 14 and all of chapter 15 to the matter of tithing. A tithe is a tenth, whether of crops, or of flocks and herds. It is an offering of thanksgiving to God for his provision, and an act of faith that he will provide all that the offerer needs. It is also the means by which the poor are helped, and the Levites are compensated for their oversight of the Tabernacle.

Those who give are called to give generously and willingly, *"...for the Lord your God will bless you in everything you do. There will always be some in the land who are poor. That is why I am commanding you to share freely with the poor and with other Israelites in need"* (Deuteronomy 15:10–11). The generosity expressed in the tithe extends also to the treatment of servants.

Finally, in chapter 16, Moses reviews the feasts and festivals Israel must celebrate in the Promised Land—the Feast of Passover, the Festival of Harvest and the Festival of Shelters.

In these chapters, the distinctive life of the people of God is drawn with sharp lines, distinguishing them from the moral, spiritual, intellectual and social depravity of the people whose land they will be occupying. Israel's national life, in all its detail, is intended to bear witness in word, deed, symbol, ceremony, and social justice to the one true God who is the Creator of the heavens and earth, and who has created men and women in his image to reflect his glory on earth.

Focus: Some may question the need for all these strange rules and restrictions regarding worship and diet. It is true that they reflect a cultural expression far removed from us. But the timeless theological insight behind them is that everything we do as God's creatures is meant to express his goodness and glory. The New Testament echoes this understanding: *"And whatever you do or say, do it as a representative of the Lord Jesus, giving thanks through him to God the Father"* (Colossians 3:17).

Prayer: Lord, we know that it is easy for others to dismiss you with skepticism in philosophical debate. It is harder to dismiss you when your people reveal the transformation of their lives brought about by your love and mercy. Help us to avoid idolatry and instead accurately reflect your holy character in this world. Amen.

Day 56   Deuteronomy 17–20

February 25

> Key Text: "The nations you are about to displace consult sorcerers and fortune-tellers, but the Lord your God forbids you to do such things." (Deuteronomy 18:14)

Moses continues to prepare the second generation of Israelites for life in Canaan by reviewing the civil laws of the Covenant which address issues of justice and impartiality. The subjects seem somewhat random as we move through the chapters, but they address the issues which the Israelites were likely to face.

There are three items of particular interest.

First, chapter 17 addresses the matter of choosing a king: *"You are about to enter the land the Lord your God is giving you. When you take it over and settle there, you may think, 'We should select a king to rule over us like the other nations around us.' If this happens, be sure to select as king the man the Lord your God chooses"* (Deuteronomy 17:14–15).

Israel's king must rule differently from the kings of other nations around them. A king must forsake tokens of wealth: *"He must not accumulate large amounts of...silver and gold."* He must not make political alliances through marriages: *"The king must not take many wives for himself, because they will turn his heart away from the Lord."*

Instead, the king of Israel must be a spiritual leader as well as a political leader. Moses says that if chosen, a king must *"copy for himself this body of instruction on a scroll in the presence of the Levitical priests. He must always keep that copy with him and read it daily as long as he lives. That way he will learn to fear the Lord his God by obeying all the terms of these instructions and decrees"* (Deuteronomy 17:18–19).

A second matter of interest concerns the function of priests, in chapter 18. They must be careful not to imitate the worship practices of the nations around them—specifically, the sacrifice of their sons and daughters as burnt offerings. And they must not practice fortune-telling, sorcery, witchcraft, casting of spells, or psychic behavior like calling forth the dead.

These kinds of practices, common in paganism, are employed by people in these nations to protect themselves from the anger of the gods, or placate the gods for favors such as fertility, or to manipulate spiritual power for the practitioner's own ambition, like gaining wealth or harming others.

Israelite worship is to be shaped by God's special revelation. He is the one true God, holy in character and Creator of the heavens and earth—the God who revealed himself to Abraham, Isaac and Jacob. He is the God who calls people into relationship through his Covenant Promise and blesses them with peace and abundance when they follow his commandments.

Therefore, to worship false gods or to worship the true God in the wrong way is to bear false witness, and to bind people in fear and moral depravity because of confusion about who God is, and consequently, what is true, right and good.

A third matter of interest, in chapter 20, are the rules of humane soldiering in the occupation of the land. We noted earlier that the unrelenting brutality and violence of ISIS in the Mideast today reminds us that some groups are so evil that they cannot be reasoned with, and must be destroyed. This was the case with the Canaanites, as we have seen.

Even so, in God's war with the Canaanites, there are humane rules that must be followed. For example: *"As you approach a town to attack it, you must first offer its people terms for peace"* (Deuteronomy 20:10).

We'll pursue this in more detail when we come to the book of Joshua, but for now we can say that God's wars against the Canaanites were to be fought with his permission only, under his rules of engagement and for his specific purposes—to bring judgment upon gross and unrepentant evil, and to repopulate Canaan with people who bear witness to the one true God.

Israel's wars are not a template for succeeding generations and certainly not an example for the Church to follow. To point to God's orders to Israel as a general sanction for future holy wars is a false reading of the text.

> **Focus:** God's strong prohibition against participating in pagan worship is essential for Israel's well-being, and consequently for God's plan to redeem the world. The Old Testament people knew very well that all religions were not the same. The theological insights, worldview, morality and practices of the Israelites were significantly different from those of the pagan religions around them. This common sense observation has been largely forgotten today. To say that all religions are equally true is a polite way of saying that all religions are equally false, or at the very least to say that no religion is to be necessarily preferred over another.

> **Prayer:** *Lord, you have called us to be different in our thinking, living and worship, so that we may faithfully reflect your character and sovereignty. Forgive us for abusing this calling at times in Church history by pursuing power instead of love and servanthood. Forgive us also for ignoring you to worship the idols of our age, whether money, power, beauty or success. Humble our hearts, Lord. Keep us theologically and practically focused on who you have revealed yourself to be. Amen.*

Day 57   Deuteronomy 21–26

February 26

> Key Text: "A newly married man must not be drafted into the army or be given any other official responsibilities. He must be free to spend one year at home, bringing happiness to the wife he has married." (Deuteronomy 24:5)

Today we speed through the last seven chapters of Moses' second sermon to the people regarding their life in the Promised Land. Many of the specific instructions concerning moral behavior, social justice, social and domestic relationships, protection of the weak, personal hygiene, and donations to God, are specific to Israel's life under the Law and to her cultural context.

So prepare to scratch your head, smile, cringe, be offended, or even be totally confused as you read through them.

The task of interpretation here is to place ourselves, as much as possible, into the story of Israel up to this point and try to see through Israelite eyes, because all of this made perfect sense to them. Many of the laws reflect issues and practices common to ancient Near Eastern people, but whether moral, legal, social or religious, the issues and practices are restated and freshly understood within Israel's understanding of God.

Take, for example, the subject of male and female relationships. Chapters 22 and 24 address a number of issues related to engagement, marriage, divorce, rape and sexual behavior. In the ancient world, wives were property owned by their husbands, and had no legal rights. The wives bore the children, but the husbands indulged in sex with temple prostitutes or concubines on the side. The old double standard has a long history.

When women were raped or otherwise used and abused, there was little recourse. But the Old Testament doctrine of creation challenged and changed the status and dignity of women, and consequently the meaning of marriage.

Remember, in Genesis 1 and 2 we learned that human beings were created in the image of God as both male and female. Both shared the dignity of God's image. Both were given the cultural mandate to rule over the earth on behalf of God. Both were called to be fruitful, multiply and fill the earth with human life.

I suppose that God could have filled the earth with life any way he pleased. He could have grown us in the ground like potatoes. But he chose to do so through the equal and loving union of gendered beings, male and female, called marriage.

Marriage is introduced in the story of creation as God's gift to humanity. He creates Eve as Adam's partner, completing humanity and bringing her to him in marriage, thereby forming the basic unit of society—the family. By creating Eve out of Adam's "side," God shows that she is part of him, but different from him in her humanity, making possible an "I and thou" relationship.

Later God will refer to his Covenant relationship with Israel as a marriage, with Israel as his bride. The New Testament echoes this picture with Christ portrayed as the groom and his Church as the bride.

Human marriage, according to Ephesians 5:21–32, is a divine creation—a holy union and a revelation (some say sacrament) of God's own nature. The early Church began to understand the nature of God as unity of diversity, a loving relationship between the persons of the Trinity—Father, Son and Holy Spirit. So the ideal of a loving, committed, "one-flesh" marriage points to the nature of God, provides for human happiness, and enables human society and culture to thrive on earth.

These and other themes within the Bible's narrative, starting with Israel's life in the Promised Land, give a new vision for human life and relationships—a recognition that men and women are equal in God's sight and co-heirs to the gifts of creation and redemption.

Of course, as we know, fallen people don't always live up to the ideal—and so the laws of Israel provided for humane ways of addressing the breakup of a marriage and providing for remarriage *(Deuteronomy 24:1–2).*

> **Focus:** The laws, traditions and ceremonies that God gave to Israel serve to make God's holy nature concrete in human society. They implement his justice and love through societal norms and legal status. They also provide for grace and mercy, allowing for human weakness and restoring those who fail. When put into practice, they provide for a united society.

> *Prayer: Lord, your Word is wisdom and truth. It passes through cultures and generations, bringing the blessings of life to all who are willing to be guided by its instruction. Help us to listen, reflect upon and apply your Word to our lives. Amen.*

Day 58   Deuteronomy 27–30

February 27

> Key Text: "If you fully obey the Lord your God and carefully keep all his commands that I am giving you today, the Lord your God will set you high above all the nations of the world. You will experience all these blessings if you obey the Lord your God."
> (Deuteronomy 28:1–2)

As mentioned earlier, the structure of Deuteronomy parallels the structure of ancient treaties between kings and their vassals. These were legal documents establishing a relationship that would result in blessings if followed and curses (consequences) if broken.

The treaty included a section specifically addressing the blessings and curses. This is what we find in chapters 27 through 30 of Deuteronomy. As Leviticus 26 put it earlier, the choice between obedience and disobedience to the Covenant is the choice between life and death. Throughout the Bible, "life" is more than mere existence; it is the fullness of life in fellowship with God, and a future resurrection life.

In a similar way, death is more than physical death. It is existence without fellowship with God. Physical death is the final consequence,

111

but death also includes living without hope in a fallen world of suffering, sorrow and loss. Since death is the default position in a fallen world, it seems familiar. It is hard to imagine life without death operating to undermine our hopes, dreams and longings.

With this understanding in mind, Moses outlines the blessings for obedience and consequences for disobedience. Keep in mind that God's desire is for the people to experience life, not death, and blessings, not curses. The blessings are summarized in Deuteronomy 28:3–6: *"Your towns and your fields will be blessed. Your children and your crops will be blessed. The offspring of your herds and flocks will be blessed. Your fruit baskets and breadboards will be blessed. Wherever you go and whatever you do, you will be blessed."*

The curses, not surprisingly, are the loss of all these blessings. If Israel violates the Covenant and does not repent, the ultimate outcome will be the loss of the Promised Land. Israel will be conquered by pagan nations and taken into exile.

Even then, however, the offer of forgiveness and restoration is available for those who repent and return to the Covenant: *"If at that time you and your children return to the Lord your God, and if you obey with all your heart and all your soul all the commands I have given you today, then the Lord your God will restore your fortunes. He will have mercy on you and gather you back from all the nations where he has scattered you"* (Deuteronomy 30:2–3).

By means of these blessings and curses, the Lord makes clear how Israel may experience "life" and how deeply he desires that they would: *"Oh, that you would choose life, so that you and your descendants might live! You can make this choice by loving the Lord your God, obeying him, and committing yourself firmly to him. This is the key to your life"* (Deuteronomy 30:19–20).

It is important to understand that God takes the curses seriously: *"Those who hear the warnings of this curse should not congratulate themselves, thinking, 'I am safe, even though I am following the desires of my own stubborn heart.' This would lead to utter ruin!"* (Deuteronomy 29:19).

He takes the curses seriously because they are part of his love. What he opposes, he curses, and he opposes all that undermines human existence. Curses, then, are expressions of "tough love" meant to soften the people's hard hearts so that they might return to the blessings of a relationship with God.

Focus: We must understand that God's love is not a codependent or sentimental emotion. It is a fierce loving—a passionate love. It is frightening to experience for those who do not take him seriously. So he says to us: *"Now listen! Today I am giving you a choice between life and death, between prosperity and disaster. For I command you this day to love the Lord your God and to keep his commands, decrees and regulations by walking in his ways. If you do this, you will live and multiply, and the Lord your God will bless you and the land you are about to enter and occupy"* (Deuteronomy 30:15–16).

Prayer: Lord, we are amazed at how passionately you desire to have a relationship with us, even to the point of allowing us to rebel against you so that we might know by experience that there is no life outside of you. Thank you for your willingness to forgive, over and over again. Amen.

Day 59   Deuteronomy 31–34

February 28

Key Text: There has never been another prophet in Israel like Moses, whom the Lord knew face to face. The Lord sent him to perform all the miraculous signs and wonders in the land of Egypt against Pharaoh, and all his servants, and his entire land. With mighty power, Moses performed terrifying acts in the sight of all Israel. (Deuteronomy 34:10–12)

Deuteronomy ends on a melancholy note. Moses is old and the time has come to transfer leadership to Joshua. In front of all the people, Moses charges Joshua: *"Be strong and courageous! For you will lead these people into the land that the Lord swore to their ancestors he would give them. ... Do not be afraid or discouraged, for the Lord will personally go ahead of you. He will be with you; he will neither fail you nor abandon you"* (Deuteronomy 31:7–8).

However, the Lord tells Moses that he *"knows the intentions of the people."* After Moses dies, the people will eventually break the Covenant and begin worshiping the gods of the nations around them. The Lord will then hide his face from them *"and they will be devoured,"* meaning that they will suffer all the consequences stipulated in the Covenant, including exile.

So the Lord directs Moses to write a song as a moral warning and a

113

witness against the people about what could happen—and, as it turns out, *will* happen. The song of chapter 32 begins with the retelling of all that the Lord has done for Israel since the Exodus in bringing them to the Promised Land. It then becomes an eerie prediction of Israel's apostasy and the terrible consequences which will follow.

What is notable about the song is its revelation of God's emotion toward Israel. She has become his bride through the Covenant Promise, so her worship of other gods is like an act of adultery. When she abandons him, he feels the emotion of a jilted lover: *"They stirred up his jealousy by worshiping foreign gods; they provoked his fury with detestable deeds. They offered sacrifices to demons, which are not God, to gods they had not known before..."* (Deuteronomy 32:16–17).

The song recalls the blessings and curses of the Covenant and paints a vivid picture of Israel's choice, and ours: Faithfulness to God is a choice for a life of blessing and abundance; unfaithfulness is a choice for a living death.

The time draws near for Moses to die. He blesses each of the twelve tribes in chapter 33, and concludes with a strong word of exhortation: *"How blessed you are, O Israel! Who else is like you, a people saved by the Lord?"* (Deuteronomy 33:29).

Don't blow it!

God gives Moses one final view of the Promised Land from Mount Nebo before he dies. The people mourn for him and promise to follow Joshua, whom Moses has anointed for leadership.

Deuteronomy ends with a fitting epitaph to one of the greatest and most influential human beings who has ever lived: *"There has never been another prophet in Israel like Moses, whom the Lord knew face to face. The Lord sent him to perform all the miraculous signs and wonders in the land of Egypt against Pharaoh, and all his servants, and his entire land. With mighty power, Moses performed terrifying acts in the sight of all Israel"* (Deuteronomy 34:10–12).

Focus: What can one say to honor the life of the great Moses? Raised and educated by Egyptian royalty, but called by God to lead his people Israel from slavery in Egypt. Moses was clearly a genius, but he was humbled by his calling. Despite his perceived weaknesses, he became a great leader, warrior and shepherd of Israel. He was also a theologian. As the principle thinker and writer behind the Pentateuch, his insights into the nature of God and his Law have changed the world.

Day 60   Reflection

February 29

Before we jump into the book of Joshua, and the conquering of the Promised Land, let's pause and think about the phenomenon of "Israel" as the chosen people. As Moses reminded the people before he died: *"How blessed you are, O Israel! Who else is like you, a people saved by the Lord?"* (Deuteronomy 33:29).

To understand the significance of "Israel," we need to look at the major themes of the first five books of the Bible, known as the Pentateuch— Creation *(where did everything come from and why are we here?)*, Fall *(why is everything so messed up?)*, and Redemption *(what, if anything, can be done about it?)*.

Regarding the subject of creation, we have learned that everything comes from the loving action of God who created the material universe for his pleasure, and called it "good." But human beings, the crown of his creation, rebelled against God and brought sin and death into the world—and therefore the need for redemption by God. Fortunately, God did not give up on the creation, but passionately pursues it with the purpose of reconciling us to himself. Beginning with Genesis chapter 3, the story of our redemption unfolds throughout the Old and New Testaments.

During the course of this long story, there are references back to the importance of understanding the Creation and Fall relative to human nature, behavior, potential and destiny. This understanding is shaped by what God has already done and continues to do, to reconcile the world to himself.

What, then, is "Israel"? When God spoke to Abraham in Genesis 12, he revealed to him that he was going to make things right in the world through the story of one special nation—Abraham's descendants, Israel. He would give Israel its own land where they could live long and prosper. The purpose of this gracious calling was that Israel would bear witness to the nations around them, through teaching, worship and holiness, of

115

the one true God, Creator of the heavens and earth.

To this end Israel was delivered from slavery in Egypt by God's mighty power, to live among the nations as God's holy people and a *"light to the Gentiles."* Israel was, in a sense, a microcosm of all humanity, and a provisional expression of what will eventually become the worldwide Church.

The connections are clearly made in the New Testament. Jesus, who establishes his Church, is a *"son of Israel"* and the fulfillment of God's Promise to Abraham. What is pictured and promised in Israel's Covenant with God—the commandments and laws, the Tabernacle and then Temple, priesthood, sacrifices, Promised Land, kings and prophets—is all fulfilled in Christ, who is Israel's prophet, King, and great High Priest. But Jesus is more than Israel's king. He belongs to the whole world, Jews and Gentiles alike.

The Church will not be a distinct nation or ethnic identity. It will be a spiritual community comprised of individuals of all times, places and ethnicities. For this reason, we find the titles given to Old Testament Israel now applied to the New Testament Church. For example, writing to congregations made up of both Jews and Gentiles, the apostle Peter writes: *"…you are a chosen people. You are royal priests, a holy nation, God's very own possession"* (1 Peter 2:9).

Because "Israel" is the provisional expression of the Church, we as contemporary Christians can learn much about who God is and what it means to be God's holy people in the world by reading the Old Testament.

> *Prayer: Lord, we are amazed as we stand back and watch the Great Story of Redemption being brought about in the Old Testament. From where we stand now, we can see how you have patiently and faithfully fulfilled your promises to Abraham through Christ, the one true Israelite. As that great story continues in the Church and its mission to the whole world, we know that the best is yet ahead, when all the promises will come to full bloom in the New Heavens and New Earth. Amen!*

Day 61   Joshua 1–5

March 1

> Key Text: The Lord told Joshua, "Today I will begin to make you a great leader in the eyes of all the Israelites. They will know that I am with you, just as I was with Moses." (Joshua 3:7)

With the book of Joshua, we move from the Pentateuch to the twelve books of history about Israel in the land. These books cover the struggles of conquering Canaan, and of living under God's authority in the land while resisting the lure of Canaanite idolatry. There comes a mostly disappointing period of Judges and then Kings. There are occasional revivals of faith, but the lure of idolatry, and the desire for national power, and political alliances, lead to the dividing of Israel into two kingdoms, north and south. Eventually, both kingdoms are conquered by superpowers and taken into exile because of their unfaithfulness to God.

The book of Joshua has been called "a tale of war and peace." With Moses dead, God now speaks to Joshua: *"Be strong and very courageous. Be careful to obey all the instructions Moses gave you. Do not deviate from them, turning either to the right or to the left. Then you will be successful in everything you do"* (Joshua 1:7).

Joshua proves to be an able leader, leading the people in three military campaigns to conquer more than thirty enemy rulers. But Israel learns that faith in God is a greater weapon than the enemies' military might.

The first battle is one of the most famous—the battle of Jericho. Spies are hidden by a pagan prostitute named Rahab, who expresses faith and respect towards the God of Israel: *"Before the spies went to sleep that night, Rahab went up on the roof to talk with them. 'I know the Lord has given you this land,' she told them. 'We are all afraid of you. Everyone in the land is living in terror. For we have heard how the Lord made a dry path for you through the Red Sea when you left Egypt. And we know what you did to Sihon and Og, the two Amorite kings east of the Jordan River, whose people you completely destroyed. No wonder our hearts have melted in fear! No one has the courage to fight after hearing such things. For the Lord your God is the supreme God of the heavens above and the earth below'"* (Joshua 2:8–11).

This is a remarkable example of pagans coming to faith in the God of Israel. Presumably many did, and Rahab's faith is early evidence that God's promise to bless the nations of the world is coming about through Israel's story.

Rahab is later spared when Jericho is taken. Amazingly, this woman—a pagan and a prostitute—is honored by being mentioned in the opening genealogy of the Messiah in the Gospel of Matthew *(Matthew 1:5).*

Joshua 2 through 5 recounts the prelude to the battle of Jericho. The

117

spies hidden by Rahab return and report to Joshua: *"'The Lord has given us the whole land,' they said, 'for all the people in the land are terrified of us'"* (Joshua 2:24).

The next morning, the Levitical priests line up to lead the army across the Jordan River. They carry the Ark of the Covenant with them, demonstrating that the Lord is leading them into battle. When the priests enter the river, the water backs up—just like the Red Sea—and the people crossed over!

There is great joy and amazement among the people: *"That day the Lord made Joshua a great leader in the eyes of all the Israelites, and for the rest of his life they revered him as much as they had revered Moses"* (Joshua 4:14).

As the army positions itself on the far side of the Jordan at Gilgal on the plains of Jericho, the uncircumcised young men are circumcised as the Covenant sign of belonging to God. After they rest and heal, the Israelites celebrate Passover and await Joshua's command.

Meanwhile, God reassures Joshua by appearing before him as *"the commander of the Lord's army"* with sword in hand. He tells Joshua: *"'Take off your sandals, for the place where you are standing is holy.' And Joshua did as he was told"* (Joshua 5:15).

Always a good idea.

Focus: As the well-known song goes, *"Joshua fit the battle of Jericho, and the walls came a-tumbling down."* But more impressive than the tumbling walls was the rising faith of some of the Canaanites like Rahab—the unlikely heroine of this story. It reminds us that God is always at work in people's hearts, even among those who have been raised in ungodly cultures. We should always be alert to where God is working in individual lives, and be prepared to share the Good News.

Prayer: *Lord, you are a warrior for your people. Thank you for fighting on our behalf, defeating the true enemies of our soul: sin, death and the demonic realm. We know that Israel's wars were but an earthly manifestation of the spiritual warfare we are presently engaged in. But because of the victory of Christ, it is a war where the outcome has already been decided. Amen!*

March 2

> Key Text: When the people heard the sound of the rams' horns, they shouted as loud as they could. Suddenly, the walls of Jericho collapsed, and the Israelites charged straight into the town and captured it. (Joshua 6:20)

The people of Jericho are very aware that Israel is camped nearby and preparing for war. Jericho was probably a military fortress and command center for oppressive rulers. As such, the gates are tightly shut— *"But the Lord said to Joshua, 'I have given you Jericho, its king, and all its strong warriors'"* (Joshua 6:2).

A holy war is about to begin. The term, as it is used today, is extremely troublesome to many. It suggests that Israel used the name of God to give sanction to their military and political ambitions. "Holy" is thus seen to be ironic.

As you might imagine, the holy wars of Israel have been subject to much scholarly inquiry and debate. Some deny that God sent Israel into war, and therefore dismiss the accounts as propaganda put into Scripture to justify their conquering and plundering. Others simply ignore "the angry, judgmental God of the Old Testament" and speak instead of "the loving and compassionate God who sent Jesus to die for our sins."

But lest we set ourselves up as judges who determine what God can or cannot do, or lest we ignore the wars of Israel altogether, we must wrestle with the idea, frequently expressed in the Old Testament, that God is a warrior who fights for his people Israel.

The battle of Jericho is well known. The Lord directs the army to walk around the walled fortress each day for six days without saying a word. Nothing is heard but the movement of people and the repeated blowing of a ram's horn. It must have been eerie and frightening!

On the seventh day, the people go around Jericho seven times and then stop. The priests sound a long blast on their horns and Joshua commands the people to shout. And then: *"Suddenly, the walls of Jericho collapsed, and the Israelites charged straight into the town and captured it. They completely destroyed everything in it with their swords—men and women, young and old, cattle, sheep, goats, and donkeys"* (Joshua 6:20–21).

How are we to understand this admittedly disturbing violence?

Old Testament historians suggest that few civilians lived in walled fortresses like Jericho or Ai, which is mentioned in chapters 7 and 8. The masses lived in hamlets and other places near the forts. Most likely, any who happened to be in Jericho would have fled before the fighting began. Rahab and her family remain because of the promise from the spies that she would be spared and welcomed to live among the Israelites.

Scholars also suggest that the inclusive phrase *"men and women, young and old"* is a stereotypical bit of hyperbole of the time, which was a way of saying "everyone." It does not necessarily describe who was killed. In fact, a careful reading of Joshua 1 through 12 indicates that no specific noncombatants are ever named among the Canaanites. The Israelites did not target nor did they kill noncombatants.

Still, we find God directing Israel to go to war. Importantly, these are God's wars, not Israel's. They are an act of divine judgment. Remember, God had told Abraham long ago that the Canaanites whose land they would occupy would be given ample warning. Indeed, God gave them 400 years to repent of their repugnant, dehumanizing idolatry and child sacrifice. They refused.

God, of course, has the right to give and take life. Thankfully, he targets his righteous anger against evil. He goes to war against the evil powers of heaven and earth, which keep people from knowing God. Sometimes, as with the Canaanites, this takes the form of historical judgment and destruction.

So God does not just look away from evil or say it doesn't matter. He goes to war against it, and we are the beneficiaries. The wars of Israel point forward to the great spiritual war that he will fight and win against sin, death and the demonic realm through the crucifixion and resurrection of Jesus. There we will see the amazing revelation that, ultimately, God defeats evil and injustice by absorbing the full fury of it—all of it—into himself on the cross of Christ.

Focus: Tragically, many have misused the wars of Israel against the Canaanites to justify acts of aggression against political or religious enemies. God's wars, however, give no such sanction. God is gracious, patient and amazingly forgiving. But there is a limit to his tolerance; the wars against the Canaanites—like the ancient flood judgment in the days of Noah—show that God will not tolerate evil forever.

✖Even so, his people are given no freedom to use his name to sanction aggression against others.

Prayer: Lord, we praise you for being our defender and a rock against our enemies. Thank you for defeating our enemy, the devil, who stirs rebellion against God in the hearts of man. Amen!

Day 63   Joshua 9–12

March 3

> Key Text: So Joshua took control of the entire land, just as the Lord had instructed Moses. He gave it to the people of Israel as their special possession, dividing the land among the tribes. So the land finally had rest from war. (Joshua 11:23)

The battle for Canaan continues. After Israel's stunning victories over the two Amorite kings of Bashan and Sihon, and then the defeat of Jericho and Ai, the word gets around to the twenty-nine other Canaanite kings that the Lord fights on behalf of his people.

One particular group, the people of Gibeon, see the handwriting on the wall and surrender by deception. They pretend that they are from outside the land God has given Israel. Then, out of fear of the Lord, they trick Joshua into making a binding peace treaty.

When he discovers their ruse, Joshua shows them mercy and allows them to live among the Israelites as woodcutters and water carriers for the community. Again we see that those, like Rahab the prostitute from Jericho, *who humble themselves before the Lord*—even if by deception— are saved from judgment.

Other kings are not so humble. In chapter 10, five Amorite kings join forces to attack Joshua but are defeated by nature miracles. Joshua surprises the kings with a sneak attack, throwing the soldiers into a panic. As he chases the fleeing enemy, *"the Lord destroyed them with a terrible hailstorm from heaven.... The hail killed more of the enemy than the Israelites killed with the sword"* (Joshua 10:11). At the same time, Joshua prays for the Lord to give the Israelites a sign: *"Let the sun stand still over Gibeon, and the moon over the valley of Aijalon. So the sun stood still and the moon stayed in place until the nation of Israel had defeated its enemies"* (Joshua 10:12–13).

✖The miraculous sign is remembered and recorded in the non-biblical book, *The Book of Jashar*: *"The sun stayed in the middle of the sky, and it did not set as on a normal day. There has never been a day like this one before or since, when the Lord answered such a prayer. Surely the Lord fought for Israel that day!"* (Joshua 10:14). It is likely that the Gibeonites worshiped the sun as a god. If so, the God of Israel is showing that he is the only God.

In chapter 11, another and larger group of kings join forces to fight against Israel: *"Their combined armies formed a vast horde. And with all their horses and chariots, they covered the landscape like the sand on the seashore"* (Joshua 11:4).

But again, God gives Israel victory over her enemies: *"So Joshua took control of the entire land, just as the Lord had instructed Moses. He gave it to the people of Israel as their special possession, dividing the land among the tribes. So the land finally had rest from war"* (Joshua 11:23).

Israel is clearly "out-manned" and "out-gunned" in every battle, yet the Lord gives them victory. Chapter 12 lists the thirty-one kings who were defeated—a sobering testimony to the power of God.

As we have suggested before, Israel's wars are not fought because God hates humans. Quite the opposite. The wars are against the proxy rebels of the powers of darkness. When humans embrace spiritual darkness and do evil on earth against fellow humans, God will intervene. God's wars point toward the larger warfare that is going on in the creation.

This becomes clearer in the New Testament when Jesus launches his ministry by being tempted by the devil. He then demonstrates the power of the Kingdom of God by casting out demons, and not by taking up arms against Israel's earthly enemies.

As the apostle Paul would later explain: *"Be strong in the Lord and in his mighty power. Put on all of God's armor so that you will be able to stand firm against all the strategies of the devil. For we are not fighting against flesh-and-blood enemies, but against evil rulers and authorities of the unseen world, against mighty powers in this dark world, and against evil spirits in the heavenly places"* (Ephesians 6:10–12).

Focus: The Old and New Testaments affirm the reality of the invisible spiritual realm. Angels and rebellious angels (called demons) who exist in the spiritual realm are not gods, but part of God's creation, over which God has complete authority. Though the Bible has little to say about the back story, it seems that demonic powers get into human minds through evil ideas, temptations, lies and shaming. Those who open their minds to the demonic realm put themselves in great danger.

Guard your heart & mind in Christ Jesus.

YES!

Prayer: Lord, thank you for being strong on our behalf. We don't have to be afraid of anything because nothing can separate us from your love. Indeed, you have already defeated our greatest enemies, sin and death, in the cross and resurrection of Jesus. Help us to live with courage and hope! Amen.

Day 64   Joshua 13–17

March 4

> Key Text: "I myself will drive these people out of the land ahead of the Israelites. So be sure to give this land to Israel as a special possession, just as I have commanded you." (Joshua 13:6)

Israel has conquered the land in fulfillment of the Covenant Promise. But now the people must "move in" and get settled.

To be honest, these chapters are rather boring to read because they are merely an account of what land was given to each tribe. However, a careful reading uncovers some interesting facts that shed further light on the wars of Israel.

To me, the most surprising fact is that much land remains to be conquered *(Joshua 13:1)* by the individual tribes within their allotted divisions, and that there are still Canaanites everywhere. For example: Joshua 15:63 says, *"But the tribe of Judah could not drive out the Jebusites, who lived in the city of Jerusalem, so the Jebusites live there among the people of Judah to this day."*

Why are these details important? They give us further clues about the use of exaggerated language in describing victory in battle. As we've noted, phrases like *"every man and woman, young and old"* were destroyed was a common way of saying "everyone," and though chilling, probably meant combatants, not civilians.

We've seen already that Rahab and her family were spared from Jericho, and also that the clever Gibeonites tricked their way into a peace agreement and were allowed to live among the Israelites *(Joshua 9:3–26)*. It's clearly stated that the Jebusites and others continued to exist around them also—even though they were a thorn in the Israelites' flesh.

These observations are important to help us understand, if not fully accept, the wars of Israel. It is important to understand that they were not random acts of aggression; they were directly connected to the redemptive Promise of God to give Abraham's descendants a land of their own and make them into a great nation. Importantly, they were God's wars, directed against unrepentant, evil cultures whose moral and religious practices were not tolerable (think ISIS today). God had given them 400 years to forsake their evil *(Genesis 15:16)*—but they refused.

God's judgment was not against Canaanite people as a race, but against the Canaanite religion. Expulsion from the land is in view, not annihilation of the people. We have described the Canaanite religion as evil and intolerable, but here is some further explanation by a professor of religious ethics:

"The Canaanite gods/goddesses encouraged all kinds of abusive sexual acts forbidden by God, including incest, bestiality and ritual prostitution—not to mention infant sacrifice and other deviant acts. In our sex-saturated culture, many people do not seem concerned about sexual immorality and the destruction it wreaks on individuals, families, and society. Our anger may flare up about racism or gender discrimination, but today's society has jaded our moral instincts when it comes to other soul-destroying activities. God's anger at a society's moral and spiritual suicide mission—his saying 'Enough!'—turns out to be a sign of moral concern." (Paul Copan)

Focus: One of the dangerous assumptions of contemporary religious pluralism is that all religions are essentially alike and equally valid. This is not the view of the Old or New Testaments. The Bible declares that there is one God, Creator of everything, to whom we owe our worship and allegiance. The gods of the pagan nations are nothing more than idols created by human imagination. Thankfully, the God of the Bible is good. He created us out of love and calls us to live in love. When we do, our lives flourish. On the other hand, to live in lust or pride or avarice or cruelty is to wreak havoc on earth and diminish human life and dignity. That is why a good God must sometimes bring judgment to stop the growth of evil, as he did with the Canaanites.

Prayer: Lord, life is messy business. Even Jesus told us that human history would be marked by wars and rumors of wars, nation rising against nation, until the end. Although you are warrior for your people when you need to be, your great redemptive purpose is to make things right in the world—no more sin or sorrow or death or tears. We long for that day! Amen.

March 5

> Key Text: As the men started on their way to map out the land, Joshua commanded them, "Go and explore the land and write a description of it. Then return to me, and I will assign the land to tribes by casting sacred lots here in the presence of the Lord at Shiloh." (Joshua 18:8)

Imagine the leaders of the twelve tribes of Israel standing in a circle, singing, "This land is *your* land, this land is *my* land, from Gath-rimmon to Shaalabbin...from Gibbethon to the land of El-te-keh. This land is made for you and me!"

Okay, that probably didn't happen. But chapters 18 through 21 do review the regions and towns assigned to each of the tribes of Israel. Mind-numbing to us, but exciting to the Israelites: *Here is our land, at last!*

Special arrangements are made for Joshua, for the Levites who care for the Tabernacle, and for providing cities of refuge in each tribal region *(Joshua 20)*. You may remember that cities of refuge allowed those who accidently killed others to be protected from irate family members seeking revenge. This was a wise provision, given humans' emotional impulses. It gave time for angry families to calm down and do their grieving before making the situation worse by committing homicide!

God has finally given Israel all the land he swore to their ancestors he would give. They have taken possession of it and settled there. And there was "rest on every side," meaning that *"none of their enemies could stand against them, for the Lord helped them conquer all their enemies. Not a single one of all the good promises the Lord had given to the family of Israel was left unfulfilled; everything he had spoken came true"* (Joshua 21:44–45).

It is interesting to note that 600 years have passed since God first gave Abraham the Promise of a great nation of his descendants, living in their own land *(Genesis 12:1–3)*. Why did it take so long? Because God chooses to work through time, space and historical processes. More importantly, God is pleased to use humans who trust him as his agents to bring about his purposes.

This is quite an honor! As followers of Jesus, we are called to help grow the Kingdom of God by taking the Gospel to the nations *(Matthew 28:19-20)* and by being partners with Christ in his sufferings *(1 Peter 4:13)*. It seems also that we will reign with Christ in the New Creation: *"If we die with him, we will also live with him. If we endure hardship, we will reign with him"* (2 Timothy 2:11–12).

It is fun to imagine what this will involve, but it will be great. God's gift of the Promised Land suggests that we are people made for the earth. It also points us to the expectation that our destiny is to spend eternity on a renewed earth, doing all the things we associate with a rich and satisfying life on this earth, except without sin and death.

Focus: The fulfillment of God's promise to give Israel the Promised Land reminds us that God always keeps his promises. The fact that it took generations shows us that God doesn't just wave a magic wand, but brings about his purposes for us through our participation with him during the course of our lives. This suggests that human history is a living drama, directed by God. We are his agents, acting in his drama, to bring about its good conclusion. Our participation means that history will have progress and setbacks, but the fact that God directs the story (and, in Jesus, enters into the story) guarantees that it will come to his intended conclusion.

Prayer: Lord, thank you for the hope of eternal life as resurrected people in a New Heaven and Earth. Israel's dwelling in the Promised Land, with you in their midst, excites our imagination about what is to come on that great day when we share your glory! Amen.

Day 66　　　　　Joshua 22–24

March 6

Key Text: "But if you refuse to serve the Lord, then choose today whom you will serve. Would you prefer the gods your ancestors served beyond the Euphrates? Or will it be the gods of the Amorites in whose land you now live? But as for me and my family, we will serve the Lord." (Joshua 24:15)

Joshua chapter 22 begins with the account of an apparent act of rebellion by the tribes of Reuben, Gad, and Manasseh. They had earlier requested to settle in an area back across the Jordan River, a request that could imply that they were not willing to enter into the Promised Land proper.

Worse, they have built a large and imposing altar, which the other tribes assume to be a violation of God's instruction to worship only at the Tabernacle. It could possibly be evidence that they are worshiping the Canaanite gods. This development stirs up fear and anger. The people remember earlier acts of disobedience by fellow Israelites that had brought God's judgment upon them all!

But a visit and conversation by a priestly delegation resolves the crisis. The others have misunderstood the motives and theological reasoning of the three tribes. These tribes have built the altar not as a statement of disobedience, but as witness of their faith in the Lord, God. The altar is a memorial, and not a functioning altar. It is meant to remind future generations that, though they were living across the Jordan River from their brothers, they too were Israelites who participated fully in the Covenant relationship with the Lord.

The successful resolution to the crisis is a good reminder of how quick we are to judge others before understanding them, even in the church.

As the years pass by, the people enjoy *"rest from all their enemies"* in the land *(Joshua 23:1)*. Joshua is very old now and calls together the leaders of the tribes of Israel. He reminds them that though they are occupying the land, there is still much work to do in order to truly *"possess"* it. Spiritual vigilance and maintenance is required!

So Joshua challenges the leaders to continue following everything Moses wrote in the book of instruction: *"Do not deviate from it, turning either to the right or to the left. Make sure you do not associate with the other people still remaining in the land. Do not even mention the names of their gods, much less swear by them or serve them or worship them. Rather, cling tightly to the Lord your God as you have done until now"* (Joshua 23:6–8).

He warns them that if they assimilate with the nations they have driven out by adopting their customs and intermarrying with them, those nations will become a *"snare and a trap,"* and the Israelites will vanish from the good land the Lord has given them.

To encourage their obedience, Joshua reviews with the tribal leaders the great story of Israel, from God's ancient Promise to Abraham, up unto the present time. He concludes with a powerful personal challenge: *"So fear the Lord and serve him wholeheartedly. Put away forever the idols your ancestors worshiped when they lived beyond the Euphrates River and in Egypt. Serve the Lord alone. But if you refuse to serve the Lord, then choose today whom you will serve. Would you prefer the gods your ances-tors served beyond the Euphrates? Or will it be the gods of the Amorites in whose land you now live? But as for me and my family, we will serve the Lord"* (Joshua 24:14–15).

After this, Joshua, the faithful and courageous servant of the Lord, dies at the age of 110. His stirring challenge still resonates today: *Whom will we serve?*

Focus: Like Moses, Joshua was a flawed leader. But also like Moses, he sincerely loved the Lord and trusted in him. When called upon, he willingly took the mantle of leadership and led the nation during the very difficult period of occupying the land. Different leaders, with different gifts, are raised up by God for different times. We always need to be asking God to raise up new leaders to meet the challenges of our own time.

Prayer: Lord, we take to heart Joshua's warning that our relationship with God must be maintained by constant vigilance. We know by experience that when we don't, we easily drift into worldly ways of thinking and behaving. With Joshua, we want you to know that we will serve you with all our hearts! Amen.

Day 67   Reflection

March 7

Moses is gone, and now Joshua also. Both of them were faithful servant-leaders who listened to God and cared about his people.

Since Genesis, we've covered a long period of salvation history, from God's Promise to Abraham to the successful occupation of the Promised Land.

Maybe you have noticed that one of the difficulties of reading the Old Testament is the tendency to get lost in the details and lose track of the bigger picture. It is not unlike staring at individual brush marks on the canvas of a famous painting. Up close it looks messy, incomprehensible— unless you are fascinated by brush marks! But step back and you see the bigger picture. All the elements of line, space, color, value and texture come together through expert brush marks to form a work of art.

That is how God works in the world. He is painting a great masterpiece called "Redemption" and he puts brush marks on the canvas of human history through people, events, processes and time. Perhaps watercolor painting is the best metaphor here, because there is a measure of freedom and unpredictability about watercolor pigment as it is placed on wet paper.

The artist prepares his work by a careful initial drawing and then lets the brush, pigment, paper and water surprise him even as he shapes his work.

So far in our reading, we have met unusual people living in a world of strange cultural practices unfamiliar to us. These details are the brush strokes. Yet, in the big picture we see people who are like us in their struggles and in their hopes and dreams. By putting ourselves in their shoes, we are able to see beyond the rough details and connect with who they are and with what God is doing in their lives.

Theologically, everything we find in the New Testament is already present in the Old Testament. God progressively reveals himself in ways that make sense within the ancient world. It is the same today. Even if the dominant secularism of our day dims our perception a bit, we can still see the "Big Picture" of the one true God, working in the world so that we can be reconciled to him and share eternal life with him.

We recognize our own sinfulness in the Fall of Adam and Eve, and the subsequent bad behavior of the Old Testament characters, including the heroes of our faith such as Abraham and Moses.

We connect with our own need of redemption and marvel at God's gracious and patient commitment to make things right in the world, even when human sinfulness threatens to undermine his Promise.

Think of the Old Testament as containing the seed of the Gospel, planted in the soil of Israel. It will eventually flower in Christ and then reproduce around the world as the Church announces the Good News.

But for now, our story continues with Israel planted in the Promised Land. What is coming next? Well, as you might suspect, based on what we've seen so far, what is coming next is the inconsistent, stumbling forward path of God's people. There will be inspiring moments of faith and heroism, along with stomach-churning moments of cowardice and evildoing.

In other words—kind of like life now.

Prayer: Lord, thank you for always speaking to us in ways we can understand— like a new mother speaks to her infant. We feel like children in our understanding

129

and behavior. Continue to grow us up into mature faith, through the twists and turns of our lives, as you did with Israel. Amen.

Day 68   Judges 1–5

March 8

> Key Text: Then the Lord raised up judges to rescue the Israelites
> from their attackers. Yet Israel did not listen to the judges but
> prostituted themselves by worshiping other gods. How quickly
> they turned away from the path of their ancestors, who had
> walked in obedience to the Lord's commands. (Judges 2:16–17)

The period of Israel's history immediately following the death of Joshua is called the period of the judges. It is a long, discouraging period of national decline.

Although the Israelites conquered the land under Joshua's leadership, there were still plenty of Canaanites around to lure them back into paganism. Keep in mind that pagan worship appealed to human sensuality, and thus to the sinful nature of these mostly young men and women. By contrast, the requirements of the Covenant with God were difficult, calling them to act contrary to their sinful nature.

This is not unlike the tension we feel today between secular society and the claims of Christ. Our culture is saturated with appeals to me-first materialism, consumerism and sexual licentiousness. Against this, the cost of discipleship is difficult.

During this period of generational change, Israel is led by judges, who are military and spiritual leaders. But Israel develops an abysmal pattern of unfaithfulness to God. The narrator says, *"After [Joshua's] generation died, another generation grew up who did not acknowledge the Lord or remember the mighty things he had done for Israel. The Israelites did evil in the Lord's sight and served the images of Baal. They abandoned the Lord, the God of their ancestors, who had brought them out of Egypt. They went after other gods, worshiping the gods of the people around them. ... This made the Lord burn with anger against Israel"* (Judges 2:10–14).

This description of the people's struggle with idolatry is a snapshot of the next 350-year period of national deterioration. The book of Judges follows a pattern of events through seven cycles of decline: The people fall into sin and God disciplines them with foreign oppression. In time, the people cry out to God for forgiveness and so God sends a "judge" to deliver them. During the period of the judge, the people return to God, but when the judge dies, the people return to paganism—and the cycle starts over.

It is important to observe that whenever the Israelites embrace the Canaanite religion, they experience the same judgment from God as the Canaanites. Israel is not a special "race" of people whom God favors over others, no matter what they do. They are a people called to faithfulness to the one true God who made himself known and entered into Covenant with them. It is a privilege, but also a burden and a struggle.

So we find, along the way, pagans like Rahab who believe and receive God's blessings, while Israelites, who are God's chosen people, act like pagans and receive God's judgment.

Israel's suffering in the book of Judges is self-inflicted. Its stories give us a glimpse of how horribly twisted, dark and brutal people can become when they rebel against God.

As one scholar describes it, *"Murder, rape, idolatry, perversion and betrayal become the backdrop for theology. Irony pervades the whole. Major character flaws appear in persons who are supposed to lead the people back to God or at least away from the enemy. Failure abounds. Defeats are normal."* (Paul House)

And so we learn that the more we understand about God and his commandments, the more accountable we become. The fact that we willfully break his commandments shows how deeply rooted our sinful nature is—and how greatly we need God's grace and mercy.

> **Focus:** The period of the judges (and the period of the kings which follows) is very disheartening. As the prophet Jeremiah would later say, the human heart is deceitful above all things, and desperately wicked. Who can know it? For pagans, who are ignorant of the one true God, there is room for tolerance and understanding. But these stories are about the "chosen people," to whom God specially revealed himself through many acts of deliverance, provision and insight through moral instruction.
>
> What are we to make of this? One thing: Salvation is all of grace. The New Testament is emphatic: *"God saved you by his grace when you believed. And you can't take credit for this; it is a gift from God. Salvation is not a reward for the good things we have done, so none of us can boast about it"* (Ephesians 2:8–9).

131

Day 69   Judges 6–8

March 9

> Key Text: "But Lord," Gideon replied, "how can I rescue Israel? My clan is the weakest in the whole tribe of Manasseh, and I am the least of my entire family!" The Lord said to him, "I will be with you. And you will destroy the Midianites as if you were fighting against one man." (Judges 6:15–17)

Judges 6 begins with a report that will become all too common in this book: *"The Israelites did evil in the Lord's sight."*

We mentioned that the book of Judges contains seven cycles of a characteristic pattern of Israel's national life: Israel does evil through idolatry; God disciplines Israel, usually through a foreign army; Israel finally cries out for help and God sends a leader-judge; there is a period of peace and blessing which follows, until the judge dies; Israel does evil through idolatry once again.

Chapters 6 through 8 describe the cycle when Gideon becomes judge of Israel. Here is what happens: Because the Israelites had done evil in the Lord's sight, he hands them over to the Midianites for seven years: *"The Midianites were so cruel that the Israelites made hiding places for themselves in the mountains, caves, and strongholds"* (Judges 6:2).

We should note here (and in the rest of the Old Testament story) that God always holds his people accountable to the Covenant they have made with him. He doesn't just judge the pagan nations; he also disciplines his own people, like a father disciplines his children. Often, this discipline takes the form of consequences. When Israel begins worshiping other gods, he withholds his divine protection so that Israel may experience life outside of his blessing and protection.

This time, when God withholds his blessing and protection, the Midianites raid Israelite towns during planting season, destroying their crops and stealing their animals. The inhabitants are reduced to starvation. Finally, they cry out to the Lord, who sends a prophet to remind them of the Covenant Promises they had broken. God had called their ancestors to belong to him. He then delivered them from slavery in Egypt and gave them this land. They must not worship the gods of the people in whose land they now live.

During this time of discipline, the angel of the Lord appears to Gideon, calling him to rescue Israel from the Midianites. Gideon argues with the angel over theology: *"If the Lord is with us, why has all this happened to us? And where are all the miracles our ancestors told us about? Didn't they say, 'The Lord brought us up out of Egypt'? But now the Lord has abandoned us and handed us over to the Midianites"* (Joshua 6:13).

The angel doesn't answer Gideon's objections because the answer is obvious—Israel has once again broken the Covenant through idolatry. So God sends him to fight the Midianites. Gideon, like Moses, complains that he doesn't have the resources. But God says to Gideon the same thing he said to Moses: *"I will be with you. And you will destroy the Midianites as if you were fighting against one man."*

And that is exactly what happens. The story is quite interesting, but the key is found in Judges 6:34: *"Then the Spirit of the Lord clothed Gideon with power."* God's blessing and protection of Israel is now restored through Gideon.

To demonstrate to Gideon and all of Israel that the battle is won by the power of God, the Lord directs Gideon to reduce his fighting force by 90%. You can read what happens in Judges 7 and 8.

After the defeat of Midian, and throughout the rest of Gideon's life, there is peace in the land.

What Israel should have learned from this amazing victory is that their national life can only be sustained by the action of God as their shield and protector. As with their ancestors in Egypt, God is able to overcome seemingly impossible circumstances or obstacles.

But sadly, the truism that *"those who fail to learn from history are doomed to repeat it"* is confirmed once again.

Chapter 8 concludes: *"As soon as Gideon died, the Israelites prostituted themselves by worshiping the images of Baal, making Baal-berith their god. They forgot the Lord their God, who had rescued them from all their enemies surrounding them. Nor did they show any loyalty to the family of Jerub-baal (that is, Gideon), despite all the good he had done for Israel"* (Judges 8:33–35).

Focus: God's action to bless or withhold blessing from people and nations is an expression of both his sovereignty and the moral nature of his creation. The whole creation comes from him and belongs to him. Our purpose, therefore, as people and nations, is to honor the Lord our Creator and do his will on earth. We should view world events, therefore, from the perspective of divine sovereignty and not just the political maneuvering of powerful people.

Prayer: Lord, we confess that we easily forget what you have done for us. We have seen your goodness and power in our lives in so many big and little ways, and yet it seems that when the next crisis occurs, we respond as if you were not able to meet our needs. Forgive our lack of faith, and as you did with Gideon, fill us with your Spirit for the challenge at hand. Amen.

Day 70   Judges 9–12

March 10

> Key Text: God was punishing Abimelech for murdering Gideon's seventy sons, and the citizens of Shechem for supporting him in this treachery of murdering his brothers. (Judges 9:24)

Judges 9 through 12 covers the six judges of Israel who follow Gideon, including the illustrious *"Tola son of Puah, son of Dodo."* (I'm not making this up!)

The periods of Abimelech and Jephthah are given the most attention. Abimelech, one of Gideon's many sons, sees an opportunity to seize power after his father's death. He was not appointed by God as a judge, but maneuvers his way into persuading the citizens of Shechem to make him their "king." But he is a scoundrel. He hires *"some reckless troublemakers"* and kills seventy of his half-brothers to remove any possible competition. However, his youngest brother, Jotham, escapes and hides.

We are reminded that the love of power trumps family and prompts violence! If this doesn't seem like the kind of leadership transition that God would approve, you are dead right.

When Abimelech is declared king, Jotham comes out of hiding and charges the citizens of Shechem with complicity in Abimelech's treachery: *"But today you have revolted against my father and his descendants, killing his seventy sons on one stone. And you have chosen his slave woman's son, Abimelech, to be your king just because he is your relative"* (Judges 9:18).

He then pronounces a curse upon Abimelech's followers, saying that if Abimelech is not the honorable man he claims to be, they will end up destroying each other. And, of course, he wasn't—and they did.

In chapter 9, there is another episode of a power-grabber and trouble-maker. Gaal, son of Ebed, moves into Shechem and decides to challenge Abimelech to battle. Abimelech appears to be winning the battle when *"a woman on the roof dropped a millstone that landed on Abimelech's head and crushed his skull"* (Judges 9:53). He is still conscious, however, and calls his armor bearer to finish him off with his sword. He doesn't want it said that a woman killed him.

(We may be excused for saying, "Way to go, lady!")

After Abimelech dies, our friend *"Tola son of Puah, son of Dodo"* is the next rescuer, or judge of Israel. He is followed by Jair from Gilead. When Jair dies, Israel once again returns with enthusiasm to doing what is evil in the Lord's sight. Once again, God punishes Israel—this time by the Ammonites, who oppress them for eighteen years before they repent and put aside their foreign gods to serve the Lord.

Jephthah is then recruited to rescue Israel from the Ammonites. He is the son of Gilead, but his mother was a prostitute. Consequently, he has been disinherited of his father's land by his brothers. But he knows how to fight, and the elders of the city of Gilead promise to make him king if he defeats the Ammonites.

So Jephthah, who fears God, sends the Ammonite king a letter explaining why and how the Lord, the God of Israel, has taken the land from the Ammonites and given it to Israel. He concludes with a little taunt: *"Why, then, should we give it back to you? You keep whatever your god Chemosh gives you, and we will keep whatever the Lord our God gives us"* (Judges 11:23–24).

The Lord gives Jephthah victory all right, but not without a terrible loss because of a very foolish vow he made to the Lord. (Read about it in Judges 11:30–39). We also learn in chapter 12 of how an incorrect pronunciation exposes a lie and leads to the deaths of many.

We continue to see, during the period of the judges, the importance of strong, godly leaders for the well-being of Israel. The iffy ones, like Abimelech and Jephthah, fail in their primary duty as leaders to demonstrate Covenant faith. When they fail, they leave the people spiritually vulnerable to the ungodly influences around them.

Focus: The people of Israel thrive as a nation only when their leaders trust the Lord to protect and bless them. The leaders express trust in the Lord by leading the people in keeping his Covenant. But the leaders discover that the fallen world with its intrigue and violence, and the human impulse to seek power and keep control, seem more real than the life of faith. We can't judge them too severely, though, because we are like them. When faced with challenges, the Church today sometimes falls to the temptation to abandon prayer and obedience, and instead embrace worldly power and wisdom.

Prayer: Lord, we see how easy it is to assume that worldly power will keep us free and at peace, so we choose someone like Abimelech or Jephthah to lead us. Yet it is character—especially godly character—that really makes a difference. So give us leaders in the world today who are both competent and godly. Amen.

Day 71   Judges 13–16

March 11

> Key Text: Then Samson prayed to the Lord, "Sovereign Lord, remember me again. O God, please strengthen me just one more time. With one blow let me pay back the Philistines for the loss of my two eyes." (Judges 16:28)

Once again, after a judge dies (in this case it's Abdon, son of Hillel), the Israelites revert to doing evil in the Lord's sight. This time, God's judgment is administered by the Philistines, the most infamous of Israel's enemies.

About this time, an angel of the Lord appears to a barren woman and promises her a son. She is told that he must be raised as a Nazirite from birth. Among other things, this means that his hair must not be cut—a sign that he has a special calling from God. In time he will rescue Israel from the Philistines.

The angel then speaks to the woman's husband, Manoah, to reaffirm the special calling of their son when he is born. Manoah doesn't realize that this man is the angel of the Lord, suggesting that angels don't look like angels of our popular imagination. So Manoah innocently asks the man's name because he wants to honor him when his prophecy comes true. In those days, asking for a person's name was not a social courtesy; it was a request to know the person's nature—*who are you?* The angel responds: *"Why do you ask my name? It is too wonderful for you to under-*

stand" (Judges 13:18).

Does the angel mean that the nature and function of angels in the life of heaven, is beyond human understanding?

When Manoah offers a sacrifice of thanksgiving, the Lord does an amazing thing: *"As the flames from the altar shot up toward the sky, the angel of the Lord ascended in the fire. When Manoah and his wife saw this, they fell with their faces to the ground"* (Judges 13:19–20).

So who is the subject of all this angelic attention? When he is born, his mother names him "Samson." *"And the Lord blessed him as he grew up. And the Spirit of the Lord began to stir him while he lived in Mahaneh-dan, which is located between the towns of Zorah and Eshtaol"* (Judges 13:24–25).

As Samson grows up, he discovers that he possesses extraordinary strength when the Holy Spirit comes upon him. (He is the original "Incredible Hulk"!) When strengthened, he demonstrates daring feats, such as easily killing an attacking lion with his bare hands.

Unfortunately, along with his great strength, he also has a bad temper and an eye for Philistine women. One particular woman catches his eye. He simply says, *"She looks good to me,"* and he falls in love (lust?) with her. Her parents, sensing an opportunity, talk thirty young Philistine men into hanging out with Samson and influencing him. It doesn't turn out well. A little game of riddles in chapter 14 turns into an all-out brawl when Samson is tricked into giving the answer to the riddle to his Philistine fiancée, who then tells the thirty men. Samson is so angry that he misuses the physical strength God had given him to kill thirty men from a nearby town. He steals their belongings and pays off his "friends." As a parting angry gesture, Samson leaves his fiancée and returns home.

Assuming that Samson has lost interest, his fiancée's father gives her in marriage to another man—the best man at Samson's failed wedding! Sampson may not want her, but doesn't want anyone else to have her. Upon hearing of her engagement, Samson comes unhinged and does an "Incredible Hulk" on the Philistines. You can read about this in chapter 15. (Spoiler alert: It involves fire, violence and harm to animals.)

But Samson, despite protests from his parents, continues to be attracted to Philistine women. This time, he falls in lust with a woman named Delilah. Delilah betrays Samson in the end by telling his enemies that the secret to his extraordinary strength is his long hair—expressive of his Nazirite vow. So his hair is cut and his eyes gouged out, and he is thrown into prison.

The Philistines boast: *"Our god [Dagon] has given us victory over our enemy Samson!"* (Judges 16:23).

Finally, weak and humbled, Samson calls out to the Lord, asking for strength one more time. God hears his prayer and strengthens him, at which time he cries out, *"Let me die with the Philistines"* and pushes the supporting pillars of the pagan temple where he is imprisoned. The temple collapses and crushes the Philistine rulers and a large number of people.

So ends the amazing twenty-year career of Samson as judge of Israel. In the story of Samson, we learn that anger and lack of self-control can undermine our gifts and calling from the Lord. And yet, the Lord still answers when we call out to him, giving us strength to serve him in our weakness.

Focus: Sometimes our greatest strength can become our greatest weakness. The secret to living with our strengths is not to deny them—for, after all, they come from the Lord. We can joyfully and thankfully embrace our strengths, but we must do so with humility and in service of the Lord. When, as in Samson's case, a God-given strength is used to pursue a selfish ambition, it will lead to heartbreak and failure.

Prayer: *Lord, grant us the character to faithfully use the gifts you have given each one of us, lest we undermine our calling by lack of self-control. Amen.*

Day 72   Judges 17–21

March 12

> Key Text: In those days Israel had no king; all the people did whatever seemed right in their own eyes. (Judges 17:6)

This dark description frames the remainder of the book of Judges as Israel continues her downward spiral into depravity, forsaking the Covenant and Law and instead giving herself over to the paganism of her neighbors.

Chapters 17 through 21 provide snapshots of the evil that follows false religion, serving as a warning for future generations, including our own.

Chapter 17 tells about a man named Micah who creates his own pagan shrine, outfitted with idols and administered by a Levite priest-for-hire. So here we see a Levite—from the tribe of those assigned by God to oversee the Tabernacle worship—becoming complicit in this Israelite/pagan hybrid religion. With misguided confidence Micah boasts: *"I know the Lord will bless me now ... because I have a Levite serving as my priest."*

Such syncretism is not unlike what we see today in the hybrid religion of New Age thinking. Many modern, secular people want to be spiritual; they just don't want to be bound by commandments to keep and doctrines to believe!

So ironically, self-made "religion" is actually rebellion against God.

In chapter 19 we read one of the most morally repugnant stories in all of Scripture. A Levite owns a concubine whom he uses as a sexual slave. She runs away, but he finds her and takes her to the pagan city of Gibeah. An old man there offers them hospitality and a place to sleep, but word gets around that outsiders have arrived in a feral mood: *"While they were enjoying themselves, a crowd of troublemakers from the town surrounded the house. They began beating at the door and shouting to the old man, 'Bring out the man who is staying with you so we can have sex with him'"* (Judges 19:22).

The story of Sodom is repeated. The old man tries to stop the crowd by offering up his virgin daughter, but they won't listen, so the Levite throws his concubine out the door to them. The men of the town take turns raping her all night and she is found dead by the door the next morning. When the Levite finds her, he takes her body and cuts it into twelve pieces, and sends them to the twelve tribes of Israel to shock them.

We are left wondering whether there is any humanity left in this Levite, the mob, or Israel as a whole. Israel has strayed far from the Covenant and become like her neighbors. But this is too disturbing to ignore: *"Everyone who saw it said, 'Such a horrible crime has not been committed in all the time since Israel left Egypt. Think about it! What are we going to do? Who's going to speak up?'"* (Judges 19:30).

The Israelites demand that the troublemakers from Gibeah be given up. The people of the city refuse and a civil war breaks out. Thousands are killed.

The book of Judges ends with such disturbing stories that we wonder whether God's plan to bless the world through Israel has totally unraveled. It is as if we have returned to the world in the days of Noah when *"the Lord observed the extent of human wickedness on the earth, and he saw that everything they thought or imagined was consistently and totally evil"* (Genesis 6:5).

But as we have seen over and over, *"...as people sinned more and more, God's wonderful grace became more abundant"* (Romans 5:20).

Focus: Readers of the Bible are sometimes shocked at the stories they find there. The book of Judges in particular makes us wonder how deep the depravity of man runs. And yet, nothing has really changed since then. The Bible records the whole unfiltered story of humans—good, bad and ugly. It is not a book of fantasy with idealized characters, nor a utopian dream about a perfect world. It is the story of an incredibly loving God pursuing a shockingly decadent humanity, determined to make things right no matter what it costs.

Prayer: Lord, it is disturbing to think of the evil we humans are capable of doing to one another. History is full of examples and we see it today. It reminds us of our deep need for your forgiveness and of your amazing grace and patience. Heal our world, Lord! Amen.

Day 73   Ruth

March 13

> Key Text: "May the Lord, the God of Israel, under whose wings you have come to take refuge, reward you fully for what you have done." (Ruth 2:12)

The book of Judges leaves us shaken. For the most part, the people of Israel have abandoned God to do whatever seems right in their own eyes. These are some of the most difficult chapters in the Bible. How can the so-called "chosen people" commit such atrocities? For that matter, how can pagans commit such atrocities? Does faith make any difference at all?

These questions touch upon the radical nature of sin and raise the further question: What will it take to change human nature?

In the meantime, it is important to realize that not everything is dark. The terrible deeds of some tend to cast a shadow over everything and everyone. But in the midst of the darkness of the book of Judges, there is light in the book of Ruth, a beautiful and theologically rich story about love and redemption.

The book of Ruth is the story of a young Moabite woman who is a widow living with her Jewish mother-in-law Naomi, now a widow herself. Because of a severe famine in their region of Moab, Naomi decides to head back home to Judah. She relieves Ruth of any obligation to take care of her and encourages her to go back to her people and remarry. But Ruth is devoted to Naomi and insists on staying: *"Don't ask me to leave you and turn back. Wherever you go, I will go; wherever you live, I will live. Your people will be my people, and your God will be my God"* (Ruth 1:16).

By this expression of devotion, Ruth also gives herself to Yahweh God, whom Naomi follows. It is further evidence that the Canaanite people were not despised by God, even if their idolatry was. God's grace reaches out to the pagan Ruth through the Israelite Naomi.

Together they go to Bethlehem and live near a wealthy and influential relative of Naomi's late husband, a man named Boaz. As a Moabite, Ruth is an outsider to this Israelite community, but she is treated with uncommon kindness and generosity by Boaz. Boaz praises her character: *"I also know about everything you have done for your mother-in-law since the death of your husband. I have heard how you left your father and mother and your own land to live here among complete strangers. May the Lord, the God of Israel, under whose wings you have come to take refuge, reward you fully for what you have done"* (Ruth 2:11–12).

Boaz's blessing—that God rewards all who take refuge in him—is regarded by many scholars to be the central theme of the book of Ruth, and a key theme throughout the whole Old Testament.

Upon hearing that Boaz has blessed Ruth, Naomi reveals that Boaz *"is one of our closest relatives, one of our family redeemers."* It is significant to note here that Naomi says "our" closest relative and one of "our" family redeemers, since Ruth is only related by marriage. To Naomi, Ruth is now family, and so the response of Boaz as a family redeemer will benefit her as well. She will be rewarded for her kindness and loyalty to Naomi.

By the Law of Israel, a family redeemer is a role and function whereby a near relative may marry a widow and redeem the deceased's land, in order to keep it in the family and also provide for the widow. In the case of Ruth, the family redeemer role is extended to a more distant relative than normal, revealing a wider expression of mercy and redemption.

Through Naomi's encouragement, Ruth cleverly lets Boaz know that she is "available" to be redeemed! They are married and she gives birth to a son. Boaz's blessing is heard by God. And with a son, both Ruth and Naomi will be cared for in their old age, in keeping with ancient practice.

Ruth's blessing, it turns out, extends beyond her marriage to Boaz. Their child, Obed, *"became the father of Jesse and the grandfather of David."* This is King David, future king of Israel. And so we learn that the outsider, Ruth, becomes part of the story of God's Messiah, who comes from the house of David. She is mentioned in the genealogy of Jesus found in Matthew, chapter 1.

> **Focus:** Ruth's devotion to Naomi, and Boaz's generosity towards Ruth, are what make this beautiful story a refreshing oasis in the period of the judges. We shall see many times again, in the story of the Old Testament, how individuals within Israel are faithful to God, even in the midst of national corruption. These are called the "remnant of faith," and they serve to remind us that there are always faithful believers, even in the worst of times when many around them have hardened their hearts.

> **Prayer:** *Lord, thank you for the reminder that when all seems dark and hopeless in the world, you are quietly at work bringing blessing to countless ordinary people, like Ruth. Thanks also that your grace is extended to everyone, no matter what their bloodline or heritage. May we be faithful like Ruth, and generous like Boaz, to those in our lives. Amen.*

Day 74 — Reflection

March 14

The past week of reading through the Bible has taken us into arguably the most disturbing chapters found in the Scriptures. They give evidence to secularists' claim that religion is the greatest source of violence among people and nations.

The secularists have a point, but probably not the one they are trying to make. In the ancient world, everyone was religious. There was no such thing as atheism, at least among the masses. People viewed reality through the lens of religion, which was overwhelmingly polytheistic, and justified their actions accordingly.

But for the Israelites, monotheism and the Ten Commandments guided their national life. The God of Israel was holy, and required holiness of his people. The commandments outlined the moral and spiritual duties of Israel. When followed, these practices greatly elevated the moral and spiritual vision of the ancient world. By its moral vision, and intellectual force, monotheism arguably made Western Civilization possible, laying the groundwork for philosophy and science, as well as great advances in literature, arts, education, law, economics, modern medicine and the technologies that make life more humane for most people.

The Ten Commandments, likewise, laid the moral groundwork for a just society where people could live in peace with their neighbor. Their teaching inspired and enabled humanity to struggle and grow in goodness, and sometimes even reach great ethical achievements.

And yet, we have the book of Judges. Here, and in many other times in history—including our own time—evil is done in the name of God. How can this be?

It is important to realize that the problem lies not with Judeo/Christianity per se, but with the human heart. This is verified by the fact that in the 20ᵗʰ century alone, there was more brutality and death in the name of secularism than there ever has been in the name of religion. Think of the horrors of Nazism under Hitler, and Communism under Stalin, Mao, Pol Pot, and others. Hundreds of millions have been killed, hundreds of millions of others left miserable.

Furthermore, all religions are not the same. Different religions represent vastly different understandings of reality and of the nature of God, or gods. Since ideas always have consequences, toxic religion based on false notions of God, or the gods, leads to toxic behavior. It is the same with secularism and its toxic ideas.

Again, the problem is the human heart. So we see Israel in the book of Judges continually returning to a form of religious paganism that appealed to their sinful nature. It seems that even the insider information that Israel had in its covenant relationship with God, and the moral instruction they received in the commandments, were not enough to change human nature.

The problem of the human heart becomes more prominent as we move along. The prophet Jeremiah, for example, will later say to exiled Israelites: *"The human heart is the most deceitful of all things, and desperately wicked. Who really knows how bad it is?"* (Jeremiah 17:9).

But the prophets Isaiah and Joel will speak of a day when God will transform the human heart by pouring out his Spirit upon every believer, so that people will love God and their neighbor because they want to, not because a commandment tells them to. In other words, the Holy Spirit will put the love of God in our hearts in a new way, enabling us to internalize moral behavior, guided by love and not just law.

In the meantime, the Law and commandments put Israel *"in protective custody"* (Galatians 3:23) to keep the people from becoming as bad as they could be.

As we will see later, the Law serves the purpose of making us aware of our sin. By giving definition to sin, it serves a diagnostic purpose, like an x-ray reveals cancer. This function of the Law, though disagreeable, is necessary, because it shows us our need of grace. The apostle Paul further explains to Christians at Galatia that the Law was given to Israel alongside the Promise to show people their sins *(Galatians 3:19)* until the coming of Christ, who is the child of the Promise.

> *Prayer: Lord, thank you for loving us enough to tell us the truth about ourselves. We know that we must hear the bad news that we are sinners before we can receive the Good News that we are loved nevertheless, and that, by your grace, you do for us what we could not do for ourselves. We acknowledge our sin and marvel at your grace and mercy. Empower us to live by the Spirit instead of giving in to our sinful nature. Amen.*

Day 75   1 Samuel 1–3

March 15

> Key Text: "The Lord gives both death and life; he brings some down to the grave but raises others up. The Lord makes some poor and others rich; he brings some down and lifts others up."
> (1 Samuel 2:6–7)

The books of 1 and 2 Samuel are important as a transition from the chaotic period of the judges to the period of Israel as a monarchy.

The book of 1 Samuel begins with the sorrow of a childless woman, named Hannah. Her husband comforts her, but she does not understand why she is childless. Some in her community (her "enemies") mock her and say that God is judging her.

One day, while worshiping at the Tabernacle, Hannah cries out to the Lord for a son. She promises to dedicate her child to the ministry of the

Tabernacle if God hears her prayer. To her joy, God does hear her prayer and Samuel is born. Samuel's birth is a reminder that God knows our hearts and hears our prayers. He always answers in his own time, even though the answers don't always come as quickly as we would like.

Hannah's prayer of thanksgiving for her son *(1 Samuel 2:1–10)* addresses more broadly the struggles she has faced in her adult life. She has been mocked for years and she prays against those who routinely hurt others with their words: *"Stop acting so proud and haughty! Don't speak with such arrogance! For the Lord is a God who knows what you have done; he will judge your actions"* (1 Samuel 2:3).

Hannah is vindicated by God, but her experience speaks to the larger story of Israel's status as God's people. It restates an important theological theme that we saw in the book of Ruth. Even when Israel as a whole is being judged by God for unfaithfulness, there are individuals, whom Hannah calls the "faithful ones" in her prayer, who are blessed and protected by God: *"He will protect his faithful ones, but the wicked will disappear in darkness. No one will succeed by strength alone. Those who fight against the Lord will be shattered"* (1 Samuel 2:9–10).

We will see in Israel's story, as we do in our own stories today, that God is always working in the world, looking for those who seek him, blessing those who find him, honoring those who serve him, and opposing those whose actions contradict his good purposes for his creation.

Because Samuel has been dedicated by Hannah to the priestly work, he is mentored at the proper time by Eli the priest and assists Eli in his work. But Eli turns out to be a man of weak character. His two sons *"were scoundrels who had no respect for the Lord or for their duties as priests."* They harass worshipers and treat the Lord's offerings with contempt, while seducing young girls who assist at the entrance of the Tabernacle.

God holds Eli responsible for failing to stop their evil blasphemy, and a bitter judgment follows. God gives Eli a heads-up regarding the near future: *"I will raise up a faithful priest who will serve me and do what I desire. I will establish his family, and they will be priests to my anointed kings forever"* (1 Samuel 2:35).

That faithful priest will be Samuel.

Eventually, God speaks to Samuel in a dream. He reveals that Eli will be judged and that he, Samuel, will replace him. Samuel's life hereafter demonstrates the wisdom of God's choice. *"As Samuel grew up, the Lord was with him, and everything Samuel said proved to be reliable. And all Israel, from Dan in the north to Beersheba in the south, knew that Samuel was confirmed as a prophet of the Lord. The Lord continued to appear at Shiloh and gave messages to Samuel there at the Tabernacle. And Samuel's words went out to all the people of Israel"* (1 Samuel 3:19–21).

Focus: The story of Samuel illustrates that God knows our hearts. He sees our potential, and then prepares us through life experience for his calling. This story also demonstrates that God is willing to discipline and replace even the most powerful and influential religious leaders when they fail to honor him by their actions.

Prayer: *Lord, forgive us for taking worship so lightly. Since we were created to worship and enjoy you above all else, our failure to do so is a fundamental failure of our sinful nature. May we be like Samuel, and not like Eli and his sons. Amen.*

Day 76   1 Samuel 4–8

March 16

Key Text: But the people refused to listen to Samuel's warning. "Even so, we still want a king," they said. "We want to be like the nations around us. Our king will judge us and lead us into battle." (1 Samuel 8:19–20)

Today's reading fills in the details about God's discipline of Eli the priest and his two evil sons, Hophni and Phinehas, before Samuel replaces Eli as priest.

Israel's unsuccessful war against the Philistines is the catalyst for a foolish decision by the elders of Israel, which is supported by Eli and his two sons. The elders ask themselves: *"'Why did the Lord allow us to be defeated by the Philistines?' Then they said, 'Let's bring the Ark of the Covenant of the Lord from Shiloh. If we carry it into battle with us, it will save us from our enemies'"* (1 Samuel 4:3).

But using the Ark of the Covenant as a good luck charm proves to be disastrous. A messenger from the battlefield returns to report to Eli: *"Israel has been defeated by the Philistines.... The people have been slaughtered, and your two sons, Hophni and Phinehas, were also killed. And the Ark of God has been captured"* (1 Samuel 4:17).

The news is so horrifying that Eli the priest falls backward from his seat beside the city gate, breaks his neck and dies. Then Eli's daughter-in-law, the widow of Phinehas, goes into early labor and passes away during birth. Before her death, *"She named the child Ichabod (which means 'Where is the glory?') ... Then she said, 'The glory has departed from Israel, for the Ark of God has been captured'"* (1 Samuel 4:21-22).

(Tip: Don't name your child Ichabod.)

But has the glory of God really departed?

The Philistines think so. They carry the Ark into their pagan temple in the city of Ashdod and place it beside an idol of their god Dagon. Bad decision. The people awake to find that the large idol has fallen with its face to the ground in front of the Ark of the Lord. They put it back in place, but by the next morning the same thing has happened again. Then God sends a plague of tumors to infect the people of Ashdod.

Out of fear of being destroyed, the leaders move the Ark around, but with similar results. They finally send the Ark away on a cart pulled by two cows. The Israelites retrieve it but don't return it to the Tabernacle yet.

Meanwhile, Samuel, who is now considered a prophet by the people, calls them to repentance by getting rid of their foreign gods and images, and determining to obey the Lord only. So now, with their hearts right with God, and under Samuel's godly leadership, the Israelites subdue the Philistines. And there is now peace in the land.

Fast forward: As Samuel grows old, the elders of Israel plead with him to appoint a king like other nations have. They no doubt fear that Israel will return to idolatry after Samuel dies. But their faith is weak. Yes, Samuel has been a good leader, but he has been the exception. The terrible dysfunction of the period of the judges has made them cynical. So instead of trusting God to be their king, the elders of Israel decide to help themselves. They conclude that a monarchy with a strong king and a standing army is needed to keep things in order.

Samuel protests, of course, but the Lord instructs him not to take it personally and to give them what they want: *"Do everything they say to you...for they are rejecting me, not you. They don't want me to be their king any longer"* (1 Samuel 8:7).

Samuel complies, but passes on God's warning about what will follow when they choose a king. In a nutshell, they'll end up regretting it! Just see *1 Samuel 8:10–19* for details on why.

Focus: Sometimes the worst thing that can happen to us is for God to give us what we want. Just like Abraham and Sarah, long ago, gave up on God's promise of an heir and did what seemed practical (with disastrous results), so now Israel's leaders are going to plan B about who should be king of Israel. They have given up on the idea that God can be their king. Circumstances on the ground are such that they must take control. They are convinced that they need a king like other nations to rule the people firmly, form military alliances for their protection, and establish trading partners for their economic well-being. God gives them what they want, and things get worse.

Prayer: Lord, help us to resist the temptation to look to the things of this world to fill the place in our hearts that only you can fill. Thank you for not always giving us what we want! Amen.

Day 77   1 Samuel 9–12

March 17

> Key Text: Then Samuel took a flask of olive oil and poured it over Saul's head. He kissed Saul and said, "I am doing this because the Lord has appointed you to be the ruler over Israel, his special possession." (1 Samuel 10:1)

Israel's leaders insist that they must have a king like the other nations around them because they are tired of the failures of the judges, including Samuel, to bring about a lasting peace.

But the Lord sees it for what it is—a rejection of him as their king. And it is a repudiation of their calling to be a *"kingdom of priests, my holy nation"* (Exodus 19:5-6).

Because Israel has failed to live up to the Covenant agreement, her troubles are her own fault and the people only have themselves to blame. They want a king to do for them what only God can do. But since they are too stubborn to see this, God allows them to have a king anyway.

Some lessons can only be learned the hard way.

The man God chooses to be king is Saul. He comes from the smallest of all the tribes, Benjamin. But he is an impressive specimen: *"...the most handsome man in Israel—head and shoulders taller than anyone else in the land."*

How Saul learns that God has chosen him is almost comical. He and a servant are out looking for some donkeys that have strayed. Having failed, they decide to consult a local prophet to help find them. The prophet turns out to be Samuel. God has already told Samuel that the future king would be coming by. Samuel tells Saul: *"And don't worry about those donkeys that were lost three days ago, for they have been found. And* [since we're talking!] *I am here to tell you that you and your family are the focus of all Israel's hopes"* (1 Samuel 9:20).

How many people do you know that have left home in the morning to find lost donkeys and returned home later as king of a nation? None? Me neither.

Samuel soon anoints Saul as ruler over Israel, saying that Saul will receive *"the Spirit of the Lord"* upon him and be *"changed into a different person."*

To some Israelites, he seems like a seventh round draft pick: *"Can anyone become a prophet, no matter who his father is? So that is the origin of the saying, 'Is even Saul a prophet?'"* (1 Samuel 10:12).

When the time comes for Saul to be formally verified as king and presented by Samuel to the people, Saul is nowhere to be found—until someone finds him *"hiding among the baggage."*

The king is a pretty boy and a coward. Not a promising start!

In time, however, word of terrible cruelty against Israelites by the Ammonite king, Nahash, comes to Saul. Nahash has sworn to gouge out the right eye of every Israelite citizen of Jabesh-gilead. Upon hearing this, *"the Spirit of God came powerfully upon Saul, and he became very angry"* (1 Samuel 11:6). Saul mobilizes an army and routs the Ammonites. God shows that he is able to work through the most unlikely of leaders to protect his people.

The people are filled with joy over what their king has done, but Samuel reminds them in chapter 12 that their request for a king is a rejection of God as their king. Nevertheless, God has forgiven them and granted their request, showing himself to be gracious and patient with his stubborn people.

Samuel reassures them: *"You have certainly done wrong, but make sure now that you worship the Lord with all your heart, and don't turn your back on him. Don't go back to worshiping worthless idols that cannot help or rescue you—they are totally useless! The Lord will not abandon his people, because that would dishonor his great name. For it has pleased the Lord to make you his very own people"* (1 Samuel 12:20–22).

Focus: God's determination to bless Israel and make her a blessing is remarkable in light of the people's persistent stubbornness and unbelief. This has been the case since the days of Moses in the wilderness. His faithfulness to us is unshakable, revealing the generous grace that flows like a river from his loving heart into our broken lives. God's sending Jesus into the world to die for our human sin is the culmination of the story of a God who will not let us go!

Prayer: God, you are so patient with us, remaining faithful even when we are not. You give us freedom to learn obedience, even though it inevitably means that we will struggle and fail until we mature. May we learn quickly! Amen.

Day 78   1 Samuel 13–15

March 18

> Key Text: Saul was thirty years old when he became king, and he reigned for forty-two years. (1 Samuel 13:1)

Saul has it all—youth, charisma, good looks and the opportunity to lead Israel in new ways as her first king. What he lacks is a strong character. Ideally, this can be developed along the way if one has a humble heart and teachable spirit. Unfortunately, Saul proves that he has neither.

Chapter 13 tells how Saul commits a major sin through impatience and lack of trust in God. Seeing the Philistines camped nearby with superior numbers and weaponry, Saul waits impatiently for Samuel the priest to arrive and offer a sacrifice to God before engaging the enemy. He then greatly oversteps his bounds: *"Saul realized that his troops were rapidly slipping away. So he demanded, 'Bring me the burnt offering and the peace offerings!' And Saul sacrificed the burnt offering himself"* (1 Samuel 13:8–9).

Saul's presumption to take upon himself the role of priest reveals his arrogance. He thinks he can disobey God and get away with it because, after all, he is the king! Surely Samuel would understand that with the enemy at the door, Saul cannot wait any longer.

Samuel doesn't understand. He is dumbfounded when he discovers what Saul has done, and gives him an ominous rebuke: *"'How foolish!' Samuel exclaimed. 'You have not kept the command the Lord your God gave you. Had you kept it, the Lord would have established your kingdom over Israel forever. But now your kingdom must end, for the Lord has sought out a man after his own heart'"* (1 Samuel 13:13–14).

Chapter 14 gives a further example of Saul's lack of character. Saul's son Jonathan, along with his armor bearer, leave the military camp to pull off a clever raid on the Philistines. The Philistines become confused. Some run, while others mistakenly kill each other. Jonathan's gambit pays off and Israel is saved from a superior army. But Saul seems angry and perhaps envious of Jonathan's success. So he plans to take out his anger on the defeated Philistines. To this end, he foolishly forces his men to pledge that they will not eat anything until he gets *"full revenge on his enemies."*

But his men are tired from the previous battle. Without thinking about their well-being, he runs his men into the ground.

Now Jonathan is unaware of his father's dictate about eating, so he eats some honey in order to be refreshed from the fatigue of battle. When this is discovered, Saul is forced to act on his foolish pledge by condemning his own son to death. But the people intervene and say to Saul: *"'Jonathan has won this great victory for Israel. Should he die? Far from it! As surely as the Lord lives, not one hair on his head will be touched, for God helped him do a great deed today.' So the people rescued Jonathan, and he was not put to death"* (1 Samuel 14:45).

Saul's respect among his soldiers, and the people, is diminishing.

In chapter 15, Saul once again fails as a leader by disobeying God's instruction not to keep the plunder of battle for himself. He tries to rationalize his actions by claiming that the sheep, goats and cattle he keeps are to be given in sacrifice to the Lord. But Samuel strongly confronts him with his sin: *"What is more pleasing to the Lord: your burnt offerings and sacrifices or your obedience to his voice? Listen! Obedience is better than sacrifice, and submission is better than offering the fat of rams. Rebellion is as sinful as witchcraft, and stubbornness as bad as worshiping idols. So because you have rejected the command of the Lord, he has rejected you as king"* (1 Samuel 15:22–23).

Samuel never meets with Saul again, but mourns for him. Leadership carries great responsibility and accountability. Natural gifts and talents are not enough. Saul is overly impressed with himself and makes the ultimate mistake of leaders: thinking that the rules do not apply to them. So, the remainder of Saul's time as king will prove troublesome and ultimately tragic.

The tragic story of Saul shows how easy it is to misunderstand and therefore misuse leadership. In the Judeo-Christian understanding, leadership is servanthood. The role of a leader is to give of him- or herself in order to help others achieve their goals. When a leader uses their position as a means to serve their own ambition, it becomes an abuse of power.

Prayer: Lord, we are reminded that what really matters to you is our heart and will—obedience is better than sacrifice. Help us to do the right things for the right reasons: love, gratefulness, respect and humility. Amen.

Day 79   1 Samuel 16–19

March 19

Key Text: **"The Lord doesn't see things the way you see them. People judge by outward appearance, but the Lord looks at the heart." (1 Samuel 16:7)**

Now that God has made it clear to Samuel that Saul is no longer fit to be king, Samuel is sent to anoint the next king of God's choosing. He is told to summon all the sons of a man named Jesse, and God will show him which one to anoint as the coming king. One boy stands out from the others as king material—Eliab. Samuel thinks, *"Surely this is the one."*

Nope.

We're not going to do the Saul thing again. The Lord says to Samuel: *"Don't judge by his appearance or height, for I have rejected him. The Lord doesn't see things the way you see them. People judge by outward appearance, but the Lord looks at the heart"* (1 Samuel 16:7).

The "heart" God is looking at belongs to Jesse's youngest son, David. Samuel anoints him and *"the Spirit of the Lord came powerfully upon David from that day on."* At the same time, the Spirit of the Lord has left Saul, the present king. What remains is a *"tormenting spirit,"* sent by the Lord as judgment against Saul, leaving him with *"depression and fear."* We should probably understand this puzzling action to mean that, in withdrawing His Spirit from Saul, God allows Saul to harden his heart against him, and thereby open himself to demonic influence.

As his depression and paranoia grow, Saul's servants bring a talented harp player to soothe his mind. The talented young man turns out to be David! His playing does soothe Saul's mind, and he grows to trust and depend upon David. But this is about to change. We the readers know what Saul does not yet know—that God has already chosen David to replace Saul.

Chapter 17 tells the story of how young David is sent with food for his brothers who had been part of a military ruckus with some Philistines. The Israelite army is being taunted by a giant named Goliath. He is over nine feet tall, sneering and roaring at the frightened Israelite army. When David arrives with food service, he asks the soldiers, *"Who is this pagan Philistine anyway, that he is allowed to defy the armies of the living God?"* (1 Samuel 17:26).

King Saul sends for David and tells him to knock off the questioning. David replies, *"Don't worry about this Philistine.... I'll go fight him!"* Saul snaps back, *"There's no way you can fight this Philistine and possibly win! You're only a boy, and he's been a man of war since his youth."* But David persists and is finally given permission to fight Goliath.

What follows is well known. David uses a skill learned as a shepherd to protect the flock from predators. He picks up five smooth stones, but he only needs one. While Goliath is sneering, roaring and laughing at the young boy, David puts a stone in his slingshot and hurls it into the forehead of the giant. Goliath falls face down like a giant sequoia. Then David quickly grabs Goliath's massive sword and—off with his head!

The Philistines run like scared chickens, but the Israelites pursue and easily defeat them. Needless to say, David becomes a hero among the people—and King Saul becomes his enemy.

Saul makes several attempts to kill David or have him killed, but God protects him. Ironically, David and Jonathan, Saul's son, became close friends. Jonathan swears to protect David from his father, the increasingly mad king.

Focus: "David and Goliath" has become an iconic story of the little guy overcoming great odds to beat the big guy. But what it really illustrates is that when we do the will of God, with the power of God, anything is possible. God seems to take pleasure in this. The apostle Paul explains: *"God chose things the world considers foolish in order to shame those who think they are wise. And he chose things that are powerless to shame those who are powerful"* (1 Corinthians 1:27).

Prayer: Lord, once again you remind us that you are able to protect us from our enemies, no matter how threatening, and whether they come from without or within our circle of family and friends. May you find our hearts inclined toward you, like

Day 80   1 Samuel 20–23

March 20

> Key Text: David now fled from Naioth in Ramah and found Jonathan. "What have I done?" he exclaimed. "What is my crime? How have I offended your father that he is so determined to kill me?" (1 Samuel 20:1)

David is convinced that King Saul is out to kill him. Saul's son and David's close friend, Jonathan, is skeptical, but the two form a solemn pact saying that Jonathan will warn David if he suspects that his father is planning something.

The new moon festival arrives, a time when David would be expected to eat with the king. But David doesn't come. Saul asks Jonathan where he is, for he knows of their friendship. Jonathan responds with the agreed-upon story—that David is away visiting his brothers.

Saul becomes outraged. He suspects that David is maneuvering to be the next king, in place of his son, Jonathan. So he shouts at Jonathan: *"You stupid son of a whore! ... Do you think I don't know that you want him to be king in your place, shaming yourself and your mother? As long as that son of Jesse is alive, you'll never be king. Now go and get him so I can kill him!"* (1 Samuel 20:30–31).

When Jonathan protests, his father picks up a spear and hurls it at him, intending to kill him. It is a horrifying and eye-opening moment. Jonathan now knows that David was right and warns him that Saul is indeed intending to kill him. After reaffirming their friendship and trust, David flees. He finally joins his brothers and relatives and assembles a small group of fighting men. After hiding his father and mother for safekeeping from Saul, David returns to Judah.

When King Saul hears that David is back, he becomes paranoid and accuses his own officers of conspiring against him in order to follow David. He then hears that David had earlier met with the priest Ahimelech to consult with God. While David was there, Ahimelech had also given him Goliath's sword. So Saul summons the priest and accuses him, too, of conspiracy. Ahimelech knows nothing of a conspiracy, and in fact believes that David is a highly honored member of Saul's household.

But King Saul will hear nothing of this: *"'You will surely die, Ahimelech, along with your entire family!' the king shouted. And he ordered his bodyguards, 'Kill these priests of the Lord, for they are allies and conspirators with David!'"* (1 Samuel 22:16–17).

His bodyguards rightly refuse. But Doeg the Edomite doesn't refuse and kills eighty-five priests. He then goes to the town of the priests and kills their families—men and women, children and babies, along with all their cattle, donkeys, sheep and goats. Only Abiathar, one of the sons of Abimelech, escapes and flees to David, telling him the horrible thing Saul has ordered.

Soon, Saul hears of David's movements. He mobilizes his entire army to besiege David in the walled city of Keilah. After inquiring of God, David leaves Keilah and begins roaming the countryside, while King Saul attempts to hunt him down. Eventually, Saul hears that the Philistines are raiding Israel again, so he gives up the search and returns home.

The chilling story of King Saul's rage shows how a person can become so consumed by hatred and jealousy that he goes mad—destroying anything and anyone in his way. It reminds us of what Jesus said about Satan—that he is a deceiver and destroyer.

Focus: In these events, the madness of King Saul is contrasted with the bravery and loyalty of his son, Jonathan. While Saul becomes increasingly isolated by his attempts to kill David, Jonathan and David become true friends, bound by loyalty and courage. Their example inspires many others to support David and help him realize his calling and anointing to be Israel's new king. What is it that produces isolation and madness, on the one hand, or friendship and honor on the other? It is the presence or absence of godly character and sincere faith.

Prayer: Lord, we are saddened to read the story of a person, made in your image, turning himself into a monster and seeking to destroy others. The power of evil is sobering, but you have overcome evil and will one day throw the devil into a bottomless pit. We long for the day when all your creation dwells together in peace on earth. Amen.

March 21

The Old Testament presents a strange and troubling world to modern readers. It is easy to dismiss the people who occupied that world (including the Israelites) as primitive, and violent. What could the Old Testament possibly teach us?

Perhaps this attitude reflects a bias against the past. Those today who are enamored with "progress" seem certain that the world has moved on intellectually, morally and culturally. They believe, with the fervency of religious faith, that life is always evolving towards higher and better ways. They look to the future with confidence, knowing that the *next* thing is always the *best* thing.

But of course, if this way of thinking is true, and if the present world exists long enough, there will be those in the future who will similarly dismiss *us*. But let's put aside for the moment the easy dismissal of the Old Testament and its people, and consider the possibility that ancient people, at the core, were not that much different from us—or should we say that we are not that much different from them?

Acknowledging this will bring some humility and enable us to learn from the Old Testament.

The Old Testament never sugarcoats the truth about human behavior, including that of God's people. Its story plays out in a fallen world where war was a way of life and, clearly, a part of the economy. Resources for life were limited, especially good land for raising livestock and women for bearing children. Many children died at birth, and often the mothers did also, or they were killed in battles with neighboring enemies.

In such a world, your enemies were always after your stuff—your land, flocks, wealth and women. And you were after *their* stuff. It was a matter of survival, so the pagan gods were appealed to and placated with the hope that they would help by making the crops grow, the flocks reproduce, and the women get pregnant. Above all, the people hoped that the gods would give them victory in battle against their enemies.

The modern world is much different, of course. The creation of new wealth under capitalism, and thus the existence of a stable middle class, is a recent phenomenon in the world. Some say this is one of the greatest achievements of Western Civilization. In the ancient world before capitalism, economics was simple: There were those who owned everything (such as kings and the aristocracy) and those who owned practically nothing (everyone else). Wealth was inherited and little new wealth was created.

Knowing this, it is easier to understand that tribes and nations for most of history had to compete for the same limited resources. They would go to war for their neighbor's land, buildings, flocks and young women, then kill the rest of the people so they wouldn't retaliate.

In this context, we can see how the commandments of God not to lie, steal, kill, covet, or commit adultery, etc., were very relevant.

In summary, life was difficult in Old Testament times. War was common. Dangers abounded. Disease was mostly unstoppable. None of the benefits of modern science and medicine that we enjoy now were available. It is easy to understand why Israel would recognize that the Lord was a warrior on their behalf. He needed to be, and he was.

Technology was slow to develop, and it gave a decided advantage to its developers. When the Israelites took possession of the Land of Canaan, for example, they discovered that the Philistines had developed basic metallurgy, giving them an advantage in war with high- quality swords and spears, as well as an advantage in agriculture with plowshares, picks, axes and sickles. At the time, the Israelites had none of these. *(See 1 Samuel 13:19–22.)*

Israel was clearly the underdog in this story. Without the Lord leading Israel into battle to cast out the evil Canaanites by his power, Israel would not have survived. Indeed, as we have seen, whenever the Israelites refused to worship and obey God, they were defeated in battle.

So this was the world in which Israel became a nation, by God's calling. To them, that world was as rational and normal as our world is to us. This may help us understand why Israel's story took the shape it did. Israel regarded God to be a warrior on behalf of his people. The Canaanites understood and respected power. Therefore, when God gave Israel victory in war, they acknowledged and feared him.

In this context, David's victory over Goliath was a big deal. The fact that David—a boy without armor and armed only with a slingshot— could defeat the Philistine giant was a revelation.

So the Old Testament acknowledges the world for the way it was without necessarily endorsing it. It introduces us to people who are much like us. It honestly reports on the human consequences of evil as well as on the blessings when humans live in conformity with God's will.

Prayer: Lord, we long for the day when your peace will fill the earth and nations will no longer go to war. We know that you went to war on behalf of your Old Testament people and then on our behalf. You went to war through Jesus against the powers and principalities of the unseen world so that we might experience your peace now, and in the New Creation to come. We rejoice in this hope! Amen.

Day 82   1 Samuel 24–26

March 22

> Key Text: So Saul chose 3,000 elite troops from all Israel and went to search for David and his men near the rocks of the wild goats. (1 Samuel 24:2)

King Saul won't give up his obsession with hunting down David to kill him. He has gathered his elite troops to comb the wilderness of En-gedi, but God protects David. In fact, he twice gives him an opportunity to kill Saul.

The first opportunity comes when Saul goes into a cave "to relieve himself." He is, we might say, in a vulnerable position. As comic as this moment is, David refuses to kill Saul: *"'The Lord forbid that I should do this to my lord the king. I shouldn't attack the Lord's anointed one, for the Lord himself has chosen him.' So David restrained his men and did not let them kill Saul"* (1 Samuel 24:6–7).

But I imagine they laughed.

David is a man of conscience, so he leaves Saul's destiny to God: *"May the Lord judge between us. Perhaps the Lord will punish you for what you are trying to do to me, but I will never harm you. … He is my advocate, and he will rescue me from your power!"* (1 Samuel 24:12, 15).

The second opportunity to kill Saul comes when David slips into Saul's camp at night while everyone is sound asleep, including the man charged with protecting the king. David quietly takes Saul's spear, which is stuck in the ground beside his head. The spear is a message to Saul. David lets him know that he could have killed him, once again, if he wanted.

Instead, David retreats to a safe distance and wakes up the camp with a shout, letting Saul, and everyone else, know that he has spared his life. He demands to know why Saul continues to hunt him down when he means him no harm.

We gain insight into David's character here. Though Saul is unworthy to be king—and indeed, his time is short—David nevertheless will not kill Saul, because Saul is the Lord's "anointed one." David respects the position of king even if he does not respect the king.

Saul is embarrassed and humbled: *"I have sinned. Come back home, my son, and I will no longer try to harm you, for you valued my life today. I have been a fool, and very, very wrong"* (1 Samuel 26:21).

Between these two events, we meet another person of wisdom and character—a woman named Abigail. Just after Samuel the priest dies, David moves to the wilderness of Maon. A wealthy man, Nabal, lives there. He has a reputation for being wicked and ill-tempered.

One day during sheep-shearing season, David asks Nabal to return a kindness he had once shown to Nabal's shepherds. Nabal rudely refuses and insults David through his messengers. Upon hearing this, David commands his men, *"Get your swords!"*

Meanwhile, Nabal's wife Abigail intervenes by meeting David on the road with gifts and accepting blame for her husband. She says, *"Please forgive me if I have offended you in any way. The Lord will surely reward you with a lasting dynasty, for you are fighting the Lord's battles. And you have not done wrong throughout your entire life"* (1 Samuel 25:28).

Her character and humility move David to put revenge aside. David says to her, *"Praise the Lord, the God of Israel, who has sent you to meet me today! Thank God for your good sense! Bless you for keeping me from murder and from carrying out vengeance with my own hands"* (1 Samuel 25:32–33).

After Nabal sobers up from a drunken binge, Abigail tells him what she has done. A short time later, Nabal dies of a stroke. David then realizes that God has judged Nabal. Abigail has kept him from playing God and taking revenge for himself.

David couldn't forget her. In time, he sends messengers to Abigail to ask her to become his wife. It seems that people of character who fear God are drawn to one another.

Focus: In these stories, we can see what God loved about David. He was a man of character, who cared more about doing God's will than getting his revenge. As the

Lord has already told Samuel: *"The Lord doesn't see things the way you see them. People judge by outward appearance, but the Lord looks at the heart"* (1 Samuel 16:7). We learn that God is able to use people of modest abilities to do amazing things if they are people of integrity.

Prayer: Lord, grant us the faith and forbearance to leave judgment up to you and instead live lives of humility and integrity, in obedience to your will. Amen.

Day 83   1 Samuel 27–31

March 24

Key Text: The fighting grew very fierce around Saul, and the Philistine archers caught up with him and wounded him severely. (1 Samuel 31:3)

Despite David's refusal, twice, to kill King Saul, he is convinced that Saul will still keep hunting for him. So he decides to hide in Gath among the Philistines.

Living as a fugitive among the enemy Philistines is a gambit for David. He tricks Achish, the Philistine king of Gath, into thinking that he will fight with him against Israel, especially since Saul has been trying to kill him. But instead of fighting his fellow Israelites, he secretly kills off Philistine raiders *(1 Samuel 27:8–12)*.

Meanwhile, King Saul becomes frantic as vast numbers of Philistine fighters gather to attack. He asks God for help but the Lord refuses to answer, either by dreams, sacred lots or by the prophets *(1 Samuel 28:6)*.

Chapter 28 notes that *"Saul had banned from the land of Israel all mediums and those who consult the spirits of the dead,"* but nevertheless, he is desperate. Since God won't listen to his prayers, he consults a medium from Endor.

This is an all-time low for Saul, as king and leader of Israel. Scholar Paul House writes, *"Saul has become the archetypal secretive, superstitious, and sleazy political ruler."* In other words, he is pathetic and embarrassing; he has completely lost his way.

At Saul's insistence, the medium of Endor calls up the spirit of Samuel who has recently died. The spirit is agitated and says to Saul, *"Why ask me, since the Lord has left you and has become your enemy? The Lord has done just as he said he would. He has torn the kingdom from you and given it to your rival, David. ... What's more, the Lord will hand you and the army of Israel over to the Philistines tomorrow, and you and your sons will be here with me"* (1 Samuel 28:16–19).

Creepy.

The large Philistine army begins to move, with David and his men at the rear. But the Philistine commanders grow wary of David's loyalties and force King Achish to send David back home. It turns out to be a good thing. While David has been away, his town of Ziklag has been raided and burned to the ground by Amalekites. The families of David and his men have been carried away.

Fortunately, with help from an abandoned Amalekite slave, they find and defeat the raiders and get everyone back safely.

But Saul is not so fortunate. Without David, the Philistines close in on Saul and kill his sons, while injuring him seriously. Not wanting to be taken captive, Saul falls on his sword. With that, his sorry life comes to an unceremonious end. His head is cut off, his body hung on a wall, and his armor put in the pagan temple of Ashtoreth.

With this, the book of 1 Samuel comes to an end. Saul is dead; long live King David!

Focus: When the proud and violent King Saul is himself threatened by his enemies, he resorts to extreme measures to save his own life. They all fail. He has lost God's protection and blessing because of his rebellion, and his life comes to a tragic end. His life is one of many cautionary tales in the Bible. From Abel's brother, Cain, to Judas Iscariot, people have allowed evil to get a foothold in their life and finally push its way in. The Lord had warned Cain, *"Sin is crouching at the door, eager to control you. But you must subdue it and be its master"* (Genesis 4:7). We can subdue it if we will. The question is, are we willing to trust God for the conflicts in our life? Or will we allow sin to get a foothold because of jealousy, pride or anger?

Prayer: *Lord, how sad it is when a man of great potential and high calling falls into disrepute. May Saul's life warn us of the danger of willful rebellion and uncontrolled anger. May we look instead to David's example of a man of faith and character. Amen.*

161

March 24

> Key Text: Your pride and joy, O Israel, lies dead on the hills! Oh, how the mighty heroes have fallen! (2 Samuel 1:19)

The book of 2 Samuel continues the story of David's rise to become Israel's king. His reign of forty years will bring Israel to the high point of its history as a monarchy. As some have pointed out, David's reign also marks the halfway point between Abraham and Christ. Unfortunately, David's successes will be undermined by his moral failures. Despite his failures, however, he genuinely loves God and repents of his sins, making him the king who is a *"man after God's own heart."*

2 Samuel begins with David receiving news of King Saul's death in battle. His close friend and protector, Jonathan, is also dead: *"David and his men tore their clothes in sorrow when they heard the news. They mourned and wept and fasted all day for Saul and his son Jonathan, and for the Lord's army and the nation of Israel, because they had died by the sword that day"* (2 Samuel 1:11–12).

Anticipating his prolific writing of psalms later, David writes a funeral song for Saul and Jonathan, known as the Song of the Bow. Its recurring theme is *"Oh, how the mighty heroes have fallen."*

With King Saul now dead, David moves to Hebron in Judah, where he is crowned as king. Once again, David shows his respect for the position of the king as God's anointed, by blessing those who give Saul a decent burial. He then asks for Saul's family to be loyal to him as he had been loyal to Saul.

But the kindness is not returned. Saul's followers declare that Saul's surviving son, Ishbosheth, will be king. Meanwhile, the people of Judah remain loyal to David. Trouble is brewing.

Saul initiates conflicts which become the pretext for a long war between those who are loyal to Saul and those loyal to David. There are some betrayals within the Saul faction, leading Abner, who was the commander of Saul's army, to change sides and support David. David extends amnesty toward Abner, but some of David's troops, who had their own grievance against Abner, protest David's amnesty and kill Abner anyway, causing David grief and distress. What a mess.

Nevertheless, David's kindness toward Abner, a fellow Israelite, pleases the people who are tired of the intramural treacheries and revenge: *"In fact, everything the king did pleased them! So everyone in Judah and all Israel understood that David was not responsible for Abner's murder"* (2 Samuel 3:36–37).

Chapter 4 recounts one more misguided attempt by opportunists to get into David's favor, this time by killing Ishbosheth—but in his own bed at home, not in battle. Again, in character, David refuses to honor violence against a king, even though Ishbosheth had been his enemy, like Saul.

> **Focus:** David's pattern of mercy toward Saul, Abner and then Ishbosheth brings him favor with God and with the people. It bears witness to the Canaanite nations that Israel's God is a God who loves. Some regard mercy as weakness, but it is not. The willingness to forgive by not retaliating, or giving people what they deserve, is a strength that comes from God himself who is merciful and patient with all of us. The humility of knowing that one has been forgiven and rescued by God's mercy ought to move us to extend the same. As the apostle John writes in 1 John 4:10–11, *"This is real love—not that we loved God, but that he loved us and sent his Son as a sacrifice to take away our sins."*
>
> **Prayer:** *Lord, we see in King David a man of compassion, mercy and wisdom—a man after your own heart. Help us to demonstrate these same qualities, especially against our enemies, so that peace may be maintained, and your name may be honored. Amen.*

Day 85   2 Samuel 5–7

March 25

> Key Text: "Who am I, O Sovereign Lord, and what is my family, that you have brought me this far? And now, Sovereign Lord, in addition to everything else, you speak of giving your servant a lasting dynasty!" (2 Samuel 7:18–19)

When King Saul's son Ishbosheth dies, all the tribes of Israel go to David and pledge their allegiance to him as their rightful king. They say to him: *"In the past, when Saul was our king, you were the one who really led the forces of Israel. And the Lord told you, 'You will be the shepherd of my people Israel. You will be Israel's leader'"* (2 Samuel 5:2).

David is only thirty years old when he is anointed king, and will reign for forty years over Judah and then all Israel. His first action as king is to remove the Jebusites and establish his capital in Jerusalem, later called "the City of David." There, David becomes more and more powerful *"because the Lord God of Heaven's Armies* [i.e., the Lord of Hosts] *was with him."* The Lord of Hosts is a military term referring to the angels of heaven. This name for God, first appearing in 1 Samuel 1:3, declares that the Lord is Israel's true commander, fighting on their behalf.

God as the "Lord of Hosts" or "the God of Heaven's Armies," reveals that, contrary to popular imagination, angels are not little cherubs with wings and arrows, but they are powerful warriors—more like military Special Forces.

This designation of God highlights the reality of spiritual warfare which will be more fully developed theologically by the apostle Paul, and others, who saw events on earth being influenced by malevolent beings in the invisible dimension called the *"heavenly realms."*

For example, Ephesians 6:12 says: *"For we are not fighting against flesh-and-blood enemies, but against evil rulers and authorities of the unseen world, against mighty powers in this dark world, and against evil spirits in the heavenly places."*

Related to the subject of spiritual warfare is the claim that God is the Lord of all creation, visible and invisible. All the nations belong to him, but have been occupied by enemy forces serving false gods and powered by the demonic. In effect, the wars of Israel are physical manifestations of spiritual warfare. So as distasteful as they are to modern sensibility, the wars of Israel make clear that human life is caught up in a bigger struggle than it imagines.

Having established the capital in Jerusalem, David, with some difficulty, now brings the Ark of the Covenant into the city and sets it inside a special tent prepared for it. David celebrates this event enthusiastically—a little too enthusiastically for his wife, Michal, who is Saul's daughter. She is certain that he is calling attention to himself to impress the ladies present. Her disgust for David is fueled by her father's humiliation as king: *"She said in disgust, 'How distinguished the king of Israel looked today, shamelessly exposing himself to the servant girls like any vulgar person might do!'"* (2 Samuel 6:20).

David, however, will not be deterred from celebrating before the Lord because Michal has questioned his motives. The Lord has chosen him to rule, and he celebrates out of joy: *"Yes, and I am willing to look even more foolish than this, even to be more humiliated in my own eyes!"*

David settles into a palace and enjoys a period of rest from all his surrounding enemies. He wonders if he should build a more beautiful place for the Ark of the Covenant. But God says through the prophet Nathan, don't bother. One of David's descendants will build a temple. Right now, the house that God cares about is a dynasty of righteous kings.

So David praises and thanks God for all that he has done to bring about his ancient blessing, concluding his prayer with these words: *"For you are God, O Sovereign Lord. Your words are truth, and you have promised these good things to your servant. And now, may it please you to bless the house of your servant, so that it may continue forever before you. For you have spoken, and when you grant a blessing to your servant, O Sovereign Lord, it is an eternal blessing!"* (2 Samuel 7:28–29).

God will answer his prayer one day by sending the Messiah to bless the world with forgiveness—a Messiah who will arise from the House of David as king of the earth.

> **Focus:** All who seek to serve God with a pure heart will find themselves opposed. David constantly faced the Canaanite armies around him, while having his motives attacked by people close to him. It is the way of things in a fallen world, especially when believers seek to advance the Kingdom of God in the world. But as David acknowledged in his prayer, God is the sovereign Lord. His promises are true, and his good purposes will prevail in our lives.

> **Prayer:** *Lord, we thank you for fighting and defeating the powers of darkness on our behalf, and then rescuing us from our sin through the sacrifice of Jesus, your Son and our Savior the King. Amen.*

Day 86   2 Samuel 8–10

March 26

> **Key Text:** So David reigned over all Israel and did what was just and right for all his people. (2 Samuel 8:15)

Having secured the loyalty of the people, King David now goes to work to protect Israel from her remaining enemies. No army proves to be a match against David because *"the Lord made David victorious wherever he went"* (2 Samuel 8:6).

The narrator provides a few examples of David's military success and the consequent wealth that he collects from the defeated nations and dedicates to the Lord. So David becomes famous and *"reigned over all Israel and did what was just and right for all his people"* (2 Samuel 8:15).

What distinguishes David, among all Israel's past and future kings, is that his heart is in the right place. Two examples illustrate this. The first, in chapter 9, describes how David considers a way to honor his close friend and protector, Jonathan, who had died in battle with his father Saul. After inquiring about Jonathan's surviving family, he hears of a son named Mephibosheth. Mephibosheth suffers from being crippled in both feet.

When summoned before the king, Mephibosheth can hardly believe his ears. He seems to be expecting ill-treatment, but then hears that King David is going to honor Jonathan by giving him all the property that had once belonged to his grandfather, Saul. In addition, he will eat with David at the king's table!

I imagine it took a while for all this to sink in, because Mephibosheth was not used to life going his way. But once he realizes that his station in life has just radically changed, Mephibosheth bows respectfully and exclaims, *"Who is your servant, that you show such kindness to a dead dog like me?"*

By David's goodness, a "dead dog" is blessed and honored. It is no wonder that the people love him. However, another good deed of David is not so well received. Chapter 10 begins: *"Sometime after this, King Nahash of the Ammonites died, and his son Hanun became king. David said, 'I am going to show loyalty to Hanun just as his father, Nahash, was always loyal to me.' So David sent ambassadors to express sympathy to Hanun about his father's death"* (2 Samuel 10:1–2).

But King Hanun and his commanders suspect a plot. Surely David has sent his ambassadors to spy out the city so that they can come in and conquer it! So Hanun foolishly humiliates David's men physically and sends them back in shame.

Not a good idea.

Hanun soon receives word that he has seriously miscalculated, so he hires some reinforcements and prepares for battle. But they are no match for David's forces and are soundly defeated.

David will write a number of psalms that express God's protection and victory on behalf of his people and their king. One of them says: *"Sing a new song to the Lord, for he has done wonderful deeds. His right hand has won a mighty victory; his holy arm has shown his saving power! The Lord has announced his victory and has revealed his righteousness to every nation! He has remembered his promise to love and be faithful to Israel. The ends of the earth have seen the victory of our God"* (Psalm 98:1–3).

Hanun certainly has.

> **Focus:** No higher praise can be given to a leader than to say that he did "what was just and right for all his people." When leaders use their authority to do what is good for the sake of others, they reflect the character of the One who gives us the gift of authority, the Lord himself who is infinitely good, just and loving. There are few of us as powerful as kings, of course, but we each have some power and influence over those around us, to whom we can do what is just and right.

> ***Prayer:*** *Lord, you have shown us that character is more important than power. You are with those who, like David, do what is just and right. Be with us also. Amen.*

Day 87   2 Samuel 11–14

March 28

> **Key Text:** David was furious. "As surely as the Lord lives," he vowed, "any man who would do such a thing deserves to die!"... Then Nathan said to David, "You are that man!"
> (2 Samuel 12:5,7)

Perhaps the most heartbreaking kind of story is one where a good man undermines himself in a moment of personal weakness. This is the story of King David. Though he is remembered as Israel's greatest king and a *"man after God's own heart,"* there is the matter of Bathsheba.

David's reign has been one of justice, compassion and wisdom so far. God has clearly blessed him. But chapter 11 reveals that his success has made David careless about his personal life. While his army is off fighting, David stays behind in Jerusalem.

One afternoon, while on the roof of his palace, he notices a woman of unusual beauty taking a bath. Instead of looking away, he allows himself to lust after her. Since he is the king, he can have anything he wants. He finds out who she is. She is married to one his soldiers, Uriah, who is away at war. Nevertheless, he sends for her and sleeps with her.

Some months later, David receives a personal message from Bathsheba. She is pregnant! To cover his sin, he hatches a plan to bring Uriah back on leave to Jerusalem, hoping that he will sleep with his wife so that her illicit pregnancy can be disguised. But Uriah does not go home to her. When asked why, he explains: *"The Ark and the armies of Israel and Judah are living in tents, and Joab and my master's men are camping in the open fields. How could I go home to wine and dine and sleep with my wife? I swear that I would never do such a thing"* (2 Samuel 11:11).

Thinking that he was honoring his king and fellow soldiers, Uriah has signed his own death warrant. David panics and sends Uriah back to the battle with a letter for his field commander, Joab. The honorable Uriah does not break the king's seal to sneak a look at the letter. It instructs Joab: *"Station Uriah on the front lines where the battle is fiercest. Then pull back so that he will be killed."*

Soon the report comes back to King David that Uriah has been killed. David waits a suitable amount of time for Bathsheba to mourn and then makes her one of his wives: *"Then she gave birth to a son. But the Lord was displeased with what David had done"* (2 Samuel 11:27).

To outsiders, it might seem that David has done a good deed by bringing this unfortunate widow of one of his soldiers into his household. But the Lord knows better. He sends Nathan the prophet to tell David a story about a grave injustice done to a poor man by a rich man. David gets furious at this injustice, declaring that anyone who would do such a thing deserves to die!

Then Nathan tells David: *"You are that man!"* (2 Samuel 12:7).

Nathan has done a courageous thing by speaking truth to power. He has put his life at risk, but if the king will listen to him, he may yet save his soul, if not his sterling reputation. To his credit, David doesn't deny his sin or justify himself. He breaks down and confesses to Nathan: *"I have sinned against the Lord."*

Nevertheless, there will be personal consequences for David—his child by Bathsheba will die. There will also be consequences for his family. The Lord tells David through Nathan: *"From this time on, your family will live by the sword because you have despised me by taking Uriah's wife to be your own"* (2 Samuel 12:10).

In addition to the legacy of violence, a legacy of lust will also be passed on to David's family. Chapters 13 and 14 recount how one of David's sons, Amnon, rapes his half sister Tamar. When this is found out by Tamar's brother Absalom, who is also Amnon's half brother and another son of David, he takes revenge and kills Amnon. Absalom flees, and a rift is created between King David and his son that will eventually bring about more sorrow and death.

> **Focus:** David's story illustrates that sin has consequences—sometimes serious and long lasting. Often, the *sins of the fathers are passed on to their children*, and beyond. And yet, God's grace is greater than all our sin.

> **Prayer:** *Lord, help us to be honest with ourselves and with you about our areas of temptation. Grant us clarity of mind and self-control, lest our sins overtake us and bring about needless sorrow and loss, for ourselves and others in our lives. Amen.*

Day 88   Reflection

March 28

I want to reflect on something that you have undoubtedly noticed in our reading so far—the practice of polygamy among the Israelites. Most recently, we've seen this with King David. 2 Samuel 5:13 notes: *"After moving from Hebron to Jerusalem, David married more concubines and wives, and they had more sons and daughters."* David's son, Solomon, whom we will meet in the book of 1 Kings, will become the "king of polygamy," having a harem of *"700 wives of royal birth and 300 concubines."*

What are we to make of this? Doesn't the Bible forbid it? The answer is yes, but it's a little complicated.

From the beginning, male and female together reflect the image and likeness of God *(Genesis 1:26–27)*. Therefore, marriage is understood to be a union between one male and female, who are counterparts to each other physically and emotionally, yet equal partners. As one scholar has explained it, though the woman is created *after* the man, she is created *from* the man and is therefore "the essence of his essence."

By the covenant of marriage, they become "one flesh," meaning equal partners in life. By their sexual union they produce children for the next generation *(Genesis 2:18–25)*.

However, all this was disrupted by the Fall. By our trying to reconstruct life without God, his good gifts become corrupted, including the meaning of marriage *(Genesis 3)*. One of the consequences is that men begin to dominate and exploit women, whether as objects of pleasure (concubines and slaves) or as means to an end (wives to bear their children or to make political alliances).

Thus, the meaning of marriage is changed and polygamy is born, as well as evils such as sexual trafficking. The first polygamist mentioned in the Bible is the violent man Lamech, who is reported to have married two women, Adah and Zillah *(Genesis 4:19–24)*.

After the Fall in Genesis 3, the exploitation of women grew and diversified. For example, women taken in battle became spoils of the victors. Some became legal wives, to bear legitimate children as heirs. Others became concubines to be used for sexual pleasure—the forebears of today's "mistresses."

This pattern of sinful behavior became legitimized through law and normalized through practice. And so, for example, when Abraham, as well as other Israelites after him, married more than one wife, he was following local custom rather than obeying divine decree.

What made the matter complicated, however, was that there were circumstances in life which seemed to make polygamy the lesser of two evils.

For example, there were periods of history where, because of war, there were far more women than men. Therefore, there was an urgent need to rebuild the population. Also, since women had no rights, if they became widows they had no recourse but slavery or prostitution, unless they were remarried—often to a man who already had a wife.

In the case of kings like David and Solomon, political marriages were common as a means of establishing political alliances. Remember, God warned Israel about the inevitability of these kinds of practices should they demand a king to rule them.

And so, in the matter of male and female relationships in a broken world, God was, thankfully, tolerant of human misbehavior, even as he called his people to live according to his will. All these factors aside, the ideal of Hebrew marriage continued to be monogamy. This was certainly Jesus' view. When asked about his view of divorce, Jesus reiterated the teaching of Genesis 2 *(Matthew 19:1–12)*.

So, the practice of polygamy, along with slavery, concubines and divorce were regarded as expressions of the Fall in human relationships and society. Out of mercy, God tolerated them to some degree, just as he has tolerated many other ignorant and hurtful practices of fallen humanity. Nevertheless, all behavior rooted in rebellion against God brings suffering as a natural consequence. The moral law, like the law of nature, works to bless human existence when followed, but when violated brings dysfunction and heartache.

The story of the Bible declares that God has not turned his back on us, but turned toward us in love. One day, the damage of sin will be overcome. We will be fully restored in the New Creation. In the meantime, God continues to speak to us through his commandments, showing the way to a blessed life, and along the way graciously forgiving those who fall short.

Prayer: Lord, we are painfully aware of the gap between your perfect will and our imperfect behavior. We are grateful for your amazing patience and forgiveness. At the same time, we long to grow in faith and obedience so that we can experience the abundant life you have for us, more and more. Amen.

Day 89   2 Samuel 15–18

March 29

> Key Text: "Get out of here, you murderer, you scoundrel!" he shouted at David. "The Lord is paying you back for all the bloodshed in Saul's clan. You stole his throne, and now the Lord has given it to your son Absalom. At last you will taste some of your own medicine, for you are a murderer!" (2 Samuel 16:7–8)

Violence has come to King David's house just as the Lord had warned. David's son, Absalom, kills his half brother in an act of revenge for raping his sister. He flees to his grandfather to escape possible punishment from his father.

Absalom begins to cleverly cultivate loyalty among the people until he has enough support to stir up a rebellion against David. He manages to be crowned king in Hebron: *"A messenger soon arrived in Jerusalem to tell David, 'All Israel has joined Absalom in a conspiracy against you!'"* (2 Samuel 15:13).

People begin taking sides. David sees events turning against him and he escapes from Jerusalem. As he flees, he encounters angry hostility. In one village, a man curses David and throws stones at him and his officers: *"'Get out of here, you murderer, you scoundrel!' he shouted at David. 'The Lord is paying you back for all the bloodshed in Saul's clan. You stole his throne, and now the Lord has given it to your son Absalom. At last you will taste some of your own medicine, for you are a murderer!'"* (2 Samuel 16:7–8).

Not exactly a fair accusation, but clearly the house of Saul and the house of David have begun to hate each other. Meanwhile, Absalom and his army move into Jerusalem to solidify his power. He is approached by Ahithophel, who had been David's personal counselor. Ahithophel tells Absalom that his loyalty lies with the king, whoever he is, and so he now offers his services to Absalom.

What Absalom doesn't realize is that this is a plan cooked up by David and Ahithophel to keep Absalom off balance, by giving him misleading information. But, in a strange turn of events, the wrong advice given to Absalom about attacking David, which it turns out would have been the *right* advice, is overturned by another of Absalom's counselors who suspects Ahithophel. Therefore, thinking that he is avoiding bad advice (which was the good advice!), Absalom ends up following bad advice.

Throughout this comic maneuvering, God is the One who is actually directing events. When Absalom's army arrives, it is soundly defeated by David. Absalom's arrogant gambit is over.

For Absalom personally, it ends in a most embarrassing manner. Absalom was previously described as *"the most handsome man in all Israel. He was flawless from head to foot. He cut his hair only once a year, and then only because it was so heavy. When he weighed it out, it came to five pounds!"* (2 Samuel 14:25–26).

Yes, he weighed his hair! How appropriate, then, that Absalom should experience death by hair: *"During the battle, Absalom happened to come upon some of David's men. He tried to escape on his mule, but as he rode beneath the thick branches of a great tree, his hair got caught in the tree. His mule kept going and left him dangling in the air"* (2 Samuel 18:9).

Well, you can imagine how that ended.

When David receives news that Absalom has been killed, he is overcome with emotion, crying: *"O my son Absalom! My son, my son Absalom! If only I had died instead of you! O Absalom, my son, my son"* (2 Samuel 18:33).

Now you know where William Faulkner got the title for his novel, *Ab-*

salom, Absalom!

> **Focus:** David and Absalom remind us that, once words are said and deeds are done, they can't be unsaid or undone. They can be repented of, by the one side, or forgiven by the other side, but the hurt, the scars, the memories remain. We all live with regrets. Regret makes our souls ache like the changing of seasons can make our joints ache. How much better to control our words and deeds beforehand.

> **Prayer:** *Lord, sometimes life seems like an incomprehensible pattern of random events and contradictory motives. It is hard to see your will being carried out. And yet, as we see in David's life, you are always working in, around and through various people and events to bring about your purposes and move the story of redemption forward. Help us to trust you in the confusing times! Amen.*

Day 90   2 Samuel 19–20

March 30

> Key Text: Sheba blew a ram's horn and began to chant: "Down with the dynasty of David! We have no interest in the son of Jesse. Come on, you men of Israel, back to your homes!" (2 Samuel 20:1)

After the failure of Absalom's conspiracy against his father, King David, there are a lot of awkward issues to sort out. First, David's troops are irritated because David seems more distraught over the death of Absalom than he is grateful for their bravery in saving the lives of the rest of his family. His commander Joab confronts him: *"You seem to love those who hate you and hate those who love you"* (2 Samuel 19:6).

At Joab's insistence, David goes out to congratulate his troops, lest they abandon him. We see here a second occasion when David's feelings have gotten the best of his judgment—first with Bathsheba, and now with the death of Absalom.

Sometimes our strengths can also be our weaknesses.

Meanwhile, the Israelites who had supported Absalom in his treachery flee to their homes. They are not certain of their future, but David, who is from the tribe of Judah, forgives them, hoping to reunite the Israelites under his rule as he returns to Jerusalem. Here is David at his best.

Nevertheless, there is tension between the factions of Israel and the tribe of Judah over their relationship to the king because of Absalom. Soon a troublemaker named Sheba, from one of the Israel factions, manages to rally some men to protest David's reemergence as king: *"Sheba blew a ram's horn and began to chant: 'Down with the dynasty of David! We have no interest in the son of Jesse. Come on, you men of Israel, back to your homes!'"* (2 Samuel 20:1).

So as not to be caught napping a second time, David sends some troops to kill Sheba, who has hidden in a fortified town. David's commander Joab builds a siege ramp against the town's fortifications and begins battering down the wall. However, a woman from the town asks to negotiate with Joab, saying that if he will spare their town from destruction, they will throw Sheba's head over the wall. Joab agrees, so Sheba loses his head, the people keep their city, and Joab returns to Jerusalem.

In addition to the grisly nature of ancient warfare, we see in these incidents the violent consequences of David's sin. His lust for sex and power is seen through his practice of polygamy—wives for political alliances and bearing children, and concubines for sex. It weakens his will and undermines his moral status before the people when he commits adultery with Bathsheba and then kills her husband Uriah.

Followers follow the moral example of their leaders, and so what unfolds in David's family and among his people can only be seen as God's judgment. First, David's child with Bathsheba dies. Then one of David's sons commits rape and incest against his sister and another brother takes vengeance against him. Then Absalom seeks to overthrow his father's rule and is killed. Now, the nation itself is in turmoil.

Nevertheless, God does not remove David. In fact, God will bless him even as he holds him accountable for his sins. This strange tension is inherent in God's grace. We don't deserve God's grace and blessing, yet he gives it anyway. He forgives our sins, yet he doesn't remove the consequences. In this tension of our sin and God's grace, we grow in faith and maturity—often sadder, but hopefully wiser.

Focus: The measure of a leader, whether a parent or a king, is what he leaves behind in the lives of his followers. A good leader creates a heritage of goodness. Those under his or her tutelage receive, by precept and example, the way of goodness and success. But those under the tutelage of a bad leader continue bad practices. A follower of Jesus will aspire to goodness as a leader, but acknowledge his or her failures, and seek the mercy of God.

Prayer: Lord, we continue to be amazed that you are willing to join us in the messiness of our lives. Like King David, we are so undeserving of your grace. But also,

174

Day 91   2 Samuel 21–24

March 31

> **Key Text:** "Is it not my family God has chosen? Yes, he has made an everlasting covenant with me. His agreement is arranged and guaranteed in every detail." (2 Samuel 23:5)

With these chapters, we come to the end of 2 Samuel. They contain events that appear to be topical rather than chronological, emphasizing lessons learned regarding the reign of David. David clearly has a desire to do what is right. He has a tender heart toward God, even though he is far from perfect. What distinguishes him is his humble and sincere repentance when he sins.

We also see David's sensitivity as king to matters of grave injustice. In chapter 21, David seeks to make right a past injustice by Saul against the Gibeonites: *"So the king summoned the Gibeonites. They were not part of Israel but were all that was left of the nation of the Amorites. The people of Israel had sworn not to kill them, but Saul, in his zeal for Israel and Judah, had tried to wipe them out"* (2 Samuel 21:2).

The moral outrage of the near-genocide of the Gibeonites is consequently settled by a symbolic retribution against members of Saul's family, who face capital punishment. David's somber initiative to provide justice avoids a potential bloodbath of revenge by the remaining Gibeonites, but more importantly it shows him to be, in the end, a man of integrity.

In chapter 22, we have another psalm of David. David's hymnody and rich theological writing in the Psalms give to Israel worship resources that continue to speak to us today. This particular psalm praises God for protecting David from his enemies as king. The theme is stated in the first few stanzas and repeated with variations throughout: *"The Lord is my rock, my fortress, and my savior; my God is my rock, in whom I find protection. He is my shield, the power that saves me, and my place of safety. He is my refuge, my savior, the one who saves me from violence. I called on the Lord, who is worthy of praise, and he saved me from my enemies"* (2 Samuel 22:1–4).

In addition to its theme of God protecting David in war, the psalm reveals something of David's theology. The Lord is his Savior, and the Savior of Israel. He hears the prayers of his people *(vs. 7)*, rewards them for doing what is right *(vs. 21–25)*, deals honestly and faithfully with his people *(vs. 26–30)*, keeps his promises *(vs. 31)*, is the only real God *(vs. 32)*, protects and preserves his people *(vs. 33–46)*, and shows unfailing love to his covenant people forever *(vs. 47–51)*.

A second, briefer hymn in chapter 23 highlights God's special calling of David and his family in the broader story of God's ultimate redemption: *"Is it not my family God has chosen? Yes, he has made an everlasting covenant with me. His agreement is arranged and guaranteed in every detail"* (2 Samuel 23:5).

David's reign as king over Israel among the nations, though imperfect in many ways, as we have seen, will become iconic of a perfect king whose reign aligns the nations in God's peace and justice. In this regard, he anticipates the Messiah, Jesus, who will come as Israel's true and perfect king in the last days.

Chapter 24 completes the books of Samuel. We are given one more example of David's impulsive decisions—this time, a misguided command for his military leader Joab to take a census of the capable warriors in the land, usually a prelude to war. David has acted without guidance from the Lord, and the people will pay for it, as the people always do when their leaders act foolishly.

However, David confesses his sin: *"I have sinned greatly by taking this census. Please forgive my guilt, Lord, for doing this foolish thing"* (2 Samuel 24:10).

The book ends with David buying a piece of property upon which to build an altar to the Lord. He prays for an end to a plague on Israel, and God answers by stopping the plague. Eventually, David's son Solomon will build a temple on this property—a temple that will be the center of worship and glory for Israel under Solomon, at least for a little while.

Focus: The story of David illustrates the generous grace of God. Despite David's many sins, God knows that David wants to do what is right, even when his weaknesses undermine him. The fact that God calls David "a man after my own heart" shows that God puts a great deal of stock in our heart attitude, especially humility. As we have noted before, God does not exempt us from the consequences, good and bad, of our choices, but neither does he abandon us, unless we abandon him. When we humbly call out to him for forgiveness, he forgives and restores our lives.

Prayer: Lord, you are indeed our rock, our fortress and the savior of the whole world. You are our refuge and strength. When waves of destruction threaten to sweep over us, in these dangerous days, hear our prayers for help and act from your heavenly sanctuary. Amen.

Day 92   1 Kings 1–4

April 1

> Key Text: "Now, O Lord my God, you have made me king instead of my father, David, but I am like a little child who doesn't know his way around. And here I am in the midst of your own chosen people, a nation so great and numerous they cannot be counted! Give me an understanding heart so that I can govern your people well and know the difference between right and wrong. For who by himself is able to govern this great people of yours?" (1 Kings 3:7–9)

In the books of 1 and 2 Kings, we discover how Israel's monarchy attains its greatest power under the leadership of King Solomon, David's son. However, by 587 BC, the monarchy blows apart into a divided kingdom. It is eventually conquered by powerful nations and the people are exiled. The conquering and exile of the kingdom will have *"profound historical and theological implications for the rest of scripture."* (Paul House)

At the beginning of 1 Kings, Solomon's extraordinary wisdom, vast accumulation of wealth, and impressive building programs—especially the great Temple—have made Israel the envy of nations. Chapters 1 through 4 describe how this comes about.

In chapter 1, King David is aging and one of his sons, Adonijah, is scheming for power. But the prophet Nathan warns Bathsheba, who is Solomon's mother, and urges her to have David name his successor before Adonijah gets too strong of a following. She does, and David swears before her and Nathan: *"As surely as the Lord lives, who has rescued me from every danger, your son Solomon will be the next king and will sit on my throne this very day, just as I vowed to you before the Lord, the God of Israel"* (1 Kings 1:29–30).

So Solomon is quickly anointed as king. The good news is announced to the people, and the ceremony of enthronement takes place as Solomon rides into Jerusalem on David's own mule. This is followed by joyful celebration and the loud blasting of the ram's horn.

Meanwhile, Adonijah hears the distant sounds of celebration and realizes that he has been outmaneuvered. Adonijah's supporters quickly scatter in a panic. However, what could have been another intramural bloodbath turns out well when Solomon forgives a humbled and apologetic Adonijah for his presumption.

Despite his sins, old King David has set the stage for the blossoming of Israel. He has not fallen into idolatry, but has made the worship of Yahweh and the keeping of the Covenant the center of his reign.

Before David dies, he gives this charge to Solomon: *"I am going where everyone on earth must someday go. Take courage and be a man. Observe the requirements of the Lord your God, and follow all his ways. Keep the decrees, commands, regulations, and laws written in the Law of Moses so that you will be successful in all you do and wherever you go. If you do this, then the Lord will keep the promise he made to me. He told me, 'If your descendants live as they should and follow me faithfully with all their heart and soul, one of them will always sit on the throne of Israel'"* (1 Kings 2:2–4).

Solomon takes control of the kingdom by attending to some "cold cases" that need to be closed and some injustices that need to be righted. Solomon loves God, and God rewards him with great wisdom and success. His reputation for wisdom is established by his great building projects, but also by his personal insight into human nature, as seen, for example, in the famous story of his determining which of two women had the rightful claim to the same child *(1 Kings 3:16–28)*.

Chapter 4 ends with a tribute to Solomon's wealth, power and wisdom. His fame grows among the surrounding nations. He *"composed some 3,000 proverbs and wrote 1,005 songs,"* which we will read in the books of Proverbs and the Psalms. He becomes an authority on nature and animals—so much so that *"kings from every nation sent their ambassadors to listen to the wisdom of Solomon."*

Focus: Solomon's wisdom was granted to him when he asked God for an understanding heart. God was pleased by his request and blessed Solomon with wisdom and knowledge. So much so, that his reign as king gained a national and international reputation. People came from far and wide to see his projects and hear his wisdom. The Psalms and Proverbs make clear that the source of all wisdom and knowledge is God himself. He willingly gives it to all who ask. Foolishness can make life bitter, but wisdom brings blessing. It is a lesson we need to pass on to our children.

Prayer: Lord, once again we see your plan of redemption moving forward through the messiness and complexity of human history. How kind you are to accommodate yourself to our lack of understanding, and how gracious you are to continue to forgive our sins along the way. Grant us your wisdom and understanding, like David and Solomon. Amen.

Day 93   1 Kings 5–8

April 2

> Key Text: "But will God really live on earth? Why, even the highest heavens cannot contain you. How much less this Temple I have built! Nevertheless, listen to my prayer and my plea, O Lord my God. Hear the cry and the prayer that your servant is making to you today." (1 Kings 8:27–28)

The portrayal of Solomon as a king of great learning and wisdom, grounded in the knowledge of God, continues as plans are made for building the Temple: *"But now the Lord my God has given me peace on every side; I have no enemies, and all is well. So I am planning to build a Temple to honor the name of the Lord my God, just as he had instructed my father, David"* (1 Kings 5:4–5).

Solomon comes to an agreement with King Hiram from Tyre to provide cedar for construction. This economic agreement with Hiram illustrates how significant Israel has become among the surrounding nations. Hiram even honors Israel's God: *"Praise the Lord today for giving David a wise son to be king of the great nation of Israel."*

As construction of the Temple begins, God promises Solomon that if he keeps the Covenant and obeys the commandments, he will fulfill the promise made to his father David, to live among the Israelites and never abandon them.

Chapters 6 and 7 are happy reading for architects! As with the Tabernacle in the wilderness, which was a portable temple, the outer design and interior articles of the permanent Temple are described in great detail. When the construction is completed, King Solomon fills the treasuries of the Temple with the inherited wealth of David.

In chapter 8, the leaders of Israel are summoned to a great worship service. So many sacrifices are offered that no one can keep count! All this leads up to the great moment when the priests carry the Ark of the Covenant, containing the two stone tablets of the Law given to Moses by God, into the inner sanctuary of the Temple—the most holy place—and place it beneath the wings of the cherubim.

When the priests come out, the glory of the Lord fills the Temple like a thick cloud, and King Solomon leads the people in a beautiful prayer revealing his deep understanding of God: *"O Lord, God of Israel, there is no God like you in all of heaven above or on the earth below. You keep your covenant and show unfailing love to all who walk before you in wholehearted devotion. ... Now, O God of Israel, fulfill this promise to your servant David, my father. But will God really live on earth? Why, even the highest heavens cannot contain you. How much less this Temple I have built!"* (1 Kings 8:23, 26–27).

The prayer also expresses a hopeful vision of the future where the nations of the earth will all know and fear God: *"In the future, foreigners who do not belong to your people Israel will hear of you. They will come from distant lands because of your name, for they will hear of your great name and your strong hand and your powerful arm. And when they pray toward this Temple, then hear from heaven where you live, and grant what they ask of you. In this way, all the people of the earth will come to know and fear you, just as your own people Israel do"* (1 Kings 8:41–43).

Finally, the prayer acknowledges Israel's sad track record regarding idolatry and rebellion against God. Solomon prays for God's mercy should the people sin against God in the future—and especially if they find themselves in exile by their enemies! This, of course, has always been a possible judgment of God should the people of Israel continue in idolatry. (Spoiler alert: They do and God does.)

But today, all is well in Israel. Solomon has proven to be a leader of uncommon ability and vision. Under his rule, at this point, one can imagine the day when God's Promise to Abraham is fulfilled and all the nations of the earth are blessed because of Israel. Revelation 21 speaks of this day as being one of a New Heaven and New Earth. A New Jerusalem descends from heaven to earth and the glory of God illuminates the city: *"And all the nations will bring their glory and honor into the city"* (Revelation 21:26).

Focus: Solomon's wonderful prayer regarding the Temple contains the mature insight that not even the highest heavens can contain God, let alone a single Temple. Indeed, the whole universe is his Temple, for he is present everywhere, listening to our prayers, receiving our worship, and providentially guiding human history and our individual lives. Not all nations in this fallen world presently recognize God, but one day they will. Solomon's prayer evokes a future creation that has been redeemed and restored under God's sovereign rule as King of creation.

Prayer: Lord, our hearts and minds are excited by the vision of our world renewed and healed, with the nations living in peace. As you have taught us to pray, we ask for your Kingdom to come and your will to be done, on earth as in heaven. Amen.

Day 94   1 Kings 9–11

April 3

> Key Text: Now King Solomon loved many foreign women. ...
> In Solomon's old age, they turned his heart to worship other
> gods instead of being completely faithful to the Lord his God, as
> his father, David, had been. Solomon worshiped Ashtoreth, the
> goddess of the Sidonians, and Molech, the detestable god of the
> Ammonites. In this way, Solomon did what was evil in the Lord's
> sight; he refused to follow the Lord completely, as his father,
> David, had done. (1 Kings 11:1,4–6)

After the Temple and the royal palace are constructed, the Lord speaks to Solomon about the future. He tells him that his presence will continue in the Temple as long as his name is honored there. And as for Solomon: *"...if you will follow me with integrity and godliness, as David your father did, obeying all my commands, decrees and regulations, then I will establish the throne of your dynasty over Israel forever. ... But if you or your descendants abandon me and disobey the commands and decrees I have given you, and if you serve and worship other gods, then I will uproot Israel from this land that I have given them. I will reject this Temple that I have made holy to honor my name. I will make Israel an object of mockery and ridicule among the nations"* (1 Kings 9:4–7).

Once again, we are reminded of God's Promise to Abraham and his subsequent Covenant with Israel. It is his desire to share life with his people and bless them. But they need to know that the Covenant is more than a contract. It is the basis of a relationship, and this relationship is broken by idolatry.

181

Chapters 9 and 10 survey the extraordinary blessing of God upon Solomon. His kingdom is a wonder of the age. He has accumulated great wealth and power, and has built impressive buildings. He is well organized and cultured, outfitting his officials in splendid clothing and serving an impressive table. In all things, great and small, Solomon excels—he has become a celebrity. Even the skeptical and curious Queen of Sheba, who has heard the stories, is amazed at what she sees of Solomon's kingdom upon her visit.

She exclaims to Solomon: *"Everything I heard in my country about your achievements and wisdom is true! I didn't believe what was said until I arrived here and saw it with my own eyes. In fact, I had not heard the half of it! Your wisdom and prosperity are far beyond what I was told. How happy your people must be! … Praise the Lord your God, who delights in you and has placed you on the throne of Israel"* (1 Kings 10:6–9).

But chapter 11 begins with an ominous note: *"King Solomon loved many foreign women."* In fact, he accumulates them like he accumulates gold. He knows that the Lord has forbidden Israelites to marry pagan wives, but he insists upon doing it anyway, with crazy abandonment: *"He had 700 wives of royal birth and 300 concubines. And in fact, they did turn his heart away from the Lord"* (1 Kings 11: 3).

Here is a cautionary tale. At the very apex of God's blessing, and of Israel's glory as a nation, Solomon throws it all away by willfully disobeying the Covenant. It's a familiar story.

God confronts Solomon with his willful sin and tells him that he will take the kingdom away from him. Out of respect for David, he will do so when Solomon dies, but Solomon will be known thereafter as another of Israel's spiritually failed kings.

Meanwhile, sniffing weakness and corruption, enemies of Solomon begin to stir up trouble. Hadad and Rezon are mentioned as ones who have personal motives for vengeance against Solomon. But the biggest threat is Jeroboam, one of Solomon's own officials and a gifted leader. Jeroboam is confronted one day by the prophet Ahijah, who tells him that God is going to give most of the kingdom to him.

Word gets around, and Solomon tries to kill Jeroboam, but he gets away and hides…and waits.

Focus: Once again, a key leader of Israel falls into sin and suffers the consequences. Yet, once again, we find that God does not wash his hands of us. He continues to use broken people to be partners with him in his great plan to redeem the world. None of us can boast that we deserve his favor, nor that we succeed on our own merits. God gets all the glory for whatever is accomplished. Thankfully, our future hope does not rest on our faithfulness to God, but on God's faithfulness to us.

Prayer: Lord, we know that success can make us presumptuous, entitled and ungrateful. We know that it can capture our hearts so that we desire it more than we desire you. Forgive us for surrendering to the familiar gods of money, sex and power. Teach us to see clearly what is most important, and keep you first in our lives. Amen.

Day 95   1 Kings 12–16

April 4

Key Text: During Rehoboam's reign, the people of Judah did what was evil in the Lord's sight, provoking his anger with their sin, for it was even worse than that of their ancestors. (1 Kings 14:22)

Solomon has died and been buried in the City of David. He accomplished a great deal as king, but his marriages to Canaanite women have opened the door to idolatry and spoiled his legacy. This legacy will be passed on to his son, Rehoboam.

After Rehoboam is anointed as king, Solomon's official, Jeroboam, who had fled to Egypt to escape Solomon, comes back. He and the other officials of Israel wisely urge Rehoboam to lighten the burdens of the people: *"'Your father was a hard master,' they said. 'Lighten the harsh labor demands and heavy taxes that your father imposed on us. Then we will be your loyal subjects'"* (1 Kings 12:4).

Here we discern that Solomon's great wealth has been gained on the backs of workers and by excessive taxation. It is an opportunity for Rehoboam to act with compassion and justice.

But Rehoboam chooses to listen to his younger advisors, who are flush with ambition and lust after power, but lack the benefit of wisdom and experience. He makes the heavy burden on the people even worse!

However, the people of Israel push back. They refuse to be ruled by a descendent of David any longer, especially one who makes their lives miserable. So they declare Jeroboam to be the king of Israel, leaving Rehoboam as king over the single tribe of Judah in the South. Rehoboam prepares for war, but is stopped by a prophet named Shemaiah, who gives him a word from the Lord: *"'Do not fight against your relatives, the Israelites. Go back home, for what has happened is my doing!' So they obeyed the message of the Lord and went home, as the Lord had commanded"* (1 Kings 12:24).

Meanwhile, Jeroboam makes a critical error of judgment. He assumes that the people will be influenced by Rehoboam, when they go to Jerusalem, to offer sacrifices at the Temple Solomon built. So he innovates and maneuvers. He makes two golden calves, like the ones the Israelites worshiped while Moses was on the mountain with God *(Exodus 32),* and he urges the people to worship them, calling them *"the gods who brought you out of Egypt."*

He then combines some elements of Yahweh worship with paganism and appoints his own priesthood, thereby creating a syncretistic system at Bethel for the people of Israel. This is a great sin before the Lord.

This retreat from strict monotheism, whether through syncretism (a combining of religious beliefs and practices) or outright polytheism (worshiping many gods) by the use of idols, will continue to plague both Israel and Judah.

In chapter 13, for example, two prophets warn Jeroboam about spiritual apostasy, but Jeroboam refuses to listen and continues to lead the people astray. Meanwhile, Rehoboam of Judah has also been seduced into using syncretism as a means to maintain power. Clearly, both of them fail to lead God's people in the manner God has directed them. They desire power more than they desire righteousness, and they both lead their people in doing evil before the Lord. Not surprisingly, there is constant war between the split kingdoms. When people willfully rebel against God, he removes his blessing and protection, and they are left to face the predictable consequences of their sin.

Chapters 14 through 16 outline the succession of kings in both Judah and Israel. Most of them sin against the Lord through idolatry. Yet some, like Asa *(1 Kings 15:9–24),* do what is pleasing to the Lord. Nevertheless, the war continues between the divided kingdoms of Judah and Israel.

Throughout this period, God increasingly sends prophets to speak on his behalf and warn the kings, but their warnings go unheeded. Idolatry increases and those who worship Yahweh alone become the persecuted minority, leaving us to wonder if the Mosaic faith is viable anymore.

Reading this from our present time in history strikes us that history may be repeating itself.

Focus: There is no doubt that pagan religion was a big temptation to Israel. God's commandments were difficult, whereas paganism appealed to their sinful nature. The pressure to be like the nations around them was particularly irresistible to the kings who sought political and military alliances to keep the nation safe, instead of trusting in God. It takes great humility, personal honesty, discipline and devotion to be able to resist the allure of the world around us and faithfully obey God.

Prayer: Lord, we confess that idols tempt us as they did the people of Israel. Our society continually offers alternatives to you for our comfort, safety and well-being. Make us wise to see the dangers, and strong to resist them. Amen.

Day 96   1 Kings 17–19

April 5

> Key Text: Immediately the fire of the Lord flashed down from heaven and burned up the young bull, the wood, the stones, and the dust. It even licked up all the water in the trench! And when all the people saw it, they fell face down on the ground and cried out, "The Lord—he is God! Yes, the Lord is God!"
> (1 Kings 18:38–39)

The unfortunate legacy of King Solomon, and his son Rehoboam, is a divided kingdom—Israel (the ten tribes in the north) and Judah (the two remaining tribes in the south.) The period of the divided kingdom is a story of corrupt kings, with a few notable exceptions, who lead their respective kingdoms into the idolatry of their neighbors. Each one seems to be worse than the one before.

Since the kings—especially the kings of the northern kingdom—no longer listen to God, he warns them through his prophets. Our reading today is about one such king, Ahab, and one such prophet, Elijah.

Ahab, son of Omri, *"did what was evil in the Lord's sight, even more than any of the kings before him. And as though it were not enough to follow the example of Jeroboam, he married Jezebel, the daughter of King Ethbaal of the Sidonians, and he began to bow down in worship of Baal. First Ahab built a temple and an altar for Baal in Samaria. Then he set up an Asherah pole. He did more to provoke the anger of the Lord, the God of Israel, than any of the other kings of Israel before him"* (1 Kings 16:30–33).

Chapters 17 and 18 introduce us to the ministry of the prophet Elijah, setting the context for his memorable confrontation with King Ahab and the pagan prophets of Baal. Elijah's relationship with Ahab begins when he brings God's message of a coming famine in the land. The famine is a judgment upon Ahab for his idolatry. Of course, Ahab hates the messenger because he hates the message, so God sends Elijah into hiding to Kerith Brook, in order to prepare him for what is ahead.

While there, Elijah demonstrates the power of God by praying for a miracle for a destitute widow and her son. The Lord multiplies their flour and oil and they survive. In time, however, the son becomes unexpectedly sick and dies. A confused Elijah cries out to the Lord on his behalf and the child is brought back to life, like Jesus would later do with Lazarus.

By this, Elijah sees the power of God to provide and restore even life itself. Then the widow becomes the voice of God to encourage Elijah: *"Now I know for sure that you are a man of God, and that the Lord truly speaks through you"* (1 Kings 17:24).

Through these experiences, Elijah's faith is strengthened for the time when he and King Ahab will meet face to face. When the day arrives, Ahab confronts Elijah: *"So, is it really you, you troublemaker of Israel?"* But Elijah points the finger at Ahab: *"I have made no trouble for Israel.... You and your family are the troublemakers, for you have refused to obey the commands of the Lord and have worshiped the images of Baal instead. Now summon all Israel to join me at Mount Carmel, along with the 450 prophets of Baal and the 400 prophets of Asherah who are supported by Jezebel"* (1 Kings 18:17–19).

What an encounter! 850 pagan prophets and...Elijah! Elijah calls out Ahab on his dalliance with paganism: *"How much longer will you waver, hobbling between two opinions? If the Lord is God, follow him! But if Baal is God, then follow him!"* (1 Kings 18:21). Elijah dares them to prepare a sacrifice to Baal to stand beside his sacrifice to the Lord. Both will call upon their God to set fire to the wood. The one who answers is the true God!

The prophets of Baal go first, dancing and calling upon the name of Baal for hours. No answer. Elijah mocks them. Their frenzy increases by cutting themselves and raving till nightfall. No fire. Elijah finally calls the people to stop and pay attention. He orders them to pour four large jars of water over the wood and offerings to the Lord God—three times!

Then he prays, *"Oh Lord, God of Abraham, Isaac, and Jacob, prove today that you are God in Israel and that I am your servant."* Immediately, fire flashes from heaven and burns everything, including the water. The pagan prophets are subsequently killed.

Then Elijah prays and the Lord sends rain, ending the drought and famine.

It is a great victory for the Lord, and his prophet Elijah, but Elijah isn't rejoicing. He is deeply discouraged by the sinfulness of the nation. King Ahab reports to his wife, Jezebel, that Elijah has killed all the other prophets of Baal, so now Jezebel wants to kill Elijah.

Elijah feels vulnerable and alone, even after all God has done through him.

So God lifts his spirits, and ours, by telling Elijah that despite the widespread rebellion and idolatry of the people, there is a remnant of the faithful in Israel—there are 7,000 others who have not bowed down to Baal or kissed him.

God can work with small numbers and few resources to bring about his purposes!

Focus: If you ever feel alone as a Christian, wondering if faith is disappearing on earth, remember God's word to Elijah about the remnant of faith. Despite how it may appear, there are always others who are faithful to God. You are not alone. God is always working in the world, sometimes in spectacular ways, as with the defeat of the prophets of Baal, and sometimes in quiet, nearly indiscernible ways. So don't give up! Trust in the Lord!

Prayer: *Lord, we rejoice in the great moments when your power and glory are revealed for all to see. We also rejoice in the little moments when your presence is experienced in quiet and simple ways. In either case, it is you we praise and thank. Amen.*

Day 97   1 Kings 20–22

April 6

Key Text: "So, my enemy, you have found me!" Ahab exclaimed to Elijah. "Yes," Elijah answered, "I have come because you have sold yourself to what is evil in the Lord's sight. So now the Lord says, 'I will bring disaster on you and consume you.'"
(1 Kings 21:20)

Ahab has been humbled by the power of God, demonstrated by the prophet Elijah's smackdown of the 450 prophets of Baal! We might expect that Ahab would now fear God. But he does not. The writer comments: *"No one else so completely sold himself to what was evil in the Lord's sight as Ahab did under the influence of his wife Jezebel. His worst outrage was worshiping idols just as the Amorites had done—the people whom the Lord had driven out from the land ahead of the Israelites"* (1 Kings 21:25–26).

Chapters 20 through 22 describe Ahab's wars against Ben-hadad of Aram and the thirty-two kings allied with him. The allied kings besiege Samaria, the capital of the northern kingdom. Seeing that he is vastly outnumbered, Ahab immediately tries to negotiate.

After the two kings exchange insults and threats, a prophet of God comes to see Ahab and extends God's offer to defeat Ben-hadad, so that Ahab will finally be persuaded to trust in the Lord and not the gods of the Canaanites.

Twice God gives Ahab victory even though *"the Israelite army looked like two little flocks of goats in comparison to the vast Aramean forces that filled the countryside!"* (1 Kings 20:27). But in the end, Ahab refuses to obey God's command to kill Ben-hadad. Instead, he offers to make a treaty with him, which amounts to making another compromise with idolatry.

Finally, Elijah himself shows up, much to Ahab's consternation. He tells Ahab, *"I have come because you have sold yourself to what is evil in the Lord's sight. So now the Lord says, 'I will bring disaster on you and consume you.'"*

Ahab's initial response is to humble himself before God, so his "disaster" is postponed. King Jehoshaphat of Judah then reaches out to Ahab and encourages him to listen to the Lord's prophet, Micaiah. But Ahab hates Micaiah because *"he never prophesies anything but trouble for me!"*

Sure enough, the Lord has told Micaiah that because Ahab refuses to call upon the Lord and lead the people to follow him, he will be killed.

Trying to escape God's prophesy, Ahab goes into battle in disguise. But a random arrow shot in the direction of the Israelite troops hits Ahab between the joints of his armor and he bleeds out. So Ahab dies as a judgment from God, and his son Ahaziah becomes the next king. Unfortunately, he's no better.

But Jehoshaphat, king of Judah, is a good king for the most part, following the good example of his father, King Asa. He did what was pleasing in the Lord's sight, although during his reign, *"he failed to remove all the pagan shrines, and the people still offered sacrifices and burned incense there."*

Focus: How can we explain the fact that Israelite kings, north and south, continue to trust in international politics, military alliances and religious syncretism, instead of in the Lord God, who has shown Israel time and again over their history that he is able to protect and bless them, if only they will be faithful to the Covenant?

Simply put, faith in the invisible God is difficult in a world where gods are made visible in idols. Faith is difficult also because God's commandments call us to a life and society based on justice and love. Jesus will later comment: *"You can enter God's Kingdom only through the narrow gate. The highway to hell is broad, and its gate is wide for the many who choose that way. But the gateway to life is very narrow and the road is difficult, and only a few ever find it"* (Matthew 7:13–14).

Prayer: *Lord, thank you for being patient with us, like you were with Ahab, giving him every opportunity to return to you, though he refused. Help us to be like Jehoshaphat, instead, and do what is pleasing in your sight. Amen.*

Day 98   Reflection

April 7

The story of King Solomon is truly puzzling. He was a man of vision, leadership, style and taste, presiding over Israel's golden era. He was a rock star in his time. Kings and queens came from afar to see if the rumors of his achievements were true. They were, and more so.

Solomon was also gifted with wisdom and insight. His writings, which we will read in the wisdom literature of the Old Testament, have guided and inspired the people of God for hundreds of generations.

And yet, his reign set in motion events that led to a divided kingdom, and eventually conquest and exile by nations around them.

What can we learn from Solomon's story? First, we see the danger of wealth and power. Solomon began well by listening to the Lord and leading the people wisely. But success can wreak havoc with our grip on reality. We are tempted to view success as God's unconditional endorsement of us, and perhaps think that the rules no longer apply. In Solomon's case, he violated God's commandments about relationships with the Canaanites by vigorously forming alliances through marriage.

Once the seed of paganism took root through these marriages, the weeds grew thick. The "wisest man who ever lived" began to act like a fool. Moral compromise led to a divided heart. He began to love wealth, women and the worship of idols. At the glittering apex of his success, he forgot God, whose blessing had made it possible.

Unfortunately, Solomon's halfheartedness is picked up by his son Rehoboam, who leads the nation into civil war which divides Israel into a northern kingdom of ten tribes (Israel) and a southern kingdom of two tribes (Judah).

As we shall see, despite occasional good kings in Judah, the spiritual handwriting is on the wall. God's judgment against idolatry and civil injustice will result in the loss of the land, the Temple and the kingdoms.

We might be tempted to ask at this point in our reading: Why has God taken Israel through so many challenges over all these generations, beginning with his Promise to Abraham, only to have it fall apart in the end? And why has he preserved this detailed record of Israel's failure?

Looking back from Christ, we see the value of this record of failure. We learn from Israel's story that absolutely no one is made right with God through human goodness and merit. In the New Testament, the apostle Paul makes his case for Christ by showing that even Israel, with the unique privilege of experiencing God's presence, power and provision, and being instructed by his Law, still failed to obey his commandments and keep his Covenant. His conclusion: *"...everyone has sinned; we all fall short of God's glorious standard"* (Romans 3:23).

This disheartening analysis of Israel, and of us, is the first step toward understanding grace, and, by grace through faith, toward embracing our salvation.

> **Prayer:** *Lord, even the best of us fall short of your intention for us to reflect your image and likeness. We are slaves to sin until you free us; we are lost until you find us. Thank you for seeking us out in Christ. Amen.*

Day 99 — 2 Kings 1–3

April 8

> Key Text: When they came to the other side, Elijah said to Elisha, "Tell me what I can do for you before I am taken away." And Elisha replied, "Please let me inherit a double share of your spirit and become your successor." (2 Kings 2:9)

In the book of 2 Kings, we trace the tragic fall of the divided Jewish empire.

Stepping back to see the wider picture, the books of Samuel and Kings reveal the irony that the nation chosen by God to be a witness of the one true God to the surrounding nations, has instead become just like the surrounding nations and will soon be conquered and exiled by Assyria and Babylonia.

Nevertheless, God continues to care for his people and show grace through the ministries of the prophets. In 1 Kings it was the great prophet Elijah; in 2 Kings it will be the prophet Elisha.

Elijah's ministry is winding down and he is mentoring a prophet named Elisha. When asked by Elijah what he would like to receive from him before he dies, Elisha asks for a *"double share"* of his spirit and to become his successor. A bold request! But it indicates Elisha's deep desire to be a faithful prophet of God, like his mentor.

In chapter 2, Elijah and Elisha visit a group of prophets at Bethel *(2 Kings 2:1–3)*. This *"group of prophets"* are probably young men studying the Law of Moses and the history of Israel in order to teach the people. Contrary to what you might think, the prophets were scholars of theology and history, primarily involved in "forth-telling" the word of God rather than "foretelling" the future.

When Elijah is dramatically taken away in a *"chariot of fire"* by a *"whirlwind into heaven,"* Elisha is deeply moved. He picks up Elijah's cloak, i.e., his mantle, and performs some nature miracles which show that indeed the spirit of Elijah rests upon him.

Elisha also shows that the Lord speaks through him when, in chapter 3, King Joram of Israel and King Jehoshaphat of Judah are joined by the king of Edom in teaming up to fight the king of Moab. But there is no water for the men or animals. King Joram becomes anxious because of

191

this, so Jehoshaphat recommends that they consult with a prophet of the Lord.

They choose Elisha, but Elisha is not very excited about helping them because they are not fully committed to the Lord. He sarcastically tells them, *"Go to the pagan prophets of your father and mother!"*

Finally, he relents and inquires of the Lord about the conflict with Moab. The Lord tells Elisha that he is going to send plenty of water to refresh the men and animals, and then give them victory over Moab. Sure enough, God sends water in a most unexpected way. At dawn the next day, the Moabites become confused by the reflection of the sun on the water, which is making it look red—like blood. Thinking that they are witnessing the bloody remains of a battle, they set off to grab loot. But the mirage of blood causes them to fall into a trap and they are defeated.

God has answered Elisha's prayer and given him a *"double share"* of Elijah's spirit. So, Elisha begins his ministry with miraculous signs and wonders against the enemies of God. And we see Elisha's ministry, like that of Elijah, combining the teaching of God's Word and the demonstration of God's power—a witness to both the pagan nations and the divided kingdom of the Israelites.

Focus: Elisha's desire to be a faithful prophet of the Lord, like Elijah, means that he is willing to suffer the thankless job of being God's spokesman to a people who don't want to hear it. As Elijah told Elisha, *"You have asked a difficult thing"* (2 Kings 2:10). It is true for all who seek to serve the Lord faithfully when all around them do not. But God rewards those who endure tribulation in order to serve him.

Prayer: Lord, like these two great prophets, grant your Church a ministry of the Word and power in the world today as we pursue our calling to make disciples of all nations. We cannot do it in our own strength! Amen.

Day 100   2 Kings 4–8

April 9

Key Text: "Now I know that there is no God in all the world except in Israel. … From now on I will never again offer burnt offerings or sacrifices to any other god, except the Lord." (2 Kings 5:15,17)

These chapters continue the stories of Elisha, a great and faithful prophet of God through whom he works nine miracles. Chapter 4 begins with two representative stories. In the first, the widow of a prophet who served under Elisha's leadership, who is now poverty-stricken, cries out to Elisha that creditors are threatening to take her two sons as slaves. Out of compassion, the Lord gives Elisha the power to greatly multiply the little olive oil they possessed—so much so that she could sell the oil, pay her debts and have money left over to live on.

In the second story, a wealthy, childless woman who has been supportive of Elisha's ministry becomes pregnant by the prayerful intervention of Elisha. She had never mentioned her heartbreak about childlessness, but in response to a discreet inquiry, Elisha discovers the woman's private sorrow. Her generosity and faith are rewarded by God through his prophet.

But when the child grows older, he suffers a terrible pain in his head and dies. His mother is distraught, thinking that God, who had previously lifted her hopes by enabling her to bear a child, has now crushed them, leaving her more sorrowful than ever. Who could blame her for despair and anger at God? When Elisha is notified, he comes to her home and prays earnestly to the Lord. Once again, the Lord hears the woman's anguish and Elisha's prayers. The boy is restored to life!

Elisha is able to deliver the most precious gift of all to this dear woman: *"Here, take your son!"* The woman falls on her knees before Elisha, full of gratefulness to God. *"Then she took her son in her arms and carried him downstairs."*

In chapter 5, Naaman, a foreigner and military commander, is cured of leprosy. He, a pagan, is convinced by the word of Elisha, and the power of his God, and he bears witness to the Lord: *"Now I know that there is no God in all the world except in Israel. ... From now on I will never again offer burnt offerings or sacrifices to any other god except the Lord"* (2 Kings 5:15,17).

It is ironic that a pagan outsider should bear witness to the one true God, when the Israelites themselves are breaking God's commandment by worshiping pagan idols. Already, we begin to see more evidence of God's Promise to bless the nations through Abraham coming true.

In chapters 6 through 8, we read several more stories about how God used his prophet Elisha to do miraculous signs, and confuse and defeat enemy armies. Again, we would expect that the messages and miracles of God's prophets would persuade God's people to return to him, and stop trusting in pagan gods and worldly wisdom. But not so. Kings come and go in the divided kingdoms of Judah and Israel, creating the same evil chaos that is characteristic of life apart from God's blessing.

The Elisha stories demonstrate that the Lord is not merely one religious option among many; he is the one and only God, with absolute power. Human events are under his control. He is the judge of people and nations. Yet, his covenant love is extended to non-Israelites as well, including a pagan military commander with leprosy, a poor woman who is rescued from poverty through a miracle of multiplication, and a wealthy woman who is healed from infertility, then comforted in loss by the restoring of her child's life.

The miracles of Elijah highlight the various aspects of God's loving power—his care for the helpless, control over nature, power over sickness and death, and supremacy over the false gods, like Baal.

> **Focus:** When a seemingly greater army gathers to attack God's people, Elisha's servant frantically cries out to him, *"Oh, sir, what will we do now?"* His fear in the face of overwhelming odds is understandable. Who of us hasn't felt the same in our personal lives at times, having no idea what we were going to do? But Elisha opens his eyes to see a greater reality: *"'Don't be afraid!' Elisha told him. 'For there are more on our side than on theirs!' Then Elisha prayed, 'O Lord, open his eyes and let him see!' The Lord opened the young man's eyes, and when he looked up, he saw that the hillside around Elisha was filled with horses and chariots of fire"* (2 Kings 6:16–17).

> **Prayer:** *Lord, open our eyes to see that you are in control, even when we can't see any way forward. Help us to see the world through your eyes so that we won't be afraid and are able to continue doing what you've called us to do in the world. Your victory is assured, and we are so grateful to be able to share in it. Amen.*

Day 101   2 Kings 9–12

April 10

> Key Text: "Jehu did not obey the Law of the Lord, the God of Israel, with all his heart. He refused to turn from the sins that Jeroboam had led Israel to commit." (2 Kings 10:31)

We are moving quickly through the kings of Israel and Judah now, but though the names of the kings change, their sins remain the same: idolatry and all its accompanying evils.

The prophet Elisha is still the spokesman of God to the kings. In chapter 9, he sends a young prophet to anoint Jehu as Israel's next king, replacing Joram, because under Joram's reign the people have continued to worship the idols introduced by Jezebel, Ahab's foreign wife, and Joram's mother. Once introduced, idolatry is hard to dispel.

It turns out that Joram has been wounded in war and King Ahaziah of Judah is with him making a hospital visit. Maybe they are conspiring against the Lord's decision to make Jehu king. Too bad for them, because Jehu is coming to town.

Joram demands to know of Jehu: *"Do you come in peace?"* Jehu responds, speaking for the Lord as well as for himself: *"How can there be peace as long as the idolatry and witchcraft of your mother, Jezebel, are all around us?"* (2 Kings 9:22).

Jehu then launches a coup and Joram, Ahaziah and Jezebel are all killed as judgment for their willful rebellion against God, for misleading the Lord's people, and for once plotting to kill the prophets. The rest of Ahab's household follows in a grisly manner: *"So Ahab was left without a single survivor."*

It was a mixed blessing in those days to be a member of a royal family.

Jehu continues by traveling to Samaria, where he cleverly summons and promptly kills all the prophets of Baal, finally destroying every trace of Baal worship from Israel.

It's hard to read these chapters because ancient war was brutal—*not unlike ISIS today*. Jehu was relentless and merciless in carrying out the Lord's judgment against those who defied God by worshiping the worst of the Canaanite gods, Baal. Baalism was so invasive, so horrible and so violent that only a relentless man of war could defeat it. Sometimes the force of evil can only be stopped by a counterforce. It is hard to stomach, but that is the way of things in a world rebelling against its Creator.

King Jehu was a better-than-average king in that he at least made an effort to destroy the public Baal worship in Israel. But he was not perfect: *"Jehu did not obey the Law of the Lord, the God of Israel, with all his heart. He refused to turn from the sins that Jeroboam had led Israel to commit"* (2 Kings 10:31).

After this, further intrigue and treason follow in the house of the late King Ahaziah, led by his mother. But her maneuvering is countered by the priest Jehoiada. A young boy Joash, who is from Ahaziah's family, but has been hidden and protected for several years, is crowned king. The priest Jehoiada then makes a covenant between the Lord, the king and the people, that they would be the Lord's people: *"And all the people of the land went over to the temple of Baal and tore it down. They demolished the altars and smashed the idols to pieces, and they killed Mattan the priest of Baal in front of the altars"* (2 Kings 11:18).

Joash was seven years old when he became king, and *"all his life he did what was pleasing in the Lord's sight because Jehoiada the priest instructed him."*

Focus: Keeping track of all the kings of Judah and Israel is very confusing. It is helpful to look for summary statements about their rule. In the case of King Jehu, the summary statement is less than stellar: *"Jehu did not obey the Law of the Lord, the God of Israel, with all his heart. He refused to turn from the sins that Jeroboam had led Israel to commit"* (2 Kings 10:31). The key phrase here is *"with all his heart."* Jesus later summarized the Law of Moses by two great commandments, which begin with: *"Love the Lord your God with all your heart."* When our heart is not totally into loving God (and loving our neighbor), we will find ourselves vulnerable to influence from the pressure of the world without, and the pull of our sinful nature within.

Prayer: Lord, it is unsettling to behold how relentless evil can be, and how difficult it is to destroy—like chemotherapy and radiation treatment against cancer. Even when the evil is destroyed, there is always collateral damage and continuing effects. Victory can be bittersweet. How we long for the day when there will be no more war. Amen.

Day 102   2 Kings 13–17

April 11

> Key Text: But the Israelites would not listen. They were as stubborn as their ancestors who had refused to believe in the Lord their God. ... They worshiped worthless idols, so they became worthless themselves. (2 Kings 17:14–15)

In these chapters we continue the overview of the kings of the divided kingdom of Israel and Judah. Most incorporate pagan worship into the national life of the people, perpetuating the syncretism which violates their Covenant with God. Think of it as serial, spiritual unfaithfulness to God.

Some kings—usually of Judah—were generally pleasing in the Lord's sight personally, but as a rule, they did not root out the well-entrenched practice of worshiping at pagan shrines. Not surprisingly, spiritual alienation begets family alienation, and the tribes of the formerly united nation fight each other.

The fighting between Israel and Judah continues to weaken both kingdoms. Smelling weakness, the pagan king, Tiglath-pileser of Assyria, begins invading Israel. The Israeli king, Menahem, pays the Assyrians to back off, but the Assyrians already have their foot in the door.

Later, King Ahaz of Judah ups the ante by proposing an alliance with Tiglath-pileser so that he will rescue Judah from the much larger army of Israel. But the price of the alliance is to allow Assyrian pagan worship in the Lord's Temple.

Initially, Ahaz gets what he wants: The Assyrian noose tightens around Israel's neck. The Assyrian king, Shalmaneser, attacks Israel and forces her to pay heavy tribute. In time, Hoshea, king of Israel, gets tired of this extortion and stops paying. He tries to shake loose from Assyria by forming an alliance with King So of Egypt.

But Assyria hears about this treachery. King Hoshea is put in prison, while Shalmaneser invades the entire land and besieges the capital city of Samaria: *"Finally, in the ninth year of King Hoshea's reign, Samaria fell, and the people of Israel were exiled to Assyria"* (2 Kings 17:5–6).

It's all downhill from here. The final and most severe judgment of God is coming upon his people, starting with the northern kingdom of Israel. The king of Assyria invades the entire land, and for three years lays siege to the city of Samaria. Finally, Samaria falls and the people of Israel are exiled to Assyria.

Chapter 17 provides a summary and commentary about this development, beginning with an indictment: *"This disaster came upon the people of Israel because they worshiped other gods. They sinned against the Lord their God, who had brought them safely out of Egypt and had rescued them from the power of Pharaoh, the king of Egypt. They had followed the practices of the pagan nations the Lord had driven from the land ahead of them, as well as the practices the kings of Israel had introduced"* (2 Kings 17:7–8).

This indictment continues with the observation that God again and again sent his prophets and seers to warn both Israel and Judah, but the Israelites would not listen. They were as stubborn as their ancestors who had refused to believe in the Lord their God and who worshiped *"worthless idols"* instead.

So now, only the tribe of Judah remains in the land: *"But even the people of Judah refused to obey the commands of the Lord their God, for they followed the evil practices that Israel had introduced through King Jeroboam."*

Meanwhile, Assyria repopulates the city of Samaria with people from Babylon and other pagan cities. The remaining Israelites intermarry with them, giving rise to a new mixed race of people, the Samaritans.

When we come to the New Testament, we find that the Samaritans are hated as racial and religious outsiders. This adds some controversy to Jesus' interaction with them, as with the woman at the well in John 4, and as reflected in his parable of the Good Samaritan in Luke 10:27–37.

Focus: The conquering and exile of the people of Israel is a heartbreaking and tragic development in the story of God's people. God had warned them repeatedly that this would happen if they abandoned him and pursued the paganism of their neighbors. By withholding his divine protection, God allows the people to be exposed to the political and military drama of the nations surrounding them. They experience the consequences of their stubborn refusal to trust the Lord their God, and of rejecting his Covenant and commandments. *"They even sacrificed their own sons and daughters in the fire"* (2 Kings 17:17).

Ultimately, as C.S. Lewis so memorably explained, God's judgment is to give those who refuse to love and obey him, what they have wanted all along—to be as far away from him as they can be. But, amazingly, God always stands ready to receive repentant prodigal sons and daughters who return to him.

Prayer: *Lord, with this deeply discouraging litany of failure by your people in the Promised Land, we are amazed that you don't walk away from your Covenant with them. Even when you bring judgment upon them, you do not forsake them. Ironically, their failure serves to reveal your faithfulness. It encourages us to know that you are just as patient and forgiving of us. Amen.*

April 12

> Key Text: Then Isaiah said to Hezekiah, "Listen to this message from the Lord: The time is coming when everything in your palace—all the treasurers stored up by your ancestors until now—will be carried off to Babylon." (2 Kings 20:16–17)

The southern kingdom of Judah now stands alone in the land the Lord had given Israel. The northern kingdom has been conquered and its people exiled by the brutal Assyrians. What will Judah do?

Though Judah has had marginally better kings, those kings have not been willing or able to totally eliminate the syncretistic practices of the people, even if they themselves have been faithful to worship Yahweh alone. The pagan shrines and Asherah poles remain.

But then Hezekiah becomes king: *"He did what was pleasing in the Lord's sight, just as his ancestor David had done. He removed the pagan shrines, smashed the sacred pillars, and cut down the Asherah poles. ... Hezekiah trusted in the Lord, the God of Israel. There was no one like him among all the kings of Judah, either before or after his time"* (2 Kings 18:3–5).

Hezekiah is no doubt sobered by the fate of the northern kingdom. But he genuinely fears God, and this gives him the courage he needs to provide strong leadership: *"...he carefully obeyed all the commands the Lord had given Moses. So the Lord was with him, and Hezekiah was successful in everything he did."*

Notably, Hezekiah revolts against the king of Assyria and refuses to pay tribute anymore. But in the fourteenth year of Hezekiah's reign, King Sennacherib of Assyria comes knocking. In chapters 18 and 19, Sennacherib's chief of staff taunts Hezekiah: *"What god of any nation has ever been able to save its people from my power? So what makes you think that the Lord can rescue Jerusalem from me?"*

Hezekiah knows he cannot stand against the mighty Assyrian army, so he consults the prophet Isaiah, who replies that Hezekiah should not be disturbed by this blasphemous speech. The Lord says through Isaiah, *"Listen! I myself will move against him."*

So Hezekiah prays that God will indeed help him against the threats of Sennacherib. He knows that the Assyrians have destroyed many nations and burned their gods in a large bonfire. But Hezekiah also knows that, in fact, the gods of the surrounding nations are not gods at all—only idols of wood and stone shaped by human hands. So he asks the Lord God to rescue Judah from the Assyrians' power: *"...then all the kingdoms of the earth will know that you alone, O Lord, are God"* (2 Kings 19:19).

Isaiah encourages Hezekiah by telling him that God has heard his prayer and will stop Assyria. Sure enough, the angel of the Lord strikes the Assyrian camp and its army is killed. Sennacherib returns home in defeat and shame. His sons kill him and God's prophecy through Isaiah is fulfilled.

Later, Hezekiah becomes deathly ill, so Isaiah goes to visit him. Isaiah tells him that God has heard his prayer for healing, and he will live 15 more years. But this proves to be a mixed blessing.

Hezekiah is visited by an envoy from Babylon bringing gifts and supposedly inquiring about his health. Hezekiah naively shows them everything in his kingdom, including the royal treasuries. So the Lord sends the prophet Isaiah to warn him about Babylon: *"The time is coming when everything in your palace—all the treasures stored up by your ancestors until now—will be carried off to Babylon. Nothing will be left, says the Lord"* (2 Kings 20:17).

Hezekiah dies and his son Manasseh becomes the next king. Unfortunately, he is not like his father: *"He did what was evil in the Lord's sight,"* returning the nation to paganism and social injustice. Despite Hezekiah's reforms, the future for Judah will be the same as for Israel—defeat and exile.

Focus: Outstanding leaders, like Hezekiah, lift our spirits from the cynicism and hopelessness that permeates life on earth. We know human nature well. We know *ourselves* well. We barely trust our leaders and institutions. But men and women like Hezekiah remind us that godly leaders, who desire above all to honor God, can make a great difference in history. God is always standing by, looking for such people who are willing to trust him, obey him and do great things for his glory. Each of us might ask: *Am I such a person?*

Prayer: Lord, thank you for Hezekiah's example of obedience and courage in a chaotic time with pressure all around to compromise with paganism. But we also see the need to disciple the next generation. Please raise up godly leaders in our own time. Amen.

April 13

> Key Text: Never before had there been a king like Josiah, who turned to the Lord with all his heart and soul and strength, obeying all the laws of Moses. And there has never been a king like him since. (2 Kings 23:25)

Josiah becomes king of Judah when he is only eight years old. Unlike the two kings before him, Josiah *"did what was pleasing in the Lord's sight and followed the example of his ancestor David."* In the eighteenth year of his reign, he orders the repair and restoration of the Temple. While searching the archives of the Temple, Hilkiah the high priest makes a stunning discovery. He finds the long-lost (and mostly forgotten) Book of the Law.

Note that before printing presses, all documents were laboriously hand-copied, making them rare. And, of course, few could read. To find the lost Book of the Law and rediscover the Covenant which established Israel as a nation is electrifying.

It is brought to Josiah and read to him. The king is overwhelmed with sadness, for he realizes that the Israelites have not kept the Covenant and are now experiencing God's judgment as a result. With alarm, he hears what God says he will do to Judah as a result of the people's continued idolatry. After verifying this with the prophetess Huldah, he is convinced that God will indeed bring judgment upon Judah as he did with Israel.

God, however, has seen Josiah's genuine grief and sorrow over the sins of the people, and he declares that he will not bring about his judgment during Josiah's reign.

So Josiah calls together all the prophets, priests and elders—and the people from the least to the greatest—and reads aloud the entire Book of the Law. He then renews the Covenant with God. Having done this, he orders Hilkiah the high priest and others to clean house in the Temple, destroying all the articles that were used to worship Baal and the other false gods. Then he does away with the idolatrous priests who led the people in pagan sacrifices, and tears down the living quarters of the male and female shrine prostitutes.

From there, he goes to the other towns and destroys the pagan shrines, buildings and altars that have accumulated through successive kings, including the horrible altar of Topheth in the Valley of Ben-Hinnon, where the people have killed their sons and daughters as sacrifices to Molech.

But this time of national repentance and renewal was to be the last. After Josiah dies in battle against Pharaoh Neco, the Babylonians begin to attack and finally lay siege to Jerusalem. They totally destroy the Temple and other buildings of the city, and steal all the wealth of the Israelites that remained. Most of the people are exiled to Babylon, and the rest flee to Egypt to escape the fury of King Nebuchadnezzar.

So ends the tragic story of Israel as a nation. She has been called to know the One God, who is their Creator and Redeemer, to worship and serve him in the land he has given, and to bear witness to the surrounding nations of the salvation that he is bringing to the world. Now it seems that all is lost. However, despite the people's persistent hardheartedness and unfaithfulness, God has not forgotten his promise to bless the world through Israel.

He will continue to speak to his exiled people in Assyria and Babylon, through the prophets whose writings we will come to in time. But first, in 1 and 2 Chronicles, we will take a second look at what has happened to Israel through the perspective of (probably) Ezra the priest. His perspective will help us see how God is at work even in the utter failure of his people to keep his Covenant.

Focus: The story of Israel, which we have followed since Genesis chapter 12, leaves us both amazed and frustrated—frustrated by the continuing return to idolatry, yet amazed at the gracious, longsuffering God who will not let his people go, no matter how sinful they are. He is determined to make things right in the world, no matter what it takes, because his greatest pleasure—indeed the very reason he created the heavens and earth—is to share his life with us. So while it now seems that God's Promise to Israel has been forfeited, we shall see that this is not the end of the story.

Prayer: Lord, the story of your people is the story of all of us. We are like Israel when we are distracted by the world and when we seek to remake you into a god who lets us remain in control and do whatever we want. Help us to see how doing whatever we want would be the worst thing that could ever happen to us. Teach us to trust you. Amen.

April 14

We have come a long way since God's Promise to Abraham to make his descendants into a great nation in their own land, and to eventually become a blessing to all nations. Along the way, we have gotten clues about God's plan, but also a boatload of puzzling contradictions. What have we learned about God and his plan for us so far?

First, we have learned how deeply God wants to be in relationship with us. This flows from his nature as a triune God whose very life consists of loving relationships within himself—Father, Son and Holy Spirit. To make a free and loving relationship with him possible, he gives us the unbelievable gift of his image and likeness, and later commits himself to us by means of a Covenant. Even when we sin against him by replacing him with idols of our own making, he does not abandon us, but fiercely pursues us with the loving purpose of reconciling us to himself through Christ.

We also learn that God takes his time and works out his plan of redemption through the messiness of human free will and the vagaries of human history. He speaks to ancient Near Eastern people as people of their time, and not as if they are moderns. He accommodates himself to the limits of their understanding, language and worldview. He is patient and forgiving of their many human weaknesses.

But he is also a jealous lover. He demands their loyalty and responds angrily when spurned. At the same time, he protects them against those individuals and influences that threaten them. When he goes to war like a mother bear against her children's enemies, he does so with righteousness and justice. He is not afraid to stop evil by force, nor is he reluctant to punish his children when they rebel.

He is the giver of all life; therefore, he is also the judge and has every right to take life. Our problem with this is the problem of every human, since Adam and Eve, who decides that they can do a better job of being god and deciding right and wrong for themselves. They, like us, don't so much hate the idea that God exists, but the idea that God is in control and can tell us what to do.

If you think that sounds like adolescent rebellion, congratulations, you win the Forbidden Fruit basket!

This is not to say that the story of Israel is uncomplicated and morally clear. It is not. We need to remember that these people knew far less about God, let alone Jesus, than we do. What they did know, they tended to view through the lens of their time and culture. And the Bible doesn't cover up or excuse bad behavior among the people of God.

But God knows who we are, who he is, and where he is taking human history.

Even though it seems, right now, that God's plan to redeem the world has been completely thwarted by Israel's failure, God knows where the story is going. In fact, he has known from the very beginning that mortal beings with free will could only be made right by his own efforts through Christ. As the apostle Paul put it: *"Even before he made the world, God loved us and chose us in Christ to be holy and without fault in his eyes. God decided in advance to adopt us into his own family by bringing us to himself through Jesus Christ. This is what he wanted to do, and it gave him great pleasure"* (Ephesians 1:4–5).

So, as disheartened as Israel feels at this part of the story, there is "the rest of the story" to come!

Before we get there, the Old Testament will take us through a priestly perspective and review of what has happened thus far (1 and 2 Chronicles); give us a ray of hope (Ezra and Nehemiah); tell us a wonderful story about a faithful Israelite in exile (Esther); wrestle with the universal problem of unjust suffering (Job); introduce us to Israel's worship (Psalms) and its wisdom (Proverbs); show how Solomon's extravagant success reveals that nothing can satisfy our souls except God himself (Ecclesiastes); and finally, show us how earnestly the prophets spoke to the kings of Israel on God's behalf, offering some of the most theologically profound and rhetorically beautiful expositions to be found in the Bible, of God's ways and his amazing plan for the future.

Then we get to Jesus!

Prayer: Lord, we confess that your ways are not our ways, and your thoughts are not our thoughts. Forgive us for dismissing you so easily through our limited reasoning, as if we knew what we were talking about! Instead, give us humility and faith and hope to follow you. Amen.

April 15

> **Key Text:** The people of Judah were exiled to Babylon because they were unfaithful to the Lord. The first of the exiles to return to their property in their former towns were priests, Levites, Temple servants, and other Israelites. (1 Chronicles 9:1–2)

1 and 2 Chronicles give us a different perspective on the story of Israel so far. They are written by an exiled priest, possibly Ezra, who will be one of the first to return to the land after seventy years of exile. "Ezra" recollects and reflects theologically on the events of Israel's monarchy, seeking to identify God's sovereign hand at work in it all.

1 Chronicles is mostly about King David, Israel's greatest king. You'll remember that despite his great heroics, like slaying the giant Goliath, David committed the sins of adultery and murder. He was far from a perfect man. Yet, David loved the Lord and showed sincere sorrow for his sins. In addition, he did not lead Israel into idolatry like so many other kings of Israel. God showed him grace and honored him by choosing David's family line (the tribe of Judah) to be the family line of the Messiah, Jesus.

Chapters 1 through 9 is a genealogy on steroids! It serves as an introduction, showing that the story of King David does not stand alone; it is rooted in the whole story of the Bible, beginning in Genesis. The genealogy (yes, it's boring) begins with Adam and moves forward to the story of Noah and the flood judgment that was the result of universal human sin. From there we come to the people at the forefront of God's promise of redemption—Abraham, Isaac and Jacob. Jacob's twelve sons eventually become the tribes that make up the nation and kingdom of Israel.

Genealogies for the twelve tribes are then presented, beginning—not surprisingly—with Judah, King David's tribe. Next, the genealogy for the priestly tribe of Levi is featured, followed by the others.

In chapter 9, the writer takes us to the exile, focusing on the kingdom of Judah, and then to the time when some of the exiles are permitted to go back to their homes in Jerusalem, and to the little that remained of the destroyed Temple: *"The first of the exiles to return to their property in their former towns were priests, Levites, Temple servants and other Israel-*

ites" (1 Chronicles 9:2).

It is from their perspective that the story of King David, and what follows, is to be told.

Yes, it is boring reading, so what's the point? We've seen that God's desire to have a relationship with human beings is the heart of the Bible's story. God persistently pursues this despite our continued rebellion and idolatry. Even when we run from God, seeking other gods of our own making, he runs after us. His gracious plan to make things right, no matter how long it takes, involves his promises to individuals like Abraham, Isaac, Jacob, Moses and David, who will become his agents of redemption.

By keeping track of all these people, we are reminded of how faithful God has been to keep his promises, even when we couldn't have cared less. How amazing that God will not let us go!

Focus: Each one of us belongs to a particular story that began long ago and was influenced by all of the decisions, good and bad, made by family members before us. Knowing that story—our genealogy—gives us perspective, and some clues, about how to understand our own lives presently.

The Bible explains, however, that our individual stories are connected to a much bigger story, the story of the whole human race. In a sense, Adam and Eve are the parents of us all. Their primeval choices radically impacted the history of the whole human race, in a bad way. But in time, another member of the human race, the incarnate Son of God, made choices that brought forgiveness, reconciliation and the promise of a new future.

Each of us should look to this larger genealogy to grasp something of the amazing story we are all a part of. God has been working in the world, over the generations, to take us to that glorious future he has in mind.

Prayer: Lord, there are so many facets to the events of our lives, and many possible interpretations. But though we don't always understand what is going on because we can't see the big picture of your plan, we are grateful that you faithfully keep after us, offering your presence, granting us blessings, and taking us to a glorious future with you in the New Creation. Amen!

April 16

> **Key Text:** Let the whole earth sing to the Lord! Each day
> proclaim the good news that he saves. Publish his glorious deeds
> among the nations. Tell everyone about the amazing things he
> does. Great is the Lord! He is most worthy of praise!
> (1 Chronicles 16:23–25)

The priestly writer "Ezra," who chronicles the reign of David, now turns from genealogy to the matter of how David became king. This review, however, brings a different perspective with different emphases. It is told by the priests, so let's call it the "View from the Temple."

Chapter 10 recounts the death of Saul and three of his sons at the hands of the Philistines. The Israelite army is in disarray, so the people abandon their towns while the Philistines move in and occupy them: *"So Saul died because he was unfaithful to the Lord. He failed to obey the Lord's command, and he even consulted a medium instead of asking the Lord for guidance"* (1 Chronicles 10:13–14).

David is recognized as the true hero behind Saul and is crowned king. He immediately goes to war against the Philistines who have reoccupied the Israelite cities. Notably, he conquers Jerusalem and makes his home and headquarters there. From that point on, Jerusalem is called the *"City of David."* While there, *"David became more and more powerful, because the Lord of Heaven's Armies was with him."*

Some tales are told about David's mightiest warriors, and they are introduced by name. The best of the best are honored with a story of their bravery and exploits. Soon, other warriors join David. According to 1 Chronicles 12:2, they were expert archers and ambidextrous slingshot slingers! Others were said to be *"as fierce as lions and as swift as deer on the mountains."* And lest we still are not impressed, *"the weakest among them could take on a hundred regular troops, and the strongest could take on a thousand!"*

Boasting is apparently allowed!

As word gets out to all the cities that David had been loyal to Saul, one by one Saul's warriors join with David for the *"single purpose of making David king over all Israel."* The nation slowly comes together around their new king, and people begin gathering to feast and celebrate: *"There was great joy throughout the land of Israel"* (1 Chronicles 12:40).

So all begins well. David summons his leaders to suggest that the Ark of the Covenant be brought to Jerusalem. Everyone agrees. A new transport cart is built and two priests, Uzzah and Ahio, accompany it on its journey, along with a festive group celebrating the event. But then something happens and the Ark is violated inadvertently by Uzzah, who is struck dead.

Not surprisingly, David is angry and confused by this. Why did God do this? Wasn't David trying to do something good? It appears that David tried to do the right thing, but in a way forbidden by the Law of Moses. His carelessness had unintended consequences.

Nevertheless, God blesses David's reign, and he begins to feel more confident. He builds himself a kingly palace with additional buildings, and he marries additional wives, probably to form political alliances just like other kings did. Not a good thing, as we have seen, but from the priestly perspective, God gives David a pass on this. Without exception, all of the people God calls to serve him are flawed, inconsistent and needing grace. Thankfully, God is full of grace.

"So David's fame spread everywhere, and the Lord caused all the nations to fear David" (1 Chronicles 14:17).

A second attempt to bring the Ark of the Covenant to Jerusalem is made after David consults the Law of Moses and discovers that only Levites are permitted to transport it. (So of course this Chronicle written from a Levite perspective would point this out!)

This time they do it properly and God blesses the people. David writes a psalm of praise to give to the musician Asaph and the Levite choir. It is a psalm celebrating the story of God with Israel, and a call to remember the Covenant that God made with Abraham, Isaac and Jacob. It points forward to the day when God's promise to bless the nations is fulfilled: *"Let the whole earth sing to the Lord! Each day proclaim the good news that he saves. Publish his glorious deeds among the nations. Tell everyone about the amazing things he does. Great is the Lord! He is most worthy of praise!"* (1 Chronicles 16:23–25).

Focus: God knows our hearts. He also knows that we are weak. When he sees men and women who, like King David, truly love God and repent of their sins, he is more than generous with his forgiveness. Therefore, we must humbly accept that the enemies of our faith will always be able to point to inconsistencies and hypocrisy among the people of God. But in a way, that is the whole point of our faith. God loves us and extends amazing grace our way, even when we totally don't deserve it!

Prayer: Lord, we identify with King David's good intentions but wrong actions, which bring about bad results. We are grateful, however, that with you, there are not only consequences but grace and mercy. Like David wrote, may the whole earth sing to the Lord with the Good News that he saves! Amen.

Day 108   1 Chronicles 17–21

April 17

> Key Text: Then King David went in and sat before the Lord and prayed, "Who am I, O Lord God, and what is my family, that you have brought me this far? And now, O God, in addition to everything else, you speak of giving your servant a lasting dynasty! You speak as though I were someone very great, O Lord God! ... May the house of your servant David continue before you forever." (1 Chronicles 17:16–17,24)

The chronicler continues his focus on David by recalling his earnest desire to build a temple for the Lord. The prophet Nathan agrees with David, but then God speaks to Nathan, telling him to say to David, *"You are not the one to build a house for me to live in"* (1 Chronicles 17:4).

God wants David to know that he doesn't require a temple to be built in order for him to dwell with his people. On the contrary, God is going to build something for David—a dynasty of kings on a throne that will be secure forever.

What could this mean? The chronicler clearly sees that God's promise to David is key to Israel's future. But how? We don't find out until centuries later when the angel Gabriel visits a virgin named Mary: *"You will conceive and give birth to a son, and you will name him Jesus. He will be very great and will be called the Son of the Most High. The Lord God will give him the throne of his ancestor David. And he will reign over Israel forever; his Kingdom will never end!"* (Luke 1:31–33).

So, having established the importance of David's reign in Judah in connection with God's future reign over the whole earth, the chronicler turns to recounting David's actions and exploits in chapters 18 through 20. With God's blessing and power, David defeats many of Israel's enemies and dedicates all the spoils of war to the Lord. He *"reigned over all*

209

Israel and did what was just and right for his people."

However—there's always a "however," isn't there? Chapter 21 begins, *"Satan rose up against Israel and caused David to take a census of the people of Israel."* Taking a census was always a precursor to gathering an army. The "Satan" (meaning Tempter) apparently tempts David to have a backup plan in case God can't protect Judah. It is a test of faith, which David fails.

God becomes angry at David for becoming enamored with Israelite firepower, instead of depending on his protection. After all, it has always been God's blessing and power that gave Israel victory.

If you let power and success go to your head, it can become your undoing.

Because of David's action, God judges the nation by sending a plague. Although 1 and 2 Chronicles tend to idealize David, the writer must admit that David is not without sin. But at least David has the good sense to cry out to God and take responsibility for what is happening to the suffering people: *"And David said to God, 'I am the one who called for the census! I am the one who has sinned and done wrong! But these people are as innocent as sheep—what have they done? O Lord my God, let your anger fall against me and my family, but do not destroy your people'"* (1 Chronicles 21:17).

You've got to like a stand-up king. God did.

Focus: You usually don't find the words *power* and *humility* in the same biography. Those who aspire to power normally must scratch and claw their way to the top, besting their enemies, believing in their own goodness and in the rightness of their cause. To admit failure is to appear weak. Note how national leaders panic and mumble when asked to name a personal weakness or a failure. David's heartfelt sorrow and humble repentance, therefore, are a breath of fresh air. These are qualities to look for in our would-be leaders.

Prayer: *Lord, thank you for the humility that we see in your servant David. We identify with his weaknesses, but his humility challenges us to be men and women of integrity before you and one another. Your love and mercy enable us to be honest before you about our sin. Remove the residue of defensiveness and pride that keeps us from you and hinders our ability to serve others. Amen.*

April 18

> Key Text: "Now, my son, may the Lord be with you and give
> you success as you follow his directions in building the Temple
> of the Lord your God. And may the Lord give you wisdom and
> understanding, that you may obey the Law of the Lord your God
> as you rule over Israel. For you will be successful if you carefully
> obey the decrees and regulations that the Lord gave to Israel
> through Moses. Be strong and courageous; do not be afraid or
> lose heart!" (1 Chronicles 22:11–13)

God has decided that Solomon (a man of peace) and not David (a man of war) will be the one to build a temple in Jerusalem. Humbly accepting the Lord's decision, David begins to gather and warehouse materials before his death: *"My son Solomon is still young and inexperienced. And since the Temple to be built for the Lord must be a magnificent structure, famous and glorious throughout the world, I will begin making preparations for it now."*

In time, David meets with Solomon and formally instructs him to build a temple for the Lord. He blesses him and asks that God would give Solomon wisdom and understanding. Importantly, he also prays that his son will obey the Law of the Lord. Finally, he challenges Solomon: *"Be strong and courageous; do not be afraid or lose heart."*

David summons the leaders of Israel and directs them to assist Solomon in the project, but above all to *"seek the Lord your God with all your heart and soul. Build the sanctuary of the Lord God so that you can bring the Ark of the Lord's Covenant and the holy vessels of God into the Temple built to honor the Lord's name"* (1 Chronicles 22:17–19).

For David, the building of the Temple points to the greater reality that God wants a relationship with his people, and that they should seek him with all their hearts. They should not take this for granted after the Temple is built and becomes familiar. Our relationship with God can easily regress to ritualism and tradition only.

Now since 1 Chronicles is told from a priestly perspective, we find that special attention is given, in chapter 23, to the role of the priestly tribe of the Levites in supervising the work of the Temple. With a permanent Temple in Jerusalem, the need for the Levites to supervise the portable

Tabernacle will be gone. At that time, they will assist the priests, as well as carry out various other Temple duties.

Everyone else's role with regard to the Temple will be adjusted as well. In chapter 24, the priests, who are descendants of Aaron, are assigned their roles and responsibilities. In chapter 25, the musicians who play instruments and make music before the Lord in the Temple are appointed to terms of service. In chapter 26, the gatekeepers are assigned guard duty, and in chapter 27, the Israelite generals, captains and their officers are assigned duty times throughout the year.

I suppose that David could have gotten angry with God for being passed over to build the Temple. But David knows that God has reasons for what he permits and forbids. When it's clear that Solomon will build the Temple, David does everything he can to lay the groundwork for his son to be successful in this great project so dear to David's heart.

Recognizing that Solomon is young, David gathers the vast amount of materials needed to finalize the project, and then prepares the people for their various roles in Temple ministry. It is a good example of a leader finishing well, because passing the mantle of leadership to the next generation is one of the most important tasks of a leader. It also illustrates that David's greatest concern is for God's glory, and not his own.

Focus: One of the life lessons that only comes with time is the recognition that things never quite turn out as we imagined. Dreams are crushed, visions go unfulfilled, and tragedies occur. Even when our plans succeed, they succeed differently than what we planned.

Who of us has lived the life we imagined when we were young? Some of us are wonderfully surprised with our lives, others disappointed. But in the end, like King David, we must accept that God knows what he is doing and has our best interests in mind. Most importantly, we must remember that our mortal life is only the prelude to eternal life. One day we will understand what God has been up to in our lives all along, and we will be overwhelmed with gratitude for his wisdom and grace.

Prayer: *Lord, it is hard to cheer for someone else while they do what we wanted to do. It is also hard to turn over power to others, especially to the next generation, because we fear that they will not be up to the task. Help us to trust you in these things, because you are a God who calls, gifts and blesses each generation to do* *what you've called them to do. May we all know our own time and accept our place in it. Amen.*

Day 110   1 Chronicles 28–29

April 19

> Key Text: "And Solomon, my son, learn to know the God of your ancestors intimately. Worship and serve him with your whole heart and a willing mind. For the Lord sees every heart and knows every plan and thought. If you seek him, you will find him. But if you forsake him, he will reject you forever. So take this seriously. The Lord has chosen you to build a Temple as his sanctuary. Be strong, and do the work." (1 Chronicles 28:9–10)

The final chapters of 1 Chronicles are a wonderful testimony to King David's faith, humility and spiritual insight. As the end of his life draws near, he summons the leaders of Israel in order to share his heart and give them final instructions.

David tells them of his desire to build a temple to the Lord, but that God had said no because he had been a warrior and shed much blood. Instead, his son Solomon will build the Temple.

Nevertheless, God has honored David. He testifies: *"Yet the Lord, the God of Israel, has chosen me from among all my father's family to be king over Israel forever"* (1 Chronicles 28:4).

He then challenges Israel's leaders, and his son Solomon, to learn to know God intimately, worshiping and serving him with their whole heart and a willing mind. He tells them that the Lord sees every heart and knows every plan and thought, so if they seek him, they will find him—because he wants to be found.

After giving Solomon the Temple plans and furnishings, as well as the instructions concerning the work of the various divisions of priests and Levites in the Temple, David urges him: *"Be strong and courageous, and do the work. Don't be afraid or discouraged, for the Lord God, my God, is with you. He will not fail you or forsake you. He will see to it that all the work related to the Temple of the Lord is finished correctly"* (1 Chronicles 28:20).

In chapter 29, David explains how he has prepared for the construction of the Temple by gathering together all the needed materials and supplies. In addition, David gives generously from his own private wealth, setting the example of generosity as king. Having done so, he challenges the leaders to give generously also, which they do. *"The people rejoiced over the offerings, for they had given freely and wholeheartedly to the Lord, and King David was filled with joy"* (1 Chronicles 29:9).

The outpouring of generosity moves David to praise God in the presence of the whole assembly of leaders: *"O Lord, the God of our ancestor Israel, may you be praised forever and ever! Yours, O Lord, is the greatness, the power, the glory, the victory, and the majesty. Everything in the heavens and on earth is yours, O Lord, and this is your kingdom. We adore you as the one who is over all things."*

In his prayer, David also recognizes that by building the Temple, the people aren't giving something to God that he doesn't already own. All the wealth and materials, and even the desire to build, come from him in the first place. They are only giving back what he has already given them!

After the prayer, the people continue in worship and celebration. They crown Solomon as their new king, anointing him as their leader and Zadok as the priest.

Finally, David dies *"at a ripe old age, having enjoyed long life, wealth, and honor."*

More than any of Israel's leaders, except perhaps Abraham and Moses, David understood and experienced intimacy with God. His insights into the greatness, power, goodness and faithfulness of God to his people were expressed in his prayers and in the psalms he wrote, leaving us a legacy of spiritual direction and encouragement.

Perhaps most important of all, David demonstrated humility. He was well aware of his sinfulness and was willing to own up to it before God and the people. In his weakness, he was one of the people; in his transparency and faith, he was a leader.

Focus: David's prayer, in response to the generosity of the people, is remarkable for its beauty of expression as well as its theological weight. He declares that the one true God is alone worthy of praise forever, which is the chief purpose of human existence. And how could we *not* praise him, for he has no rival. There is no greatness, power, glory, victory or majesty in the created realm that even remotely compares to his. This understanding of God is what gave David his humility, faith and obedience.

Day 111   2 Chronicles 1–5

April 20

> Key Text: God said to Solomon, "Because your greatest desire is to help your people, and you did not ask for wealth, riches, fame, or even the death of your enemies or a long life, but rather you asked for wisdom and knowledge to properly govern my people—I will certainly give you the wisdom and knowledge you requested. But I will also give you wealth, riches, and fame such as no other king has had before you or will ever have in the future!" (2 Chronicles 1:11–12)

Solomon's early years as king are very promising. He humbly asks God for the wisdom to lead the nation properly. God is pleased with Solomon's desire to help his people instead of serving himself. So he grants Solomon the wisdom and knowledge he requests, but also gives him wealth, riches and fame such as no other king has had before him.

Prompted by God, Solomon begins construction of the Temple, and also a royal palace, with the best materials and the most skilled craftsmen and artisans. Chapters 2 through 4 give a detailed overview of the design, materials and furnishings.

Even as the great project moves forward, there is a sense in which its magnificent materials, dimensions and design are, nevertheless, inadequate to express the glory of God. Solomon exclaims: *"This must be a magnificent Temple because our God is greater than all other gods. But who can really build him a worthy home? Not even the highest heavens can contain him! So who am I to consider building a Temple for him, except as a place to burn sacrifices to him?"* (2 Chronicles 2:5–6).

When the Temple is completed, Solomon brings all the wealth that his father David had dedicated to the Lord, and puts it in the Temple treasuries. Then the spiritual high point of the whole project arrives—the Levites and priests carry the Ark into the inner sanctuary of the Temple, the Most Holy Place. The Ark contains the tablets of the Law and a reminder of the unshakable Covenant of love and faithfulness which God had initiated with his people, Israel.

The Levites now play instruments and sing to the Lord their God: *"He is good! His faithful love endures forever."*

The song is an invitation for God to remember his Covenant Promise and live among his people by occupying the Temple: *"At that moment a thick cloud filled the Temple of the Lord. The priests could not continue their service because of the cloud, for the glorious presence of the Lord filled the Temple of God"* (2 Chronicles 5:13–14).

The building of Solomon's Temple illustrates the importance of art and music in God's world. It is significant that God wants to dwell in a Temple that is built to exact specifications from quality materials and with beautiful craftsmanship. And he wants music! Levites and priests are assigned as instrumentalists and singers, placing music at the heart of worship *(2 Chronicles 5:12–13)*.

From this we learn that beauty, as well as goodness and truth, are expressions of God's own nature, and therefore of our nature as well. God wants us to fill the earth with it. So let us follow our God-given impulse to create, express, build, decorate, and perform to his glory!

Focus: We are accustomed to hearing that *"pure and genuine religion in the sight of God the Father means caring for orphans and widows in their distress and refusing to let the world corrupt you"* (James 1:27). This is certainly true, but while pure and genuine religion is not less than this, there is also more to it. In the New Creation, especially, where sin and death no longer spoil human existence, the impulse to create beauty will be unleashed. Imagine the architectural wonders, the heavenly music and all the various forms of art which will blossom in the eternity to come—all to the glory of God. It will never end!

But the creating of beauty for the glory of God begins right now, in this present sinful age. For beauty, like goodness and truth, reveals the presence of God.

Prayer: *Lord, we are amazed at the beauty of all things you have made, and which you have put the desire in our own hearts to make. May we use those gifts to glorify you and enjoy your presence in our lives. Amen.*

Day 112   Reflection

April 21

Since one of the key themes of 1 and 2 Chronicles is the building of the Temple by King Solomon, as envisioned by his father King David, it will be helpful to consider what the Temple reveals about God.

The Old Testament hints at, and the New Testament more fully reveals, that the Lord God is One God, existing eternally as three persons: Father, Son and Holy Spirit—a Trinity. As such, God is not a lonely unit but a unity of fellowship. I cannot overestimate how important this is. From this fundamental reality, an expansive view of life, humanity and the universe is possible. But before pursuing this, let's consider the other options.

If a Creator God doesn't exist, nor any other spiritual entity, whether personal or impersonal (as atheism claims), then either the universe has existed forever (which the "Big Bang" calls into question) or the physical universe—along with human life—generated itself out of nothing. And then, by inconceivably good fortune, through unguided chemical and biological evolution, it developed into the vast, diverse, complex, wondrous universe that we encounter.

This would mean that there is no transcendent meaning to life and no solid foundation for human dignity and worth. Truth, goodness, justice, love and beauty are merely preferences and imagination. Reality exists only as a chemical artifact in our brains, and there is nothing beyond it. To put it cynically: life sucks, and then you die. Get over it.

If we believe that the universe has existed forever, then we could say that the universe is God (as pantheism does). God is everything and everything is God. Everything that exists, therefore, must be good—even evil. This results in moral paralysis and a brutal fatalism. Some who hold to this view believe that the goal of our existence is to lose our sense of personal identity and our individual memories, becoming part of "everything," which is God—or whatever. Like a drop of water in a vast ocean of collective consciousness. But no personal God, and no individual you.

If we allow that there is a "God" of some sort outside of the universe (as deism does) who is essentially a clockmaker who winds up the universe and then disappears, and has no contact with us, then we are in the unhappy position of never being able to know God or understand ourselves. We might guess about God and ourselves, but we can never know. It is forever a mystery. We are orphans abandoned by "God," whoever he or she, or it, is. For all practical purposes, deism is not much different in outcome than atheism or pantheism. In all three, we ultimately lose our "self," whether to nothingness, assimilation or uncertainty.

But the triune God of the Bible is a game changer, and Solomon's Temple gives us a big clue about why. The Temple will be God's dwelling place on earth among his people, because God is a person who loves and communicates and desires to have a relationship with us.

The Israelites understood, of course, that the Temple could not contain God, but his presence was real nevertheless. The Temple was the special place where God came close in order to forgive our sins, hear our prayers, receive our worship and bless us with his grace.

Skipping ahead a bit to Solomon's prayer of dedication for the Temple, we read these wonderful declarations about the God who wants to be in fellowship with us: *"O Lord, God of Israel, there is no God like you in all of heaven and earth. You keep your covenant and show unfailing love to all who walk before you in wholehearted devotion. ...*

"But will God really live on earth among people? Why, even the highest heavens cannot contain you. How much less this Temple I have built! ...

"May you hear the humble and earnest requests from me and your people Israel when we pray toward this place. ... Yes, hear us from heaven where you live, and when you hear, forgive" (2 Chronicles 6:14–21).

The God of the Bible—the God of Abraham, Isaac and Jacob—has bound himself to us through a Covenant of faithfulness. He loves us unconditionally, and his plan of redemption, which will ultimately be fulfilled in Christ, takes us to a future where we humans and all creation will flourish in ways that we cannot imagine now in our brokenness. God will be with us in the fullest possible way, as anticipated by the Temple.

Prayer: God, thank you for not hiding yourself from us, but revealing yourself to be a God of compassion and love, beyond our expectation. There is indeed no God like you in all heaven and earth! Amen!

Day 113   2 Chronicles 6–9

April 22

Key Text: "Then if my people who are called by my name will humble themselves and pray and seek my face and turn from their wicked ways, I will hear from heaven and will forgive their sins and restore their land. My eyes will be open and my ears attentive to every prayer made in this place."
(2 Chronicles 7:14–15)

218

Solomon now leads the entire community of Israel in worship at the Temple he has built to honor the name of the Lord. By means of this beautiful prayer, the people dedicate themselves to order their lives around the presence of God.

The prayer of chapter 6 begins with a confession: *"...there is no God like you in all of heaven and earth. You keep your covenant and show unfailing love to all who walk before you in wholehearted devotion"* (2 Chronicles 6:14).

Solomon marvels that God will limit himself to live on earth among them, but then recognizes that the Temple does not limit God: *"Why, even the highest heavens cannot contain you. How much less this Temple I have built!"* By praying this, he confesses that God is both revealed and hidden to them. He can be known, but not fully known.

Then Solomon asks God to always hear the prayers that he and the people of Israel make, especially prayers for forgiveness.

In response to Solomon's prayer, God's glorious presence fills the Temple and ignites the offerings and sacrifices. The people are filled with awe. They fall face down on the ground and worship the Lord, while the Levites sing, *"his faithful love endures forever!"*

The people celebrate for seven more days and go back home joyful and glad because the Lord had been so good to David, to Solomon and to his people Israel.

The Lord appears to Solomon later and reaffirms his Covenant Promise to hear the people's prayers for forgiveness: *"Then if my people who are called by my name will humble themselves and pray and seek my face and turn from their wicked ways, I will hear from heaven and will forgive their sins and restore their land. My eyes will be open and my ears attentive to every prayer made in this place"* (2 Chronicles 7:14–16).

At the same time, God warns Solomon that he will not bless him or the people if they serve and worship other gods. If they do, he will uproot the people from the land he has given them and reject the Temple.

It is important to distinguish two issues regarding Israel's relationship with God. First, they are made right with God only by grace through faith. He has chosen Israel and given them his presence because it pleased him do so, not because the people are righteous or deserving.

However, as God's chosen people, they will prosper or stumble in life based upon their obedience to the Covenant—especially the First and

Second Commandments against worshiping other gods and using idols in worship.

For the first part of Solomon's reign, he keeps the Covenant and commandments, and his kingdom flourishes. Other nations marvel at Solomon's wisdom, wealth, buildings and administration. In chapter 9, the queen of Sheba visits and exclaims that everything she had heard about Solomon was true, and even far beyond what she was told.

Interestingly, the book of 2 Chronicles is kinder to Solomon than the book of 1 Kings. The writer of 1 Kings feels free to lay out all the tragic details of Solomon's life. In 1 Kings, chapter 11, Solomon is said to have been influenced by the many foreign women of his harem to worship other gods, unlike David his father. So the Lord tells Solomon that he will take the kingdom away from him and give it, not to a son, but to one of his servants. However, out of respect for King David's legacy, he will not do this until Solomon dies.

We hear none of this in 2 Chronicles, where Solomon dies at the end of chapter 9. And you may have noticed that 1 Chronicles does not mention David's sin with Bathsheba either. The priestly chronicler is more interested in the theology of the Temple than reporting on the sins of Israel's leaders.

Perhaps there is a lesson here about being gracious concerning the sins of leaders and staying focused on the greater matters of God's Kingdom.

Focus: Critics of Christianity frequently point (often gleefully) to the moral failures of Christian leaders. The point seems to be that their failures show that these people are no better than anyone else, and therefore discredit the truth of Christianity. But as we have seen in our reading thus far, all human beings are sinners. As Christians, we are *forgiven* sinners. Far from discrediting Christianity, the fact that God calls sinners to be partners with him on earth—even when we fail—is exhibit A to the essential message of our faith: God loves sinners. He forgives us and uses us to do his work on earth, even though we don't deserve it and even when we fail.

Prayer: Lord, your ways are often not clear to us, and your thoughts are way beyond our understanding. Yet we cannot deny that you graciously choose us and then use us even though we are weak and prone to wander. May the favor you bestow move us to gratefulness and obedience. Amen.

April 23

> Key Text: Because Rehoboam humbled himself, the Lord's anger
> was turned away, and he did not destroy him completely. There
> were still some good things in the land of Judah.
> (2 Chronicles 12:12)

When Solomon dies, his son Rehoboam is crowned king and very quickly gets off to a rocky start. He forsakes the wisdom of his old counselors about being kind to the people, and instead follows the advice of his young, ambitious advisers. They influence him to act abusively by callously adding to the people's heavy burdens.

This hubris not only hurts the people; it also angers the older advisers. They decide to split off from the two southern tribes, now called Judah, and follow Jeroboam, one of Solomon's former managers, as their king. After this, the ten northern tribes, now called Israel, refuse to be ruled by a descendent of David.

So begins the breakup of the Promised Land into two kingdoms: Israel and Judah. The writer of 2 Chronicles comments: *"This turn of events was the will of God, for it fulfilled the Lord's message to Jeroboam son of Nebat through the prophet Ahijah from Shiloh"* (2 Chronicles 10:15).

The revolt against Judah and King Rehoboam takes an ominous turn. The newly appointed King Jeroboam ignores the Law of Moses and establishes his own priesthood to serve at pagan shrines. In response to this outrage, all the Hebrew priests and Levites abandon the northern kingdom and side with Rehoboam in Judah: *"From all the tribes of Israel, those who sincerely wanted to worship the Lord, the God of Israel, followed the Levites to Jerusalem, where they could offer sacrifices to the Lord, the God of their ancestors."*

King Rehoboam wants to go to war against the northern tribes to restore them to himself, but God says, *"Do not fight against your relatives. Go back home, for what has happened is my doing!"* (2 Chronicles 11:4).

Rehoboam's record as king of Judah is mixed. He starts well, but like so many others he becomes complacent after he is firmly established and strong. He abandons the Law of the Lord, and all of Judah follows him in this sin.

But why abandon God's Law after all this? Because, compared to Canaanite religion, God's commandments were demanding and difficult. The Law required impulse control when paganism encouraged lack of control!

So God sends the Egyptians to attack Jerusalem. But the king and the leaders of Judah humble themselves and acknowledge: *"The Lord is right in doing this to us."* God sees their change of heart and stays his anger. So, Rehoboam reigned seventeen years in Jerusalem. Nevertheless, when the final appraisal is made: *"He was an evil king, for he did not seek the Lord with all his heart."*

It is certainly difficult to be the son of a celebrity, as Rehoboam was to Solomon. He did not demonstrate the wisdom of his father, nor his talents. So, what does a young man do who doesn't have great talent or character, but possesses the power to do whatever he wants? He lets his passion run wild.

> **Focus:** Rehoboam's reign as king of Judah is a mixed bag. There is much to commend him, especially early on. But success and power become his undoing. Perhaps he grew weary of the discipline of keeping God's commandments and was lured away by pagan temptations. However, he maintained a humble heart before the Lord, and accepted the Lord's discipline for his sin. In the end, his reign as king was undermined because he did not seek the Lord with all his heart. But at least his heart was not hard towards the Lord, and that's something.

> **Prayer:** *Lord, teach us to be wise and obedient so that we don't have to learn the hard way, like Rehoboam. Amen.*

Day 115   2 Chronicles 13–16

April 24

> Key Text: The eyes of the Lord search the whole earth in order to strengthen those whose hearts are fully committed to him.
> (2 Chronicles 16:9)

Today's reading is about two kings of Judah—Abijah and his son Asa. Abijah honors the Lord, although the chronicler does not mention (as does 1 Kings 15:3) that he is not as faithful to the Lord God as his ancestor David had been.

We can probably understand from this that, while Abijah was personally faithful to God, he did not ensure that the people of Judah stopped their idolatry. As we have seen before, there was widespread syncretism among the Israelites—the blending of Israelite worship with pagan worship.

Nevertheless, God uses Abijah to defeat a far worse king, Jeroboam of Israel, even though Abijah is outnumbered two to one. Abijah shouted to Jeroboam in battle: *"Do you really think you can stand against the kingdom of the Lord that is led by the descendants of David? You may have a vast army, and you have those gold calves that Jeroboam made as your gods. ... But as for us, the Lord is our God, and we have not abandoned him"* (2 Chronicles 13:8–10).

After being defeated by Abijah, Jeroboam of Israel never regains his power and is finally struck down by the Lord and dies.

When King Abijah dies, his son Asa becomes the next king. He exceeds his father's faith and zeal for God: *"Asa did what was pleasing and good in the sight of the Lord his God. He removed the foreign altars and the pagan shrines. He smashed the sacred pillars and cut down the Asherah poles. He commanded the people of Judah to seek the Lord, the God of their ancestors, and to obey his law and his commands. Asa also removed the pagan shrines, as well as the incense altars from every one of Judah's towns. So Asa's kingdom enjoyed a period of peace"* (2 Chronicles 14:2–5).

God is clearly with Asa when Judah is attacked by a huge Ethiopian army of one million men! Asa cries out to the Lord for deliverance and the Ethiopians are defeated.

The chronicler includes two incidences where God speaks words of wisdom to Asa through a prophet or seer. The first is in chapter 15 when Azariah, who may be a prophet, speaks God's words to Asa, saying that *"the Lord will stay with you as long as you stay with him! Whenever you seek him, you will find him. But if you abandon him, he will abandon you"* (2 Chronicles 15:2).

The second incidence is in chapter 16 when Hanani the seer tells King Asa: *"The eyes of the Lord search the whole earth in order to strengthen those whose hearts are fully committed to him"* (2 Chronicles 16:9).

These words of wisdom to Asa reveal that God desires partnership with us on earth. He wants us to be his agents, acting with his authority, and thereby sharing in his blessing. Therefore, those who freely seek him with all their hearts will find him. Yet he gives freedom to abandon him and try life without his blessing and protection.

It had always been God's desire that the kings trust in him alone for the nation's well-being. But even Asa, the good king that he is, loses sight of the Lord and seeks a political alliance with a pagan king, Aram, to protect him against threatening actions by king Baasha of Israel. Fear overcame faith. When this is later pointed out to Asa by the prophet and seer, Hanani, Asa gets angry and defensive. He throws the prophet into prison and begins oppressing some of his people *(2 Chronicles 16:10)*.

This is notable because Hanani the seer becomes the first prophet to be persecuted by a Jewish king. Once again we discover that a "good" king of Judah is nevertheless a flawed man. And once again we learn that God is gracious to his people, even when the people do not experience his blessing because they fail to keep the Covenant.

Hanani's wise words to Asa reveal that God keeps searching, hoping to find men and women of faith so that he can stay close to them, and strengthen and bless them.

Focus: While the stories of First and Second Chronicles are about the kings of Israel and Judah, they reveal truth about God that is applicable to the average believer. We each are known by God and called by him to a life of worship and service. It is encouraging to know that God searches everywhere for men and women of faith so that he may bless and use them. Most of us are imperfect people who live simple lives in small places with little influence in the big scope of things. We are exactly the people God is looking for to be his partners and make a difference in the world!

Prayer: *Lord, we may not be kings and queens, but we wish to be used by you to bless the world. So help us to follow the pattern of Asa's early life, by boldly identifying and removing the idolatry in our hearts and keeping them fully committed to you. Amen.*

Day 116   2 Chronicles 17–20

April 25

Key Text: Early the next morning the army of Judah went out into the wilderness of Tekoa. On the way Jehoshaphat stopped and said, "Listen to me, all you people of Judah and Jerusalem! Believe in the Lord your God, and you will be able to stand firm. Believe in his prophets, and you will succeed."
(2 Chronicles 20:20)

The next four chapters are devoted to the righteous reign of Jehoshaphat, King Asa's son. Chapter 17 begins with an impressive resume: *"The Lord was with Jehoshaphat because he followed the example of his father's early years and did not worship the images of Baal. He sought his father's God and obeyed his commands instead of following the evil practices of the kingdom of Israel. So the Lord established Jehoshaphat's control over the kingdom of Judah. All the people of Judah brought gifts to Jehoshaphat, so he became very wealthy and highly esteemed"* (2 Chronicles 17:3–5).

Jehoshaphat initiates a wise, and I think unprecedented, program of instruction. He sends leaders throughout the towns of Judah with copies of the Book of the Law and teaches the people. The spiritual effect is powerful. The fear of the Lord falls over all the surrounding kingdoms so that none of them want to go to war against Jehoshaphat.

As a follow-up to the spiritual instruction, Jehoshaphat institutes teaching about justice throughout the towns. He appoints judges among the people and urges them to fear God and judge the people with integrity because *"the Lord our God does not tolerate perverted justice, partiality, or the taking of bribes"* (2 Chronicles 19:7).

By adding accountability to biblical teaching, Jehoshaphat blesses the people with good governance as well as peace with their enemies.

However, he makes one puzzling mistake during his reign. Chapter 18 says that the *"rich and highly esteemed"* king of Judah makes an alliance with King Ahab, the spiritually corrupt ruler of Israel. Perhaps he thinks that an alliance might lead to a reuniting of the northern and southern kingdoms. But it is a naïve notion.

In time, after wining and dining him, Ahab *"enticed Jehoshaphat to join forces with him to recover Ramoth-gilead."* Jehoshaphat quickly agrees, but suggests that they consult the Lord's prophet for confirmation from God. For his part, Ahab summons his 400 pagan prophets and (surprise!) they all agree that God will give their king his victory. But much to Ahab's annoyance, a true prophet of God, Micaiah, is summoned by Jehoshaphat. Ahab hates Micaiah because he always prophesies trouble for Ahab. This time is no different and Ahab has him arrested.

So with the encouragement of the pagan prophets, the kings join forces against Ramoth-gilead. In a cowardly act, Ahab decides to disguise himself, perhaps thinking that the enemy will kill Jehoshaphat instead.

But God has other plans—Ramoth-gilead wins. King Jehoshaphat is spared and a "random" arrow shot in the air at the Israelites hits Ahab right between the joints of his armor! By evening he is dead.

Despite his naïve lapse in judgment, Jehoshaphat is a good king and God spares him from his enemies. In fact, during one particular war against a vastly superior army, Jehoshaphat wins, by God's intervention, without Judah's army even lifting a bow (see chapter 20). After this unusual victory Jehoshaphat says, *"Listen to me, all you people of Judah and Jerusalem! Believe in the Lord your God, and you will be able to stand firm. Believe in his prophets, and you will succeed"* (2 Chronicles 20:20).

Good advice. Though he was not perfect, on balance Jehoshaphat exceeded even his father Asa as one of the best kings of Judah.

> **Focus:** Jehoshaphat was a remarkable king in many ways. He strengthened the spiritual life of the nation by his initiative to have the Law of Moses read before all the people. This united the nation and put fear in the hearts of their enemies. He listened to God's counsel and led by example. This is a good example for all of us. Such a life influences others and brings glory to God.
>
> **Prayer:** *Lord, thank you for those leaders who truly excel in faith and obedience as good shepherds of your people. May we demonstrate the same faith and trust in your Word as did Jehoshaphat, so that we also may succeed in life. Amen.*

Day 117   2 Chronicles 21–25

April 26

> Key Text: **"This is what God says: Why do you disobey the Lord's commands and keep yourselves from prospering? You have abandoned the Lord, and now he has abandoned you!"** (2 Chronicles 24:20)

Since faith and character are not heritable traits, good parents sometimes raise a child who does not follow their example. Such is the case with good King Jehoshaphat. Before Jehoshaphat dies, he designates his oldest son Jehoram to become the next king. Bad things follow: *"But when Jehoram had become solidly established as king, he killed all his brothers and some of the other leaders of Judah"* (2 Chronicles 21:4).

Jehoram's reign is only eight years. He follows the example of the kings of Israel and is as wicked as King Ahab, one of the really bad guys. This is not surprising, because he has married one of Ahab's daughters. Like father, like daughter! So Jehoram squanders the inheritance of a wealthy and powerful kingdom from his father by allowing his heart to be drawn away by paganism.

Here we go again!

Despite Jehoram's sin, God does not destroy David's dynasty because of the promise he had made to David that his descendants would continue to reign. Instead, he sends the prophet Elijah to tell Jehoram that his sin would be his personal undoing—and sure enough his whole family, except his youngest son, is killed by pagan enemies. Jehoram himself dies a horrible and painful death from intestinal disease. And... *"No one was sorry when he died"* (2 Chronicles 21:20).

Jehoram's only surviving son, Ahaziah, becomes the next king. However, since he does what is evil like his father, he doesn't last long as king. None of the surviving members of Ahaziah's family are capable of ruling the kingdom, so a power struggle follows with Ahaziah's mother, Athaliah, a pagan wife through political marriage, brutally taking control for a few years.

However, an infant son of Ahaziah has been hidden away and is not killed in the purge of the royal family. In time, a group led by Jehoiada the priest rebels against Athaliah, and the young boy Joash is produced and made king at age seven by a secret plan enacted by five army commanders. Once again, a descendent of David reigns on the throne of Judah.

In time, King Joash and the priest Jehoiada begin repairing the damaged Temple, as well as the spiritual damage that had been done by King Ahaziah and his mother: *"So all the people of the land rejoiced, and the city was peaceful because Athaliah had been killed"* (2 Chronicles 23:25).

Joash reigns for forty years and does what is pleasing in the Lord's sight, as guided by Jehoiada the priest. When Jehoiada dies, he is buried among the kings of Judah because he has done so much good in Judah for God and his Temple.

Unfortunately, Joash, who had depended on Jehoiada, comes under the counsel and influence of ungodly leaders who beg him to compromise with paganism and get rid of the Temple worship. God sends a prophet, Zechariah, to warn Joash, but Joash is now under the influence of pagan counselors and has Zechariah killed. Ironically, Zechariah was the son of Joash's late mentor, Jehoiada the priest! *"That was how King Joash repaid Jehoiada for his loyalty—by killing his son"* (2 Chronicles 24:22).

Shortly thereafter, Judah is attacked by an Aramean army and Joash is seriously injured. His own officials then assassinate him while he lies in bed, because he had murdered the beloved priest's son, Zechariah.

Joash's son, Amaziah, becomes the next king and he does what is pleasing in the Lord's sight, but not wholeheartedly. In time, he turns to the gods of Edom and brings judgment upon himself and Judah.

Do you see a pattern emerging?

We see the dynamics of God's Covenant at work in the stories of the kings. Whenever a king keeps the Covenant and commandments, he is blessed by God and the land is given peace. But when a king disobeys the Lord's Covenant and commandments, and worships other gods, he is kept from prospering and the nation is at war.

When will they learn? When will *we* learn?

Focus: If the stories of the kings of Israel and Judah sound just like the palace intrigue of ancient pagan kingdoms, there is a reason—they have forsaken God and begun to think and behave just like their pagan neighbors. The constant challenge for them, and for us, is to faithfully serve God in the midst of a contrary world. As the apostle Paul later writes to the Roman believers: *"Don't copy the behavior and customs of this world, but let God transform you into a new person by changing the way you think. Then you will learn to know God's will for you, which is good and pleasing and perfect"* (Romans 12:2).

Prayer: *Lord, we thank you for your amazing grace and abundant mercy. You continue to love us and strive with us even though so many times we frustrate your blessing by our disobedience. We want our lives to honor you, so open our eyes to our sin and empower us to obey. Amen.*

Day 118   2 Chronicles 26–28

April 27

Key Text: But when [Uzziah] had become powerful, he also became proud, which led to his downfall. He sinned against the Lord his God by entering the sanctuary of the Lord's Temple and personally burning incense on the incense altar.
(2 Chronicles 26:16)

The next king of Judah is Uzziah—the Uzziah that the prophet Isaiah famously mentions when speaking of his calling from God: *"It was in the year King Uzziah died that I saw the Lord..."* (Isaiah 6:1).

Because the Old Testament books are not chronological, we will hear about the various kings of Israel and Judah again when we come to the prophets, because they were God's spokesmen to the kings and bring rich theological perspective to all the events we have been following in Samuel, Kings and Chronicles.

Uzziah becomes king at age 16 and rules for 52 years. During most of his reign he does what is pleasing in the eyes of the Lord. He is an able leader and his fame spreads far and wide: *"But when he had become powerful, he also became proud, which led to his downfall"* (2 Chronicles 26:16). A particular offense noted by the chronicler is Uzziah's presumption to enter the Temple by assuming priestly prerogatives for himself. This is clearly a sin against God's explicit instructions regarding priests.

When confronted by the priests, Uzziah becomes furious. Yet, as he stands in the Temple raging against the priests, leprosy suddenly breaks out on his forehead. He lives in isolation the rest of his life and dies from leprosy.

Uzziah's son Jotham follows him as king, and like his father, is pleasing in the Lord's sight—but without the Temple presumption. He becomes a powerful king and reigns 16 years.

But then the third generation arrives—Ahaz. We know about him. He does not do what is pleasing in the sight of the Lord. Instead of following the example of his father and grandfather, Ahaz goes full-out pagan: *"He cast metal images for the worship of Baal. He offered sacrifices in the valley of Ben-Hinnom* [also known as Gehenna], *even sacrificing his own sons in the fire. In this way, he followed the detestable practices of the pagan nations the Lord had driven from the land of the Israelites. He offered sacrifices and burned incense at the pagan shrines and on the hills and under every green tree"* (2 Chronicles 28:2–4).

Ahaz's evil brings God's judgment, and Judah is brought to her knees by King Tiglath-pileser of Assyria. Even in this time of personal and national trouble, Ahaz does not return to the Lord. Instead he goes down as one of Judah's worst kings. When he dies, he is buried in Jerusalem, but not in the royal cemetery of the kings of Judah.

What a terrible heritage to leave behind. Given the stories so far, the occasional good kings like Jotham stand out as men of strong faith, able to resist the lure of paganism. But the more common story of the kings is one of failure—or at least of mixed success. It illustrates that even with all the advantages Israel had as the people of God, especially the long history of God's gracious dealing with her, the people and their kings were not able to live consistently righteous lives.

Paul will summarize this very human problem of sin in Romans 3 when he makes the case that *"all have sinned and fall short of the glory of God."* He makes this point to show beyond any doubt that we are saved by God's grace and not by our personal merit.

The story of Israel is the story of every nation and every individual. We all sin and fall short of the glorious humanity for which God created us. We all need Christ to be forgiven and made right with God. Thankfully, this forgiveness is made available to anyone who repents of their sin and receives God's grace through Christ.

> **Focus:** King Uzziah is the next of a number of Judah's kings who served God faithfully at the beginning, but gradually were undone by pride, as money and power increased. Malevolent pride—the kind that not only wants to win, but wants to see all rivals lose—turns our hearts away from God. C.S. Lewis explains why in *Mere Christianity:* *"If I am a proud man, then as long as there is one man in the world more powerful, or richer, or cleverer than I, he is my rival and my enemy. And of course my greatest enemy is God himself, because in God I have come up against something which is in every respect immeasurably superior to me."* Beware of pride!

> **Prayer:** *Lord, keep us from the pride which led to King Uzziah's fall, let alone the complete abandonment to paganism that brought down King Ahaz. Let King Jotham be our guide in humbly clinging to grace and living to please you. Amen.*

Day 119   Reflection

April 28

First and Second Chronicles provide us with a different perspective on the reign of Israel's kings, focusing primarily on King David's story in 1 Chronicles, and then his descendants who rule over the southern kingdom of Judah in 2 Chronicles.

Evil kings such as Ahab, who lead the people back into wholehearted paganism, are balanced by reformer kings like Jehoshaphat, Joash, Uzziah and Jotham. They lead the people in reform and seek to minimize, if not eliminate, the practices of pagan worship.

The fact that the chronicler doesn't whitewash the sins of bad leaders, nor idealize the obedience of good leaders, gives us a realistic portrayal of the constant struggle we face against idolatry—even when we know better.

Today, our idols are not wood or stone, but idols of the heart. Notable among these idols are money, sex and power. But anything—especially good things—can become idols when they replace God at the center of our lives. We know they have become idols when we turn to them for comfort or happiness or security—or when we can't imagine life without them.

We may find it difficult to understand why the Israelites would prefer to worship Canaanite gods through shrines, idols and Asherah poles, but these things represented the "norm" of the ancient world. They were just as important and real to them as Wall Street is important and real to us.

It is the struggle of every generation of believers to resist the allure of idols. The apostle John ends his first epistle to the Christian community he oversees by saying, *"Dear children, keep yourselves from idols,"* or as one translation renders it, *"Dear children, keep away from anything that might take God's place in your hearts"* (1 John 5:21).

The reason God takes this so seriously is explained by the purpose for which God created us in the first place. He wants a relationship with us. He wants us to know, enjoy and worship him as he truly is. We can only be truly human in relationship to our Creator.

Idolatry presumes to reimagine and reshape God into a god we can control. In doing so, we not only lose God, we lose ourselves as well. Such a god will inevitably disappoint, disillusion and even destroy us.

This is why God was so angry at Israel about idolatry. He loved them too much to let them go insane by worshiping false gods. After all, not living in reality is the very definition of insanity.

Prayer: Lord, we acknowledge our struggle against idolatry. Keep our hearts and minds fixed on you, as you are, so that we may experience the purpose for which we were made. We honor you as the one true God, Creator of the heavens and earth, and redeemer of our wayward hearts. Amen

Day 120   2 Chronicles 29–32

April 29

> Key Text: In the very first month of the first year of his reign, Hezekiah reopened the doors of the Temple of the Lord and repaired them. He summoned the priests and Levites to meet him at the courtyard east of the Temple. He said to them, "Listen to me, you Levites! Purify yourselves, and purify the Temple of the Lord, the God of your ancestors." (2 Chronicles 29:3–4)

During the regrettable reign of King Ahaz, the doors of the Lord's Temple were shut so that no one could worship the Lord God there. Then Ahaz set up altars to pagan gods in every corner of Judah.

But dark and discouraging times are not too much for the Lord. Ahaz's son, Hezekiah, chooses a different path as Judah's next king who reopens the doors of the Temple!

Consistent with the priest-centered account of Chronicles, the priests and Levites are front and center at Hezekiah's command to cleanse and reopen the Temple for worship. *"They were careful to follow all the Lord's instructions in their work."* Once again the sacrifices are made at the Temple as required by the Lord, and the Levite choir leads the worshipers in songs of praise. The people came in droves with their offerings: *"So the Temple of the Lord was restored to service. And Hezekiah and all the people rejoiced because of what God had done for the people, for everything had been accomplished so quickly"* (2 Chronicles 29:35).

King Hezekiah then sends word to all Israel and Judah, inviting everyone to return to the Lord and come to the Temple at Jerusalem to celebrate the Passover. The response is weak in Israel but strong in Judah, as a huge crowd assembles. With the requirements of worshiping the Lord God long forgotten, the people do not purify themselves for worship. But King Hezekiah prays for them and they are allowed to participate anyway: *"'May the Lord, who is good, pardon those who decide to follow the Lord, the God of their ancestors, even though they are not properly cleansed for the ceremony.' And the Lord listened to Hezekiah's prayer and healed the people"* (2 Chronicles 30:18–20).

The joyous festivities surrounding this spiritual renewal continue to a second week as the people celebrate and the priests offer thousands of sacrifices: *"There was great joy in the city, for Jerusalem had not seen a celebration like this one since the days of Solomon, King David's son."*

After the festival ends, the people are spiritually alive and refreshed. They go back to their towns and begin to remove and destroy all the pagan elements and artifacts from their communities. The people reinstate their tithing to the Temple storehouse. Their generosity makes it possible to fully redeploy the priests and Levites to their Temple duties.

The reinvigorating of Israelite faith and worship catches the attention of King Sennacherib of Assyria. He regards Judah's spiritual awakening as a threat and promptly invades Judah and lays siege to the fortified towns. Hezekiah digs in to resist the sieges, telling the people, *"Don't be afraid or discouraged because of the king of Assyria or his mighty army, for there is a power far greater on our side! He may have a great army, but they are merely men. We have the Lord our God to help us and to fight our battles for us!"* (2 Chronicles 32:7–8).

Sennacherib tries to terrify the Israelites by boasting and mocking them, but the Lord sends an angel to destroy the Assyrian army. We don't know how—Was it disease or miraculous feats of war? Nevertheless, Sennacherib returns home beaten and disgraced. He is killed by his own sons.

All in all, Hezekiah is a courageous and faithful leader of Judah. The renewal of faith under his leadership is emblematic of a future Day when the Lord will be honored in his Temple by all the nations.

> **Focus:** Spiritual renewal is a gift of God. It usually follows a period of decline or abandonment of faith, and is accompanied by the joy of finding something precious that has been long misplaced or forgotten. In Kings and Chronicles, renewal is usually marked by a leader who is strong in faith who reintroduces people to the Word of God. Hearing the Word of God is then followed by national repentance, along with a recommitment to honor the Lord God alone, and in the manner he has prescribed.
>
> Renewal also happens on a personal level. It too includes a response to God's Word through repentance and recommitment. Faith needs to be maintained, because like everything else in our fallen world, things tend to move from order to disorder. Spiritual entropy is overcome by disciplined attention to the means of grace God has given us, including Scripture, prayer, corporate worship, fellowship and service.

Day 121   2 Chronicles 33–36

April 30

> Key Text: "This is what King Cyrus of Persia says: 'The Lord, the God of heaven, has given me all the kingdoms of the earth. He has appointed me to build him a Temple at Jerusalem, which is in Judah. Any of you who are the Lord's people may go there for this task. And may the Lord your God be with you!'"
> (2 Chronicles 36:23)

Hezekiah's son Manasseh becomes king at age twelve. One wonders who or what shaped his thinking as he grew up, because in the end he becomes one of Judah's most evil kings. In fact, the chronicler states: *"Manasseh led the people of Judah and Jerusalem to do even more evil than the pagan nations that the Lord had destroyed when the people of Israel entered the land"* (2 Chronicles 33:9).

His evil deeds include *"bowing before all the powers of the heavens and worshiping them."* These "powers" are understood to be demonic, which explains something else Manasseh does—he sacrifices his own sons in the fire in the Valley of Ben-Hinnom. The ritual killing of children in the name of religion was common in the ancient world.

After ignoring all God's warnings, which were probably given to him through prophets, Manasseh is punished by God when he is taken prisoner by Assyrian armies. He is humiliated by his captors and locked away. Finally, he humbles himself before the Lord, realizing that the Lord alone is God. God sees his sincerity and brings him back to Jerusalem and his kingdom, where Manasseh restores Judah to the worship of the Lord God.

In considering Manasseh's life, one is impressed to see that the Lord is more merciful than most of us would be. Though much of Manasseh's life as king is wasted, God still hears him at the end when he humbles himself and asks for forgiveness. We are reminded of the wideness of God's mercy, and that it is accessed through humility and repentance.

After Manasseh, his son Amon is made king. Unlike his father, Amon does not humble himself before the Lord: *"Instead, he sinned even more."*

He is assassinated in the palace by his own officials.

Amon's son Josiah, who is only eight years old, is then made king. It must have been difficult to keep track at times! However, Josiah eventually chooses to follow the example of his ancestor David. By age twenty, he has implemented a widespread program of reform throughout Judah, especially in the city of Jerusalem. Next, he sets about repairing the damage to the Temple and finally restores all that earlier kings of Judah had allowed to fall into ruin. In the course of repair, the Book of the Law of the Lord, which was written by Moses, is found and read to the king.

Josiah is horrified. He tells the Temple officials to go and pray for him and the people: *"For the Lord's great anger has been poured out on us because our ancestors have not obeyed the word of the Lord. We have not been doing everything this scroll says we must do"* (2 Chronicles 34:21).

What Josiah does is honorable and courageous. However, the pattern of Israel's sin over the generations has already merited God's judgment. Exile will come just as God had warned all along, but because of Josiah's alarm and genuine humility, judgment will be delayed until Josiah dies and is resting in peace.

After Josiah dies, King Nebuchadnezzar of Babylon begins to harass Judah and politically takes over the appointment of kings. Not surprisingly, the kings all do evil. The priests and people follow, becoming more and more unfaithful by returning to paganism, desecrating the Temple and ignoring the words of the prophets. Babylon becomes the instrument of judgment. The Temple is burned to the ground, the walls of Jerusalem are torn down, and everything else is completely destroyed.

The people of Judah are exiled to Babylon and it seems as if all is lost.

But is it? Jeremiah prophesies: *"This is what the Lord says: 'You will be in Babylon for seventy years. But then I will come and do for you all the good things I have promised, and I will bring you home again. For I know the plans I have for you,' says the Lord. 'They are plans for good and not for disaster, to give you a future and a hope'"* (Jeremiah 29:10–11).

Focus: As 2 Chronicles concludes, the prophecy of Jeremiah is fulfilled in a most interesting manner. God stirs the heart of a pagan king, Cyrus of Persia, to rebuild a Temple in Jerusalem *"for the Lord, the God of heaven."* Cyrus gives written permission for any Hebrews to return to Jerusalem and begin the task. It is fascinating to learn that God uses foreign nations both to execute his judgment, and to bring about his hopeful future. We need to keep in mind that God is sovereign over all the nations on earth, and may choose to accomplish his purposes in the most unexpected ways, and with the most unexpected nations!

Prayer: Lord, life is full of reasons to be discouraged and give up. Our hopes are crushed; utopian dreams come to nothing; evil always seems to follow good. And yet, the prophet Jeremiah gives us reason to believe that evil will not triumph, because you are faithful to fulfill your promises in the most surprising ways! So, Lord, bring this world home again, as you did with your people of Judah. Amen.

Day 122   Ezra 1–3

May 1

Key Text: When the builders completed the foundation of the Lord's Temple, the priests put on their robes and took their places to blow their trumpets. And the Levites, descendants of Asaph, clashed their cymbals to praise the Lord, just as King David had prescribed. With praise and thanks, they sang this song to the Lord: "He is so good! His faithful love for Israel endures forever!" (Ezra 3:10–11)

The book of Ezra picks up the story of Judah seventy years after the end of the events covered in 2 Chronicles. Judah, the southern kingdom, has been taken to Babylon into exile, just as Israel, the northern kingdom, was taken into exile earlier by Assyria.

The exile is God's judgment against his people because of the hardness of their hearts and their continued violation of the Mosaic Covenant. In particular, their hearts were drawn away from God to worshiping idols, and to otherwise behaving like the pagan nations around them.

This is the beginning of the "diaspora"—the dispersing of the Jews away from Israel, especially from Jerusalem and the Temple, to live among the nations of the world.

During this period of time, the prophets speak to the exiled peoples of both the northern and southern kingdoms about judgment and hope. When we get to the prophetic writings, we will see that this is a period of soul-searching and anguish over difficult, unresolved issues: What does it mean to be the people of God outside of the land promised to Abraham? Has their breaking of the Covenant placed them outside of God's grace? What about God's promise to David about an eternal Kingdom? Is there any hope for the future?

But the prophets offer hope. They remind the people that God is the Lord of history. Even though other nations now occupy the Promised Land, God has not forgotten his promises. There is restoration for those who repent of their sins and return to the Lord.

Remarkably, after seventy years have passed, God prompts the pagan King Cyrus of Persia to let any Jews who wish, to return to Jerusalem and rebuild the Temple *(Ezra 1:1–4)!*

This stirs the hearts of the priests and Levites and other Jewish leaders. They return with all the wealth that Nebuchadnezzar had taken from the Temple, plus an abundance of gifts from their neighbors. In all, over 42,000 people return to their towns throughout Israel.

The present occupiers of the Promised Land are not happy about King Cyrus's proclamation to allow the Jews to return. These surrounding tribes had moved into the land once the Israelites were forced to leave. Even though the Jews are afraid of these local residents, they begin rebuilding the altar at its original site in the Temple ruins so that they can begin sacrificing burnt offerings to the Lord.

The leaders start by gathering materials and hiring masons and carpenters. Finally, two years after their return, the people begin rebuilding the Temple itself. When the foundation is completed, there is a great celebration: *"And the Levites, descendants of Asaph, clashed their cymbals to praise the Lord, just as King David had prescribed. With praise and thanks, they sang this song to the Lord: 'He is so good! His faithful love for Israel endures forever!'"* (Ezra 3:10–11).

It is a bittersweet moment. The ruins of the Temple remind the older Jews of their failure to keep the Covenant and commandments. They lament the greatness of what was lost. But the younger Jews, who have been born in exile, shout for joy. A new generation is able to hope because God is faithful.

Focus: The events covered in Ezra were but a minor blip on the screen of Persian politics. Yet they stand as a signal to all Jews who have remained faithful to the Lord God that he has not forgotten them, nor his ancient promises. Ezra illustrates that God can be powerfully at work in little things, even as he is the Lord of the broader sweep of history. In comparison to the population of the whole earth, individual lives seem like little things, but God is focused on you and me. He calls us to forsake the gods of this world and worship him alone. He invites us to be partners with him in declaring the Gospel to the world. He looks forward to the Day when he rules once again as King of the whole earth, together with us.

Prayer: Lord, again we are struck by your grace and mercy. Your love simply will not let go of us, even when we let go of you. Like the Israelites, we feel the pain of the consequences for our sins, yet there is also the sweetness of your gracious forgiveness and new beginnings. We sing with those who returned to the land: "You are so good! Your faithful love for your people endures forever!" Amen.

Day 123   Ezra 4–6

May 2

> Key Text: There was great joy throughout the land because the Lord had caused the king of Assyria to be favorable to them, so that he helped them to rebuild the Temple of God, the God of Israel. (Ezra 6:22)

The rebuilding of the Temple by the Jewish returnees from exile in Babylonia is met with fierce resistance from the local inhabitants. They employ clever and then increasingly more hostile tactics to get the Jews to stop building.

First, they pretend to want to help with construction. When that ploy fails, they try to discourage and frighten the workers. They bribe agents to undermine the project and write letters of accusation and fearmongering to the kings of Persia. King Artaxerxes finally takes the bait and issues a stop order on the project. This remains in effect for fifteen years, until Darius becomes king.

At this time, the prophets Haggai and Zechariah are encouraging the leaders of the Jews to restart the building project. Once again, the locals protest by writing to King Darius, questioning whether there ever was permission granted by King Cyrus for the Jews to rebuild the Temple.

But the gambit fails. Darius orders the Babylonian archives to be searched, and sure enough the memorandum is found, giving them permission. Darius responds with an order to allow the construction of the Temple: *"Let it be rebuilt on its original site, and do not hinder the governor of Judah and the elders of the Jews in their work. Moreover, I hereby decree that you are to help these elders of the Jews as they rebuild this Temple of God. You must pay the full construction costs, without delay, from my taxes collected in the province west of the Euphrates River so that the work will not be interrupted. … May the God who has chosen the city of Jerusalem as the place to honor his name destroy any king or nation that violates this command and destroys this Temple"* (Ezra 6:7–12).

When the Temple is completed and dedicated, the priests and Levites return to their tasks of service at the Temple, as prescribed in the Law. Then, all the returned exiles celebrate Passover—the defining moment of the people of God—giving hope that God has not forgotten his people.

The irony here, not lost on the Jews, is that God once again uses a foreign nation to carry out his will for Israel—first Assyria and Babylonia to bring his judgment against Israel's sin, and now the kings of Persia, who had since conquered the Assyrian and Babylonian empires, to help restore God's people to the land.

These big events, involving the decisions of kings and nations, show that God is in control of history and can use anything and anyone to carry out his will. It also anticipates the day when all the nations of the world will worship the God of Israel, the one true God.

Focus: The Old Testament repeatedly reveals the Lord God to be the one true God who is sovereign over all the nations of the earth, and who uses them to achieve his good purposes. The nations have him alone—their Creator—to thank for their very existence. As their Redeemer, they have only him to look to for salvation and hope. Knowing this, it is important that Christians not abandon or minimize the material realm. Above all others, we ought to faithfully pursue justice for its peoples, wisely manage nature's resources, carefully study history, diligently pursue reason, and joyfully create art, music, literature and all forms of beauty, goodness and truth. And all of this with grateful hearts, for it is on this good earth, fully renewed, that we shall forever enjoy and serve God our Creator.

Prayer: Lord, we are once again reminded that the earth belongs to you. By your sovereign power you bring about all your good purposes. What seems to us a hopeless situation is nothing to you. You are the Lord of history and nations. Help us not to be afraid. Amen.

May 3

> Key Text: "And you, Ezra, are to use the wisdom your God has given you to appoint magistrates and judges who know your God's laws to govern all the people in the province west of the Euphrates River. Teach the law to anyone who does not know it." (Ezra 7:25)

During the reign of King Artaxerxes of Persia, a second group of exiles returns to Jerusalem. They are led by Ezra, a scribe well versed in the Law of Moses and well respected by Artaxerxes.

The gracious hand of God is upon Ezra, who is determined to study and obey the Law of the Lord, and to teach those decrees and regulations to the people of Israel. The rebuilding of the Temple in Jerusalem is one thing, but rebuilding the people's spiritual lives is quite another. And for this task, *God has prepared Ezra.*

He leaves Babylon with King Artaxerxes' blessing, a letter of passage in hand and abundant resources, including more stolen wealth taken during the destruction of Jerusalem, to be returned to the Temple. Artaxerxes encourages Ezra to use the wisdom God has given him to appoint magistrates and judges who know the Mosaic Law.

Ezra rejoices at the unexpected favor shown him by the king, saying: *"Praise the Lord, the God of our ancestors, who made the king want to beautify the Temple of the Lord in Jerusalem! And praise him for demonstrating such unfailing love to me by honoring me before the king, his council, and all his mighty nobles! I felt encouraged because the gracious hand of the Lord my God was on me. And I gathered some of the leaders of Israel to return with me to Jerusalem"* (Ezra 7:27–28).

Chapter 8 lists all who leave with Ezra and safely arrive in Jerusalem because God's hand of protection is upon them. Ezra testifies: *"...we had told the king, 'Our God's hand of protection is on all who worship him, but his fierce anger rages against those who abandon him.' So we fasted and earnestly prayed that our God would take care of us, and he heard our prayer"* (Ezra 8:22–23).

There is a sense of joy and expectation in the story of Ezra so far. God is clearly at work through the surprising actions of the pagan kings of

Persia—Cyrus, Darius and now Artaxerxes—as well as through Jewish leaders like Ezra—to return a remnant of Israel to the land.

Persia plays an interesting role in the story of Israel, not only because of these three kings, but also later when three magi out of Persia come to worship the child born in Bethlehem!

Focus: Ezra's contribution to the returned exiles, and their project of restoring the Temple, was his gift of teaching. Because he was well versed in the Law of Moses, he was able to teach and to prepare others to assist in teaching. Israel as a people cannot be understood apart from God's call, Covenant and Law. They are people of the Book—the Old Testament. They are a "holy" people, not in the sense of being perfect (they are not!), but in the sense of being uniquely "set apart" to know, serve and bear witness to the Lord God. Christians too are people of the Book—the New Testament. Christ as a Jew "under the Law" fulfills what God intended Israel to become. However, he came for the whole world, not just for Israel. So all who believe in him become part of the story of Israel, God's holy people.

Prayer: *Lord, it is exciting to live, like Ezra and the exiles, during days of blessing when it is clear to all that you are at work in the world. Of course, you are always at work, even when times are difficult and confusing. Give us eyes to see you at work in our lives and in our times, so that we will not be afraid or disillusioned, but confident that all your gracious promises to us will be fulfilled! Amen.*

Day 125   Ezra 9–10

May 4

Key Text: "From the days of our ancestors until now, we have been steeped in sin. That is why we and our kings and our priests have been at the mercy of the pagan kings of the land. We have been killed, captured, robbed, and disgraced, just as we are today. But now we have been given a brief moment of grace, for the Lord our God has allowed a few of us to survive as a remnant." (Ezra 9:7–8)

The need for Ezra to give spiritual guidance to those in Jerusalem is apparent as soon as he arrives. The Jewish leaders on the scene approach Ezra to say: *"Many of the people of Israel, and even some of the priests and Levites, have not kept themselves separate from the other people living in the land. They have taken up the detestable practices of the Canaanites, Hittites, Perizzites, Jebusites, Ammonites, Moabites, Egyptians and Amor-*

241

ites" (Ezra 9:1).

So the old sinful practices have returned, especially the practice of marrying pagan wives. God's Law specifically forbade it and Moses warned the people against it *(Exodus 34:10–17)*, not for reasons of race, but of faithfulness to the Covenant. Marrying pagan wives has inevitably resulted in a return to idolatry.

To make things worse, the leaders are leading the way!

Ezra becomes deeply troubled: *"Then all who trembled at the words of the God of Israel came and sat with me because of this outrage committed by the returned exiles. And I sat there utterly appalled until the time of the evening sacrifice"* (Ezra 9:4).

But great challenges reveal great leaders. Ezra takes the burden of the people upon himself and intercedes for them in a heartfelt prayer of confession. He acknowledges God's grace in the face of the people's history of sin: *"We come before you in our guilt as nothing but an escaped remnant, though in such a condition none of us can stand in your presence"* (Ezra 9:15).

We notice in Ezra's prayer three references to the *"remnant."* The presence of a remnant of faithful people shows that even in Israel's darkest moments as a nation, there are faithful Israelites who do not harden their hearts against God. But even this *remnant of faith* sin against the Lord and need to repent. So in chapter 10, Ezra leads the people in a recommitment of their lives to obey the Law, and to give evidence of this by the painful act of divorcing their pagan wives and sending them home.

The people must remember that their calling from God, as codified in the Covenant, means that they are to lead a different life and not assimilate into the world. It is a difficult calling. As Jesus will later say, *"narrow is the road and few there are that find it."* The road is not narrow in the sense that it is hard to find, but rather that it is difficult to travel, so the half-hearted do not prevail.

So Ezra leads the people back to the narrow road of the Covenant and to the way of blessing. But, as we shall see in Nehemiah, the struggle will continue.

Focus: Israel in exile is becoming assimilated among the pagan nations. Nevertheless, some Jews remain faithful to God. Many of these are counted among the ones who return to live in the Promised Land and rebuild the Temple. Though the land is now occupied and controlled by Israel's ancient enemies, and the returnees are a small population, they survive as a "remnant of faith." However small and insignificant, they still bear witness to the Lord God. The "remnant of faith" becomes important in the messages of the prophets, which we shall come to, because it is for them that God remains faithful to his promises. We should not despise small things, or equate the present status of the Church with God's promise and power. He is always faithful even when we are not.

Prayer: Lord, we understand that even faithful believers struggle with temptation and with the fear of opposition. Help us to be vigilant, humble, repentant, and persevering in the walk of faith. Though the road is narrow, your blessings are abundant! And though we often feel small and powerless, you are able to do unimaginably more than all we ask or think. Amen.

Day 126   Nehemiah 1–2

May 5

> Key Text: "Please remember what you told your servant Moses: 'If you are unfaithful to me, I will scatter you among the nations. But if you return to me and obey my commands and live by them, then even if you are exiled to the ends of the earth, I will bring you back to the place I have chosen for my name to be honored.'" (Nehemiah 1:8–9)

The book of Nehemiah is written in the first person by Nehemiah, a personal assistant, confidant and food taster to King Artaxerxes of Persia. He is a contemporary of Ezra the scribe, who took the second group of Jewish exiles from Babylon back to Jerusalem to rebuild the Temple.

Nehemiah receives word that things are not going well for the returnees to Jerusalem. It has been nearly a century since the first group of exiles returned to the ruined city. Though the Temple has been rebuilt, the walls protecting the city of Jerusalem still lie in ruins. This makes the Jews vulnerable to mischief, bullying and violence by their hostile neighbors. And the ruins remind everyone of Israel's shame and Babylon's conquest.

After a period of fasting and prayer, Nehemiah is deeply impressed by the words of God to Moses long ago regarding Israel. God had said: *"If you are unfaithful to me, I will scatter you among the nations. But if you return to me and obey my commands and live by them, then even if you are exiled to the ends of the earth, I will bring you back to the place I have chosen for my name to be honored"* (Nehemiah 1:8–9).

Nehemiah is moved to ask King Artaxerxes for permission to return to Judah and rebuild the city of his ancestors. Artaxerxes shows him favor and gives him passage and a letter of permission to rebuild the walls.

Knowing, as before, that this mission will not be received well by Israel's neighbors, Nehemiah keeps his purpose for returning quiet. But the neighbors are wary, nonetheless. In particular, Sanballat the Horonite, Geshem the Arab, and Tobiah the Ammonite official are very displeased when they hear that Nehemiah has come to help the people. It seems that the memory of Israel's past greatness under her good kings is a cause for concern.

Three days after arriving, Nehemiah and a few others slip out at night to quietly inspect the broken walls and burned gates. He finally meets with the Jewish leaders to tell them of his plan to rebuild the walls of Jerusalem, and of how God had been with him and given him favor with Artaxerxes.

The leaders agree at once, and begin the good work. But the neighbors scoff contemptuously. Tension is in the air; it is clear that Nehemiah's mission will be resisted.

There is more going on here than disputes over zoning and conflict over building codes. The pagan nations don't want Jerusalem restored with Israel's God back in the neighborhood! Ancient people had long memories, and they remembered that their ancestors had been judged by God because of their unrepentant idolatry and gross immorality. They were consequently removed from the land (the land "vomited them up") and the land was given to Israel. Now that the Canaanites have returned to the land, and are once again comfortably reestablished in their idolatry and gross immorality, they don't want a repeat.

As Jesus would later say regarding people who love darkness: *"God's light came into the world, but people loved the darkness more than the light, for their actions were evil. All who do evil hate the light and refuse to go near it for fear their sins will be exposed. But those who do what is right come to the light so others can see that they are doing what God wants"* (John 3:19–21).

> **Focus:** In our reading of the Old Testament, it has become clear that God's redemptive plan will always be resisted by the fallen world. We may scratch our heads and wonder why the Canaanites would reject God's love and mercy, especial-

ly in light of the brutal practices of pagan idolatry, including the sacrifice of their children! As Jeremiah the prophet will say, *"The human heart is the most deceitful of all things, and desperately wicked. Who really knows how bad it is?"* (Jeremiah 17:9). We need to be prepared for resistance, and sometimes outright hostility. The good news is that God's offer of forgiveness and eternal life still stands; it is available for anyone who will humble themselves, forsake their sins and follow Jesus.

Prayer: *Lord, your people around the world are finding that the darkness hates the light, and consequently it hates those who talk about Jesus, the Light of the World. We pray for your suffering Church worldwide, and also for ourselves, that we will not be shamed or bullied into hiding the light of the Gospel. Amen.*

Day 127   Nehemiah 3–4

May 6

Key Text: Then as I looked over the situation, I called together the nobles and the rest of the people and said to them, "Don't be afraid of the enemy! Remember the Lord, who is great and glorious, and fight for your brothers, your sons, your daughters, your wives, and your homes!" (Nehemiah 4:14)

Nehemiah's vision to rebuild the walls around the city of Jerusalem proceeds in the face of threats and plots by Israel's enemies. Nehemiah designs a clever plan to divide the wall into sections, and assigns those who live closest to each section to do the building. Everyone is motivated, of course, to build their assigned section, in order to protect their homes.

The success of the project irritates Jerusalem's enemies. Nehemiah writes: *"Sanballat was very angry when he learned that we were rebuilding the wall. He flew into a rage and mocked the Jews, saying in front of his friends and the Samarian army officers, 'What does this bunch of poor, feeble Jews think they're doing? Do they think they can build the wall in a single day by just offering a few sacrifices? Do they actually think they can make something of stones from a rubbish heap—and charred ones at that?'"* (Nehemiah 4:1–2).

Well, yes they do!

Nevertheless, Nehemiah takes their threats seriously. He prays that God would frustrate their plans, and he does. The work continues at a rapid pace and is completed to half its original height around the entire city, because the people work with enthusiasm.

By repairing the gaps in the walls of Jerusalem—even if only to half as high as they should be—the Jews put themselves in a much better position to protect themselves as they finish up. Their success is perceived by their enemies as more than an irritation now. It is a threat: *"They all made plans to come and fight against Jerusalem and throw us into confusion. But we prayed to our God and guarded the city day and night to protect ourselves"* (Nehemiah 4:8–9).

Nehemiah takes steps to make sure that armed guards are always present, day and night. The workers themselves *"carried on their work with one hand supporting their load and one hand holding a weapon."* Because the work is spread out, a trumpeter is employed to sound the alarm if there is an incident anywhere along the wall.

In addition to implementing security protocols, Nehemiah gathers the leaders and people to spiritually encourage them: *"Don't be afraid of the enemy! Remember the Lord, who is great and glorious, and fight for your brothers, your sons, your daughters, your wives, and your homes!"* (Nehemiah 4:14).

Nehemiah proves to be an able leader. He has a great vision, an effective plan, and the ability to manage threats. His spiritual leadership and encouragement enable the people to safely complete the project.

Focus: When we ask God to help us with a project, great or small, it doesn't mean that we ourselves are passive. God uses humans as his *agents* to accomplish his purposes. God desires partnership with us. Each of us, like Nehemiah, is called to use our gifts and life experiences as wisely as possible to make things happen on earth for the glory of God. Prayer is not an abnegation of responsibility, but a recognition that the truly great achievements on earth arise from partnership with God. We pray, we trust, we work, and together make things happen that would not have happened had we not prayed, trusted and worked. What an honor it is to be used by God to accomplish great things!

Prayer: Lord, thank you for the privilege of being your agents in the world. Thank you also for giving leaders to your Church to organize people and accomplish the dreams and visions you place in our hearts. We trust that you will protect us from our enemies, as you did with Nehemiah and the remnant, as we faithfully do your work. Amen.

May 7

As we have noted, an important new element in Ezra and Nehemiah is the idea of a *remnant of faith.* Though Israel as a whole had rejected God's Covenant, some had remained faithful.

The remnant, which defined itself by the Word of God, returned to Israel in three migrations to rebuild the city, worship God at the rebuilt Temple, and renew the ancient Covenant. Though Israel has lost its statehood, she has not lost her calling or identity as God's people.

The remnant is a small percentage of the former Israel; nevertheless, it is the inheritor of God's promises. God said through the prophet Isaiah, *"I will preserve a remnant of the people of Israel and of Judah to possess my land. Those I choose will inherit it, and my servants will live there"* (Isaiah 65:9).

The prophet Micah suggests that the existence of a remnant proves the unfailing love of God: *"Where is another God like you, who pardons the guilt of the remnant, overlooking the sins of his special people? You will not stay angry with your people forever, because you delight in showing unfailing love"* (Micah 7:18).

Chronologically, Nehemiah deals with the final status of Old Testament Israel, meaning that Israel is mostly scattered among the nations, although some have returned to the land. This situation is not a fulfillment of God's Promise to Abraham. The ancient Promise still awaits fulfillment.

So, there was an "Israel" within Israel, just as today there is a "Church" within the church. Those who are Christian in name only are not the Church known to God. Jesus once said, *"Not everyone who calls out to me, 'Lord! Lord!' will enter the Kingdom of Heaven. Only those who actually do the will of my Father in heaven will enter"* (Matthew 7:21).

The mark of authentic faith is always the fruit it produces: *"A good tree produces good fruit, and a bad tree produces bad fruit. A good tree can't produce bad fruit, and a bad tree can't produce good fruit"* (Matthew 7:17–18).

The continuing fact of the remnant of faith shows that God is able to bring about his plan of redemption with the smallest of resources. Over and over again in our reading of the Old Testament we see God's working in, around and against great earthly powers. We see him overcome impossible circumstances. He does the exact opposite of what we would expect. There is no great divine power play from heaven, obliterating all human resistance. Instead, God uses what is weak, little, insignificant and despised.

The apostle Paul makes special note of this in writing to the Christians at Corinth: *"Remember, dear brothers and sisters, that few of you were wise in the world's eyes or powerful or wealthy when God called you. Instead, God chose things the world considers foolish in order to shame those who think they are wise. And he chose things that are powerless to shame those who are powerful. God chose things despised by the world, things counted as nothing at all, and used them to bring to nothing what the world considers important. As a result, no one can ever boast in the presence of God"* (1 Corinthians 1:26–29).

We should keep this in mind when we are tempted to despair, when it seems that the Church makes so little headway in its mission in the world. We will always be facing impossible odds. But this is not a problem, for *"nothing is impossible with God"* (Luke 1:37).

> **Prayer:** *Lord, may we be people who genuinely love you from the heart, and not pretenders. Even in our weakness and failures, look inside us and know that our spirit is willing even when our flesh is weak. Show us that everything is possible with you. Amen.*

Day 129   Nehemiah 5–8:1

May 8

> Key Text: I [Nehemiah] replied, "There is no truth in any part of your story. You are making up the whole thing." They [the enemies of the Jews] were just trying to intimidate us, imagining that they could discourage us and stop the work. So I continued the work with even greater determination. (Nehemiah 6:8–9)

By now, we are aware that God's story of redemption through Israel does not go unchallenged. The fallen world resists the authority of God, and proudly defies his Word, so the enemies of Israel infiltrate, seduce, attack and destroy.

But the enemy is sometimes within. Though the Israelites have received God's grace, they still struggle with their sinfulness and their proneness to return to the practices of idolatry—the very thing the Lord says over and over again they must not do.

This is not to point a finger at the Israelites, for we are all just as sinful. Rather, this is to say that sin runs deep in the human heart and the fallen world. The work of God will always be resisted and undermined—especially, as we shall see, when the work progresses.

As the project to rebuild the ruined walls of Jerusalem progresses under the leadership of Nehemiah, the enemies of the people are frustrated by their inability to stop it. However, a problem develops within the Jewish remnant itself. Burdened by taxes imposed by the Persians, and aggravated by a famine, many of the families are becoming destitute and forced to borrow money. What makes it worse is that fellow Jews with resources are charging interest on loans to their brothers. The people complain: *"We belong to the same family as those who are wealthy, and our children are just like theirs. Yet we must sell our children into slavery just to get enough money to live"* (Nehemiah 5:5).

Nehemiah strongly confronts this injustice, stopping the usury and returning the properties used as equity against loans. Furthermore, unlike previous governors, he refuses to exploit his position and indulge in unethical, self-serving practices.

No sooner have the problems *within* been addressed than the people face a threat from *without*. Local leaders from among their enemies, Sanballat and Tobiah, falsely claim that Nehemiah is going to declare himself king of Jerusalem and lead the Jews in rebellion against their Persian lords. Nehemiah doesn't bite and avoids their traps.

When the walls are finished and the doors installed in the gates, Nehemiah sets up a governing structure for the city and an effective security system to guard the walls. Jerusalem is ready to once again function as a city!

> **Focus:** When great challenges arise within a community, it challenges the integrity of its leaders. Where there is credibility and trust, the challenges can be met because the people will believe and follow their leaders. Nehemiah was a leader worthy of respect because he led by example, refusing to take advantage of his position even when he had the right to do so. Nehemiah's challenge to the people to stop taking advantage of each other is taken seriously because the people knew

that he lived by the same standards that he was calling them to live by. In Nehemiah 5:9–19, he follows his challenge with a testimony of his own practices as governor of Judah. It is an impressive statement. So much so, that he is able to say to God out loud before the people: *"Remember, O my God, all that I have done for these people, and bless me for it"* (Nehemiah 5:19).

Prayer: Lord, keep us alert to the schemes of the enemy of our souls, and to the power of our sinful nature to lead us astray. Grant great leaders to your Church, who lead its mission by example and protect it from the forces of this world that try to stop or silence it. Amen.

Day 130   Nehemiah 8:2–10

May 9

Key Text: "But our ancestors were proud and stubborn, and they paid no attention to your commands. They refused to obey and did not remember the miracles you had done for them. Instead, they became stubborn and appointed a leader to take them back to their slavery in Egypt! But you are a God of forgiveness, gracious and merciful, slow to become angry, and rich in unfailing love." (Nehemiah 9:16–17)

With the walls around Jerusalem now rebuilt, Ezra the priest leads the people to the more important rebuilding, the rebuilding of their faith. He calls the people together and reads to them for hours from the Book of the Law. The Levites then continue with instruction: *"They read from the book of the Law of God and clearly explained the meaning of what was being read, helping the people understand each passage"* (Nehemiah 8:8).

When the people hear the Word of God being read and interpreted for them, they begin to weep, both for joy and sorrow. They rejoice to hear God's Word proclaimed, but are convicted of their sins at the same time.

This text illustrates that the Israelites are faithful to their calling only when they keep God's Word at the center of their lives. The Old Testament is their story. Therefore, it needs to be regularly read and interpreted so that all can understand and respond to its powerful claim on their lives.

The most powerful claim upon their lives is God's election and grace. God chose Israel to be his people, not because they deserved it, but because it pleased him to do so. And he remains faithful to them even when they are not faithful to him. Therefore, Nehemiah the governor, Ezra the priest, and all the Levites encourage the people not to mourn but celebrate: *"'Hush! Don't weep! For this is a sacred day.' So the people went away to eat and drink at a festive meal, to share gifts of food, and to celebrate with great joy..."* (Nehemiah 8:11–12).

And so the people celebrate and feast with great joy because *"they had heard God's words and understood them."* The more they understand, the more they are able to reintroduce the commandments of the Lord into their life together.

Chapter 9 recalls that later that month, on October 31, the people assemble again for the reading of the Law, confession and worship. The Levites lead the people in a magnificent prayer that is both a historical overview of Israel's relationship with God and an acknowledgment of his mighty acts as Creator, Redeemer, deliverer, law-giver, judge and warrior on Israel's behalf *(Nehemiah 9:1–38)*.

There is also a confession of the people's perpetual hardheartedness and disobedience that have brought Israel to the present sad state of affairs: *"So now today we are slaves in the land of plenty that you gave our ancestors for their enjoyment! We are slaves here in this good land. The lush produce of this land piles up in the hands of the kings whom you have set over us because of our sins. They have power over us and our livestock. We serve them at their pleasure, and we are in great misery"* (Nehemiah 9:36–37).

At the conclusion of the prayer, the people make a solemn promise to obey the Law of God as issued by his servant Moses, and in particular not to neglect the Temple of the Lord.

Chapter 9 is worth reading carefully as a summary and analysis of the lessons learned in the story of Israel, from Abraham to the exile. If we had only this chapter in the whole Old Testament, we would have a good synopsis of the story of Israel.

Focus: The New Testament describes God's Word as "alive and powerful." It resonates with us like nothing else. We hear God's voice in its words, like the people did when Nehemiah read and interpreted the Old Testament story. The New Testament book of Hebrews begins with the declaration that God speaks to his people, and has spoken most clearly in his Son, Jesus: *"Long ago God spoke many times and in many ways to our ancestors through the prophets. And now in these final days, he has spoken to us through his Son. God promised everything to the Son as an inheritance, and through the Son he created the universe. The Son radiates God's* *own glory and expresses the very character of God, and he sustains everything by the mighty power of his command"* (Hebrews 1:1–3).

Prayer: Lord, thank you for the gift of your Word, which above all reveals Jesus to us. From the perspective of his death, resurrection and teaching, we see more clearly what you have been up to in the story of your people Israel, and how it points forward to our great redemption in Christ. Thanks for those in our lives who have faithfully read and interpreted the Scriptures to us. Amen.

Day 131   Nehemiah 11–13

May 10

> Key Text: For the dedication of the new wall of Jerusalem, the Levites throughout the land were asked to come to Jerusalem to assist in the ceremonies. They were to take part in the joyous occasion with their songs of thanksgiving and with the music of cymbals, harps, and lyres. The singers were brought together from the region around Jerusalem…. (Nehemiah 12:27–28)

Nehemiah's time as governor of Jerusalem is coming to an end, so he takes care of a last few important matters. His first task is to repopulate Jerusalem with Israelites. Lots are cast, and ten percent of the towns of Judah and Benjamin are chosen to move to Jerusalem. These people, along with the priests and Levites who serve in the Temple, are listed in chapter 11.

In chapter 12, at the dedication of the new wall of Jerusalem, we get a picture of how important music is to Israelite faith and worship. Among their other duties, the Levites are singers. They sing accompanied by cymbals, harps, lyres and trumpets. Choirs are formed to sing songs of thanksgiving. Worship is joyous and usually loud.

Nehemiah makes an interesting comment that will give insight to the book of Psalms later on: *"The custom of having choir directors to lead the choirs in hymns of praise and thanksgiving to God began long ago in the days of David and Asaph"* (Nehemiah 12:46). We'll see David's and Asaph's names, along with others, credited as writing various psalms used in Israel's worship.

Nehemiah mentions in chapter 13 that he had been gone from Jerusalem for a period of time while traveling to King Artaxerxes of Babylon. After receiving permission to return, he discovers several lapses of discipline as well as corruption and violations of the Law in the administration of the Temple.

So Nehemiah confronts the violators and demands that everything and everyone be brought back into conformity with God's will—at least as much as is possible with stiff-necked people!

Because the Old Testament books are not arranged in chronological order, it is important to note that these reforming events under Ezra and Nehemiah happen at the end of the period covered in the Old Testament when Israel and Judah are still in exile, except for the remnant that has returned to Jerusalem. The prophets have been active all along, but soon there will be 400 years of prophetic silence until one day a man named John the Baptist will begin to preach!

But we are getting ahead of ourselves. For now, we readers of the Old Testament are left with hope, but also a sense of incompleteness. Scholar Paul House writes:

"God has restored Israel to the promised land, to the chosen site of worship, to a secure defensive position, to a set priesthood, to societal purity and to doctrinal normativeness. Yahweh's sovereignty, mercy, compassion and faithfulness have all once again been proven in real historical circumstances. The people have responded well to these divine attributes and the works that necessarily attend them. A serious remnant serves Yahweh now. Still, long-term promises await fulfillment. It is clear, though, that the source of further blessing is the God of Scripture, who inspires the remnant's adherence to their relationship to Yahweh and Yahweh's word."

Before moving on to the New Testament, we are going to pause and savor the rich wisdom literature, Israel's hymnbook, and the writings of the prophets that nurtured the people's lives during the period of the exile and return.

Focus: Who could have guessed, after the stories of Abraham concerning God's Promise to raise up a special people with land of their own, and the subsequent stories of the Exodus from Egypt across the Red Sea, and the eventual conquering of Canaan, that the Old Testament story would end like this? It seems hopeless. And after 70 years of captivity and exile, only a small number of Jews go back to Jerusalem to patch up the Temple and city walls. The glory days are over! Or are they?

Spoiler alert: Just when it seems that all is lost, God shows up in a most unexpected way.

Day 132   Esther 1–2

May 11

Key Text: And the king loved Esther more than any of the other young women. He was so delighted with her that he set the royal crown on her head and declared her queen instead of Vashti. (Esther 2:17)

Not all exiled Jews chose to go back to Jerusalem with Zerubbabel, Ezra or Nehemiah. In fact, only about 50,000 returned—a *remnant of faith.* Most were reluctant to return to the Promised Land and stayed in Persia, because after 70 years it now seemed like home.

The story of Esther takes place among those who stayed in Persia. Her remarkable story shows that God is present to protect and bless his people even in a foreign land. The story begins at a banquet thrown by King Xerxes for his nobles and officials. It is quite a celebration, lasting *"180 days—a tremendous display of the opulent wealth of his empire and the pomp and splendor of his majesty."*

Following the banquet for his nobles and officials is a banquet for all the common people, from the greatest to the least. And Queen Vashti gives a banquet for the women in the royal palace of the king. After all this partying and a lot of wine, the king is in high spirits. On a whim, he commands that Queen Vashti be summoned because he wants all the men to jealously *"gaze on her beauty, for she was a very beautiful woman."*

There is nothing more flattering than being displayed as the object of male lust, right? Not surprisingly, the queen refuses! So the king, being denied this opportunity to show off his "trophy wife," is furious—and hell hath no fury like a narcissistic king scorned! So Xerxes (shall we say Jerkzies?) summons his advisors to determine a suitable penalty for a queen who refuses to obey.

The advisors, of course, are outraged! They say: *"Queen Vashti has wronged not only the king but also every noble and citizen throughout your empire. Women everywhere will begin to despise their husbands when they learn that Queen Vashti has refused to appear before the king. Before this day is out, the wives of all the king's nobles throughout Persia and Media will hear what the queen did and will start treating their husbands the same way. There will be no end to their contempt and anger"* (Esther 1:16–18).

So, at his advisors' advice, Xerxes issues a written decree—a law of the Medes and Persians that cannot be revoked—that Queen Vashti will be forever banished from the king's presence, so that a *"more worthy"* (i.e., controllable) queen may be found.

So the king's eunuchs search the empire and assemble a royal harem of beautiful young virgins, none more beautiful than a young Jewish woman named Esther. Her cousin Mordecai has raised her after her parents' death, and he has instructed her not to tell anyone of her nationality or background as an exiled Jew.

All the women are given 12 months of special diets and beauty treatments, but Esther stands out from the group. She is given additional pampering, seven maids to serve her, and the best room in the harem.

Without going into the creepy details, Esther is brought to the king, like the rest of the girls, for a "test drive." Xerxes is enthralled with Esther and requests she visit a second time in his private rooms.

Despite this dehumanizing process, Esther manages to keep her dignity and composure. So, *"the king loved Esther more than any of the other young women. He was so delighted with her that he set the royal crown on her head and declared her queen instead of Vashti"* (Esther 2:17).

As queen, Esther continues to keep her nationality and family identity a secret. Meanwhile, her cousin Mordecai is providentially made a palace official and is able, thereafter, to secretly advise her. One day, Mordecai overhears an assassination plot by two of Xerxes' guards. Mordecai tips off Queen Esther, who tells the king, giving Mordecai the credit.

The book of Esther is noteworthy for the fact that God is not mentioned outright, but is seen to be providentially at work throughout, controlling events by strategically positioning his people for a critical moment that is soon to come!

> **Focus:** All who have experienced sexual exploitation and harassment will cringe with empathy for Esther, who gets caught up in the king's wrath, lust and abuse of power. Unfortunately, these kinds of stories happen all the time in the fallen world.

Yet, even here, in the dark shadows of lust and sexual abuse, God is at work to bring dignity and freedom to the exploited and—as we shall see—justice to those who do evil.

Prayer: Lord, thank you once again for the reminder that you see all things, even the darkest affairs of men and nations. Thank you also for the assurance that you are at work in all things for the good of those who love you and are called according to your purposes, like Esther. The story of Esther encourages us to remain strong and faithful to you, even when we are caught in situations that we have no power to avoid. Amen.

Day 133   Esther 3–4

May 12

> **Key Text:** Then Haman approached King Xerxes and said, "There is a certain race of people scattered through all the provinces of your empire who keep themselves separate from everyone else. Their laws are different from those of any other people, and they refuse to obey the laws of the king. So it is not in the king's interest to let them live." (Esther 3:8)

Sometime later, King Xerxes promotes a man named Haman to a position which makes him the most powerful official in the empire. Haman also has the biggest ego in the empire. He leverages his new position by demanding that all the kings' officials show him respect and bow down to him.

But Mordecai, Queen Esther's cousin and a faithful Jew, refuses. This fills Haman with rage. The palace officials try to persuade Haman to tolerate this refusal, since Mordecai has told them that he is a Jew. But Haman refuses the refusal of this Jew. In fact, the more he thinks about it, the more his malevolent pride consumes him: *"...he decided it was not enough to lay hands on Mordecai alone. Instead, he looked for a way to destroy all the Jews throughout the entire empire of Xerxes"* (Esther 3:6).

So Haman stirs up a Persian pogrom against the Jews. Lots (called *purim* in Hebrew) are cast in front of Haman, and the date of March 7 of the following year is chosen for the slaughter.

Haman persuades Xerxes to let him proceed, saying, *"There is a certain race of people scattered through all the provinces of your empire who keep themselves separate from everyone else. Their laws are different from those of any other people, and they refuse to obey the laws of the king."*

So a decree is written in the name of the king, and messengers are sent throughout all the kingdom giving the order that all Jews—young and old, including women and children—must be killed, slaughtered and annihilated on a single day.

And to sweeten the pot, the property of the Jews will be given to those who kill them.

When Mordecai learns what Haman has done, he tears his clothes, puts on burlap and ashes, and cries out in grief. Word of Mordecai's mourning reaches Queen Esther, and upon her inquiry, Mordecai asks her to appeal to the king about what has been decreed. She hesitates, saying that she cannot approach the king without his permission, but Mordecai responds to her with a strong exhortation: *"Don't think for a moment that because you're in the palace you will escape when all other Jews are killed. If you keep quiet at a time like this, deliverance and relief for the Jews will arise from some other place, but you and your relatives will die. Who knows if perhaps you were made queen for just such a time as this?"* (Esther 4:13–14).

So in the face of possible annihilation, Mordecai does not cave in but chooses to act. And Esther, in response to Mordecai's example, chooses to act as well. She will be bold: *"...though it is against the law, I will go in to see the king. If I must die, I must die."*

What happens next is one of the great turns of events to be found in the Bible!

Focus: Moral clarity and boldness in the face of evil are a grace that comes only from God. Mordecai and Esther are found to be trapped in Haman's horrifying plot—a pogrom to annihilate the Jews. Instead of surrendering to fear, they resist this evil and thereby reveal the character of God, who is their deliverer. The coming victory of God over Haman anticipates the final victory of God over sin and death, at the end of history.

Prayer: Lord, thank you for the example of Mordecai and Esther as courageous people of faith who risk their lives for the sake of their brethren. Their exceptional example reminds us of Jesus, who was willing to die for us even while we were still sinners. Amen.

May 13

> Key Text: Then Haman gathered together his friends and Zeresh, his wife, and boasted to them about his great wealth and his many children. He bragged about the honors the king had given him and how he had been promoted over all the other nobles and officials. (Esther 5:10–11)

At Mordecai's suggestion, Queen Esther takes the huge risk of going before King Xerxes without being summoned. But she finds that God has prepared the king to receive her kindly. She tells him that she would like to prepare a banquet for both him and Haman, his highest official. After the meal, the king is pleased, so Esther invites them both back for a second banquet, at which time she will tell him of her request.

Haman goes away from the banquet feeling pretty good about himself. He gathers his friends and wife together to boast about his position, power and wealth—and he has been invited to dine with the king alone, twice! But then his mind turns dark. He cannot enjoy his power while Mordecai won't show him honor. So the group brainstorms and comes up with the cruel idea of erecting a sharpened pole seventy-five feet high. They will ask the king for permission to impale Mordecai on it.

But that night the king cannot sleep, so he pulls out the book of the history of his reign to be read to him. The narrative comes to the plot against his life some time ago, which Mordecai had reported and thus saved the king's life. Xerxes realizes that he hasn't rewarded Mordecai. Meanwhile, Haman happens to be coming to see the king to discuss his own plan for Mordecai. Xerxes asks Haman what he, the king, should do to honor a man who truly pleases him. Thinking that the king is referring to him, Haman suggests royal robes, a special horse which the king himself has ridden, a royal emblem to wear on his head, and an official to precede him in the streets as he proudly rides, calling out, *"This is what the king does for someone he wishes to honor!"*

"'Excellent!' the king said to Haman. 'Quick! Take the robes and my horse, and do just as you have said for Mordecai the Jew....'" And so, Haman's evil plan is frustrated. He returns home dejected and humiliated. His wife, who no doubt has been enjoying Haman's prestige and good fortune

until now, heaps further humiliation on him: *"Since Mordecai—this man who has humiliated you—is of Jewish birth, you will never succeed in your plans against him."*

Of course, Haman still has a banquet to go to, which Esther has prepared. After the meal, the king asks about her request. She tells him that an order has been given to kill her and all her people. Then, she asks that they be spared. Xerxes demands to know who would be so presumptuous as to touch his queen and her people. She replies, *"This wicked Haman is our adversary and our enemy."*

Xerxes is furious about what Haman has done. An attending eunuch points out that Haman has erected a seventy-five-foot pole in order to impale Mordecai. Well, you can guess what happens next! Haman gets the point.

So the story ends as a wonderful example of God's sovereign work, even in the affairs of pagan nations and their leaders. Justice is served and God is able to protect his people from danger through the moral courage and godly wisdom of Mordecai and Esther.

Focus: Why do we love stories like this, where evil is found out and turned on itself? I believe we love these stories because justice is sweet. We intuitively understand good and evil, even when we fail to consistently do good and avoid evil. God has given all people, created in his image, a conscience which bears witness to moral truth. The apostle Paul argues this point when he says, *"Even Gentiles, who do not have God's written law, show that they know his law when they instinctively obey it, even without having heard it. They demonstrate that God's law is written in their hearts, for their own conscience and thoughts either accuse them or tell them they are doing right"* (Romans 2:14-15).

Prayer: Lord, thank you for reminding us that you see all things and can frustrate the evil plans of wicked people. We long for that great day when you will reveal all things and bring final judgment and justice to the whole world. Amen.

Day 135   Esther 8–10

May 14

> Key Text: Mordecai the Jew became the prime minister, with authority next to that of King Xerxes himself. He was very great among the Jews, who held him in high esteem, because he continued to work for the good of his people and to speak up for the welfare of all their descendants. (Esther 10:3)

Queen Esther's courage has caused Haman to be killed for his terrible plan to exterminate the Jews. It also results in Mordecai being appointed manager of Haman's property.

However, the matter of revoking the decree to kill the Jews, which had been sealed with the king's signet ring, is a bit tricky because it is an *"irrevocable law of the Medes and Persians."* But there is always a way around the impossible if one is clever enough. A new decree is written by Xerxes, giving permission for the Jews to fully defend themselves against any who might seek to kill them and take their property. In addition, the Jews can take the property of those they defeat.

This has a sobering effect. Everyone is now afraid of the Jews, whose status has changed in the kingdom because of Queen Esther and Mordecai.

The Jewish people themselves *"were filled with joy and gladness and were honored everywhere. In every province and city, wherever the king's decree arrived, the Jews rejoiced and had a great celebration and declared a public festival and holiday. And many of the people of the land became Jews themselves, for they feared what the Jews might do to them"* (Esther 8:16–17).

So when the day of the original (and irrevocable) decree comes about, there is quite a different outcome than that planned by Haman. The enemies of the Jews—primarily Haman's sons and the soldiers they could employ—now have free rein to attack the Jews on March 7th. But the Jews are prepared, and their enemies are overpowered at every turn. Ironically, the nobles, officers and governors of King Xerxes help the Jews out of fear of Mordecai, who is now a high official.

The Jews win in a big way in all the cities throughout the king's provinces. Xerxes allows one more day of fighting, on March 8th, so that the

Jews can finish the fight. All their enemies are destroyed, but the Jews take no plunder. The ten sons of Haman are killed by impalement on poles, reaping tenfold what their father had sown.

Mordecai records these events and sends letters to the Jews near and far throughout the provinces of King Xerxes, calling on the people to celebrate an annual two-day festival on March 7–8. It will be called the Festival of Purim. The word purim means "lots," referring to Haman having cast lots to determine which day he would carry out his evil plan to exterminate the Jews.

From then on, Purim commemorated the time when the Jews gained relief from their enemies, when their sorrow was turned into gladness and their mourning into joy. *"The Festival of Purim would never cease to be celebrated among the Jews, nor would the memory of what happened ever die out among their descendents"* (Esther 9:28).

They would learn that the Lord God was with his people, even in exile, scattered among the nations.

As for Mordecai, King Xerxes imposed a tribute to him throughout his empire. His achievements were recorded in the official state history so as to never be forgotten.

Meanwhile, *"Mordecai the Jew became the prime minister, with authority next to that of King Xerxes himself. He was very great among the Jews, who held him in high esteem, because he continued to work for the good of his people and to speak up for the welfare of all their descendants"* (Esther 10:3).

So ends the story of Esther.

Focus: The story of Esther is a brilliant example of the quiet sovereignty of God. Though he is never explicitly mentioned in the story, he is at work everywhere in the circumstances which bring about justice and peace for his people. We don't always get to see the outcome of God's working—as we will in the final judgment at the end of history—but in Esther we do get to rejoice at a provisional victory. It points forward to what God will one day do for the whole world.

Prayer: *Lord, grant us all the protection you showed your people in Persia through Mordecai and Queen Esther. May we feel safe and secure in your arms, now and forever. Amen.*

May 15

The Books of Ezra, Nehemiah and Esther are satisfying to read because they make clear what is sometimes hard to see in the moment: God is always working on behalf of his people. He is a just God and his justice *will* prevail. He *will* make things right in the world. This is the case with Israel, even though Israel as a nation has failed God and is dispersed among the nations.

In the stories of Ezra and Nehemiah, God works on behalf of the Jews who have returned to Jerusalem, but are still under Persian rule. Their enemies seek to undermine the repair of the Temple, and later the rebuilding of the walls around Jerusalem, but God frustrates their plans.

With Esther, God works on behalf of his exiled people who live in Persia. In this case, the malignant pride of a power-obsessed man threatens to annihilate the Jews, but God intervenes through the courage of a young Jewish woman and her wise cousin. So we see that God often chooses to do his work through people of faith and courage.

I like to think of human history as a living drama, working itself out in each generation. We each are real players, acting out our lives in real time as the plot moves forward towards its inevitable conclusion—God's redemption of the world.

Another way to think of history is as a vessel which God is piloting. Like a giant passenger ship, moving from one destination to another, the outcome of the journey is certain. However, as the ship moves, there is plenty of drama onboard, as people go about their lives making choices, good and bad, and having experiences together.

But however life aboard ship may seem at any given moment, one thing is certain: God is the pilot and so the ship will arrive at its destination. This is the Bible's point of view. God, the author of our story, and who at a point in time enters into the story himself through Jesus, will ensure that his intended happy ending comes about.

It is important to keep this in mind when we are tempted to grow cynical or lose faith in those times and circumstances when evil seems to be winning. When we are tempted to hide, or look the other way, or give up, or doubt God, we must remember that God's loving purpose and his sovereign working in the world will always have the last word.

In the meantime, we are called to do our part and play our role in response to God's calling, like Ezra, Nehemiah, Esther and Mordecai.

> **Prayer:** *Lord, we are inspired by such great examples of faith and courage as Ezra, Nehemiah, Esther and Mordecai. Help us not to be afraid or disheartened in the circumstances of our own life, but instead persevere in faith and service, knowing that you are with us and for us. Amen.*

Day 137   Job 1–3

May 16

> Key Text: **"I came naked from my mother's womb, and I will be naked when I leave. The Lord gave me what I had, and the Lord has taken it away. Praise the name of the Lord!"** (Job 1:21)

The ancient book of Job, examines a question that is both ancient and contemporary: Why does God allow the innocent to suffer, especially those of his people who wholeheartedly worship and serve him? The story seems to be written as a theological drama in heaven. The opening scene in heaven is a legal setting where *"members of the heavenly court,"* like prosecuting attorneys, present themselves before the Lord with evidence against the behavior of people on earth. They are said to patrol the earth, watching everything that is going on.

On this day, *"the Accuser, Satan,"* is also present. (Is he the chief prosecutor?)

The book opens with the circumstances of a man named Job, who is introduced as *"a man of complete integrity. He fears God and stays away from evil."* Job is the wealthiest man of his community and is a good father and model citizen. With the Accuser before him, God asks Satan: *"Have you noticed my servant Job? He is the finest man in all the earth."*

As Sherlock Holmes might say, "The game is afoot!"

Satan responds with an evil glint in his eye and a broad accusation: *"Yes, but Job has good reason to fear God. You have always put a wall of protection around him and his home and his property. You have made him prosper in everything he does. Look how rich he is! But reach out and take away everything he has, and he will surely curse you to your face!"* (Job

1:9–11).

This is quite an accusation against Job, and by implication against all human beings. Perhaps Satan and his fellow accusers are jealous of human beings, or angry at God for favoring them?

Whatever the motives, God says to Satan: *"All right, you may test him.... Do whatever you want with everything he possesses, but don't harm him physically"* (Job 1:12).

It's important to note that God is in control of this whole narrative. Satan is *"before him"* like a prosecutor before a judge, and he is given permission to test Job and to gather evidence for his accusation, but only within God's stated limits.

The limits, however, are pretty broad—this is going to be an epic moral and spiritual challenge to the *"finest man in all the earth."*

With God's permission, Satan begins to wreak havoc in Job's life. Messenger after messenger arrives with tragic news of natural disasters and criminal behavior. Job has lost his sheep and all his shepherds, his camel and all his servants, his house and all his children. How would Job respond to this furious first blow?

"Job stood up and tore his robe in grief. Then he shaved his head and fell to the ground in worship. He said, 'I came naked from my mother's womb, and I will be naked when I leave. The Lord gave me what I had, and the Lord has taken it away. Praise the name of the Lord!'" (Job 1:20–21). Wow!

In chapter 2, the heavenly court assembles again before the Lord. Having failed to make his case, Satan changes the terms regarding Job: *"... take away his health, and he will surely curse you to your face!"* Again, God gives permission, but forbids Satan to take Job's life. So Job is stricken with terrible boils all over his body. To make things worse, his wife turns on him, telling Job to *"curse God and die."* Again Job shows remarkable faith: *"Should we accept only good things from the hand of God and never anything bad?"*

Eventually, three friends arrive—the people who inspired the phrase, "with friends like these, who needs enemies?!" After a period of silence, Job finally speaks. His pain is overwhelming. In a long monologue, he basically says, I wish I'd never been born. At least when you are dead, you are at rest, where the wicked can no longer afflict you. *"What I have always feared has happened to me. What I dreaded has come true. I have no peace, no quietness. I have no rest; only trouble comes"* (Job 3:25–26).

Job speaks for many who have suffered great loss in this life.

Focus: As the story of Job begins, it appears that Satan has the advantage. His accusations sting and call into question human motivation for believing in God. Perhaps religion is a crutch after all. Those who live in comfort and isolation from the misery of common people may find it easy to indulge themselves in religious fantasies, presuming themselves to be righteous because they are rich. Job's initial response to the terrible losses in his life takes Satan by surprise. His arguments are proved false and he quickly disappears from the story. Cynicism and unbelief are easy, but quickly evaporate in the presence of persevering faith. The story now is not about Satan's accusation, but Job's faith in the midst of suffering.

Prayer: *Lord, we are just as amazed at Job's faith in the midst of suffering and loss, as we are familiar with the emotional trauma that it brings. Grant us the grace to be able to gratefully receive what you give, and spiritually accept what you take away. Amen.*

Day 138   Job 4–7

May 17

Key Text: "At least I can take comfort in this: Despite the pain, I have not denied the words of the Holy One." (Job 6:10)

Now that Job has lost almost everything, including his health and the sympathy of his wife, he becomes depressed and wishes he had never been born. This is a normal reaction to grief and loss. Furthermore, Job's three friends don't have the bedside manner to let him grieve in peace, at least for now. Instead, they engage him in theological debates throughout the rest of the book.

The first of his three friends, Eliphaz the Temanite, now steps up to the mound to throw Job a hardball. Eliphaz is going to argue in poetic fashion and from his own experience in life. He begins by telling Job to suck it up. Job has encouraged many others in their misfortunes, and now, Eliphaz lectures, he must practice what he preaches.

Eliphaz thinks he knows something: *"My experience shows that those who plant trouble and cultivate evil will harvest the same"* (Job 4:8). He learned in a vision at night that no one is innocent before God. So Job may as well go before God and admit that he is guilty and take his medicine: *"But consider the joy of those corrected by God! Do not despise the disci-*

265

pline of the Almighty when you sin. For though he wounds, he also bandages. He strikes, but his hands also heal" (Job 5:17–18). Eliphaz counsels Job to acknowledge the truth and let God restore him, for *"we have studied life and found all of this to be true."*

Job responds strongly in chapter 6: *"Stop assuming my guilt, for I have done no wrong. Do you think I am lying? Don't I know the difference between right and wrong?"* (Job 6:29–30).

Job rebukes Eliphaz for so confidently assuming that Job is guilty and jumping on him with advice instead of listening to his pain. Job is utterly miserable and out of strength. He wishes he were dead. He needs a kind word, but his friend is tone deaf, lecturing him on theology. Job says to the three: *"My brothers, you have proved as unreliable as a seasonal brook that overflows its banks in the spring when it is swollen with ice and melting snow. But when the hot weather arrives, the water disappears. The brook vanishes in the heat"* (Job 6:15–17).

In chapter 7, Job prays, asking God to have compassion for his terrible sufferings. He asks God why he has made him such a target. What has he done? Can't God just leave him alone? Or, if he is somehow guilty, forgive him and let him die.

In times of terrible loss and sorrow, we must allow the suffering person to express his or her grief and anger, even if it is expressed in shocking ways uncharacteristic of them. Rational explanations, even if they are true, are not helpful to someone in deep pain. The only thing we can do with pain is feel it, and over time, let it pass through us. The best gift we can give suffering friends is the gift of presence and a listening ear.

Eliphaz may be right about Job, or not. Job may be right, or have a blind spot. Or perhaps, as we readers of Job know, it may not have anything to do with Job's behavior. How could Job or his friends know that God has given Satan permission to strike Job down to test his faith?

Focus: By beginning the story of Job in heaven, and not on earth, the author tips us off that there are realities and reasons beyond our awareness which influence events on earth. A materialist would deny this, of course. For him, there is no God, and consequently no spiritual realities and reasons. In one sense, he has an easier time of it, saying that there simply is no answer to the question of unjust suffering, so deal with it! The person who believes in God, however, has to wrestle with the seeming dichotomy of a good God who allows evil on earth. The question "why?" is particularly difficult, and often painful. Yet in the end—difficult though it may be—the mystery of God's ways at least allows for the possibility that there *is* an answer, and that if we knew what God knows, we would be in full agreement with what he is doing. With the materialist, there is no answer, only silence.

Prayer: Lord, there are things we can know, and things we cannot know. Our lives are enveloped in mystery as much as clarity. We want to trust you in the dark. Give us friends who will listen and care, and help us all to be such a friend. Amen.

Day 139   Job 8–10

May 18

Key Text: "I am innocent, but it makes no difference to me—I despise my life. Innocent or wicked, it is all the same to God. That's why I say, 'He destroys both the blameless and the wicked.'" (Job 9:21–22)

The second of Job's friends, Bildad the Shuhite, now steps up to make his case against Job. Like Eliphaz, Bildad assumes that Job's sufferings are punishment for sin, either Job's or his children's. Instead of arguing from the perspective of personal experience, like Eliphaz, he argues about God's justice from the historical perspective of those before us: *"Does God twist justice? Does the Almighty twist what is right? … Just ask the previous generation. Pay attention to the experience of our ancestors. For we were born but yesterday and know nothing. Our days on earth are as fleeting as a shadow. But those who came before us will teach you. They will teach you the wisdom of old"* (Job 8:3–10).

What we learn from those before us, Bildad insists, is that a just God will not reject a person of integrity.

While Job agrees to this in principle, he raises the question: How could anyone who feels wrongly accused by God, presume to ask him about this? Job clearly feels innocent, but says that no one can defend himself before God: *"For God is so wise and so mighty. Who has ever challenged him successfully?"* (Job 9:4).

Who is Job that he should try to answer God or even reason with him? There is no real court of appeal to what is said to be God's justice: *"Even if I were right, I would have no defense."* The fact that Job is being punished, even though he insists he is innocent, suggests to him that there can be no fair trial. God will do whatever he wants, so why should Bildad suggest that Job would get a fair hearing? *"I am innocent, but it makes no difference to me—I despise my life. Innocent or wicked, it is all the same to God. That's why I say, 'He destroys both the blameless and the wicked'"* (Job 9:21–22).

Job tells Bildad to look around. The guilty clearly get away with sin and the whole earth is in the hands of the wicked. Who can confidently point to the justice of God and say that the wicked are always punished and the innocent are always blessed? It seems that no matter what the truth may be, Job will be found guilty: *"God is not a mortal like me, so I cannot argue with him or take him to trial. If only there were a mediator between us, someone who could bring us together. The mediator could make God stop beating me, and I would no longer live in terror of his punishment"* (Job 9:32–34).

Job instinctively raises a great issue: If only there *were* a mediator between him and God. The good news is that there is a mediator indeed! It will be the role one day of Jesus the Messiah, who will stand between Holy God and a sinful race, to bear its sin upon himself. And we will be the benefactors.

In the meantime, Job feels wronged; he has no recourse and no power to resist. He wonders out loud whether God is just after all: *"If I am guilty, too bad for me; and even if I'm innocent, I can't hold my head high, because I am filled with shame and misery. … Why, then, did you deliver me from my mother's womb? Why didn't you let me die at birth?"* (Job 10:15–18).

We may ask whether Job could be comforted by the hope of resurrection life. But the clarity and nature of resurrection life really don't appear until after the resurrection of Jesus. In the Old Testament, the nature of life after death is rather vague and uncertain. So Job laments: *"I have only a few days left, so leave me alone, that I may have a moment of comfort before I leave—never to return—for the land of darkness and utter gloom"* (Job 10:20–21).

Indeed, there is a mystery to God's justice that Job senses in his misery and self-pity. He cannot see what is going on in heaven right now, nor can he imagine any good outcome. He surely would be surprised to know that his story would be instructing people thousands of years later!

Focus: Job appears to be cynical when he expresses the hopelessness of questioning God. But he is actually saying this out of a deep humility. Who, indeed, would presume to question God? Who would dare to shake his fist and rage against God's will? Only a fool. Job feels crushed beneath it. How can he resist it? He can only accept it. The brutal truth is, God does what he wants and we must accept it. At least that is how we feel, and as Job says, *"my bitter soul must complain."*

Prayer: Lord, your justice is an issue that is often hard to get into focus, especially when we, or those we know and love, are hurting unfairly. We know there is a bigger picture to this matter, but like Job, we find it hard to find comfort in that knowledge when we are suffering. Help us to trust you when we hurt, and learn to play through the pain! Amen.

Day 140   Job 11–14

May 19

> Key Text: "You claim, 'My beliefs are pure,' and 'I am clean in the sight of God.' If only God would speak; if only he would tell you what he thinks! If only he would tell you the secrets of wisdom, for true wisdom is not a simple matter. Listen! God is doubtless punishing you far less than you deserve!" (Job 11:4–6)

Zophar, the third friend, now steps forward to tell Job what he thinks about the reason for his suffering and, unquestionably, he is the most critical! He not only judges Job, but does so with sarcasm and mean-spiritedness: *"Should I remain silent while you babble on? When you mock God, shouldn't someone make you ashamed? ... Listen! God is doubtless punishing you far less than you deserve! ... If only you would prepare your heart and lift up your hands to him in prayer!"* (Job 11:3–13).

Zophar is a know-it-all who confidently judges others. He points his finger at Job to tell him what he has done wrong and how to fix it. So far, Job's three friends have given a textbook display of how to make things worse and look like jerks doing it!

Understandably, Job is getting angrier. He responds to Zophar with a three-chapter lecture of his own, because he knows a thing or two also! *"You people really know everything, don't you? And when you die, wisdom will die with you! Well, I know a few things myself—and you're no better than I am. Who doesn't know these things you've been saying?"* (Job 12:2–3).

Job goes on to say that those in ease find it easy to tell those in pain what is the matter with them. Their platitudes reveal they know nothing. Job insists again that he is a just and righteous man. What he knows is that we don't understand God's ways. God can do whatever he wants and no one can stop him—even when it seems unjust. For his friends to resort to the "truism" that "God always blesses the righteous and judges the unrighteous," therefore, simply reveals that they have a superficial view of life. If only they would look around, they would see that sometimes the evil prosper and the righteous suffer.

Job is losing patience. At this point, he doesn't want to argue with his friends about God; he wants to argue with God about his case.

So Job again addresses God, saying: *"O God, grant me these two things, and then I will be able to face you. Remove your heavy hand from me, and don't terrify me with your awesome presence"* (Job 13:20–21). In other words, ease up on the suffering and let's talk!

He finishes his lament before God by acknowledging that life is short and full of trouble. Must God keep a close eye on such a frail creature as Job? We humans are weak and sinful, completely at God's mercy, so why doesn't he leave us alone? Let us cope as best we can with the mysteries of our lives and then let us die in peace.

But perhaps there is a larger framework from which to think about the sufferings of this present life. Job wonders whether the dead can live again: *"If so, this would give me hope through all my years of struggle, and I would eagerly await the release of death. You would call and I would answer, and you would yearn for me, your handiwork. For then you would guard my steps, instead of watching for my sins. My sins would be sealed in a pouch, and you would cover my guilt"* (Job 14:14–17).

One again, Job is almost prescient. He has said how good it would be if there were a mediator between man and God to bring them together *(Job 9:33).* Now he imagines that the struggles of life would be bearable if he knew that there was hope of life after death, when God would not only forgive sins but also yearn for a relationship with man, his handiwork.

Job's terrible pain seems to give him a spiritual understanding that his accusers lack. His inclination to argue with God is not a lack of respect, but a deep desire for moral clarity. He wants to know God, not just talk about him. This is man in the image and likeness of God!

Focus: If wisdom and insight are gained through pain more than pleasure, then Job is enrolled in the Graduate School of Wisdom and Insight. His angry outbursts, and occasional sullen self-pity episodes, are balanced by genuine insights which open new vistas of understanding. Perhaps pain and suffering do have a purpose in the larger human story, after all. No one seeks it out, but if it comes, there is opportunity for growth through suffering. Perhaps the end of it is forgiveness of sin and everlasting life in fellowship with God!

Prayer: Lord, may we be as determined as Job to know you, and not be satisfied with a superficial faith of easy answers. Amen.

Day 141 Job 15–17

May 20

> Key Text: "My spirit is crushed, and my life is nearly snuffed out. The grave is ready to receive me. I am surrounded by mockers. I watch how bitterly they taunt me. You must defend my innocence, O God, since no one else will stand up for me."
> (Job 17:1–3)

Job's three friends line up again for a second round of attacks against his insistence that God has unjustly punished him. Eliphaz begins first by intensifying his accusation. He calls Job a windbag: *"Your sins are telling your mouth what to say. Your words are based on clever deception. Your own mouth condemns you, not I"* (Job 15:5–6).

Eliphaz is off to the rhetorical races now. He accuses Job of thinking he is wiser than everyone else, having inside information *"at God's secret counsel."* Nothing in heaven or on earth is pure, yet Job thinks he is righteous. Suffering always marks the way of a sinner like Job. And like Job, sinners live in fear and shake their fists at God, defying the Almighty. The wicked will lose their wealth, and all they have greedily accumulated will be lost, just like Job has lost everything. In the end, they will be cut down in the prime of life. Their branches will never again be green. So watch out, Job!

Job responds to Eliphaz in chapter 16: *"I have heard all this before. What miserable comforters you are! Won't you ever stop blowing hot air? What makes you keep on talking? I could say the same things if you were in my place. I could spout off criticism and shake my head at you. But if it were me, I would encourage you. I would try to take away your grief. Instead, I suffer if I defend myself, and I suffer no less if I refuse to speak"* (Job 16:2–6).

Then Job returns to his lament: *"O God, you have ground me down and devastated my family. ... God hates me and angrily tears me apart. ... God has handed me over to sinners. He has tossed me into the hands of the wicked. ... Then he set me up as his target, and now his archers surround me"*

271

(Job 16:7–13). Even allowing for poetic excess, Job clearly feels wronged and defenseless. There is the silent God on one side, and three noisy friends on the other!

He doesn't back down regarding his guilt: *"I have done no wrong, and my prayer is pure"* (Job 16:17). It may seem that Job is contradicting himself by acknowledging earlier that no mortal can be pure and just *(Job 15:14)* and yet continuing to insist on his own innocence. Perhaps Job is saying, as we might say, that within the limits of human mortality, and in accordance with the accepted rules of moral behavior and religious practice, he has not erred. (We don't want to judge Job by the measure of Pauline theology on righteousness just yet! It would not be fair to him nor to the thrust of the story about Satan's test of Job.)

Once again, Job wishes for a mediator between God and him—to translate to God what he feels and then to hear from God what he is thinking. Without such a mediator, Job himself must defend his innocence before God. No one else will stand up for him! It appears that God has closed his friends' minds to understanding. All they can offer is criticism, mockery and platitudes.

Finally, he addresses his friends again: They need to come back with a better argument, because he finds no wisdom among them. Just the opposite. Darkness is light to them, and light is darkness. And so, there is no hope for Job, not even in the dust of death.

Job's wrestling with God over his suffering, and his friends' hurtful attempts to make sense of guilt and righteousness, leaves him thrashing and gasping in a large pool of sorrow. Our own sorrows may not be as severe as Job's, nor our friends as unhelpful, yet we all feel despair in our own ways. At times, when we feel very much alone and misunderstood, it seems like we are drowning in sorrow.

Focus: It is very significant that the Old Testament boldly and honestly faces this issue right from the beginning. God's Word rings true to us because it is real and gritty. It doesn't look away from the human crisis of life in a fallen world.

Prayer: Lord, we ask you again to help us trust you in the dark days of our soul, when nothing makes sense and we feel that you do not answer our prayers. Amen.

May 21

Walking silently through the Buchenwald concentration camp, I had a hard time comprehending what I was hearing through the digital device describing the horrors that happened there. Photos of American troops liberating the camp at the end of the war reveal looks of similar incomprehension, stunned as they stare at piles of dead bodies and the emaciated bodies of the living. The more I learn of the cold, efficient methods of the "final solution," committed by educated, disciplined humans who believed themselves to be the Master Race, the more irrational it all seems.

Many point to the Holocaust and similar horrors to explain their atheism. How could a good and all-powerful God allow this to happen? Either he is not good, or he is not all-powerful, or he does not exist. It is a compelling argument and there is no easy answer.

The book of Job narrows the problem of evil to the story of one man who believes himself to be unjustly accused and punished by God through terrible suffering. We know the backstory. It is a test, permitted by God and executed by Satan, to see whether this man will remain faithful to God in the midst of suffering. Satan clearly believes that Job will eventually curse God.

Knowing this, however, does not lessen the unfairness of it. Why does God agree to go along?

After all is said and done in the story of Job, we will not receive a clear and simple answer. There is a resolution, and Job accepts it, but that is for later. In the meantime, we can wonder about the presence of evil in the world and consequently the problem of unjust suffering. Many ideas have been proposed, but let me suggest three:

First, God's gift of free will to humans means that evil must be theoretically possible, because if not, the choice to do good and not evil is meaningless. Doing good would not be a free moral choice because doing evil would not be an option. We would be like puppets, able to do only what God directs.

Second, if evil becomes possible through free will, it also becomes inevitable because some will freely choose it. Of course, Genesis chapter 3 tells us that this is exactly what happened when we freely doubted and disobeyed God's word to us. Evil came into the world not of its own accord, but as a consequence of human choice. We opened the door. Thereafter, humans became evildoers. One of the many consequences of evildoing, as I learned at Buchenwald, is moral darkness. What happened there was done by humans who felt they were morally justified and rational. Such moral darkness, in greater and lesser degrees, is present everywhere on earth, and in each of our lives.

Third, what God has chosen to do about evil is *not* to take away human free will, even though our acts of free will have condemned the whole human race before God. To lose our ability to freely choose to love God would be to lose our full humanity as the image of God. Instead, God responded to our crisis by joining us in our suffering through Jesus. One of the purposes of God becoming man was to be the mediator that Job alluded to. He would represent sinful humans before a holy God. As such, he took our suffering, sin and brokenness upon himself and offered his life in our place so that our sin, no matter how awful, would not be the last word. Sin and death—including Buchenwald and all such horrific acts—are *"swallowed up in victory."* Satan may condemn our sins by his accusing finger, but Christ has guaranteed that grace will have the last word. We shall not be condemned but reconciled and restored to God, to one another and to nature.

In the end, the problem of goodness is even more mysterious than the problem of evil.

Prayer: Lord, human sin is a mystery to us. We don't even understand our own sin, let alone that of others. But righteousness is a greater mystery yet. How could you love the human race so much as to forgive an earth-load of sin? Your forgiveness of us through Christ is totally unexpected and undeserved! We give you all the glory! Amen.

Day 143 Job 18–19

> Key Text: "I cry out, 'Help!' but no one answers me. I protest, but there is no justice. God has blocked my way so I cannot move. He has plunged my path into darkness. He has stripped me of my honor and removed the crown from my head. He has demolished me on every side and I am finished. He has uprooted my hope like a fallen tree." (Job 19:7–10)

Bildad returns for his second go at Job. He ups the emotional ante by giving Job what we would call a hellfire and brimstone message: *"Surely the light of the wicked will be snuffed out. The sparks of their fire will not glow. The light in their tent will grow dark. ... Their own schemes will be their downfall. ... They will be thrust from light into darkness, driven from the world"* (Job 18:5–18).

So take that, Job!

I don't know what Bildad's dad did to him, but it couldn't have been good. Most would agree that using fear to motivate change seldom works, and even if it does work, it leaves behind emotional and spiritual damage. Hellfire and brimstone imply that God is always angry and eager to hurt and punish. So, you better watch out!

What can Job say in response to Bildad's vitriol, except to protest his cruel words: *"How long will you torture me? How long will you try to crush me with your words? You have already insulted me ten times. You should be ashamed of treating me so badly"* (Job 19:2–3).

Job won't back down from his main contention: *"But it is God who has wronged me, capturing me in his net."* Now, it could be that Job has a huge blind spot about his sin, but none of his detractors have been able to point to a specific example. They merely assume that because of Job's sufferings, he is guilty. In fact, Job has cried out to God, over and over again, without results: *"I cry out, 'Help!' but no one answers me. I protest, but there is no justice. God has blocked my way so I cannot move"* (Job 19:7–8).

We readers, who know what is going on, feel sympathy for Job. He has gone from a position of wealth, respect, happiness and a good reputation, to a position of total loss. God is against him, and so now are his family, relatives, friends and servants. He even says, *"My breath is repul-*

sive to my wife."

From his position of ignorance about the test of faith that is being played out in heaven, Job's anger at God and his friends is understandable. Who of us has not been angry about injustice in our life or frustrated at the silence of God? As we have noted before, the issue of God's silence in the face of injustice on earth is the reason many cite for their unbelief.

And yet, for all his anger, Job does not curse God. His confidence in his innocence has not diminished. He knows that there is another reason for his horrible suffering, even though he cannot discern it. If only he could hash it out with God face to face! He believes that he will be vindicated, if only after he dies. Only then, perhaps, will he get his day in court.

He ends his response to Bildad with a confident assertion: *"But as for me, I know that my Redeemer lives, and he will stand upon the earth at last. And after my body has decayed, yet in my body I will see God! I will see him for myself. Yes, I will see him with my own eyes. I am overwhelmed at the thought!"* (Job 19:25–27).

In the ancient world, a redeemer or kinsman-redeemer (as in the story of Ruth) is a close relative who comes to one's defense and aid. Since no one, including family members, are taking Job's side, could Job see God as his redeemer? It would not seem likely, given Job's anger at him. But who else could it be? As Job has already noted, only God has unquestioned knowledge and power.

So a likely understanding is that Job believes that God will eventually stand up for him, if not in this life, then at least in the heavenly court after he dies. Of course, Job does not know that God has already spoken for him, but we readers do. God is his redeemer.

Focus: We all know that earthly justice is imperfect. The meaning of events is disputed. The heroes and villains are differently labeled, depending on who is writing the history. Will the truth about things ever be known and justice satisfied? The book of Job would say, yes it will. The God who sometimes hides from us, and refuses to answer our questions, is nevertheless the Judge of the whole earth. People will be ultimately held accountable for the things they do. The truth will come out. The living ought to take this to heart.

Prayer: *Lord, we are once again taken by surprise at Job's faith, arising out of his misery and loss. Forgive us for being so ungrateful to you even in the midst of our abundance and ease. Amen.*

May 23

> Key Text: "But who can teach a lesson to God, since he judges
> even the most powerful? One person dies in prosperity,
> completely comfortable and secure, the picture of good health,
> vigorous and fit. Another person dies in bitter poverty, never
> having tasted the good life. But both are buried in the same dust,
> both eaten by the same maggots." (Job 21:22–26)

Zophar makes his final appearance before Job and fills the air with empty clichés. What he says is more of the same, but you've got to hand it to him and his two friends for their inventive ways of making the same point over and over again.

He is *"greatly disturbed"* that Job is not taking his input to heart. He has *"had to endure"* Job's insults, he says, so it seems Zophar is now playing the victim. Perhaps, this final time, Job will listen to his instruction about the fate of the wicked and soften his heart?

Zophar begins by asserting that from the beginning of time, *"the triumph of the wicked has been short-lived and the joy of the godless has been only temporary ... they will vanish forever, thrown away like their own dung."* The wicked savor the sweet taste of their sin for a while, but then it turns sour in their stomachs. Their evil lives of injustice toward the poor suddenly turn on them and unravel: *"Nothing is left after they finish gorging themselves. Therefore, their prosperity will not endure. ... May God give them a bellyful of trouble"* (Job 20:21–23).

After losing everything, the wicked will die and finally face the judgment of God, and it will be broadcast throughout heaven and earth: *"The terrors of death are upon them. Their treasures will be thrown into deepest darkness. A wildfire will devour their goods, consuming all they have left. The heavens will reveal their guilt, and the earth will testify against them"* (Job 20:25–27).

Zophar confidently makes his final point and sits down: *"This is the reward that God gives the wicked. It is the inheritance decreed by God."* End of case, Job. This is your life.

But Job hasn't lost confidence in his case yet, and puts Zophar in his place: *"Bear with me, and let me speak. After I have spoken, you may resume mocking me. My complaint is with God, not with people. I have good reason to be so impatient. Look at me and be stunned. Put your hand over your mouth in shock."*

Job believes that Zophar's empty clichés don't hold up under inspection. Zophar assumes that the prosperity of the wicked is always short lived and their judgment certain, yet if we are honest, this is not what we see: *"Why do the wicked prosper, growing old and powerful? They live to see their children grow up and settle down, and they enjoy their grandchildren. … They sing with tambourine and harp. They celebrate to the sound of the flute. They spend their days in prosperity, then go down to the grave in peace. And yet they say to God, 'Go away. We want no part of you and your ways. Who is the Almighty, and why should we obey him?'"* (Job 21:7–15).

After living full lives and prospering from their wickedness, they die with full honors: *"A great funeral procession goes to the cemetery. Many pay their respects as the body is laid to rest, and the earth gives sweet repose"* (Job 21:33).

So, Job convincingly makes the case that life is *not* as Zophar presents it. Zophar should not be so confident about judging Job's situation. There are mysteries concerning the ways of God that must be accepted without resorting to easy judgments and empty clichés.

Try as he and his friends may, Zophar has not given Job, or us, any further insights into the problem of unjust suffering.

Focus: The more a person talks, the quicker an unconvincing argument loses the wind in its sails. Repeating the same limp arguments with different words does not make the wind blow. Human reasoning goes only so far. Only the simple are confident in their arguments about the mysteries of life and the ways of God. The wise know what they don't know.

Prayer: *Lord, we admit that it is frustrating to see the evil prosper, while so many suffer hardships that could be relieved with generosity, justice and love. Help us not to forget them, because you haven't forgotten them. You minister to them through us as your agents of justice and love. So many things in this life are mysterious to us. Help us to be faithful to you, even when we don't understand what you are doing. Amen.*

May 24

Key Text: "Why doesn't the Almighty bring the wicked to judgment? Why must the godly wait for him in vain?" (Job 24:1)

The third and final round of the debate with Job begins with Eliphaz. He has run out of arguments and ideas, but that doesn't stop him from finding another angle. God has brought his judgment on Job, Eliphaz claims, because of his wickedness, even if that wickedness has not been identified. So Eliphaz helpfully suggests some possible sins: *"For example, you must have lent money to your friend and demanded clothing as security. Yes, you stripped him to the bone. You must have refused water for the thirsty and food for the hungry. You probably think the land belongs to the powerful and only the privileged have a right to it! You must have sent widows away empty-handed and crushed the hopes of orphans"* (Job 22:6–9).

With Job's hypothetical sins enumerated, Eliphaz now challenges him to quit doing them! Stop ignoring God's judgment. Submit to God and he will give you peace; you will be restored. Give up your lust for money and the Almighty himself will be your treasure. Then when you pray, God will hear your prayers and you will succeed in whatever you choose to do.

So Eliphaz not only points out hypothetical sins, he also counsels Job on some hypothetical steps toward reconciliation!

Nothing yet has caused Job's friends to pause a moment and think about what they are saying. None have taken him seriously. Job's protest has remained consistent: He complains that he cannot find God despite his earnest efforts. He believes that if he could find him and present his case, God would give him a fair hearing. Then Job would listen and understand.

But wherever Job looks—north, east, south and west—he cannot find God. But God surely knows where Job is, and Job is confident that when God tests him, he *"will come out as pure as gold. For I have stayed on God's paths; I have followed his ways and not turned aside"* (Job 23:10–11). There doesn't seem to be anything Job can do. It seems that God has made up his mind to allow Job to suffer for reasons he has not shared, so Job has no recourse but to wait in fear.

Still the central question about God remains: *"Why doesn't the Almighty bring the wicked to judgment? Why must the godly wait for him in vain?"* Waiting for justice seems to be the big issue. On the issue of God judging the wicked, Job and his friends are in agreement—God *will* judge the wicked. Where they still disagree—and this is the tension of the story— is over Job's innocence before God. Is Job one of the wicked? They cannot believe that God would allow a righteous man to suffer.

Job obviously disagrees. He is a righteous man, and he is suffering!

Judgment *is* coming, though not necessarily right now or even in this life. In chapter 24, Job lists all the sins of the wicked against the poor and then describes how their thoughts and behavior are controlled by darkness, and their lives end in judgment. *"They may be allowed to live in security, but God is always watching them. And though they are great now, in a moment they will be gone like all others, cut off like heads of grain. Can anyone claim otherwise? Who can prove me wrong?"* (Job 24:23–25).

It is a small consolation, but the wicked who prosper will eventually die, just as certainly as the poor whom they exploit will die.

We do not have any further insight into what Satan the Accuser is muttering before God and the other members of the heavenly court regarding Job's test to date *(Job 1:6–11)*. I cannot imagine that Satan comprehends Job. Job's faith and humility, even with the loss of everything and without any understanding of what is going on, vindicate God's sovereign choice to honor man-in-the-image-of-God over all other created life, even the angels of heaven.

Focus: As Job and his friends argue back and forth about the matter of Job's innocence, one point of agreement rises to the surface: God sees all that happens on earth and will finally judge the wicked and the innocent when they die. Sometimes that is the only satisfaction and hope we get. "Justice is mine," says the Lord. "I will repay them." Accepting this by faith, and refusing to become judge and jury in God's place, saves a lot of additional misery in our lives.

Prayer: Lord, each of us has a life story in which you are allowing tests of faith. Sometimes we think we understand, and other times we are perplexed. But give us the grace we each need to trust and obey you in the hard times as well as the good times. Amen.

May 25

> Key Text: "And this is what [God] says to all humanity: 'The fear of the Lord is true wisdom; to forsake evil is real understanding.'" (Job 28:28)

All of the arguments by Job's friends against his innocence have been made. Bildad now delivers another angry screed as the closing statement, and the prosecution rests its case.

Bildad impatiently reminds Job that God is powerful and dreadful, with a mighty heavenly army. No mortal can be innocent before him, despite what Job claims. *"God is more glorious than the moon; he shines brighter than the stars. In comparison, people are maggots; we mortals are mere worms"* (Job 25:5–6).

After firing off his final rhetorical load, the prosecuting maggot sits down, no doubt with a satisfied and smug look on his face.

The patience of Job has been severely tested. He responds once again, even though it is like casting pearls before swine—which, as Jesus will later remind us, has very little chance of being appreciated by the swine.

Job points out the obvious, that his friends have been no help to him at all. Of course God is powerful. If anything, he is more powerful than Bildad seems to understand. Job continues with a moving exposition of God as Creator and how the whole of creation comes from him, depends on him and trembles in his presence: *"These are just the beginning of all that he does, merely a whisper of his power. Who, then, can comprehend the thunder of his power?"* (Job 26:14).

Certainly not Bildad. If anything, Job has an even greater understanding of God's sovereign power and knowledge, and of the certainty of his judgment. Nevertheless, he insists on his innocence. He will not make a false confession just to get his friends off his back: *"As long as I live, while I have breath from God, my lips will speak no evil, and my tongue will speak no lies. I will never concede that you are right; I will defend my integrity until I die. I will maintain my innocence without wavering. My conscience is clear for as long as I live"* (Job 27:3–6).

People know where to dig for treasures in the earth, Job notes, but they can't seem to find the wisdom of heaven. The wisdom we seek does not come from the earth, and it cannot be purchased. But God knows where to find it because wisdom comes from him. Therefore, we can only find wisdom by fearing God: *"The fear of the Lord is true wisdom; to forsake evil is real understanding"* (Job 28:28).

For Job, fearing God means keeping his commandments, for in them we discover wisdom for life. The rebel thinks that he becomes free by shaking off the chains of God's Law, but he is only deceiving himself. Such a person is a fool, for *"only fools say in their hearts, 'There is no God.'"* Job's friends think *he* is a fool, but he knows in his heart that he does fear God and has kept his commandments.

His anger at God is not disrespect for God. It arises from the conviction that he is being treated unjustly. If indeed he has done something wrong, God has not revealed what it is. Why is God silent? Why does Job suffer?

Focus: Why is fear (or profound respect) for God the beginning of wisdom? Because without God, there is no ultimate truth, upon which wisdom is built. God has expressed himself in his creation. There are spiritual laws which inform and govern human flourishing, just as there are physical laws which inform and govern the operation of the material world. As we live life as God intended (i.e., follow his commandments), we discover by experience that they are wise and we are blessed by them. It is trendy in our culture to be a lawbreaker—to color outside the lines—but in the end, the rebel against God becomes a fool.

Prayer: Lord, despite how frustrated Job was with you for your silence, he never ceased to believe that wisdom is found in keeping your commandments. May we, in our ease and pleasure, always remember the same, lest we, in apathy or pride, cease to fear you. Amen.

Day 147   Job 29–31

May 26

Key Text: "I long for the years gone by when God took care of me, when he lit up the way before me and I walked safely through the darkness. When I was in my prime, God's friendship was felt in my home. The Almighty was still with me, and my children were around me. My cows produced milk in abundance, and my groves poured out streams of olive oil." (Job 29:1–6)

Job's three friends have made their case against Job, insisting that he is suffering because he deserves it. He has sinned and God is punishing him—it is as simple as that. The sooner he acknowledges his sin and repents of it, the sooner Job's suffering will end. Sadly, their tone has been mocking and condescending. They think they know more than Job about his situation and let him know it, without kindness or compassion.

Understandably, Job has met this assault with anger and a stubborn defense of his innocence before God. We are supportive of Job because, unlike his friends, we know what is going on. Job is indeed innocent. But while we are on Job's side, we wonder why God has given permission to Satan to test Job so severely.

So now, in chapters 29 through 31, Job reflects on his life and does a moral inventory. He remembers the life he lost—a life of contentment, abundance, and respect. He was praised by others for his help to the poor, his honest dealings, and his pursuit of justice for the weak. When he spoke, people listened to his wisdom.

He once lived like a good and righteous king among his people, but now he is mocked by those who are in no position to judge him. His young moralist friends have sought to tutor him about righteousness, while immoral neighbors find his humiliation to be a source of glee, taunting him with vulgar songs, like an ancient version of "Saturday Night Live."

This has left Job depressed and in great physical pain: *"With a strong hand, God grabs my shirt. He grips me by the collar of my coat. He has thrown me into the mud. I'm nothing more than dust and ashes. I cry to you, O God, but you don't answer. I stand before you, but you don't even look. You have become cruel toward me. You use your power to persecute me. You throw me into the whirlwind and destroy me in the storm"* (Job 30:18–22).

In time, God will finally speak to Job from a whirlwind, but for now he is silent.

Job summons the courage to do a rigorous moral inventory to see if there is some sin he has possibly overlooked. He adds self-imprecation to this exercise, calling for punishment if indeed he is guilty of any of these sins against God's Law. So he asks himself, in the presence of God: Have I lusted, lied, committed adultery, been unfair to servants, refused to help the poor, used my influence to sway a judge, put my trust in money, committed idolatry, rejoiced over the misfortunes of others, sought revenge, refused hospitality to a stranger, or tried to hide secret sins in my heart?

Having rigorously searched his heart and found no guilt, he cries out: *"If only someone would listen to me! Look, I will sign my name to my defense.*

Let the Almighty answer me. Let my accuser write out the charges against me. I would face the accusation proudly. I would wear it like a crown" (Job 31:35–36).

This is all Job has to say.

Focus: When all is said and done in our earthly life, we will stand alone before God. Others have been our friends or enemies along the way, but in the end God is the only one we will answer to. He is the Judge of all the earth. Christians will not be judged regarding heaven or hell. That judgment already took place when Jesus died on the cross. By faith in him, we received forgiveness and everlasting life. But we will have to give an account for the stewardship of our lives as Christians. What did we do with the grace given us? In light of that heavenly performance appraisal, we might follow Job's example by regularly doing a rigorous moral inventory. To use a computer analogy, think of this moral inventory as defragmenting your life and relationships.

Prayer: *Lord, you are indeed the Judge of all the earth. While we make our moral arguments and defenses, you alone see everything and know the truth. Despite the anguish we feel when truth seems not to triumph on earth, you will judge all things one day, and all things will be made right. In this, like Job, we take our comfort. Amen.*

Day 148 Job 32–34

May 27

> **Key Text:** Then Elihu son of Barakel the Buzite, of the clan of Ram, became angry. He was angry because Job refused to admit that he had sinned and that God was right in punishing him. He was also angry with Job's three friends, for…their inability to answer Job's arguments. (Job 32:2–3)

Job has said all he has to say, and his three "friends" have given up because of Job's insistence that he is innocent. For all their talk, they are nowhere closer to understanding the reason for Job's suffering.

Unfortunately, the blessed silence of their departure is broken by a new voice—that of a younger man named Elihu, who has kept his silence out of respect for his elders. So now Job's life will be picked apart by someone with even *less* life experience and wisdom than his three omniscient friends!

Like everyone else in this debate, Elihu is angry: *"He was angry because*

Job refused to admit that he had sinned and that God was right in punishing him. He was also angry with Job's three friends, for they made God appear to be wrong by their inability to answer Job's arguments" (Job 32:2–3).

What, if anything, does Elihu have to contribute? Well, despite his youth, he thinks he has a lot to say. He is frustrated with Job and his elders, and *"full of pent-up words."* He thinks the others have been too easy on Job, and so with the uber-confidence that only youth and inexperience can muster, he plunges in, daring Job to answer him if he can! (But he promises not to come down too hard on Job!)

His first argument: Job is wrong in saying that God does not answer his demand for reasons for his suffering. The fact is, Elihu says, *"God speaks again and again, though people do not recognize it"* (Job 33:14).

How does God speak? Elihu says that he speaks through dreams, visions and whispers. He even disciplines sinners with pain on their sickbeds. He may then send an angel to intercede for the suffering one. When confession is made, forgiveness comes and health returns. The suffering one will admit to his friends that he had sinned after all, and it was ultimately not worth hiding it.

There it is! So Job, have you got anything you want to say? No? Then listen to me and I will teach you wisdom!

Elihu now backs up and dumps a truckload of wisdom on Job.

He accuses Job of being unprecedented in his irreverence, blaming God for doing wrong: *"Everyone knows that God doesn't sin! The Almighty can do no wrong. He repays people according to their deeds. He treats people as they deserve. Truly, God will not do wrong. The Almighty will not twist justice"* (Job 34:10–12).

God watches how people live; he sees everything they do. No one can hide from him. In the night, he overturns and destroys them. He strikes them down because they are wicked, doing it openly for all to see—*are you listening, Job?* If God chooses to remain quiet, who can criticize him—*does the shoe fit, Job?* Must God tailor his justice to your demands—*sound familiar, Job?*

Elihu is wound up pretty tight with anger by now, and finally delivers what he hopes will be the strikeout pitch: *"Job, you deserve the maximum penalty for the wicked way you have talked. For you have added rebellion to your sin; you show no respect, and you speak many angry words against God"* (Job 34:36–37).

And Job responds to this angry, young know-it-all with the most irritating response of all—he says nothing. Elihu needs to catch his breath, but he'll be back one more time.

> **Focus:** No one likes an insufferable know-it-all, especially a young one. When we are young, we are omniscient. We see clearly what older people have forgotten or never figured out in the first place. But with age—and lots of suffering—comes wisdom. Suddenly we don't know so much anymore. We become more tolerant of others and more open to hearing from them. The gifts of listening, empathy and tolerance come later in life for most of us. When they come, use them generously.
>
> **Prayer:** *Lord, keep us from being know-it-alls. Give us humility and the willingness to wait until you make things clear in our lives. Even when the clarity doesn't come, help us to trust you and praise you in our suffering. Amen.*

Day 149   Reflection

May 28

The enduring value of the book of Job is its unflinching honesty about human suffering. The portrayal is real and unrelenting; there is no easy resolution. Instead, there is debate and angry disagreement about possible reasons, including the injustice of God.

Someone has described Judaism as a continuing argument with God. If so, Job provides the template: *"God might kill me, but I have no other hope. I am going to argue my case with him. But this is what will save me—I am not godless. If I were, I could not stand before him"* (Job 13:15–16).

Job's protest is not the easy debate of skeptics and academics, but the agonizing search of suffering believers who truly want to know the mind of God and seek his justice. The verbal swordfight between Job and his friends may seem off-putting, especially when accusations and mockery fly back and forth. But what other human emotions are appropriate in facing the horror of unjust suffering?

It is morally satisfying to see good people succeed in life, and bad people get what's coming to them. But many experiences in life are not so morally clear. The tension within Job is not a disagreement over whether God will one day judge everyone: *"For God watches how people live; he sees everything they do. No darkness is thick enough to hide the wicked from his eyes. We don't set the time when we will come before God in judg-*

ment" (Job 34:21–23).

The question for Job is why God allows innocent people to suffer now on earth. Job is convinced that his suffering is unjust because he is innocent before God. He has rigorously searched his heart to discern hidden sin, and finding none, he has asked, begged and screamed at God to tell him why he is suffering!

But so far, there is nothing but silence from heaven.

We, the readers, have to decide what we are going to do about this. Some may say there is no God, or if there is, he does not see what goes on, so don't expect that justice will come. Others would say that God is not good and does not care, so we must reject him and fend for ourselves.

But surprisingly, Job stubbornly refuses to go down either of those roads. Yes, he is angry at God, and so miserable that he wants to die, but he never walks away from faith: *"But as for me, I know that my Redeemer lives, and he will stand upon the earth at last. And after my body has decayed, yet in my body I will see God! I will see him for myself. Yes, I will see him with my own eyes. I am overwhelmed at the thought!"* (Job 19:25–26).

This is Job's test. There is tension in believing in a God who is good. Will we believe God even if everything is taken from us *(Job 1:9–11)?* Can we trust God in the dark? Can we live with mystery? Will we survive the anguish of not knowing? Job's life is offered by God as the supreme example of one whose faith is severely tested and yet prevails.

> **Prayer:** *Lord, the mystery of suffering is great, especially unjust suffering. When you permit it in our lives, grant us also the courage and faith to trust you in the dark and live with the tension. Amen.*

Day 150   Job 35–37

May 29

> Key Text: Then Elihu said: "Do you think it is right for you to claim, 'I am righteous before God'? For you also ask, 'What's in it for me? What's the use of living a righteous life?'" (Job 35:2–3)

After taking a breather, Elihu returns to continue his "wisdom dump" on Job. He begins by addressing two of Job's persistent complaints.

The first: Where is the justice of living a righteous life if you're going to suffer anyway? His answer is that whether or not you live a righteous life, it has no effect on God's justice. A righteous life doesn't benefit or alter God—it only benefits you and those around you.

The second: Why doesn't God hear us when we pray, especially when we are oppressed? His answer is that God always hears our prayers, except when they come from pride.

Neither answer satisfies Job, because his contention all along is that he doesn't deserve God's punishment and he can't seem to get God's attention. Elihu basically tells him, too bad!

Next Elihu, a self-proclaimed "man of great knowledge," instructs Job about the righteousness of God. God is surely not mistreating him because God is mighty in power and understanding, and he always gives justice to the afflicted. He never takes his eyes off the innocent *(so you must not be innocent, Job)*, and those who listen to God will be blessed with prosperity throughout their lives *(so apparently you haven't been listening, Job)*.

Stop being obsessed with judgment and justice, Job. Instead, accept this suffering from God as a means to keep you from a life of evil: *"Look, God is all-powerful. Who is a teacher like him? No one can tell him what to do, or say to him, 'You have done wrong.' Instead, glorify his mighty works, singing songs of praise"* (Job 36:22–24).

All true, and eloquently stated. Elihu is sincere, even if arrogant in his youth and annoying in his presumption. He says, *"My heart pounds as I think of this. It trembles within me."*

Elihu concludes his exhortation by reminding Job that *"God is greater than we can understand."* He then points to more than thirty illustrations from the natural world of God's wisdom and power, urging Job to pay attention. Stop and consider the wonderful miracles of God: *"We cannot imagine the power of the Almighty; but even though he is just and righteous, he does not destroy us. No wonder people everywhere fear him. All who are wise show him reverence"* (Job 37:23–24).

So with this, all of Job's counselors are done. They have said much that is true about God and generally true about human life on earth. And yet, the tension remains. There is a truckload of uncertainty that has not been explained by the certainties of Job's friends. His sufferings remain and his questions have not been answered. All that can be said has been said. The only hope is for God himself to speak.

And speak he will.

Day 151   Job 38–39

May 30

Key Text: Then the Lord answered Job from the whirlwind:
"Who is this that questions my wisdom with such ignorant
words? Brace yourself like a man, because I have some questions
for you, and you must answer them." (Job 38:1–2)

For 37 chapters, God has been silent as Job and his interrogators debate the reasons for Job's suffering. In this debate, both the nature of God and the nature of man have been explored. At times the debate has touched upon profound mysteries about God with rhetorical eloquence. At other times, the debate has fallen into churlish name-calling and angry flame-throwing between the participants.

Job and his friends are, as someone has described it, caught in history between harsh reality and a fuller revelation of God's ways. Job doesn't have the benefit of Moses' teaching, let alone that of Jesus. So we, the readers, watch with anticipation as they try to figure out the puzzle with several key pieces not yet on the table.

The key question of the debate has been God's justice. Job's friends are convinced that Job has sinned and that is why he has suffered—suffering is God's righteous punishment. Job has insisted that he has not sinned and that God's punishment has been unjust. He recognizes that God is Almighty and can do whatever he wants, but Job demands to know why. Hard issues are raised in the book of Job, and God is presented as one who may be questioned.

Finally, God speaks to Job.

He doesn't speak in the way Job had hoped, because he doesn't explain himself. He answers Job from a storm—*"the whirlwind"*—using a powerful force of nature to indicate his greatness. Job has questioned God, but God now questions Job: *"Who is this that questions my wisdom with such ignorant words? Brace yourself like a man, because I have some questions for you, and you must answer them"* (Job 38:2–3).

The questions are rhetorical, but probing, beginning with: *"Where were you when I laid the foundations of the earth? Tell me, if you know so much. Who determined its dimensions and stretched out the surveying line? What supports its foundations, and who laid its cornerstone as the morning stars sang together and all the angels shouted for joy?"* (Job 38:4–7).

For two full chapters, God barrages Job with questions about the mysteries of nature. The questions are meant to establish God as the sole Creator and sustainer of material and biological life. Can the creation put the Creator on trial?

He is impressing upon Job that his ways are beyond our understanding and his power is far greater than we ever imagined. God gets in Job's face a bit with comments like, *"But of course you know all this! For you were born before it was created, and you are so very experienced"* (Job 38:21). But he is not trying to humiliate Job—quite the opposite. By speaking directly to Job, and revealing his greatness—as he does with Moses in another way—God is expressing his love for Job. He does not condemn Job as a sinner like his friends were certain God would do, but he ennobles Job by taking him seriously.

Job is learning that God is on his side after all, even when he allows Job to suffer. He can be trusted.

Focus: The great reversal has begun in the story of Job: God begins to question Job. It is remarkable that God speaks. By doing so, he shows his regard for Job and for all the creation. If God did not exist, or did not care to involve himself with his creation, then we would only be left with silence from heaven and endless, fruitless debate on earth. But the God of the Bible not only exists; he speaks and acts in human history, because his greatest purpose and pleasure in bringing the universe into existence is to have a relationship with us!

Prayer: Lord, it is amazing to think that you would want to make yourself known to us as you did when you spoke to Moses and Job. We are so honored to know you, even though our knowledge is so incomplete—like seeing in a glass, darkly. We look forward to the day when we shall see you with clarity. Amen.

Day 152   Job 40–42

May 31

> Key Text: "I had only heard about you before, but now I have seen you with my own eyes. I take back everything I said, and I sit in dust and ashes to show my repentance." (Job 42:5–6)

The story of Job comes to a conclusion with God breaking his silence and questioning Job. God makes the case for his power and wisdom, to which Job humbly replies, *"I am nothing—how could I ever find the answers? I will cover my mouth with my hand. I have said too much already. I have nothing more to say"* (Job 40:4–5).

God presses Job on his presumption to discredit God's justice. While he acknowledges Job's strong concern for justice, he shows Job that he doesn't really understand what he is talking about—a reality we can all appreciate when probing the mysteries of God. Two examples from nature are given to show Job that God's moral reasoning and just actions are superior.

God points to the strongest earthly creatures Job would be familiar with: the Behemoth (perhaps the hippopotamus) and the Leviathan (maybe the crocodile). The descriptions of these powerful, almost mythic creatures are extravagant, but it's to make a point—God is too powerful and frightening to injure, capture or tame, although plenty of philosophers have tried!

You can't put a ring in the nose of Behemoth, nor can you make Leviathan a pet like a bird: *"No, it is useless to try to capture it. The hunter who attempts will be knocked down. And since no one dares to disturb it, who then can stand up to me? Who has given me anything that I need to pay back? Everything under heaven is mine"* (Job 41:9–11).

When God finishes talking, Job is totally humbled and overwhelmed. He says to God, *"You asked, 'Who is this that questions my wisdom with such ignorance?' It is I—and I was talking about things I knew nothing about, things far too wonderful for me"* (Job 42:3).

Job is changed, persuaded, and repentant—not because he understands, but because now he realizes that he didn't understand anything. But how does Job know this? It is a rational conclusion, but it goes beyond reason. He is more than convinced; he is overwhelmed. Something deeper has happened. A beam of light has pierced the darkness; Job has experienced God personally! *"I had only heard about you before, but now I have seen you with my own eyes. I take back everything I said, and I sit in dust and ashes to show my repentance"* (Job 42:5–6).

Job has suffered to the point of death, yet he still believes. This is the very thing Satan denied he would do, but Job has proven him wrong and passed the test. Something profoundly important has been revealed in Job's test—the spiritual capacity of human beings to suffer without understanding and still believe. It is the glory of man and woman in the image of God!

In the end, Job's fortunes and reputation are restored to him.

We learn from the book of Job that a loving God may allow his people to suffer for a while, sometimes for reasons we don't understand. We also learn that those who trust God will not be put to shame. This has been a comfort for the legions of Christians throughout the ages who have suffered even to the point of death because of their faith.

The book of Job implies that there is a depth of experience with God that only those who suffer much will experience. This will be a recurring theme as we move through the Bible.

From one perspective, the fact of suffering is itself evidence, not of God's absence, but of God's presence in our lives and therefore a reason for hope. 1 Peter 1:6–7 says, *"So be truly glad. There is wonderful joy ahead, even though you have to endure many trials for a little while. These trials will show that your faith is genuine. It is being tested as fire tests and purifies gold—though your faith is far more precious than mere gold. So when your faith remains strong through many trials, it will bring you much praise and glory and honor on the day when Jesus Christ is revealed to the whole world."*

Focus: There is no intellectual argument that can absolutely prove God's existence. One can convincingly argue that all the evidence strongly points to that conclusion, but skeptics can always find plausible reasons to doubt. Indeed, doubting is easy. Faith is difficult. Rational evidence is important to faith, but in the end, faith is a letting go of doubt and trusting that the Other is there to catch you. In other words, faith in God is a relationship; in fact, it is the most fundamental of all relationships—of Creator to creature! God has brought us into existence and sustains us in life, moment by moment. Because God is good, he can be trusted. The "letting go" of faith, therefore, is the most rational thing we can do. When Job says, *"now I have seen you with my own eyes,"* he means that he has finally "gotten it." He doesn't understand it all, but he joyfully, humbly embraces the mystery.

Job becomes the forefather of all theologians whose task is, as the great Medieval thinker, Anselm of Canterbury, put it: *faith seeking understanding.*

Prayer: *Lord, the mystery of suffering and pain is great. It tests our faith and resolve. But as we ponder this mystery through Job's experience, we see where human suffering is not inconsistent with your love for us. In the end, the suffering of your Son on our behalf—a suffering far greater than Job's—is what leads us to glory and the New Creation. Give us the strength we need to pass the tests you permit. Amen.*

Day 153   Psalms 1–6

June 1

> Key Text: "Oh, the joys of those who do not follow the advice
> of the wicked, or stand around with sinners, or join in with
> mockers. But they delight in the law of the Lord, meditating on
> it day and night. They are like trees planted along the riverbank,
> bearing fruit each season. Their leaves never wither, and they
> prosper in all they do." (Psalm 1:1–3)

The book of Psalms is perhaps the most loved and frequently read book of the Bible. The Psalms are known for their theological depth and historical breadth, spanning one thousand years of Israel's history—from the time of Moses to the return from exile in Babylonia. They were used as the Temple hymnbook, assisting Israel in her worship and confession of faith.

There are many themes in the Psalms, but according to one scholar, they all tend to fall under the overall theme of *"the God who rules in good-*

ness, majesty and power." It is this God that Israel celebrates, confesses and worships.

Their usefulness in worship, both personal and corporate, lies in the richness of thought and human emotion expressed through the features of Hebrew poetry.

The book of Psalms begins with two important declarations. Psalm 1 declares that God can be known through his Word by those who *"delight in the law of the Lord, meditating on it day and night."* His Word plants us in life like a fruit-bearing tree. It is the way to wisdom and the key to success in life. The wicked ignore his Word at their peril.

Psalm 2 adds that God can also be known by his "son," who proclaims the "Lord's decree." In the Psalms, the "son" is usually a reference to King David, who represents and points forward to the true Son and King, Jesus Christ. The pagan kings of the earth are warned: *"Serve the Lord with reverent fear, and rejoice with trembling. Submit to God's royal son, or he will become angry, and you will be destroyed in the midst of all your activities—for his anger flares up in an instant. But what joy for all who take refuge in him!"* (Psalm 2:11–12).

According to Psalm 3, the Lord will protect his people. David bears testimony that he cried out to the Lord and the Lord answered him from his holy mountain. Though David is threatened by his enemies, he is confident of the Lord's protection: *"But you, O Lord, are a shield around me; you are my glory, the one who holds my head high"* (Psalm 3:3).

In Psalm 4, the Lord hears the urgent prayers of his people when they are troubled. Instead of being enslaved by anger and frustration, we can trust in the Lord for better times, because he is ultimately the object of our security and happiness: *"You have given me greater joy than those who have abundant harvests of grain and new wine. In peace I will lie down and sleep, for you alone, O Lord, will keep me safe"* (Psalm 4:7–8).

Psalm 5 assures us that the wicked will not prevail. When it seems that the wicked are winning, we can pray for wisdom about what to do: *"Lead me in the right path, O Lord, or my enemies will conquer me. Make your way plain for me to follow"* (Psalm 5:8).

Psalm 6 adds that when we are weakened by life, sick at heart, and worn out with grief and sorrow, we can depend upon the compassion of the Lord. He will heal us when our bones are in agony, and save us because of his unfailing love. All who do evil will be judged and the righteous restored.

Day 154   Psalms 7–12

June 2

> Key Text: "When I look at the night sky and see the work of your fingers—the moon and the stars you set in place—what are mere mortals that you should think about them, human beings that you should care for them? Yet you made them only a little lower than God and crowned them with glory and honor. You gave them charge of everything you made, putting all things under their authority...." (Psalm 8:3–6)

Psalm 7 is song of praise to God because he is just. Like King David, we can ask God to vindicate us against the accusations of our enemies: *"God is my shield, saving those whose hearts are true and right."* David is confident that God is an honest judge, who undermines the plans of the wicked: *"The wicked conceive evil; they are pregnant with trouble and give birth to lies. They dig a deep pit to trap others, then fall into it themselves. The trouble they make for others backfires on them. The violence they plan falls on their own heads"* (Psalm 7:14–16).

Psalm 8 is a celebration of the creation. God's majesty fills the earth. Even infants sense God's majesty as Creator. Studying nature creates a sense of awe and gratefulness, especially for our place in the creation: *"...what are mere mortals that you should think about them, human beings that you should care for them? Yet you made them only a little lower than God and crowned them with glory and honor. You gave them charge of everything you made..."* (Psalm 8:4–6).

Psalms 9 and 10 are about King David's enemies, which is a common

295

theme. Psalm 9 is joyful praise for God defeating his enemies: *"The enemy is finished, in endless ruins; the cities you uprooted are now forgotten."* He declares that *"the Lord reigns forever, executing judgment from his throne. ... The wicked will go down to the grave. This is the fate of all the nations who ignore God."*

In Psalm 10, David challenges God to punish the wicked because of their many injustices against the innocent. In their arrogance, *"the wicked are too proud to seek God. They seem to think that God is dead. ... They think, 'Nothing bad will ever happen to us!'"* But the Lord is king forever and ever. The godless nations will vanish from the land, and justice will come to the orphans and the oppressed.

Psalm 11 recalls a time of trouble, when the foundations of law and order had collapsed, when David sought the Lord for protection. He was warned by some to *"fly like a bird to the mountains for safety!"* But David stood firm: *"The Lord is in his holy Temple; the Lord still rules from heaven. ... The righteous Lord loves justice. The virtuous will see his face."*

Psalm 12 expresses confidence that in times when it seems that the godly are fast disappearing, being deceived by a *"lying generation,"* God will rise up to rescue them and preserve them forever *"...even though the wicked strut about and evil is praised throughout the land."*

This grouping of psalms points to the majesty of God, as seen by his power in creating the world, and in his moral power as the Judge of the wicked.

Focus: The Psalms reflect what we might call the "two books of God." The first is the book of nature. Here we see God's power, creativity and even whimsical humor, revealed in the things he has made. The gift of science has widened the worship book of nature significantly over the centuries, as we have come to understand more and more of the astonishing complexity and diversity of life. The second book is the written Word of God, the Bible. If the book of nature paints in a broad stroke, the Word of God brings special insights into the nature and ways of God. Together, general revelation and special revelation enable us to worship God with all our heart, mind, soul and strength!

Prayer: Lord, when we consider the things you have made, we are struck by your power and majesty. Thankfully, your awesome power is tempered by justice and love. You protect those who love you, and oppose those who despise and dismiss you. We are grateful to know that the future belongs to those who serve you! Amen.

June 3

> **Key Text:** "You rescue the humble, but you humiliate the proud.
> You light a lamp for me. The Lord, my God, lights up my
> darkness." (Psalm 18:27–28)

Sometimes our enemies have the upper hand. In those times, we wonder *how long?* Psalm 13 says that we can ask God for answers, and pray that our enemies' plans to defeat us be undermined. But above all, we should trust in God because he cares for us: *"But I trust in your unfailing love. I will rejoice because you have rescued me. I will sing to the Lord because he is good to me"* (Psalm 13:5–6).

Ultimately, the enemies of God and his people are fools: *"Only fools say in their hearts, 'There is no God.'"* Fools are not clowns, but morally corrupt people who do no good. History reveals that the most destructive fools among us have been brilliant, charismatic people. There is no natural correlation between a high I.Q. and a high moral character.

Psalm 14 says that God looks down from heaven and sees lots of fools: *"He looks to see if anyone is truly wise, if anyone seeks God. But no, all have turned away; all have become corrupt. No one does good, not a single one!"* (Psalm 14:2–3). Paul will later quote this psalm in Romans 3 to make the case that *"everyone has sinned; we all fall short of God's glorious standard"* (Romans 3:23).

This is important because only those *"who lead blameless lives and do what is right, speaking the truth from sincere hearts"* can worship God in his Temple in Jerusalem *(Psalm 15:2)*. They must be people who forsake harming others with unjust actions, but instead love God and their neighbors with their words and deeds. Since no one lives a perfect life, the truth of this psalm depends upon God's grace being given to his sinful people so they may worship in his sanctuary.

Indeed, we sinners must take refuge in God's grace and mercy. At the same time, we must resist doing evil and worshiping idols: *"Troubles multiply for those who chase after other gods. I will not take part in their sacrifices of blood or even speak the names of their gods"* (Psalm 16:4). God has given Israel the Promised Land as their inheritance, and has promised to be with them if they remain faithful to him. King David prays, *"The land you have given me is a pleasant land. What a wonderful inheritance! … I know the Lord is always with me. I will not be shaken, for he is right beside me. No wonder my heart is glad, and I rejoice. My body rests in safety."*

Nevertheless, we have enemies. We must sometimes pray for God's help, deliverance, justice and protection from our enemies, because he loves us *(Psalm 17).* Our enemies can be dangerous and without pity, like hungry lions ready to devour us. When our hearts are right and we seek to do God's will, we can expect God to hear our prayers and arise on our behalf.

God is worthy of our praise because he is our protection and strength in all the dangers of life: *"He is my shield, the power that saves me, and my place of safety. I called on the Lord, who is worthy of praise, and he saved me from my enemies"* (Psalm 18:2–3). To the faithful, God shows himself faithful. He is a light in the darkness. His way is perfect and all his promises prove true. He enables us to be as surefooted as a deer standing on mountain heights.

Psalms like these reflect both God's unconditional grace and his conditional blessing. He loves us and will always forgive us when we sin and make a mess of our lives. When we keep his commandments and forsake sin, he is free to bless and establish our lives. When we are unfaithful to him and disobey his commands, he allows us to experience the painful consequences which inevitably follow.

Focus: Enemies feature prominently in the Psalms. As king, David had many of them, but all of us have experienced people who for some reason don't like us nor want us to succeed. They are *against* us. Political, military enemies are one thing, but a neighbor or coworker who is against us is more complicated. We need wisdom to know how to respond to our enemies with grace. After all, Jesus said that we must love our enemies. This is perhaps the most demanding moral imperative of all. But God is not demanding of us anything that he has not already demonstrated. Remember, Jesus died on the cross for his enemies.

***Prayer:** Lord, we praise you for your grace and mercy toward us. We commit ourselves to keeping your commandments so that we may live wisely and experience your blessing in our lives. Help us to stand strong against those who oppose you, and bear faithful witness. At the same time, give us the grace we need to forgive our enemies and not seek revenge. Amen.*

June 4

> Key Text: "The Lord is my shepherd; I have all that I need.
> He lets me rest in green meadows; he leads me beside peaceful
> streams. He renews my strength. He guides me along right paths,
> bringing honor to his name." (Psalm 23:1–3)

These six psalms express different ways that God reveals himself and participates in human life.

Psalm 19 returns to the theme of the two books of God. It begins by declaring that God reveals himself through what some call general revelation. General revelation is that which all people, everywhere, can know about God through observation and reason: *"The heavens proclaim the glory of God. The skies display his craftsmanship. Day after day they continue to speak; night after night they make him known"* (Psalm 19:1–2). Romans, chapter 1, makes the same observation and argues that at minimum, nature ought to create a sense of awe and thankfulness for the powerful God who created the universe.

Think of it as God 101.

Special revelation is further, specific knowledge of God, which he gives to those of his choosing, in this case Israel. God gave Israel his commandments and instructions so that they would know him personally and understand more specifically how to worship, serve and represent him in the world: *"The instructions of the Lord are perfect, reviving the soul. The decrees of the Lord are trustworthy, making wise the simple. The commandments of the Lord are right, bringing joy to the heart"* (Psalm 19:7–8).

Psalm 20 is a benediction for believers that God may hear their prayers, grant their hearts' desires and make all their plans succeed.

Psalm 21 is King David's grateful praise to God for victory and success. He expresses his heartfelt trust in the Lord, whose unfailing love will keep him from stumbling. Future victories are assured because God has a *"strong right hand."*

Psalms 22 and 23 contain messianic references, used by Jesus and the New Testament writers as pointers toward our ultimate redemption through Christ, Israel's true king and Savior.

Christ quotes Psalm 22:1 while on the cross: *"My God, my God, why have you abandoned me?"* David's sufferings anticipate the sufferings of Jesus: *"I am scorned and despised by all! Everyone who sees me mocks me. They sneer and shake their heads, saying, 'Is this the one who relies on the Lord? Then let the Lord save him!' ... They have pierced my hands and feet. ... They divide my garments among themselves and throw dice for my clothing"* (Psalm 22:6–8, 16, 18).

The great and beloved 23rd Psalm reveals God to be the Shepherd of his people, a title that Jesus takes for himself, saying, *"I am the Good Shepherd."* As Shepherd, God provides for, guides, protects and blesses his "sheep." Even in dangerous places and in the presence of our enemies, we can rest assured that he is close by and that his goodness and unfailing love will be with us in life and in death, forever.

Psalm 24 makes clear that the whole earth and all its people belong to God, for there is only one true God: *"For he laid the earth's foundation on the seas and built it on the ocean depths"* (Psalm 24:2). He makes himself known on earth and shows how people may have a right relationship with him so that they may *"stand in his holy place."* His commandments explain that all those who have clean hands and pure hearts, forsake idols and tell the truth to their neighbor, may worship in his presence.

The composer Handel used this psalm in his musical text for the *Messiah* oratorio: *"Open up, ancient gates! Open up, ancient doors, and let the King of glory enter. Who is the King of glory? The Lord of Hosts—he is the King of glory"* (Psalm 24:9–10).

In all these ways, God makes himself known and enters into relationship with all who open their hearts to him, just as Israel opened the ancient gates of the Temple to him.

Focus: You may notice that the Psalms seem to ask for perfection on the part of those who worship God in his Temple: *"Who may climb the mountain of the Lord? Who may stand in his holy place? Only those whose hands and hearts are pure, who do not worship idols and never tell lies"* (Psalm 24:3–4).

It is important to remember that God's grace permeates his Law and commandments. God never expected that his people could perfectly keep the commandments. For this reason, he also gave the priesthood and sacrifices to make atonement for sin. In some instances, the purity required is ceremonial and symbolic. What God is looking for in the ritual and symbolism is the intent of our hearts. Grace is always operating in the background of our life with God, like a firewall against judgment. Therefore, we sinners we can read the Psalms with a sense of desire to have clean hands and be pure of heart, forsaking idols and always telling the truth. With these desires, we may worship in his presence.

Prayer: Lord, you are the King of Glory! We are so grateful for the ways you make yourself known to us. Your creation fills us with awe. Your Word instructs us in the way of the blessed life. Your answers to prayer encourage us, and your invitation to worship fills us with joy. But above all, the suffering and death of Jesus for our sin shows us how much we are loved. Amen!

Day 157   Psalms 25–30

June 5

Key Text: "The Lord is good and does what is right; he shows the proper path to those who go astray. He leads the humble in doing right, teaching them his way. The Lord leads with unfailing love and faithfulness all who keep his covenant and obey his demands." (Psalm 25:8–10)

Psalm 25 begins with a pledge of personal commitment to God that expresses the heart of worship and frees God to bless us: *"O Lord, I give my life to you. I trust in you, my God!"*

When we entrust our lives to God, he is able to guide us: *"Show me the right path, O Lord; point out the road for me to follow."* He is able to restore us: *"The Lord is good and does what is right; he shows the proper path to those who go astray."* He is free to forgive us: *"For the honor of your name, O Lord, forgive my many, many sins."*

Psalm 26 continues the theme of personal commitment and the spiritual freedom it brings to live openly and honestly: *"Declare me innocent, O Lord, for I have acted with integrity; I have trusted in the Lord without wavering. Put me on trial, Lord, and cross-examine me. Test my motives and my heart."* As we purposely choose to follow the Lord and reject the influence of sinners, we put ourselves in the place of integrity where we stand on solid ground.

Psalm 27 declares that the fully committed need not live in fear. God is our protector and helper: *"The Lord is my light and my salvation—so why should I be afraid?"* We find our confidence and delight by being in God's presence: *"...delighting in the Lord's perfections and meditating in his Temple."* The Lord hears our prayers, and we hear his voice: *"My heart* has heard you say, 'Come and talk with me.' And my heart responds, 'Lord, I am coming.'" The Lord will never abandon us!

In Psalm 28, David recalls a time when he cried out for mercy in the Lord's sanctuary, and the Lord heard his cry. The wicked go about their evildoing without the slightest twinge of conscience, but the Lord will give them the punishment they deserve, so we should not fret that they are getting away with it. By trusting the Lord to take care of matters of justice, we can stop trying to do it for him: *"The Lord is my strength and shield. I trust him with all my heart. He helps me, and my heart is filled with joy."*

Psalm 29 declares that God's powerful voice thunders throughout the creation, over which he is the ruler. It is a call for heaven and earth, and angels, animals and people, to praise him: *"In his Temple everyone shouts, 'Glory!'"*

Psalm 30 affirms that when we give God our lives and trust in him, he is faithful to deliver us from our enemies. Therefore, we should give thanks and praise God continually: *"Sing to the Lord, all you godly ones! Praise his holy name. For his anger lasts only a moment, but his favor lasts a lifetime! Weeping may last through the night, but joy comes with the morning."*

Focus: Everyone trusts someone or something, even if the only thing we trust is our own thoughts. But most things are not worthy of our trust. The Psalms insist, in fact, that only God is worthy of our trust. To trust in ourselves only, is to live in perpetual fear and uncertainty. It is a minimal existence, getting ever smaller as more doubts and fears arise. To trust in God, however, is to expand life. If God the Creator loves us and has our best interests in mind, then we are free to live with joyful abandonment to God's will for us. Thus, David is able to shout out: *"O Lord, I give my life to you. I trust in you, my God!"* Can you make these *your* words as well?

Prayer: Lord, we joyfully give you our lives and trust that you will walk with us through all the challenges of our lives—our joys and our sorrows—and bring us through safely on the other side. Amen.

Day 158   Psalms 31–35

June 6

Key Text: "O Lord, I have come to you for protection; don't let me be disgraced. Save me, for you do what is right. Turn your ear to listen to me; rescue me quickly. Be my rock of protection, a fortress where I will be safe." (Psalm 31:1–2)

The Psalms tend to repeat themes, such as prayers for protection, rescue and forgiveness. This is reflected in our reading today. The repetition reminds us that the same challenges tend to follow us through life!

In Psalm 31, King David shares some very personal descriptions of his distress as king. They are evidence of the strain of war: *"Tears blur my eyes. My body and soul are withering away. I am dying from grief; my years are shortened by sadness. Sin has drained my strength; I am wasting away from within. I am scorned by all my enemies and despised by my neighbors—even my friends are afraid to come near me"* (Psalm 31:9–11).

Psalm 32 describes the joy of forgiveness and the strain of unconfessed sin: *"Oh what joy for those whose disobedience is forgiven, whose sin is put out of sight!"* Harboring sin has physical and emotional consequences: *"When I refused to confess my sin, my body wasted away, and I groaned all day long."* When we finally confess the sin we have stubbornly denied, the burden of guilt is lifted and joy is restored: *"Finally, I confessed all my sins to you and stopped trying to hide my guilt. I said to myself, 'I will confess my rebellion to the Lord.' And you forgave me! All my guilt is gone."*

Psalm 33 is a call to praise the Lord with joyful song—to write new songs and play skillfully—because God can be trusted and he loves justice and truth. God spoke the heavens into being, so let all the nations fear him. The nations who do will rejoice; those who don't will be frustrated and thwarted because fear of the Lord, and not the size of the king's warhorse, is what brings victory.

The beautiful Psalm 34 is written, the notation says, at a time when David was on the run and needed to resort to cleverness to stay alive. *"In my desperation, I prayed, and the Lord listened; he saved me from all my troubles."* It is a hymn of praise, encouraging others also to *"Taste and see that the Lord is good. Oh, the joys of those who take refuge in him!"* Those who do right are heard when they pray, and God protects them.

303

Psalm 35 is another prayer asking for protection and assistance—and for joy to those who come to David's defense. David asks that those who want to harm him (because they don't respect Israel's God) be turned back and humiliated for their presumption. No other god acts with justice and mercy like Yahweh: *"Lord, who can compare with you? Who else rescues the helpless from the strong?"*

Focus: David's earnest prayers for protection and victory over his enemies, are not just for his own sake. Israel's king was understood to be God's representative on earth. When Israel's king was slandered, mocked, plotted against and targeted for assassination, it was as if all things were being done to God himself. So we see a strong commitment to protecting the reputation of God's name. In a polytheistic culture, where gods were understood to have territorial powers and reputations, this would have been a big issue. There is a little bit of "my god is stronger than your god" going on here. Of course, King David knows that Israel's God, Yahweh, is the one and only God, Lord of all nations and peoples—but that is an insight that required a huge paradigm shift. It is *not* what the neighboring nations thought. The only thing they respected was strength, and so the Lord God is presented as a warrior who defends his people—offensive, perhaps, to modern sensibilities, but totally credible to ancient sensibilities.

Today, in some parts of the world, this kind of thinking persists. In the secular West, however, God's reputation is defended more by the moral character of his people than by military strength. So we should pray that our churches honor God's name and reputation in local communities by the way Christians live.

Prayer: Lord, we tend to come to you with the same confessions and requests, over and over again. Thankfully, you never tire of our prayers, nor do you get fed up with our weakness. Your love is without limits. Thank you for the assurance that we can always come to you and find the protection, rescue and forgiveness we need. We want your name to be honored in our communities, so above all, teach us how to love. Amen.

Day 159   Reflection

June 7

The Psalms are a remarkable resource for worship. They give words to the raw feelings of the worshiper as he or she processes life.

There is anger with God: *"O Lord, how long will you forget me? Forever?*

How long will you look the other way?" (Psalm 13:1).

There is desperation: *"O Lord, hear my plea for justice. Listen to my cry for help"* (Psalm 17:1).

There is personal testimony: *"The ropes of death entangled me; floods of destruction swept over me. The grave wrapped its ropes around me; death laid a trap in my path. But in my distress I cried out to the Lord; yes, I prayed to my God for help. He heard me from his sanctuary; my cry to him reached his ears"* (Psalm 18:4–6).

There is awesome wonder: *"The heavens proclaim the glory of God. The skies display his craftsmanship. Day after day they continue to speak; night after night they make him known"* (Psalm 19:1–2).

There is humble contrition: *"For the honor of your name, O Lord, forgive my many, many sins"* (Psalm 25:11).

There is spontaneous joy: *"I will praise the Lord at all times. I will constantly speak his praises. I will boast only in the Lord; let all who are helpless take heart. Come, let us tell of the Lord's greatness; let us exalt his name together"* (Psalm 34:1–3).

There is life wisdom: *"Does anyone want to live a life that is long and prosperous? Then keep your tongue from speaking evil and your lips from telling lies! Turn away from evil and do good. Search for peace, and work to maintain it"* (Psalm 34:12–13).

We could go on, but the various emotions of the Psalms, expressed in the form of Hebrew poetry, enable us to identify with believers of all times and places, who faced the same struggles as we do. The fact that they are so honest—even shouting at God or questioning him—reveals that God welcomes us just as much in our doubt and anger and fear, as he does in our joyful devotion. The Psalms are an invitation to come to him, just as we are.

Let's take him up on his invitation! Make the words of the Psalms your words, in heartfelt worship and thanksgiving.

Prayer: *Lord, thank you for your amazing tolerance of our humanity. In our ignorance and weakness, we reach out to you in worship and prayer. Thank you for giving us the words! Amen.*

June 8

> Key Text: "I waited patiently for the Lord to help me, and he turned to me and heard my cry. He lifted me out of the pit of despair, out of the mud and the mire. He set my feet on solid ground and steadied me as I walked along. He has given me a new song to sing, a hymn of praise to our God." (Psalm 40:1–3)

The next six psalms are both testimony and teaching. They recount various times when King David asked for and found strength in God's mercy, love and protection.

Psalm 36 reflects on the blind conceit of the wicked. In their ignorance, they have no fear of God. By contrast, David testifies that he finds his strength in God's vast, unfailing love. He says to God: *"For you are the fountain of life, the light by which we see."*

In Psalm 37, David counsels us not to worry about the wicked who prosper. The Lord laughs at them. Their Day of Judgment is coming. Instead: *"Trust in the Lord and do good. Then you will live safely in the land and prosper. Take delight in the Lord, and he will give you your heart's desires. Commit everything you do to the Lord. Trust him, and he will help you."*

Psalm 38 is filled with distress. King David's health is broken by overwhelming guilt and an anguished heart. His friends stay away, fearing his disease. Meanwhile, his enemies lay traps to kill him. So, in his weakness he calls for help: *"Do not abandon me, O Lord. Do not stand at a distance, my God. Come quickly to help me, O Lord my savior."*

In Psalm 39, King David is experiencing God's punishment by having to suffer the mockery of fools. He is aware of the shortness of life; he is *"a traveler passing through,"* as his ancestors before him. He asks God for help: *"Hear my prayer, O Lord! Listen to my cries for help! Don't ignore my tears."*

And God is merciful. In Psalm 40, David reports: *"I waited patiently for the Lord to help me, and he turned to me and heard my cry. He lifted me out of the pit of despair, out of the mud and the mire. He set my feet on solid ground and steadied me as I walked along. He has given me a new song to sing, a hymn of praise to our God. Many will see what he has done and be amazed. They will put their trust in the Lord."*

The Lord has taught David to listen patiently so that he might learn, and "write new songs." He shares in song the good news of God's justice with others: *"May all who search for you be filled with joy and gladness in you. May those who love your salvation repeatedly shout, 'The Lord is great!'"*

Again, in Psalm 41, David asks for the Lord's mercy, because of his continuing sickness. Meanwhile, his enemies speak evil against him and hope that he will die soon. Even his best friend has turned against him. But since God has not allowed his enemies to triumph over him, David knows that the Lord is pleased with him: *"You have preserved my life because I am innocent; you have brought me into your presence forever. Praise the Lord, the God of Israel, who lives from everlasting to everlasting. Amen and amen!"*

Focus: The life of faith is often a life of waiting and listening. Impatience gets in the way of spiritual growth. But those who learn to wait and listen are rewarded. Trusting, delighting in, and committing everything to God is the way to prosper and find our deepest desires met. When our desires align with God's will, good things follow as a general rule. However, they don't necessarily come quickly or in the way we had anticipated. So along with waiting and listening, God wants us to trust him for the answers he gives.

Prayer: Lord, we identify with King David. We all have, at times, needed your love, your help or your mercy, but have been impatient and complaining when the answers didn't come quickly. How wonderful it is to know that you always have our best interests in mind. When your answers to our prayers are slow in coming, please teach us to wait and listen. Amen!

Day 161   Psalms 42–49

June 9

Key Text: "Come everyone! Clap your hands! Shout to God with joyful praise! For the Lord Most High is awesome. He is the great King of all the earth." (Psalm 47:1–2)

Here we begin Book Two of the Psalms, which includes Psalms 42 through 72, a collection attributed (mostly) to Levites known as the *"descendants of Korah."* These family members were singers and musicians in the Temple choir *(1 Chronicles 6:31–47)*.

Psalm 42 is a song of longing for closeness with God: *"As the deer longs for streams of water, so I long for you, O God."* The writer remembers the days when God seemed present, as he *"walked among the crowds of worshipers, leading a great procession to the house of God, singing for joy and giving thanks amid the sound of a great celebration!"* In this present time of discouragement, when others mock him in his grief, he puts his hope in God, convinced that he will praise him again.

Psalm 43 continues the theme of discouragement. The writer has been lied about by his enemies, perhaps about his not being worthy of priestly functions. He wants the truth to come out so that he can attend to his priestly function with joy. *"Why am I discouraged? Why is my heart so sad?"* We don't always know. Sometimes we need to simply pass through it and put our hope in God, knowing that while our feelings are changeable, God remains close at hand. He will defend us.

Psalm 44 recalls the stories of Israel's ancestors, and of God's victory over the pagan nations of Canaan. If God did it once, he can do it again, especially since Israel is presently being defeated by her enemies: *"But for your sake we are killed every day; we are being slaughtered like sheep."* Why does God look the other way? It seems like God has rejected them. Help!

Psalm 45 is song of praise about the king of Israel and his family, perhaps a bit idealized if referring to David, but more appropriate as a picture of Christ as King. *"Your throne, O God, endures forever and ever. You rule with a scepter of justice"* (Psalm 45:6).

Psalm 46 declares God to be *"our refuge and strength, always ready to help in times of trouble."* In times of trouble, our greatest enemy is fear. Our greatest antidote to fear is faith: *"So we will not fear when earthquakes come and the mountains crumble into the sea."* The Lord of Heaven's Armies is here: *"Be still, and know that I am God! I will be honored by every nation. I will be honored throughout the world."*

Psalm 47 is a call for all the nations of the earth to clap their hands and shout to God with joyful praise, for all the earth belongs to him, and all the rulers must answer to him.

Psalm 48 is a song praising Jerusalem, where God dwells in his Temple and defends his people. Armies advanced against it and were stunned. They ran away, gripped by terror: *"We had heard of the city's glory, but now we have seen it ourselves—the city of the Lord of Heaven's Armies* [i.e., the Lord of Hosts]."

Psalm 49 offers words of counsel to the foolish, who trust in their wealth. Like everyone else, they must finally die, just like animals, and take nothing with them. What is gained? So don't envy the rich. In contrast, the psalmist writes, *"God will redeem my life. He will snatch me from the power of the grave."* Those who place their trust in the Lord need not fear the injustices of mortal life.

> **Focus:** The Psalms call us to celebrate even when it seems contrary to the "facts on the ground." Two realities make celebrating a rational thing to do: First, evil and injustice on earth are limited by death; Second, God has the last word. He is the great King of all the earth. So when it seems that evil is winning and the righteous are suffering, we are called to forsake fear and celebrate instead! *"Come, everyone! Clap your hands! Shout to God with joyful praise! For the Lord Most High is awesome. He is the great King of all the earth"* (Psalm 47:1–2).

> **Prayer:** *Lord, give us an unquenchable thirst for you, and only you. Keep us from foolishly trusting in wealth or living in fear about the troubles of life. Redeem our lives, O Lord, and snatch us from the power of the grave through the greater power of Christ's resurrection! Amen.*

Day 162   Psalms 50–54

June 10

> Key Text: "Create in me a clean heart, O God. Renew a loyal spirit within me. Do not banish me from your presence, and don't take your Holy Spirit from me." (Psalm 51:10–11)

These five psalms focus on human sin and God's righteous judgment.

They begin, in Psalm 50, with a strong statement of God's moral authority over creation: *"The Lord, the Mighty One, is God, and he has spoken.... He calls on the heavens above and earth below to witness the judgment of his* [covenant] *people."*

His charges against Israel are familiar to us. God wants more than outward religion, because he doesn't need sacrifices, but requires obedience from the heart: *"Make thankfulness your sacrifice to God, and keep the vows you made to the Most High."*

Psalm 51 is a powerful song of confession: *"Against you, and you alone,* have I sinned; I have done what is evil in your sight." Since Adam and Eve fell, all children born on earth are born sinners: *"For I was born a sinner—yes, from the moment my mother conceived me."* Original sin has been passed on, so all children of Adam and Eve need forgiveness and cleansing: *"Purify me from my sins, and I will be clean; wash me, and I will be whiter than snow. ... Create in me a clean heart, O God. Renew a loyal spirit within me. Do not banish me from your presence, and don't take your Holy Spirit from me."*

Psalm 52 is a painful recollection about a betrayal by a friend. David says of Doeg, *"You love evil more than good and lies more than truth. You love to destroy others with your words, you liar!"* Even the mighty warrior, Doeg, is subject to God's judgment when he turns on God's anointed one.

Psalm 53 is a virtual repeat of Psalm 14, a calling out of the foolish who say there is no God. It seems as if the entire human race has become foolish. *"God looks down from heaven on the entire human race; he looks to see if anyone is truly wise, if anyone seeks God."* But the foolish will be singled out by God: *"Terror will grip them, terror like they have never known before."* The wise, however, who believe in God will be rescued and restored, and then shout with joy!

Psalm 54 is a prayer of King David for protection and rescue because he is being threatened by those who want to kill him. He confesses his faith that God is his helper, and asks him to turn the evil plans of his enemies against them. He praises God in advance, because God has rescued him from his troubles and defeated his enemies many times before.

Focus: Repentance is an essential part of worship, and Psalm 51 is a great psalm to use for this purpose. Repentance keeps the nature of our salvation where it belongs—on God's grace and not human merit. It also acknowledges the need to address areas in our lives which hinder our relationship with God. Unrepentant (meaning unacknowledged) sin becomes like barnacles on the bottom of a boat. Hidden from view, they nevertheless create drag and slow the boat down. Using a different analogy, Hebrews 12:1–2 compares the Christian life to a long distance run. We are urged to *"strip off every weight that slows us down, especially the sin that so easily trips us up. And let us run with endurance the race God has set before us."*

Prayer: *Lord, we remember that sin is first of all an offense against you, our Maker. Forgive us for our idolatry and rebellion. Restore us to the joy of our salvation. We*

Day 163   Psalms 55–59

June 11

> Key Text: "O God, have mercy on me, for people are hounding me. My foes attack me all day long. I am constantly hounded by those who slander me, and many are boldly attacking me. But when I am afraid, I will put my trust in you. I praise God for what he has promised. I trust in God, so why should I be afraid? What can mere mortals do to me?" (Psalm 56:1–4)

We've noticed that the Psalms are useful for worship and prayer because they give words to human emotion—especially for the times we are in distress or trouble.

Reading Psalm 55, one can almost hear David's heart pounding with fear. He cries out to God: *"My enemies shout at me, making loud and wicked threats. They bring trouble on me and angrily hunt me down."* What makes it worse is that his "enemy" was once his close friend: *"What good fellowship we once enjoyed as we walked together to the house of God."* How sad to see friends walk away from God! David calls on God to frustrate the plans of his enemies, even if his enemy was once his friend!

Psalm 56 is a prayer for mercy because David is being hounded and slandered. Who doesn't experience fear when people are out to get you? When your words are twisted and people watch your every step in order to harm you if possible, it creates great anxiety. But David summons his faith and takes comfort in this: *"I trust in God, so why should I be afraid? What can mere mortals do to me?"* As Jesus later said, *"Don't be afraid of those who want to kill your body; they cannot touch your soul. Fear only God, who can destroy both soul and body in hell"* (Matthew 10:28).

As David fled from King Saul, who wanted to kill him, he took refuge in a cave. Psalm 57 was written regarding this time of being hunted and threatened. Again David prays for God's mercy and deliverance, but his heart is confident. He knows that he will once again be free to return to Jerusalem and thank God in his Temple among all the people.

In Psalm 58, David calls out to his enemy kings and accuses them of injustice and violence. *"They spit venom like deadly snakes; they are like cobras that refuse to listen,"* so David asks God to *"break off their fangs"* and cause them to become, among other things, *"like snails that dissolve into slime."* He looks forward to the final judgment when those who live for God experience his reward.

Finally, in Psalm 59, David prays for the Lord to wake up and punish the hostile nations that try to destroy Israel's king. To oppose the King of Israel, is to oppose the God who appointed him as king. David believes that their destruction will let the whole world know that God reigns in Israel. *"O my Strength, to you I sing praises, for you, O God, are my refuge, the God who shows me unfailing love."*

Focus: The Bible's instruction on dealing with one's enemies is complex. The Psalms, especially, capture the emotions of those who are being attacked by their enemies. When the enemy is another nation or hostile group intent upon destroying us, we are encouraged to depend on God to be our defender, and also to be our strength, if we must stop evil, injustice and violence. When the enemy is an individual who is lying about us, or slandering us, we are called to ask God to make the truth known—to stop and punish the perpetrator. In either case, God is the Judge of all men and nations, and the avenger of evil. When Jesus calls us to love our enemies, he isn't asking us to *like* them, but to refuse to retaliate in kind, and if possible to do good to them, as David did repeatedly to King Saul when Saul sought to kill him. This is the most demanding moral imperative in life! But whatever we face from our enemies, the bottom line is: *"What can mere mortals do to me?"* (Psalm 56:4).

Prayer: *Lord, your enemies have always sought to silence or destroy your people, thinking that in doing this, they are destroying you. But you laugh at them from heaven; you frustrate their plans and will bring them to judgment. In this we take comfort, O Lord. Amen.*

Day 164   Psalms 60–66

June 12

Key Text: "Your unfailing love is better than life itself; how I praise you! I will praise you as long as I live, lifting up my hands to you in prayer. You satisfy me more than the richest feast. I will praise you with songs of joy." (Psalm 63:3–5)

The next seven psalms begin, in Psalm 60, with a song of lament regarding a setback in battle, then a plea to be restored to favor, and finally a confession of faith in God's power to deliver his people: *"With God's help we will do mighty things, for he will trample down our foes."*

Psalm 61 is a petition for protection during David's reign: *"Lead me to the towering rock of safety, for you are my safe refuge, a fortress where my enemies cannot reach me."* What he wishes for is a long life devoted to faithfully fulfilling his spiritual commitments to God: *"Add many years to the life of the king! May his years span the generations! ... Then I will sing praises to your name forever as I fulfill my vows each day."*

Psalm 62 is about waiting quietly in the presence of God, who is our rock and salvation. While enemies plot and maneuver, David finds comfort in his faith and urges others to do the same: *"O my people, trust in him at all times. Pour out your heart to him, for God is our refuge."*

Psalm 63 is a hymn of spiritual thirst and heartfelt worship: *"O God, you are my God; I earnestly search for you. My soul thirsts for you; my whole body longs for you in this parched and weary land where there is no water."* David remembers worshiping in the sanctuary when he grasped something more of God's power and glory. God's power and glory are seen most clearly in his love for his creation, and for his special people Israel: *"Your unfailing love is better than life itself; how I praise you! I will praise you as long as I live, lifting up my hands to you in prayer."*

Psalm 64 is a prayer for protection from an *"evil mob...this gang of wrongdoers."* David lists their treacherous ways, but expresses confidence that *"God himself will shoot them with his arrows, suddenly striking them down."* Their defeat will sober other enemies, but cause the godly to rejoice.

Psalm 65 is a song of praise to God who answers the prayers of his people and gives them joy and hope. *"Though we are overwhelmed by our sins, you forgive them all. What joy for those you choose to bring near, those who live in your holy courts."* God's mighty deeds are seen in his providential protection and provision, making the land and flocks fertile all over the earth: *"The meadows are clothed with flocks of sheep, and the valleys are carpeted with grain. They all shout and sing for joy!"*

Psalm 66 is a song of praise about God's mighty acts on behalf of Israel, such as delivering her from Egypt across the Red Sea. The psalm invites all the nations of the world to *"come and see what our God has done, what awesome miracles he performs for people!"* It asks the whole world to join Israel in her worship of Yahweh: *"Let the whole world bless our God and loudly sing his praises. Our lives are in his hands, and he keeps our feet from stumbling."* A testimony is given to all who will hear: *"Come and listen, all you who fear God, and I will tell you what he did for me."*

Focus: A recurring theme in Psalms, and in the rest of the Old Testament story, is God's invitation for all the nations of the fallen earth to come to him for his mercy, and then to worship him and experience his blessing. Yes, God sometimes moves to stop nations from doing evil, but not because he enjoys inflicting pain, and never with the intent to wipe them off the face of the earth. He demonstrates his power not to harm but to stop those who would harm others, just as, in their unbelief, they are harming themselves. All the blessings of this life and eternity are offered to all who will receive them by repentance and faith.

Prayer: *Lord, you are the one true God of all the earth. You invite us to meet you at the Temple for worship. Though our enemies seek to harm us, you are our comfort and hope. Nothing can separate us from you. Our salvation is kept for us in heaven, pure and undefiled, beyond the reach of change and decay. Help us to love our enemies in this world the way you love them, and show them that your love is better than life itself! Amen.*

Day 165   Psalms 67–72

June 13

> Key Text: "O Lord, you alone are my hope. I've trusted you, O Lord, from childhood. Yes, you have been with me from birth; from my mother's womb you have cared for me. No wonder I am always praising you!" (Psalm 71:5–6)

Book Two of the Psalms concludes with six psalms about God's relationship with Israel, the king, and the nations—many of which are God's enemies.

Psalm 67 calls for the nations to praise God because he is the just King of all the earth: *"Let the whole world sing for joy, because you govern the nations with justice and guide the people of the whole world."*

Psalm 68 asks for God to rise up and scatter those who hate him. A scattered group does less damage! (Remember the Tower of Babel scattering in Genesis 11:1–8.) The Psalm next asks for the godly to rejoice because the Lord cares about them, granting abundant rain and bountiful harvests. He is a just God: *"Father to the fatherless, defender of widows—this is God, whose dwelling is holy."* He is a God who saves, rescuing Israel from Pharaoh and the Red Sea. He is a God who is close at hand, carrying his people in his arms, and dwelling among them in his Temple. The Lord is awesome in his sanctuary, and eventually all the kings of the earth will bow before him.

Psalm 69 is a plea for a life preserver! David's enemies are trying to drown him with lies, and the floodwaters are up to his neck! He worries about giving God a bad reputation: *"Don't let those who trust in you be ashamed because of me...."* He is personally offended when Yahweh God is insulted: *"Passion for your house has consumed me, and the insults of those who insult you have fallen on me."* (This is quoted by Jesus when he cleanses the Temple in John 2:17.) David is in deep despair because his enemies are mocking him. He needs to be kept afloat and promises to praise God among the people when his enemies are defeated.

Psalm 70 is a similar, briefer prayer for God's help. An exhausted King David asks that God do to his enemies what his enemies are doing to him, so that Jerusalem will not be destroyed, nor the towns of Judah, but that those who love the Lord will continue to live in the land.

Psalm 71 is a request for protection from the power of the wicked. God has been with David from birth, and so his whole life is an example to many of God's strength and protection, even now in David's old age: *"Now that I am old and gray, do not abandon me, O God. Let me proclaim your power to this new generation, your mighty miracles to all who come after me."*

Psalm 72, written by King Solomon, is a request that God would give him a love of justice so that he may judge the people in the right way and treat the poor fairly. He wants the people to feel refreshed by his rule *"like spring rain on freshly cut grass,"* and therefore be able to flourish in life. Even more: *"May all nations be blessed through him and bring him praise."* The intent of the prayer is that God would be praised among the nations as Israel flourishes under the wise and capable leadership of its king.

Focus: Psalm 71 beautifully expresses the fact of God's intimate knowledge of us, from conception and birth to old age. Throughout his lifetime, the psalmist has been aware of God's presence. This has shaped his life. His faith, wisdom and joy have influenced others: *"My life is an example to many, because you have been my strength and protection. That is why I can never stop praising you."* Now in his old age, David wants to end well by passing on to the next generation what he knows

315

and has experienced. Wise words! What better ending could there be for any of us who love God, than to pass what we know to the next generation?

Prayer: Lord, we rejoice to know that you have known us from the very beginning. You have been with us throughout our lives, revealing yourself and giving us the wisdom to better know and serve you. May we be faithful to teach the next generation of believers! Amen.

Day 166 — Reflection

June 14

One of the important recurring themes in the Psalms is that Yahweh is the God of all nations, not just the God of Israel within the boundaries of the Promised Land. Israel's neighbors, by contrast, were henotheists, meaning that each nation had its own god or gods which were said to exercise power over a particular geographical region.

So, when God revealed himself to Abraham in Genesis 12, and promised that his descendants would have a land of their own, God was establishing the fact that he was the Creator (and Landlord, so to speak) of the whole earth. This is celebrated in Psalm 33: *"The Lord merely spoke, and the heavens were created. He breathed the word, and all the stars were born. He assigned the sea its boundaries and locked the oceans in vast reservoirs."*

As Creator, God is the ruler of all the earth and every nation. This was codified into the Ten Commandments, which began with the acknowledgement of monotheism: there are no other gods besides him.

Monotheism was the root of the Jewish "Shema" (meaning "Listen"): *"Listen, O Israel! The Lord is our God, the Lord alone. And you must love the Lord your God with all your heart, all your soul, and all your strength"* (Deuteronomy 6:4–5).

This theology permeates the Psalms, expressing itself in Israel's worship. There are repeated references to God as Creator; to the danger of worshiping false gods; to the essential goodness and blessing of the earth and our relationship to it; and, to the fact that creation declares the glory of God.

The Psalms offer an invitation to all nations to worship God: *"Let the whole world fear the Lord, and let everyone stand in awe of him. For when he spoke, the world began! It appeared at his command"* (Psalm 33:8–9).

With this invitation comes accountability. To those who oppose or ignore him, *"the Lord frustrates the plans of the nations and thwarts all their schemes."* But to those nations who fear him and follow him: *"What joy for the nation whose God is the Lord, whose people he has chosen as his inheritance."*

The vision expressed in the Psalms is that one day the whole earth will finally be taken from the wicked and given to the righteous. Then, all creation and every nation will be united in worshiping God the Creator. The earth will be filled with his glory: *"Praise the Lord God, the God of Israel, who alone does such wonderful things. Praise his glorious name forever! Let the whole earth be filled with his glory. Amen and amen!"* (Psalm 72:18–20).

> *Prayer: Lord, what a vision—the whole earth united in worship and service of you, our Creator! Until that great day comes, we pray with the psalmist that you would frustrate the plans of those nations who oppose you, and prosper the work of your people in all nations around the world. Amen and amen!*

Day 167　　　　Psalms 73–77

June 15

> Key Text: "I cry out to God; yes, I shout. Oh, that God would listen to me! When I was in deep trouble, I searched for the Lord. All night long I prayed, with hands lifted toward heaven, but my soul was not comforted. I think of God, and I moan, overwhelmed with longing for his help." (Psalm 77:1–3)

Book Three of the Psalms begins with several psalms written by Asaph, a singer, choir director and fine musician *(1 Chronicles 15:16–17, 19).*

Asaph writes in Psalm 73 about his difficulty with envy of the wicked who prosper despite their wickedness. On the surface, they *"seem to lead such painless lives,"* proudly strutting their stuff even as they badmouth others. They mock God, causing the faithful to wonder whether obedience to God is worth it: *"Did I keep my heart pure for nothing? Did I keep myself innocent for no reason?"*

In the end, however, the proud die like everyone else and then face the judgment of God. Better to resist envy and instead keep the Lord in mind: *"Whom have I in heaven but you? I desire you more than anything on earth."*

In Psalm 74, Asaph lets his anger show in protest to God: *"O God, why have you rejected us so long? Why is your anger so intense against the sheep of your own pasture?"* The people are suffering. Jerusalem is in ruins. The enemy has destroyed the sanctuary and all the places where God was worshiped. The prophets are gone. There are no more miraculous signs. Why is God holding back his powerful fists? Asaph prays that God will arise and defend his cause.

In Psalm 75, it is acknowledged that God is near and has a plan for justice—but in his own time. The wicked will inevitably drink the cup of judgment. In the meantime, Asaph will remain faithful. He knows that God is the judge. He decides who will rise and who will fall. *"But as for me, I will always proclaim what God has done; I will sing praises to the God of Jacob."*

Psalm 76 rejoices in God's victory in battle: *"God is honored in Judah; his name is great in Israel. Jerusalem is where he lives; Mount Zion is his home. There he has broken the fiery arrows of the enemy, the shields and swords and weapons of war."* No wonder God is greatly feared. He judges those who do evil. Human defiance only enhances God's glory, for it turns back upon the defiant ones like an errant rocket of self-destruction.

In Psalm 77, Asaph recalls a sleepless night of earnest prayer. Yet, his soul was not comforted. Has the Lord rejected him? He begins to lose hope, but then remembers and is encouraged by all of God's wonderful deeds of long ago, especially the miracle of the Red Sea. He cries out: *"O God, your ways are holy. Is there any god as mighty as you?"*

Focus: In personal and corporate worship, we bring our strong emotions before God. The Psalms give us permission to speak openly about what we feel, and so we encounter words of joy and thanksgiving as well as words of protest, lament and anger. In Psalm 74:3, God is invited by the worshipers to look at the destruction that has been done by their enemies: *"Walk through the awful ruins of the city; see how the enemy has destroyed your sanctuary."* It is startling to see how free the Israelites were to say whatever they felt to God—even to blame him for their sufferings. This freedom is encouraged by God, giving us insight into his empathy and love. Like a parent, he is willing to listen to the emotions of his children out of love for them. Don't be afraid to be honest with God!

Day 168   Psalms 78–83

June 16

> Key Text: "O God, pagan nations have conquered your land, your special possession. They have defiled your holy Temple and made Jerusalem a heap of ruins. ... O Lord, how long will you be angry with us? Forever?" (Psalm 79:1,5)

This selection of psalms completes the contribution of the musician, Asaph. They address Israel's troubled history of disobedience and bitter consequences.

Psalm 78 recalls how God gave his laws to Israel with the expectation that each generation would teach the next so that it *"should set its hope anew on God, not forgetting his glorious miracles and obeying his commands."* Time and time again, however, God provides for his people only to have them rebel. Yet, God is merciful. He protects them from their enemies, and takes them into the Promised Land, enabling them to build a Temple and providing David as their shepherd-king.

Nevertheless, Psalm 79 laments that pagan nations have conquered the Promised Land, killing many, defiling the Temple and leaving Israel an object of scorn. This is the consequence of Israel rebelling against God and turning away from his protection. Asaph cries out, *"O Lord, how long will you be angry with us? Forever?"* He begs God to help, for the glory of his name: *"Let your compassion quickly meet our needs, for we are on the brink of despair."* He asks God to pour out his judgment upon their enemies.

Psalm 80 continues the lament: *"You have fed us with sorrow and made us drink tears by the bucketful. You have made us the scorn of neighboring nations. Our enemies treat us as a joke."* Asaph pleads with God to *"take care of this grapevine,"* Israel, that he has planted but now has been chopped up and burned by enemies: *"Turn us again to yourself, O Lord God of Heaven's Armies. Make your face shine down upon us. Only then will we be saved."*

Psalm 81 is a call to festival in order to sing praises to God! He rescued Israel from Egypt and called her to never bow down before a false god. But Israel didn't listen. God's judgment was to let the Israelites follow their own stubborn desires, living according to their own ideas. He says: *"Listen to me, O my people, while I give you stern warnings. O Israel, if you would only listen to me! You must never have a foreign god; you must not bow down before a false god."* God longs for Israel to return to him so that he may subdue her enemies, and then feed and satisfy her.

Psalm 82 calls for God to give justice to the poor and the orphans by rescuing them from the grasp of evil people. The oppressors are ignorant of God and consequently walk in darkness. They will surely face God's judgment when he judges the earth, because all the nations belong to him.

Psalm 83 asks God not to be silent in response to the uproar of his enemies, but to look, listen and act. Enemies have aligned themselves to wipe out Israel as a nation and destroy the very memory of its existence. Asaph pleads with God to utterly destroy Israel's enemies because only then will they learn *"that you alone are the Most High, supreme over all the earth."*

Focus: Do the recurring themes of revenge, judgment and destruction trouble you? They should, because they are meant to. In a moral universe, created by a holy God, where men and women act on their free will to do good or evil, there are going to be consequences. Our culture rejects the idea of a God who gives us commandments to keep, and who holds the world accountable for its actions. Malevolent pride rejects this and presumes for itself (thanks to Adam and Eve) the right to be a little god, deciding good and evil for itself. Thus the world's constant conflict. Part of worship, therefore, is to beseech God to stop evil.

Prayer: *Lord, we admit it—we get angry for revenge when we see the wicked hurting the poor and defenseless. We want you to do to them what they have done to others. But you are a righteous judge, and more merciful than we are. Lord, do what must be done for your name's sake, and for your Kingdom to come on earth, as it is in heaven. Amen.*

June 17

> Key Text: "Teach me your ways, O Lord, that I may live
> according to your truth! Grant me purity of heart, so that I may
> honor you." (Psalm 86:11)

Psalm 84 is about longing for God: *"How lovely is your dwelling place, O Lord of Heaven's Armies. I long, yes, I faint with longing to enter the courts of the Lord. With my whole being, body and soul, I will shout joyfully to the living God."* There is great joy in trusting him: *"A single day in your courts is better than a thousand anywhere else! I would rather be a gatekeeper in the house of my God than live the good life in the homes of the wicked."* The Lord God is our sun and our shield. He gives us grace and glory. The Lord will withhold no good thing from those who do what is right.

Psalm 85 is a request for the restoration of Israel's fortunes, yet again: *"You held back your fury. You kept back your blazing anger. Now restore us again, O God of our salvation. Put aside your anger against us once more."* The psalmist begs God not to allow his people to return to their foolish ways. *"Surely his salvation is near to those who fear him, so our land will be filled with his glory. Unfailing love and truth have met together. Righteousness and peace have kissed!"* Don't be angry with us forever.

Psalm 86 is a prayer of David, calling for mercy and protection: *"O God, insolent people rise up against me; a violent gang is trying to kill me."* At the same time, it is a request for a pure and undivided heart, so that David may praise God because: *"No pagan god is like you, O Lord. None can do what you do! All the nations you made will come and bow before you, Lord; they will praise your holy name. For you are great and perform wonderful deeds. You alone are God."*

Psalm 87 is a unique psalm of praise for the significance of Jerusalem. It is God's city: *"O city of God, what glorious things are said of you!"* Ultimately, the citizens of all the cities on earth will become citizens of Jerusalem, because all the people on earth belong to God. Jerusalem, as a metaphor, points forward to the New Creation when the heavenly Jerusalem will descend from heaven and be united with earth, where God will dwell forever among all believers *(Revelation 21:1–2).*

Psalm 88 is a prayer of a sick and dying man: *"Now hear my prayer;*

listen to my cry. For my life is full of troubles, and death draws near. I am as good as dead, like a strong man with no strength left." He wonders and frets about the status of the dead: "Do the dead rise up and praise you?" Death seems like rejection and a place of terrors. But the ultimate answer to this prayer is the resurrection of Jesus. It declares that, yes, those who have died can and will rise up to praise him!

Psalm 89 is a hopeful song: "I will sing of the Lord's unfailing love forever! Young and old will hear of your faithfulness. Your unfailing love will last forever. Your faithfulness is as enduring as the heavens." The Kingdom of God will last forever and all heaven with its angels will praise God's glory. Indeed, the heavens and earth come from God and belong to God! The psalm reminds God that he promised to make David's reign eternal because it represents the Kingdom of God on earth. So now, at a time when David's enemies have gained the advantage, the psalm asks for God to keep his promise and stop the enemies of Israel.

Focus: David's request of God is an example for all who seek to honor him: *"Teach me your ways, O Lord, that I may live according to your truth! Grant me purity of heart, so that I may honor you"* (Psalm 86:11). All living things exist for God's glory and pleasure, especially human beings created in his image. To live according to our Creator's truth is our highest calling and aspiration. Anything less than that is living a lie and missing out on the meaning of life!

Prayer: Lord, your presence in our lives is transforming. It gives us hope for the future of this world, when it will become the New Creation, and all the nations of earth will unite in worship and service. We join the angels by celebrating your glory, even in the midst of our present troubles. Amen.

Day 170   Psalms 90–97

June 18

Key Text: "Sing a new song to the Lord! Let the whole earth sing to the Lord! Sing to the Lord; praise his name. Each day proclaim the good news that he saves. Publish his glorious deeds among the nations. Tell everyone about the amazing things he does." (Psalm 96:1–3)

Book Four contains the oldest psalms, one of which is attributed to Moses.

Psalm 90 is the prayer of Moses during the time of Israel's wandering in the wilderness—a time of both joy and pain. It begins with grateful-ness to eternal God whom he calls Israel's true home, even before the world began. But human life is brief: *"Seventy years are given to us! Some even live to eighty. But even the best years are filled with pain and trouble."* Moses asks God to impress upon the people the brevity of life so that they may grow in wisdom while they can. And along the way, to *"satisfy us each morning with your unfailing love, so we may sing for joy to the end of our lives."*

Psalm 91 speaks about the many fears we face. It declares: *"Those who live in the shelter of the Most High will find rest in the shadow of the Al-mighty."* God is our refuge. He protects us from the terrors of the night as well as the dangers of the day. And though many around us are dying, we will not be afraid of disease. God protects us from the plague: *"For he will order his angels to protect you wherever you go."* He promises to rescue those who love him: *"When they call on me, I will answer; I will be with them in trouble. ... I will reward them with a long life and give them my salvation."*

Psalm 92 declares that it is a good thing to give thanks to God in the morning for his unfailing love, and then give thanks in the evening for his faithfulness. We can sing for joy, morning and evening, because of all God has done for us. One day, God's enemies will perish, but his people will exalt him forever. Therefore, they will flourish like palm trees and grow strong like the cedars of Lebanon, declaring that the Lord is just.

Psalm 93 declares that *"the Lord is king!"* and therefore, *"the world stands firm and cannot be shaken."* God has reigned as king from the *"ev-erlasting past."* Nothing on earth can threaten his reign.

Psalm 94 makes clear that God is the judge of the earth and punishes the wicked. Though the wicked seem to go unpunished, and claim that God isn't looking, they are fools: *"[God] punishes the nations—won't he also punish you? He knows everything—doesn't he also know what you are doing?"*

Psalm 95 is an invitation for God's people to sing to the Lord with psalms of praise and thanksgiving. The Lord is a great God, a great King above all gods. He is our Creator and we are the flock under his care. We must not harden our hearts as the Israelites did in the wilderness. Instead, we must listen to his voice today!

Psalm 96 invites the whole earth to sing a *"new song,"* praising God's name and proclaiming the good news that he saves. He alone is worthy. He is to be feared above all gods. *"The gods of other nations are mere idols, but the Lord made the heavens!"* So, nations of the world— *"Give to the Lord the glory he deserves!"* So, heaven and earth—rejoice and be glad; shout his praise! Fields, produce your crops with joy! Trees, rustle your branches with praise! The Lord is coming with justice and truth!

Psalm 97 calls for all the earth to rejoice in the righteousness and justice of God—his fire and lightening! His glory is plain for all to see. Idol worshipers are disgraced; every god must bow to him. *"For you, O Lord, are supreme over all the earth; you are exalted far above all gods."*

Focus: Worship should be fresh and inventive, anticipating the coming freedom of the whole creation to worship God. Psalm 96 invites us to *"sing a new song to the Lord!"* New songs reflect new insights, and new experiences, giving new words to draw attention to the greatness of God. Because God's attributes are without limit, we will never run out of new things to say. In fact, to help us out, even nature will participate—the sea and everything in it will shout his praise! The fields and their crops will burst out with joy! The trees of the forest will rustle with praise *(Psalm 96:11–12).*

Prayer: *Lord, we are your people, created to praise you. Keep us from false gods. Give us the reassurance of knowing that justice will ultimately prevail, and the whole earth will rejoice in you! Amen.*

Day 171   Psalms 98–103

June 19

> **Key Text:** "He has removed our sins as far from us as the east is from the west. The Lord is like a father to his children, tender and compassionate to those who fear him." (Psalm 103:12–13)

These psalms jump off the page with praise for God!

Psalm 98 celebrates a victory of God for his people—*"His right hand has won a mighty victory; his holy arm has shown his saving power!"* God has remembered his promise to love his people, Israel. Therefore, let all the earth *"break out in praise and sing for joy,"* like a joyful symphony before the Lord. Let the seas, rivers and hills join in because *"he will judge the world with justice, and the nations with fairness."*

Psalm 99 declares that *"the Lord is king! Let the nations tremble!"* The

Lord reveals himself to Israel, giving her his laws and decrees. He disciplines her when she goes wrong, but forgives her when she repents.

Psalm 100 is also a moving call for the whole earth to shout with joy to the Lord: *"Worship the Lord with gladness. Come before him, singing with joy. Acknowledge that the Lord is God! He made us, and we are his. We are his people, the sheep of his pasture."* Using the language of the Covenant, the psalmist points to God's unfailing love and faithfulness that continue to each generation. The Gospel of John uses the same Covenant language to describe the incarnate Christ, who was *"full of unfailing love and faithfulness"* (John 1:14).

Psalm 101 is a psalm of David, who sings God's praise and promises to live a blameless life of integrity, forsaking evil and associating with those who do good.

Psalm 102 is the prayer of a middle-aged person overwhelmed with trouble—perhaps a prisoner suffering with a debilitating illness: *"Because of my groaning, I am reduced to skin and bones. ... My life passes as swiftly as the evening shadows. I am withering away like grass."* Then he speaks of Jerusalem as a broken and debilitated city, asking God to rebuild the city even as he hears the groans of prisoners.

Psalm 103 is a prayer remembering all the good things that God does for us. He forgives sins, keeps us safe, and fills our life with good things. His unfailing love is great: *"He has removed our sins as far from us as the east is from the west. The Lord is like a father to his children, tender and compassionate to those who fear him. For he knows how weak we are; he remembers we are only dust."* Let everything he has created praise the Lord, even his armies of angels who serve him and do his will.

Focus: While it seems at times that the psalmists are preoccupied with God's judgment against their enemies, they are also acutely aware of their own sins. It is a good reminder for us as well. It may keep us from being as hard on others, and as easy on ourselves, as we are tempted to be. Psalm 103 gives us a good perspective on the compassion and forgiveness of God. He is patient with our sins out of compassion. His love is unfailing, his punishment is less than we deserve, and his forgiveness is total. *"He has removed our sins as far from us as the east is from the west. The Lord is like a father to his children, tender and compassionate to those who fear him."* God is sympathetic to our human weakness, like a parent is sympathetic to their toddler's lack of self-control. Meditate on Psalm 103 and make its words your own.

Prayer: Lord, we run out of words to praise you for your unfailing love and faithfulness. Thanks for removing our sins as far as the east is from the west, and for your compassion in remembering that we are dust. May we, like David, seek to forsake evil and join the company of those who do good. Amen.

Day 172   Psalms 104–106

June 20

Key Text: "Like our ancestors, we have sinned. We have done wrong! We have acted wickedly! Our ancestors in Egypt were not impressed by the Lord's miraculous deeds. They soon forgot his many acts of kindness to them. Instead they rebelled against him at the Red Sea." (Psalm 106:6–7)

Book Four of the Psalms concludes with praise for the Covenant and for the God of creation who patiently stays with his people even when they reject him.

Psalm 104 is a psalm of praise about the greatness of God revealed in the creation. The psalm proceeds along the themes of Genesis 1 when God created the heavens and earth, with the sun, moon and stars to rule the sky. He separated land from sea, planted grass and trees, and then populated the earth with birds, fish and animals: *"O Lord, what a variety of things you have made! In wisdom you have made them all. The earth is full of your creatures."* All life, including man's, is animated and sustained by God's breath and so, *"I will sing to the Lord as long as I live. I will praise my God to my last breath!"*

Psalm 105 is a psalm of praise about God's special creation—the Covenant people of Israel: *"He always stands by his covenant—the commitment he made to a thousand generations. This is the covenant he made with Abraham and the oath he swore to Isaac. ... 'I will give you the land of Canaan as your special possession.'"* The psalm recalls key events in the story of Israel, notably the stories of the Promise to Abraham, the life of Joseph in Egypt, the Exodus out of Egypt into the wilderness under Moses, and finally the Promised Land: *"All this happened so they would follow his decrees and obey his instructions."*

Psalm 106 is a psalm for the exiled Israelites in Babylon. It recalls the story of Israel from the point of view of her stubbornness and sinfulness. Despite God's powerful deliverance from Egypt, and his miracles of provision in the desert, the people quickly forgot and rebelled against him

326

over and over again. Even worse, they returned to the paganism of their ancestors by worshiping idols. So when they finally occupied the land, they failed to destroy the nations as God had commanded them. In fact, they repeatedly acted just like these nations, doing the same evil. As a result, God handed them over to exile by pagan nations so that they were ruled by those who hated them.

The retelling of the story leads the present exiled people to confess their sins: *"Like our ancestors, we have sinned. We have done wrong! We have acted wickedly!"* (Psalm 106:6). Their repentance then moves them to pray for a return to Jerusalem: *"Save us, O Lord our God! Gather us back from among the nations, so we can thank your holy name and rejoice and praise you. Praise the Lord, the God of Israel, who lives from everlasting to everlasting! Let all the people say, 'Amen!'"* (Psalm 106:47–48).

Focus: It is interesting to note that the psalmists frequently review Israel's past sins as part of their worship. Naming the sins, confessing their stubborn rebellion, and acknowledging that their behavior broke the Covenant they had made with God, enabled them to receive God's forgiveness and hope. Our gracious God always holds open the possibility of forgiveness and restoration for those who confess their sins and desire to do what is right. Their example encourages us to regularly confess our sins as part of our personal and corporate worship.

Prayer: *Lord, when we consider the story of Israel as a whole, we are moved by your patience and grace, despite the repeated sin of your people. You did it for them so that you could do it for us, your New Covenant people. We thank you that you didn't give up on us but sent Jesus to make things right with you, and to give us new life and a new future. Amen.*

Day 173   Reflection

June 21

The Psalms, which continue to be useful as aids in personal and corporate worship, are also useful for theological reflection. In particular, psalms like 105 and 106, which retell the story of Israel from different perspectives, are useful for understanding God and ourselves.

In psalms like these we learn that God has an unrelenting determination to be in fellowship with us. Though he gets angry and frustrated—even heartbroken—over Israel's unfaithfulness, and ours, he will not walk away from the Covenant of faithfulness he made through Moses. Even his punishment of Israel's sins, though sometimes harsh, was not intended as revenge, but discipline for the sake of reconciliation. Tough love.

And so, even after recalling all the ways that Israel was unfaithful to God, the psalmist will still write: *"Give thanks to the Lord, for he is good! His faithful love endures forever"* (Psalm 106:1).

God won't give up, but will go to any length necessary to make things right with us, and right in the world. As New Testament believers, we know this ultimately means the cross.

What we learn about ourselves in the Psalms is how weak and sinful we are: *"Like our ancestors, we have sinned. We have done wrong! We have acted wickedly!"* (Psalm 106:6). And so, when the psalmist reviews the sinful history of the Israelites, it is not to condemn their ancestors, but to identify with them.

It is the same in our present day reading of the Psalms. We too are like Israel. Despite all God does for us, we continually forsake his commandments and wisdom, and follow our passions into idolatry. Yet God continues to show us his grace and mercy.

The apostle Paul draws upon the story of Israel, as told in the historical books and recounted in the Psalms and by the prophets, to make his case for Christ in Romans. He begins by showing how the pagans and then the Roman moralists are all sinners. Then he recounts Israel's story to argue that even they who had every advantage, including God's Law, are also sinners: *"For everyone has sinned; we all fall short of God's glorious standard. Yet God, with undeserved kindness, declares that we are righteous. He did this through Christ Jesus when he freed us from the penalty for our sins"* (Romans 3:23–24).

By reading straight through the Bible, we observe how consistently it addresses the major themes of Creation, Fall, Redemption and New Creation. The Psalms, in particular, enrich our theological understanding of God and ourselves, by placing its teaching into the context of worship, where our emotions are engaged as well as our minds.

Prayer: Lord, we identify with the Israelites in their struggle with sin. We, like they, are powerless to keep your commands. So thank you for Jesus, who died in our place to set us free from the guilt of sin, and who gave us his Spirit to keep us free from the power of sin. May we always choose to obey you. Amen.

June 22

> **Key Text:** "Give thanks to the Lord, for he is good! His faithful love endures forever. Has the Lord redeemed you? Then speak out! Tell others he has redeemed you from your enemies."
> (Psalm 107:1–2)

Psalm 107 is filled with testimonies about those who suffered for various reasons but found help from the Lord. They are each encouraged to *"praise the Lord for his great love and for the wonderful things he has done for them."* Some were homeless, lost and hungry; some imprisoned because of their lawlessness; some were fools who rebelled and suffered for their sins; some faced terrors on the seas while in ships. The Lord gives and takes away: *"Those who are wise will take all this to heart; they will see in [Israel's] history the faithful love of the Lord"* (Psalm 107:43).

Psalm 108 is both a hymn of praise for God's unfailing love and faithfulness, as well as a cry for deliverance. David knows that *"with God's help we will do mighty things, for he will trample down our foes."* Therefore, his heart is confident in the Lord. He sings God's praises among the unbelieving nations: *"Be exalted, O God, above the highest heavens. May your glory shine over all the earth."*

Psalm 109 asks God for the truth to come out because David's enemies slander him without reason. What makes it worse is that these enemies were once friends: *"I love them, but they try to destroy me with accusations even as I am praying for them! They repay evil for good, and hatred for my love."* He is cursed because he allegedly *"refused all kindness to others."* Such is the life of leaders. Inevitably, leaders disappoint others. They face criticism, opposition and even hostility. But the Lord is the defender of those who are wrongly accused.

Psalm 110 contains Messianic references. King David writes, *"The Lord said to my Lord* [i.e., the Lord said to me], *'Sit in the place of honor at my right hand until I humble your enemies, making them a footstool under your feet.'"* This is quoted by Jesus in Mark 12:36, and then again by Peter on the Day of Pentecost in Acts 2:34–35. In saying this, David was pointing toward a future king, and that king and Messiah was Jesus. King David never literally sat at the right hand of God, but the resurrected, glorified Jesus does.

Day 175   Psalms 111–118

June 23

Key Text: "Their idols are merely things of silver and gold, shaped by human hands. ... And those who make idols are just like them, as are all who trust in them." (Psalm 115:4,8)

Here are eight psalms which give more reasons to praise God:

Psalm 111 praises God for his amazing deeds because *"all he does is just and good, and all his commandments are trustworthy."* Therefore, *"fear of the Lord is the foundation of true wisdom."*

Psalm 112 praises God that his commandments give wisdom which, when lived consistently and passed on to our children, brings success to the next generation. The good deeds of the next generation will be like light shining in the darkness, giving them honor and influence that will be remembered.

Psalm 113 gives lavish praise to the Lord who is *"high above the nations; his glory is higher than the heavens."* He looks down to earth and lifts up the poor from the dust and sets them among princes.

Psalm 114 praises God who delivered his people from slavery in Egypt and chose to dwell among them. So amazing was this act of power that *"the Red Sea saw them coming and hurried out of the way! ... The mountains skipped like rams. ... Tremble, O earth, at the presence of the God of Jacob."*

Psalm 115 praises God for his *"unfailing love and faithfulness."* The God of Israel does what he wishes, while the idols of the surrounding nations are lifeless pieces of wood—and those who make them become like them. The Lord blesses those who praise him: *"The heavens belong to the Lord, but he has given the earth to all humanity."*

Psalm 116 praises God for hearing our prayers. He hears them *"because he bends down to listen."* In times of danger or sorrow, or even when we are facing death, *"the Lord protects those of childlike faith."* In life, we should keep God's promises. In growing old, we should remember that *"the Lord cares deeply when his loved ones die."*

Psalm 117, in two short verses, urges all the nations of the earth to praise God: *"Praise the Lord, all you nations. Praise him, all you people of the earth. For his unfailing love for us is powerful; the Lord's faithfulness endures forever. Praise the Lord!"* He never forgets his Covenant promises to his people.

Psalm 118 urges all of Israel to praise God for his Covenant love: *"His faithful love endures forever."* The Lord is greater than the hostile nations surrounding Israel and her king: *"My enemies did their best to kill me, but the Lord rescued me. The Lord is my strength and my song; he has given me victory."*

Focus: The Psalms reflect the theology and preaching of Israel's prophets when mentioning the subject of idolatry. Idols are forbidden in the Second Commandment as a means of worshiping God, and are exposed as powerless. Psalm 115 explains the obvious— that they are *"merely things of silver and gold, shaped by human hands. They have mouths but cannot speak, and eyes but cannot see. They have ears but cannot hear, and noses but cannot smell. They have hands but cannot feel, and feet but cannot walk, and throats but cannot make a sound."* Instead, idols are merely projections of fallen humanity. They are the reversal of creation—gods made in man's image, if you will. In the modern world, idols are not ordinarily images of silver and gold, but anything (good or evil) that replaces God in our lives. All "God substitutes" inevitably disappoint and sometimes seriously harm us. Worst of all, they keep us distracted from the one true God.

Prayer: *Lord, we never run out of reasons to praise and thank you, in hard times as well as good times. Help us to keep our balance in life by staying focused on your Covenant commitment of unfailing love and faithfulness. Above all, keep us from idols. Amen.*

June 24

> Key Text: "Your word is a lamp to guide my feet and a light for
> my path." (Psalm 119:105)

This magnificent psalm of 176 verses is the longest chapter of the Bible, and is organized as an acrostic of the 22 letters of the Hebrew alphabet—from Aleph to Taw. It is an exposition of the nature and function of God's Word as law, decree, commandment, and instruction, and the believer's response to it.

Aleph: *"Joyful are those who obey his laws and search for him with all their hearts."*

Beth: *"I have hidden your word in my heart, that I might not sin against you."*

Gimel: *"Open my eyes to see the wonderful truths in your instructions."*

Daleth: *"Keep me from lying to myself; give me the privilege of knowing your instructions."*

He: *"Make me walk along the path of your commands, for that is where my happiness is found."*

Waw: *"I will walk in freedom, for I have devoted myself to your commandments."*

Zayin: *"I reflect at night on who you are, O Lord; therefore, I obey your instructions."*

Heth: *"O Lord, your unfailing love fills the earth; teach me your decrees."*

Teth: *"I used to wander off until you disciplined me; but now I closely follow your word."*

Yodh: *"You made me; you created me. Now give me the sense to follow your commands."*

Kaph: *"In your unfailing love, spare my life; then I can continue to obey your laws."*

Lamedh: *"I will never forget your commandments, for by them you give me life."*

Mem: *"Your commandments give me understanding; no wonder I hate every false way of life."*

Nun: *"Your word is a lamp to guide my feet and a light for my path."*

Samekh: *"You are my refuge and my shield; your word is my source of* hope."

Ayin: *"Truly, I love your commands more than gold, even the finest gold."*

Pe: *"The teaching of your word gives light, so even the simple can under-stand."*

Tsadhe: *"Your promises have been thoroughly tested; that is why I love them so much."*

Qoph: *"I rise early, before the sun is up; I cry out for help and put my hope in your words."*

Resh: *"Many persecute and trouble me, yet I have not swerved from your laws."*

Shin: *"Those who love your instructions have great peace and do not stumble."*

Taw: *"I have wandered away like a lost sheep; come and find me, for I have not forgotten your commands."*

Focus: As you have no doubt noticed on our journey through the Bible, God's Word is central to Judeo-Christianity. This arises from God's nature; he is a God who speaks. He spoke the universe into being, and continues to speak through general revelation (nature, reason, and human conscience) and special revelation (his specific self-disclosure to his Covenant people). One of the defining moments of Israel was God's gift of his commandments through Moses. By his command-ments, God made himself known, as well as his will for human life and community. His Word gives us knowledge and wisdom: *"Your word is a lamp to guide my feet and a light for my path"* (Psalm 119:105). In worship, the Holy Spirit makes God's written Word alive and active in our lives.

Prayer: Lord, we rejoice that you are a God who speaks! Thanks for the gift of your Word, for by it we find life and understanding, so that we may serve you faithfully and make you known to others. Amen!

Day 177 — Psalms 120–127

June 25

> Key Text: "Restore our fortunes, Lord, as streams renew the desert. Those who plant in tears will harvest with shouts of joy. They weep as they go to plant their seed, but they sing as they return with the harvest." (Psalm 126:4–6)

The titles of Psalms 120 through134 indicate that they are traveling songs sung by pilgrims on their way to celebrate the festivals of Passover, Harvest and Shelters. The themes represent what people on a long and dangerous journey to Jerusalem might be feeling.

Psalm 120 is about the threat from liars and all deceitful people along the way, who deserve to have their tongues *"pierced with sharp arrows and burned with glowing coals."* It is tiresome, they say, to live far away from Jerusalem *"among people who hate peace"* and want war.

Psalm 121 reflects the pilgrim walking in the heat of the sun as the walls of Jerusalem come into view, high on the hill: *"I look up to the mountains—does my help come from there? My help comes from the Lord, who made heaven and earth!"* The Lord who watches over Israel never sleeps; he protects us from all harm as a shade protects from the heat of the sun: *"The sun will not harm you by day, nor the moon at night."*

Psalm 122 expresses the joy of the pilgrimage to worship in Jerusalem: *"I was glad when they said to me, 'Let us go to the house of the Lord.' And now here we are, standing inside your gates, O Jerusalem."* All the tribes make their pilgrimages as required by the Law: *"Pray for peace in Jerusalem. May all who love this city prosper."*

Psalm 123 is a prayer addressed to God, enthroned in heaven, on whom we depend for mercy: *"We have had more than our fill of the scoffing of the proud and the contempt of the arrogant."*

Psalm 124 ponders the chilling thought: *"What if the Lord had not been on our side when people attacked us?"* Israel would have been swallowed alive, but the Lord did not let their enemies' teeth tear them apart: *"Our help is from the Lord, who made heaven and earth."*

Psalm 125 takes comfort in the realization that *"those who trust in the Lord are as secure as Mount Zion; they will not be defeated but will endure forever."* As Judge, God will not allow the wicked to rule forever in the *"land of the godly."* The psalm concludes with a prayer that still resonates today: *"May Israel have peace!"*

Psalm 126 rejoices in the return of the exiles to Jerusalem. It was like a dream! The people were filled with laughter and sang for joy, while the other nations watched in amazement at what God had done. Yet moments of joy, in this life, are often preceded and followed by times of testing and seasons of drought. Thus the psalm asks for a season of renewal: *"Restore our fortunes, Lord, as streams renew the desert. Those who plant in tears will harvest with shouts of joy."*

Psalm 127 declares that God alone establishes our life and well-being, giving us families to enjoy and food to eat. He protects our lives, like he protected his city, Jerusalem: *"Unless the Lord builds a house, the work of the builders is wasted. Unless the Lord protects a city, guarding it with sentries will do no good."*

Focus: Pilgrimage was a necessary spiritual discipline in Israel, since the tribes lived away from Jerusalem. The journey itself was a time of fellowship and spiritual reflection. The songs expressed the joys and sorrows of their daily lives, as well as the joyful anticipation of worshiping the Lord in his holy Temple. In many ways, our life on earth is a pilgrimage. The joy awaiting us in the New Jerusalem, our future home, gladdens our hearts and helps us to persevere in faith, here and now. Worship itself, is like a weekly (or even daily) festival of fellowship with God, our Creator and Redeemer.

Prayer: *Lord, we can imagine the thrill of pilgrims seeing the walls of Jerusalem and the Temple after a long, dangerous journey. We too look forward to seeing the heavenly Jerusalem at the end our weary lives on earth, rejoicing at the end of our mortal journey and the beginning of our everlasting life. Amen.*

Day 178   Psalms 128–134

June 26

Key Text: "How wonderful and pleasant it is when brothers live together in harmony! For harmony is as precious as the anointing oil that was poured over Aaron's head, that ran down his beard and onto the border of his robe." (Psalm 133:1–2)

These psalms complete the pilgrim psalms section. They are meditations and songs of faith for Israelites on their journeys to Jerusalem.

Psalm 128 is praise for the blessings of God, especially the simple blessings of work, prosperity and family life: *"May the Lord continually bless you from Zion. May you see Jerusalem prosper as long as you live. May you live to enjoy your grandchildren. May Israel have peace!"*

The writer of Psalm 129 testifies that, though enemies have persecuted him from his youth, they have never defeated him. He expresses the wish that all who hate Jerusalem (i.e., resist the presence of God) be turned back in shameful defeat.

In Psalm 130, the writer cries out from the depths of despair for help from God as he draws near to Jerusalem—to God's presence in his Temple. He is aware of his sin: *"Lord, if you kept a record of our sins, who, O*

Lord, could ever survive? But you offer forgiveness, that we might learn to fear you." Confident in God's forgiveness and unfailing love, he testifies: *"I am counting on the Lord; yes, I am counting on him. I have put my hope in his word."*

Psalm 131 expresses a childlike faith: *"I don't concern myself with matters too great or too awesome for me to grasp. Instead, I have calmed and quieted myself, like a weaned child who no longer cries for its mother's milk. Yes, like a weaned child is my soul within me."*

Psalm 132 recalls King David's desire and promise to build a Temple for God to dwell in, where the Ark of the Covenant would rest. In the end, it was built by his son, King Solomon. The psalm concludes with a prayer that God's promise to maintain and bless a royal line from the house of David would be fulfilled: *"For the sake of your servant David, do not reject the king you have anointed."* The answer to this prayer came with King Jesus.

Psalm 133 is a celebration of unity and brotherhood: *"How wonderful and pleasant it is when brothers live together in harmony! For harmony is as precious as the anointing oil that was poured over Aaron's head, that ran down his beard and onto the border of his robe."* Unity and brotherhood is ultimately fulfilled in the New Jerusalem, where there is blessing and life everlasting.

Psalm 134 concludes the pilgrim psalms with an all-hands-on-deck call for those who serve in the house of the Lord to *"lift your hands toward the sanctuary, and praise the Lord. May the Lord, who made heaven and earth, bless you from Jerusalem."*

Focus: Thematically, the Psalms move back and forth from this world to the next, from the present moment to the glorious future when Israel's King will reign forever on the earth, and all the nations of the earth will gather together to worship him. There is an obvious tension between the "now" and the "then." So the Psalms call us to faith, perseverance and obedience in the struggles of the "now." By keeping God's commandments, even when others don't, we strive to live "now," in this present evil age, as we shall live "then," when God's ancient plan of redemption is fully realized. Until that the day, we wait and hope. The capacity for hope is one of the great gifts of God. His Word opens our imagination to what the future will look like: There will be peace on earth; unity in worship; harmony among peoples. Can't wait!

Day 179   Psalms 135–139

June 27

> Key Text: "Search me, O God, and know my heart; test me and
> know my anxious thoughts. Point out anything in me that
> offends you, and lead me along the path of everlasting life."
> (Psalm 139:23-24)

Today's five psalms bring fresh expression to familiar themes.

Psalm 135 encourages those who lead worship in the Temple to *"cele-brate his lovely name with music."* The God who has chosen Israel as his special people, and delivered her from slavery in Egypt, is greater than any other god. He has sovereign power to create and destroy in accordance with his redeeming purpose. The Lord lives and reigns among his people in Jerusalem. He has no rivals, for the idols of the nations are merely man-made objects of silver and gold, not able to think or speak, and those who make them are just like them.

Psalm 136 is song of God's Covenant love. The twenty-six calls to the congregation to give thanks to God are met with the same antiphonal response: *"His faithful love endures forever."* The repetition in this psalm drives home the truth of God's greatness and his enduring love for his weak people: *"He remembered us in our weakness. His faithful love endures forever."* His people may forsake him, but God remains faithful to his Covenant promise.

Psalm 137 is a lament, written from exile in Babylon by those who long for Jerusalem as they endure bitter lives enforced by their conquerors: *"Beside the rivers of Babylon, we sat and wept as we thought of Jerusalem. ... For our captors demanded a song from us. Our tormentors insisted on a joyful hymn: 'Sing us one of those songs of Jerusalem!' But how can we sing the songs of Lord while in a pagan land?"* But sing they must, even if in their darker moments of despair and humiliation they wish for their captors what their captors have done to them: *"Happy is the one who pays you back for what you have done to us. Happy is the one who takes your*

337

babies and smashes them against the rocks!"

Psalm 138 gives heartfelt thanks to God who keeps his promises and answers the prayers of his people. One day, the whole earth will sing about the Lord's ways. In the meantime, God leads his people by his powerful right hand: *"The Lord will work out his plans for my life...."*

Psalm 139 is a remarkable psalm by King David, of God's intimate knowledge of us from the moment we are conceived until the moment of our last breath. During the course of our lives, God keeps a diary: *"Every day of my life was recorded in your book."* He watches over the details—he examines our hearts and knows everything about us, including where we go and what we do. David becomes overwhelmed thinking about these things: *"Such knowledge is too wonderful for me, too great for me to understand!"*

As he marvels at the mysteries of the Lord, David is suddenly struck with the irony of the wicked. How could they hate a God like the Lord? Perhaps David should set his heart against the wicked because of the way they dishonor God. But, of course, God is able to defend himself. Besides, who can know one's motives when he sets out to defend God? He concludes with a prayer of introspection: *"Search me, O God, and know my heart; test me and know my anxious thoughts. Point out anything in me that offends you, and lead me along the path of everlasting life."*

Focus: Psalm 137:9 is a shocking sentence: *"Happy is the one who takes your babies and smashes them against the rocks!"* It is raw and it is real. The sympathetic reader will understand dark thoughts of revenge by those who have been brutalized themselves in this way. Imagine an invading army cruelly moving through your town, killing your friends, destroying your property and yes, even slaughtering children in the most horrifying way imaginable. Who could not have dark thoughts of revenge?

Of course, the expression of these raw emotions is not license to pursue them. God is judge; revenge is his. But how can we ever find healing from such brutality? Perhaps never in this life. Those who have experienced war never entirely get over it. What we cling to is the knowledge that Jesus understands. He loved us so much that he came to join us in our mortal sufferings. And he experienced horrors that no human could understand—for our sake. One day this messy world will be sorted out and made right. Meanwhile, the work of faith is to cling to this hope.

Day 180   Reflection

June 28

You have no doubt noticed that a common complaint in the Psalms is the behavior of one's enemies. Usually this refers to the enemies of King David who wanted to kill him, or failing that, to discredit him, because discrediting the king of Israel supposedly discredits the God of Israel as well. So we see, on many occasions, that King David is angry with his enemies out of concern for the Lord's reputation.

It's true that our enemies today will probably not be rival warrior kings, intent on killing us, but rather people who oppose us or emotionally hurt us because of jealousy, competitiveness, revenge, or any other number of reasons.

But as often as David prays for terrible things to happen to his enemies, they continue to afflict him throughout the Psalms. Observing this, we might ask ourselves why God allows our enemies to continue to afflict us.

One reason could be that God wants us to have a clearer picture of ourselves. Critics criticize, and no one likes to be criticized, but it is always good to listen to one's critics, because there is often a kernel of truth to be discovered. If we are humble enough, we might learn something about ourselves that will help us to be more effective in life.

Another purpose for our enemies is to reveal the power of God. Without the threat of enemy opposition, we might never learn that God is our protector. David prays, *"Though I am surrounded by troubles, you will protect me from the anger of my enemies"* (Psalm 138:7).

Probably the most obvious (and unwanted) reason for God to allow our enemies to afflict us is to allow our endurance to grow. This trait of mature faith, like other traits, is only discovered and developed in situations which require it.

James 1:2–4 says, *"Dear brothers and sisters, when troubles come your way, consider it an opportunity for great joy. For you know that when your faith is tested, your endurance has a chance to grow. So let it grow, for when your endurance is fully developed, you will be perfect and complete, needing nothing."*

We must remember that God sees all things on earth. The fool says that God doesn't notice or doesn't care, but God does care and he does notice. My expectation is that in the Last Judgment, God will expose all the secrets, good and evil, of men and women. He will condemn those who have done evil and commend those who have done good. In this way, history will be sorted out, wrongs will be righted, and God himself will be vindicated as the good and righteous Lord of history.

> **Prayer:** *Lord, you have commanded us to love our enemies. This doesn't mean that we must like them, but that we recognize that they are made in your image. We acknowledge you as the righteous Judge of all the earth. So help us not to presume that role for ourselves. Keep us from entertaining revenge in our hearts, for you have said that you will forgive our debts as we forgive our debtors. Amen.*

Day 181   Psalms 140–145

June 29

Key Text: "Lord, do not let evil people have their way. Do not let their evil schemes succeed, or they will become proud." (Psalm 140:8)

Today we have the final psalms of King David about his hopes and fears and faith.

Psalm 140 is an earnest prayer for God to protect him and the vulnerable citizens of Israel from the blots and traps set by evil, violent people. David asks God to frustrate the plans of his enemies: *"Let my enemies be destroyed by the very evil they have planned for me."* He is confident of God's help: *"But I know the Lord will help those they persecute; he will give justice to the poor."*

Psalm 141 is a cry for help—another prayer for protection from David's enemies. He asks God to take control of what he does and says, so that his enemies cannot accuse him of hypocrisy. He asks that the wicked will fall into their own nets while he escapes.

Psalm 142 is a prayer arising from a time when David felt overwhelmed and alone, hiding in a cave from Saul who sought to kill him. He sees traps set by his enemies everywhere. He begs for God to rescue him so that as a free man, he can thank him before the people.

Psalm 143 is another prayer from the cave where David's enemy has knocked him to the ground and forced him *"to live in darkness like those in the grave."* His fear and depression deepen, and so he asks for rescue: *"May your gracious Spirit lead me forward on a firm footing."*

Psalm 144 is a meditative prayer, reflecting on the wonderful fact that God notices mere mortals—especially David himself. God has made him strong in battle and feared among the nations. His enemies lie, but David will sing a new song to the Lord, celebrating his victory. *"Save me!"* he cries out. Let the sons of Israel flourish in life, happily married with children and with barns filled with crops, fields filled with flocks and no cries of alarm in the town squares.

Psalm 145 is David's last. Appropriately, it is a psalm exalting the Lord as his God and King forever. The Lord is great, and worthy of praise! May each generation hear and pass on the mighty acts of God so that everyone may know about the goodness of God: *"The Lord is merciful and compassionate, slow to get angry and filled with unfailing love. The Lord is good to everyone. He showers compassion on all his creation."* Furthermore, God's Kingdom is everlasting; he protects those who love him and destroys the wicked: *"I will praise the Lord, and may everyone on earth bless his holy name forever and ever."*

Focus: How do we pray about those who do evil in the world? I find the words of Psalm 140:8 helpful: *"Lord, do not let evil people have their way. Do not let their evil schemes succeed, or they will become proud."* I don't believe that this is a prayer of revenge—i.e., asking God to make them suffer. But it does ask that God would frustrate their plans so that they cannot bring misery upon others. There are lots of ways that God could do this and, perhaps in so doing, open their eyes to the self-defeating nature of evil. Not to mention the larger issue of their accountability to God for doing evil. When God intervenes by frustrating their plans, he acts with compassion toward their potential victims, and at the same time opens the door to possible repentance and a change of heart. The Lord's Prayer directs us to pray for deliverance from evil, and from the Evil One. This would surely involve God frustrating the plans of the Evil One! The greatest defeat of the Evil One is for those who do evil to be converted to faith! Let's pray for that outcome!

Prayer: *Lord, like King David, may we be energized by a vision of your everlasting Kingdom and the promise of blessing and sheer joy therein. May those who have*

Day 182   Psalms 146–150

June 30

> Key Text: "Let everything that breathes sing praises to the Lord! Praise the Lord!" (Psalm 150:6)

The book of Psalms concludes with five songs of—what else?—*praise!*

Psalm 146 begins with the strongest possible commitment to a life of praise: *"Let all that I am praise the Lord. I will praise the Lord as long as I live. I will sing praises to my God with my dying breath."* Only God is worthy of such praise. He is the Eternal One, Creator of heaven and earth. He is just and loving, the protector of the weak and the keeper of his promises. He will reign forever!

Psalm 147 is a song of praise about the return of Jewish exiles from Babylonia to rebuild Jerusalem. The brokenhearted are given hope. Clearly the Lord delights in those who fear him. Therefore: *"Glorify the Lord, O Jerusalem! Praise your God, O Zion!"* God has done for Israel what he has not done for any other nation: *"He has revealed his words to Jacob, his decrees and regulations to Israel."*

Psalm 148 summons the angels of heaven, as well as the sun, moon and stars, to praise the Lord. In fact, *"Let every created thing give praise to the Lord."* This includes every land creature, sea creature, and bird—even the mountains and their trees. And, of course, all people: *"kings of the earth and all people, rulers and judges of the earth, young men and young women, old men and children."* Why this great summons to praise God? *"For his name is very great; his glory towers over the earth and heaven!"*

Psalm 149 calls the *"assembly of the faithful"* in the Temple to sing God's praises. Use dance and instruments: *"Praise his name with dancing, accompanied by tambourine and harp."* And when called by God to do so, worship him by being his agent of judgment. God is honored also when his enemies are frustrated in their evil plans.

Psalm 150 concludes the psalter like the final volley of a fireworks display—everything is shot into the air, exploding with the sights and sounds of worship. There is praise with human singing and dancing in the sanctuary, accompanied by the blast of the ram's horn, the rattling of the tambourine, the sultry vibrations of the lyre and harp, the clash of cymbals—loud clanging cymbals! And lest we think that anyone or anything is excluded: *"Let everything that breathes sing praises to the Lord! Praise the Lord!"*

Focus: Hopefully you have a new appreciation for how the Psalms can help you live out the highest calling upon your life—to praise the Lord with all that you are and for as long as you live! Of course, this does not mean that praising God only takes place in devotions or liturgy or in public services. Praising God is something we do with our whole selves, all day long.

The apostle Paul writes (with the Old Testament clearly in mind): *"I plead with you to give your bodies to God because of all he has done for you. Let them be a living and holy sacrifice—the kind he will find acceptable. This is truly the way to worship him"* (Romans 12:1). The vision of Psalms, and of the whole Bible, is that everything comes from God and belongs to him, including ourselves. Therefore, all that we do, in work and in play, is in grateful response to his blessings in our lives.

Prayer: *Lord, may we live the spirit of the Psalms by dedicating our lives to praise you always and in every situation, for there is no other god besides you. Amen!*

Day 183 — Proverbs 1–4

July 1

> Key Text: These are the proverbs of Solomon, David's son, king of Israel. Their purpose is to teach people wisdom and discipline, to help them understand the insights of the wise. Their purpose is to teach people to live disciplined and successful lives, to help them do what is right, just, and fair. (Proverbs 1:1–3)

We come now to the book of Proverbs, attributed in the text to King Solomon, David's son. In the historical books of the Old Testament, King Solomon is widely celebrated for his wisdom *(1 Kings 10:23).*

While the book of Psalms guides us in worship with great theology, Proverbs guides us in wise living by the practical application of theological knowledge. Think of proverbs as truisms which express the way life works, by God's decree. Consequently, as Proverbs 1 makes clear: *"Fear of the Lord is the foundation of true knowledge, but fools despise wisdom and discipline"* (Proverbs 1:7).

Specifically, God's commandments establish the boundary markers for life wisdom, and the Proverbs guide us to practical application for a happy and successful life. This is not magic, however, nor automatic. Proverbs express general outcomes. We need to take into consideration other factors at work in the world and in our personal lives. These would include the actions of others, random events, and the power of sin. The power of sin, in particular, undermines our best efforts and tempts us, like fools, to despise wisdom and discipline.

Therefore, godly people are not always successful and happy at every moment. But in general, God's way works, and most of the time our lives are blessed when we follow the insights of the Proverbs: *"Their purpose is to teach people to live disciplined and successful lives, to help them do what is right, just, and fair."*

You'll discover that reading Proverbs is like facing a machine gun load of advice—verse after verse hitting us like bullets. There are broad themes, but hundreds of applications. Therefore, as we go through Proverbs we will focus mainly on broad themes, and then particular proverbs. You'll need to read the text itself to fully benefit.

Proverbs are meant to be passed on as instruction, so there are a lot of exhortations like Proverbs 1:8: *"My child, listen when your father corrects you. Don't neglect your mother's instruction."* Good advice for our children, and for all of us.

Often wisdom is personified in the Proverbs: *"Wisdom shouts in the streets. She cries out in the public square"* (Proverbs 1:20). Many believe that the personified Wisdom of the Proverbs is a precursor to Jesus as the Word of God in John 1:1–14.

Here are some highlights from Proverbs 1–4:

Proverbs 1 reminds us that wisdom cannot be gotten in the moment of a crisis. It takes time and thought: *"When they cry for help, I* [wisdom] *will not answer. Though they anxiously search for me, they will not find me."*

Proverbs 2 urges us to search for wisdom as we would for hidden treasure. By seeking, we will find what is truly profitable for us. Wisdom will fill us with joy and keep us safe, especially from evil people and seductive situations.

Proverbs 3 is loaded with great truths about trust: *"Trust in the Lord with all your heart; do not depend on your own understanding. Seek his will in all you do, and he will show you which path to take."* And: *"Honor the Lord with your wealth and...he will fill your barns with grain."*

Proverbs 4 is a plea for the wise to listen to wisdom's counsel: *"If you prize wisdom, she will make you great. ... The way of the righteous is like the first gleam of dawn, which shines ever brighter until the full light of day. But the way of the wicked is like total darkness."* Therefore: *"Guard your heart above all else, for it determines the course of your life."*

> **Focus:** God's wisdom will only prove itself true if you trust in him and discipline yourself to keep his commandments. Many people believe in wisdom's ideals, but don't discipline themselves to actually act on what they believe. So they live in suspended animation, between belief and unbelief—the worst place to be.
>
> The book of James makes clear that when you ask God for wisdom, he will give it to you, but only if you trust in him: *"But when you ask him, be sure that your faith is in God alone. Do not waver, for a person with divided loyalty is as unsettled as a wave of the sea that is blown and tossed by the wind. Such people should not expect to receive anything from the Lord. Their loyalty is divided between God and the world, and they are unstable in everything they do"* (James 1:5–8).
>
> ***Prayer:*** *Lord, thank you for your abundant wisdom. Now, give us the good sense and discipline to live by it! Amen.*

Day 184   Proverbs 5–9

July 2

> Key Text: Listen as Wisdom calls out! Hear as understanding raises her voice! On the hilltop along the road, she takes her stand at the crossroads. By the gates at the entrance to the town, on the road leading in, she cries aloud, "I call to you, to all of you!" (Proverbs 8:1–4)

The next five Proverbs, which are cast as a father mentoring his son, lay out the struggle between wisdom and foolishness, especially for the young. The choices are presented with frank, worldly illustrations.

Proverbs 5 is a parental call: *"pay attention to my wisdom."* Foolishness is introduced as a prostitute. (Both wisdom and foolishness are feminine in the Proverbs.) Immoral sexual pleasure is a strong temptation and a deadly trap. It can undermine your reputation, consume your body, and destroy relationships *(Proverbs 5:8–14)*. Instead, direct sexual desire toward your marriage: *"Let your wife be a fountain of blessing for you. Rejoice in the wife of your youth. She is a loving deer, a graceful doe. Let her breasts satisfy you always."*

Chapter 6 is a warning against laziness: *"Take a lesson from the ants, you lazybones. Learn from their ways and become wise!"* Laziness leads to debt, and debt corrupts the soul. It leads to deceitfulness and manipulation of others. So let wisdom and self-discipline be your guide; it will protect you from other temptations as well.

Proverbs 7 returns to the warning against sexual temptation. The seduction of a foolish young man by a wayward wife is described in uncomfortable detail: *"Come, let's drink our fill of love until morning. Let's enjoy each other's caresses, for my husband is not home. He is on a long trip."* She was dressed to lure him; her bed perfumed with myrrh, aloes, and cinnamon: *"So she seduced him with her pretty speech and enticed him with her flattery. He followed her at once, like an ox going to the slaughter."* Don't let the allure of forbidden sex lead you down the road of ruin.

Wisdom is introduced in chapter 8. She is the woman whose words lead us to a successful and abundant life. She gives us great advice, worth more than pure gold, or rubies. Her commonsense advice is to love righteousness but hate evil. Stay away from pride, corruption and perverse speech. Wisdom has been with God from the beginning, when he shaped the heavens and earth. She was *"the architect at his side...his constant delight, rejoicing always in his presence...with the human family."* Wisdom is the way the world works, by God's design. Wisdom rewards those who love her. Listen to her and be wise.

Proverbs 9 takes us to Wisdom's house, where she has prepared a great banquet. Everyone is invited to come and eat: *"Leave your simple ways behind, and begin to live; learn to use good judgment."* Mockers aren't interested in Wisdom; therefore, she instructs the wise so that the wise become even wiser, while fools become even more foolish. Wisdom will add years to your life. But *"the woman named Folly is brash. She is ignorant and doesn't know it. She sits in her doorway.... She calls out to men going by who are minding their own business."* Forbidden pleasure is a powerful lure, but leads to death.

Focus: When we are young, we are driven by our emotions (and hormones) into situations where our lack of experience and maturity makes us vulnerable, and we fall into traps. Some traps result in "lesson, learned—never again," while others leave us damaged. The book of Proverbs suggests that the old have a responsibility to give wisdom to the young—and the young have the responsibility to listen to them! Of course, it doesn't always work out that way. Most of us have regrets about warnings we have ignored and choices we have made. So while Wisdom cries aloud in the streets, warning us against danger, Grace also stands by to bring forgiveness and healing.

Prayer: Lord, sometimes your Word shocks us by speaking plainly about the secrets of our minds and hearts, so that our vulnerabilities are exposed and fortification can begin. May we be so bold as to do the same for one another. We all need your wisdom and strength to resist temptation and choose wisdom instead. Amen.

Day 185   Proverbs 10–13

July 3

> Key Text: Doing wrong is fun for a fool, but living wisely brings pleasure to the sensible. (Proverbs 10:23)

As we can see, Proverbs is not a narrative, but a collection of individual wise sayings. Think of them as "wisdom bites." Most are written as Hebrew parallelism, a literary device used to emphasize a point by saying it again in a different way or by contrasting it with its opposite, often by the use of a comma, semicolon or the conjunction "but."

Remember that proverbs are truisms which reflect the way life works by God's decree and plan. In this sense, they are the moral equivalent to the physical laws of nature. But unlike nature, human beings have free will and live complex lives. The law of gravity cannot choose not to be the law of gravity, but a free moral agent can choose to pursue wisdom or foolishness, with their different outcomes. So think of these wisdom bites as bite-size applications of God's wisdom in a particular situation for a good outcome.

The following is a sampling of wisdom bites from chapters 10 through13.

Proverbs 10 begins by noting that our choices have consequences, not just for the individual, but for everyone around them. For example, there is a lot at stake for parents and children in the task of imparting wisdom: *"A wise child brings joy to a father; a foolish child brings grief to a mother."*

From chapter 10 we also read:

- *"People with integrity walk safely, but those who follow crooked paths will be exposed."*
- *"Hatred stirs up quarrels, but love makes up for all offenses."*

- *"Doing wrong is fun for a fool, but living wisely brings pleasure to the sensible."*
- *"When the storms of life come, the wicked are whirled away, but the godly have a lasting foundation."*

From chapter 11:

- *"Riches won't help on the day of judgment, but right living can save you from death."*
- *"Upright citizens are good for a city and make it prosper, but the talk of the wicked tears it apart."*
- *"Without wise leadership, a nation falls; there is safety in having many advisers."*
- *"Give freely and become more wealthy; be stingy and lose everything."*
- *"Trust in your money and down you go! But the godly flourish like leaves in spring."*

From chapter 12:

- *"To learn, you must love discipline; it is stupid to hate correction."*
- *"Wickedness never brings stability, but the godly have deep roots."*
- *"A fool is quick-tempered, but a wise person stays calm when insulted."*
- *"Truthful words stand the test of time, but lies are soon exposed."*

From chapter 13:

- *"Those who control their tongue will have a long life; opening your mouth can ruin everything."*
- *"Some who are poor pretend to be rich; others who are rich pretend to be poor."*
- *"The instruction of the wise is like a life-giving fountain; those who accept it avoid the snares of death."*
- *"Walk with the wise and become wise; associate with fools and get in trouble."*

Focus: Even people who have never heard of Moses or Jesus can come to broadly similar conclusions about life simply by trial and error. God's wisdom makes life work and can be discovered by any thoughtful person, whether or not they know God. It is part of the General Revelation of God, which we have commented upon. One common example is the Golden Rule: *"Do unto others as you would have them do unto you."* Life simply works better when the Golden Rule is applied. And whether we know it or not, this is true because it reflects the character of God. How good it is to know the God whose character is seen in things he has made! How motivating it is to choose to live wisely because it pleases him!

Day 186   Proverbs 14–17

July 4

> Key Text: A cheerful heart is good medicine, but a broken spirit saps a person's strength. (Proverbs 17:22)

You'll notice that, like the Psalms, the book of Proverbs revisits themes again and again. Repetition is a way to emphasize importance. It is also a way to communicate more broadly. Everyone learns differently, so different ways of saying the same things connect with a broader audience.

Here is another basketful of wisdom bites. You'll recognize some familiar ones:

From Proverbs 14:

- *"A fool's proud talk becomes a rod that beats him, but the words of the wise keep them safe."*
- *"Fools make fun of guilt, but the godly acknowledge it and seek reconciliation."*
- *"There is a path before each person that seems right, but it ends in death."*
- *"A peaceful heart leads to a healthy body; jealousy is like cancer in the bones."*
- *"Those who oppress the poor insult their Maker, but helping the poor honors him."*

From Proverbs 15:

- *"A gentle answer deflects anger, but harsh words make tempers flare."*
- *"The tongue of the wise makes knowledge appealing, but the mouth of a fool belches out foolishness."*
- *"Mockers hate to be corrected, so they stay away from the wise."*
- *"Better to have little, with fear for the Lord, than to have great treasure and inner turmoil."*
- *"A bowl of vegetables with someone you love is better than steak with someone you hate."*

- *"The Lord is far from the wicked, but he hears the prayers of the righteous."*

From Proverbs 16:

- *"We can make our own plans, but the Lord gives the right answer."*
- *"People may be pure in their own eyes, but the Lord examines their motives."*
- *"Pride goes before destruction, and haughtiness before a fall."*
- *"Gray hair is a crown of glory; it is gained by living a godly life."*
- *"We may throw the dice, but the Lord determines how they fall."*

From Proverbs 17:

- *"Better a dry crust eaten in peace than a house filled with feasting—and conflict."*
- *"Love prospers when a fault is forgiven, but dwelling on it separates close friends."*
- *"If you repay good with evil, evil will never leave your house."*
- *"A cheerful heart is good medicine, but a broken spirit saps a person's strength."*

Focus: Living according to God's wisdom not only makes us happier; it also makes us healthier: *"A peaceful heart leads to a healthy body...."* The Proverbs illustrate that we humans are created as physical / spiritual beings, where each aspect affects the other. We know, for example, that many physical illnesses are psychosomatic in origin. When we experience great stress or grief or anger, it manifests itself in physical symptoms. Our secular society emphasizes body care by proper eating, exercising, etc. But we also need to give attention to soul care, by attending to our relationship with God and others. One aspect of soul care is living wisely—the foundation of a peaceful heart, and consequently a healthy body. In this way, we can truly worship God with all our heart, mind, soul and strength!

Prayer: Lord, teach us to live wisely, in accordance with your Word, so that with body and soul we may worship you and experience an abundant life. Amen.

Day 187 — Proverbs 18–21

July 5

Key Text: No human wisdom or understanding or plan can stand against the Lord. (Proverbs 21:30)

The book of Proverbs makes sense to us in the West because our worldview—especially the idea of the wise and good life—has been shaped by Judeo-Christianity. Proverbs assumes that a loving God created a moral universe where human beings with free will may thrive if they live according to his will. Or, they may flounder if they don't. In any event, there will be a final judgment.

So, the freedom to choose is a gift of God which grants us a dignity, power and accountability not afforded other creatures.

Such a view of life contrasted significantly with the nations around Israel at the time. There was no idea of a rational, loving God who created everything and loved human beings. The gods of paganism were irrational, selfish, combative and dismissive of human beings. Human life was fatalistic and lived in fear of the gods. There was no incentive for moral virtues like love, compassion and mercy.

Not surprisingly, therefore, Judaism was a revelation to the ancients, providing a moral and spiritual vision that lifted the ancient world from its fear and moral chaos. So what may seem like sophomoric truisms to us today, were truly game-changing insights about the good life to Israel's neighbors.

So let's consume another bowl of wisdom bites from chapters 18–21:

From chapter 18:
- *"It is not right to acquit the guilty or deny justice to the innocent."*
- *"Spouting off before listening to the facts is both shameful and foolish."*
- *"There are 'friends' who destroy each other, but a real friend sticks closer than a brother."*

From chapter 19:
- *"People ruin their lives by their own foolishness and then are angry at the Lord."*
- *"Sensible people control their temper; they earn respect by overlooking wrongs."*
- *"If you help the poor, you are lending to the Lord—and he will repay you!"*
- *"Discipline your children while there is hope. Otherwise you will ruin their lives."*

From chapter 20:
- *"Wine produces mockers; alcohol leads to brawls. Those led astray by drink cannot be wise."*
- *"Who can say, 'I have cleansed my heart; I am pure and free from sin'?"*

- *"Don't say, 'I will get even for this wrong.' Wait for the Lord to handle the matter."*
- *"The Lord detests double standards; he is not pleased by dishonest scales."*

From chapter 21:

- *"The Lord is more pleased when we do what is right and just than when we offer him sacrifices."*
- *"Watch your tongue and keep your mouth shut, and you will stay out of trouble."*
- *"No human wisdom or understanding or plan can stand against the Lord."*

Focus: There have been many attempts in history to silence Judeo-Christianity. The most insidious has been Enlightenment Rationalism, which for over 400 years has sought to replace Christianity as a source of truth and morality, with human reason guided by science. The Enlightenment, following the "wisdom" of the Fall, determined that humans don't need God for truth and morality because we can figure it out for ourselves. How freeing! No commandments to keep; no doctrines to believe!

But Proverbs 21:30 begs to differ: *"No human wisdom or understanding or plan can stand against the Lord."* The apostle Paul concurs in 1 Corinthians 1:18–25: Though God's wisdom seems like foolishness to the enlightened world, it always prevails. Enlightenment Rationalism is running out of gas because it does not explain reality, and because it has failed, in many respects, to give us wisdom.

Prayer: *Lord, forgive us for hurtful or lying words that destroy others. Take control of our tongues so that with them we may praise you and build up our loved ones and friends. Amen.*

Day 188   Proverbs 22–24

July 6

> Key Text: Listen to the words of the wise; apply your heart to my instruction. For it is good to keep these sayings in your heart and always ready on your lips. I am teaching you today—yes, you—so you will trust in the Lord. (Proverbs 22:17–19)

We have defined proverbs as "wisdom bites." Most of them are couplets, written using Hebrew parallelism, which present a brief truism *("A gentle answer deflects anger")* and then supports it by stating its opposite *("but harsh words make tempers flare").*

But this is not the only form of parallelism. Sometimes the second thought simply restates the first, in a different way: *"Pride goes before destruction, and haughtiness before a fall."* Still another form reinforces the proverb by offering a positive outcome of living this way: *"The godly walk with integrity; blessed are their children who follow them."*

In Proverbs 22 through 24, we encounter yet a different form of proverb—an extended exposition with a warning. These are more than wisdom bites; they are more like wisdom meals. The following are three examples:

A Warning Against Abusing Alcohol:

"Who has anguish? Who has sorrow? Who is always fighting? Who is always complaining? Who has unnecessary bruises? Who has bloodshot eyes? It is the one who spends long hours in the taverns, trying out new drinks. Don't gaze at the wine, seeing how red it is, how it sparkles in the cup, how smoothly it goes down. For in the end it bites like a poisonous snake; it stings like a viper. You will see hallucinations, and you will say crazy things. You will stagger like a sailor tossed at sea, clinging to a swaying mast. And you will say, 'They hit me, but I didn't feel it. I didn't even know it when they beat me up. When will I wake up so I can look for another drink?'" (Proverbs 23:29–35)

A Challenge to Speak Out Against Injustice:

"Rescue those who are unjustly sentenced to die; save them as they stagger to their death. Don't excuse yourself by saying, 'Look, we didn't know.' For God understands all hearts, and he sees you. He who guards your soul knows you knew. He will repay all people as their actions deserve." (Proverbs 24:11–12)

A Warning Against Laziness:

"I walked by the field of a lazy person, the vineyard of one with no common sense. I saw that it was overgrown with nettles. It was covered with weeds, and its walls were broken down. Then, as I looked and thought about it, I learned this lesson: A little extra sleep, a little more slumber, a little folding of the hands to rest—then poverty will pounce on you like a bandit; scarcity will attack you like an armed robber." (Proverbs 24:30–34)

Focus: A life directed by wisdom does not come naturally, or easily. It requires a diligent effort: *"Listen to the words of the wise; apply your heart to my instruction. For it is good to keep these sayings in your heart and always ready on your lips. I am teaching you today—yes, you—so you will trust in the Lord"* (Proverbs 22:17–19). Many of us, when we were young, did not want to listen, let alone memorize and apply God's wisdom for life. We wanted to do whatever we wanted to do! Then, having become fools, and with our tails between our legs—like the Prodigal Son—we concluded that obeying God's Word was not such a stupid idea after all! Wisdom must be learned; it requires desire, discipline and humility. In other words, you must *want it and pursue it with all your heart.* Listen to your teachers!

Prayer: Lord, you have said repeatedly through your Word that you discipline your children because you love them. Thank you for telling the truth to us. Thank you for our parents and teachers and friends who didn't give up on us. Our pride makes it hard to listen, so soften our hearts. Give us ears to hear and eyes to see, so that we do not become morally deaf and spiritually blind. Amen.

Day 189   Reflection

July 7

The book of Proverbs is a ringing endorsement of wisdom, and a stern warning against foolishness. At stake is the well-being of our lives, and the lives of our children.

But some people say that truth, like beauty, is only in the eye of the beholder. They believe that there is no universal truth outside the laws of nature. Therefore, what is morally wrong for you may be right for me. We cannot judge another person's point of view, and it is wrong to try and convert others to your way of thinking, especially religious thinking.

Most who hold this view don't believe in a personal Creator who has revealed his will. So they conclude that there is no universal truth, outside of scientific truth. Reality only exists inside our individual minds, and it is there that we must find truth and wisdom for ourselves.

The problems with this view are well known. If there is no God who reveals his will to us, we can't know anything for certain. And if there is no final judgment of right and wrong, then we can't be held accountable for our actions. There is nothing to restrain human impulses. What this means in practice is that right and wrong are determined by those in power, and therefore the danger of tyranny grows.

Furthermore, the atheist's claim that there is no God, and consequently no moral absolutes, is a self-defeating argument. Here's why: An atheist can't absolutely prove that there is no God any more than a theist can absolutely prove that there is. So his underlying assumption that there is no God is a statement of faith, not a statement of proven fact.

Finally, the argument that there are no absolutes is itself an absolute statement—the very kind of statement that they deny to others. The argument defeats itself.

But just because we cannot "prove" the existence of God does not mean that there are no strong clues that there is a personal, moral God. There are many. One clue, for example, is that every culture ever studied has some variation of the "Golden Rule"—*Do unto others as you would have others to do unto you.* Moral awareness seems to be coded in our DNA!

Christianity argues that there are strong clues from human experience, intuition, reason, and the study of science which point to the existence of God and to moral absolutes. So the book of Proverbs echoes what we instinctively, experientially and rationally suspect: *"Fear of the Lord is the foundation of true knowledge, but fools despise wisdom and discipline."*

In the end, "the proof is in the pudding," as they say. Generations of believers have experienced a happy and successful life (though not a perfect life, without pain) by following the wisdom of God's Word, including the wisdom of Proverbs.

Christianity literally gave birth to Western Civilization. All that we consider right and good—whether the triumph of reason, the defeat of tyranny, the insights of science, the growth of the university, human freedom, representative government, legal justice, compassion for the poor, the rights of women, charitable institutions, and the creation of new (uninherited) wealth, making the middle class possible and lifting countless people out of poverty—has come directly or indirectly through the teaching and moral vision of Christianity. And this does not even touch upon the supreme gifts of art, music, sculpture, literature, and countless manifestations of beauty and goodness in the world.

Prayer: Lord, thank you for giving us so many ways to access your wisdom and knowledge—the ways of reason, emotion, intuition, experience, and of course your revealed Word and Spirit. May we discover joy and freedom in life through keeping your commandments. Amen.

July 8

> **Key Text:** Wounds from a sincere friend are better than many
> kisses from an enemy. (Proverbs 27:6)

Today's chapters are a collection of Solomon's proverbs by the advisors of King Hezekiah of Judah, perhaps 250 years after they were written. Their wisdom has continuing value for the flourishing of individuals and society. So here again are selected wisdom bites, this time from chapters 25–29.

From Proverbs 25:
- *"It is God's privilege to conceal things and the king's privilege to discover them."*
- *"Do you like honey? Don't eat too much, or it will make you sick!"*
- *"Singing cheerful songs to a person with a heavy heart is like taking someone's coat in cold weather or pouring vinegar in a wound."*
- *"If your enemies are hungry, give them food to eat. If they are thirsty, give them water to drink. You will heap burning coals of shame upon their heads, and the Lord will reward you."*

From Proverbs 26:
- *"As a dog returns to its vomit, so a fool repeats his foolishness."*
- *"Lazy people take food in their hand but don't even lift it to their mouth."*
- *"Fire goes out without wood, and quarrels disappear when gossip stops."*
- *"If you set a trap for others, you will get caught in it yourself. If you roll a boulder down on others, it will crush you instead."*

From Proverbs 27:
- *"Wounds from a sincere friend are better than many kisses from an enemy."*
- *"A prudent person foresees danger and takes precautions. A simpleton goes blindly on and suffers the consequences."*
- *"As iron sharpens iron, so a friend sharpens a friend."*
- *"As a face is reflected in water, so the heart reflects the real person."*

From Proverbs 28:
- *"When there is moral rot within a nation, its government topples easily. But wise and knowledgeable leaders bring stability."*
- *"Better to be poor and honest than to be dishonest and rich."*

- *"People who conceal their sins will not prosper, but if they confess and turn from them, they will receive mercy."*
- *"In the end, people appreciate honest criticism far more than flattery."*

From Proverbs 29:

- *"When the godly are in authority, the people rejoice. But when the wicked are in power, they groan."*
- *"The godly care about the rights of the poor; the wicked don't care at all."*
- *"Discipline your children, and they will give you peace of mind and will make your heart glad."*
- *"Fearing people is a dangerous trap, but trusting the Lord means safety."*

Focus: A friend is a precious gift, and wisdom makes us better friends. A true friend knows us as we are and accepts us, but also tells us the truth. And we would do the same for them. *"Wounds from a sincere friend are better than many kisses from an enemy."* Sadly, many people—especially men—don't have such a friend. The relationships they do have are superficial and changeable. Earlier, in Proverbs 18:24, it says, *"There are 'friends' who destroy each other, but a real friend sticks closer than a brother."* Those who have such a friend are blessed. Those who are such a friend to others are a blessing.

Prayer: *Lord, your wisdom enables us to form deep and meaningful friendships by showing us what such friendships look like. Thank you for those in our lives who have been faithful, honest friends through thick and thin. May we always have time to be such a friend to another! Amen.*

Day 191   Proverbs 30–31

July 9

Key Text: Who can find a virtuous and capable wife? She is more precious than rubies. Her husband can trust her, and she will greatly enrich his life. She brings him good, not harm, all the days of her life. (Proverbs 31:10–12)

The final two chapters of the book of Proverbs are written by men named Agur and Lemuel, respectively.

Agur writes chapter 30 with the same themes we have encountered before in this book, but with a distinctive personality and style. Here are some examples to chew on:

"I am weary, O God; I am weary and worn out, O God. I am too stupid to be human, and I lack common sense. I have not mastered human wisdom,

nor do I know the Holy One."

"O God, I beg two favors from you; let me have them before I die. First, help me never to tell a lie. Second, give me neither poverty nor riches! Give me just enough to satisfy my needs. For if I grow rich, I may deny you and say, 'Who is the Lord?' And if I am too poor, I may steal and thus insult God's holy name."

"There are three things that amaze me—no, four things that I don't understand: how an eagle glides through the sky, how a snake slithers on a rock, how a ship navigates the ocean, how a man loves a woman."

King Lemuel is the source for chapter 31. The wisdom here is said to have been learned from his mother. The whole chapter is a wisdom feast about one thing, a suitable wife. His mother warns Lemuel, as a king, to avoid alcohol and wild women—*"those who ruin kings."* Instead, search for a *"virtuous and capable wife. She is more precious than rubies."*

A virtuous woman is a blessing to her husband and brings him *"good, not harm, all the days of her life."* She is industrious, smart and capable. She is able to manage the operation of her household and family, and at the same time able to invest in property, run a business, and still have energy to open her arms to the needy.

"She is clothed with strength and dignity, and she laughs without fear of the future. When she speaks, her words are wise, and she gives instructions with kindness. She carefully watches everything in her household and suffers nothing from laziness. Her children stand and bless her. Her husband praises her."

Her character, dignity and hard work make her husband look smart for marrying her!

He praises her in public: *"There are many virtuous and capable women in the world, but you surpass them all!"*

The very last wisdom bite of the book of Proverbs, therefore, is noteworthy: *"Charm is deceptive, and beauty does not last; but a woman who fears the Lord will be greatly praised. Reward her for all she has done. Let her deeds publicly declare her praise."*

Focus: Chapter 31 stands out in the book of Proverbs for its honoring of the *"virtuous and capable wife."* The Old Testament greatly elevated the status of women in the ancient world, where they were little more than property and baby makers, with no legal rights. Genesis chapters 1 and 2 explain that women equally share the image of God with men, and are to be honored and cared for as equal partners in life. They are protected by the Seventh Commandment, which forbids adultery because conjugal marriage is sacred. Neither men nor women are sexual objects to be used.

Women like Ruth and Queen Esther are prominent people in the Hebrew Bible, and examples of godly character, courage and strength. Proverbs 31 praises the "virtuous and capable" woman, who is wife, mother, entrepreneur, and compassionate friend to the poor and needy. She is blessed by her children and praised by her husband. She embodies wisdom, and anchors the book of Proverbs with her superb example of what wisdom does.

Prayer: Lord, perhaps the most important decision we make on earth is the person whom we marry. May we and our children choose well, so that together we all may bless our families, our friends and the nation with the greatest gift of all—a happy, loving home. Amen.

Day 192   Ecclesiastes 1–6

July 10

> Key Text: So I set out to learn everything from wisdom to madness and folly. But I learned firsthand that pursuing all this is like chasing the wind. (Ecclesiastes 1:17)

The book of Ecclesiastes probes deeply into the complexity, mystery and frustration of our brief existence on earth.

Reading Ecclesiastes is a challenge, because on the surface it seems almost nihilistic. Its recurring analysis is that life is *"meaningless,"* as some translate the Hebrew word. As we will see, a better and more helpful translation is *transient* or *elusive*, because the writer, while dark at times, is surely not saying that life is meaningless for those who believe in God.

However, the writer, who identifies himself as the "Teacher," forces us to look at the truth about *"life under the sun."* He relentlessly explores every pretentious attempt to find meaning in life apart from God. Before he comes to his final conclusion, he takes us with him to the playgrounds of the rich and famous, as well as to every dark alley, cul-de-sac and dead end of miserable humanity. If it sounds depressing, it is. But it's also real. Once we stop pretending that the material world is enough, we can deal with the brevity of life by faith in God and gratefulness to him for life's simple blessings.

The truth is, without God, nothing does matter. At life's end, we come to a precipice and stare into the darkness. All we've accomplished will be forgotten. All we've accumulated will be lost. All we've experienced will be for naught. But if God is with us—*everything* matters and *nothing* is lost, no matter how transient and elusive life might seem!

Ecclesiastes begins in chapter 1 with the Teacher introducing his thesis: *"Everything is meaningless...completely meaningless!"* It is like *"chasing the wind."* As mentioned above, "meaningless" is not a helpful translation of the Hebrew word, "hebel." Dr. Iain Provan convincingly suggests that a better translation is "breath." Breath suggests brevity, elusiveness, and transience, rather than meaninglessness.

Generations quickly come and go on earth, but the earth ever changes. History repeats itself with the same outcome—frustration. The Teacher, who boasts that he is wiser than any of the kings who ruled in Jerusalem before him, will make his case by setting out *"to learn everything, from wisdom to madness and folly."* He's taking nothing for granted. He's going to try everything and hold it up for examination. But we are given a spoiler alert: What he learned only increased his grief and sorrow. It was indeed like *"chasing the wind."*

In chapter 2, the Teacher reports on his pursuit of pleasure without limits. He spent money on wine, women and song: *"Anything I wanted, I would take. I denied myself no pleasure."* But he concludes that it was elusive—like grasping after air. Trying the opposite—to live with self-discipline and self-denial—got no better results. So he concludes that if both hedonism and asceticism are dissatisfying in the end, he might as well be a hedonist! But then, a glimmer of insight: *"Then I realized that these pleasures are from the hand of God. For who can eat or enjoy anything apart from him?"* (Ecclesiastes 2:24–25).

In chapter 3, the Teacher reflects on the fact that *"for everything there is a season, a time for every activity under heaven."* Does this imply that life is an endless cycle, or does it suggest an order designed by God? He follows with this thought: *"I have seen the burden God has placed on us all. Yet God has made everything beautiful for its own time. He has planted eternity in the human heart, but even so, people cannot see the whole scope of God's work from beginning to end."* So then, perhaps we should eat, drink and be merry, and consider that all the pleasures of life are gifts of

God. But keep in mind: *"In due season, God will judge everyone, both good and bad, for all their deeds."*

Chapter 4 explores the varieties of human tragedy. There are *"the tears of the oppressed, with no one to comfort them."* There is the case of those who are *"all alone."* There is also the emptiness of success.

Chapter 5 surveys thoughtless religion, restless activity, rash promises, abuse of power, and the perils of wealth. There is the sobering conclusion that *"people leave this world no better off than when they came."*

Chapter 6 revisits the perils of wealth. A man works hard to earn it and then dies young before he can enjoy it. But even if he lives to an old age, he may finish his life an unhappy man. Again, we see that we have no control over these things. There's no use arguing with God about our destiny: *"Enjoy what you have rather than desiring what you don't have. Just dreaming about nice things is meaningless* [or better, elusive]*—like chasing the wind."*

> **Focus:** There is clearly a tension between the "eternity" that God has put in our hearts, and the brevity of life. We find that we have more desire than fulfillment, more ideas than opportunity. We run out of time before we are ready to go. Part of wisdom is accepting the fact that there is a certain measure of dissatisfaction to life, even in the best of circumstances. Accepting this, while enjoying the pleasures of life that God gives, is the first step to making sense of it all.

> ***Prayer:*** *Lord, we are reminded that we have far less control over our lives than we think. Help us to accept what you give and find pleasure in the life you have ordained for each of us. There is so much we don't understand, but we trust in you. Amen.*

Day 193   Ecclesiastes 7–12

July 11

> Key Text: Young people, it's wonderful to be young! Enjoy every minute of it. Do everything you want to do; take it all in. But remember that you must give an account to God for everything you do. (Ecclesiastes 11:9)

The Teacher continues his arduous analysis of human experience *"under the sun."* He holds up life and death to the light of the sun, like a faceted precious stone, turning it in his hand to investigate every angle and note every reflection of light. His analysis is both profound and wearisome! Is it possible to overanalyze life?

Chapters 7 through 12 drive us to his final conclusion about the whole matter, but there are plenty of exit ramps and on-ramps before we get there. Chapter 7 begins with odd ruminations about death:

- *"And the day you die is better than the day you are born."*
- *"Better to spend your time at funerals than at parties."*
- *"A wise person thinks a lot about death, while a fool thinks only about having a good time."*

By that analysis, the world is full of fools! But why the preoccupation with death? It's obvious when you think about it. Death is the elephant in the room for each of the living. It's inevitable, just like taxes. The Grim Reaper stalks us. So we put off thinking about our death until the last possible moment. Better to party, right? The Teacher observes, *"It seems so wrong that everyone under the sun suffers the same fate. Already twisted by evil, people choose their own mad course, for they have no hope. There is nothing ahead but death anyway"* (Ecclesiastes 9:3).

Nevertheless, the Teacher sees value in sober reflection about inevitabilities: *"Sorrow is better than laughter, for sadness has a refining influence on us"* (Ecclesiastes 7:3). We simply have to take the fact of death into account in any reckoning of life. This is the way to wisdom, even though *"wisdom is always distant and difficult to find."*

Honesty and humility are a good starting place for the journey—especially acknowledging that *"God created people to be virtuous, but they have each turned to follow their own downward path"* (Ecclesiastes 7:29). In particular, *"the wicked will not prosper, for they do not fear God"* (Ecclesiastes 8:13).

If one's life is tempered by the awareness of God, and the inevitability of death and judgment, one is then, ironically, free to enjoy life: *"So I recommend having fun, because there is nothing better for people in this world than to eat, drink and enjoy life. That way they will experience some happiness along with all the hard work God gives them under the sun"* (Ecclesiastes 8:15).

So enjoy life, but don't be foolish. The Teacher acknowledges that *"the words of the wise are like cattle prods—painful but helpful"* (Ecclesiastes 12:11).

He encourages the young: *"Young people, it's wonderful to be young! Enjoy every minute of it. Do everything you want to do; take it all in. But remember that you must give an account to God for everything you do"* (Ecclesiastes 11:9).

So the Teacher has seen it all and done it all. He is a realist, but not a nihilist. Although there is a lot of sadness in the world, we should not deny it or avoid it, but allow ourselves to feel it—to let it temper us. As he has already warned us: *"The greater my wisdom, the greater my grief. To increase knowledge only increases sorrow."*

The Teacher has now given us all the wisdom he has: *"That's the whole story. Here now is my final conclusion: Fear God and obey his commands, for this is everyone's duty. God will judge us for everything we do, including every secret thing, whether good or bad"* (Ecclesiastes 12:13–14).

Focus: When we take into consideration that the Teacher had far less understanding of God, and no understanding of redemption through Christ, his insights into the status of our mortal life are quite profound, but realistic. He tells the truth. He walks to the precipice and stares into the darkness, but he pulls back. Upon further reflection, the light of understanding begins to illuminate his dark mind. God exists, and though his ways are mysterious, he has made himself known to us. He has given us his commandments as a lamp to light our path in the brief journey of mortal life.

During the journey, we should receive the pleasures God gives with joy. As for death—well, God has put eternity in our hearts. Why would he give us a desire that nothing can fulfill? Our longing for heaven gives us hope that that which is temporary will blossom into eternity, and that which is elusive will be made clear. The Teacher doesn't know it yet, but he is longing for the resurrection which is ours through Christ!

Prayer: Lord, the Teacher certainly describes life as we experience it, with all its joys and sorrows, as well as its mysteries and irony. But we know from the vantage point of the cross that you are with us. In Jesus, you have joined us in our sorrow and suffering, and in the limitations of our humanity. His victory over death becomes our victory as well. Help us to live out our brief days with purpose and hope. Amen!

Day 194   Song of Songs

> Key Text: Place me like a seal over your heart, like a seal on your arm. For love is as strong as death, its jealousy as enduring as the grave. Love flashes like fire, the brightest kind of flame. Many waters cannot quench love, nor can rivers drown it.
> (Song of Songs 8:6–7)

The Song of Songs is a Hebrew love poem about the beauty, joy, pain and holiness of married love.

King Solomon is identified as the author and is the main character, along with a Shulammite girl who is his fiancée and then bride. It is likely, however, that Solomon is the foil of the story, not the author, for his well-known polygamy is the antithesis of the love between one man and one woman in marriage, which the author wants to commend.

In the song, the lovers are identified as the *"young man"* and *"young woman."* We also hear from some other women, identified as the *"young women of Jerusalem,"* and once from some other men called the *"young woman's brothers."*

Chapter 1 begins by claiming that this love song is the *"song of songs,"* more wonderful than any other ever written! Though written nearly three thousand years ago, we instantly recognize the sweet hyperbole of young love. The young woman longs for her beloved, wanting to kiss him and be alone with him.

The young women of Jerusalem express their giddy crush on the king, like a crowd of girls with a rock star. They will appear several times, almost as a chorus, encouraging the lovers and pushing the story along.

The poem moves thematically toward the *"most joyous day"* of their wedding *(Song of Songs 3:6–11),* followed by the sexual celebration of married life.

Most of the song is sensual love talk, sometimes quite explicit. The focus of their talk is the beauty of their bodies and the strong feelings of attraction they have for one another. The modern reader smiles at the archaic metaphors: *"Your navel is perfectly formed like a goblet filled with mixed wine."* ... *"Your teeth are as white as sheep, recently shorn and freshly washed."* And then there are the humorous erotic references that you might be tempted to borrow, just for the fun of it: *"Between your thighs lies a mound of wheat."* ... *"I was a virgin, like a wall; now my breasts are like towers."*

But setting aside the anachronistic language, we notice the surprising affirmation here of sexual love within marriage. By contrast, we can perceive that the widespread abuse of nonconjugal sex, including the horrors of rape and sexual trafficking, is a blight on human history.

So contrary to stereotype, Judeo-Christianity is neither prudish nor hostile toward sex. But sex is more than an appetite, like hunger and thirst. It is a precious gift and holy union. Man and woman are created by God for one another. In the intimacy of marriage, two genders become one flesh, and in the mystery of childbirth, they experience God's joy in creating life.

The Bible celebrates sex as a wonderful gift of God, but one that must be kept holy and protected. It is the most intimate gift one can give another. It can bring great joy or inflict terrible emotional pain. A recurring plea in the Song of Songs is to not *"awaken love until the time is right."*

The song concludes in chapter 8 with a moving description of the bond that love creates between a husband and wife. The young woman says: *"Place me like a seal over your heart, like a seal on your arm. For love is as strong as death, its jealousy as enduring as the grave. Love flashes like fire, the brightest kind of flame. Many waters cannot quench love, nor can rivers drown it"* (Song of Songs 8:6–7).

> **Focus:** The sexual revolution of the 60s in the Western World has proven to be a bitter and ironic sort of "freedom." There has been a tsunami of sexually transmitted diseases and a steep rise in rape, pregnant teenagers, single parent households, and the ultimate expression of sexual idolatry, abortion on demand. As the revolution unwinds to its ultimate logic, the meaning of marriage itself has been rewritten. Gender is now considered fluid; you can be whatever you imagine yourself to be. The conceit of the sexual revolution has left collateral damage everywhere—emotional, physical and spiritual.
>
> Rediscovering sex as a joyful gift of God, and marriage as a holy union, requires that we rediscover the wise teaching of the Bible and trust God that his ways are good. The Song of Songs is a good place to start.

Day 195   Isaiah 1–4

July 13

> Key Text: Listen, O heavens! Pay attention, earth! This is what the Lord says: "The children I raised and cared for have rebelled against me. Even an ox knows its owner, and a donkey recognizes its master's care—but Israel doesn't know its master. My people don't recognize my care for them." (Isaiah 1:2–3)

With the book of Isaiah, we come to the section of the Bible known as the major and minor prophets, a reference to their length, not importance. The book of Isaiah, with its 66 chapters, is first among its peers, both in length and depth of writing.

The stereotype of a prophet as a wild-haired, eccentric predictor of coming doom is contradicted by their theologically and historically profound messages. Their first calling was to speak God's truth to power, in this case to the kings of Israel and Judah. Unfortunately, neither the kings nor the people listened to them very often.

Some prophets, like Isaiah, wrote during the turbulent kingdom period when Israel was still in the Promised Land, flagrantly breaking God's commandments and violating his Covenant by participating in the pagan practices of their neighbors. Other prophets wrote later, during the time of Israel's exile in Assyria and then Babylonia.

Chapter 1 begins, *"These are the visions that Isaiah son of Amoz saw concerning Judah and Jerusalem."* What follows is an accusation by God against Judah, speaking through Isaiah: *"The children I raised and cared for have rebelled against me."*

The nature of their sin is idolatry. They still go through the motions of worshiping God, all right, but their heart is not in it, and they haven't kept the commandments about doing good, seeking justice and helping the oppressed. Nevertheless, God invites the people to be reconciled to him: *"'Come now, let's settle this,' says the Lord. 'Though your sins are like scarlet, I will make them as white as snow.'"*

Indeed, Isaiah has a vision in chapter 2, that in the last days the nations of the world will come together to worship the Lord. The nations will *"hammer their swords into plowshares and their spears into pruning hooks. Nation will no longer fight against nation, nor train for war anymore."*

But today is not that day.

Chapter 3 says that today, the leaders are inept, corrupt and childish. The people follow them and are unfaithful to God. They act like a wealthy, haughty woman, finely dressed, bejeweled and strutting around, flirting with her eyes. However, a terrible day of reckoning is coming when *"the Lord takes his place in court and presents his case against his people!"* Sadly, *"Jerusalem will stumble, and Judah will fall, because they speak out against the Lord and refuse to obey him."*

Chapter 4 adds that on the terrible day of judgment, when Judah falls, some among them will survive nevertheless. They will be a remnant of faith, and the Lord will provide for them.

Focus: The prophets were called to a hard task for the Lord—to deliver his warning and instruction to kings and people who didn't want to hear it. Their hearts were hard, so the prophets were generally laughed at by the people, even as they indulged in pagan revelry. But Isaiah was faithful to his calling. His brilliant insights into Israel's history and theology, along with his bold obedience to God, were hard to ignore. As we see, his words still speak to the Church today, and remind the Church of its prophetic, as well as its pastoral, role in the world.

Prayer: *Lord, it must break your heart and test your will to see your people rebel against you. And yet, you continue to invite us to come together so that you may make our sins white as snow. How gracious you are! And how thankful we are that you did not give up on us! Amen.*

Day 196   Reflection

July 14

The book of Isaiah begins with God's judgment of Israel: *"Oh, what a sinful nation they are—loaded down with a burden of guilt. They are evil people, corrupt children who have rejected the Lord. They have despised the Holy One of Israel and turned their backs on him"* (Isaiah 1:4).

Verses like these offend people. The consensus of our age is that judging people is not right. Therefore, if God were good and loving, he would not judge people.

Do you see the double irony here? First, the very definition of a judge is to determine and protect what is right. Second, to dismiss this as unworthy of God our Creator is itself a judgment—doing yourself what you condemn God for doing.

What is going on here is that we have, in our minds, changed places with God. Secular man now presumes the prerogative of God to determine what is right and wrong. If this sounds familiar, it should. It was the aspiration which caused Adam and Eve to rebel against God.

Genesis 3:1–7 describes how the first humans fell for the lie that God was lying to them about the reason for his commandment not to eat from the Tree of the Knowledge of Good and Evil: *"'You won't die!' the serpent replied to the woman. 'God knows that your eyes will be opened as soon as you eat it, and you will be like God, knowing both good and evil.'"*

Hmmm…*"be like god."* Judge for myself what is right and wrong!

Unfortunately, as we have seen over and over again in our journey through the Bible, playing God never turns out well for us. We are alienated from our Creator, and at war with our neighbor. As a human race, we have fallen down and we can't get up! History repeats itself over and over again—second verse same as the first.

Someone needs to intervene and stop us from our self-defeating behavior! Someone needs to tell us what is wrong, so that we can come to our senses, acknowledge our sin, and rediscover what it means to be God's sons and daughters on the earth. In other words, we need a Judge.

Through Isaiah, God is judging Israel, as well as the world, with words that are hard to hear: "sinful," "evil," "guilty," "corrupt." It is divine truth-telling, without which we are lost. God's judgments are his warnings, given with sufficient pain as to be heard.

To hear this makes us wince. But we know it's true. We cannot be healed until the infection is exposed and cleansed. This is God's end game. His anger and condemnation are those of a jealous lover, not a cruel tyrant. He wants reconciliation, so he relentlessly pursues us with passionate love, offering us his grace and mercy, and being willing to let us hurt until we stop the madness and give up trying to be god.

The prophets, more than any other of the Old Testament books, reveal the passion of God. You may be surprised to discover how strongly he feels about you.

Day 197   Isaiah 5–8

July 15

> Key Text: What sorrow for those who say that evil is good and good is evil, that dark is light and light is dark, that bitter is sweet and sweet is bitter. (Isaiah 5:20)

Isaiah 5 begins with an extended song about a vineyard—a metaphor about God and the people of Judah: *"The nation of Israel is the vineyard of the Lord of Heaven's Armies* [or the Lord of Hosts]. *The people of Judah are his pleasant garden"* (Isaiah 5:7). (Remember from Kings and Chronicles that Judah is the southern kingdom after the nation was divided into North and South. When speaking of both, it is just Israel.)

God "planted" Israel expecting sweet grapes, but what grew instead were the bitter grapes of oppression, violence and injustice. Instead of righteousness, there were grand parties of flaming drunkenness. Therefore, *"what sorrow for those who say that evil is good and good is evil."*

Isaiah sadly announces that the consequence of Judah's evil will be defeat by the foreign nation of Assyria and subsequent exile. When God's people fail to respond to his patient and gracious exhortations to return to him, he withdraws his protection from their enemies. Again, we see God's tough love in action. He will allow his people to suffer consequences in order to soften their hearts so that they can be reconciled to him.

In chapter 6, Isaiah describes his well-known vision and calling to be a prophet: *"It was in the year King Uzziah died that I saw the Lord. He was sitting on a lofty throne, and the train of his robe filled the Temple. Attending him were mighty seraphim, each having six wings...calling out to each other, 'Holy, holy, holy is the Lord of Heaven's Armies!'"* In this vision, God asks whom he should send as a messenger to his people, and Isaiah responds, *"Here I am. Send me."*

So Isaiah is sent to preach to the people, but he is warned that they won't listen. Judah and Jerusalem will become a wasteland. But all hope is not lost. A *"remnant of faith"* will survive like *"a stump when it is cut down."* From that stump (the remnant), a new shoot will begin to grow.

In chapter 7, a sign is given to King Ahaz, the grandson of Uzziah, to confirm this judgment and hope: *"Look! The virgin will conceive a child! She will give birth to a son and will call him Immanuel (which means 'God with us')"* (Isaiah 7:14). This prophecy, you probably know, is a sign pointing to the birth of Jesus, and is why Jesus is called *"Immanuel."* He is our ultimate hope.

In its immediate context, however, the sign of a virgin conception is a message saying that, even if the nation falls to Assyria, there will be a *remnant of faith* who will survive because God is with them.

Chapter 8 gives more detail about Judah's fate: *"The Lord will overwhelm them with a mighty flood from the Euphrates River—the king of Assyria and all his glory."* The fear of Assyria causes Judah's king to consult mediums for guidance. Isaiah challenges him to look instead *"to God's instructions and teachings! People who contradict his word are completely in the dark."*

Focus: Isaiah makes clear, even as God gives notice that his judgment will fall upon Judah by Assyrian armies, that the way back to the Land from exile will come about by the "remnant of faith." The seed has already been planted in Israel's stump, and it will grow. God's story is always about reconciliation and hope. Even his tough-love discipline of his people is always about getting their attention so that they may return to him. It is the same with us. God is at work *in all things, good and bad,* for the good of those who love him and are called according to his purposes *(Romans 8:28).* He is willing to show you and me tough love if that is what it takes to bring us home to him.

Prayer: *Lord, even when national events seem out of control, and many look to other authorities for answers, we will look to you and your Word. Give us a vision of your greatness and glory so that we will remain faithful to you, no matter what happens around us. Amen.*

Day 198   Isaiah 9–12

July 16

> **Key Text:** For a child is born to us, a son is given to us. The government will rest on his shoulders. And he will be called: Wonderful Counselor, Mighty God, Everlasting Father, Prince of Peace. His government and its peace will never end. He will rule with fairness and justice from the throne of his ancestor David. (Isaiah 9:6–7)

The prophets of Israel always balanced God's judgment for Israel's sin, with his amazing promise for the future. Isaiah is no exception.

After delivering a grim assessment of the spiritual and moral corruption of the people of the southern kingdom of Judah, and then explaining that Assyria will conquer and exile the people as the judgment of God, Isaiah finally brings words of comfort and hope. Israel's darkness and despair will not go on forever: *"The people who walk in darkness will see a great light. For those who live in a land of deep darkness, a light will shine."*

The hope of the people is that Israel can be reunited and restored, ruled by a king from the house of David. Thus the hopeful song: *"For a child is born to us, a son is given to us. The government will rest on his shoulders. And he will be called: Wonderful Counselor, Mighty God, Everlasting Father, Prince of Peace. His government and its peace will never end. He will rule with fairness and justice from the throne of his ancestor David"* (Isaiah 9:6–7).

But who is such a king? He seems larger than life.

In chapters 9 and 10, Isaiah returns to the depressing present, this time for the people of the northern kingdom of Israel. As with Judah, God brings his case against Israel and then offers hope of an ideal king to lead them: *"Out of the stump of David's family will grow a shoot—yes, a new Branch bearing fruit from the old root. And the Spirit of the Lord will rest on him…"* (Isaiah 11:1–2).

Isaiah continues to describe this larger-than-life person as one who gives justice to the poor and makes fair decisions for the exploited. The earth will shake at the force of his word and the wicked will be destroyed: *"In that day the wolf and lamb will live together; the leopard will lie down with the baby goat. The calf and the yearling will be safe with the lion, and a little child will lead them all."*

371

In that great day, *"the earth will be filled with people who know the Lord."*

The scattered people of God in exile will be brought back to Jerusalem: *"He will make a highway for the remnant of his people, the remnant coming from Assyria, just as he did for Israel long ago when they returned from Egypt."* Their return to the land will be a signal of hope that God has not forgotten his ancient Promise to save his people, and through them, save all peoples of the earth. He will make all things new.

In that day, chapter 12 concludes, there will be great joy, for God has done wonderful things for his wayward people: *"With joy you will drink deeply from the fountain of salvation!"*

All the nations of the earth will hear about the wonderful things the Lord has done.

In these chapters, Isaiah uses what some call "prophetic foreshortening," which means seeing in current events an anticipation of something much greater in the future. In this case, the child who is born to us, and who will be granted the unique titles of Wonderful Counselor, Mighty God, Everlasting Father, and Prince of Peace, is none other than Jesus Christ. He is the shoot who grows out of the stump of David—the tree of Israel cut down by the judgment of God—seemingly dead, but now coming alive.

Christ's coming portends the ultimate hope of the people of God for the time when God makes all things new—when the nations of the earth are united in worshiping him, and even nature is transformed, with the wolf lying down with the lamb.

The Judeo-Christian view of history is eschatological, meaning that it is being guided by God to a glorious predetermined end. Therefore, we are able to find a reason for hope even in the most disheartening present.

Focus: God gave Isaiah a vision of a great future in a New Creation, where the order of things in the present fallen world have been reversed: *"The wolf and the lamb will live together; the leopard will lie down with the baby goat."* To those living in the present days of darkness, it must have seemed impossible, even ridiculous, to believe such a thing. Nevertheless, our hearts respond to the vision of a world (and even nature) at peace, where justice and goodness reign under the gracious rule of a loving God. It seems too good to be true. And it would still seem that way were it not for Jesus. His suffering for our sins, and his victory over death, have made Isaiah's vision not only plausible, but joyfully inevitable. It is rational and liberating to put our hope in God's New Creation!

Prayer: Lord, give us eyes to see! While we struggle with the issues of the moment, both in our personal lives and with national concerns, grant us a bigger perspective, grounded in your sovereign plan for our future when you will make all things new. Thank you that Jesus' resurrection to new life is the promise and guarantee of that future. Amen.

Day 199   Isaiah 13–16

July 17

> Key Text: When oppression and destruction have ended and enemy raiders have disappeared, then God will establish one of David's descendants as king. He will rule with mercy and truth. He will always do what is just and be eager to do what is right. (Isaiah 16:4–5)

God, who is sovereign over history, sometimes uses ungodly nations to judge his people. He reveals to Isaiah that both Assyria and Babylon will conquer the northern and southern kingdoms, sending his people into exile. The reasons for their judgment, and the Promise that God will one day heal the divided nation and bring them back from exile, are explained in Isaiah's preaching.

However, chapters 13 through 16 reveal that even when God uses evil nations for his purposes, it doesn't mean that they themselves are exempt from his judgment. As we have seen, God's judgment arises from his holy character as expressed in his commandments. Life works, and God is glorified, when people and nations align themselves with his will. But when the nations refuse, and instead act out of greed, injustice, idolatry and a love of violence, life unravels. God is patient with the nations, but he will not stand by forever. Isaiah is sent by God to bring this message to Babylon.

In chapter 13, God tells Isaiah that he is raising an army against Babylon, from the kingdom of Medes: *"They are the Lord's weapons to carry out his anger."*

Babylon's coming Day of Judgment is called *"the day of the Lord"* and it is described with apocalyptic language: *"For I will shake the heavens. The earth will move from its place when the Lord of Heaven's Armies displays his wrath in the day of his fierce anger."* The merciless terror Babylon has heaped upon others will be visited upon them.

At the same time, we learn that God will have mercy on the rebellious-but-humbled Israelites: *"He will choose Israel as his special people once again. He will bring them back to settle once again in their own land. ... Those who captured Israel will themselves be captured, and Israel will rule over its enemies"* (Isaiah 14:1–2).

Isaiah speaks here of Israel's ultimate deliverance from her *"sorrow and fear, from slavery and chains"* as if it has already happened. He imagines Israel taunting the king of Babylon, saying that the evil he has done to others will be now done to him and his nation.

Interestingly, the king of Babylon, who is the embodiment of human arrogance, is mocked in terms that some see as an echo of the fall of Satan from heaven: *"How you are fallen from heaven, O shining star, son of the morning! You have been thrown down to the earth, you who destroyed the nations of the world. For you said to yourself, 'I will ascend to heaven and set my throne above God's stars. ... I will climb to the highest heavens and be like the Most High.' Instead, you will be brought down to the place of the dead, down to its lowest depths"* (Isaiah 14:12–15).

A similar prediction of doom for the land of Moab is given in chapters 15 and 16. Babylon, and those who align themselves with her, will certainly fall because nothing can stop God's redemptive plan: *"When oppression and destruction have ended and enemy raiders have disappeared, then God will establish one of David's descendants as king"* (Isaiah 16:4–5).

As mentioned above, the destruction of Assyria and Babylon are described in cosmic, larger-than-life terms. This language was commonly used to taunt the enemy and exaggerate the significance of their defeat. In this case, Babylon's judgment by God anticipates and points to the greater reality that one day the whole world system, which stands in opposition to God, will fall.

> **Focus:** The biblical view of the creation includes a spiritual realm as well as a material realm. The spiritual realm is invisible to us, but is just as real. We might think of it as God's space. There are also created beings, called angels, who are spiritual and share God's space. Some seem to be occupied in continual glorious worship and praise. Others, *"heaven's armies,"* are involved in spiritual warfare against fallen angels—those led by Lucifer in rebellion against God. We can only speculate about that story, but we discern that their war against God in heaven is connected to the rebellion against God on earth. Perhaps the serpent's lie to Adam and Eve was meant to gain their allegiance, and ours, to his campaign.

God's commitment to reoccupy earth as its King, as played out in the great story of redemption, is furiously resisted in heaven and on earth. Thus, the story of the Bible is presented as a deadly serious great struggle against powerful foes, regarding the ultimate outcome of the whole creation. Since we New Testament believers know how the conflict ends, we can fight the good fight, in the present day—like Isaiah—with courage and hope!

Prayer: Lord, once again we take comfort in the wonderful vision of a world where evil is destroyed, once and for all, and your sons and daughters can live together with you in the joy and peace of the New Creation. Please come soon, Lord. Amen!

Day 200   Isaiah 17–20

July 18

> Key Text: Then at last the people will look to their Creator and turn their eyes to the Holy One of Israel. They will no longer look to their idols for help or worship what their own hands have made. They will never again bow down to their Asherah poles or worship at the pagan shrines they have built. (Isaiah 17:7–8)

As a nation, Judah is faced with the choice to trust in the Lord for her protection, or to politically align herself with the pagan nations that surround her. Isaiah has begun a prophetic preaching tour of those pagan nations to show how weak they are, and how foolish Judah's leaders are, to think that their hope lies in alliances with them.

While it may seem like a taunting tour, it is meant to be both a warning and an invitation. This is interesting because it illustrates God's desire for all nations to be reconciled with him through repentance and faith—not just Israel. This can only happen in centers of idolatry and power, when that power is defeated and those gods are exposed as false. Until their abusive pride is conquered, the nations will not humble themselves before God.

So, having already announced God's judgment of the city of Moab, Isaiah now does the same for Damascus *(chapter 17)*, Ethiopia *(chapter 18)*, and the nation of Egypt *(chapter 19)*. If the Israelites think that they will find safety by embracing the pagan gods of their neighbors and counting on those nations' armies to protect them, they will soon be disappointed. Israel's fate will follow the inevitable judgment of God against the pagan nations.

The Lord God is the powerful Lord of history, yet Israel has forgotten this and is now more impressed by the size of armies and the wealth of nations. Even the memory of God's victory over Pharaoh and the gods of Egypt, followed by his deliverance through the Red Sea into Canaan, has faded.

Isaiah's preaching in these chapters identifies idolatry as the root of Israel's fatal miscalculations. Those who trust in idols find that idols do not respond when people look to them for help. How can they? The idol worshiper merely worships what his own hands have made!

There is no power in them except perhaps the limited power of demons that enslave those who *"plead with their idols for wisdom and call on spirits, mediums, and those who consult the spirits of the dead"* (Isaiah 19:3). But fighting against those demonic powers are the Lord of Heaven's armies of angels. As we have noted, the Old Testament views the spiritual realm as influencing earthly affairs. This is explained further in the New Testament: *"Put on all of God's armor so that you will be able to stand firm against all strategies of the devil. For we are not fighting against flesh-and-blood enemies, but against evil rulers and authorities of the unseen world, against mighty powers in this dark world, and against evil spirits in the heavenly places"* (Ephesians 6:11–12).

The demonic realm must be taken into account by resisting it, but it is no match for God's kingdom because the devil is not a rival god—he is nothing more than a rebellious angel, another kind of creature created by God. Remember, the Lord easily defeated the gods of Egypt *(Exodus 8–15);* the prophet Elijah confronted and easily defeated the pagan god Baal who was summoned to fight against the Lord *(1 Kings 18:25–39);* and Jesus easily confronted and cast out demons during his public ministry *(Matthew 9:32–34).*

Israel repeatedly turned to paganism as an attempt to find power and protection, but it always ended badly. But whenever she returned to the Lord and remembered that the Lord God alone was worthy of worship, her fortunes changed and her national life was blessed.

Focus: It is easy to forget that God loves the whole world, and not just Israel. Israel was originally chosen to be God's people, not because Abraham or his descendants were better or more numerous than other people, but just because God said, *"I choose you."* But this choosing proves to be a burden. Israel is called to bear witness to the nations, of the God who has revealed himself to them and shown himself to be the one true God by his mighty acts of power. In bearing witness, Israel must live a *different* life, ordered and expressed through the commandments and the Covenant. This different way of life also proves be a *difficult* way of life. It is a life of servanthood and obedience *for the sake of witness.* Israel is to make God known to the nations because God loves them too. The Church must also keep this in mind, lest we fall into the trap of judging others because we feel we are better than they are.

Prayer: Lord, we confess that it is easier to trust something we can see and feel and hold in our hand—like an idol. But our idols only end up disappointing us and sometimes ruining our lives. We want to worship you alone. Show yourself to us through the glory of Jesus, the one who makes you known. Give us a love for those who don't know you. May we live in such a way that they may see something of the glory of Jesus in us. Amen.

Day 201   Isaiah 21–23

July 19

> Key Text: Then the watchman said, "Babylon is fallen, fallen! All the idols of Babylon lie broken on the ground!" (Isaiah 21:9)

Isaiah continues with his warning to the southern kingdom of Judah that she should not align herself with the pagan nations nearby, because those nations are under God's judgment. His message, in short, is that the crisis they face will not be solved by looking to the unbelieving world for solutions.

Chapter 21 is an eerie warning about the fall of Babylon, the nation which Judah was depending on to protect her from Assyria: *"Disaster is roaring down on you from the desert, like a whirlwind sweeping in from the Negev. I see a terrifying vision: I see the betrayer betraying, the destroyer destroying."*

Isaiah's vision of what is coming for Babylon makes him physically ill: *"My stomach aches and burns with pain. Sharp pains of anguish are upon me, like those of a woman in labor. I grow faint when I hear what God is planning; I am too afraid to look."*

At last the prophetic vision comes to its inevitable and terrifying climax: *"Babylon is fallen, fallen! All the idols of Babylon lie broken on the ground!"* What little remains of Babylon will be crushed by Edom and Arabia. What will Israel do now?

377

In chapter 22, Isaiah shares a further vision, which anticipates the terrible fate of Jerusalem because the leaders have aligned themselves with the Babylonians for protection. The vision is a heartbreaking picture of chaos and violence: *"The whole city is in a terrible uproar. ... Bodies are lying everywhere, killed not in battle but by famine and disease. All your leaders have fled. They surrendered without resistance. The people tried to slip away, but they were captured, too. That's why I said, 'Leave me alone to weep; do not try to comfort me. Let me cry for my people as I watch them being destroyed'"* (Isaiah 22:2–4).

The rest of the chapter illustrates the failure of Judah's leaders and its people to repent of their sin and turn in faith to the Lord: *"The Lord... called you to weep and mourn...to show your remorse. But instead, you dance and play.... You say, 'Let's feast and drink, for tomorrow we die!'"*

In chapter 23, Isaiah completes his series of prophecies against particular nations by turning to the city of Tyre. Where Babylon, the first nation of his series, was known for its military might and cultural achievements, Tyre was known for its commercial wealth. Together, they symbolize all that is alluring about the wealth and power of the world.

The message begins with the reaction of the Mediterranean nations to the shocking financial and trade implications of the fall of Tyre: *"Wail, you trading ships of Tarshish, for the harbor and houses of Tyre are gone! The rumors you heard in Cyprus are all true."*

Why is God bringing judgment on Tyre? Secondary causes are brushed aside—the root of their fall is pride: *"Who has brought this disaster on Tyre? ... The Lord of Heaven's Armies has done it to destroy your pride and bring low all earth's nobility"* (Isaiah 23:8–9).

Focus: Isaiah's vision of what is to come is eerily presented as if it were now happening. In his vision of the fall of Babylon, Judah is exposed. She has long since rejected the Covenant with the Lord God, and now the nations whose wealth and power she has depended on for safety, through political alliances, are crumbling. She is helpless and alone in the world. Sometimes it takes the loss of all that gives us confidence to become aware of our spiritual need. When we do, we discover that God has been patiently waiting for us to turn (or to return) to him. Everyone eventually figures out that the world cannot save us. It is just as lost as we are. Only God can find us when we are lost.

Prayer: *Lord, we feel overwhelmed by the powerful forces of culture, politics and wealth, which seem to push our lives to places we don't want to go. We continue to* *pray, as you taught us to pray, that "your Kingdom may come and your will be done on earth as in heaven." Amen.*

Day 202   Isaiah 24–27

July 20

Key Text: Then the glory of the moon will wane, and the brightness of the sun will fade, for the Lord of Heaven's Armies will rule on Mount Zion. He will rule in great glory in Jerusalem, in the sight of all the leaders of his people. (Isaiah 24:23)

A superficial understanding of God as Judge leaves some people offended, confused and incapable of seeing why God's judgment is actually the best thing that can happen to the world.

God's judgment is his emphatic "NO!" to all that obscures his glory and undermines the goodness of his creation. At the center of his creation are human beings, created in his image to reflect his glory, and called to love and serve him as our highest purpose. But as we have seen during our read through the Bible, our sin has obscured his glory and undermined the goodness of his creation. God cannot tolerate evil to coexist with him, so he must either destroy *us* or destroy *it*. Thankfully, he has chosen the latter.

This decision is God's emphatic "YES!" to us. But just as a condemned building must first be demolished before it can be rebuilt, so the sin of the world must first be judged before the world can be renewed. We know that this involves the sacrifice of Jesus, in which he takes the judgment of the world upon himself. Consequently, he is the foundation upon which God rebuilds.

Isaiah doesn't know about Jesus, of course, but God tells him through visions that as Judge, he (God) is going to renew the whole earth and bless his people beyond imagination.

Isaiah presents this by stretching the limits of human language and imagination. He begins chapter 24 with an alarming vision: *"Look! The Lord is about to destroy the earth and make it a vast wasteland. He devastates the surface of the earth and scatters the people."* The earth will be completely emptied and looted. Everything will be lost. Only a few people—a remnant— will be left alive because a curse has consumed the earth: *"Its people must pay the price for their sin."* The earth has broken

379

up. It has utterly collapsed; it is violently shaken. The language is figurative, but the event is real. In that day, God will punish the gods in the heavens and the proud rulers of the nations on earth.

But after this terrible, cleansing judgment, chapter 24 suddenly pivots to a picture of great hope: *"Then the glory of the moon will wane, and the brightness of the sun will fade* [the sun and moon were worshiped as gods], *for the Lord of Heaven's Armies will rule on Mount Zion. He will rule in great glory in Jerusalem, in the sight of all the leaders of his people."*

A song of praise follows, and then in chapter 25, a further statement of cosmic transformation: *"In Jerusalem, the Lord of Heaven's Armies will spread a wonderful feast for all the people of the world. It will be a delicious banquet with clear, well-aged wine and choice meat. There he will remove the cloud of gloom, the shadow of death that hangs over the earth. He will swallow up death forever! The Sovereign Lord will wipe away all tears"* (Isaiah 25:6–8).

This is a sneak peek of the New Creation at the end of history. Isaiah moves back and forth between NOW and THEN, earth and heaven, seeing in the present situation an anticipation of the final judgment and the Day of Salvation.

Accordingly, in response to this great hope, the rest of chapters 26 and 27 are songs of praise and sober reflection.

Focus: Isaiah's picture of God spreading a wonderful feast for all the people of the world is as good a word-picture as we could choose to illustrate the nature of God's future. In God's future, the ravages of sin and death are gone; he wipes away all tears. And the nations which fought each other nonstop for power and resources are now sitting around the same table, enjoying a feast prepared by God himself—*"a delicious banquet with clear, well-aged wine and choice meat."*

Can you imagine the joy of the peoples of the earth united in their diversity, by love and the grace of God? Think of what redeemed humanity could do! It is the undoing of the Tower of Babel, where the unity of peoples served only evil. Read Isaiah when you've become weary of the world and have given up!

Prayer: Lord, give us ears to hear and eyes to see the bigger story of where history is going. The present problems seem so hopeless, yet your promise of a world restored, refreshed and reunited in Christ enables us to not lose hope, but to persevere in the ministry of your Church, of making your Good News known. Amen.

Day 203   Reflection

The book of Isaiah reflects a view of history that is typical of the whole Bible. It is called "eschatological," referring to the "end" or goal toward which history is moving by God's will and power. It also refers to the things which define the end, such as death, judgment, heaven and hell.

Israel's pagan neighbors held a very different view of history. There were gods, but no overall plan for the end—at least not for a good end. Human life was fatalistic and full of fear because the gods were immoral and unpredictable. Each nation had its own territorial gods, which were always at war with one another. History was shaped by those who were the most powerful and ruthless.

A secular version of the pagan view today is a materialistic account of history, which denies any transcendent purpose for life and any divine guidance to the events of history. There is no particular "end" or destination to life. Events just happen randomly, one thing after another. When you die, there is nothing. The light switches off and you are gone.

By introducing an eschatological view of history, Judeo-Christianity provides a sound basis for human hope and progress. Despite our sin, God has not given up on us. The future will be wonderful, beyond imagination. This is why, as we have noted, the future is described with fantastic and figurative language—like a *"delicious banquet...for all the people of the world."* There the *"shadow of death"* is removed and all tears are wiped away. The natural world is also at peace, with the predator lying down beside the prey.

Such a worldview counters the nihilism of our time. It declares that the best days lie ahead for all who trust in the Lord. We can be truly glad because *"there is wonderful joy ahead, even though you must endure many trials for a little while"* (1 Peter 1:6).

When we read the prophets, we get plenty of bad news, but bad news is never the last word—it is the necessary prelude to good news. The prophets unanimously proclaim that there is a "Day" coming, the great and terrible Day of the Lord, a Day of Judgment and salvation. God says through Isaiah: *"Look! I am creating new heavens and a new earth, and no* one will even think about the old ones anymore. Be glad; rejoice forever in my creation! And look! I will create Jerusalem as a place of happiness. Her people will be a source of joy. I will rejoice over Jerusalem and delight in my people. And the sound of weeping and crying will be heard in it no more" (Isaiah 65:17–19).

> *Prayer: Lord, help us to see life as you see it—as moving toward that great Day when the troubles of the world are over, and the New Creation begins. Our imaginations are not enough to grasp it, but we feel it in our bones. It keeps us hoping, believing and obeying. Amen!*

Day 204　　　　Isaiah 28–30

July 22

> Key Text: And so the Lord says, "These people say they are mine. They honor me with their lips, but their hearts are far from me. And their worship of me is nothing but man-made rules learned by rote." (Isaiah 29:13)

In these messages, Isaiah once again expresses God's anguish about the spiritual emptiness and moral corruption of the northern and southern kingdoms. Beginning with Samaria, the capital city of Israel, Isaiah lays out the evidence for God's judgment against them.

Samaria, he says, is *"the glorious crown of the drunks of Israel. It sits at the head of a fertile valley, but its glorious beauty will fade like a flower. It is the pride of a people brought down by wine"* (Isaiah 28:1). The priests and prophets are so drunk they can't walk straight, but *"stagger with alcohol"!* Their plan to escape God's judgment by creating military alliances with pagan nations is delusional: *"You boast, 'We have struck a bargain to cheat death and have made a deal to dodge the grave. The coming destruction can never touch us, for we have built a strong refuge made of lies and deception'"* (Isaiah 28:15).

The leaders of Samaria grow weary of Isaiah's preaching, protesting that God is treating them like little children and telling them everything over and over again— one line at a time.

But God has measured them, using the plumb line of righteousness, and their lives are not morally or spiritually straight. One day, however, God will place a foundation stone in Jerusalem that *is* straight, a precious cornerstone that is safe to build on. Peter identifies that cornerstone:

"You are coming to Christ, who is the living cornerstone of God's temple" (1 Peter 2:4).

Next, in chapter 29, Isaiah addresses Jerusalem, which is called "Ariel" by the prophet, and is the capital of Judah. Of Judah he says: *"You are stupid, but not from wine! ... For the Lord has poured out on you a spirit of deep sleep. He has closed the eyes of your prophets and visionaries"* (Isaiah 29:9–10). In a verse which is later cited by Jesus in Matthew 15:8 about the Pharisees, Isaiah says: *"These people say they are mine. They honor me with their lips, but their hearts are far from me. And their worship of me is nothing but man-made rules learned by rote."*

Finally, in chapter 30, the Lord warns Israel specifically not to make an alliance with Egypt because Egypt's promises are worthless. Israel, however, refuses to listen to the Lord. They don't want to hear from Isaiah or anyone else about the matter.

Nevertheless, with God's judgment—his "NO!"—against Israel's stubborn unbelief, he continues to offer the opportunity of forgiveness: *"'Only in returning to me and resting in me will you be saved. In quietness and confidence is your strength.' ... So the Lord must wait for you to come to him so he can show you his love and compassion. For the Lord is a faithful God. Blessed are those who wait for his help."*

Blessed indeed. Because in the end, the Lord will strike down his people's enemies and then *"...the people of God will sing a song of joy, like the songs at the holy festivals"* (Isaiah 30:29).

Focus: Why does God refuse the worship of some who do the rituals properly, and say the right things? Because what God desires—what he has wanted from the very beginning—is a relationship with us. He wants to know that our "heart" is in it. Pretending to love and respect God, by rote ritual, is as empty for him as it is for the fake worshiper. We can't do love by rote.

Prayer: Lord, we are perplexed at the persistent stubbornness of your Old Testament people, and of we ourselves. Forgive us for the times when our worship is on autopilot and we sing empty words without paying attention. Stir our hearts with your love! We are so grateful for your amazing grace and willingness to wait for us to return to you. Only in you do we find salvation! May sincere faith and worship be our strength. Amen.

July 23

> Key Text: The heavens above will melt away and disappear like a rolled-up scroll. The stars will fall from the sky like withered leaves from a grapevine, or shriveled figs from a fig tree. (Isaiah 34:4)

Isaiah has spoken words of judgment which, as we have said, is God's "NO!" to all that undermines his creation. But judgment is not an end in itself; it is the prelude to hope. Words of judgment are always followed by words of eschatological hope, meaning that God has an end game of unbelievable joy for those who love and worship him. Chapters 31 through 35 tilt to the hope side.

Chapter 31 reminds the people that God's judgment is temporary. His purpose is to turn their hearts back to him, for there they will find their life and future. The Egyptians to whom they have turned for help and protection *"are mere humans, not God!"*

God's compassion shines through the cloud of his judgment, revealing its purpose: *"Though you are such wicked rebels, my people, come and return to the Lord. I know the glorious day will come when each of you will throw away the gold idols and silver images your sinful hands have made"* (Isaiah 31:6–7).

The anticipation of their return fills God with joy. The Assyrian captivity will end with the hope of the promised righteous king in view. He has been previously identified as the son of the virgin *(Isaiah 7:14)* and called *"Wonderful Counselor, Mighty God, Everlasting Father, Prince of Peace"* (Isaiah 9:6).

Chapter 32 adds that the reign of this righteous king will bring about a transforming event—the Spirit will be poured out on us from heaven: *"Then the wilderness will become a fertile field, and the fertile field will yield bountiful crops."*

The agricultural metaphor speaks about a future that is abundant and joyful, characterized by God's presence through his Spirit. Consequently, there will be justice and righteousness: *"My people will live in safety, quietly at home. They will be at rest"* (Isaiah 32:18).

Chapter 33 returns to God's judgment of Assyria. It is a brutal nation, but justice will come in the form of proportional retribution—what they have done to others will be done to them. The prospect of this fills the Assyrians with terror: *"'Who can live with this devouring fire?' they cry. 'Who can survive this all-consuming fire?'"*

God's people will be restored and the ways of God vindicated: *"For the Lord is our judge, our lawgiver, and our king. He will care for us and save us"* (Isaiah 33:22). The humiliation and suffering of exile will become a distant memory.

Now in Chapter 34, all the nations of the earth are summoned to hear God's warning of universal judgment at the end of history. The vision draws a bleak picture of the future for those people and nations who resist God and face his judgment. It is hard to imagine such things, even though our hearts tell us that justice must be satisfied in the end.

Again, in prophetic fashion, the near events of judgment against Assyria are placed on top of the expectation of Final Judgment, because the same God who works in the details of history today will bring history to its conclusion: *"The heavens above will melt away and disappear like a rolled-up scroll. The stars will fall from the sky like withered leaves from a grapevine, or shriveled figs from a fig tree"* (Isaiah 34:4).

Isaiah concludes his vision of future judgment and salvation with a frenzy of joyful expectation in chapter 35. The whole creation will rejoice: *"Even the wilderness and desert will be glad in those days. ... There the Lord will display his glory."* This news will strengthen weary people who have weak knees and tired hearts. The Lord is coming to save us by defeating our enemies, which are really his enemies. We will ultimately see that our true enemies are sin and death, but they are defeated by Christ in his cross and resurrection: *"Sorrow and mourning will disappear, and [God's people] will be filled with joy and gladness"* (Isaiah 35:10).

Focus: The Bible's vision of the end of history has been a source of both terror and comfort. The biblical writers often employ the genre of "apocalyptic" to speak of these final things which God has revealed. They speak of a final victory, at last, for the people of God. Sin will be judged, the devil defeated and death overcome. The whole creation will be renewed, and humanity at last will enter the full joy of its salvation.

Such things are, by definition, beyond human experience, so apocalyptic writings employ symbolism and vivid imagination to tell the story. It will be epic and cosmic in scale. The modern world, with technologies capable of wreaking nuclear, environmental, and biological havoc on a large scale, makes the apocalyptic language of the Bible quite believable. The Good News is that the End is not final destruction, but a New Creation!

Prayer: Lord, your description of our future seems almost too good to be true. And yet, it is what we have always longed for. We sense that we were made for this, and that the troubles of the world are an intrusion into your good plan. Help us to be strong and not fear. May we live with joy and gladness. Amen.

Day 206   Isaiah 36–39

July 24

> Key Text: Then the Assyrian king's chief of staff told them to give this message to Hezekiah: "This is what the great king of Assyria says: What are you trusting in that makes you so confident? Do you think that mere words can substitute for military skill and strength? Who are you counting on, that you have rebelled against me?" (Isaiah 36:4–5)

These four chapters are considered to be the pivot on which the book of Isaiah turns, and a bridge between the first and second divisions of Isaiah. The chapters focus on the key question of the book—*what are you trusting in?*

The events that follow occur in the fourteenth year of the reign of Hezekiah, the godly, reforming king of Judah.

Chapter 36 begins with the announcement that the Assyrian king, Sennacherib, has conquered the fortified towns of Judah, and is now positioned near Jerusalem, ready to lay siege. When officials go out to meet with Assyrian leaders, they are given a message to take back to Hezekiah: *"What are you trusting in that makes you so confident?"* This is followed by a whole bunch of boasting, taunting, and minds games, back and forth. Finally, Judah is given the option to either align themselves with Assyria, or be destroyed.

To instill more fear in the people, the Assyrian chief of staff stands on a wall and shouts in Hebrew to the people nearby: *"Don't let Hezekiah deceive you. He will never be able to rescue you. Don't let him fool you into trusting in the Lord by saying, 'The Lord will surely rescue us.' ... What god of any nation has ever been able to save its people from my power? So what makes you think that the Lord can rescue Jerusalem from me?"*

King Hezekiah reports this to the prophet Isaiah, asking for his prayers

386

and counsel. Isaiah responds that the Lord says: *"Do not be disturbed by this blasphemous speech against me from the Assyrian king's messengers. Listen! I myself will move against him...."*

Hezekiah receives another message from King Sennacherib warning him not to be deceived by the Lord, because Assyria will not be stopped. Sennacherib seems to think that the Israelite God is no different from the gods of the other nations.

This time, Hezekiah lays the letter out before the Lord in prayer, addressing him as the one true God—the Creator of the heavens and the earth. He asks: *"Now, O Lord our God, rescue us from his power; then all the kingdoms of the earth will know that you alone, O Lord, are God"* (Isaiah 37:20).

The Lord responds with strong words to Sennacherib for defying and mocking the *"Holy One of Israel."* The Lord declares: *"His armies will not enter Jerusalem. They will not even shoot an arrow at it."*

Sure enough, that night the angel of the Lord goes into the Assyrian camp and kills 185,000 soldiers. A stunned Sennacherib returns home, and not long thereafter is killed by his own sons.

The story of Hezekiah continues in Chapter 38. Hezekiah becomes deathly ill, but after he prays for healing, God gives him fifteen more years: *"Think of it—the Lord is ready to heal me! I will sing his praises with instruments every day of my life in the Temple of the Lord."*

Unfortunately, the story does not end well for Hezekiah. Visitors from Babylon come during his illness with well wishes and a gift. Assyria is their common enemy, and Hezekiah, with his guard down, foolishly shows the Babylonians everything in his royal treasuries. It will prove to be a tragic mistake.

Focus: The Assyrian taunting of Hezekiah about his military weakness, contrasted with the Assyrian army's reputation for brutality and success, would make any leader nervous and quick to look for a way out. This is David and Goliath again on a national level! The Assyrians even claim that the Lord God himself has told them to attack Judah and destroy it! The question for Hezekiah, and for all of us who are tempted to give in to pressure from the world, is: *"Who are you trusting in?"* Do I believe that God is able to protect me and provide for me? It is the same question that has been asked of Abraham, Moses, David and others at different stages of the Story. So, who are you trusting in?

Day 207   Isaiah 40–43

July 25

> Key Text: "Look at my servant, whom I strengthen. He is my chosen one, who pleases me. I have put my Spirit upon him. He will bring justice to the nations." (Isaiah 42:1)

It is widely accepted that the tone and focus of Isaiah changes noticeably at chapter 40 until the end of the book. So much so, that some have suggested two authors. But there is sufficient evidence to regard it as the writing of one prophet.

From chapter 40 on, Isaiah changes his focus from warning corrupt Israelite kings and the surrounding pagan nations about the judgment of God, to encouraging God's people about his gracious future for them notwithstanding.

Now we hear Isaiah speaking words of hope into the misery of a people whose lives have been shattered: *"'Comfort, comfort my people,' says your God. 'Speak tenderly to Jerusalem. Tell her that her sad days are gone and her sins are pardoned'"* (Isaiah 40:1–2). This opening thought, immortalized in Handel's *Messiah* oratorio, begins a theological journey that is one of the highlights of the Old Testament.

God calls them "my people." He has not forsaken them!

Chapter 40 is a magnificent celebration of the glory of God. He is coming to save his people, and everyone will see it. And who is this Lord? He is the sovereign God of creation. His knowledge and power surpass all earthly thrones: *"...all the nations of the world are but a drop in the bucket. ... He picks up the whole earth as though it were a grain of sand."*

It is laughable to compare the man-made idols of the nations to him: *"'To whom will you compare me? Who is my equal?' asks the Holy One."*

God is all powerful, and yet tender: *"He will feed his flock like a shepherd. He will carry the lambs in his arms, holding them close to his heart."*

The chapter concludes with the much-loved declaration: *"Have you never heard? Have you never understood? The Lord is the everlasting God, the Creator of all the earth. He never grows weak or weary. No one can measure the depths of his understanding. He gives power to the weak and strength to the powerless. Even youths will become weak and tired, and young men will fall in exhaustion. But those who trust in the Lord will find new strength. They will soar high on wings like eagles. They will run and not grow weary. They will walk and not faint"* (Isaiah 40:28–31).

In chapter 41, we are given a courtroom drama of God summoning all the nations of the world before him to prove that they, with their false gods, are the ones who shape history. They cannot: *"Not one gave any answer when I asked."*

In chapter 42, the mysterious *"servant of the Lord"* is introduced. The servant seems to be a figure who embodies all that Israel is supposed to be, but is not. The Lord says of him: *"He is my chosen one, who pleases me. I have put my Spirit upon him. He will bring justice to the nations."* His identity is a secret at this point, but will be revealed later in Isaiah.

For now, the Lord calls his people to trust him. He will bring them back from captivity and suffering, because he has made them for his glory and he will not forget them: *"You are my witnesses, O Israel! ... You have been chosen to know me, believe in me, and understand that I alone am God. There is no other God—there never has been, and there never will be"* (Isaiah 43:10).

Focus: When the Jewish-Christian leaders of the first and second generations of the Church read the prophet Isaiah in the light of Christ, their eyes were opened. They realized that God had been dropping hints all along about how he was going to fulfill his Promise to Abraham. Christ was his plan all along! The apostle Paul wrote: *"Even before he made the world, God loved us and chose us in Christ to be holy and without fault in his eyes. God decided in advance to adopt us into his own family by bringing us to himself through Jesus Christ. This is what he wanted to do, and it gave him great pleasure"* (Ephesians 1:4–5).

I can imagine God, then and now, patiently working out his plan. Yes, it grieves him to see the suffering in the world, but it pleases him to see his plan for our salvation now made known to the whole world through the Gospel. I bet there is a smile on his face as he anticipates where all this is going!

Prayer: *Lord, the revelation of your glory is like the visible glory of the heavens in the night sky. It is beyond description. We revel in the vastness of it. Its power and beauty bring us comfort. You show us by your treatment of Israel that you are* *patient and forgiving of us. You could have walked away, but you showed mercy instead. How wonderful you are! May we indeed honor you before the world! Amen.*

Day 208   Isaiah 44–48

July 26

> Key Text: "Oh, that you had listened to my commands! Then you would have had peace flowing like a gentle river and righteousness rolling over you like waves in the sea. ... Yet even now, be free from your captivity! Leave Babylon and the Babylonians. Sing out this message! Shout it to the ends of the earth! The Lord has redeemed his servants, the people of Israel." (Isaiah 48:18–20)

Through Isaiah's words, God continues "comforting" his people. He reassures them that though they are presently captive to nations who worship other gods, they must not be afraid or believe the lies of their captors. Their enemies boast that Israel's God is weak, and that their gods are strong. But the Lord says that these gods don't exist. Idols are nothing but wood and stone fabrications—objects of rebellion against the one true God: *"All who worship idols will be disgraced along with all these craftsmen—mere humans—who claim they can make a god"* (Isaiah 44:11).

Isaiah, like others before him, considers the foolishness of idolatry. He notes that a woodcarver takes a block of wood and uses it to make a fire so that he can warm himself and bake some bread. He then takes the rest of it and makes an idol, and bows down in front of it: *"'Rescue me!' he says. 'You are my god!'"*

This reduction of God to a piece of wood or metal is stupidity, Isaiah says. Those who worship idols are ignorant. Their minds are shut and they cannot think straight.

Against this, the Lord says: *"For there is no other God but me, a righteous God and Savior. There is none but me. Let all the world look to me for salvation!"* These are not empty claims, but are backed up by his mighty works on Israel's behalf, time after time.

Israel's God is all-powerful, all-knowing and everywhere present. The whole world, even all the nations, belong to him as Creator of the heavens and earth. To demonstrate his sovereignty, he announces that he is going to raise up a pagan leader, King Cyrus of Persia, to defeat the Babylonians.

390

Cyrus will then show favor to the Jews and allow them to return to Jerusalem, rebuild the Temple, and repair the broken walls around the city *(Isaiah 44:26–28)*. We know this story already from the books of Ezra and Nehemiah.

In chapter 45, the Lord speaks directly to Cyrus, saying that he will empower him for the sake of Israel: *"I will raise up Cyrus to fulfill my righteous purpose, and I will guide his actions."* God's use of the Persian king for his own purposes is a sign that, ultimately, all nations will worship him: *"Every knee will bend to me, and every tongue will confess allegiance to me."*

Then, in chapters 46 and 47, the Lord turns to Babylon. He tells them that he has punished his people by letting them fall into Babylon's hands: *"But you, Babylon, showed them no mercy. … So disaster will overtake you …"* (Isaiah 47:6–11).

Finally, in chapter 48, the Lord addresses his people, reminding them that this calamity has come upon them because of their persistent obstinacy, just as he predicted long beforehand: *"That is why I told you what would happen; I told you beforehand what I was going to do."*

Through defeat and exile, God has humbled and refined his people in the *"furnace of suffering."* But now, for the honor of his name, he will rescue them: *"The Lord has chosen Cyrus as his ally. He will use him to put an end to the empire of Babylon and to destroy the Babylonian armies."*

All this was so unnecessary: *"Oh, that you had listened to my commands! Then you would have had peace flowing like a gentle river and righteousness rolling over you like waves in the sea. … Yet even now, be free from your captivity! Leave Babylon and the Babylonians. Sing out this message! Shout it to the ends of the earth! The Lord has redeemed his servants, the people of Israel"* (Isaiah 48:18–20).

Focus: Every life is marked by at least a few significant *"what ifs."* What if I had done this instead of that? We can never know. We can only live out the consequences of our choices. God gives us broad freedom to choose how we will live—where we will go to college, what we will do for a vocation, whom we will marry, and so forth. We can't know the outcome of those choices, but we can choose to honor God within them.

Israel made some monumentally bad choices, over and over again, and faced the bitter consequences. God watched them and grieved: *"Oh, that you had listened to my commands!"* Yet, there is always opportunity to make things right with God, to *"be free from your captivity!"* The Gospel always holds out the possibility of forgiveness and new beginnings! That is what makes it "Good News"!

Prayer: Lord, we are such stubborn and rebellious children. We deserve your judgments, yet even your discipline comes from love. It grows us up and shapes our character and will. So we acknowledge, Lord, that our present suffering becomes the means of our future glory. Thank you for caring enough to hold us accountable, and then welcome us home when we repent of our sins. We will shout it to the ends of the earth! Amen.

Day 209   Isaiah 49–51

July 27

> Key Text: Sing for joy, O heavens! Rejoice, O earth! Burst into song, O mountains! For the Lord has comforted his people and will have compassion on them in their suffering. (Isaiah 49:13)

We return in these chapters to the mysterious *"servant"* who was first introduced in chapter 42. There, he was presented as an ideal king who will bring justice, not just to Israel, but to all the nations.

In chapter 49, he appears as a prophet who speaks God's truth. So, is he a king or a prophet? Or both? Even more puzzling, he is called *"my servant, Israel"* by the Lord. How can this be? Israel is in rebellion against God and needs to be reconciled to him. Perhaps the *"servant"* is what we might call a true Israelite—a leader who embodies all that Israel was called, but failed, to be. If so, he is God's *"perfect servant,"* greater than any of Israel's kings or even the prophet Isaiah himself.

From the perspective of the New Testament, we know who this is, but let's go with the puzzle for now and wait for Isaiah's clues.

First clue: The servant is commissioned to bring Israel back to God. He will also be *"a light to the Gentiles,"* bringing God's salvation to the ends of the earth. When the world sees God comforting Israel and restoring her to blessing, they will learn that God's comfort is for them too: *"All the world will know that I, the Lord, am your Savior and your Redeemer, the Mighty One of Israel"* (Isaiah 49:26).

Second clue: The servant will be resisted and will face suffering: *"I offered my back to those who beat me and my cheeks to those who pulled out my beard. I did not hide my face from mockery and spitting. Because the Sovereign Lord helps me, I will not be disgraced. Therefore, I have set my*

392

face like a stone, determined to do his will. And I know that I will not be put to shame" (Isaiah 50:6–7).

By his servant, the Lord will comfort Israel again and have pity on her ruins: *"Her desert will blossom like Eden, her barren wilderness like the garden of the Lord. ... Those who have been ransomed by the Lord will return. They will enter Jerusalem singing, crowned with everlasting joy"* (Isaiah 51:3, 11).

I think we can see where this is going.

The return of the Lord's people to Jerusalem is a picture of the final return of a rebellious world to the Lord, the glorious end of the redemptive plan which started with Abraham. When this occurs, everyone will recognize that Jesus, God's Son, is the ultimate *"servant"* of Isaiah. Jesus is the one true Israelite, the *"perfect king"* from David's line—the leader who embodies all that Israel was called, but failed, to be. And as we shall see even more vividly in Isaiah, he is the *"Suffering Servant"* of God.

Focus: Some things can only be seen in retrospect. Like finishing a good detective novel and realizing that the clues were there all along, but you didn't recognize them until the bigger picture was revealed. So it is with Jesus in Isaiah. Actually, Jesus has been a hidden character in the whole story of the Old Testament so far. We'll discover from the apostles John and Paul that Jesus was with the Father in the beginning when the universe was created. He may have appeared as the mysterious "angel of the Lord" in the Abraham stories. He was prefigured in great leaders, like Moses and King David. He was Israel's everlasting King in the Psalms, Wisdom personified in the Proverbs, the child of the virgin and the Suffering Servant of Isaiah—and of course he was the Word of God, who in the beginning was with God and was God, and who became flesh and lived among us! He is now the resurrected Lord reigning in heaven and returning again for his Church! Jesus is everywhere in the Bible. The Bible's greatest purpose is to reveal Jesus to the world!

Prayer: Lord, in retrospect, it amazes us how you prepared for hundreds, even thousands of years, for the coming of Jesus, your faithful servant, to fulfill your plan of redemption. What a privilege it is to participate in that redemption now, and to look forward to the Day when everything is finally and fully made right, so that your glory fills the earth as well as our individual lives. Thank you for your faithfulness! Amen.

July 28

So far in our reading through the Bible, the four great biblical themes of Creation, Fall, Redemption and New Creation have been introduced, illustrated and analyzed from various perspectives. Along the way, God has revealed himself progressively, like the dimmer switch on a light.

Each new layer of understanding builds on and clarifies the last. Several foundational truths have been established along the way, themes that come together in the brilliant book of Isaiah. For example: There is one God, the Creator of the heavens and earth and Lord of all the nations of the world. So Isaiah says: *"For there is no other God but me, a righteous God and Savior. There is none but me. Let all the world look to me for salvation! For I am God; there is no other"* (Isaiah 45:21–22).

We humans are created in the image of God and are therefore unique among all the creatures God has made. To be fully human means to know, enjoy and serve the one true God. But tragically, we have become lost souls and rebels who have walked away from our Creator. We have fallen short of our glorious calling. So Isaiah says: *"What sorrow awaits those who argue with their Creator. Does a clay pot argue with its maker? Does the clay dispute with the one who shapes it, saying, 'Stop, you're doing it wrong'?"* (Isaiah 45:9).

Despite our obstinacy and sinfulness, and the bitter consequences which follow, God has not given up on us. Yes, he is our judge and disciplinarian, because we need to be stopped from our self-defeating behavior. But he is also our faithful and loving redeemer who comes to make things right between us. Isaiah says: *"'Come now, let's settle this,' says the Lord. 'Though your sins are like scarlet, I will make them as white as snow. Though they are red like crimson, I will make them as white as wool'"* (Isaiah 1:18).

The salvation God brings is taking us and the whole creation to a new future. Isaiah says: *"And when he comes, he will open the eyes of the blind and unplug the ears of the deaf. The lame will leap like a deer, and those who cannot speak will sing for joy! Springs will gush forth in the wilderness, and streams will water the wasteland. The parched ground will become a pool, and springs of water will satisfy the thirsty land. ... And a great road will go through that once deserted land. It will be named the Highway of Holiness. Evil-minded people will never travel on it. It will be only for those who walk in God's ways..."* (Isaiah 35:5–8).

We have noted that the prophets take an eschatological view of history, meaning that history is moving toward a God-intended end. There are hints along the way of what this end will be like, especially in small moments, as when bursts of light shine out of the darkness through acts of love, forgiveness, compassion, beauty and truth—a sneak peek of that great day when all of creation is redeemed, restored and refocused around its glorious purpose of being the stage upon which the glory of God is narrated and celebrated. Isaiah says: *"Sing, O heavens, for the Lord has done this wondrous thing. Shout for joy, O depths of the earth! Break into song, O mountains and forests and every tree!"* (Isaiah 44:23).

> **Prayer:** *Lord, give us eyes to see the evidence in front of us that you are at work in our lives, and in the broader events of history, bringing about your glorious future when you will make all things right, and the earth will be full of the knowledge and glory of God! Amen.*

Day 211   Isaiah 52–57

July 29

Key Text: All of us, like sheep, have strayed away. We have left God's paths to follow our own. Yet the Lord laid on him the sins of us all. (Isaiah 53:6)

We come now to the heart of Isaiah's message of hope. God's glorious plan is coming into focus. The people of God, beaten down and shamed by their enemies and captors, can now raise their heads: *"Rise from the dust, O Jerusalem. Sit in a place of honor. Remove the chains of slavery from your neck."*

Israel's shame has been removed, and her sins forgiven, by God's grace and love.

His act of delivering Israel from captivity and returning her to Jerusalem will be understood by surrounding nations as evidence of God's salvation: *"How beautiful on the mountains are the feet of the messenger who brings good news, the good news of peace and salvation, the news that the God of Israel reigns!"* (Isaiah 52:7). T h i s verse is quoted by the apostle Paul when he announces in Romans 10:13–15 the Good News that *"everyone who calls on the name of the Lord will be saved."*

After these encouraging words, the mysterious "servant" returns to the forefront in Isaiah 52:13. Now he is revealed to be a Suffering Servant, bearing the sins of the people. Jews have long puzzled over who this could be.

But the remarkable description of the Suffering Servant in chapter 53 was recognized by the early Church as being fulfilled in the Passion of Christ: *"He was despised and rejected—a man of sorrows, acquainted with deepest grief. We turned our backs on him and looked the other way. ... Yet it was our weaknesses he carried; it was our sorrows that weighed him down. And we thought his troubles were a punishment from God, a punishment for his own sins! But he was pierced for our rebellion, crushed for our sins. He was beaten so we could be whole. ... All of us, like sheep, have strayed away. We have left God's paths to follow our own. Yet the Lord laid on him the sins of us all"* (Isaiah 53:3–6).

No doubt, the resurrected Christ discussed Isaiah's prophesy at length with his disciples, pointing out how it explained the meaning of his crucifixion, which was then verified by his resurrection. Isaiah could only wonder about the Suffering Servant—but we have the privilege of knowing his name!

Jesus' suffering gives us insight into the nature of God. Incredibly, he is a God who is willing to humble himself and suffer unjustly on behalf of his people. The injustice done to him becomes, by God's grace, his justice applied to us. Justice is satisfied because Jesus paid the debt of our sins.

What a transforming thought! As the apostle John writes in his first epistle: *"This is real love—not that we loved God, but that he loved us and sent his Son as a sacrifice to take away our sins. Dear friends, since God loved us that much, we surely ought to love each other"* (1 John 4:10–11).

Isaiah continues in chapters 54 through 57 to pour out words of praise about the mercy of God: *"'My covenant of blessing will never be broken,' says the Lord, who has mercy on you."* God's goodness is beyond our understanding: *"'My thoughts are nothing like your thoughts,' says the Lord. 'And my ways are far beyond anything you could imagine'"* (Isaiah 55:8).

Furthermore, the blessings that he pours out on Israel are for outsiders, as well, *"who commit themselves to the Lord, who serve him and love his name, who worship him and do not desecrate the Sabbath day of rest...*

because my Temple will be called a house of prayer for all nations" (Isaiah 56:6–7).

Focus: It is sobering to think that at the center of human existence is a God who is willing to suffer on behalf of those he loves. God's action in Creation and Redemption reveals *love* to be the willingness to sacrifice oneself for the sake of another. How different this is from a fallen, upside-down, inside-out world, where we allow others to suffer so that we can gratify ourselves. God's love fuels life in the New Creation, beginning here and now, when by faith we humbly receive God's love and forgiveness, and then extend it to others.

Prayer: *Lord, we are struck once again by the sheer scale of your loving plan to restore the whole creation to yourself. This has been your plan from the beginning and you have been gracious to include anyone who believes. Truly, your ways are beyond our imagination! Amen.*

Day 212   Isaiah 58–62

July 30

> Key Text: "No, this is the kind of fasting I want: Free those who are wrongly imprisoned; lighten the burden of those who work for you. Let the oppressed go free, and remove the chains that bind people. Share your food with the hungry, and give shelter to the homeless. Give clothes to those who need them, and do not hide from relatives who need your help." (Isaiah 58:6–7)

After several chapters regarding God's comfort and restoration of his people through Cyrus, the Persian king, and then the ministry of the Suffering Servant, Isaiah now returns to the sinful attitudes of Israel that led them into exile in the first place.

You might think, wait a minute! Why is God returning to a message of judgment after reassuring the people of his grace and mercy? Well, it isn't a message of judgment so much as an in-your-face challenge to become the kind of people God created them to be. And there is a lot of work to be done!

Chapter 58 is an indictment of Israel's spiritual pretentiousness. They go through the motions of a righteous nation, such as Temple worship, fasting and penance. But all the while they are oppressing their workers, and fighting and quarreling among themselves. Their injustice, greed and oppression of the poor trump any pretense of righteousness: *"Feed* the hungry, and help those in trouble. Then your light will shine out from the darkness, and the darkness around you will be as bright as noon" (Isaiah 58:10).

The people don't seem to get the fact that truth and goodness must be lived. Faith is a verb, not a noun. Faith *does*. Therefore, when Israel goes through the motions of righteousness but behaves like the unrighteous, it is deeply offensive to God. Isaiah puts it bluntly: *"It's your sins that have cut you off from God. Because of your sins, he has turned away and will not listen anymore."*

Sadly, not all Israelites will listen to the Lord's challenge—but there is a *remnant of faith* within Israel. There always has been, but now the identity of the remnant comes to the fore. These are the ones, in the midst of unbelieving Israel as a whole, who God knows have humble, repentant hearts: *"Yes, we know what sinners we are. We know we have rebelled and have denied the Lord. We have turned our backs on our God. We know how unfair and oppressive we have been, carefully planning our deceitful lies"* (Isaiah 59:12–13).

So for the sake of the *remnant of faith*, God now acts: *"'The Redeemer will come to Jerusalem to buy back those in Israel who have turned from their sins,' says the Lord."* Those who are the people of God in fact, and not just in name, will receive the Lord's blessing. They will rebuild Jerusalem and prosper: *"Arise, Jerusalem! Let your light shine for all to see. For the glory of the Lord rises to shine on you. Darkness as black as night covers all the nations of the earth, but the glory of the Lord rises and appears over you"* (Isaiah 60:1–2).

Isaiah makes clear that things on earth will not go on forever as they have. The Lord will judge evil and bring salvation to all who will receive him by faith. This will come about provisionally for the remnant of faith by their return to Jerusalem. Their return will serve as a sign of what will come finally and fully for all the earth.

We now live in the in-between times, between the "already" and the "not yet" of God's eternal Kingdom rule on earth.

Focus: The New Testament book of James is a riff on the message of God through Isaiah about the meaning of faith. James sounds like an Old Testament prophet when he insists that faith is not just an intellectual abstraction; it is what we do, how we live: *"What good is it, dear brothers and sisters, if you say that you have faith but don't show it by your actions? Can that kind of faith save anyone? Suppose you* *see a brother or sister who has no food or clothing, and you say, 'Good-bye and have a good day; stay warm and eat well'—but then you don't give that person any food or clothing. What good does that do? So you see, faith by itself isn't enough. Unless it produces good deeds, it is dead and useless"* (James 2:14–17).

Prayer: *Lord, we praise you that sin and death are not the final words in our lives, or in the whole creation. One day you will make everything right. Until then, we will live into that future, by living holy lives and letting your love leak out into the world through us. Amen.*

Day 213   Isaiah 63–66

July 31

> Key Text: "Look! I am creating new heavens and a new earth, and no one will even think about the old ones anymore."
> (Isaiah 65:17)

The book of Isaiah now concludes with a vision of God returning from battle on behalf of his people, his clothing stained with the blood of Israel's captors. It is a disturbing picture of the reality of evil and the cost of stopping it. Using the conventional language of ancient Near Eastern accounts of war, it is described with visceral explicitness: *"In my anger I have trampled my enemies as if they were grapes. In my fury I have trampled my foes. Their blood has stained my clothes. For the time has come for me to avenge my people, to ransom them from their oppressors"* (Isaiah 63:3–4).

This act is both judgment and subsequent salvation, echoing the message of Isaiah 61:2 where the prophet says, *"He has sent me to tell those who mourn* [Israel] *that the time of the Lord's favor has come, and with it, the day of God's anger against their enemies."* Unlike human wars, God's wars of judgment lead to restoration.

As we have noted, God's wars are troubling to modern readers, especially for those who think of God in more sentimental terms. But his holiness is not the same as niceness. His hatred of evil is as intense as his love of good. Without divine vengeance, there could be no moral universe; the malignancy of evil would infect the whole creation, unchecked. Think of it as chemotherapy and radiation treatment against sin, for the sake of the whole creation.

Having announced the defeat of Israel's enemy and her subsequent restoration, Isaiah begins to pray for Israel. It is one of the great prayers of the Bible. In chapters 63 and 64, it takes the form of narration and intercession, beginning: *"I will tell of the Lord's unfailing love. I will praise the Lord for all he has done. I will rejoice in his great goodness to Israel, which he has granted according to his mercy and love"* (Isaiah 63:7).

He continues with praise: *"For since the world began, no ear has heard and no eye has seen a God like you, who works for those who wait for him!"* (Isaiah 64:4). And then with confession: *"We are all infected and impure with sin. When we display our righteous deeds, they are nothing but filthy rags"* (Isaiah 64:6).

Finally, in chapters 65 and 66, the Lord responds. He acknowledges that despite Israel's sins as a nation, there are faithful Israelites: *"For just as good grapes are found among a cluster of bad ones ... I still have true servants there. I will preserve a remnant of the people of Israel and of Judah to possess my land."* Those among the people who continue to forsake him will be carried away in the flood of judgment against the evil nations. But the *remnant of faith* will be protected.

Theirs is the promise of a new future: *"Look! I am creating new heavens and a new earth, and no one will even think about the old ones anymore. Be glad; rejoice forever in my creation! And look! I will create Jerusalem as a place of happiness. Her people will be a source of joy. ... And the sound of weeping and crying will be heard in it no more"* (Isaiah 65:17–19).

So the Lord is coming in both judgment and salvation. Those who believe will be sent to tell all the nations who have not heard of his fame or seen his glory: *"'As surely as my new heavens and earth will remain, so will you always be my people, with a name that will never disappear,' says the Lord. 'All humanity will come to worship me from week to week and from month to month'"* (Isaiah 66:22–23).

Focus: Judgment and salvation, war and peace, despair and hope—these are the dichotomies of life in a fallen world where God is on the move. One the one hand, the sea is roaring and man is overboard! On the other, a Rescuer appears throwing a lifeline. The question is, will we grab hold of the lifeline? Will we allow God to rescue us? If we deny our peril, thinking that the roaring sea of our sin is merely a wading pool we are sitting in—no big deal. But if we see clearly and sense the danger, we may reach out to God and discover that life can be different now. And more than that, a New Heavens and New Earth are coming—a reality so all-encompassing that *"no one will even think about the old ones anymore."*

Day 214   Jeremiah 1–6

August 1

> Key Text: "When will you stop running? When will you stop panting after other gods? But you say, 'Save your breath. I'm in love with these foreign gods, and I can't stop loving them now!'" (Jeremiah 2:25)

Jeremiah is another great Hebrew prophet called by God to speak to the southern kingdom of Judah during the years leading up to the cruel Babylonian captivity. As a mouthpiece for God to his stubborn and rebellious people, the prophets were often tasked with being the bearers of bad news, and as such received the abuse of those who didn't want to hear it. (Now you know where the saying, "Hey, I'm just the messenger," comes from.)

Jeremiah was "just the messenger" for more than forty years. His impassioned call for Judah to repent of her sins and return to the Lord went largely unheeded. Not surprisingly, therefore, Jeremiah is known as the weeping prophet. He senses and communicates the passion of God for his wayward people.

Chapter 1 begins with an account of Jeremiah's call: *"The Lord gave me this message: 'I knew you before I formed you in your mother's womb. Before you were born I set you apart and appointed you as my prophet to the nations.'"* In response to Jeremiah's protests that he is too young, God assures him that he must simply be faithful and God will do the rest. And what a calling it turns out to be—speaking truth to power: *"Look, I have put my words in your mouth! Today I appoint you to stand up against nations and kingdoms"* (Jeremiah 1:9–10).

God reveals that he is sending Babylon to conquer Jerusalem: *"I will pronounce judgment on my people for all their evil—for deserting me and burning incense to other gods. Yes, they worship idols made with their own hands!"*

God sends Jeremiah to stand against the whole nation of Judah—the

401

kings, officials, priests and people. He warns Jeremiah: *"They will fight you, but they will fail. For I am with you, and I will take care of you. I, the Lord, have spoken!"* (Jeremiah 1:19).

Jeremiah is given a forceful message from God for the people. It is first of all a heart-wrenching account of God's feeling of betrayal by Judah—a betrayal as painful as the unfaithfulness of a wife. God says of Judah: *"I remember how eager you were to please me as a young bride long ago...."* But now, she has prostituted herself by bowing down to the idols of the nations around her.

In anguish God demands, *"When will you stop running? When will you stop panting after other gods? But you say, 'Save your breath. I'm in love with these foreign gods, and I can't stop loving them now!'"* (Jeremiah 2:25).

But even in his anguish, God offers a way home: *"'O Israel,' says the Lord, 'if you wanted to return to me, you could. You could throw away your detestable idols and stray away no more'"* (Jeremiah 4:1). Her return, even after all she has done, would restore the hope of God's ancient Promise to Abraham: *"Then you would be a blessing to the nations of the world, and all people would come and praise my name."*

But alas, it is not to be. The sins of the people have become deeply formed ruts because idolatry is addictive; Judah has become like *"well-fed, lusty stallions, each neighing for his neighbor's wife."*

So, God tells his prophet that his ministry will be tough and deeply discouraging: *"Jeremiah, I have made you a tester of metals, that you may determine the quality of my people. They are the worst kind of rebel, full of slander. They are as hard as bronze and iron, and they lead others into corruption. The bellows fiercely fan the flames to burn out the corruption. But it does not purify them, for the wickedness remains. I will label them 'Rejected Silver,' for I, the Lord, am discarding them"* (Isaiah 6:27–30).

Focus: Jeremiah is called by God to be *"a tester of metals."* It will test his own mettle! But Jeremiah recognizes that God has been preparing him for this difficult calling since his conception—yes, his conception! The Lord tells him: *"I knew you before I formed you in your mother's womb. Before you were born I set you apart and appointed you as my prophet to the nations."* We can rightly assume that God worked in all the variables of Jeremiah's life growing up, granting him experiences and influences that shaped his personality and character in such a way that he could fulfill his calling. We are the beneficiaries.

Day 215   Jeremiah 7–10

August 2

Key Text: "The people of Judah have sinned before my very eyes," says the Lord. "They have set up their abominable idols right in the Temple that bears my name, defiling it."
(Jeremiah 7:30)

Jeremiah's messages to the kingdom of Judah now focus on the subject of worship, since worship is at the heart of a relationship with God. In the case of the Israelites, that relationship was initiated by God long ago, first through his Promise to Abraham, and later through his Covenant with the people through Moses.

Through most of the Old Testament, worship is defined by Covenant stipulations, and guided by the moral imperatives of the Ten Commandments. In effect, God says, "This is how you should love me, with all your heart, mind, soul and strength."

But God's ongoing argument with the Israelites is that they have repeatedly violated both the Covenant and the commandments, thereby breaking relationship with him. The Temple in Jerusalem has come to represent a kind of good luck charm, rather than a holy place where God meets with his people in heartfelt worship.

So in chapter 7, Jeremiah's message from God is delivered at the entrance of the Temple: *"Don't be fooled into thinking that you will never suffer because the Temple is here. It's a lie! Do you really think you can steal, murder, commit adultery, lie, and burn incense to Baal and all those other new gods of yours, and then come here and stand before me in my Temple and chant, 'We are safe!'—only to go right back to all those evils again?"* (Jeremiah 7:8–10).

God has been extraordinarily patient with Israel, but a line has been crossed by the nation as a whole. He no longer wants to dwell in the Temple which the people have tainted by their idolatry—in fact, he doesn't want them in his presence at all: *"And I will send you out of my sight into exile, just as I did your relatives, the people of Israel."* He even tells Jeremiah to weep no more for Judah nor pray for them, for he will not listen to his prayers.

Serious action will be taken to break the people's addiction to idolatry. Several things are highlighted in Jeremiah's series of messages about idolatry in chapters 7 through 10:

First, idolatry dehumanizes. It moves people to horrible acts of evil, such as burning their sons and daughters as offerings in pagan fires.

Second, idolatry places the people in conflict with God and forces his judgment. Remember, God's judgment is his emphatic opposition to all that dishonors him and destroys his good creation. When the people and their leaders disregard God, they lose his protection and are vulnerable to the evil actions of the nations around them.

Third, when God's Word is ignored, and his laws and commandments violated, the people lose their insight and wisdom, falling into traps of their own foolishness and immorality. These are tragic, self-inflicted wounds worthy of weeping and sorrow.

Fourth, idolatry breaks down community. When life is about self-gratification, unhinged from moral boundaries, people turn *on* one another instead of turning *to* one another. Civil society breaks down.

Fifth, idols are nothing more than man-made, fake gods: *"These idols have no breath or power. Idols are worthless; they are ridiculous lies! On the day of reckoning they will all be destroyed. But the God of Israel is no idol! He is the Creator of everything that exists, including Israel, his own special possession. The Lord of Heaven's Armies is his name!"* (Jeremiah 10:14–16).

Focus: One of the besetting sins of the Fall is idolatry—worshiping created things as gods instead of the Creator himself. Jeremiah, along with other Old Testament writers, probes the nature and consequences of idolatry in order to warn the people that they are harming themselves, and alienating God their Creator. Idolatry at its root is rebellion against God. We fallen humans still have spiritual feelings, so we create gods for ourselves, or obsess over earthy things, in order to fill the spiritual vacuum. We get our spiritual "fix," and—importantly—we stay in control over our lives. We make God over into our own image, guaranteeing that he is just fine with whatever we think or do. None of that uncomfortable doctrine to believe, nor moral rules to keep, especially about our sex lives.

Day 216   Jeremiah 11–15

August 3

> Key Text: "I have seen your adultery and lust, and your disgusting idol worship out in the fields and on the hills. What sorrow awaits you, Jerusalem! How long before you are pure?" (Jeremiah 13:27)

A necessary component of teaching children about bad behavior is to make the consequences clear: "Johnny, if you hit your little sister, you will spend the day in your room and cannot play with your friends."

Of course, adult bad behavior has more serious consequences. God tells Jeremiah in these chapters to make this clear: *"Broadcast this message in the streets of Jerusalem. Go from town to town throughout the land and say, 'Remember the ancient covenant, and do everything it requires. For I solemnly warned your ancestors when I brought them out of Egypt, "Obey me!" I have repeated this warning over and over to this day, but your ancestors did not listen or even pay attention. Instead, they stubbornly followed their own evil desires. And because they refused to obey, I brought upon them all the curses described in this covenant'"* (Jeremiah 11:6–8).

The curses, or consequences, cannot be avoided because the people *"actually rejoice in doing evil."* Their unrepentant idolatry—especially worshiping the horrible god, Baal—has exhausted the Lord's patience. Furthermore, false prophets among them aid in their rebellion by sharing fake messages and visions that God did not give them. They speak foolishness which is made up in their own lying hearts.

The leaders of Judah are even making plans to kill the true prophet, Jeremiah, to shut him up.

There is no doubt now that Judah will be uprooted: *"I have seen your adultery and lust, and your disgusting idol worship out in the fields and on the hills. What sorrow awaits you, Jerusalem! How long before you are pure?"* (Jeremiah 13:27). The sermons of Jeremiah here focus on the evidence of Judah's sin and the justice of God's judgment. Jeremiah takes no

405

pleasure in his preaching. He cares deeply about the public shame that Judah's sin has brought upon God, and he cares about how idolatry has harmed the people's souls.

Jeremiah weeps for Judah, interceding for her even though God has told him to stop. A line has been crossed; nothing will change God's mind: *"Even if Moses and Samuel stood before me pleading for these people, I wouldn't help them. Away with them!"*

So it has been decided. Judah's judgment will be exile at the hands of the Babylonians: *"I will destroy my own people, because they refuse to change their evil ways."* Meanwhile, Jeremiah pleads with God not to let the people kill him in response to his preaching, and the Lord kindly responds: *"They will fight against you like an attacking army, but I will make you as secure as a fortified wall of bronze. They will not conquer you, for I am with you to protect and rescue you. ... Yes, I will certainly keep you safe from these wicked men. I will rescue you from their cruel hands"* (Jeremiah 15:20–21).

Comforting words to Jeremiah, the faithful preacher—and for any preacher for that matter!

Focus: Jeremiah's tears represent God's tears for his people. More than anywhere in the Bible, the prophets reveal God's deep emotion. Some have questioned this idea, saying that God could not have negative human emotions. Okay, not human emotion. But his speaking to us through Jeremiah's tears points to something real and mysterious that God feels. Clearly he loves his creation. And just as clearly, by giving us free will, he opens himself up to being rejected, betrayed and disregarded—in other words, to being hurt. We need to be careful so as not to make God a mere projection of ourselves, like the gods of paganism. On the other hand, we cannot deny that God is a person and feels deeply for his people—*God-feelings* to be sure, but real. Let us take his passionate love for us to heart!

Prayer: Lord, again we are taken aback by your anger as well as your love. Your passion is frightening. Help us to take your Word seriously. Keep us from making you nothing more than an extension of ourselves. Indeed! There is no one like you. You are Holy God! Amen!

August 4

> Key Text: "The human heart is the most deceitful of all things, and desperately wicked. Who really knows how bad it is? But I, the Lord, search all hearts and examine secret motives. I give all people their due rewards, according to what their actions deserve." (Jeremiah 17:9–10)

Jeremiah has been given the somber ministry of preparing Judah for the coming judgment of military defeat and exile by Babylon. Ancient wars with their sieges on cities and body-to-body warfare were terrible spectacles. This horror is coming because Judah has forsaken God and will not repent. Consequently, God has removed his protection and favor from Judah.

For Jeremiah, it is a chilling prospect—but the people seem to shrug it off.

The removal of God's protection and favor is the final acknowledgement that, despite all God's patience, warnings and forgiveness, Judah has forsaken the Lord to follow other gods. Her heart is hardened. Her leaders are confident in their ability to protect the people through strategic alliances with pagan nations. So now God will give Judah what she demands—freedom to walk away and face life on her own.

Jeremiah once again explains why the Lord's judgment is coming: *"It is because your ancestors were unfaithful to me. They worshiped other gods and served them. They abandoned me and did not obey my word. And you are even worse than your ancestors! You stubbornly follow your own evil desires and refuse to listen to me. So I will throw you out of this land and send you into a foreign land where you and your ancestors have never been. There you can worship idols day and night—and I will grant you no favors!"* (Jeremiah 16:11–13).

To draw attention to his warning, Jeremiah performs what we may call "acted parables." In acted parables, unusual behavior becomes part of the message. In chapter 16, Jeremiah says that God has instructed him not to get married and enjoy a family life, nor to bother going to funerals and showing sympathy. Neither should he go to feasts and parties. Jeremiah is acting out the alarming truth that all of these normal events of human life will be disrupted by what is to come.

In chapter 19, Jeremiah takes a clay pot to the garbage dump in the Valley of Ben-Hinnom and shatters it in front of the people. It is a dramatic act of mourning, warning the people of coming judgment.

The messages start to annoy the religious leaders of Judah: *"Now Pashhur son of Immer, the priest in charge of the Temple of the Lord, heard what Jeremiah was prophesying. So he arrested Jeremiah the prophet and had him whipped and put in stocks at the Benjamin Gate of the Lord's Temple."*

All of this becomes too much for Jeremiah. In chapter 20 he gives a long, depressed lament about the misery of his life, and what it feels like to be hated and considered a household joke among his own people: *"Why was I ever born? My entire life has been filled with trouble, sorrow, and shame"* (Jeremiah 20:18).

Jeremiah's suffering, at the hands of his own people, reveals how a hard heart toward God leads to abusive behavior toward others, even those who love us enough to tell us the truth: *"The human heart is the most deceitful of all things, and desperately wicked. Who really knows how bad it is?"* (Jeremiah 17:9).

Focus: Jeremiah's comment about the human heart is a sober reminder of how deep the roots of sin go into human thought and behavior. Evil, in particular, is irrational. In the aftermath of a particularly evil event, people express disbelief that such a thing could have happened. Who can understand why? On a lesser scale, there are the nagging realities of human behavior. Why do we hurt the ones we love? Why do we continue in behavior that is self-defeating? Why do we find it so hard to tell the truth, or to forgive those who have hurt us? So, as Jeremiah suggests, we are constantly faced with a mystery—the mystery of the human heart. Thankfully, there is a solution—the grace of God which is greater than all our sin!

Prayer: Lord, it is tragic that we humans keep repeating the folly of Adam and Eve by choosing to live outside your will and authority. We tend to think well of ourselves, and blind ourselves to the shocking reality of evil within us. Soften our hearts; open our eyes to our sin and move us to repentance before it wraps us tight in its spider's web. Amen.

Day 218   Jeremiah 21–25

> Key Text: "What sorrow awaits the leaders of my people—the
> shepherds of my sheep—for they have destroyed and scattered
> the very ones they were expected to care for," says the Lord.
> (Jeremiah 23:1)

Chapter 21 brings us twenty years forward from chapter 20. Babylon is now at the gates of Jerusalem. Jeremiah arranges his messages thematically rather than chronologically. So don't be confused if it seems like we are moving back and forth in time, because we are!

Now that Jeremiah's prophecies about Babylon are coming true, the leaders of Judah come begging Jeremiah to pray to God so that he will force Nebuchadnezzar to withdraw his armies. But Jeremiah tells them that it is way too late. The Lord says that the only hope for the people is to surrender: *"Take your choice of life or death! Everyone who stays in Jerusalem will die from war, famine, or disease, but those who go out and surrender to the Babylonians will live"* (Jeremiah 21:8–9).

Jeremiah is sent to Jehoakim, the present king of Judah, to confront him with his failed leadership. Jehoakim loves the privileges of office—the palace, the parade of attendants and subjects—but his spiritual arrogance has brought him down. His legacy is ruined: *"People from many nations will pass by the ruins of this city and say to one another, 'Why did the Lord destroy such a great city?' And the answer will be, 'Because they violated their covenant with the Lord their God by worshiping other gods'"* (Jeremiah 22:8–9).

Next, Jeremiah pulls back the curtain on the sins of the prophets and priests of Judah, bringing this warning from God: *"'What sorrow awaits the leaders of my people—the shepherds of my sheep—for they have destroyed and scattered the very ones they were expected to care for,' says the Lord"* (Jeremiah 23:1). They have done this by their personal immorality, false prophesies, and lying about receiving visions from the Lord, when in fact they are only saying what the corrupt leaders want to hear. Some of them even prophesy in the name of the horrible pagan god, Baal, leading people into grave sin.

After the exile of Jews begins, God gives a vision to Jeremiah about two baskets of figs. The bad, inedible figs represent the king of Judah, his officials, and others whose hearts are hard against the Lord. They will experience the full measure of God's judgment. However, the basket of good figs represents other exiles, which we have called the *remnant of faith*. Of them, God says: *"I will watch over and care for them, and I will bring them back here again. I will build them up and not tear them down. I will plant them and not uproot them. I will give them hearts that recognize me as the Lord. They will be my people, and I will be their God, for they will return to me wholeheartedly"* (Jeremiah 24:3–10).

An earlier message from the Lord to all the people of Judah is now presented in chapter 26. God tells them that their judgment of exile will last seventy years. Judgment begins first with the people of God who should know better. But then God will bring judgment upon the nations of the world. Jeremiah will visit the various nations who enslaved God's people over the years and who tempted them with idolatry. He will bring an object lesson—a cup in his hand, called the *"cup of the Lord's anger."* His message: *"Drink from this cup of my anger. Get drunk and vomit; fall to rise no more, for I am sending terrible wars against you"* (Jeremiah 25:27).

Focus: Events sometimes come to the point of no return. What was once ignored or dismissed has now become inevitable. This was the case for Judah's leaders when they finally realized that Babylon was going to attack them, just as Jeremiah had warned for years. Now they come begging for God to *"do a mighty miracle"* on their behalf. But it is too late.

Pride and stubbornness run so deep in us that we are often unwilling to listen to those who tell us the truth. We always assume that things will work out. So, for example, we spend and don't save. The day arrives when we can't pay our bill, or we can't retire. We've been warned for years, but we've just put it off.

Or what about those who say, "I'll sow my wild oats when I am young, and then when I am old, I'll get religious"? If this were true, nursing homes would be filled with people of vibrant faith—but they are not. Better to humble ourselves before God, now.

Prayer: Lord, the willful sinning of your own people is so grievous that it is hard to fathom. We who know Christ, know so much more than even your Old Testament people, and yet we sin against you also. How sad that we wait until it is too late. How sad that you must sometimes tear down before you can rebuild. But Lord, we pray that you will rebuild. Amen.

Day 219 Jeremiah 26–29

August 6

> Key Text: "And work for the peace and prosperity of the city where I sent you into exile. Pray to the Lord for it, for its welfare will determine your welfare." (Isaiah 29:7)

Jeremiah's sermon in the courtyard in front of the Temple, in chapter 26, is similar to the one in chapter 7. It also moves us chronologically back again. After making clear that the Lord is planning to give Judah over to the Babylonians for judgment, unless the people repent and return to him, Jeremiah receives a swift response: "...the priests and prophets and all the people at the Temple mobbed him. 'Kill him!' they shouted. ... 'What do you mean, saying that Jerusalem will be destroyed and left with no inhabitants?' And all the people threatened him as he stood in front of the Temple" (Jeremiah 26:8–9).

A prophet with a similar message, Uriah son of Shamaiah, is arrested and killed, but Jeremiah is spared by the intervention of a friend.

In another message, Jeremiah warns the people that the Babylonian army is coming. He tells them not to listen to the false prophets, fortune-tellers, interpreters of dreams, mediums or sorcerers who are telling them that the king of Babylon will not conquer them.

Chapter 28 offers a related story of the false prophet Hananiah, who repudiates Jeremiah and gives false hope to the people by his false prophecies. The Lord confronts him with his sin, through Jeremiah, and within two months he is dead.

Jeremiah urges the people to accept exile as judgment from God, and then submit to Nebuchadnezzar so that they may be allowed to live.

Moving forward again to the time of the Babylonian exile, Jeremiah writes a letter to the elders, priests, prophets and all the people who have been taken by King Nebuchadnezzar. His message is one of hope. Yes, they will be in Babylon for a generation—seventy years. While there, Jeremiah says that they should not be troublemakers nor give up and dwindle away: "And work for the peace and prosperity of the city where I sent you into exile. Pray to the Lord for it, for its welfare will determine your welfare" (Isaiah 29:7).

By contributing to the well-being of their enemies, even while in exile, the Lord's people can demonstrate the Lord's concern for all the nations of the world. Israel, in a sense, is a microcosm of all humanity. What he does for them, he wants to do for all nations. And so, to his people and to us, the Lord says: *"'I will come and do for you all the good things I have promised, and I will bring you home again. For I know the plans I have for you,' says the Lord. 'They are plans for good and not for disaster, to give you a future and a hope. In those days when you pray, I will listen. If you look for me wholeheartedly, you will find me. I will be found by you,' says the Lord. 'I will end your captivity and restore your fortunes'"* (Jeremiah 29:10–14).

Focus: Sometimes what gets lost in all of the admittedly long narrative sections about God's judgment, are remarkable statements about God's plan for his creation. Remember, God's judgments are meant to stop us in our self-destructive tracks, and bring us back to him again. His plan for us—for the whole creation—is for *good,* to give us *a future and a hope,* to *restore our fortunes.* If he has to discipline us to get our attention, so be it. But don't think of God as an angry deity looking everywhere to find someone doing wrong, so that he can throw him into hell. There is nothing further from the truth. God's plan is to bring us home to him. He will heal our hearts, forgive our sins, outfit us with resurrection bodies, and prepare us for an amazing eternity of fellowship with him. That is good news! Why don't we believe it?

Prayer: Lord, we are surprised again, in the midst of Israel's arrogant defiance of you, that you follow your word of judgment with a word of hope for the future. You do not turn your back on us when you are angry, but desire to engage us so that we may be reconciled. What a gracious and patient God you are! Of course, we have expressed this over and over again as we have read through your Word. Help us to truly believe it with all our heart. Amen.

Day 220   Reflection

August 7

As we have noted, a central issue in the Old Testament, from the book of Exodus through the prophets, is God's revulsion toward idolatry. Our present prophet, Jeremiah, speaks for God when he says of the people of Judah: *"I will double their punishment for all their sins, because they have defiled my land with lifeless images of their detestable gods and have filled my territory with their evil deeds"* (Jeremiah 16:18).

The issue of idolatry is present at the very beginning of Israel's story when God calls Abraham to believe in him. Abraham was an idol worshiper at the time. Everyone was. Most anthropologists and historians assume that polytheism and idol worship preceded monotheism in human evolution. Humans, they say, eventually began to believe in one God because it was advantageous to them.

But it is more likely—and consistent with the biblical story—that polytheism is a corruption of an original monotheism. In this view, the memory of the Creator God faded within human culture after the Fall in Eden. Rebellion led to confusion, until eventually God was replaced by gods of human imagination. Polytheism and idolatry would therefore be evidence of human foolishness. As we have seen, the Old Testament prophets make fun of idolaters, who with one piece of wood heat their home and cook a meal, then make a god with what remains and worship it!

The New Testament echoes this critique. The apostle Paul addresses the paganism of Rome by arguing: *"Yes, they knew God, but they wouldn't worship him as God or even give him thanks. And they began to think up foolish ideas of what God was like. As a result, their minds became dark and confused. Claiming to be wise, they instead became utter fools. And instead of worshiping the glorious, ever-living God, they worshiped idols made to look like mere people and birds and animals and reptiles"* (Romans 1:21–23).

So the position of the biblical writers is consistent. Idolatry is an offense against God the Creator because it refuses to give him our most fundamental obligations as created beings— worship and thanksgiving. As such, it is the most egregious form of denial, causing the human race to lose track of reality. And there is a word for this: insanity.

We have said that God's judgment against sin is his loud "NO!" to all that undermines his creation and dehumanizes men and women. He knows that idolatry is self-defeating. It confuses us, and keeps us from the life he offers. Even more, God says through Jeremiah that it *"defiles my land."* This is a striking statement. In its context, I take it to refer to the Promised Land given to Israel. But more broadly it can apply to the whole creation. The defilement comes, God says, by *"filling my territory with evil deeds."*

We see, therefore, that idolatry is an unraveling of God's creation. It leads to foolish thinking and evildoing. Therein lies the root of God's revulsion against it. Like a parent watching his child's life unravel because of drug addiction, God grieves the unraveling of his creation. And he relentlessly pursues us with justice and love.

> **Prayer:** *Lord, we are so accustomed to the unreality of our broken lives in this fallen world that we find it hard to imagine anything else. So we wonder what life would be like if the created realm had never fallen and we were fully engaged in living life as a human race in worship and thanksgiving to you. We hope to experience this one day, but for now Lord, open our eyes to see reality—to understand you as you are, so that we may become what you have created us to be. Amen.*

Day 221   Jeremiah 30–33

August 8

Key Text: "But this is the new covenant I will make with the people of Israel after those days," says the Lord. "I will put my instructions deep within them, and I will write them on their hearts. I will be their God, and they will be my people." (Jeremiah 31:33)

Jeremiah's message in chapter 30 predates the exile. Again, there is movement back and forth in time in Jeremiah's collection of messages. Jeremiah tells the people that terrible trouble is coming and nothing can stop it *"because your sins are many and your guilt is great."*

But typical of the Bible's story, judgment is not the last word. God tells the people: *"For the time is coming when I will restore the fortunes of my people of Israel and Judah."* This restoration is envisioned as a return to Jerusalem. The city will be restored, the Temple rebuilt and a new king, descended from David, will be raised up. This will happen after the seventy years of captivity when Persia will overthrow Babylon and then look favorably upon the Jewish exiles. They will be permitted to return to Jerusalem and rebuild.

But even this will not fulfill the Restoration of God. The promise, *"you will be my people and I will be your God,"* looks further ahead to the great Day of Salvation when God restores his creation once and for all. On this day, God will make a New Covenant with his people, not like his Old Covenant: *"'But this is the new covenant I will make with the people of Israel after those days,' says the Lord. 'I will put my instructions deep within them, and I will write them on their hearts. I will be their God, and they will be my people. And they will not need to teach their neighbors, nor will they need to teach their relatives, saying, "You should know the Lord." For everyone, from the least to the greatest, will know me already,' says the Lord. 'And I will forgive their wickedness, and I will never again remember their sins'"* (Jeremiah 31:33–34).

In chapter 32, we move ahead in time. Jeremiah writes to Israelites in Jerusalem who are under siege by Babylon. He prays a beautiful, humble prayer recognizing God's goodness to Israel over the generations and then confessing the people's sins: *"Our ancestors came and conquered it* [the land] *and lived in it, but they refused to obey you or follow your word. They have not done anything you commanded. That is why you have sent this terrible disaster upon them"* (Jeremiah 32:23).

But again, hope follows judgment. God says, *"I will bring them* [the Israelites] *back to this very city and let them live in peace and safety. They will be my people, and I will be their God. And I will give them one heart and one purpose: to worship me forever, for their own good and for the good of all their descendants. And I will make an everlasting covenant with them: I will never stop doing good for them. I will put a desire in their hearts to worship me, and they will never leave me. I will find joy doing good for them and will faithfully and wholeheartedly replant them in this land"* (Jeremiah 32:37–41).

Focus: This is the first mention in the Old Testament that God is going to establish a "New Covenant" with his people one day. When Jesus, in the upper room with his disciples, took the cup of the Passover meal, and said "this cup is the New Covenant in my blood," he was referring to Jeremiah's prophecy. That prophesy is being fulfilled in the life, death, resurrection and ascension of Jesus. The New Covenant is a fresh restating of the old, announcing that the first Covenant has been fulfilled in Jesus. The people of God, Jew and Gentile alike, have received the blessing of salvation through the broken body and shed blood of Jesus. What was provisionally structured with the nation of Israel, in its laws, rituals and institutions, has been restructured. Whereas the life of the people of God was ordered by ritual and law under the Old Testament, it will now be ordered by the Holy Spirit under the New.

So the difference between the Old and New Testaments is *not* law and grace—as is sometimes misunderstood—but law and Spirit. The Spirit of Jesus working in the heart of the believer, to fulfill the commandment to love, is what describes the life of the New Testament believer.

Day 222　　　　Jeremiah 34–36

August 9

> **Key Text:** Each time Jehudi finished reading three or four columns, the king took a knife and cut off that section of the scroll. He then threw it into the fire, section by section, until the whole scroll was burned up. Neither the king nor his attendants showed any signs of fear or repentance at what they heard. (Jeremiah 36:23–24)

For the next several chapters Jeremiah moves from a written account of his preaching to a written account of his personal experiences during the nation's last days. Both his messages and his experiences are prompted by God speaking to him.

In chapter 34, during the Babylonian siege of Jerusalem, God tells Jeremiah to speak to Zedekiah, the wavering king of Judah. Zedekiah has issued a legal proclamation directing the people to free their Hebrew slaves.

This is the right thing to do—in accordance with the Mosaic Covenant—but like many right things, it is done with mixed motives. Because it is only ordered after the siege is in effect, it is probably motivated by the wealthy slaveholders' wanting to have fewer mouths to feed during the terrible ordeal of a prolonged siege, when food supplies would be impossible to get.

Not surprisingly, then, when the siege is interrupted while the army attends to another matter, the people quickly "un-free" their slaves. With the Babylonian army gone, they no longer have a food problem, but a servant problem! This story gives further evidence of God's righteous judgment against the disobedience of Judah.

In chapter 35, Jeremiah recalls God sending him, during the reign of King Jehoiakim, to meet with an unusual nomadic clan of Israelites called the Recabites. They were the Amish of their day, remaining faithful to their roots of tending flocks and living in tents, rather than adopting the more settled life of farms and vineyards. When called together to meet with Jeremiah, the leaders refuse the wine offered. They tell Jeremiah that their ancestor Jehonadab had given them a command to never drink wine, nor build houses, nor plant crops or vineyards. And they never had.

Jeremiah contrasts their obedience to a distant ancestor with the disobedience of other tribes of Judah to God's Covenant: *"Come and learn a lesson about how to obey me. The Recabites do not drink wine to this day because their ancestor Jehonadab told them not to. But I have spoken to you again and again, and you refuse to obey me"* (Jeremiah 35:13–14).

In chapter 36, Jeremiah tells of a revealing event which happened later in the reign of Jehoiakim. While Jeremiah has been put in prison so the people won't have to listen to him, the Lord tells Jeremiah to write down on a scroll all the messages about the coming judgment that he has ever delivered against Israel, Judah and other nations.

His scribe is then sent to read the scroll at the Temple during a religious holiday when Jerusalem is filled with pilgrims. God wonders out loud: *"Perhaps the people of Judah will repent when they hear again all the terrible things I have planned for them. Then I will be able to forgive their sins and wrongdoings."* They didn't.

Word finally gets to the king about what has happened. He sends for the scribe and orders him to read the messages column by column: *"Each time Jehudi finished reading three or four columns, the king took a knife and cut off that section of the scroll. He then threw it into the fire, section by section, until the whole scroll was burned up."*

To emphasize that the Word of the Lord cannot be stopped, God orders Jeremiah to write it all again on a new scroll, and then say to the king: *"You burned the scroll because I said the king of Babylon would destroy this land and empty it of people and animals"* (Jeremiah 36:29).

As a consequence of his arrogant presumption, King Jehoiakim of Judah is killed and his family name removed from the kingly line of David.

Focus: Again we see Jeremiah's comment on the human heart illustrated by the dismissive behavior of the people and their leaders. It takes an odd group of outsiders, the Recabites, to shame the insiders about their proud and stubborn disobedience. Nothing illustrates this pride like King Jehoiakim cutting and burning Jeremiah's messages to the people, one by one. The cutting and burning that will follow when Babylon attacks will not be so amusing. Meanwhile, King Jehoiakim's name is removed from the Davidic line Hall of Fame.

Day 223   Jeremiah 37–39

August 10

> Key Text: Later King Zedekiah secretly requested that Jeremiah come to the palace, where the king asked him, "Do you have any messages from the Lord?" "Yes, I do!" said Jeremiah. "You will be defeated by the king of Babylon." (Jeremiah 37:17)

The next events take us back to a time before the events of the past three chapters. (Reading Jeremiah is like experiencing time travel!)

In the events of chapter 37, when Jedekiah is king of Judah, Egypt's army has approached the southern border of Jerusalem during the Babylonian siege. This forces the Babylonians to abandon their siege and respond to the Egyptians.

After the army leaves, Jeremiah is sent by the Lord to warn King Jedekiah about any false confidence that God's judgment has been abated. He tells the king: *"Pharaoh's army is about to return to Egypt, though he came here to help you. Then the Babylonians will come back and capture this city and burn it to the ground"* (Jeremiah 37:7–8).

The patience of the king and his officials with Jeremiah wears out. He is arrested under false pretenses, flogged, and then imprisoned in a dungeon cell for many days. Then, hoping that prison has "cleared up" Jeremiah's prophecies, the king secretly brings him to the palace to ask if he has any new messages from the Lord: *"'Yes, I do!' said Jeremiah. 'You will be defeated by the king of Babylon.'"*

This is not what the king wanted to hear. Jeremiah is sent back to prison, though his room is upgraded to the courtyard of the guard in the royal palace. *"The king also commanded that Jeremiah be given a loaf of fresh bread every day as long as there was any left in the city."*

But the officials are concerned about what Jeremiah has already said to the people—that if they surrender to the Babylonians, their lives will be spared and the city will not be burned. But those who stay in Jerusalem to fight will die from war, famine or disease.

The officials appeal to the king for permission to kill Jeremiah as a traitor, and he lets them do *"whatever they wanted."* They take Jeremiah from the palace prison and lower him into an empty cistern, where he sinks into a thick layer of mud and is left to die.

However, an important court official, Ebed-melech the Ethiopian, hears about what has happened and quickly appeals to the king. The king capitulates when presented with the Ethiopian's wishes. Jeremiah is rescued and taken back to the palace prison.

King Zedekiah then secretly promises not to let him be killed. Upon receiving this good news, Jeremiah once again urges the king to surrender himself to the Babylonians so that he and his family may live.

But of course, Zedekiah doesn't listen. When the Babylonians return and break through the walls of Jerusalem, he flees but is captured and taken to the cruel Babylonian king, Nebuchadnezzar. What happens to him is not a pretty picture. Zedekiah is forced to watch as his sons and noblemen are killed, and then they gouge out his eyes.

Meanwhile the Babylonians burn Jerusalem, including the palace, and tear down the walls of the city. Most of the people are exiled to Babylonia, although a few of the poorest are left behind and assigned to care for the vineyards and fields. After all, the Babylonians want their meat and wine!

In the midst of this terrible violence and widespread loss, there is a moment of grace. The Lord speaks to Jeremiah about Ebed-melech, the Ethiopian hero, saying that because Ebed-melech has trusted God and rescued his prophet, he will be spared from death by the Babylonian army.

Focus: King Zedekiah makes the suffering of his people far worse by his refusal to accept God's word through Jeremiah. Instead, he continues to fight against Babylonia. Jeremiah has made it clear that the Babylonian army is the agent of God's judgment against Judah for their willful and unrepentant idolatry. Zedekiah's pride produces a far worse defeat than would have been the case had he obeyed God and surrendered in the first place. Even in the face of certain defeat, Zedekiah can't humble his heart before God. Pride is his undoing.

Prayer: Lord, this story about King Zedekiah reminds us of your warning about a divided heart. Such a heart is as unsettled as a wave in the sea that is blown and tossed by the wind. You say that people like this are unstable in all they do. Their loyalty is divided between you and the world, and they should not expect to receive

419

anything from you. So Lord, grant us a strong heart and a settled faith that will sustain us in the hard times. Amen.

Day 224   Jeremiah 40–45

August 11

> Key Text: "Do not fear the king of Babylon anymore," says the Lord. "For I am with you and will save you and rescue you from his power. I will be merciful to you by making him kind, so he will let you stay here in your land." (Jeremiah 42:11–12)

After the fall of Jerusalem, Jeremiah is released by the Babylonian captain of the guard. Interestingly, he comments to Jeremiah: *"The Lord your God has brought this disaster on this land, just as he said he would. For these people have sinned against the Lord and disobeyed him. That is why it happened"* (Jeremiah 40:2–3).

How ironic that the enemy has more respect for Israel's God than Israel!

Jeremiah chooses to stay behind in Jerusalem with Gedaliah, the Jewish governor appointed by Babylon. Gedaliah is tasked with directing the poor people left behind to work the land and serve the Babylonians. He proves to be a good man, winning the trust of the "Judean guerrillas" who had retreated to the hills after the war, but have now returned.

Unfortunately, one of them, Ishmael, is from the royal family and has ambitions to rule. So in an act of treachery he kills Gedaliah and takes captive those left under his care. This so shocks the other guerrilla leaders that they pursue Ishmael, who abandons the people and escapes.

The guerrillas now began to worry about what will happen to them when the Babylonian king finds out that Gedaliah is dead. They think about fleeing to Egypt, but first seek out Jeremiah to ask for prayers for wisdom and protection.

The Lord tells them through Jeremiah: *"Do not fear the king of Babylon anymore... For I am with you and will save you and rescue you from his power. I will be merciful to you by making him kind, so he will let you stay here in your land."*

Notice the willingness of God to save them if only they will trust him. The Lord knows that Egypt will be destroyed by Babylonia. His warning not to flee to Egypt reminds us of the book of Exodus, where the Israelites complain about their lives in the wilderness and threaten to return to Egypt from where the Lord had delivered them.

Sadly, the people still do not trust God about submitting to the Babylonians. Contrary to God's explicit promise, they are convinced that if they stay in Jerusalem they will be killed. So like their leaders before them, they choose to trust in political alliances and go to Egypt and worship their gods. Jeremiah is sent to confront them with their idolatry. God says through Jeremiah: *"Why provoke my anger by burning incense to the idols you have made here in Egypt? You will only destroy yourselves and make yourselves an object of cursing and mockery for all the nations of the earth"* (Jeremiah 44:8).

The people make their feelings clear: *"We will not listen to your messages from the Lord! We will do whatever we want"* (Jeremiah 44:16).

Sadly, for them, the Lord gives them what they want. And they will all be destroyed when King Nebuchadnezzar returns.

Focus: Throughout the story of these events, there is incredible denial going on. Zedekiah won't accept the Babylonian victory as God's judgment against Judah, and instead continues to resist. Ishmael, the guerilla hiding in the hills, entertains fantasies about leading an underground rebellion. And the people, despite Jeremiah's warnings, place their hopes in an alliance with Egypt. Once again, they illustrate Jeremiah's comment that *"the human heart is the most deceitful of all things, and desperately wicked. Who really knows how bad it is?"* At its root, sin is irrational. It deceives us into making foolish decisions, leading to self-defeating behavior.

Prayer: *Lord, we confess that in times of great stress we fall back to old patterns of running to everything but you for help. We listen to any voice but yours. We do what feels right instead of obeying you. Lord, open our eyes to your sovereign power, for you who created the universe can surely take care of us. Amen.*

Day 225   Jeremiah 46–52

August 12

> Key Text: "For the Lord of Heaven's Armies has not abandoned Israel and Judah. He is still their God, even though their land was filled with sin against the Holy One of Israel." (Jeremiah 51:5)

The book of Jeremiah ends with seven chapters outlining wars between the nations around Judah—the ungodly nations of Egypt, Philistia, Moab, Ammon and Babylon. The last chapter, however, gives hope to the *remnant of faith* who are living in the fallen city of Jerusalem.

The description of judgment for the nations reflects the taunting and florid language characteristic of the time, but with a moral and spiritual slant. These are not random events. Behind them, the Lord of history is working. The nations believe that they control their own destinies, but they rise and fall with God's permission. The unbreakable law of history is that sin will be judged.

Reading these chapters is like listening to Jeremiah as God's prosecuting attorney, bringing his case against the nations. Every bit of evidence is presented, and every creative metaphor employed, to show that the day of reckoning is coming for these nations whose idolatry, injustice and cruelty are so offensive to the Lord God.

The broader message is twofold: First, the earthly powers who defy God, and wreak havoc on human life, are powerless before God's sovereign will. They only exist by his permission, and are brought down by his word. Second, God's special favor continues toward his people, even in their sinfulness: *"For the Lord of Heaven's Armies has not abandoned Israel and Judah. He is still their God, even though their land was filled with sin against the Holy One of Israel"* (Jeremiah 51:5).

As we have noted along the way, Israel is not special because of her merit or superiority, but only because God in his sovereignty has chosen her for a special purpose—a purpose that will eventually be a blessing to all the nations of the earth—as long as those nations don't destroy her first!

The word of judgment against Babylon in chapter 51 is representative of God's case against all nations: *"The whole human race is foolish and has no knowledge! The craftsmen are disgraced by the idols they make, for their carefully shaped works are a fraud. These idols have no breath or power. Idols are worthless; they are ridiculous lies! On the day of reckoning they will all be destroyed. But the God of Israel is no idol! He is the Creator of everything that exists, including his people, his own possession. The Lord of Heaven's Armies is his name!"* (Jeremiah 51:17–19).

If, in our own day, we were to substitute intellectuals and filmmakers for the word "craftsmen" above, and then philosophy, politics, economics and media for the "idols" they make, then we could see where God might speak to our culture today. Culture based on idolatry, old or new, is based on "ridiculous lies" and is therefore foolish.

The essence of idolatry is not wood and stone, but ideas that are unworthy of God. The apostle Paul says that the ministry of the Church is to confront ideas with the Gospel. He takes the language of war and translates it into spiritual conflict: *"We [Christians] are human, but we don't wage war as humans do. We use God's mighty weapons, not worldly weapons, to knock down the strongholds of human reasoning and to destroy false arguments. We destroy every proud obstacle that keeps people from knowing God"* (2 Corinthians 10:3–5).

Today, the Church is on the front line of a spiritual war for the hearts and minds of people and nations. Even though the Church is imperfect, and often sinful, it is the means God has chosen to bear witness to the Good News of new life in Christ.

So it is appropriate that the prophet Jeremiah, at the end of his brutally honest appraisal of the sins of God's people, nevertheless leaves Israel with hope that God still loves his people and is going to bring good out of the mess they have made.

Focus: In a fallen world, nations have a life cycle ending in defeat. This has been true of every great nation in history. Whatever vision brought them into being, eventually dissipates, and is replaced by complacency, moral corruption, decline and death. Today a person can walk through the ruins of the mighty Roman Empire, the greatest nation the earth had ever seen at the time, and wonder about its fall. This is the way of things in a fallen world. But one day, God will create a permanent nation, made up of all the redeemed peoples of the world, where there is no more war or death or sorrow. Then all will see what a redeemed humanity, living in peace with God and one another, will be able to accomplish!

Prayer: *Lord, we confess that it is discouraging to read the prophets. They are relentless in their brutal honesty about human sinfulness. But without acknowledging the truth, we cannot find redemption and new life in Christ. Help us to apply this insight to our own personal lives and relationships as well. Amen.*

Day 226   Lamentations

August 13

> Key Text: The faithful love of the Lord never ends! His mercies never cease. Great is his faithfulness; his mercies begin afresh each morning. (Lamentations 3:22–23)

The little book of Lamentations, written by Jeremiah, is a hard read. It is a book of sorrow about extreme human suffering brought on by the utter devastation of Jerusalem by the Babylonians.

Imagine your own city burned to the ground. Imagine your neighbors being raped and killed, your home and all your possessions taken from you by an invading army. Imagine being forcefully moved to another country where you are not wanted, have no rights and can't speak the language.

This is the drama of Lamentations. It is a scream of pain from Jeremiah, who witnessed all these things happening to his own people. Chapter 1 begins: *"Jerusalem, once so full of people, is now deserted. She who was once great among the nations now sits alone like a widow. Once the queen of all the earth, she is now a slave. She sobs through the night; tears stream down her cheeks. … Judah has been led away into captivity, oppressed with cruel slavery"* (Lamentations 1:1–3).

Jeremiah laments the failure of the Israelites to be the people of God: *"Jerusalem has sinned greatly, so she has been tossed away like a filthy rag. All who once honored her now despise her, for they have seen her stripped naked and humiliated. All she can do is groan and hide her face. She defiled herself with immorality and gave no thought to her future. Now she lies in the gutter with no one to lift her out. 'Lord, see my misery,' she cries"* (Lamentations 1:8–9).

As is often the case, the guilty ask for mercy only when it is too late: *"'The Lord is right,' Jerusalem says, 'for I rebelled against him.'"* They try to blame God: *"Without mercy the Lord has destroyed every home in Israel."* But they have brought all this misery upon themselves. They were warned and warned, and warned again, given grace upon grace, but didn't take it seriously.

The fact that they are responsible, however, doesn't lessen Jeremiah's grief: *"I have cried until the tears no longer come; my heart is broken. My spirit is poured out in agony as I see the desperate plight of my people. Little children and tiny babies are fainting and dying in the streets. They cry out to their mothers, 'We need food and drink!' Their lives ebb away in the streets like the life of a warrior wounded in battle. They gasp for life as they collapse in their mothers' arms"* (Lamentations 2:11–12).

In his grief and horror at witnessing the siege of Jerusalem, Jeremiah shouts at God: *"You have killed them in your anger, slaughtering them without mercy."* Jeremiah bitterly remembers God's calling to be his prophet; he is like a drafted soldier who now sees the horrors of war: *"He has led me into darkness, shutting out all light."*

How tragic to be both the rejected prophet and the witness to the judgment he warned about repeatedly. But the people have hardened their hearts.

Still, even in his darkest moment, Jeremiah does not lose hope: *"Yet I still dare to hope when I remember this: The faithful love of the Lord never ends! His mercies never cease. Great is his faithfulness; his mercies begin afresh each morning. … For no one is abandoned by the Lord forever. Though he brings grief, he also shows compassion because of the greatness of his unfailing love. For he does not enjoy hurting people or causing them sorrow"* (Lamentations 3:21–33).

The book of Lamentations ends with a plaintive prayer: *"Restore us, O Lord, and bring us back to you again! Give us back the joys we once had! Or have you utterly rejected us? Are you angry with us still?"*

Focus: In the worst moment imaginable, when Jeremiah's heart is breaking and he is angrily shouting at God about what he sees happening to his people, there emerges an unexpected benediction. It has been made into a worship song: *"The steadfast love of the Lord never ceases; his mercies never come to an end. They are new every morning, new every morning. Great is thy faithfulness, O Lord, great is thy faithfulness!"*

Despair gives way to hope. What might those "new mercies" mean? We find out in another "worst moment imaginable," hundreds of years later. In the dead silence of the third day after Jesus' crucifixion, as two women go the tomb to attend to the body of Jesus, two men appear to them in dazzling robes. They say to the terrified women, and to us: *"Why are you looking among the dead for someone who is alive? He isn't here! He is risen from the dead!"* (Luke 24:5–6). Great is thy faithfulness, O Lord!

Day 227 — Reflection

August 14

Lamenting, or crying, is characteristic of human beings alone. God has given us the capacity to react to disappointment, tragedy or outright horror with tears of sorrow. Tears are cleansing, an escape valve to release our pain.

Tragedy or loss is like an assault against our soul. Our thoughts and feelings are overwhelmed. We need to express them or we will explode. Instinctively, our face reflects the sorrow as our muscles tighten, and tears come to our eyes. In biblical times, lamentation would be ritually expressed by the tearing of a garment and/or covering oneself in ash. Among friends, or even bystanders, lamentation can quickly ignite compassion and move them to join us in our lament.

As such, lamenting is a gift of God to help us process pain and sorrow—a necessary capacity in a fallen world. This ability to lament helped Jeremiah, the "weeping prophet," to process the horror of the Babylonian siege and destruction of Jerusalem. War is perhaps the greatest assault against the human soul. The widespread destruction of life, property and cultural treasures can never be forgotten. Tears are sometimes the only consolation that remain.

For this reason, we may think of lamenting as a form of worship—of communion with God. Sometimes all we can do is make an inarticulate cry of sorrow or pain. This is received by God as worship and it stirs within him a response of compassion. One of the most amazing things about the God of the Bible is that he resonates with the feelings of his creation. Through the incarnation of Christ, he enters into our pain and sorrows as a human being.

In his Passion, Christ experienced the full measure of human suffering, crying out from the cross, *"My God, my God, why have you abandoned me?"* (Matthew 27:46).

The apostle Paul adds that when we are unable to pray because of our

426

weakness (either in the body or the soul), *"the Holy Spirit prays for us with groanings that cannot be expressed in words"* (Romans 8:26).

So, lamentation as a God-given means to express sorrow, is a way of worshiping the God who joins us in our sorrows. When used as worship, our sorrows can draw us closer to God rather than push us away.

Lamentation can also draw us closer to one another. When we allow ourselves to feel what others feel and draw near to them—like God did with us in his incarnation—we are able to help with healing. The New Testament epistles encourage us to *bear one another's burdens,* and to laugh and cry together.

Even though Israel's sufferings are the result of her willful, perpetual sin, God is present in her pain through the tears of his prophet Jeremiah, offering consolation and hope, and calling for her to return to him. Jeremiah still speaks today to the people of God.

Prayer: It is comforting, Lord, to know that when we pray, especially in our sorrow, you are able to feel our pain because you made us to have fellowship with you. Thank you that our pain and sorrows will one day give way to everlasting joy! Amen.

Day 228   Ezekiel 1–6

August 15

> Key Text: "They will know that I alone am the Lord and that I was serious when I said I would bring this calamity on them." (Ezekiel 6:10)

The prophet Ezekiel is given a tough assignment from God: to live and minister among the first Judeans exiled to Babylon, a people suffering from all the terrible effects of catastrophic dislocation.

His people are also traumatized from the horrors of war and of the loss of their homeland, possessions and identity. Most have not heeded the words of the prophets—that Jerusalem would be destroyed. Now they must face the reality that it is happening.

In addition to the psychological issues, there are theological ones. Where is God in all this? Was he defeated by the Babylonian gods, or has he really done this to his own people? Is he still in control of events, and if so, is there any future for Israel?

A further issue is how, if at all, the Israelites can maintain their faith and worship while surrounded by paganism. To help them, Ezekiel is called to be their watchman.

His famous "vision" call is outlined in Ezekiel 1: *"On July 31 of my thirtieth year, while I was with the Judean exiles beside the Kebar River in Babylon, the heavens were opened and I saw visions of God."* The vision he describes is fantastical and symbolic, like wildly inventive special effects in a movie. The details are interesting, but their intent is to present the glory of God. Ezekiel says: *"This is what the glory of the Lord looked like to me. When I saw it, I fell face down on the ground, and I heard someone's voice speaking to me. 'Stand up, son of man,' said the voice. 'I want to speak with you'"* (Ezekiel 1:28–2:1).

God proceeds to call Ezekiel to live among the exiled people and speak to them on his behalf, even though, as God warns, they won't listen: *"Do not be dismayed by their dark scowls, even though they are rebels. You must give them my messages whether they listen or not. But they won't listen, for they are completely rebellious!"* (Ezekiel 2:6–7).

What an assignment!

But God has made Ezekiel just as stubborn as the people. He is "a watchman for Israel," taking God's message to them, warning them about their sins of idolatry and Covenant breaking, and urging them to repent. Once Ezekiel has delivered God's message, the responsibility then lies with the people.

So in chapters 4 through 6, God directs Ezekiel to perform symbolic acts, as well as deliver pointed messages of warning. His first act, using props, dramatizes the horrors of the Babylonian siege against the city of Jerusalem, warning the people of the famine and disease which a siege brings about.

The second act is shaving his head and beard with a sharp sword, like a razor, and then, in three little dramas of judgment, burning his hair: *"This is an illustration of what will happen to Jerusalem. I placed her at the center of the nations, but she has rebelled against my regulations and decrees and has been even more wicked than the surrounding nations. She has refused to obey the regulations and decrees I gave her to follow"* (Ezekiel 5:5–6).

Israel's judgment will be a warning to all the surrounding nations of what happens when the Lord punishes a nation in righteous anger:

"They will know that I alone am the Lord and that I was serious when I said I would bring this calamity on them" (Ezekiel 6:10).

Focus: As you have noticed (and maybe gotten tired of), the Old Testament devotes a lot of time to the events leading up to and following the conquering and exile of Israel and then Judah, by foreign nations. Many questions are raised by these traumatic events through the preaching of the prophets. Since the prophets are the mouthpiece of God, the questions are in effect raised and answered by God himself. His answers are clear, but they aren't easy. In the end, we have to trust him that he knows what he is doing, and that he has our best interests in mind—not only in the story of Israel, but in our individual stories as well.

Prayer: Lord, you have given us a hard calling, first to trust you, and then to be your witnesses in the world. Telling the truth to a world that doesn't want to hear it, is hard work. Help us to love one another enough to be willing to tell the truth and be held accountable for our lives, so that we may live what we preach as your people in the world. Amen.

Day 229   Ezekiel 7–11

August 16

> Key Text: "And I will give them singleness of heart and put a new spirit within them. I will take away their stony, stubborn heart and give them a tender, responsive heart, so they will obey my decrees and regulations. Then they will truly be my people, and I will be their God." (Ezekiel 11:19–20)

Ezekiel's next message from God is a searing indictment of Israel's sins: *"Son of man, this is what the Sovereign Lord says to Israel: 'The end is here! Wherever you look—east, west, north, or south—your land is finished. No hope remains, for I will unleash my anger against you. I will call you to account for all your detestable sins'"* (Ezekiel 7:2–3).

"Detestable" is a strong word, reserved for the most outrageous and unjust sins against God and one's neighbor. These must be accounted for, meaning that they must be listed, weighed and measured so that proportionate retribution may be given. In Israel's case, there is a lot of tonnage! The Lord says: *"I will bring on them the evil they have done to others, and they will receive the punishment they so richly deserve. Then they will know that I am the Lord"* (Ezekiel 7:27).

Some readers of the Bible may consider the idea of divine retribution to be unseemly, perhaps beneath God. But we must keep in mind that God's anger against sin is entirely justified. Even we humans who are sinful ourselves get angry at injustice. How much more so, a holy God who is perfectly loving and just? He cannot tolerate evil in his creation because evil corrupts and destroys creation like cancer destroys the life of the body. Think, for example, of the dehumanizing and destructive power of drugs, poverty, crime, injustice and war. For human life to thrive, these evils must be stopped.

And so we see that if God did not love us, he would not get angry. He would remain impassive, allowing human evil to grow unchecked. But that is not the holy God of the Bible. His anger is the red-hot emotion of a betrayed lover, not the cool indifference of a God who doesn't care. Keep in mind also that God has known from the beginning that he would ultimately deal with human sin, not by destroying his creation, but by taking the penalty of sin upon himself through Christ.

In chapter 8, Ezekiel recalls a vision where he is transported in the sky to the city of Jerusalem. He is shown a large idol near the altar of the Temple that makes the Lord jealous. He is taken to other dark places to observe the leaders of Israel engaging in secret idol worship: *"Son of man, have you seen what the leaders of Israel are doing with their idols in dark rooms? They are saying, 'The Lord doesn't see us; he has deserted our land!'"*

After visiting several scenes where his Temple is being desecrated by idol worship, the Lord says: *"Have you seen this, son of man? ... Is it nothing to the people of Judah that they commit these detestable sins, leading the whole nation into violence, thumbing their noses at me, and provoking my anger? Therefore, I will respond in fury"* (Ezekiel 8:17–18).

Ezekiel's terrible vision continues in chapters 9 through 11. Those Israelites who detest these sins are spared; the rest are not. In the vision, the glory of the Lord moves through the Temple, and the Lord points out prominent men of Jerusalem who are planning evil and giving wicked counsel. Ezekiel is told to warn them of their judgment so that when it comes, they will know that the Lord is God.

But God also tells Ezekiel to visit the exiles who will be spared. He is to give them a message of hope for the future: *"And I will give them singleness of heart and put a new spirit within them. I will take away their stony, stubborn heart and give them a tender, responsive heart, so they will obey my decrees and regulations. Then they will truly be my people, and I will be their God"* (Ezekiel 11:18–20).

> **Focus:** It is a good thing that we cannot read each other's minds, or know everything others are doing at any given moment. Too much information! Yet God must deal with this information because he does know our thoughts and actions, even if we do them in darkness, thinking that no one sees. Unlike in our legal system, where guilty people get off because there is not sufficient evidence to convict, God has all the evidence. If we knew everything that he knew, we would be overwhelmed, and probably horrified. Imagine for a moment that you could see all of the microscopic bugs and creatures that exist in your home, hiding in dark corners and crawling around on your hair and skin, for example. You would probably be a little freaked out at what hides in plain sight! There is nothing hidden from God. He sees it all. In light of this, it is amazing that he still wants to have a relationship with us!

> *Prayer: Lord, we see in Ezekiel's vision that you do see what is going on, and you are present among us as Judge. We acknowledge that you love us passionately. Therefore, you take our sin seriously. But we praise you for the Good News that Jesus has taken our sins upon himself so that we might be spared. Thank you for your amazing grace! Amen.*

Day 230   Ezekiel 12–15

August 17

> Key Text: "This will happen because these evil prophets deceive my people by saying, 'All is peaceful' when there is no peace at all! It's as if the people have built a flimsy wall, and these prophets are trying to reinforce it by covering it with whitewash! Tell these whitewashers that their wall will soon fall down."
> (Ezekiel 13:10–11)

Ezekiel faces a high hurdle in getting the Israelites to listen to his message from God that Jerusalem will be destroyed. Ironically, the hurdle is false prophecy. The false prophets among the people are literally making up prophecies, allegedly from God, telling people what they want to hear. They say that Ezekiel's predictions will never come to pass. Of course, telling people what they want to hear has been the practice of false prophets, scoundrels and politicians from time immemorial!

We have a great capacity for denial and are predisposed to believe what we want to hear. To get past these hurdles, God directs Ezekiel to juice up his messages with dramatic depictions. In chapter 12, Ezekiel is told to pretend, in front of everyone, that he is being sent into exile. So he goes through the actions that an exile would take before leaving. His actions elicit questions from his neighbors. He responds by declaring that they all will soon need to be taking these actions, because they will be driven into exile as captives.

Ezekiel then addresses the false prophets: *"This is what the Sovereign Lord says: What sorrow awaits the false prophets who are following their own imaginations and have seen nothing at all!"* (Ezekiel 13:3). Israel is in the tragic position of experiencing the Lord's judgment in part because their own prophets mislead them: *"It's as if the people have built a flimsy wall, and these prophets are trying to reinforce it by covering it with white-wash! Tell these whitewashers that their wall will soon fall down."*

The net effect is to discourage the righteous remnant among Israel with their lies, and at the same time to encourage the wicked by promising them life.

Further messages to the leaders of Israel, and then to the people themselves, repeat God's case against Israel for its idolatry and consequent moral and social corruption. The message is always the same: Do a 180-degree turn and walk away from idolatry and all the detestable sins which follow it. If you don't, terrible consequences will follow—war, famine, wild animals, and disease that will destroy human and animal life.

The important point of God's argument with his rebellious people is this: Human life, as well as the whole creation, can only function and flourish when it is rightly connected with God. When people—even God's chosen people—rebel against him, go their own way, and then worship and serve gods of their own imagination, everything comes unhinged. At stake, therefore, is the future of the human race. Will the people ever listen?

Focus: False prophets are whitewashers, Ezekiel says. Whitewashing covers up and hides what is really going on beneath the surface, whether on rotting wood or world events. Whitewashing deceives people into thinking all is well, until they are surprised by unexpected destruction. Our sinful minds are capable of denying almost anything, for fear of being exposed and facing consequences. Consequently,

432

we are drawn to those who tell us what we want to hear. But love tells the truth, no matter how uncomfortable. Be thankful that our God is both truthful and gracious.

Prayer: Lord, how terrible it is when the leaders of the people and the prophets who presume to speak on your behalf, refuse to listen to you, and continue to deceive their listeners. We ask you to raise up godly leaders and pastors who will faithfully guide and protect your people. Amen.

Day 231   Ezekiel 16–19

August 18

> Key Text: "It is I who makes the green tree wither and gives the dead tree new life. I, the Lord, have spoken, and I will do what I said!" (Ezekiel 17:24)

God gives Ezekiel a disturbing message to agitate the people, so that they will pay attention. Ezekiel is told to *"confront Jerusalem with her detestable sins."* For they have become just like the pagans around them— they have become Canaanites!

It is hard to fathom how this has come about, given the grace God has shown them. Here is how God describes it: Israel once was like an abandoned newborn child, dumped in a field, bloody with its umbilical cord still attached. But the Lord came by and saw her helplessness. He picked her up so that she could live.

He helped her grow into a beautiful young woman. Then, at the proper age, he declared his marriage vows: *"I made a covenant with you, says the Sovereign Lord, and you became mine"* (Ezekiel 16:8). As his bride, God made her a queen. She ate the finest foods and wore beautiful clothes so that her beauty became legendary.

But then, *"you thought your fame and beauty were your own. So you gave yourself as a prostitute to every man who came along. Your beauty was theirs for the asking. ... Then you took your sons and daughters—the children you had borne to me—and sacrificed them to your gods"* (Ezekiel 16:15–20).

So she commits adultery and infanticide against the Lord.

This disturbing story, based on the common practice of the Canaanites for unwanted children, is how God sees Israel's idolatry. God rescued Israel as an abandoned child, and then later married her as his beloved bride. Yet she has broken covenant with God in spiritual adultery, and

433

she who was rescued has subsequently killed her own children.

Yet, amazingly, God will remain faithful to her: *"I will remember the covenant I made with you when you were young, and I will establish an everlasting covenant with you. ... You will remember your sins and cover your mouth in silent shame when I forgive you of all that you have done. I, the Sovereign Lord, have spoken!"* (Ezekiel 16:60–63).

This story will have a greater impact on the reader if we keep in mind that Israel is a microcosm of the human race. We all fall short of God's calling; we're all unfaithful to God our Creator. Yet we are all offered his amazing grace and forgiveness.

A second disturbing story is delivered to Israel in chapter 17. The Lord says that Israel is like a cedar tree whose top is broken off by a great eagle with broad wings. It is carried far away and replanted, but then is uprooted again and withers away. This is a parable about exile. Here we learn that "replanted" Israelites make a treaty with Babylon to serve her as a conquered nation. If only Israel had stayed faithful to her promise, she would have survived. But of course Israel doesn't have a good track record with promises. She breaks her treaty with Babylon and looks to Egypt for rescue. Egypt is subsequently defeated by Babylon, and Babylon takes out her fury against Israel.

But yet again, there is a message of hope following the message of judgment. God will plant another cedar on top of Israel's highest mountain, and it will become majestic: *"It is I who makes the green tree wither and gives the dead tree new life. I, the Lord, have spoken, and I will do what I said!"* (Ezekiel 17:24).

God's message of hope is clarified in chapter 18. Though the nation as a whole is under God's judgment, individuals who repent of their sin and seek, by faith, to keep God's Law will be forgiven. The children will not be condemned because of their parents' sin, and vice versa: *"Therefore, I will judge each of you, O people of Israel, according to your actions, says the Sovereign Lord. Repent, and turn from your sins. Don't let them destroy you! Put all your rebellion behind you, and find yourselves a new heart and a new spirit. For why should you die, O people of Israel? I don't want you to die, says the Sovereign Lord. Turn back and live!"* (Ezekiel 18:30–32).

Focus: In the aftermath of a terrible tragedy, people sometimes show concern by identifying with the victims. After 9/11, for example, people from around the world declared, "We are all Americans." This wonderful, albeit temporary, declaration expressed empathy. This could happen to us too! Now, imagine the opposite—imagine that in a moment of national failure and shame, the other nations of the world identified with that shame. Yeah, hard to imagine. You never heard, after World War II, "We are all Nazis."

Yet the truth is, there is a solidarity of sin. When God tells Israel, through Ezekiel, that they have become "Canaanites," he is clarifying that they are no better than their enemies. They are sinners, just the same. Their confidence and hope—as well as that of their enemies—are in the grace of God, who freely gives us what we do not deserve.

Prayer: Lord, we are so grateful that, though you see through all of our pretension, denial and stubbornness, you continue to pursue us anyway. Your love just won't let go of us. Despite everything, there is always a way back to you through repentance and faith. We take hope in this truth and will seek to share it with others! Amen.

Day 232   Ezekiel 20–23

August 19

Key Text: "When I chose Israel—when I revealed myself to the descendants of Jacob in Egypt ... I took a solemn oath that day that I would bring them out of Egypt to a land I had discovered and explored for them—a good land, a land flowing with milk and honey, the best of all lands anywhere. Then I said to them, 'Each of you, get rid of the vile images you are so obsessed with. Do not defile yourselves with the idols of Egypt, for I am the Lord your God.'" (Ezekiel 20:5–7)

Chapter 20 reports that some of the leaders of Israel ask to meet with Ezekiel *"to request a message from the Lord."* Perhaps this reflects an attitude of repentance, seeking God's mercy. More likely, they are coming to plea-bargain.

But God's message for them is not encouraging. He reminds them of their original calling and their promise to leave idol worship behind: *"When I chose Israel—when I revealed myself to the descendants of Jacob in Egypt—I took a solemn oath that I, the Lord, would be their God. I took a solemn oath that day that I would bring them out of Egypt to a land I had discovered and explored for them—a good land, a land flowing with milk and honey, the best of all lands anywhere. Then I said to them, 'Each of you, get rid of the vile images you are so obsessed with. Do not defile yourselves*

435

with the idols of Egypt, for I am the Lord your God'" (Ezekiel 20:5–7).

Despite God's gracious commitment to be their God and bless their lives, Israel would not let go of her obsession with idols. The rest of the chapter is a review of her history of unfaithfulness to God. In the end, he challenges Israel's leaders: *"Do you plan to pollute yourselves just as your ancestors did? Do you intend to keep prostituting yourselves by worshiping vile images? For when you offer gifts to them and give your little children to be burned as sacrifices, you continue to pollute yourselves with idols to this day. Should I allow you to ask for a message from me, O people of Israel? As surely as I live, says the Sovereign Lord, I will tell you nothing"* (Ezekiel 20:30–31).

Nevertheless, God's merciful patience will win the day. A day is coming when Israel will return to God and he will accept them. He will honor his name by treating them mercifully in spite of their wickedness. Again, we hear from God that his grace will be greater than Israel's sin. The last word for Israel—and for all human history—will not be extinction, but eternal life for all who receive his grace. That is where the long and perplexing story of Israel is moving.

In the meantime, God stands opposed to Israel's sin. He doesn't say that her sin doesn't matter, but instead holds Israel accountable by handing her over to the consequences of her evil. And the immediate consequence is defeat and captivity.

If this all seems like much ado about nothing—what's the big deal about idols?—remember that people's view of God and his character shapes their moral vision and behavior, and consequently the development of human society. In the case of paganism, it produces a violent, unjust and morally contemptible society. Chapter 22 describes what Israelite society became when it pivoted back to paganism. It's a sordid depiction of moral depravity.

To show how this appears to God, Ezekiel is given a message telling a story about two sisters, Oholah and Oholibah who, at a young age, became prostitutes in Egypt. The Lord says, *"I married them, and they bore me sons and daughters. I am speaking of Samaria and Jerusalem, for Oholah is Samaria and Oholibah is Jerusalem"* (Ezekiel 23:1–4).

Even after they were "married," they continued in prostitution and depravity, abandoning themselves to lust. Foolishly, Oholah (Israel) chased after lovers from the Assyrian army. Following her example, Oholibah

(Judah) chased after lovers from the Babylonian army. In the end, they were both used up, brutalized, left naked and humiliated. A tragic consequence of willful human rebellion.

> **Focus:** Ezekiel's depiction of Israel's sin is particularly disturbing. The people have, indeed, become like Canaanites in their behavior. Their kings, priests, prophets and common people are corrupt to the core. These pictures of depravity, though wincing, are familiar to us. This is the way the world is. It is what we know. If only we could see what God sees. He will not accommodate himself to it. To do so would be to deny his nature and character. Our challenge, as his people, is to avoid the Canaanite option of shaping God to our wishes, and to embrace the Covenant option of shaping our wishes to God's will.

> **Prayer:** *Lord, may we keep your holy character before us always, so that our thoughts and imagination may be shaped by truth, goodness, beauty and love. May we experience your blessing as we increasingly conform our lives to your will. Amen.*

Day 233   Ezekiel 24–28

August 20

> Key Text: "This is what the Sovereign Lord says: Because you clapped and danced and cheered with glee at the destruction of my people, I will raise my fist of judgment against you. I will give you as plunder to many nations. I will cut you off from being a nation and destroy you completely. Then you will know that I am the Lord." (Ezekiel 25:6–7)

On the 15th of January, 588 BC, King Nebuchadnezzar of Babylon began his siege of Jerusalem. After 18 months, the Babylonian army captures the city, sets it on fire and destroys it.

Ezekiel, and the other Hebrew prophets, had warned the people repeatedly, but they refused to listen. So now, God directs Ezekiel to perform a dramatic message: *"Put a pot on the fire, and pour in some water. Fill it with choice pieces of meat.... Bring the pot to a boil, and cook the bones along with the meat."* This is a picture of the judgment of the people. God himself is the wood fuel beneath the pot.

But the dramatic message is to no avail either: *"I tried to cleanse you, but you refused"* (Ezekiel 24:13). So the time of judgment has arrived and it is too late for the people.

Ezekiel is then given tragic news from the Lord—his wife will soon die. However, he is not to mourn her death: *"Groan silently, but let there be no wailing at her grave. Do not uncover your head or take off your sandals. Do not perform the usual rituals of mourning or accept any food brought to you by consoling friends."* When people ask what is going on, Ezekiel is to tell them that his response to his wife's death is a message from God about his response to Jerusalem's death. Therefore, when the death of Jerusalem has occurred, the people are not to wail or offer consolation to one another. They will not be objects of sympathy, because this has come about by their own doing.

Next, in chapter 25, God speaks to the surrounding nations who mock Israel in her time of desolation: *"Because you clapped and danced and cheered with glee at the destruction of my people, I will raise my fist of judgment against you."* Israel deserves her judgment, but it is given as a call to repentance and restoration, not as an opportunity to humiliate and laugh.

In chapters 26 through 28, the nations of Tyre and Sidon are singled out for judgment because of their particularly offensive boasts. Ezekiel says to the prince of Tyre: *"In your great pride you claim, 'I am a god! I sit on a divine throne in the heart of the sea.' But you are only a man and not a god, though you boast that you are a god. You regard yourself as wiser than Daniel and think no secret is hidden from you. ... Because you think you are as wise as a god, I will now bring against you a foreign army, the terror of the nations. They will draw their swords against your marvelous wisdom and defile your splendor!"* (Ezekiel 28:2–7).

Though God judges his people, he does not mock them as do the nations around them. He doesn't rejoice in their pain. Instead, he announces that the people of Israel will live in their own land again, the land he gave them. He will gather them from exile in the distant countries where he has scattered them: *"I will reveal to the nations of the world my holiness among my people. They will live safely in Israel and build homes and plant vineyards. And when I punish the neighboring nations that treated them with contempt, they will know that I am the Lord their God"* (Ezekiel 28:25–26).

Focus: It is one thing for a parent to discipline their child; it is another to rejoice over it and enjoy their pain. This is the difference between the judgment of God against his people, and the mockery and rejoicing of the surrounding nations.

Though it is a parental cliché, it may be properly said of God, that his judgment against Israel hurt him as much as it hurt her.

We see this also in Jesus' lament over the Jewish refusal to repent: *"O Jerusalem, Jerusalem, the city that kills the prophets and stones God's messengers! How often I have wanted to gather your children together as a hen protects her chicks beneath her wings, but you wouldn't let me"* (Matthew 23:37). God's sorrow and anger against our hard hearts is something only love can produce.

Prayer: Lord, remind us that the pain and sorrow of your temporal judgments for our sin is not an indication that you despise us. Quite the opposite—we know that it is an indication of your love, and of your intention to bring us home to you. Like a parent, you discipline the children you love. Amen.

Day 234   Reflection

August 21

Ezekiel's warning to the pagan nation of Tyre is singled out in chapter 28 because of the excessive pride of its leader: *"In your great pride you claim, 'I am a god! I sit on a divine throne in the heart of the sea'"* (Ezekiel 28:1). How much haughtier can a man become than to consider himself a god?!

Proverbs 6:17 names haughtiness as first among six things the Lord hates.

How could any person develop such a grotesquely exaggerated view of himself? The prince of Tyre became this way through wealth and power. He had the gift of intelligence and the good fortune of his circumstances, to advance himself over others. Ezekiel says to him: *"With your wisdom and understanding you have amassed great wealth—gold and silver for your treasuries. Yes, your wisdom has made you very rich, and your riches have made you very proud"* (Ezekiel 28:4–5).

Ezekiel tells the king that he had it all—he was in Eden, the Garden of the Lord! However, his pride brings him down: *"Your rich commerce led you to violence, and you sinned. ... Your heart was filled with pride because of all your beauty. Your wisdom was corrupted by your love of splendor. So I threw you to the ground and exposed you to the curious gaze of kings"* (Ezekiel 28:16–17).

C.S. Lewis echoes Proverbs 6:17 and names pride as the worst of human sins. He is not referring to the loving pride that a parent has for their child, but to the narcissistic pride that wants to win at all costs, and takes pleasure in others' defeat. Such pride does not share the stage with anyone. It is a form of violence. It must always assert itself and defend itself from potential rivals. As such, it violates the image of God in humanity and turns the creation against itself.

But someone might say, "Isn't God proud because he demands our worship?" God cannot be proud because he has no competition—in reality, there are no other gods. They only exist in the delusions of fallen minds. For mortals to acknowledge and worship immortal God is an act of sanity and rationality, for it perceives the world as it really is.

Remember, it was pride that caused the fall of the devil. It was pride that caused Adam and Eve to embrace the devil's cause and break fellowship with God. They despised their humanity and grasped for deity. As we have learned over and over again, when individuals and groups presume the power of God for themselves, terrible things follow.

What is at stake, then, is the well-being of the human race.

Astrophysicists teach us that black holes form in the universe when large stars die in a supernova. The collapse of these stars creates a gravitational force so strong that nothing can escape, including light. Thus, "black" holes. In the universe of human beings, narcissistic pride is a black hole. Nothing good comes from it; everything around it is destroyed. More than any sin, pride is the greatest obstacle keeping us from faith in God.

The greatest obstacle to spiritual growth, too, is the presence of pride. It can only be removed by humility before God. *"Blessed are the meek,"* says Jesus, *"for they shall inherit the earth."*

Prayer: Lord, we have seen what selfish, ambitious pride can do in our relationships, and in the wider world. It always leads to conflict and the destruction of things. Thank you for coming to us with tough love, to tell the truth and hold us accountable to live life as you demand. For you are the eternal God, our Creator—infinite and perfect in your attributes, loving and just in your ways! Amen.

August 22

> Key Text: "Weep and wail for that day, for the terrible day is almost here—the day of the Lord! It is a day of clouds and gloom, a day of despair for the nations." (Ezekiel 30:2–3)

Ezekiel's next message from God is for Israel's old nemesis, Egypt. You'll remember that Israel was born as a nation after being delivered out of Egypt. There, the Lord God revealed himself to be the one true God by routing the gods of Egypt and taking Israel across the Red Sea into the wilderness, where she grew up for forty years before occupying the land of Canaan.

But as Ezekiel and the other prophets testify, Israel gradually turned back to those old familiar gods and once again became captive to idolatry. Despite God's extraordinary patience, power and provision on her behalf, Israel would not return to her Covenant promises, so God removed his protection and gave her up over the years to the political whirlwinds of her pagan neighbors.

When attacked by Babylon, as God had long warned would happen, Israel again failed to turn to God. Ironically, she turned to a political alliance with Egypt, thinking that Egypt's gods could now deliver her. What foolishness! Besides, Egypt cared nothing for Israel.

So God says to Egypt: *"I am your enemy, O Pharaoh, king of Egypt—you great monster, lurking in the streams of the Nile. ... I will bring an army against you, O Egypt, and destroy both people and animals. The land of Egypt will become a desolate wasteland, and the Egyptians will know that I am the Lord"* (Ezekiel 29:3–9).

In time, the scattered Egyptians will return back to their land, but thereafter it will remain a minor kingdom, *"the lowliest of all the nations, never again great enough to rise above its neighbors. Then Israel will no longer be tempted to trust in Egypt for help. Egypt's shattered condition will remind Israel of how sinful she was to trust Egypt in earlier days. Then Israel will know that I am the Sovereign Lord"* (Ezekiel 29:15–16).

What dominates the following chapters is the theme of God's sovereignty over Egypt and Babylon, as well as Israel. He is Lord of all nations. For example, Babylon defeats Tyre, an old enemy of Israel, but gains no plunder. Therefore, Ezekiel says that God gives the land of Egypt as plunder to Nebuchadnezzar, king of Babylon, *"as a reward for his work ... because he was working for me when he destroyed Tyre."*

Whatever the great nations of the earth think they are doing, it is God who is in control of history!

Later, Ezekiel says to Pharaoh that Egypt is like mighty Assyria, which he compares to a cedar of Lebanon—a great tree which towered high above other trees around it. No tree in the garden of God came close to it in beauty. And most significantly, God made this tree beautiful. So, he is saying to Pharaoh that God alone makes the nations great. The rise and fall of nations is controlled by the sovereign Lord, despite the boasting of their leaders!

For confirmation, look at history. Once-great nations who put terror in the hearts of their enemies, now lie defeated themselves, the object of scorn by other nations: *"Once a terror, they have been put to shame. They lie there as outcasts with others who were slaughtered by the sword. They share the shame of all who have descended to the pit"* (Ezekiel 32:30).

Focus: We need to be careful about the idolatry of nationalism. God is the Lord of all nations. No nation, however strong at the moment, should presume that they are God's nation. Israel, as God's people, was not called to be just another ancient Near Eastern nation; she was called to be different—to stand outside the family of other nations in order to bear witness to them of the one true God. But she was not exempt from God's judgment. When she turned from God and his special calling, she was taken down. And God's judgment of the surrounding nations should caution us not to presume that we could not be next.

Prayer: Lord, when we are afraid because of world events, wondering what will become of us if this nation or that country grows more powerful, remind us that you are in control of history. What seems confusing and frightening to us, is clear to you. The future of this world is not chaos, but the New Creation. You are the Sovereign Lord! Amen.

Day 236   Ezekiel 33–36

August 23

> Key Text: "Now, son of man, I am making you a watchman for the people of Israel. Therefore, listen to what I say and warn them for me." (Ezekiel 33:7)

The city of Jerusalem has fallen. God's warning has come true. Israel has experienced the full measure of God's judgment in her exile. As this reality sets in, there are differing responses: Some blame God, while others repent of their sins.

And what does God think about all this? *"As surely as I live ... I take no pleasure in the death of wicked people. I only want them to turn from their wicked ways so they can live. Turn! Turn from your wickedness, O people of Israel! Why should you die?"* (Ezekiel 33:11).

The Lord appoints Ezekiel as a spiritual watchman for the people, to warn them of the consequences of the sins they will not forsake. It will be a thankless job, because the people have no intention of doing what Ezekiel says: *"They hear what you say, but they don't act on it! But when all these terrible things happen to them—as they certainly will—then they will know a prophet has been among them."*

The strongest words of judgment are given, in chapter 34, to Israel's spiritual leaders, who are called false shepherds because they abuse or neglect their calling: *"Therefore, you shepherds, hear the word of the Lord: As surely as I live, says the Sovereign Lord, you abandoned my flock and left them to be attacked by every wild animal. And though you were my shepherds, you didn't search for my sheep when they were lost. You took care of yourselves and left the sheep to starve."*

God will cast the false shepherds aside and give the people a suitable shepherd, instead—a king like David. Here again the expectation of a coming Messianic King from David's family line is raised. Who will this Messiah be?

Ezekiel's message now turns to the future. Despite Israel's sin, God will forgive and restore his people from the inside out: *"For I will gather you up from all the nations and bring you home again to your land. Then I will sprinkle clean water on you, and you will be clean. Your filth will be washed away, and you will no longer worship idols. And I will give you a new heart, and I will put a new spirit in you. I will take out your stony, stubborn heart and give you a tender, responsive heart. And I will put my Spirit in you so that you will follow my decrees and be careful to obey my regulations"* (Ezekiel 36:24–27).

Here is another prophetic reference to the ministry of Christ. After his resurrection and ascension, the Holy Spirit will be poured out from heaven on the Day of Pentecost, as described in Acts, chapter 2. In this way Ezekiel's words will come true: *"I will put my Spirit in you."*

The gift of the Holy Spirit for every believer will make it possible to be the people of God in a new way. The new people of God, the Church, will be made up of Jews and Gentiles alike, who have believed in Jesus as their King and have received his Spirit in their hearts.

And so it will be that, in Christ, God's Promise of redemption to Abraham, and all that was pictured in the provisional institutions, rituals and practices of Israel as a nation, will be fulfilled.

Focus: What God wants most of all for us is to turn from our life of rebellion so that we can truly live. There is existence, and there is life—a rich and satisfying life, as Jesus says in John 10:10. None of the gods of the ancient world would ever have said such a thing. Humans were of no concern to them, except as slaves to feed them. When Jesus, as King, finally unites heaven and earth under his gracious reign, there will be love, joy and peace such as we have never seen. Who can imagine it? But this is the Promise of blessing that God gave Abraham at the beginning of our story.

Prayer: *Lord, more than anything, we long for the rich and satisfying life that you offer. Sometimes, it seems too good to be true. Other times—especially when your people fail to love and serve you—it seems impossible to attain. But grant us the grace we need to remain faithful to you and your Kingdom work, no matter the troubles of the day. Amen.*

Day 237　　　　Ezekiel 37–39

August 24

Key Text: "Look! I am going to put breath into you and make you live again! I will put flesh and muscles on you and cover you with skin. I will put breath into you, and you will come to life. Then you will know that I am the Lord." (Ezekiel 37:5–6)

The final section of Ezekiel, beginning with chapter 37, changes focus from mostly warnings of disaster that will befall the people of Israel and her neighbors, to the restoration and hope that is to come. Of course, this theme has been mentioned several times along the way, but now it is front and center.

The final section begins with a bang, or perhaps we should say, a "rattle." Chapter 37 is the most memorable chapter of Ezekiel. If you've ever sung, *"The foot bone's connected to the ankle bone; the ankle bone's con-*

nected to the leg bone...," then you have sung a song based on the following vision of Ezekiel.

Ezekiel reports that he was carried away by the Spirit of the Lord to a valley filled with bones, which represent the people of Israel under God's judgment: *"They were scattered everywhere across the ground and were completely dried out. Then he asked me, 'Son of man, can these bones become living people again?'"* (Ezekiel 37:2–3). Ezekiel is unsure.

The Lord then directs Ezekiel to speak a prophetic word to the scattered bones, saying: *"I am going to put breath into you and make you live again! I will put flesh and muscles on you and cover you with skin. I will put breath into you, and you will come to life. Then you will know that I am the Lord."*

Suddenly, there is a rattling noise all across the valley. The bones of each body come together and attach themselves as complete skeletons. As Ezekiel watches, muscles and flesh form over the bones. Skin forms to cover their bodies, but they still have no breath in them.

Then Ezekiel commands the four winds to breathe into these dead bodies so that they may live again. And they come to life! They stand on their feet as a great army. He speaks the Lord's words to them: *"I will put my Spirit in you, and you will live again and return home to your own land. Then you will know that I, the Lord, have spoken, and I have done what I said"* (Ezekiel 37:14).

The Lord will make a New Covenant with them, an everlasting Covenant of peace, and he will dwell among them in his Temple forever.

The Lord warns the people in chapters 38 and 39 that there will still be opposition to them when they return from exile, but that he will now protect and deliver them from all their enemies.

Israel's restoration will serve to highlight God's faithfulness to his Covenant. He will accept the people not because of their goodness, but because of his amazing grace.

So the long, often scandalous story of Israel's unfaithfulness will resolve itself in reconciliation before the watching world, to the glory of God. The pagan nations will also be forced to acknowledge that the Lord is God, and they must come to terms with him.

We have spoken a few times about Jesus as the fulfillment of Israel. He is the obedient Son that Israel never was. He is humanity as God intended. As such, he is the first of a New Humanity able to fully realize what it means to be man and woman in the image of God.

The vision of the revived bones of Israel points forward, in the short view, to the return of the remnant of faith to Jerusalem. But its fulfillment doesn't end there. The revived bones point, in the long view, all the way to the bodily resurrection of Jesus and, thereafter, to the bodily resurrection of all believers in the New Creation.

Focus: For men and woman created in the image of God, life means more than having a pulse and breathing. It means having a right relationship with God, one another, and the whole creation. Such a life—a rich and satisfying life—is possible because God wants it. He wanted it when he first created us in his image. He wanted it when we ran from him, and he pursued us all the way to Christ. It gives him pleasure now to think about spending eternity with you and me. Who knows what joy lies ahead?

Prayer: *Lord, what an awesome vision of hope we have been given! We feel ourselves to have been scattered like the desiccated bones of Israel, but then made alive again by your Spirit. We thank and praise you for giving us new life and hope through the cross and resurrection of Jesus. Amen.*

Day 238   Ezekiel 40–43

August 25

Key Text: The Lord said to me, "Son of man, this is the place of my throne and the place where I will rest my feet. I will live here forever among the people of Israel. They and their kings will not defile my holy name any longer by their adulterous worship of other gods...." (Ezekiel 43:7)

Ezekiel's final vision from God places him atop a very high mountain in the land of Israel. Before him, in the distance, is the Temple of the Lord. Drawing near through dream transportation, Ezekiel sees a man *"whose face shone like bronze,"* and who instructs him to watch and listen so that he can return to the people of Israel and tell them everything he has seen.

The man takes him on a tour of the inside and outside of the Temple, now restored. He carries measuring instruments and makes a detailed measurement of everything, just like a blueprint.

But it is more than a blueprint: *"To use a modern analogy, what we are given is like a three-dimensional, computer generated virtual reality tour of the Temple. The impact of the vision is not so much the measurements themselves but the cumulative effect of the perfect numerical symmetries and geometric design."* (Christopher J. H. Wright)

Ezekiel is deeply moved by the dimensions and beauty of this idealized Temple.

Once the measurement of the idealized Temple is concluded, the man brings Ezekiel back around to the east gateway to watch what happens next: *"Suddenly, the glory of the God of Israel appeared from the east. The sound of his coming was like the roar of rushing waters, and the whole landscape shone with his glory."*

God's glorious presence is back in his Temple, among the people: *"The Lord said to me, 'Son of man, this is the place of my throne and the place where I will rest my feet. I will live here forever among the people of Israel. They and their kings will not defile my holy name any longer by their adulterous worship of other gods...'"* (Ezekiel 43:7).

At this point, we might ask why the presence of the Lord on earth among his people was such an important matter to Israel, and why it should be to us today. Consider this: If there is not one God, but many—as many as there are nations—then we inhabit a world of continual conflict between rival gods.

In our secular world today, we prefer not to speak of gods. But if we substitute economic, political and military power for "gods," then we can see what is at stake. In a world without God, all that would remain, said the modern philosopher Nietzsche, is the "will to power." Whoever has the most power, wins.

So then, if God is not honored among us as the One who brings order, sanity, truth, beauty and moral clarity to life, we are sentenced to perpetual conflict.

This is the legacy of our presumption to be "gods" ourselves, the bitter fruit of the Fall.

But on the other hand, imagine what would be possible if we humans were all at peace with one another, and aligned in worship of the one true God who is present among us. Imagine what we could accomplish if we all sought to glorify him through our enterprise, creativity, learning, building, traveling and discovery! As the apostle Paul put it: *"No eye has seen, no ear has heard, and no mind has imagined what God has prepared for those who love him"*

(1 Corinthians 2:9).

Focus: Ezekiel's vision of an ideal, restored Temple, rising out of the debris of a destroyed Jerusalem, and filled with the glorious presence of God, would have given the exiled Israelites a sense of hope and a future—a reason to confess their sins and return to God. Our own rebellion against God has produced nothing but destruction as well. In our present world, we see the rubble and remains of the secular City of Man with its Temple of the Self lying in ruins. For us, too, Ezekiel's vision stands as an indictment of the mess we have made of things, but also as a reassurance that God has not left us in exile, without hope.

Prayer: Lord, it excites our imagination to think of what life could be like—will be like—when your presence transforms earth from warring nations to a united humanity! What joy to live life in its fullness as a daily act of worship to you! Amen.

Day 239   Ezekiel 44–48

August 26

> Key Text: "The distance around the entire city will be 6 miles. And from that day the name of the city will be 'The Lord Is There.'" (Ezekiel 48:35)

Ezekiel's vision of a renewed Temple with renewed worship now continues in chapters 44 through 48, with a renewed priesthood leading proper worship in the Promised Land. This vision gives assurance and hope that God's ancient Promise to Abraham *(Genesis 15:18–21),* which was fulfilled by God but then forfeited by Israel's idolatry, will be renewed by God.

What God wants more than anything—the very reason he created us in the first place—is to enjoy fellowship with us. So the encouraging words at the end of the previous chapter, where the Temple is renewed, leap out at us: *"I will accept you."*

We should hear it as God's welcome: *"This is the language of love, of welcome, of warmth and invitation. This word smiles out at us and greets us with open arms. The altar was the place that actualized that welcome."* (Christopher J.H. Wright)

By this vision we are reminded again that God will not be deterred from giving his blessing to the world, even though the world does everything it can to reject his gracious gift. Ezekiel's vision of a renewed Temple and restored people is symbolic in its form. We know, from the New Testament, that the fulfillment of Ezekiel's vision will come about differently than envisioned here. However, the vision of an ideal Temple and priesthood prepares us for Christ, who is the embodiment of the high priest, the sin offering, the Temple, and the glorious presence of God.

In chapter 44, the vision restates the proper functions of the priest in the restored Temple. Previously, Israel's priests had actually encouraged the people in their idolatry. Now they will faithfully keep God's Law regarding their personal behavior and ministry.

In chapter 45, the land is redistributed to the tribes. It was forfeited by idolatry, but is now restored by grace in response to repentance and faith. A portion of the land must be allocated to the Lord for the use of the priesthood: *"They will use it for their homes, and my Temple will be located within it."* The prince or king will have his own land as well, so that he will not be tempted to oppress and rob the people of their possessions.

The requirements for the prince or king regarding his offerings in the Temple, followed by some instruction about giving the gift of land to a relative or a servant, are outlined in chapter 46.

The mundane details of the Temple vision and land division are interrupted suddenly in chapter 47. Ezekiel writes: *"In my vision, the man brought me back to the entrance of the Temple. There I saw a stream flowing east from beneath the door of the Temple and passing to the right of the altar on its south side."* They walk along the river, noting that the further the river flows, the deeper it gets. Returning back along the bank, Ezekiel notices *"many trees growing on both sides of the river,"* perhaps a reference to the Tree of Life in Genesis, but here they are growing into a forest of life.

The river flows east through the desert into the Valley of the Dead Sea, making the sea fresh and pure. Living things abound where the water flows, even fish in the formerly dead water. Fruit trees of all kinds grow along both sides of the river with fruit-laden branches: *"There will be a new crop every month, for they are watered by the river flowing from the Temple. The fruit will be for food and the leaves for healing."*

The text returns now to the division of the renewed and refreshed land among the tribes, ending finally with these words: *"The distance around the entire city will be 6 miles. And from that day the name of the city will be 'The Lord Is There.'"* The presence of the Lord is, of course, the source of the life-giving river which flows from his presence—the gift of his Spirit—refreshing his people and the whole world.

Focus: It has been noted that the book of Ezekiel offers an emphasis on the empowering nature of God's Spirit, that is unparalleled in the Hebrew Scriptures: *"To Ezekiel, the Spirit inspires prophecy, empowers the remnant, creates the future community of faith, changes human hearts and raises Israel from the dead.... As long as the Lord is present there is hope for the future."* (Paul R. House)

Prayer: *Lord, your powerful message through Ezekiel's vision causes our hearts to race! How encouraging to know that dead bones can live again, and desert land and salty seas can bloom and be refreshed with life. Lord, give us your Spirit's fullness so that we may remain spiritually energized for worship and service. Amen.*

Day 240   Daniel 1–3

August 27

Key Text: "O Nebuchadnezzar, we do not need to defend ourselves before you. If we are thrown into the blazing furnace, the God whom we serve is able to save us. He will rescue us from your power, Your Majesty. But even if he doesn't, we want to make it clear to you, Your Majesty, that we will never serve your gods or worship the gold statue you have set up." (Daniel 3:16–18)

The wonderful book of Daniel is listed under the prophets, but is part narrative, part autobiography, and part apocalyptic literature. As a narrative, chapters 1 through 3 tell how the Babylonians take some of the young men of Judah's royal family, and other noble families, to Babylon as captives. Only the strong, healthy, good-looking and educated young men are selected, like Daniel and three of his friends. His friends are renamed Shadrach, Meshach and Abednego.

Daniel and his friends are strong of faith and do not defile themselves as Jews by eating forbidden foods given them by the king. But since they demonstrate unusual aptitude for literature and wisdom, they are consulted by the king and treated favorably.

Daniel is also given the special ability by God to interpret the meaning of visions and dreams.

Sometime later, King Nebuchadnezzar has disturbing dreams. He summons his own magicians, sorcerers and enchanters, unfairly demanding that they give him an interpretation without his actually telling them what he dreamed about. When they cannot, he threatens them all with death.

Daniel is told about this and requests time from the king to discern his dreams and their interpretation. So Daniel and his friends ask the Lord to intervene, and he reveals the meaning of the king's dream to them. Daniel tells the king that there is a God in heaven who reveals secrets. God has told Nebuchadnezzar through his dreams about what will happen in the future, and revealed its meaning to Daniel. Daniel tells him, in summary, that kingdoms will rise and fall, but *"the God of heaven will set up a kingdom that will never be destroyed or conquered. It will crush all these kingdoms into nothingness, and it will stand forever"* (Daniel 2:44).

Though not a favorable interpretation for Nebuchadnezzar, he falls down before Daniel out of fear and cries out, *"Truly, your God is the greatest of gods."* Daniel and his friends are then appointed to high positions in his government.

However, Nebuchadnezzar's fear of Israel's God fades in time. He makes a ninety-foot-tall statue out of gold and insists that everyone bow down to worship it or be thrown into a blazing furnace.

Shadrach, Meshach and Abednego refuse, and are ratted out and brought before the king. They say, *"O Nebuchadnezzar, we do not need to defend ourselves before you. If we are thrown into the blazing furnace, the God whom we serve is able to save us. He will rescue us from your power, Your Majesty. But even if he doesn't, we want to make it clear to you, Your Majesty, that we will never serve your gods or worship the gold statue you have set up"* (Daniel 3:16–18).

Nebuchadnezzar is furious! He demands that the furnace be heated seven times hotter than usual and orders that the three men be thrown in. But suddenly, Nebuchadnezzar jumps up, horrified. He sees FOUR men walking around in the fire unharmed: *"And the fourth looks like a god!"* (Daniel 3:25).

Again, Nebuchadnezzar is forced by circumstances he cannot understand to praise the God of Israel and the courage of the three Jews. He decrees that no one can speak against them, and then promotes them to even higher positions in the province of Babylon.

Focus: Daniel and his friends are obedient to God under the most threatening circumstances. Their absolute confidence in God makes them strong in faith. Nebuchadnezzar, on the other hand, is driven to acknowledging God by his fear. When his fear subsides, so does his faith. So we see that fear is not a good foundation for faith. Motivating people to believe in Jesus out of fear of going to hell, for example, may get temporary results, but when the fear goes away, so does the faith. Authentic faith arises in response to understanding God's love. If any fear is needed in a person's life, let God's Spirit do the scaring!

Prayer: Lord, how encouraging it is to hear of men who faithfully obeyed you, even in the face of death, resisting the temptation to simply go along with sin. Again, we are encouraged to remember that you alone are God, and all nations and powers must answer to you. Raise up more believers like Daniel and his friends to lead us through perilous times! Amen.

Day 241 Reflection

August 28

The story of Daniel and his friends, like other stories we have read so far, reminds us that even when God's chosen people as a whole strayed far away from God, there were always individuals who remained faithful. Often in difficult circumstances, and with far less understanding of God's plan than we have today, they were amazing examples of what the Bible has been calling the *remnant of faith*.

With all of the time given to the matter of Israel's failures and God's judgment, it is good to remember this remnant.

Looking back, many stood out: Abraham, who demonstrated great faith in the unknown God, Yahweh; Joseph, who forgave and protected his brothers after their treachery; Moses, who persevered in leadership through constant complaining and resistance; Rahab, the prostitute who protected the Israelite spies while they checked out Jericho; Joshua, who declared in the face of criticism, *"As for me and my family, we will serve the Lord"*; good judges and kings who resisted pressure and led the people in righteousness; Queen Esther and Mordecai, who showed courage in threatening times; Job, who remained faithful through unjust suffering; the prophets, who faithfully spoke truth to power and suffered for it; and, of course, Daniel and his friends, who refused to bow before an idol, even though it meant being thrown to the lions or into an oven!

With Daniel, as with Joseph, Esther and Mordecai, we have an interesting example of a faithful Jew who serves pagan leaders with distinction. It would have been easy for them to compromise their faith in order to fit in, avoid suffering and enjoy all the perks of power and wealth. Instead, they serve as examples of what God can accomplish in us if we maintain our faith and integrity in the midst of unbelief, temptation and danger.

Beyond this, they anticipate and point to the One whose perfect faith and obedience earned righteousness for us all—Jesus, whom we have identified as the "One true Israelite." All of the virtues of the great men and women of faith in the Old Testament come together with perfection in him. The apostle Paul says of him: *"Though he was God, he did not think of equality with God as something to cling to. Instead, he gave up his divine privileges; he took the humble position of a slave and was born a human being. When he appeared in human form, he humbled himself in obedience to God and died a criminal's death on a cross"* (Philippians 2:6–8).

It is motivating to think that our willingness to suffer out of obedience to Christ, makes us *"partners with Christ in his suffering,"* and therefore we *"will have the wonderful joy of seeing his glory when it is revealed to all the world"* (1 Peter 4:13).

In the day of Christ's "glory," all of the other things of history will be sorted out; all the questions will be answered, and there will be no one who can say that God has not been just and gracious beyond all expectation.

Those who have lived in humble obedience, like Daniel and the others, will especially share the joy of that Day!

> *Prayer: Lord, we are energized when we read of these men and women who at all costs, and in the most difficult of circumstances, remained faithful to you. Grant us all the grace we need to be like them as we follow Christ. Amen.*

Day 242   Daniel 4–6

August 29

> Key Text: "Now I, Nebuchadnezzar, praise and glorify and honor the King of heaven. All his acts are just and true, and he is able to humble the proud." (Daniel 4:37)

King Nebuchadnezzar of Babylon is a fascinating study. As his kingdom grows through military conquest, he develops a kind of megalomania—a madness wherein he begins thinking of himself as a god. One day while walking on the roof of his royal palace, he indulges in some dangerous delusional thinking: *"Look at this great city of Babylon! By my own mighty power, I have built this beautiful city as my royal residence to display my majestic splendor"* (Daniel 4:30).

His frightening dreams, narrated in chapters 1 and 2, and now recounted in chapter 4, are a warning from the Lord that Nebuchadnezzar will be humbled by his megalomania in a bout of insanity. Daniel explains, *"You will be driven from human society, and you will live in the fields with the wild animals. You will eat grass like a cow, and you will be drenched with the dew of heaven ... until you learn that the Most High rules over the kingdoms of the world and gives them to anyone he chooses."*

Daniel warns Nebuchadnezzar: *"Stop sinning and do what is right. Break from your wicked past and be merciful to the poor. Perhaps then you will continue to prosper."*

But of course, Nebuchadnezzar does not listen, and the madness comes upon him as foretold in his dream. (His behavior of acting like an animal is, in fact, a rare mental disorder called *insania zoanthropia*.) In time, his sanity returns. Humbled by this demonstration of his weakness, Nebuchadnezzar worships the Most High. He praises and honors God by confessing, *"his rule is everlasting, and his kingdom is eternal. All the people of the earth are nothing compared to him. He does as he pleases among the angels of heaven and among the people of the earth. No one can stop him or say to him, 'What do you mean by doing these things?'"* (Daniel 4:34–35).

Many years later, Nebuchadnezzar's grandson, King Belshazzar, gives a great feast for 1,000 of his nobles. When everyone is lit up with wine, he decides to mock the God of the Jews, and perhaps his grandfather Nebuchadnezzar, who now worships this God. So Belshazzar gives orders that the gold and silver cups that had been taken from the Temple in Jerusalem be brought out so that he and his nobles, wives and concubines can drink from them while praising Babylonian idols!

Suddenly, everyone sees the fingers of a human hand writing on the plaster wall of the king's palace near a lampstand. None of the king's wise men can interpret the writing, but the queen mother reminds Belshazzar of Daniel, who had interpreted dreams for his grandfather, and so he is summoned.

Daniel reminds Belshazzar of his grandfather's faith, and warns him about this idolatrous act: *"You have not honored the God who gives you the breath of life and controls your destiny! So God has sent this hand to write this message.... Mene, Mene* [meaning 'numbered'—the days of your reign are over], *Tekel* [meaning 'weighed'—you have been weighed in the balance and not measured up], *and Parsin* [meaning 'divided'—your kingdom will be divided and given to the Medes and Persians]."

That very night Belshazzar is killed. And Darius the Mede takes over the kingdom.

Daniel thrives under Darius' rule and is given favor and power. This creates jealousy, and a plan is hatched to trick Darius into issuing an irrevocable law for 30 days that forbids worship and prayer to any god. Daniel ignores it, of course, and is arrested and thrown into a lions' den. But much to Darius' relief, Daniel is discovered alive and well the next morning. His conspirators are themselves thrown into the lions' den and eaten.

Meanwhile, Darius issues another irrevocable law: *"I decree that everyone throughout my kingdom should tremble with fear before the God of Daniel. For he is the living God, and he will endure forever. His kingdom will never be destroyed, and his rule will never end"* (Daniel 6:26).

Focus: Once again, pagan kings—like Nebuchadnezzar and Darius—honor Israel's God, even when the Israelites themselves do not! It reminds us of Jesus' statement to the religious leaders of Israel, during his entry into Jerusalem when the crowds are praising him as Israel's Messiah, that even if the crowds were silenced, *"the stones along the road would burst into cheers!"* (Luke 19:40). No matter what people or nations do to try to stop it—or what the Church does to mess it up—the fact is that God will become King of the whole creation, through Jesus, and *"every knee [will] bow, in heaven and on earth and under the earth, and every tongue confess that Jesus Christ is Lord, to the glory of God the Father"* (Philippians 2:10–11).

Prayer: Lord, what a wonderful story of your power to save your people, and your authority over the rulers of the earth. We affirm Darius' decree that you are the living God who endures forever. Your Kingdom will never be destroyed and your rule will never end! Amen.

August 30

> Key Text: I saw someone like a son of man coming with the
> clouds of heaven. He approached the Ancient One and was
> led into his presence. He was given authority, honor, and
> sovereignty over all the nations of the world, so that people of
> every race and nation and language would obey him. His rule is
> eternal—it will never end. His kingdom will never be destroyed.
> (Daniel 7:13–14)

Daniel now recalls an earlier dream, during the first year of King Belshazzar's reign in Babylon. It is similar in form to Nebuchadnezzar's dream in chapter 2, where apocalyptic imagery of beasts representing kings opposed to the God of Heaven are brought to nothing by him.

Here, in chapter 7, more beasts appear out of the sea when it is churned by a great storm blowing from every direction (literally "from heaven"). This suggests that the activity of God lies behind even the most troubling and fearful events.

Daniel sees a vision of God in heaven, on a throne with wheels of blazing fire and millions of angels attending him. The scene is a courtroom. As the *"Ancient One"* sits down to judge, the court begins its session and the books are opened, containing the facts of history. During this vision, one of the most important moments in the book of Daniel occurs: *"I saw someone like a son of man coming with the clouds of heaven. He approached the Ancient One and was led into his presence. He was given authority, honor, and sovereignty over all the nations of the world, so that people of every race and nation and language would obey him. His rule is eternal—it will never end. His kingdom will never be destroyed"* (Daniel 7:13–14).

Daniel is describing a heavenly being who is worthy and able to rule over the Kingdom of God. As such, he is sovereign over all people, nations and powers, and will reign forever. This is important to note because Jesus almost certainly identifies with this heavenly *son of man*. His favorite reference to himself is as *"son of man,"* which simply means, human. But Jews who knew the book of Daniel would have understood the reference: Jesus was referring to himself as the *heavenly son of man* from Daniel.

For example, in Mark 14, Jesus is arrested and brought before the Jewish High Council to find evidence to execute him: *"Then the high priest* asked him, 'Are you the Messiah, the Son of the Blessed One?' Jesus said, 'I AM. And you will see the Son of Man seated in the place of power at God's right hand and coming on the clouds of heaven'" (Mark 14:61–62).

When Jesus identifies himself with Daniel's dream, he proclaims himself to be Israel's Messiah. But more than that: He is the divine Son who comes from heaven to become human and rule as King forever in the New Creation.

Another earlier vision, during the reign of Belshazzar, is presented in chapter 8. It is a fuller and broader picture of the struggles that Daniel speaks to as a prophet. The vision goes beyond what Daniel can see "on the ground," to reveal these events as part of a cosmic struggle between the kingdoms of this world and the Kingdom that God is establishing. A two-horned ram is seen, representing the kings of Mede and Persia, and a single-horned goat, representing the coming power of Greece by Alexander the Great. The growing conflict between these powerful nations, and their ultimate fates, is a picture of the fate of all earthly kingdoms, except for that of the Most High God. The description of what nations do to one another—especially the terrible blasphemy of the Assyrian king, Antiochus Epiphanes, who commits blasphemous acts against the Temple of God—reveals the nature of evil, showing how in its pride and falsehood, it destroys human life and opposes God. It shall be like this to the end!

Hope is seen, however, in the midst of the chaos of history. While history books focus on the events of great empires, the Bible focuses on Israel and its mission—and more importantly, on the faithfulness of God to help them achieve it. In chapter 9, Daniel reveals that he has learned from the prophet Jeremiah that Israel must suffer exile for 70 years for her sins. This moves Daniel to a heartfelt prayer of repentance on behalf of the nation: *"O Lord, hear. O Lord, forgive. O Lord, listen and act! For your own sake, do not delay, O my God, for your people and your city bear your name"* (Daniel 9:19).

Focus: Daniel's prayer of confession is a model of humility, and a testament to God's amazing grace: *"O Lord, we and our kings, princes, and ancestors are covered with shame because we have sinned against you. But the Lord our God is merciful and forgiving, even though we have rebelled against him"* (Daniel 9:8–9).

Prayer: Lord, we join our prayers with those of Daniel, confessing our personal and national sins, and asking for your mercy. We are grateful to know the secret of the heavenly son of man—it is Jesus, who is given authority, honor, and sovereignty over all the nations of the world. Come soon, Lord Jesus! Amen.

Day 244   Daniel 10–12

August 31

> Key Text: Only I, Daniel, saw this vision. The men with me saw nothing, but they were suddenly terrified and ran away to hide. So I was left there all alone to see this amazing vision. (Daniel 10:7–8)

In the final chapters of Daniel, he shares a remarkable and life-changing vision which came during the third year of the reign of King Cyrus of Persia.

Daniel is with others, perhaps on a spiritual retreat, when the vision occurs: *"I looked up and saw a man dressed in linen clothing, with a belt of pure gold around his waist. His body looked like a precious gem. His face flashed like lightning, and his eyes flamed like torches. His arms and feet shone like polished bronze, and his voice roared like a vast multitude of people"* (Daniel 10:5–6).

"Vision" may be an inadequate description of what happens. He is not asleep and it doesn't occur in his imagination; it is more like a visitation. Daniel's friends do not see the man, but are suddenly frightened and run. Daniel himself becomes weak and passes out.

Some believe that Daniel has been visited by the pre-incarnate Christ, who is visibly present but not physically incarnate. Daniel would have considered him to be, in some way, the presence of the Lord.

Whatever the case, Daniel is awakened by another being who lifts him, trembling, to his feet. It turns out to be an angel. The angel tells Daniel that he is very precious to the Lord. His humble prayers for understanding have been heard in heaven and the angel has come in response.

However—and this is very intriguing—the angel has been *"blocked"* from coming for twenty-one days by the *"spirit prince of the kingdom of Persia."* He says that the archangel Michael was sent to help him, and is even now still fighting the spirit prince. After that battle is over, *"the spirit prince of the kingdom of Greece will come"* (Daniel 10:13–21).

What this reveals to Daniel is that God's people on earth and the angels of heaven are deeply involved together in one and the same conflict.

458

In other words, earthly conflicts have analogues in the spiritual realm—they are also cosmic conflicts. Dark spiritual forces, opposed to the reign and rule of God, stir up wickedness in the minds of human beings who are receptive. They are agitated to oppose the Lord and his people and to destroy goodness, beauty, love and truth. So angels are not only messengers of the Lord, they are also *"patrons and guardians of communities and nations, and possibly of individuals on earth."* (Ronald S. Wallace)

The connection between the conflicts in heaven and on earth is a key insight into how the Bible understands human history in a fallen universe. Occasionally evil breaks out in such irrational and horrific ways on earth that even secular people use the word *evil,* for there is no other word to describe it. Evil has demonic contours that are recognizable, if not rational.

Daniel's experience reveals how the angels depend upon human intercession in their conflicts with evil spirits, and that the angels in turn are our *"patrons and guardians on earth."*

With this perspective in view, the prophecy of what is to come in Israel's near future, as outlined in chapters 11 and 12, takes on a far more serious and cosmic perspective. The prophetic view of history, as we have noted before, sees in the present struggle an anticipation of the Final Struggle at the end of history. Thankfully, this struggle does not end in death, but in life—the ultimate triumph of the Kingdom of God in history.

Focus: The book of Daniel gives us a peek "behind the curtain" of history that is quite riveting. Its portrayal of the struggles on earth having direct correlation to struggles in heaven offers a holistic view of reality, both spiritual and material. For many, the Enlightenment's assault on Christianity has effectively discredited the supernatural, as a childlike myth to explain life before science gave us the grown-up truth. Science is our new religion, and scientists the new priesthood. Ironically, the evidence of science itself is making the materialistic critique of Christianity look like a myth. It appears that Daniel's visions are on to something!

Prayer: Lord, the perspective of Daniel about the connection of the spiritual and material realms in our struggle with evil is chilling. There is something much bigger going on than we understand. We thank you, Lord, for the invisible presence of your heavenly host to protect us on earth. And we pray that the angel forces will defeat the demonic realm in its opposition to you and your creation. May your Kingdom come, and will be done on earth as it is in heaven. Amen!

Day 245   Hosea 1–3

September 1

> Key Text: "I will make you my wife forever, showing you righteousness and justice, unfailing love and compassion. I will be faithful to you and make you mine, and you will finally know me as the Lord." (Hosea 2:19–20)

The prophet Hosea is the first of what are called the "minor prophets." As with the "major prophets," this designation has to do with the length of the books, not their importance.

The prophet Hosea ministered before the exile, during the reigns of the last six kings of Israel, the northern kingdom, and four kings in Judah, the southern kingdom. This meant that he had a broad geographical audience for his very unusual calling: *"When the Lord first began speaking to Israel through Hosea, he said to him, 'Go and marry a prostitute, so that some of her children will be conceived in prostitution. This will illustrate how Israel has acted like a prostitute by turning against the Lord and worshiping other gods'"* (Hosea 1:2).

If you are shocked and offended by this action, then you have gotten the point. It was meant to show what Israel had done and how God felt about her serial unfaithfulness with the pagan nations around her.

Hosea marries a prostitute named Gomer. Yes, Gomer. She bears three children, one through Hosea, and two through other lovers. The second child was named Lo-ruhamah, meaning "not loved," and the name of the third, Lo-ammi, means "not my people."

Hosea quickly mentions here that the judgment of exile is coming, but one day the Lord will bring his people back to himself in the land. And then the children's names will change to *"My people"* and *"The ones I love"* (Hosea 1:10–11).

But that does not diminish the pain the Lord feels now as Israel ignores her marriage vows and continues to prostitute herself by idolatry. She gives herself to any god in exchange *"for clothing of wool and linen, and for olive oil and drinks."* Not until she can find no more willing partners does she return to her husband, the Lord God.

God's heart has been broken and humiliated, so consequences will follow: *"I will punish her for all those times when she burned incense to her images of Baal, when she put on her earrings and jewels and went out to look for her lovers but forgot all about me"* (Hosea 2:13).

Nevertheless, God still loves her and will win her back: *"She will give herself to me there, as she did long ago when she was young, when I freed her from her captivity in Egypt."*

Hosea demonstrates amazing humility (and obedience) by acting out this drama of redemption through marriage to his unfaithful wife Gomer. As the people watch—and cringe—at how Gomer treats Hosea by prostituting herself, they are hit with the raw footage of how they are treating God by their idolatry. And how faithful God is to his people, nonetheless. Despite her sin, God promises: *"I will make you my wife forever, showing you righteousness and justice, unfailing love and compassion. I will be faithful to you and make you mine, and you will finally know me as the Lord"* (Hosea 2:19–20).

Focus: God's "unfailing love and faithfulness" to Israel, a phase repeated throughout the prophets, is expressive of the Covenant agreement he made with Israel through Moses way back in the book of Exodus. The prophet Hosea's story shows how this Covenant was more than a legal document; it was a marriage license, a pledge of love and faithfulness.

The so-called "angry, vengeful God of the Old Testament" reflects a complete misunderstanding of the story. As we have seen, God's anger is the jealous passion of a betrayed lover. His judgment is his fierce "NO!" to all that undermines his beloved creation. Its purpose is not *destruction,* but *reconstruction.* Or to use the analogy of marriage, it is for the purpose of reconciliation. God will not be deterred from his fierce love. He will do whatever is necessary to win back his beloved. Christ, hanging on the cross, declares how far God was willing to go. In other words, Jesus is God's fulfillment of his Covenant Promise to bless the world. As the Gospel of John says of Jesus: *"He was full of unfailing love and faithfulness"* (John 1:14).

Prayer: Lord, we are humbled by your faithfulness to us. We are so grateful that you have dealt with your righteous anger toward us, not by giving us what we deserved, but by graciously bearing within yourself the pain and sorrow of unrequited love. Amen.

September 2

> Key Text: "Leave Israel alone, because she is married to idolatry. When the rulers of Israel finish their drinking, off they go to find some prostitutes. They love shame more than honor. So a mighty wind will sweep them away. Their sacrifices to idols will bring them shame." (Hosea 4:17–19)

The most striking feature of the book of Hosea is its willingness to speak of God's relationship with his people as that of a husband with his wife, rather than a king and his subjects or a master and his servants. This perspective frames Israel's idolatry not so much as religious perversion, which it is, but as the betrayal of love and commitment. Sins against love are particularly painful, because they violate a relationship, not just break a rule.

As such, the healing process requires more than a quick "I'm sorry," or a hasty promise not to do it again. It requires genuine sorrow and deep repentance, along with a change of behavior. The rest of Hosea probes into the details of Israel's sin against the Lord, and then points the way back to a restored relationship.

Chapter 4 makes the claim that Israel is "married to idolatry." Idol worship itself involved drunkenness, rampant sexual immorality with Temple prostitutes, and the breaking of many other of the commandments of the Lord, including lying, killing, and stealing.

Priests are singled out as more culpable than the people. They have led the people into idolatry by their example. They encourage sin so that the people will bring more food offerings, which the priests eat. *"So the priests are glad when the people sin!"* (Hosea 4:8).

The fact is, longing after idols has made the people stupid: *"They ask a piece of wood for advice! They think a stick can tell them the future!"* (Hosea 4:12).

Chapter 5 outlines how the people's sin has caused God to react: *"The leaders of Judah have become like thieves. So I will pour my anger on them like a waterfall. The people of Israel will be crushed and broken by my judgment because they are determined to worship idols"* (Hosea 5:10–11).

In chapter 6, Hosea begs the people to return to the Lord. Though the Lord has injured his people, he will bandage their wounds and heal them, if they are willing. He has sent his prophets to speak to them—convict them if necessary—but their response has been nil or short-lived.

A harvest of punishment is awaiting Judah and Israel: *"I want you to show love, not offer sacrifices. I want you to know me more than I want burnt offerings. But like Adam, you broke my covenant and betrayed my trust. ... O Judah, a harvest of punishment is also waiting for you, though I wanted to restore the fortunes of my people"* (Hosea 6:6–7,11).

Focus: There are many metaphors given in the Old Testament by which we understand the relationship of God with his people: he is a king to his subjects; a warrior on behalf of his people; a shepherd to his sheep; a Savior to the lost—to name a few. But no metaphor is more striking and deeply personal than God as a husband to his wife. In a similar manner, no relationship on earth is better able to express our relationship to God than the marriage of a man and woman.

In the New Testament book of Ephesians, the apostle Paul says to married couples that a husband should love his wife as Christ loved the church and gave himself for it. And a wife should respond to her husband's self-giving love by respecting him and trusting him to take responsibility for her and the family (see Ephesians 5:21–33). Christ is the example for both the husband and wife, for he sacrificed himself for the sake of us all, in submission to the will of the Father. As Paul admits, *"This is a great mystery, but it is an illustration of the way Christ and the church are one."*

Prayer: *Lord, we see your broken heart as you confront your unfaithful people. We see that you want our love and not just outward religiosity. Forgive us for our failure to understand that at the heart of creation and redemption is a longing for relationship. Amen.*

Day 247   Hosea 7–8

September 3

Key Text: "Worshiping foreign gods has sapped their strength, but they don't even know it. ... Their arrogance testifies against them, yet they don't return to the Lord their God or even try to find him. ... The people of Israel have sold themselves—sold themselves to many lovers." (Hosea 7:9–10; 8:9)

Hosea has been called by God to a difficult life—a marriage to an unfaithful prostitute that is an enacted parable of Israel's unfaithfulness to God. Hosea's humiliation and anger at his unfaithful wife is God's humiliation and anger at Israel's idolatry.

We move now from drama to narrative. God speaks to his people about his pain at their unfaithfulness through Hosea: *"I want to heal Israel, but its sins are too great. … Its people don't realize that I am watching them. Their sinful deeds are all around them, and I see them all"* (Hosea 7:1–2).

It must greatly pain God to watch us being unfaithful to him. Like video tapes from a private detective hired to spy on a suspected spouse, the visual evidence breaks through mere suspicion, piercing the heart. But unlike us, God cannot hide in denial, or be fooled by naiveté. He sees everything we do, and feels it.

What does he see? Spiritual adulterers *"always aflame with lust."* To describe the nature of Israel's sin, Hosea piles metaphor upon metaphor: The people have made themselves *"as worthless as a half-baked cake"*; they are *"as useless as a crooked bow"*; they *"lie among the nations like an old discarded pot"*; they are like a wild donkey in heat, *"looking for a mate."*

At the root of it all is a broken promise. The people *"have broken my covenant and revolted against my law"* (Hosea 8:1). By walking away from the Covenant and Law, which provided moral and spiritual boundaries, the people have become unhinged and swept along by their lusts. These currents have taken them to places that are self-defeating and hurtful to others, not to mention God himself.

Idolatry has taken a toll on Israel. Hosea says: *"Worshiping foreign gods has sapped their strength, but they don't even know it. … Their arrogance testifies against them, yet they don't return to the Lord their God or even try to find him. … The people of Israel have sold themselves—sold themselves to many lovers"* (Hosea 7:9–10; 8:9).

With any addiction, the addict has lost control and become a slave to the behavior they have turned to for comfort or happiness. No appeal to change their behavior will work; no promise they make is believable; no forgiveness offered will create a change of heart. At this point, the only hope is for tough love, through intervention, to enforce the pain of consequences. This is the meaning of God's judgment.

The Lord says: *"I will hold my people accountable for their sins, and I will punish them. They will return to Egypt"* (Hosea 8:13). The reference to Egypt, of course, is a reminder of their former suffering as slaves under Pharaoh. After all this time, and the countless manifestations of God's provision, power, protection and forgiveness, it is as if Israel has returned to place where she started.

> **Focus:** To come "full circle" is not a good thing if the place where you started was slavery. But that is the story of Israel. What has this story told us so far? It has told us, as Tim Keller puts it, that *"our sin is far worse than we ever imagined, but God's grace is far greater than we could ever have hoped for."* This is the Gospel. We see it clearly in the Old Testament. All that's missing is the resolution to the mystery: How will God, once and for all, resolve the problem of sin and death so that his ancient Promise can be fulfilled? Any guesses?

> **Prayer:** *Lord, these are sobering thoughts. How tragic for Israel to go all the way back to the starting line. How heartbreaking for any of us to forsake your grace and return to being slaves to sin. We are amazed at how much you put up with and yet remain faithful to us. Your grace and mercy are amazing, even in the pain you allow to wake us from our spiritual sleep. Thank you for not giving up! Amen.*

Day 248 — Hosea 9–11

September 4

> **Key Text:** "When Israel was a child, I loved him, and I called my son out of Egypt. But the more I called to him, the farther he moved from me, offering sacrifices to the images of Baal and burning incense to idols. I myself taught Israel how to walk, leading him along by the hand. But he doesn't know or even care that it was I who took care of him." (Hosea 11:1–3)

Hosea writes in chapter 9 that *"the time of Israel's punishment has come; the day of payment is here. Soon Israel will know this all too well."* The nation has defiled itself by repeated unfaithfulness to God, and will lose everything God has given—her land, identity and fruitfulness as a nation and culture.

Hosea says that the Lord remembers when Israel was a young nation, like fresh grapes and ripe figs. But soon after the euphoria of her deliverance from Egypt, she abandoned the Lord: *"They deserted me for Baal-peor, giving themselves to that shameful idol. Soon they became vile, as vile as the god they worshiped"* (Hosea 9:10).

As we have noted, Baal worship was vile indeed. Its frenzied worship was unhinged with *"horrendous and repulsive sexual perversity,"* including bestiality and the burning of children as an offering to Baal. All of the boundaries God gave in the commandments were crossed. The people behaved like animals. They no longer reflected the image of God in their behavior.

It does not take much imagination to understand how such worship damaged the people's souls, and turned their hearts away from God. As a result, Israel will wander as lost in the world: *"My God will reject the people of Israel because they will not listen or obey. They will be wanderers, homeless among the nations"* (Hosea 9:17).

Chapter 10 is a series of observations and warnings. Israel is prosperous in her rebellion, rationalizing that God doesn't care about her idolatry, but they are wrong. They think that having a king like other nations will benefit them, but it doesn't. They trust in foreign idols, believing they will protect them, but they can't. They create political alliances with foreign nations for safety, but to no avail.

Hosea says that Israel's failure to trust God, and her arrogant breaking of the Covenant and commandments, are coming down upon her head. The people will experience the terror of war.

Israel is proving the adage that we don't break God's commandments; they break us.

So the Lord says, *"I will call out the armies of the nations to punish you for your multiplied sins"* (Hosea 10:10).

Chapter 11 is a sorrowful remembrance of Israel as a child: *"When Israel was a child, I loved him, and I called my son out of Egypt. But the more I called to him, the farther he moved from me, offering sacrifices to the images of Baal and burning incense to the idols"* (Hosea 11:1–2).

But again we hear that God will not give up on his people. Yes, judgment is coming. Painful consequences will wake people up to the wrong they have done, and will move them to repent and return to God their lover: *"Oh, how can I give you up, Israel? How can I let you go? … My heart is torn within me, and my compassion overflows. No, I will not unleash my fierce anger. I will not completely destroy Israel, for I am God and not a mere mortal. I am the Holy One living among you, and I will not come to destroy. For someday the people will follow me. I, the Lord, will roar like a lion. And when I roar, my people will return trembling from the west"* (Hosea 11:8–10).

Focus: One of the important contributions of the prophets is to give us insight into God's feelings about his prodigal world. We may be surprised to learn how deeply he feels, even allowing for the fact that God speaks through the words and personalities of the various prophets. Who could have known how deeply our sins wound him? Those who look at God through the lens of philosophy tend to shy away from the idea that anything can really impact God, for if so, it would make him less than perfect. But we cannot deny that the witness of the Old and New Testaments, taken at face value, reveal God to have genuine feelings towards us. He feels love, and therefore he feels anger and jealousy when spurned. Unless we are prepared to dismiss much of the Old Testament witness to God, we must accept the wonderful mystery that God allows himself to have feelings towards us! *"When Israel was a child, I loved him...."* Amazing!

Prayer: *Lord, the story of your people is heartbreaking, but it rings true to what we know of ourselves and this present world. How easily we ignore you and turn to idols. How natural it feels to follow our corrupted passions and then rationalize it as doing what is right for us. Impress upon us how our sins affect you, especially in light of how much you love us. Help us to see clearly how grave a sin it is to reject the true and living God. Amen.*

Day 249   Hosea 12–14

September 5

> Key Text: Return, O Israel, to the Lord your God, for your sins have brought you down. Bring your confessions, and return to the Lord. Say to him, "Forgive all our sins and graciously receive us, so that we may offer you our praises." (Hosea 14:1–2)

The book of Hosea ends with Hosea's messages that address familiar themes. Hosea's heart has been broken by the unfaithfulness of his wife, who has prostituted herself with as many men as she could find. His heartbreak echoes the heartbreak of God over the unfaithfulness of Israel.

In chapter 12, God compares the Nation of Israel's story to the story of Jacob (later renamed Israel in Genesis 35:10), who, from the beginning of his existence, struggled with God and man, and even wrestled with an angel! But where is that struggler now who pleaded for a blessing from God? What has become of the nation?

Israel has forsaken the struggle to be blessed by God, and instead has

467

gone after the soft comforts and easy immorality of the pagan nations. Injustice, cheating, theft, violence, lying—and of course idolatry—all come naturally. The Ten Commandments are a distant memory, a forsaken commitment.

God sent his prophets to warn the people with many visions and parables, but they did not listen: *"Now they continue to sin by making silver idols, images shaped skillfully with human hands. 'Sacrifice to these,' they cry, 'and kiss the calf idols!' Therefore, they will disappear like the morning mist, like dew in the morning sun, like chaff blown by the wind, like smoke from a chimney"* (Hosea 13:2–3).

The only way back is for Israel to remember her birth as a people. The Lord God delivered her out of Egypt, demonstrating by his mighty power that there is no God but him, and no other savior. He took care of them in the wilderness, but when they had *"eaten and were satisfied,"* they became proud and forgot him.

He had pursued them with numerous attempts to win them back. Finally, God has let them go. He has removed his protection, freeing them to chase after the religious and political novelties that appeal to their pride and lusts.

Now, the consequences are coming, and they will be terrifying: *"They will be killed by an invading army, their little ones dashed to death against the ground, their pregnant women ripped open by swords"* (Hosea 13:16).

But while God lets Israel go, he does not harden his heart toward them. There is an open invitation to return to him: *"Return, O Israel, to the Lord your God, for your sins have brought you down. Bring your confessions, and return to the Lord"* (Hosea 14:1–2).

If they return, he will heal them of their faithlessness: *"...my love will know no bounds, for my anger will be gone forever. I will be to Israel like a refreshing dew from heaven. Israel will blossom like the lily; it will send roots deep into the soil like the cedars in Lebanon"* (Hosea 14:4–5).

Hosea concludes with a final heartfelt plea to Israel from God her lover: *"'O Israel, stay away from idols! I am the one who answers your prayers and cares for you. I am like a tree that is always green; all your fruit comes from me.' Let those who are wise understand these things. Let those with discernment listen carefully. The paths of the Lord are true and right, and righteous people live by walking in them"* (Hosea 14:8–9).

Day 250   Joel

September 6

> Key Text: Let everyone tremble in fear because the day of the Lord is upon us. It is a day of darkness and gloom, a day of thick clouds and deep blackness. Suddenly, like dawn spreading across the mountains, a great and mighty army appears. Nothing like it has been seen before or will ever been seen again. (Joel 2:1–2)

The prophet Joel is a bit of a mystery. Other than the fact that Joel is the son of Pethual, we know nothing for certain of who he is or when he prophesied. One thing we do know—his message is riveting.

It arises out of a horrible crisis in the southern kingdom of Judah, where a swarming locust plague of unprecedented severity has devastated the agriculture of the region: *"A vast army of locusts has invaded my land, a terrible army too numerous to count. Its teeth are like lions' teeth, its fangs like those of a lioness. … Despair, all you farmers! Wail, all you vine growers! Weep, because the wheat and barley—all the crops of the field—are ruined. The grapevines have dried up, and the fig trees have withered. The pomegranate trees, palm trees, and apple trees—all the fruit trees—have dried up. And the people's joy has dried up with them"* (Joel 1:6, 11–12).

Historical accounts of swarming locusts report that they can contain

469

up to ten billion insects, covering 2,000 square miles. They can block out the sun as they travel, with a noise that has been likened to a jet engine. When they die, they give off a revolting stench, and their bodies breed typhus and other diseases. When the carcasses are burned, the fires consume whatever plants remain.

Nothing is left, except fear and famine: *"How the animals moan with hunger! The herds of cattle wander about confused, because they have no pasture. The flocks of sheep and goats bleat in misery. ... Fear grips all the people; every face grows pale with terror"* (Joel 1:18, 2:6).

Joel sees this devastation of locusts as a judgment from God, but it is also a portent of the coming great and terrible "day of the Lord" at the end of history, the day of final judgment and the destruction of sin. He describes the locust swarm as an invading army, and then seamlessly begins speaking of it as a real army of soldiers: *"The Lord is at the head of the column. He leads them with a shout. This is his mighty army, and they follow his orders. The day of the Lord is an awesome, terrible thing. Who can possibly survive?"* (Joel 2:11).

In light of God's imminent judgment of Judah, Joel urges his people to return to the Lord while there is time: *"Return to the Lord your God, for he is merciful and compassionate, slow to get angry and filled with unfailing love"* (Joel 2:13).

In light of the final day of the Lord, the book of Joel serves as a warning for every generation of believers to return to the Lord. But, as with all the Hebrew prophets, Joel sees hope for the future. He says that in the last days, God will pour out his Spirit upon all people: *"Your sons and daughters will prophesy. Your old men will dream dreams, and your young men will see visions. In those days I will pour out my Spirit even on servants—men and women alike"* (Joel 2:28–29).

This prophecy was fulfilled on the Day of Pentecost, as noted by the apostle Peter in Acts 2:16–18. So when we read in Joel about "those days," remember that they are referring to our days.

Focus: Events in nature are often used as metaphors of God's greatness. The psalmist writes that *"the heavens proclaim the glory of God."* Thunder and lightning express his power, as do frightening beasts on land and the huge, mysterious creatures of the sea. For Joel, the terrifying destruction of the locusts speaks of God's judgment. They are an invading army of destruction, like Babylon, and a portent of the final judgment at the end of history. Nature speaks, if only we will listen.

Prayer: Lord, human life has been shaken over and over again by natural disasters, like the plague of locusts. These disasters remind us of the disasters that we ourselves bring about because of greed, lust, anger and the need for power. We look forward to the day when all creation is healed, but until then we rejoice in the promise of Joel—that your Holy Spirit has been poured out into our hearts, empowering us to worship and serve you in the world. Amen.

Day 251   Reflection

September 7

There is no question that the writings of the prophets have contributed to the misperception that the God of the Old Testament is an angry deity who hunts down sinners to condemn and destroy them. The prophets speak for God with language that sometimes is hauntingly beautiful and deeply moving, and other times reflects the common idioms of speech of the time—hyperbole, war taunts, symbolism and dramatic gesture.

It must be admitted that prophetic words can be florid and disturbing, especially to cultures like ours, whose language is more measured and literal. The reader of the prophets has to do some interpretation—understanding first what the words would have meant to the original hearers, and then translating that meaning and emotional impact into our present culture and thought forms.

It sounds complicated, but it is necessary if we want to avoid misleading and sometimes flat-out wrong interpretation. The truth is that we ourselves interpret and translate all the time, even in ordinary conversation with friends. Human communication is filled with cultural references, metaphors, irony, exaggeration, double meanings and so forth—and we understand each other perfectly well.

So when you read the prophets, hear it as God speaking with an ancient Near Eastern accent, within an ancient frame of reference!

As we have noted along the way, God accommodates himself to the limited understanding and experiences of the people he addresses. We might think of it as a parent who speaks to her children in age-appropriate ways at different stages of their lives. To this point, Martin Luther, the Reformation leader, once wrote that when God speaks to us, he lisps, meaning that he talks "baby talk" to us.

The New Testament book of Hebrews reflects this process: *"Long ago God spoke many times and in many ways to our ancestors through the prophets. And now in these final days, he has spoken to us through his Son"* (Hebrews 1:1–2). The apostle Paul adds that with the coming of Jesus, a mystery has been made known that was not understood before: *"As I briefly wrote earlier, God himself revealed his mysterious plan to me. As you read what I have written, you will understand my insight into this plan regarding Christ. God did not reveal it to previous generations, but now by his Spirit he has revealed it to his holy apostles and prophets"* (Ephesians 3:3–5).

But even though Christ makes God's plan of salvation much clearer to us than Abraham, Moses, or King David ever understood, there still is much we do not know. Paul wrote that our present understanding is partial: *"When I was a child, I spoke and thought and reasoned as a child. But when I grew up, I put away childish things. Now we see things imperfectly, like puzzling reflections in a mirror, but then we will see everything with perfect clarity. All that I know now is partial and incomplete, but then I will know everything completely, just as God now knows me completely"* (1 Corinthians 13:11–12).

The important point here is that God wishes to be understood. For this reason, he accommodates himself to each place and time of history, progressively revealing more and more. Age-appropriate can also be taken to mean appropriate to each Age of history.

When we take all these things into consideration, we begin to see that the so-called "Old Testament God of Wrath and Judgment" is the same God of mercy and love who, for the sake of a relationship with us, sent Jesus to take upon himself the judgment for our sin.

***Prayer:** Lord, help us to read the Old Testament with Jesus-colored glasses, so that we may see, starting in the book of Genesis, that you have always acted with love and mercy, and with incredible patience so that we may exist and enjoy fellowship with you forever. May those who avoid you by appealing to the angry-God argument, see in your anger the passion of one who loves them deeply and eternally. Amen!*

September 8

> Key Text: This is what he saw and heard: "The Lord's voice will roar from Zion and thunder from Jerusalem! The lush pastures of the shepherds will dry up; the grass on Mount Carmel will wither and die." (Amos 1:2)

Amos was a shepherd who lived in Judea during the reign of King Uzziah in Judah, and of King Jeroboam II in Israel. When called by God to be a prophet, he receives this message in a series of visions *"two years before the earthquake."*

Amos hears the Lord's voice: *"The Lord's voice will roar from Zion and thunder from Jerusalem!"*

The visions begin with a message of judgment upon the nations surrounding the Promised Land: Damascus, Gaza, Tyre, Edom, Ammon, Moab, Judah and Israel. As we have seen in the prophetic books already, the nations around Judah and Israel were a constant temptation to them, luring the people into pagan worship and its accompanying social pathologies, including rampant injustice and violence.

God's warning through Amos begins with Damascus: *"The people of Damascus have sinned again and again, and I will not let them go unpunished!"* This declaration of divine intent is repeated as a formula by Amos as he addresses the six pagan nations. In each case, divine intent is revealed by a description of the nation's sins—usually sins against the Israelites—and then the form of punishment God will bring. For example: *"The people of Tyre have sinned again and again, and I will not let them go unpunished! They broke their treaty of brotherhood with Israel, selling whole villages as slaves to Edom. So I will send down fire on the walls of Tyre, and all its fortresses will be destroyed"* (Amos 1:9–10).

These warnings and consequences are consistent with the Old Testament's teaching that God is the Lord and judge of all nations on earth, not just Israel. He will not allow evil to continue unchecked forever.

So again, what is sometimes viewed as a negative message of judgment in the Bible is actually good news, especially for the victims of injustice, violence and bigotry. It reassures them that God does see what happens on earth and that everyone will be held to account.

The loss of fear about the judgment of God has encouraged tyrants throughout history to do evil, thinking they will never answer for their sins.

But remember Psalm 14:1–2: *"Only fools say in their hearts, 'There is no God.' They are corrupt, and their actions are evil; not one of them does good! The Lord looks down from heaven on the entire human race; he looks to see if anyone is truly wise...."*

When Amos finishes his warning to Israel's neighbors, we might think that his message is over, but it is not. He concludes his prophetic warning with God's own people in Judah and Israel, and with the same formulaic statement: they have *"sinned again and again, and I will not let them go unpunished!"* (Amos 2:4).

But their sins are worse, for they are not sins of ignorance as with the pagan nations. They have sinned despite their knowledge of God's will: *"They have rejected the instruction of the Lord, refusing to obey his decrees."* Their society does not reflect the will of God as provided for in the Ten Commandments. As a result, Israel is no different than the pagan societies around them, full of injustice, oppression and immorality.

Through Amos we see the painful irony of Israel's sin. She has become just like the sinful nations who were driven out of the land she inherited from God. Even though God gives her everything necessary for flourishing as a society, she throws it all away in order to be like everyone else, because it is too difficult to be different.

Jesus once said, *"You can enter God's Kingdom only through the narrow gate. The highway to hell is broad, and its gate is wide for the many that choose that way. But the gateway to life is very narrow and the road is difficult, and only a few ever find it"* (Matthew 7:13–14).

Few find it, not because it is hidden, but because it is hard. It is hard to be different.

Focus: God's judgment comes upon the pagan nations because of their brutal and unjust treatment of the poor and defenseless, *again and again.* Israel's culpability is far worse, for they know better. They know what God requires, and that he sees from heaven what the nations do, and holds them accountable. Knowing these things, Israel's sin seems irrational. The truth is, all sin is irrational. It is contrary to God's nature and Law, and it is counterproductive to human well-being. And it inevitably brings God's judgment. He will not let it have the last word on earth, and eventually it will be destroyed forever. So why do individuals, groups and societies continue to sin against the Lord?

> *Prayer: Lord, you have said that judgment begins with the household of faith. Help us, who know your Law, to carefully walk in your ways so that we do not find ourselves condemned—a condemnation made worse by the fact that we know better. Grant us the willingness to be different out of loyalty to you. Amen.*

Day 253   Amos 3–5

September 9

> Key Text: Hate evil and love what is good; turn your courts into true halls of justice. Perhaps even yet the Lord God of Heaven's Armies will have mercy on the remnant of his people.
> (Amos 5:15)

When people don't care, what do they do? They walk away; they fail to get involved or give assistance. The opposite of love is indifference.

On the other hand, people who care get angry with those who betray them, especially when they are people whom they love. Loving parents discipline their children when they rebel. This is Amos' message to God's people: *"Listen to this message that the Lord has spoken against you, O people of Israel and Judah—against the entire family I rescued from Egypt: 'From among all the families on the earth, I have been intimate with you alone. That is why I must punish you for all your sins'"* (Amos 3:1–2).

Amos tells them ahead of time what the Lord is going to do, so that when he does it, they will know that it is the Lord's judgment—not merely circumstances or bad luck. They must understand that through their spiritual rebellion and moral corruption, they have brought this trouble upon themselves. Perhaps then they will repent and return to the Lord.

Israel's moral corruption is public and embarrassing. While mistreating the poor, the wealthy live in beautiful mansions filled with expensive possessions. The women are as corrupt as the men: *"Listen to me, you fat cows living in Samaria, you women who oppress the poor and crush the needy, and who are always calling to your husbands, 'Bring us another drink!'"* (Amos 4:1).

Their moral laziness is rooted in spiritual corruption and hypocrisy: *"'Go ahead and offer sacrifices to the idols at Bethel. Keep on disobeying at Gilgal. Offer sacrifices each morning, and bring your tithes every three*

475

days. Present your bread made with yeast as an offering of thanksgiving. Then give your extra voluntary offerings so you can brag about it everywhere! This is the kind of thing you Israelites love to do,' says the sovereign Lord" (Amos 4:4–5).

Amos points out that God has repeatedly tried to get their attention through his discipline and punishment over the years, but to no avail—the people would not return to him. So Amos sings a "funeral song" to the people: *"The virgin Israel has fallen, never to rise again! She lies abandoned on the ground, with no one to help her up"* (Amos 5:2). She is vulnerable and unprotected—the picture of a nation who, Amos prophesies, will be *"dragged off into exile."* The judgment of exile will be like a fire roaring through Israel, devouring her completely: *"Your gods in Bethel won't be able to quench the flames"* (Amos 5:6).

And yet, God once again extends his gracious invitation to return to him: *"Come back to the Lord and live! … Do what is good and run from evil so that you may live! … Perhaps even yet the Lord God of Heaven's Armies will have mercy on the remnant of his people"* (Amos 5:6,14–15).

What the Lord wants is not *"noisy hymns of praise"* … but *"a mighty flood of justice, an endless river of righteous living"* (Amos 5:23–24).

Focus: Imagine a world washed clean by *"a mighty flood of justice, an endless river of righteous living."* One company that cleans up after disasters advertises its service quite convincingly: "Just as if it never happened." This is God's redeeming vision for his fallen creation. The New Creation will be constantly refreshed by a river of righteousness—a flood of justice. Isn't that what we long for today? God put that longing in our hearts because it is an echo of his own character. We want to live in such a world, and God is going to bring it about in the end. In the meantime, he calls his people to live this way as best we can in the present fallen world.

Prayer: Lord, the Old Testament prophets reveal you to be the Hound of Heaven. You never stop pursuing us, trying to get our attention so that we can be reconciled to you. Your faithfulness, in the face of our sinfulness, is amazing. We are so grateful that, through Jesus, you have gone all the way to open the door to eternal life and to flood that life with justice and righteousness. Amen.

September 10

> Key Text: What sorrow awaits you who lounge in luxury in Jerusalem, and you who feel secure in Samaria! (Amos 6:1)

Careless self-indulgence can ruin a life, or even the life of a nation. So says Amos to the people of Israel: *"What sorrow awaits you who lounge in luxury in Jerusalem, and you who feel secure in Samaria!"*

Financial good times have made the Israelites spiritually lazy and morally self-indulgent. They think that God has given them their wealth and, therefore, he must be okay with them. But the Lord says, *"How terrible for you who sprawl on ivory beds and lounge on your couches, eating the meat of tender lambs from the flock and of choice calves fattened in the stall. You sing trivial songs to the sound of the harp and fancy yourselves to be great musicians like David. You drink wine by the bowlful and perfume yourselves with fragrant lotions. You care nothing about the ruin of your nation. Therefore, you will be the first to be led away as captives. Suddenly, all your parties will end"* (Amos 6:4–7).

The Lord despises the arrogance and indifference of Israel and so he will give Jerusalem, and everything in it, to their enemies.

We learn in what follows that Amos has been earnestly praying for the people, asking God to delay his judgment. Chapter 7 recounts two visions of disaster coming upon the people. The first is a swarm of locusts over the land, and the second is a great fire that burns up the depths of the sea and then devours the land. In each case, Amos intercedes by praying, *"O Sovereign Lord, please stop or we will not survive."* Each time, God hears Amos' prayer and relents.

But then Amos is given a third vision. He sees the Lord standing beside a wall that has been built using a plumb line. He is using a plumb line to see if it is straight. The Lord tells Amos, *"I will test my people with this plumb line. I will no longer ignore all their sins. The pagan shrines of your ancestors will be ruined, and the temples of Israel will be destroyed; I will bring the dynasty of King Jeroboam to a sudden end"* (Amos 7:8–9).

Amos' prophecy reached King Jeroboam, but was reported as a plot against the king by Amos himself, instead of a word from the Lord: *"What [Amos] is saying is intolerable. He is saying, 'Jeroboam will soon be*

477

killed, and the people of Israel will be sent away into exile.'"

So Jeroboam's corrupt priest Amaziah tries to push Amos out of Israel, telling him to go and prophesy somewhere else! Amaziah seems to be saying that if Amos wants to earn a living preaching, he might make more money elsewhere.

But Amos says, *"I'm not a professional prophet, and I was never trained to be one. I'm just a shepherd.... But the Lord called me away from my flock and told me, 'Go and prophesy to my people in Israel'"* (Amos 7:14–15).

So Amos stays and continues to warn them of what is to come because of their unrepentance: *"The people of Israel will certainly become captives in exile, far from their homeland"* (Amos 7:17).

> **Focus:** Wealth and ease can be the worst things that ever happen to us if they lead us to conclude that God must think we're special. It's a short journey from presumption to corruption, where we live as though the rules don't apply to us. We must take heed to Jesus' warning about wealth—that it has a power over us and can become our master. And no one, Jesus says, can serve two masters. The quickest way for us to be free from wealth's power is to be generous to the needy out of love for God.

> **Prayer:** *We see, O Lord, how easily wealth and success can diminish our sense of spiritual need. When things are good, we assume that you must be pleased with us, and so we continue along without any honest self-examination, even to the point where we drop worship and prayer altogether. May your Holy Spirit keep us alert to the lure of riches, and ever mindful of our need of humility and faith, in the good times as well as the hard times. Amen.*

Day 255   Amos 8–9

September 11

> Key Text: Listen to this, you who rob the poor and trample down the needy! You can't wait for the Sabbath day to be over and the religious festivals to end so you can get back to cheating the helpless. (Amos 8:4–5)

Reading the prophets is like beginning to listen to classical music. At first, you hear only the main melodies and shifts of tempo and mood. Listen again and again, and you begin to catch the variations on themes that you missed and perhaps more of the instrumental voices. Become a student of music and all the subtleties are opened to you. What once was merely a nice tune played by a bunch of instruments, becomes a seamless, multi-layered work of brilliant music that grabs your mind and heart.

Now, it's true that most readers wouldn't consider the themes of idolatry, judgment and redemption, played over and over again, to be "nice tunes." However, taken together, the prophets present a brilliant and compelling message about a forsaken and heartbroken God, who persistently pursues his lost people in order to bring them home. He will not give up and allow his creation be lost forever in its sin.

The main prophetic themes and variations on those themes provide a peek into God's heart, and are the outline of what we might call the Gospel in the Old Testament. Amos illustrates that point.

In chapter 8, God speaks to the people through Amos to establish the facts of their rebellion and sin. They have not kept the Covenant they made to worship God alone and they have not lived lives pleasing to him. The Lord gives Amos a vision of a basket filled with ripe fruit, and tells him that Israel is ripe for punishment. Why? Because the people routinely *"rob the poor and trample down the needy!"* They can't wait for the Sabbath day to be over and the religious festivals to end so that they can get back to cheating the helpless: *"You measure out grain with dishonest measures and cheat the buyer with dishonest scales. And you mix the grain you sell with chaff swept from the floor. Then you enslave poor people for one piece of silver or a pair of sandals"* (Amos 8:5–6).

Because the Lord is holy, and the whole creation belongs to him, he cannot and will not tolerate injustice, especially among his called people: *"I will never forget the wicked things you have done! The earth will tremble for your deeds, and everyone will mourn."*

To convince his people that they are lost, God will send a famine to the land—not a famine of bread or water but *"of hearing the words of the Lord. People will stagger from sea to sea and wander from border to border searching for the word of the Lord, but they will not find it"* (Amos 8:11–12). They will be left only with their mute idols, and those idols will tip over and break apart, never to rise again. They will be spiritually adrift with no prophet to bring them God's word.

The nation will suffer the consequences of defeat and exile—the loss of their national identity, their personal possessions and their homeland. Everything will be gone. However, though God will destroy the nation, he promises: *"I will never completely destroy the family of Israel.... In that day I will restore the fallen house of David. I will repair its damaged walls. From the ruins I will rebuild it and restore its former glory. ... I will bring my exiled people of Israel back from distant lands"* (Amos 9:8, 11, 14).

So once again, we hear the great themes of the prophets: The people have forsaken God and pursued idols. Practicing idolatry has led to grievous and unrepentant moral corruption. The behavior must be stopped, so terrible consequences will follow, but God will not let his people go.

The final movement of the symphony of Israel's story, and indeed the story of the whole creation, will be the joyous celebration of forgiveness and new life in Christ.

Focus: We've all heard the saying, "ripe for punishment." Did you know that it came from the book of Amos? In a vision, God shows Amos a basket filled with ripe fruit. The fruit represents the nation of Israel, which is "ripe for punishment." The figure of speech suggests that sin has grown so "ripe" that God must act before it does even greater damage. A parent intervenes, for example, in a dispute between two children when the teasing and hitting reaches a certain threshold, and the screaming hits a certain frequency! Left unchecked, damage is certain to follow with many tears and protests of injury. Discipline hurts too, but the purpose of this pain is to stop greater pain. As we have said all long, God's discipline is an act of tough love.

Prayer: Lord, we are surprised that the discordant, chaotic noise of human sinfulness has not caused you to put your hand over your ears and walk away in disgust. You know the very worst about us, yet you still pursue us to win us back so that we may enjoy eternal life together in sweet harmony. You are amazing, and we praise your holy name! Amen.

Day 256   Obadiah

September 12

> Key Text: This is the vision that the Sovereign Lord revealed to Obadiah concerning the land of Edom. (Obadiah 1:1)

Blood is thicker than water, right? Not always, at least not in the ancient story of Isaac's twin sons, Jacob and Esau. You may remember from Genesis 25 through 36 that Jacob and Esau fought as brothers, and that Jacob came out the winner because of his unique gifts of deception and manipulation. Not surprisingly, their descendants—the nations of Israel (Jacob) and Edom (Esau)—didn't exactly get along.

This is not too unusual in families where old hurts are never forgotten or forgiven. But in the case of these two families, the conflict boils over at times in hateful ways. One such time is during the wilderness wanderings after God has delivered Israel from slavery in Egypt. In Numbers 20:14–21, Moses sends ambassadors to the king of Edom, humbly asking permission to travel through their land, being careful to protect their fields and vineyards and not drink their well water. But the king angrily refuses and mobilizes an army against them.

Fast-forward to the era of the prophets, and we find Edom acting hatefully against Israel again. This time, they commit treachery by supporting an enemy nation who has invaded Israel and then is gloating over her defeat.

This ancient family feud is the context for the writing of the little-known prophet Obadiah, who is sent by God with judgment against Edom: *"Because of the violence you did to your close relatives in Israel, you will be filled with shame and destroyed forever. When they were invaded, you stood aloof, refusing to help them. Foreign invaders carried off their wealth and cast lots to divide up Jerusalem, but you acted like one of Israel's enemies. ... You should not have rejoiced when the people of Judah suffered such misfortune"* (Obadiah 1:10–12).

Obadiah warns them that their treachery against Israel will come back to bite them: *"All your allies will turn against you. They will help to chase you from your land. They will promise you peace while plotting to deceive and destroy you. Your trusted friends will set traps for you, and you won't even know about it"* (Obadiah 1:7).

By going against Israel, Edom has gone against God's chosen nation. (You will remember from Genesis 12 that Israel was chosen to be the nation from which the Messiah would come to bless the nations of the earth.) Therefore, *"the people of Israel will come back to reclaim their inheritance"* (Obadiah 1:17), while Edom will lose its national identity and disappear from history.

The subplot of Jacob and Esau's conflict over the generations, and how it eventually destroys Edom, illustrates the tragic consequences of unresolved sin, in families and in nations. It is also a microcosm of the larger conflict of the whole world with its Creator. But thankfully, this conflict has a resolution. God himself will bear the penalty of the world's sin. He will make things right. Israel's exile will end, as will the exile of the world from God. In that day, as Obadiah strongly concludes his message: *"The Lord himself will be king!"*

Focus: Sometimes I think the greatest invention possible would be a chemical in the water supplies of the world that causes people to forget the past! Most conflicts today are enflamed by ancient feuds between peoples and nations who have long memories of past injustices, real or imagined. Over the generations, those injustices have fueled hostile acts of revenge which become vicious circles of revenge, without end. The only possible end to this vicious circle—short of my imagined chemical in the water—is confession and forgiveness. It is true of nations as well as of families, friends, neighbors, and even spouses. There is a great difference between human judgment as a vehicle to inflict pain, and God's judgment as a means to stop evil and bring about reconciliation. Peacemaking is God's work, and so as Jesus said, *"Blessed are the peacemakers, for they shall be called children of God."*

Prayer: *Father, we look forward to that great day when everything is put back in order—when you will reign as king and all the nations of the earth are peacefully united in worshiping and serving you, the one true God and Creator. In the meantime, Lord, help us to be peacemakers, promise keepers, and truth tellers in our world of conflict, treachery and deceit. Amen.*

Day 257   Jonah

September 13

> **Key Text:** "That is why I ran away to Tarshish! I knew that you are a merciful and compassionate God, slow to get angry and filled with unfailing love. You are eager to turn back from destroying people. Just kill me now, Lord! I'd rather be dead than alive if what I predicted will not happen." (Jonah 4:2–3)

Jonah is probably the best-known prophet in popular culture today, but usually as a myth or cartoon. The book of Jonah, however, is not a children's story. It gives us unique insight into God's compassion, even toward the worst kinds of people.

The story proceeds as follows: God directs the prophet Jonah to go Nineveh, the great city of the cruel Assyrian nation and Israel's hated enemy. Why? To warn the city of God's coming judgment for its wickedness and to call the people to repentance.

But Jonah hates the Assyrians and wants no part in their possible repentance and avoidance of God's judgment. So he *"got up and went in the opposite direction to get away from the Lord"* (Jonah 1:3).

While Jonah is on a ship headed for Tarshish, a violent storm arises and threatens to break the ship apart: *"Fearing for their lives, the desperate sailors shouted to their gods for help and threw the cargo overboard to lighten the ship."*

Jonah finally acknowledges that he is Hebrew and worships *"the God of heaven, who made the sea and the land."* But he is presently running away from God. So, fearing that they would all die for Jonah's sin, the crew throws him into the sea.

However, *"the Lord had arranged for a great fish to swallow Jonah. And Jonah was inside the fish for three days and three nights"* (Jonah 1:17).

While inside the fish, Jonah prays to the Lord, calling for his help *"from the land of the dead."* He confesses that this living death in the belly of the fish is a judgment from God for his disobedience, but at the same time it is his salvation.

When Jonah promises to worship and obey God, *"the Lord ordered the fish to spit Jonah out onto the beach."*

Once again, the Lord tells Jonah to go and preach to the Ninevites, and this time he obeys. But just as he fears, *"the people of Nineveh believed God's message, and from the greatest to the least, they declared a fast and put on burlap to show their sorrow"* (Jonah 3:5). Even the king repents. He sends a decree throughout the city that everyone should *"turn from their evil ways and stop all their violence. Who can tell? Perhaps even yet God will change his mind and hold back his fierce anger from destroying us."*

When the Lord sees how they have put a stop to their evil ways, he changes his mind and does not destroy them.

Jonah gets angry at God because he just knew that God would let Nineveh off the hook: *"I knew that you are a merciful and compassionate God, slow to get angry and filled with unfailing love. You are eager to turn back from destroying people"* (Jonah 4:2).

So Jonah seethes and pouts. While camping out and waiting to see whether God will judge the city, a silly thing happens—a shade plant dies, and Jonah gets very upset about it. God then confronts him with his hypocrisy—he cares more about a plant dying than he does about the 120,000 people of Nineveh living in spiritual darkness.

The story of Jonah ends with God making a statement by asking a question: *"Shouldn't I feel sorry for such a great city?"*

The historicity of Jonah, especially the three days in the belly of a great fish, is plausible or not, depending on one's presuppositions. Those who do not believe in the supernatural, or that God occasionally intervenes in human history for his own purposes, will dismiss Jonah as myth. Those who are open to the supernatural because of their faith in all-powerful God, who created the heavens and earth, are more open to seeing God's hand in it. And those who believe in an all-powerful Creator but believe that the fish story is meant to be, by God's inspiration, a metaphor, will see it as a powerful storytelling device.

But whether the great fish is meant to be history or metaphor, the book of Jonah challenges us to feel compassion for all people, even our enemies.

Focus: The story of Jonah is by all accounts a brilliant and memorable story of God's love for the world. The disturbing revelation here is that he loves those, like the Ninevites, whom most would regard as unworthy of love and forgiveness—perhaps even beyond the possibility of grace. Will we be surprised at who meet in heaven? Perhaps.

Jonah also illustrates the ironic fact that sometimes unbelievers demonstrate greater character and respect for God than believers. This suggests that God's judgment may be different from what we would expect. Just when we think we have all the good guys and bad guys sorted out, a story like Jonah's comes along and makes us rethink what we "know."

Prayer: *Lord, we find it hard to love our enemies, but then we think of how you loved us while we were still your enemies. Give us the ability to see others through your eyes and to grant them the same compassion that we would wish from them. Amen.*

Day 258   Reflection

September 14

Those who feel a need to identify the good guys and bad guys may be puzzled that God would direct Jonah to extend the opportunity for forgiveness to the bad guys—the Assyrian nation. It was the most brutal and bloodthirsty nation of its day, without mercy for civilians, women or children.

Jonah is certainly shocked and offended. He can't tolerate the idea that God might love Israel's enemies just as he loves Israel. We can sympathize.

But God wants Jonah to see the Ninevites through his eyes, not as monsters, but as fellow human beings created in his image. They are lost, but God wants to find them, like he found Israel. This is a theme we have noticed throughout the Old Testament. God's Promise to restore and bless the creation includes all nations, not just Israel.

Sometimes the Old Testament is regarded as inferior to the New Testament with its focus on Jesus. But as careful readers of the Bible will notice, Jesus is not a change of direction in the story. Jesus brings the ancient Promise of God to Abraham to its ultimate fulfillment. Since the tragedy of the Fall, God has been active in the world, seeking and finding the lost, bringing the spiritually dead back to life, rescuing the world from destruction.

As Old Testament scholar John Goldingay points out, *"God had been letting humanity do its worst. He had especially been letting the people he adopted as his own to do its worst, refusing to be overcome by its rejection and rebellion, declining to abandon it or destroy it."*

God will not allow his creation to be undone by sin and death. Some may refuse his offer of grace and mercy, but it is offered to all, even to the Ninevites. Jesus expresses this indiscriminate love in one of the most loved and memorized verses of the Bible: *"For this is how God loved the world: He gave his one and only Son, so that everyone who believes in him will not perish but have eternal life"* (John 3:16).

Because God loves the whole world, Jesus instructs his followers not to love their friends only, but also to love their enemies. Through this counterintuitive action, God's grace can be seen and heard by those who would otherwise be antagonistic. At the very least, it allows for a more humane world.

To say this doesn't mean that it is easy to do. Who wants to love their enemies? There may be good reason for a person or a nation to hate their enemies. Some wrongs are almost impossible for humans to forgive. Nevertheless, God offers his grace and mercy to all who will receive it.

To protest that someone else should be denied grace is to minimize our own need of grace. Even if it is true that some humans live better lives than others, we are not saved or lost by this measure. The apostle Paul, echoing the Old Testament, makes clear that God's measure is the standard of humanity for which he created us, of which we all fall short: *"For everyone has sinned; we all fall short of God's glorious standard"* (Romans 3:23).

> **Prayer:** *Lord, we identify with Jonah's resistance to taking a message of hope and forgiveness to Israel's enemies. We admit that we too are quick to judge others, but exempt ourselves. Help us to follow Jesus' example of forgiving his enemies. And when that is emotionally impossible, help us at least to accept that your love and mercy are greater than ours. And this is good news for everyone. Amen.*

Day 259   Micah 1–2

September 15

> Key Text: "Don't say such things," the people respond. "Don't prophesy like that. Such disasters will never come our way!"
> (Micah 2:6)

The prophet Micah lived during the time of the divided kingdom, and prophesied to Samaria, the capital city of the northern kingdom of Israel, and to Jerusalem, the capital city of the southern kingdom of Judah.

Micah focuses his message on these two capital cities because they are the centers of power and culture in the divided kingdom. Idolatry has taken root and is growing like a noxious weed throughout the two kingdoms, spreading moral corruption and social injustice.

In chapter 1, the Lord speaks as King and Judge of the whole earth: *"Attention! Let all the people of the world listen! Let the earth and everything in it hear. The Sovereign Lord is making his accusations against you; the Lord speaks from his holy Temple"* (Micah 1:2).

The Lord then leaves his throne, and with the Assyrian army as his proxy, *"tramples the heights of the earth. The mountains melt beneath his feet and flow into the valleys like wax in a fire."*

Samaria's defeat and exile is the focus of God's judgment here: *"So I, the Lord, will make the city of Samaria a heap of ruins."* But Judah's towns are also summoned and named as co-conspirators in idolatry, one city after another. As each town is named, a play on words follows as an omen of their destruction. For example, in verse 10, the people of the town of

Beth-leaphrah, which means "house of dust," are told to *"roll in the dust to show your despair."*

Here, as in many places of the Old Testament, literary symmetry and word play are used to describe God's moral order.

Chapter 2 contains an oracle of doom, beginning with the sad warning, *"what sorrow awaits you"*—i.e., woe unto you. The woe is pronounced first on Jerusalem's greedy landowners who use their power to dream up evil plans to swindle others out of their land and family inheritance.

The woe is then pronounced on lying false prophets who tell the people to ignore the warnings of Micah, which are the warnings of God. These prophets preach *"the joys of wine and alcohol"* instead. That is just the kind of prophet the people like! But Micah raises the question, *"Will the Lord's Spirit have patience with such behavior?"* The answer, of course, is no.

Once again, however, a word of hope follows the word of woe: *"Someday, O Israel, I will gather you; I will gather the remnant who are left. I will bring you together again like sheep in a pen, like a flock in its pasture"* (Micah 2:12).

This is an reference back to shepherd psalms like 23, 95:6–7, and 100:3, as well as a prelude to Jesus' shepherd sayings in the Gospel of John: *"I am the good shepherd; I know my own sheep, and they know me, just as my Father knows me and I know the Father. So I sacrifice my life for the sheep"* (John 10:14-15).

Focus: Those who are spiritually lost or confused, but nevertheless seekers after God, normally respond well to the story of the Bible. It is like a glass of cold water for their thirsty souls. It has the ring of truth to it, and they are drawn in to hear more. Others, however, can't bear to hear its story. It sets off an alarm. The doors of their hearts are double-bolted and the shades of their minds pulled down. They don't have, as Jesus put it, eyes to see or ears to hear. It is a mystery, really.

I understand why a guilty person would want to hide from God, and only after being assured that God loves and forgives them, be willing to come out of hiding. But a hard heart and a closed mind are different. Can we wander so far away from God and be so enamored with idolatry that there is no way back? It seems that some do. In the end, they choose hell—they choose to be as far away from God as they can get. And God gives them what they want.

Prayer: Lord, you are our Good Shepherd, and consequently we have all we need in you. Help us to drown out the many voices of the world, and the lure of idols, so that we may hear the welcoming word of your voice, and follow you to the green pastures and quiet streams of your leadership in our lives. Keep us from hard hearts and closed minds. Amen.

Day 260 — Micah 3–5

September 16

> **Key Text:** Listen to me, you leaders of Israel! You hate justice and twist all that is right. You are building Jerusalem on a foundation of murder and corruption. (Micah 3:9–10)

There is a moral and spiritual component to leadership. So the worst thing that can happen to any group is for their leaders to become corrupt. Sadly, this is the case with Israel. Micah challenges the leaders: *"Listen, you leaders of Israel! You are supposed to know right from wrong, but you are the very ones who hate good and love evil"* (Micah 3:1–2).

Among its leaders, Israel's prophets are false prophets, telling the people what they want to hear so that they will financially support them. And the kings hate justice and twist all that is right. Micah accuses them of building Jerusalem on a foundation of murder and corruption. The rulers make decisions based on bribes, and the priests teach God's Law only for a price.

Their corruption has rendered them delusional: *"No harm can come to us,"* they say, *"for the Lord is here among us."* But he is not. The whole nation will suffer the judgment of defeat and exile, which Micah, like all the prophets, makes known. But like them also, he brings a strong word of hope for the future.

In the *"last days,"* Micah says, *"the mountain of the Lord's house will be the highest of all—the most important place on earth"*—where people from many nations will come to worship. They will listen to God's teaching and walk in his ways. The outcome will be amazing: *"They will hammer their swords into plowshares and their spears into pruning hooks. Nation will no longer fight against nation, nor train for war anymore. Everyone will live in peace and prosperity, enjoying their own grapevines and fig trees, for there will be nothing to fear"* (Micah 4:3–4).

In this Day, the Lord will finally and fully reign as King on earth forever.

To this end, Micah makes a prophecy that is fulfilled in the birth of Jesus and quoted twice in the New Testament. He says: *"But you, O Bethlehem Ephrathah, are only a small village among all the people of Judah. Yet a ruler of Israel, whose origins are in the distant past, will come from you on my behalf"* (Micah 5:2).

So in the same city in which King David was born, the King and Savior of the world will also be born.

The Gospel of John mentions that the Jews were expecting their Messiah to come from Bethlehem, based on this prophecy of Micah: *"For the Scriptures clearly state that the Messiah will be born of the royal line of David, in Bethlehem, the village where King David was born"* (John 7:42).

We have noticed in the prophetic books that there are a number of prophecies about the coming of the Messiah, which Jesus himself said were speaking of him, and which the Church later used as evidence that Jesus was the Messiah.

Jesus confronts the unbelief of the religious leaders of first century Israel with verses like these: *"You search the Scriptures because you think they give you eternal life. But the Scriptures point to me! Yet you refuse to come to me to receive this life"* (John 5:39–40).

Focus: Spiritual leaders have a unique calling, not to power, but servanthood. They stand between God and his people to lead them, by example, to follow Jesus. To use one's position as a means to profit, or to pursue selfish ambition, or to fulfill the need to control others, is to invite God's judgment. Tragically, the bad behavior of leaders is multiplied because they lead others astray also. Many who have believed them, trusted them and followed them, suffer also when they fall. Cynicism follows, and the betrayed often never trust spiritual leaders again. No wonder God's judgment of leaders is so severe.

Prayer: Lord, we ask you to raise up men and women of influence to lead the Church with integrity and humility. Grant them the self-control needed to resist the temptations of leadership. Keep them close to you. Protect them from the Enemy who wants to bring them down. Honor them for their faithfulness and sacrifice in helping your Kingdom grow. Amen.

September 17

> Key Text: O people, the Lord has told you what is good, and this is what he requires of you: to do what is right, to love mercy, and to walk humbly with your God. (Micah 6:8)

Micah ends his message with a courtroom scene, a common prophetic theme. God summons the mountains and hills to bear witness to the trial.

The trial opens with the Lord bringing his charges against Israel: *"O my people, what have I done to you? What have I done to make you tired of me? Answer me! For I brought you out of Egypt and redeemed you from slavery. I sent Moses, Aaron, and Miriam to help you"* (Micah 6:3–4).

Through Moses, the Lord had given them instructions on how to worship him, but had made clear that the liturgy was not the end he was looking for, but the means to the end. What is he looking for? *"O people, the Lord has told you what is good, and this is what he requires of you: to do what is right, to love mercy, and to walk humbly with your God"* (Micah 6:8).

But the people fail miserably, so he warns them: *"Fear the Lord if you are wise! His voice calls to everyone in Jerusalem: 'The armies of destruction are coming; the Lord is sending them.'"*

Evidence for the prosecution is presented. The rich among them have become wealthy through financial corruption by using dishonest scales and weights. Extortion and violence are also common, as is habitual lying. The proceeds of their injustices fund a lavish lifestyle.

The Lord cannot tolerate it: *"Therefore, I will wound you! I will bring you to ruin for all your sins. You will eat but never have enough. Your hunger pangs and emptiness will remain."* All of their ill-gotten gain will be taken away from them by their conquerors.

Chapter 7 is a lament. God is miserable as he looks in vain for the righteous. He feels like a fruit picker after the harvest who finds nothing to eat. There is no fruit left—not even a grape or fig: *"The godly people have all disappeared; not one honest person is left on the earth. ... Even the best of them is like a brier; the most honest is as dangerous as a hedge of thorns"* (Micah 7: 2,4).

But Micah steps back from his prophecy against the people and now assumes the voice of a personified Jerusalem: *"I will be patient as the Lord punishes me, for I have sinned against him. But after that, he will take up my case and give me justice for all I have suffered from my enemies. The Lord will bring me into the light, and I will see his righteousness"* (Micah 7:9).

Micah expresses the confident hope of the remnant of faith that they will return to the Promised Land, where in time, all the nations of the earth will honor God: *"In that day, Israel, your cities will be rebuilt, and your borders will be extended. People from many lands will come and honor you—from Assyria all the way to the towns of Egypt, from Egypt all the way to the Euphrates River, and from distant seas and mountains"* (Micah 7:11–12).

Saying this, Micah ends his prophecy appropriately, with praise: *"Where is another God like you, who pardons the guilt of the remnant, overlooking the sins of his special people? You will not stay angry with your people forever, because you delight in showing unfailing love"* (Micah 7:18).

How amazing that God's righteous anger at human evil is overcome by his unfailing love. Grace will always triumph over evil, not by saying that evil doesn't matter, but by absorbing its offense into Jesus' life while he hangs on a cross and dies for the sins of the world.

No matter how much we resist God, he will show us his Covenant faithfulness and unfailing love, as he promised to Israel's ancestors Abraham and Jacob long ago.

Focus: While all the prophets address the same issues of Israel's sin, judgment and restoration, each brings his own insights and perspectives, as inspired by God. Micah puts his own stamp on the larger message of the prophets by asking a rhetorical question of God: Where is another God who pardons guilt, overlooks sin, and holds his anger in check because he *"delights in showing unfailing love"*?

God *delights* in loving us, despite our sin! Who can fathom such love? Nothing can cause God to give up and change his mind. On the other hand, who can understand why anyone would refuse such love? Only a willful, persistent, and conscious repudiation of God's gracious love can separate us from him. A person has to *really* want that separation. Recognizing this, C.S. Lewis famously remarked that *"the gates of hell are locked on the inside."* The damned, he wrote, are successful rebels to the end in that God finally gives them what they want—to be as far away from him as possible. Two mysteries, indeed!

Prayer: Lord, we are so glad that you are the judge before whom we will one day stand and give account of our lives. How wonderful to know that the Judge who would condemn us is the same One who loves us and died for our sins. Because of that, we are forgiven and freed from all condemnation. We give you thanks and offer our lives to you as a living sacrifice. Amen.

Day 262 Nahum

September 18

> Key Text: The Lord is slow to get angry, but his power is great, and he never lets the guilty go unpunished. (Nahum 1:3)

Every new generation suffers memory loss about the past. In this way, history is repeated. In the book of Nahum, the recent past refers to the Assyrian city of Nineveh, to which the prophet Jonah had been sent by God to call them to repentance. One hundred years has passed, and the current generation of Ninevites has forgotten their encounter with the one true God and the forgiveness shown them when their ancestors repented of their evil behavior long ago.

They are back to their old behavior—as wicked as ever. As the current world power, they feel invincible and think, *"Maybe our ancestors had to humble themselves before the Hebrew God, but times have changed."* So God sends another prophet, Nahum, to warn them.

Nahum's message begins with a refresher course on God and his ways:

As Holy God, *"The Lord is slow to get angry, but his power is great, and he never lets the guilty go unpunished"* (Nahum 1:3).

As Creator, God is Lord of the whole earth and the forces of nature: *"At his command the oceans dry up, and the rivers disappear. ... In his presence the mountains quake, and the hills melt away; the earth trembles, and its people are destroyed. Who can stand before his fierce anger? Who can survive his burning fury?"* (Nahum 1:4–6).

As Redeemer, the Lord *"is close to those who trust in him."*

As Judge, *"he will sweep away his enemies in an overwhelming flood."* So, Nahum poses a simple question to the city of Nineveh: *"Why are you scheming against the Lord? He will destroy you with one blow; he won't need to strike twice!"*

This is good news for God's people in exile. Their conqueror will be conquered, and they will be restored to Jerusalem. But it is bad news

492

for the Ninevites. Chapters 2 and 3 paint a vivid picture of the coming destruction of Nineveh with the ugly sights and sounds of war: *"Soon the city is plundered, empty, and ruined. Hearts melt and knees shake. The people stand aghast, their faces pale and trembling"* (Nahum 2:10).

When the surrounding nations see her ruin, there is a strange silence: *"Where are the mourners? Does anyone regret your destruction?"* (Nahum 3:7).

Nahum's message ends with a somber obituary: *"There is no healing for your wound; your injury is fatal. All who hear of your destruction will clap their hands for joy. Where can anyone be found who has not suffered from your continual cruelty?"*

As you have no doubt noticed, the ancient nations did not fight by the principles of just war. Their intent was to terrorize, humiliate and utterly destroy. Women and children were not spared. In Nineveh's case, God has been exceptionally patient. The Ninevites have been warned that he will not tolerate their evil forever. They once repented of it and God spared them. Yet they have now returned to their evil more defiantly than ever.

The Holy God stops them as he will eventually stop all evil, so that righteousness may blossom and spread to cover the whole earth.

Focus: Nahum makes the point that God *"never lets the guilty go unpunished."* That hardly sounds like a loving God. But think about it: How can Holy God allow sin to coexist in his creation? Sin is by definition a rejection of God, so it cannot continue to exist in God's good creation. Think of God's judgment against sin as the work of an immune system in the human body. When disease threatens the health of the body, the immune system goes right to work to protect the body and stop the disease.

A healthy body, by definition, has no disease. In a similar way, a holy God and a moral universe cannot tolerate sin. It must be stopped. This would be very bad news, except for the Gospel. Since God cannot allow the guilty to go unpunished, he takes punishment upon himself, so that we may live! And that is the very definition of a loving God!

Prayer: *Lord, sin is a mystery to us. It is irrational. So, why do we resist your love and rebel against your commandments? Why do we repeat the same mistakes, generation after generation, with the same results? We are so grateful that you are a patient and loving God! Amen.*

Day 263   Habakkuk

> Key Text: "Look at the proud! They trust in themselves, and their lives are crooked. But the righteous will live by their faithfulness to God." (Habakkuk 2:4)

The book of Job wrestled with the question, "Why do the innocent suffer?" The prophet Habakkuk struggles with the opposite but equally vexing question, "Why are the guilty not punished?"

His three-chapter message, written during Judah's last days as a kingdom, is a dialogue with God, followed by a hymn of praise.

The dialogue is initiated by a complaint about the wicked among God's chosen people going unpunished: *"How long, O Lord, must I call for help? But you do not listen! 'Violence is everywhere!' I cry, but you do not come to save. … Wherever I look, I see destruction and violence. … The wicked far outnumber the righteous, so that justice has become perverted"* (Habakkuk 1: 2–4).

God responds by informing Habakkuk that he is going to judge the Israelites by sending the nation of Babylon to conquer them: *"I am raising up the Babylonians, a cruel and violent people. They will march across the world and conquer other lands. They are notorious for their cruelty and do whatever they like."*

But Habakkuk protests that the cure seems worse than the disease, wondering if God is planning to wipe Israel out. Israel deserves judgment, but this seems too much. Habakkuk asks God, *"Should you be silent while the wicked swallow up people more righteous than they? … Are we only fish to be caught and killed? … Will [the Babylonians] succeed forever in their heartless conquests?"* (Habakkuk 1:13–17).

So, the question of God's goodness has taken a new turn. Habakkuk was initially concerned that the wicked of Israel were getting away with it; now he is concerned that the even more wicked Babylonians will get away with their sin.

God's response in chapter 2 is to assure Habakkuk that justice for Israel, and later for Babylon, will be coming, but that he must be patient and trust the Lord in his sovereign decisions and timetable. Furthermore, he should be more concerned with cultivating righteousness and less concerned with how God will judge evil. To that end, Habakkuk says: *"The righteous will live by their faithfulness to God"* (Habakkuk 2:4).

This verse is the key to the book of Habakkuk, and is quoted three times in the New Testament. It was also a key text for Martin Luther and the Reformation leaders who pointed to the source of righteousness as faith in God, not in human merit through good works.

After a lengthy description of the sorrows that await Babylon when the Lord's judgment finally comes upon her, Habakkuk finishes in chapter 3 with a song of praise. The song declares that God can be trusted no matter what: *"Even though the fig trees have no blossoms, and there are no grapes on the vines; even though the olive crop fails, and the fields lie empty and barren; even though the flocks die in the fields, and the cattle barns are empty, yet I will rejoice in the Lord! I will be joyful in the God of my salvation!"* (Habakkuk 3:17–18).

Focus: It is interesting to note that Habakkuk is given a vision from God that begins with a protest against the way God is delaying judgment: *"How long, O Lord, must I call for help? But you do not listen! 'Violence is everywhere!' I cry, but you do not come to save. Must I forever see these evil deeds? Why must I watch all this misery?"* God is not the least bit resistant to our hard questions and intense emotions; in fact, he encourages us to tell him exactly how we feel. This is a manifestation of the freedom we are given by God to inquire, search, protest, and complain. Jesus echoed this when he encouraged us: *"Keep on asking, and you will receive what you ask for. Keep on seeking, and you will find. Keep on knocking, and the door will be opened to you"* (Matthew 7:7). Understanding is a quest, and a struggle. The joy of arriving at our destination is preceded by the effort required to get there.

Prayer: *Lord, we are grateful to know that we, like Job and Habakkuk before us, can argue, complain and even disagree with you without fear of reprisal. At the same time, we acknowledge that you are Sovereign God who works your will in your own time and in your own way. Teach us to be patient, and to live by faith in your good plans for us. Amen.*

September 20

> Key Text: Stand in silence in the presence of the Sovereign Lord, for the awesome day of the Lord's judgment is near. (Zephaniah 1:7)

The end is coming! And that's a good thing.

The prophet Zephaniah is laser-focused on the coming *"awesome day of the Lord's judgment"*—the end of fallen human history when God will finally judge evil and all who cling to it. The cry for justice and the longing for righteousness that have characterized human history will finally be satisfied. The truth about all things will be revealed. Life will be sorted out.

This is a good thing because the cleansing of creation from evil and injustice will free it for a fresh start, to become what God intended in the beginning. But before the wound can be healed, it must be exposed, cleansed and treated, which can be painful.

Zephaniah, like all the prophets, is a bringer of pain. His message is that God will *"sweep away everything from the face of the earth"* (Zephaniah 1:2). This is hyperbole, of course, but it vividly expresses the fact that the whole world is a mess that needs to be cleaned up.

Zephaniah's present focus is on God's own people. As the apostle Peter writes: *"For the time has come for judgment, and it must begin with God's household. And if judgment begins with us, what terrible fate awaits those who have never obeyed God's Good News?"* (1 Peter 4:17).

Like other prophets, Zephaniah lays out the case for God's judgment against his people. The Israelites have broken covenant with God by turning to idol worship. By worshiping other gods, who are really not gods at all, their moral compass has been damaged. They have broken the commandments of the Lord. This national sin is an open wound, infected and threatening the life of the nation.

Since Israel's leaders no longer turn to God for direction, they have forfeited his wisdom and protection, exposing the nation to the evil intentions of the nations around them.

So Zephaniah preaches with urgency: *"Gather together—yes, gather together, you shameless nation. Gather before judgment begins, before your time to repent is blown away like chaff. Act now, before the fierce fury of the Lord falls and the terrible day of the Lord's anger begins"* (Zephaniah 2:1–2).

The prophetic message of judgment is not a catharsis for the prophets' anger. Certainly, none of them found pleasure in delivering it. Judgment is God's intervention and his cleansing of the wound of sin, even though it hurts. Their fervent hope is that Israel will once again recognize the Lord as their King.

There is great hope ahead for Israel and for all those who repent and return to the Lord: *"And the Lord himself, the King of Israel, will live among you! At last your troubles will be over, and you will never again fear disaster. On that day the announcement to Jerusalem will be, 'Cheer up, Zion! Don't be afraid! For the Lord your God is living among you. He is a mighty savior. He will take delight in you with gladness. With his love, he will calm all your fears. He will rejoice over you with joyful songs'"* (Zephaniah 3:15–17).

Focus: Ironic though it seems, pain is a gift of God. The missionary-doctor, Paul Brand, worked in India among the lepers, discovering that the scourge of leprosy is the deadening of nerves, removing all sensations of pain. The lack of pain enables injuries to worsen because the body's alarm system—pain—is disabled. Without awareness, otherwise treatable injuries may become infected with gangrene, requiring amputation and other disfiguring treatments. In a fallen world, pain is necessary for our well-being, physically and spiritually. The good news is that pain is temporary. If it grabs our attention and leads to healing and reconciliation with God, it produces eternal joy. Outside of God's presence and blessing, there is nothing but pain.

Prayer: *Lord, show us our sin so that we may repent of it. We don't want the days of our lives to blow away like chaff. Even if it causes pain, Lord, cleanse and heal our wounds that we may be among those who welcome you as King on that awesome day when you return. Amen.*

Day 265   Reflection

September 21

Who of us has not been in a heated conversation with someone and discovered, in the end, that they meant the exact opposite of what we understood them to mean? This is often true with readers of the prophets.

A casual and selective reading can result in a complete misunderstanding of their message. They require careful thought and interpretation to unpack their message properly.

For example, we may perceive *ourselves* to be victims in a world where God allows terrible things to happen to people, and in some cases causes them to happen. Like Job, we demand to know why the innocent suffer, and like Habakkuk, we are offended that the guilty seem to get away with sinning.

Our questions are legitimate, and God invites them, but until we stop seeing ourselves as victims and consider how the world's sinfulness has wounded God, we will remain stuck in our self-righteous indignation.

It may seem odd to say that we have wounded God. Some Christian thinkers believe God to be impassive to human response, even untouchable. But you can't read the prophets without seeing the joys and sorrows of God.

Let's review what we have learned so far.

We have seen that God joyfully spoke the universe into being. It reflects his loving purpose and was carefully designed to please him. Significantly, he made human beings in his image and then revealed himself to them, because he wanted a relationship. When Adam rebelled against God, the relationship was broken. But it was God who immediately moved toward reconciliation, which launched the rest of the story of the Bible.

Beginning with Abraham, God has worked within human history to redeem and restore the creation. Israel, his chosen people, is a microcosm of the world. While the rest of the nations watched, God revealed himself to Israel in unprecedented ways. None of the gods of pagan nations had ever done such a thing.

The Lord rescued Israel from slavery in Egypt, defeating Egypt's gods, and drowned Pharaoh's army in the Red Sea. He then formed a Covenant with Israel—like a covenant of marriage, promising to be faithful and bless her.

But soon into the marriage, Israel began an ugly pattern of serial adultery. She habitually broke her vows and ignored God's commandments by turning to pagan idolatry and the horrible practices of the neighboring nations. Seen by ancient standards, she spit in God's face, repudiated his love, disregarded all that he had done for her, and willfully prostituted herself to false gods.

"But," John Goldingay writes, "*God refuses to be overcome by humanity's rejection or rebellion. He is insistent on bringing to a consummation the purpose he has initiated from the beginning. To use Jesus' language, God was insistent on establishing his Kingdom. He was determined to reign in the world and not let humanity get away from him. So while he allowed Israel to do its worst, he refused to be overcome by its rejection and rebellion, and declined to abandon or destroy it.*"

All along, God had been paying the price for his people's attitude toward him, sacrificing himself for them and bearing their sin. Who can imagine any king allowing himself to be treated this way, let alone God?! Yes, he disciplined his people, but even his discipline was within the context of an ongoing relationship, stopping them with tough love from destroying themselves. In the end, by allowing Jesus to die, God counters all human self-assertion with an amazing act of divine self-giving.

So God is not cruel and unjust after all. Just the opposite—he is gracious and forgiving beyond belief. That is the message of the prophets, if we have eyes to see and ears to hear.

Prayer: Lord, open the eyes of our hearts to see you clearly and receive your amazing grace and continued faithfulness with gratefulness. Forgive us for playing the victim by ignoring our sin and blaming you for our self-inflicted wounds. We long for the day when your loving purposes are fully implemented. For now, we submit to your working in our lives. Amen.

Day 266 — Haggai

September 22

> Key Text: Then the Lord sent this message through the prophet Haggai: "Why are you living in luxurious houses while my house lies in ruins?" (Haggai 1:3–4)

With Haggai we come to the first of the three post-exilic prophets that complete the thirty-nine books of the Old Testament. Each prophet writes to those who have been permitted to return to Jerusalem following the Babylonian exile, in order to rebuild the Temple and city walls.

When the exiles arrive in Jerusalem, they are overwhelmed with the level of destruction. It is disheartening, to say the least. To make matters worse, they face opposition from the locals who are not pleased that the Jews have come back to rebuild.

The prophet Haggai writes to the governor of Judah and to the high priest, concerning a developing problem—the people have stopped working on the Temple. Instead they have built luxurious houses for themselves. It seems as if the people don't care whether the Lord lives among them or not! The Lord says through Haggai: *"Why are you living in luxurious houses while my house lies in ruins?"* (Haggai 1:4).

Haggai points to an ongoing drought as a message from the Lord about their spiritual deafness. The earth has produced few crops. It's almost as if heaven and earth are in agreement, and working together to grab the people's attention.

Surprisingly, the leaders hear and obey the message of the Lord. This encourages the people to go back to working on rebuilding the Temple. After that, Haggai is able to bring a word of encouragement: *"I am with you, says the Lord!"* (Haggai 1:13).

A couple of months after the people resume construction, Haggai comes with another message from the Lord. He says to the governor and high priest, and to the remnant of faith: *"Be strong ... get to work.... My Spirit remains among you, just as I promised when you came out of Egypt"* (Haggai 2:4–5). This word from God reassures the remnant that they are still God's people, and he is still honoring his ancient Covenant, with all its promises, with them.

Haggai speaks of the future when God will shake up the entire heavens and earth, and all the nations. The wealth of all the nations will be brought to God's holy Temple, and it will be filled with the glory of God. And the future glory of the Temple will be greater than its past glory: *"And in this place I will bring peace. I, the Lord of Heaven's Armies, have spoken!"* (Haggai 2:9).

The remainder of the letter contains Haggai's rhetorical questions to the priests regarding defilement, according to the Mosaic Law—i.e., that an unclean person makes anything he touches unclean. The application Haggai makes is that their previous indifference to repairing the Temple points to an indifference about the Lord's presence.

This indifference, like the ceremonial defilement in the Mosaic Law, has spoiled not only their offerings, but everything else they do. Their indifference also prompts God's judgment by means of the drought, in the hopes that they will return to him.

Thankfully they do return to him. Their repentance has resulted in fresh grace from God, and new hope for the fruitfulness of their land and their national future. The Lord will make Zerubbabel, the governor of Judah, his *"signet ring,"* meaning that he has been entrusted by God to carry out his will.

> **Focus:** The prophet Haggai speaks to the recurrent issue we all face, of allowing the work of God's Kingdom to take second or third place in our lives. We so easily become invested in our own comfort, like the returnees to Jerusalem who had set aside the task of rebuilding the Temple in order to build "luxurious houses" for themselves. Jesus promises that he will take care of all our needs if, by faith, we keep our priorities straight: *"Seek the Kingdom of God above all else, and live righteously, and he will give you everything you need"* (Matthew 6:33).

> **Prayer:** *Lord, we praise you for your abundant grace toward your people. Were it not for this, we would be forever lost in our sin. You are the God who brings life out of death, and hope out of despair. You are the God who takes care of the needs of your people. Help us to keep your Kingdom at the top of our priority list. Amen.*

Day 267   Zechariah 1–2

September 23

> Key Text: The other angel said, "Hurry, and say to that young man, 'Jerusalem will someday be so full of people and livestock that there won't be room enough for everyone! Many will live outside the city walls. Then I, myself, will be a protective wall of fire around Jerusalem, says the Lord. And I will be the glory inside the city!'" (Zechariah 2:4–5)

Someone has defined preaching as "divine truth mediated through human personality." At one level, God speaks to all those who love him and seek to know him better through prayer and Scripture. Then, through their witness and testimony, he speaks to others.

But God has also chosen people like Zechariah to bring a special message with his authority to a particular context. This message is recognized by the community of faith as being from God because it is consistent with God's character and his previous words and deeds. As such, it is understood to faithfully record and correctly interpret what God said and did.

This "word of the Lord" became part of the written text of Scripture, which successive generations preserved and looked to for an authoritative word from God for their own times. With the Holy Spirit's guidance, the Church learned to recognize divine inspiration. Through a rigorous process of discernment, the canon of Scriptures that we know as the Old and New Testaments was formed.

Since God chose to speak *through* human beings *to* human beings, it is not surprising that the life, personality and experiences of each speaker shape his message. This benefits the Church by providing a variety of perspectives, literary forms and particular emphases, by which to understand God and his will for our lives.

Zechariah was one of those people whom God chose and inspired to bring a faithful message from him to the people.

He is the second prophet who speaks to the post-exile community in Jerusalem. But unlike Haggai, Zechariah brings a message of comfort and encouragement instead of rebuke. We need both!

Zechariah begins his messages with a reminder of God's faithfulness to his word: *"Where are your ancestors now? They and the prophets are long dead. But everything I said through my servants the prophets happened to your ancestors, just as I said. As a result, they repented and said, 'We have received what we deserved from the Lord of Heaven's Armies. He has done what he said he would do'"* (Zechariah 1:5–6).

Zechariah's second message comes in a vision which reveals God's love for his people and his anger at the other nations who have *"inflicted harm on them far beyond my intentions."* I believe this means that the nations that have been the mechanism for God's judgment of Israel for her idolatry have violated even their own low standards of justice, and have acted with extreme cruelty. So, God will show mercy to his people and punish the other nations.

Two angels appear next in the vision and begin measuring Jerusalem. Why? Because Israel will once again overflow with prosperity: *"Jerusalem will someday be so full of people and livestock that there won't be room enough for everyone!"* (Zechariah 2:4).

The Lord promises to be *"a protective wall of fire"* around Jerusalem and *"the glory inside the city."* So the Lord who scattered his people to the four winds is now gathering them back. The Lord has disciplined his stubborn and rebellious people, but he has not forgotten them. The time of exile is over and the Lord will be their protector: *"Anyone who harms you harms my most precious possession"* (Zechariah 2:8).

This redeeming act foreshadows the great redemption coming to the whole world: *"The Lord says, 'Shout and rejoice, O beautiful Jerusalem, for I am coming to live among you. Many nations will join themselves to the Lord on that day, and they, too, will be my people'"* (Zechariah 2:10–11).

> **Focus:** It seems impossible that the nations of the world could ever be united in worshiping the one true God who made himself known to Abraham. And yet, Abraham himself came from a pagan, idol-worshiping culture. God is able to make himself known in natural and supernatural ways to people of all nations, races, languages and cultures. Indeed, the picture we have of the future is not that of bland uniformity, but of a diversity of races and cultures worshiping their Creator and living life on the New Earth. Who can imagine such a world, united in its diversity around their common love of God and their neighbor? Who can imagine a world cleansed of evil and filled instead with goodness beyond description? But such is the picture the prophets paint!
>
> **Prayer:** *Lord, it is so amazing that you want to make yourself known to us and live among us in joyful fellowship! You have always loved your people, even in the times of severe discipline, for by our suffering we recognize that there is no life apart from you. Thanks for watching over us and leading us into your good future! Amen.*

Day 268 Zechariah 3–4

September 24

> Key Text: "It is not by force nor by strength, but by my Spirit, says the Lord." (Zechariah 4:6)

Zechariah has been given a message from God composed of eight visions. The first three focus on the whole community and are about the priority of rebuilding the Temple. The next two visions, in chapters 3 and 4, are focused on two key leaders: Joshua, or Jeshua, the high priest, and Zerubbabel, the governor. So the concern shifts here from the task itself to the human instruments God is using to complete it.

In chapter 3, Zechariah shares his vision of a courtroom trial about to begin. Again, we have a courtroom scene, reminding us that what is at stake is divine justice. The defendant is Joshua, the high priest, and the prosecuting attorney is Satan, the accuser. This is a serious matter, because according to the Law of Moses, the high priest is the one person designated to represent the people in standing before Holy God. In God's presence, he would offer sacrifices of repentance and receive atonement for sin.

Only the high priest could enter the Holy of Holies in the Temple, and only once a year. In the vision, Joshua's clothing is filthy, meaning that he is spiritually unfit for this role—a fact which Satan the Accuser is only too happy to point out. Joshua represents the condition of all of us.

But then something unexpected and wonderful happens! God rejects Satan's accusations and declares Joshua to be a saved man and righteous in his sight: *"This man is like a burning stick that has been snatched from the fire"* (Zechariah 3:2).

What happens to Joshua is important to understand because it reflects the heart of the biblical story: *"See, I have taken away your sins, and now I am giving you these fine new clothes"* (Zechariah 3:4). This is what God's grace does. It makes unworthy people righteous in his eyes. But this also raises questions. Does God's grace imply that our sins don't matter? Does God simply ignore them and let us go free? Not at all!

Verses 8 through 10 mention that our sins are removed by the agency of God's servant, *"the Branch."* This is a technical term for the Messiah, who would be the ideal future king of David's line and who would remove sin. So God's grace is offered to sinful people because his servant bears all sin.

Satan the Accuser is right. Joshua, and all of us, are sinful and unworthy of standing before God. But by God's grace, the force of his accusations is dismissed and we are set free.

In chapter 4, another vision is given. This time, it is of a solid gold lampstand with a bowl of oil on top of it. Around the bowl are seven lamps, each with seven spouts and wicks. One olive tree stands on each side of the bowl.

The two olive trees represent Joshua and Zerubbabel. The lampstand represents the people. The olive oil in the bowl, which flows to the seven lamps, comes from the olive trees. Therefore, the vision reveals that Joshua and Zerubbabel are the leaders through whom the Lord will lead and nourish the community in their work of rebuilding.

The lampstand will be kept burning by Spirit-directed leadership. It is the way God always leads his people and does his work in the world. As the Lord famously says to Zerubbabel: *"It is not by force nor by strength, but by my Spirit, says the Lord"* (Zechariah 4:6).

So the work of rebuilding begins again. A humble beginning perhaps, but we are cautioned: *"Do not despise these small beginnings, for the Lord rejoices to see the work begin..."* (Zechariah 4:10).

Focus: How do we get the work of the Lord done? Zechariah makes clear that we cannot do it in our own strength—we cannot even want to do it in our own strength. It is the Spirit of the Lord that gives us the willingness and ability to do his work. Paul echoes Zechariah's claim when he says to the Philippians: *"For God is working in you, giving you the desire and the power to do what pleases him"* (Philippians 2:13). The dynamic of God in partnership with humans, by his Spirit and our cooperation, to do his work on earth, is the "secret sauce" of the Christian faith. We need not *despise small beginnings* when God is at work in us!

Prayer: Lord, thanks for reminding us that you do big and small things in the world through human agency. You have honored us by including us as your partners in bringing new life to a broken world. We are unworthy for this task, but you have made us worthy through Christ. Thank you for your continuing mercies. Amen.

Day 269 Zechariah 5–6

September 25

> Key Text: "Tell him, 'This is what the Lord of Heaven's Armies says: Here is the man called the Branch. He will branch out from where he is and build the Temple of the Lord. Yes, he will build the Temple of the Lord. Then he will receive royal honor and will rule as king from his throne. He will also serve as priest from his throne, and there will be perfect harmony between his two roles.'" (Zechariah 6:12–13)

Zechariah's next vision, in chapter 5, contains a flying scroll which is about thirty feet long and fifteen feet wide. It has a message on both sides, like a banner pulled behind a plane, but the message is a curse directed at *"those who steal"* and *"those who swear falsely"* in the Lord's name.

It is likely that these two messages summarize the deeds of all evildoers who break the commandments of God. They will be banished from the land.

Next in the vision, an angel points Zechariah's attention to a basket used for measuring grain. The basket is not filled with grain, however, but with the sins of everyone throughout the land. Sitting in the basket under a lead cover is a woman whose name is Wickedness.

Suddenly two women with wings like storks come flying in and pick up the basket, lifting it into the sky. When Zechariah asks where the basket is being taken, the angel replies, *"To the land of Babylonia, where they will build a temple for the basket. And when the temple is ready, they will set the basket there on its pedestal"* (Zechariah 5:11).

The vision pictures the cleansing of God's people. The basket full of wickedness has no place among them, but fits right in with Babylonian paganism.

The next vision, in chapter 6, contains four chariots pulled by red, black, white and dappled-gray horses. The angel explains to Zechariah that these are the four winds, or spirits of heaven, who are sent everywhere—north, south, east and west—to do God's work of patrolling the earth.

They represent God's invisible but inescapable presence in the world, perhaps echoing the sentiment of Psalm 139: *"I can never escape from your Spirit! I can never get away from your presence! If I go up to heaven, you are there; if I go down to the grave, you are there. If I ride the wings of the morning, if I dwell by the farthest oceans, even there your hand will guide me, and your strength will support me"* (Psalm 139:7–10).

Zechariah and the people are comforted by the fact that even in the darkness of exile, the Lord has never abandoned them.

A further message from the Lord says that silver and gold will be brought back with the exiles who leave Babylon to return to Jerusalem. The people will make a crown from the precious metals for the high priest, Jeshua, to be placed in the Temple.

At this point the person called the "Branch" is mentioned again. As we noted before, this title was associated with the Messiah. It is said of him here that he will rebuild the Temple of the Lord. He will receive royal honor and will rule as king from his throne. And surprisingly, he will take the position of priest as well, so he will rule as priest and king and *"there will be perfect harmony between his two roles"* (Zechariah 6:13).

While the dual role of priest and king was forbidden for Israel's rulers, when the prophecy is applied to Jesus, the details fall into place. The New Testament reveals Jesus to be both king and high priest.

As high priest, he stands before Holy God on behalf of sinful humanity, offering sacrifices on their behalf. But with Jesus, atonement for our sins comes not by sprinkling the blood of animals on the altar, but from his own shed blood on the cross.

And as king, the resurrected Jesus rules over all the earth, having put an end to our enemies—sin, death and the devil.

As our high priest and king, Jesus becomes the Savior and Lord of his people who will serve him eternally in the New Heavens and New Earth.

Focus: Zechariah's "Branch," like Isaiah's "Servant," are prefigures of Christ— the latter anticipating his suffering and atonement for our sins, and the former adding the role of king. Jesus is both our Savior and Lord, everything we need to be made right with God and share in his everlasting Kingdom.

Prayer: Lord, thank you for the prophecies which guided the imagination and expectation of your people until the coming of your Son. Looking back, from the cross and resurrection of Jesus, we can see how you prepared us all along for this great salvation. We serve you faithfully as our King! Amen.

Day 270   Zechariah 7–8

September 26

> Key Text: "The traditional fasts and times of mourning you have kept in early summer, midsummer, autumn, and winter are now ended. They will become festivals of joy and celebration for the people of Judah. So love truth and peace." (Zechariah 8:19)

Two years have passed since Zechariah's last visions. Now the Lord commands him to deliver four more messages to the remnant of Jews who have returned to Jerusalem.

The first message is given in response to a question about fasting: *"Should we continue to mourn and fast each summer on the anniversary of the Temple's destruction, as we have done for so many years?"* (Zechariah 7:3).

Fasting is the spiritual discipline of going without food for the purpose of prayer. It may be for a meal, a day, or longer, but the purpose is to redirect one's hunger for food to hunger for God, especially when there is an important matter to pray about. For the Jews, fasting was accompanied by mourning for the destruction of Jerusalem and the Temple. This had been their habit four times a year for the past seventy years.

The Lord's response to their question is to challenge the people and their spiritual leaders about their motives: *"...Was it really for me that you were fasting? And even now in your holy festivals, aren't you eating and drinking just to please yourselves?"*

How easily we fall back into our old habits! Selfish religion without justice or mercy, and fueled by idol worship, was Israel's undoing in the first place, and the ultimate reason for the exile.

So, the second message of the Lord says: *"Judge fairly, and show mercy and kindness to one another. Do not oppress widows, orphans, foreigners, and the poor. And do not scheme against each other"* (Zechariah 7:9–10).

The Lord had said the same things to their ancestors, but they *"stubbornly turned away and put their fingers in their ears to keep from hearing. They made their hearts as hard as stone, so they could not hear the instructions or the messages that the Lord of Heaven's Armies had sent them by his Spirit through the earlier prophets."* Since they would not listen, the Lord scattered them like a whirlwind among the distant nations, and this is exactly what they deserved.

In a third message, however, the Lord moves on to something totally undeserved. He restates his passion for Jerusalem, the city where his Temple is being rebuilt and where he will once again be present with his people. Once again the city will be filled with people—former exiles—because they have been brought home *"from the east and from the west"* to live safely. He will be faithful and just toward them as their God. In other words, he is determined to remain faithful to his Covenant with Israel.

In response, the people are required to *"tell the truth to each other. Render verdicts in your courts that are just and that lead to peace. Don't scheme against each other. Stop your love of telling lies that you swear are the truth. I hate all these things, says the Lord"* (Zechariah 8:16–17).

A fourth message returns to the original question about fasting. The Lord tells them that the years of fasting and mourning for Jerusalem are ended. Instead, *"they will become festivals of joy and celebration for the people of Judah. So love truth and peace"* (Zechariah 8:19).

It is the faithfulness of God that turns our mourning into joy, and his judgment into blessing.

Day 271   Zechariah 9–11

September 27

> Key Text: Rejoice, O people of Zion! Shout in triumph, O people of Jerusalem! Look, your king is coming to you. He is righteous and victorious, yet he is humble, riding on a donkey—riding on a donkey's colt. (Zechariah 9:9)

Beginning in chapter 9, Zechariah changes imagery, language and focus, but with the same concerns. Some scholars believe it is the word of a disciple of Zechariah's, while others believe that the chapters belong with Malachi. In either case, these chapters bring a strong, consistent prophetic message.

Chapter 9 begins with a series of warnings and judgments for Israel's neighbors. Though the Lord has judged his own people Israel through the agency of pagan nations, he will not again allow his Temple to be destroyed: *"I am watching closely to ensure that no more foreign oppressors overrun my people's land"* (Zechariah 9:8).

Indeed, he is sending his king, his Messiah. Zechariah 9:9 is the best-known verse of this book: *"Rejoice, O people of Zion! Shout in triumph, O people of Jerusalem! Look, your king is coming to you. He is righteous and victorious, yet he is humble, riding on a donkey—riding on a donkey's colt."*

Since the Lord sends no new king to his people after the exile until the New Testament times, it is assumed that this is a prophecy about Christ. And, of course, that is how the gospel writers understood it. It is quoted in the narrative of Christ's kingly "triumphal entry" into Jerusalem in all

509

four gospels.

The day of this king's coming is a day of victory, freedom and peace for God's people. Although it is described here as an actual battle against earthly enemies, the New Testament recognizes that our true enemies are not flesh and blood, but sin, death and demonic forces. And, our True King is not another military leader, but a Suffering Servant who is God's Son.

Chapter 10 is a hopeful vision of national flourishing. The Lord will look after his people like a shepherd looks after his sheep. He will strengthen and restore them because of his compassion. He promises: *"It will be as though I had never rejected them, for I am the Lord their God, who will hear their cries"* (Zechariah 10:6).

Meanwhile, chapter 11 is a lament, which returns to the theme of the coming judgment for Israel's neighbors who have oppressed her and opposed God's purposes. The Lord will let these nations *"fall into each other's hands and into the hands of their king. They will turn the land into a wilderness, and I will not rescue them."*

Zechariah then speaks allegorically (probably) of being sent as a shepherd to the people of Israel, but finding they hate him and show it by means of a dismissive payment for his services: *"So they counted out for my wages thirty pieces of silver"* (Zechariah 11:12).

This verse comes to mind in the New Testament when Judas is paid thirty pieces of silver—the cost of a slave—for betraying Christ.

Focus: It can get confusing when the Old Testament speaks of future events as if they are already here—a conflation of the present and future. Whether speaking of judgment or salvation, the fact is declared by God as a present reality as well as a future event. This makes more sense when we remember that God does not exist within time, as we created beings do. We experience time as a series of events, a flow or sequence. For God, things simply "are" because they are in his mind. Paul, for example, reflects this when he speaks of God loving us and choosing us as his redeemed people *"even before he made the world"* (Ephesians 1:4).

When God decides something, such as to make us holy in Christ, he makes a "legal" decision. It is legally true before it becomes actually true. So we live in the tension of being called *holy* and *saints* when in fact we still struggle with sin in our mortal bodies. But once God has ruled, it is real, and we need to learn to think of it as real for us, right now.

510

Day 272 — Reflection

September 28

One of the most remarkable facts about the God of the Bible is that he allows human beings to say "no" to him. "No" is a word that introduces tension into a relationship because it challenges authority and power.

Genesis 3 tells us that the human race said "no" to God's authority right at the beginning by believing the lie of Satan, when he told Adam and Eve that humans didn't need God but were free and able to determine good and evil for themselves.

How did God respond to this presumptuous rebellion? He exposed the lie of Satan and judged the sin of Adam and Eve. But significantly, he did not destroy human life.

He had every right to. By definition, Almighty God who created all things, has all power and authority. He can do anything he wants. That is why it is silly for us mortals to dismiss God by saying that we don't believe in him or don't agree with him. Logically, if God exists, it doesn't matter what we think. He has all power and authority.

But as we have seen in our reading of the Old Testament, God does not dismiss us when we say "no" to him. In fact, Genesis says that after the Fall, God immediately launched a plan to redeem the world to himself. As you remember, he chose Abraham to be the head of a great nation through which he would bless and restore the world. As Abraham's descendants multiplied, they were enslaved by a mighty pharaoh. But God heard their prayers and delivered the people from slavery in Egypt, entered into covenant with them, and enabled them to take possession of the Promised Land.

Despite all these blessings, his people routinely disregarded the Covenant and broke his commandments. Still, God remained faithful to them. Over and over again, he sent his prophets to call the people back to him, but they wouldn't listen. He made them face consequences for continuing idolatry and moral corruption, but the people hardened their hearts even more.

Nevertheless, God continued to extend unmerited grace so that the people could return to him.

Behind God's dogged faithfulness was his determination to have a relationship with us—to reign as King over the whole earth so that we could enjoy the many blessings of his riches for eternity.

The story of the Gospel is so unlike other stories of gods or the writings of philosophers. As revealed by the Law and prophets, the God of the Bible created the universe with a loving purpose, and created human beings in his image. It pleased him to do so because, as we have noted over and over again, he desired to share his life with us. He was determined to bring this about, no matter what it cost, through the free choice of human beings responding to his love and mercy.

C.S. Lewis wrote that God's choosing to create a species with free will, capable of resisting him, was the most amazing thing he had ever heard. What God wants from us—no matter what the cost to him—is the glad and grateful response of our saying "YES!" to his love.

Of course, we know what the ultimate cost will be for him, and he gladly bears it: *"Because of the joy awaiting him, [Jesus] endured the cross, disregarding its shame. Now he is seated in the place of honor beside God's throne"* (Hebrews 12:2).

> *Prayer: Lord, the world still can't get over the message of the cross. For some, it is an amazing statement of love and an invitation to share his life, which they freely choose. For others, it is a frightening challenge to their own story which says that they don't need God and can choose right and wrong for themselves. Thank you for opening our eyes to see your undaunted love and faithfulness to us. Amen.*

Day 273   Zechariah 12–14

September 29

> Key Text: And the Lord will be king over all the earth. On that day there will be one Lord—his name alone will be worshiped. (Zechariah 14:9)

Zechariah ends his prophecy with an inspiring message *"concerning the fate of Israel."*

There have been plenty of hints in the writings of the prophets about what is ahead for the people of God, within history and beyond it.

Presently Israel, as a historical entity, is scattered among the nations, while Jerusalem and the Temple lay in ruins. There are tensions between the returning exiles and the few Israelites that had stayed behind, as well as their neighbors who are not happy to see any Jews return. It is a tragic mess and a mockery of the former days of Israel's greatness.

But a "day" is coming when God's people will be reestablished by God's forgiveness and blessing. Jerusalem, the city of God, will become *an immoveable rock. All the nations will gather against it to try to move it, but they will only hurt themselves*" (Zechariah 12:3).

On that day, Zechariah prophesies, Israel's enemies will be destroyed. Idols and false prophets will be gone. God will pour out *"a spirit of grace and prayer"* upon the royal family line of King David—which is the Messianic line, remember—and upon the people of Judah. Then, its leaders will be like faithful shepherds to the people.

But in Zechariah's account, something mysterious and troubling happens in this victory. God himself is somehow wounded—by his own people: *"They will look on me whom they have pierced and mourn for him as for an only son."* How can this be? No answers are given here, except that the piercing of God is followed by the pouring out of a *"spirit of grace,"* as noted above.

We will see in the New Testament that this piercing anticipates the piercing of Jesus on the cross. The disciples quoted this passage as a prophecy of Jesus' suffering and death, which became a fountain of grace flowing into the world. His resurrection became the prelude to God's pouring out of his Spirit on the Day of Pentecost.

"On that day"—a phrase repeated several times in these chapters—the sin that has marred Israel's life with God from the beginning will be washed away, and the relationship restored. Even the earth itself will be cleansed from its defilement from idolatry and false prophets.

The prospect of the whole creation being cleansed and ruled, as God intended, by his redeemed people, is inevitable because God wills it.

In short, the Lord says: *"I will bring that group through the fire and make them pure. I will refine them like silver and purify them like gold. They will call on my name, and I will answer them. I will say, 'These are my people,' and they will say, 'The Lord is our God'"* (Zechariah 13:9).

513

Zechariah concludes in chapter 14 with the eschatological hope of the coming Kingdom of God: *"And the Lord will be king over all the earth. On that day there will be one Lord—his name alone will be worshiped"* (Zechariah 14:9).

That "day" will bring the troubles and turmoil of the creation to an end. Only then will sin and death be judged forever and humans returned to the Garden of Eden. They will live in peace with one another and in perfect, eternal fellowship with God.

Focus: From the very beginning, God's Promise to Abraham has been something of a mystery. God reveals himself to Abraham, promising to make him into a great nation with its own land, and that somehow this nation will produce a descendant by whom all the nations of the earth will be blessed. As the generations go by, God is found faithful, yet the people themselves struggle, doubt, complain, rebel and ultimately fail God. The holy fire that was Israel becomes a smoldering ruin dispersed throughout the nations, as a judgment from God. But out of the warm embers of God's faithfulness, a small flame reignites through the preaching of the prophets. God has not forgotten his Promise, nor has he lost his love for his people. He declares once again: *"The Lord will be king over all the earth. On that day there will be one Lord—his name alone will be worshiped."*

Prayer: *Lord, we continue to marvel at the hints you have given us of the details of Jesus' life and mission. We are so grateful that you were willing to be pierced for our transgressions. It encourages us also to know that you have been in control of history since the beginning, and will be faithful to the end, because your love for your people never ends. Amen.*

Day 274   Malachi

September 30

Key Text: The Lord of Heaven's Armies says, "The day of judgment is coming, burning like a furnace. ... But for you who fear my name, the Sun of Righteousness will rise with healing in his wings. And you will go free, leaping with joy like calves let out to pasture." (Malachi 4:1–2)

We finally come to Malachi, the last book of the Old Testament!

After all these years and tears, Israel is sadder but wiser (well, at least sadder), given all the events, good and bad, that have occurred since God first revealed himself to Abraham in Genesis 12. There have been notable moments of faith and obedience to God by individuals, but the prevailing pattern has been disobedience. In the end his people fail him.

The great nation promised to Abraham, formed in deliverance from Egypt, shaped in the wilderness and established as a kingdom, has now been scattered among the nations. The Promised Land, graced by Jerusalem and the Temple, has been conquered and destroyed. And even though the pagan King Darius has allowed exiles to return to Jerusalem after seventy years of captivity and begin rebuilding, the project has fallen flat.

Incredibly, Malachi reveals that the returnees to Jerusalem have returned to the very sins that brought about their captivity in the first place. Once again, they have hardened their hearts toward God. So Malachi is given the disheartening task of warning the people one final time of their need to return to God in repentance and faith.

Malachi points out that, while the people go through the motions of worship, their indifference to God's Law, especially about the offerings, shows contempt for God's name. The animals offered as sacrifices are blind, crippled and diseased—in other words, the leftovers: *"You say, "It's too hard to serve the Lord," and you turn up your noses at my commands,' says the Lord of Heaven's Armies. 'Think of it! Animals that are stolen and crippled and sick are being presented as offerings! Should I accept from you such offerings as these?' asks the Lord"* (Malachi 1:13).

The Mosaic Law had carefully specified how the religious leaders and the people should worship him. They were taught to give the right offerings in the right way by leaders who were living righteous lives. But once again, they have ignored the Covenant stipulations.

The Israelite men have violated God's command by participating in the sexual immorality associated with pagan worship. The illicit affairs corrupt the men. They divorce their wives and leave their children in order to marry pagan women and continue in idolatry.

They have wearied the Lord with their excuses, Malachi says. So he is coming in judgment against them, *"like a blazing fire that refines metal, or like a strong soap that bleaches clothes. He will sit like a refiner of silver, burning away the dross ... so that they may once again offer acceptable sacrifices to the Lord"* (Malachi 3:2–3).

They will be put on trial. All their sins, personal and public, will be judged: *"'I will speak against those who cheat employees of their wages,* who oppress widows and orphans, or who deprive the foreigners living among you of justice, for these people do not fear me,' says the Lord of Heaven's Armies."

Yes, God is angry at his people for their willful and persistent sin. But, nevertheless, he will not relent in his determination to keep them from falling away beyond recovery. He will pursue them and win them back, no matter what the cost: "'They will be my people,' says the Lord of Heaven's Armies. 'On the day when I act in judgment, they will be my own special treasure. I will spare them as a father spares an obedient child'" (Malachi 3:17).

Thus, we end the Old Testament, as we began it, with God announcing his resolve to redeem his people. Despite everything, he will still send his king, his Messiah. We don't know when, but as Malachi 4:5–6 notes, the day of his arrival will be announced by the preaching of a prophet like Elijah. (Spoiler alert: It will be John the Baptist.)

God's redeeming plan, begun with Abraham, is not completed yet, but neither is it abandoned.

There is Good News coming!

Focus: Congratulations! You have persevered through the entire Old Testament! No doubt, at times you have found it confusing, boring, offensive or hard to believe. But I hope that the bigger picture has become clearer. I trust that the four great themes of the Bible—Creation, Fall, Redemption and New Creation—are beginning to make sense so that you can see why the Bible is the greatest story ever told.

But above all, I hope that you have been persuaded that the God of the Old Testament is far from being the angry God who loves to punish sinners, as some have claimed. Yes, he gets angry, but it is the anger of a betrayed lover, as well as the anger of a holy God against the sin that threatens his creation.

I hope that you have seen his passionate love, relentless faithfulness, amazing patience and generous grace, far beyond what we deserve. I hope you see that, more than anything, God our Creator wants a relationship with us, forever! The best days are ahead.

Prayer: Lord, we praise you for the unforgettable story of your Old Testament people. We see ourselves in them, for we too have stubborn and divided hearts with misplaced affections. We too quickly turn to idols to find what we think we need. But what we need is your grace and mercy, for we are unable to be righteous in our own strength. We rejoice that you did not give up on Israel, for it shows that you

Day 275   Matthew 1–4

October 1

> **Key Text:** As he considered this, an angel of the Lord appeared to him in a dream. "Joseph, son of David," the angel said, "do not be afraid to take Mary as your wife. For the child within her was conceived by the Holy Spirit. And she will have a son, and you are to name him Jesus, for he will save his people from their sins." (Matthew 1:20–21)

Four hundred years have passed since God spoke through the prophet Malachi to the Jewish exiles who returned to Jerusalem and the Temple under the benevolent policies of the Persian king, Cyrus. Most of the Israelites, however, remain scattered and assimilated among the other nations.

Worship for the exiled Jews has become centered around small worship places called synagogues, where prayer, and Torah reading and interpretation, keep their Jewish identity alive.

Eventually, Israel's captors, the Persians, were conquered by the Greeks, led by Alexander the Great, and Judaism began to be shaped by Greek culture.

This is the status of God's people when the four hundred years of God's silence is broken by a miracle, the conception of a child by a young Jewish virgin named Mary. Yes, a virgin. Does this sound familiar? Remember Isaiah's prophecy: *"The Lord himself will give you the sign. Look! The virgin will conceive a child! She will give birth to a son and will call him Immanuel (which means 'God is with us')"* (Isaiah 7:14).

An angel arrives to help Joseph, Mary's fiancé, make this connection. He tells a confused Joseph that the child conceived in her is by the Holy Spirit, and shall be named Jesus (which means "God saves")—*"for he will save his people from their sins."* In Matthew's telling, Jesus is subsequently introduced to Israel, and then to the whole world, as the promised Messiah (king). He is so designated by miracles, dreams, angelic visitations, prophetic messages, and by pagan foreigners following a star that they believe will lead them to a child born to be king of the Jews.

Matthew begins his account of Jesus' life, in chapter 1, by establishing

517

his messianic credentials through a genealogy. He is writing to a primarily Jewish audience, for whom the genealogy is important because they were told by God that the coming Savior would be a descendent of King David as fulfillment of God's ancient Promise to Abraham. So Matthew begins his gospel by stating: *"This is a record of the ancestors of Jesus the Messiah, a descendant of David and of Abraham"* (Matthew 1:1).

Mary's conception of Jesus is explained as the ultimate fulfillment of Isaiah's prophecy, which is quoted in Matthew 1:23: *"Look! The virgin will conceive a child! She will give birth to a son, and they will call him Immanuel, which means 'God is with us'"* (Matthew 1:23).

Chapter 2 explains how Jesus was born in Bethlehem, in fulfillment of the prophecy of Micah 5:2. The universal significance of his birth is shown by the visit of Magi from Persia, who worship the child as a king. God then delivers Jesus from the wrath of King Herod, just as he delivered Moses long ago from the wrath of Pharaoh.

Chapter 3 fast-forwards 30 years to the time of the preacher, John the Baptist, who is Jesus' cousin. John is sent by God to call Israel to repentance because the promised and long-awaited day of God's rule, the Kingdom of Heaven, is near. Matthew regards John as the fulfillment of Isaiah's prophecy of a *"voice shouting in the wilderness, 'Prepare the way for the Lord's coming! Clear the road for him!'"* (Matthew 3:3).

We might think it surprising that Jesus is baptized, since John's baptism was about repentance. But Jesus submits to baptism in order to identify with us in our need. He is sinless, but we are not, so he has come to take the debt of our sin upon himself.

Jesus begins his public ministry as one of us.

His ministry is verified during his baptism when the Holy Spirit descends upon Jesus, like a dove, and the Father's voice from heaven says, *"This is my dearly loved Son, who brings me great joy"* (Matthew 3:17).

In chapter 4, Jesus is tempted by the devil to reject his messianic mission and seek power, riches and glory for himself instead. Unlike Adam and Eve, Jesus says no to the tempter. *"Get out of here, Satan,"* he commands. *"For the Scriptures say, 'You must worship the Lord your God and serve only him'"* (Matthew 4:10).

Jesus now commits himself to the mission that God the Father has had in mind all along when he first promised Abraham that he would one day make things right by bringing salvation to the whole world. According to Jesus, this "day" has begun. The Kingdom has come, and everyone is invited to repent and believe the Good News.

Significantly, Jesus invites twelve Jewish men to be his companions and associates, an allusion to the twelve tribes of Israel and a sign that "Israel" is being renewed.

Focus: At long last we discover what God has been up to all along. He is going to create a new humanity in Jesus. Jesus is the fulfillment of God's ancient Promise to redeem the world, and his message to you is the same as it was to Abraham long ago—"Follow me."

Prayer: Lord, as your ancient Promise now comes into focus through Jesus, we are amazed again at your faithfulness. You move slowly but persistently. You accommodate yourself to the pace of human history, and to our slowness to learn. Your grace takes up the enormous slack of our sinfulness. Oh how great are your riches and wisdom and knowledge! How impossible it is for us to understand your decisions and your ways! Amen.

Day 276   Matthew 5–7

October 2

Key Text: "Seek the Kingdom of God above all else, and live righteously, and he will give you everything you need." (Matthew 6:33)

After calling twelve disciples to be his companions and apprentices, Jesus begins traveling throughout the region of Galilee, announcing the Good News about the Kingdom of Heaven, and performing miracles of healing and exorcism. Matthew reports that large crowds follow him wherever he goes.

Think of the Kingdom of Heaven (or alternately the Kingdom of God) as God's reign and rule in the hearts of those who love him. One day, God's rule will be universal. He will destroy sin and death, once and for all. He will raise those who love him from the dead in order to live under his reign forever in a renewed creation. Jesus' words and deeds indicate that the transforming power of the Kingdom has already begun.

Jesus' miracles not only demonstrate that the power of God is with him, but they also reveal the nature of the Kingdom of Heaven. When

God rules as King over his creation once again, the present order of things will be reversed. Everything that sin has broken will be fixed—no more sickness, sorrow, spiritual torment, human conflict or general human misery.

But Jesus is not just a miracle worker; he is also "Immanuel"—God with us—revealing God to us and teaching us about his Kingdom, especially about how our lives are transformed when we follow him. The most famous of all Jesus' teachings is called "The Sermon on the Mount." This is what Matthew now recounts for us in chapters 5 through 7.

The Sermon begins with an overview of the blessings of the Kingdom known as the Beatitudes. They are addressed to the *"poor in spirit"*—those who humbly realize their need for God. All the blessings of the future Kingdom are open to them, even if their present life is marked by sorrow, poverty, injustice and suffering for doing what is right. We must remember that the good deeds of Jesus' followers have a positive impact in the world now, like salt and light.

Jesus then calls his followers to a life of integrity in the world, living consistently with what we preach and teach others. This stands in contrast to the hypocrisy common among even the religious leaders of the time. Jesus ups the ante concerning God's commandments, by explaining that outward acts, like murder and adultery, are first of all attitudes of the heart—anger and lust. Therefore, we need to pay attention to our inner life, where sin is conceived and grows to become an outward act.

In chapter 6, Jesus warns his followers about their motives: *"Watch out! Don't do your good deeds publicly, to be admired by others, for you will lose the reward from your Father in heaven"* (Matthew 6:1). He then gives them what we know as "the Lord's Prayer" to guide them in praying properly about God's Kingdom and their daily needs.

Further warnings follow against the dangers of materialism, a divided heart and worrying about everyday needs. Jesus gives them this great promise: *"Seek the Kingdom of God above all else, and live righteously, and he will give you everything you need"* (Matthew 6:33).

In chapter 7, the sermon concludes with teaching about not judging others and about persevering in prayer for what we need. In summary, Jesus says: *"Do to others whatever you would like them to do to you. This is the essence of all that is taught in the law and the prophets"* (Matthew 7:12).

Jesus is honest about challenges we will face in following him, because it is a difficult life: *"The highway to hell is broad, and its gate is wide for the many who choose that way. But the gateway to life is very narrow and the road is difficult, and only a few ever find it"* (Matthew 7:13–14).

He also warns: *"Beware of false prophets who come disguised as harmless sheep but are really vicious wolves"* (Matthew 7:15). They will seek to mislead others in order to gain power over them, but their behavior will give them away.

The Sermon on the Mount concludes with a challenge for everyone to hear and follow Jesus' teaching. All who do so are wise, like a person who builds a house on solid rock.

Focus: Jesus has come to give us a great and everlasting future. He has outlined the solid foundation upon which to build our lives. We embrace this life by repentance and faith. We pursue it with love and prayer. We endure troubles with confidence, knowing that God will give us all we need when we make his Kingdom our first priority.

Prayer: Lord, thank you for sending Jesus to us so that we may know what is ahead, and how to live faithfully in the meantime. Amen.

Day 277   Matthew 8–11

October 3

> Key Text: Jesus traveled through all the towns and villages of that area, teaching in the synagogues and announcing the Good News about the Kingdom. And he healed every kind of disease and illness. When he saw the crowds, he had compassion on them because they were confused and helpless, like sheep without a shepherd. (Matthew 9:35–36)

A key theme of Matthew is that Jesus has genuine compassion for our suffering, and that the Good News of forgiveness and salvation is for the whole world, not just ethnic Israel.

Chapter 8 shows how the Kingdom of Heaven compassionately breaks down social, racial and religious barriers. Jesus touches and heals a leper—a person that no devout Jew would come near, let alone touch. He heals the servant of a Roman soldier—a Gentile who no devout Jew would associate with. (Surprisingly, Jesus commends the Gentile for his great faith and predicts that many Gentiles will enter the Kingdom of

Heaven.) He also casts out evil spirits from demonized people who were considered unclean and were typically shunned.

In chapter 9, Jesus creates a controversy by forgiving a man's sins before he heals him. The religious leaders are outraged, because only God can forgive sins. Who does Jesus think he is? Not only does he forgive sins, he also forgives *notorious* sinners—like Matthew, the despised tax collector and writer of the present gospel, whom he invites to be one of the twelve disciples!

Even worse, Jesus goes to Matthew's house to have dinner with him and his other tax collector friends. When the Pharisees see this, they protest to Jesus' disciples: *"'Why does your teacher eat with such scum?' When Jesus heard this, he said, 'Healthy people don't a need a doctor—sick people do. ... For I have come to call not those who think they are righteous, but those who know they are sinners'"* (Matthew 9:11–13).

Chapter 10 introduces the twelve disciples of Jesus. As noted earlier, the twelve disciples represent the twelve tribes of the Old Testament Israel, suggesting that Jesus is now creating a new Israel. The disciples are first called "apostles" here. The word apostle means *"sent one."* This is an appropriate title because Jesus sends them out to proclaim the message of the Kingdom, beginning with the Jews. They are instructed on how to respond to every situation they may encounter. Jesus warns them that there will be conflict when the Gospel is proclaimed, and all nations will hate them because they are his followers. He is sending them out as *"sheep among wolves,"* so they must be *"as shrewd as snakes and harmless as doves."* They must not be afraid and cling to their lives when faced with threats.

Finally, chapter 11 introduces John the Baptist's ministry as preparing the way for the Lord and his Kingdom. Jesus identifies him as the prophet like Elijah who would come, as prophesied in Malachi 4:5–6. Starting with John's preaching, and continuing with Jesus and his disciples, the Kingdom of Heaven is *"forcefully advancing"* in the world. Jesus adds, ominously: *"...and violent people are attacking it."*

They still are, all over the world. But there is comfort and strength in Jesus' invitation to Kingdom workers: *"Come to me, all of you who are weary and carry heavy burdens, and I will give you rest"* (Matthew 11:28).

Focus: With the coming of Jesus, and the launching of his Kingdom ministry, something new has come into the world, and the world has forever changed. God's power and authority are being seen in new ways as his Kingdom advances through preaching and Kingdom work. It is a force for good, confronting and resisting evil with unstoppable love. It can't be ignored. It sheds light in the darkness. It forces us to declare ourselves. Jesus has come to reclaim God's rightful rule over his creation, and he calls us to make his Kingdom our first priority.

Prayer: Lord, the presence of your Kingdom is good news for all who will receive it! We are so grateful that you love us and want to lead us into the amazing future you have for us. May the prayer you taught us be our constant concern—that your Kingdom would come and your will be done on earth, as it is in heaven. Amen.

Day 278   Matthew 12–15

October 4

Key Text: "But if I am casting out demons by the Spirit of God, then the Kingdom of God has arrived among you."
(Matthew 12:28)

It was inevitable that Jesus would face hostility from the religious leaders of Israel. His miracles attracted widespread attention from their congregations; his teaching and practices contradicted their authority in these matters; and he was not shy about pointing out their hypocrisy and lack of compassion for the people.

Matthew reports that when Jesus heals a man on the Sabbath, the leaders accuse him of breaking the Sabbath law of no work on the Sabbath. Jesus challenges their understanding of the Law by saying that the Law of Moses permits a person to do good on the Sabbath.

Later, when Jesus heals a demon-possessed man and the amazed crowd wonders out loud if Jesus could be the Messiah, the religious leaders accuse him of casting out demons by the power of Satan *(Matthew 12:22–24).*

After showing how silly it is to think that Satan would cast out his own evil colleagues, Jesus offers an alternative explanation: *"But if I am casting out demons by the Spirit of God, then the Kingdom of God has arrived among you."*

The implications of this are stunning. By making this slanderous accusation against Jesus, the religious leaders could actually be resisting the very Kingdom of God which they are waiting for, and blaspheming the Messiah by attributing the work of God's Spirit to Satan!

So Jesus warns them to very careful in what they say: *"Anyone who speaks against the Son of Man can be forgiven, but anyone who speaks against the Holy Spirit will never be forgiven, either in this world or in the world to come"* (Matthew 12:32).

Having been stymied by Jesus, the religious leaders demand a sign to prove his authority. Quoting the book of Jonah, Jesus says the only sign their hard hearts will recognize will be his resurrection: *"For as Jonah was in the belly of the great fish for three days and three nights, so will the Son of Man be in the heart of the earth for three days and three nights."*

In chapter 13, Matthew includes another group of Jesus' teachings. He notes that Jesus makes use of stories called parables, which use everyday circumstances to teach about the Kingdom of God. These make his teachings vivid and memorable. Parables also provide a gentle way of probing the spiritual interest of the hearer.

Jesus tells a long parable about a farmer who scatters seeds on different kinds of soils, with differing results. He explains the parable to be about proclaiming the Kingdom of God to different kinds of people—some of whom listen and believe, others of whom believe and then fall away, and still others who aren't interested at all.

Jesus tells several other parables about letting God determine, at the end of history, who is a believer and who isn't.

Chapter 14 describes what happens after Herod Antipas, the ruler of Galilee, arrests and then beheads John the Baptist as a favor to his wife and daughter.

Upon hearing the news, Jesus goes to a remote area to be alone, but the crowds find him. Out of compassion, he heals many, and then later that evening performs the miracle of feeding 5,000 with five loaves and two fish. According to John's gospel, this miraculous feeding is a sign pointing to Jesus as the Bread of Life.

As the disciples head home across the sea after these events, they are beset with a strong storm producing heavy waves. In the midst of this crisis, as they push at the oars, Jesus suddenly appears—walking on the water! To reassure them that he is not a ghost, he invites Peter to walk out toward him. Peter does, but then reacts with fear to the strong wind and waves, and sinks! Little faith.

Focus: We need to be prepared for the fact that the Good News of God's Kingdom will not be welcomed by everyone—humans or demons. Sometimes there will be

524

angry pushback, even martyrdom, as for John the Baptist, so we need to be strong in faith, knowing that Jesus is with us in the present storm.

Prayer: Lord, grant us the wisdom, grace and protection we need as we live and share the Kingdom life in a hostile world. Amen.

Day 279   Matthew 16–19

October 5

> Key Text: Then Jesus said to his disciples, "If any of you wants to be my follower, you must turn from your selfish ways, take up your cross, and follow me. If you try to hang on to your life, you will lose it. But if you give up your life for my sake, you will save it. And what do you benefit if you gain the whole world but lose your own soul?" (Matthew 16:24–26)

Both the religious leaders of Israel, and Jesus' followers, fail to grasp that his miracles are not meant to be ends in themselves. The religious leaders demand a sign to prove his authority, but Jesus refuses. The people are poor and often hungry, so their thoughts return to Jesus' ability to make bread. Jesus sighs: *"Why can't you understand that I'm not talking about bread?"* (Matthew 16:11).

Later, the disciples do understand, sort of. A breakthrough occurs when Jesus asks them, *"Who do you say that I am?"* Peter, speaking for the group, confesses, *"You are the Messiah, the Son of the living God"* (Matthew 16:16). Jesus tells Peter that he is blessed because this recognition has come from God. Then he declares that he will build his Church upon the truth of Peter's confession. All the powers of hell cannot not conquer it.

He begins talking about his need to suffer and die and then be raised from the dead. When Peter strongly objects to his saying such a thing, Jesus rebukes him: *"Get away from me, Satan! You are a dangerous trap to me. You are seeing things merely from a human point of view, not from God's."*

Jesus knows he cannot avoid the cross. Neither can his disciples, in a manner of speaking: *"If any one of you wants to be my follower, you must turn from your selfish ways, take up your cross, and follow me. If you try to hang on to your life, you will lose it. But if you give up your life for my sake, you will save it"* (Matthew 16:24–25).

Chapter 17 says that six days after this, Jesus takes Peter, James and

John to a high mountain to be alone. There, Jesus' appearance is transformed so that his face shines like the sun, and his clothes become as white as light. Suddenly Moses and Elijah appear, representing the Old Testament Law and prophets, and begin talking with Jesus. Like at Jesus' baptism, the voice of God speaks from heaven: *"This is my dearly loved Son, who brings me great joy. Listen to him."* This event is called the Transfiguration and is a glimpse at Jesus' glory. Jesus is the One of whom Moses and the prophets had written, and God's eternal Son who can exist in both the material and spiritual realms which make up the whole creation.

Chapters 18 and 19 return to a collection of Jesus' teachings, mostly about honoring children and having the willingness to forgive. Jesus regularly notices and blesses children, saying that *"anyone who welcomes a little child like this on my behalf is welcoming me."* He also urges believers to forgive one another when they are wronged. How often? A lot! The great debt of sin for which God has forgiven us ought to be reflected in the generosity of our forgiveness of one another.

Chapter 19 begins with some Pharisees intending to trap Jesus with a "gotcha" question about divorce and remarriage. In response, Jesus clarifies God's original intention for marriage from Genesis, chapter 2—one man and one woman becoming "one flesh" for a lifetime: *"Since they are no longer two but one, let no one split apart what God has joined together"* (Matthew 19:6).

Divorce happens—and sometimes needs to happen because of human sinfulness—but it is not God's will for people to treat marriage as a disposable relationship of self-gratification.

Another difficult issue Jesus raises is wealth. A wealthy young ruler walks away from Jesus when it becomes obvious that his money possesses him. Jesus challenges him to give his wealth to the poor and then follow him. He can't let go of it.

Jesus assures his disciples that nothing we sacrifice in this life will be lost; indeed, it will be multiplied beyond imagination in heaven.

Focus: Most would agree that "money is power." We control it, or it controls us and becomes our master. Jesus says that no one can serve two masters. Inevitably, you must choose. The rich young ruler made his choice and walked away. Bad decision. The economics of the Kingdom of God teach us that whatever we lose in this life by following Jesus, we will gain a hundredfold in return, and will inherit eternal life!

Prayer: Lord, grant us the grace to turn from our selfish ways and take up the cross of obedience, even suffering for your sake, so that we may find the life is that truly life! Amen.

Day 280   Matthew 20–23

October 6

Key Text: "**W**hoever wants to be a leader among you must be your servant, and whoever wants to be first among you must become your slave. For even the Son of Man came not to be served but to serve others and to give his life as a ransom for many." (Matthew 20:26–28)

We learn from two events in chapter 20 that God operates by a different understanding of merit. First, Jesus tells a story about God's generosity that causes concern among those who feel offended when others get what they don't deserve. The story, or parable, is about a landowner who hires men throughout the day to work in his vineyard. At the end of the day, he pays them all the same, regardless of how many hours they worked. Unfair? The early workers think so, but the landowner says to them: *"Take your money and go. I wanted to pay this last worker the same as you. ... Should you be jealous because I am kind to others?"* (Matthew 20:14–16).

From this Jesus draws a Kingdom principle which turns on its head the common sense of the world: *"Those who are last now will be first then, and those who are first will be last."*

Next, the mother of two of Jesus' disciples, James and John, lobbies for her sons to sit in places of honor when Jesus becomes king. Jesus cautions their enthusiasm, saying that his Kingdom is different from the kingdoms of this world: *"Whoever wants to be a leader among you must be your servant.... For even the Son of Man came not to be served but to serve others and to give his life as a ransom for many"* (Matthew 20:26–28).

What a remarkable statement of the mission of God in the world!

Jesus later illustrates this by entering Jerusalem in a humble manner, on a colt. This act was understood by the cheering people to be a Messianic sign, because the prophet Zechariah predicted that such a thing would happen. But Jesus' humility is puzzling. Instead of calling for a revolution against Rome, as Israel expected the Messiah to do, Jesus goes into the Jewish Temple and protests religious corruption.

The crowd's enthusiasm, and Jesus' protest, cause the religious leaders to become indignant. Later, when Jesus teaches the people, the leaders try to trip him up with another "gotcha" question, this time about John the Baptist's preaching—whether or not it was from God. Jesus cleverly turns it back on them and shows them to be hypocrites: *"I tell you the truth, corrupt tax collectors and prostitutes* [whom the leaders judged and shamed] *will get into the Kingdom of God before you do"* (Matthew 21:31).

He tells another parable about a landowner who goes away, leasing his vineyard to tenant farmers. Whenever he sends a servant to collect his share of the crop, per the agreement, the farmers kill him. Finally, the landowner sends his own son, and they kill him too. By this and other parables, Jesus illustrates the spiritual blindness of the leaders, who do not recognize Jesus as the Messiah and are planning in their hearts to kill him.

They have decided to arrest him when they think the time is right.

In chapter 22, Jesus tells a parable about the Kingdom of Heaven wherein a king prepares a great wedding feast for his son, but those invited to celebrate refuse to come. A second invitation results in the messenger being insulted and killed. In response to their non-response, the king invites people off the street—*"good and bad alike, and the banquet hall was filled with guests."* This was a criticism of the religious leaders of Israel for failing to acknowledge God's Son, while ordinary people recognized him right away and entered the Kingdom of Heaven by their faith.

The chapter ends with the religious leaders seeking to trap Jesus with some more "gotcha" questions. The first is about paying taxes to Caesar as king, to which he famously replies, *"give to Caesar what belongs to Caesar, and give to God what belongs to God."* The second question is a wildly hypothetical question about the Old Testament Levitical law requiring a brother to marry his widowed sister-in-law in order to guarantee the survival of the family line. If such a woman married a series of brothers, who all died, then whose wife would she be *"in the resurrection?"* they asked. (Those who asked the question, the Sadducees, didn't believe in the resurrection). Jesus basically tells them that they don't know what they are talking about. The resurrection will bring about a whole new order of existence and relationships, where there will be no marriage.

In chapter 23, Jesus warns the crowds and his disciples to beware of the religious teachers who don't practice what they preach. Instead, learn humility, because in the Kingdom of God, *"those who exalt themselves will be humbled, and those who humble themselves will be exalted"* (Matthew 23:12). Again, the Kingdom of God turns the ways of the world upside down.

Jesus then gives a stern warning to the religious leaders that they are in danger of failing to enter the Kingdom themselves. They are "blind guides" and "hypocrites." Great sorrow awaits them because they ignore the true meaning of the Law, which is justice, mercy and faith. They are like their ancestors, who hardened their hearts towards God and killed the prophets he sent to them.

Focus: The most dangerous of all sins is malignant pride, because those who exalt themselves close their hearts to both God and people. Skepticism is an easy out for lazy minds who don't want to change, and for proud people who don't want to admit that they don't know everything. In his fantasy, *The Great Divorce*, C.S. Lewis imagines hell to be populated by self-satisfied, skeptical people who regard themselves as smarter than others because they don't believe in God nonsense. On a bus trip to the outskirts of heaven to meet friends they knew on earth, they discover that they have no weight, while the people of heaven are larger and substantial. All the hell-dwellers are offered the chance to remain and grow, but in the end they refuse. They get back on the bus and return to hell. Who can understand the mystery of unbelief?!

Prayer: *Lord, keep our hearts honest and humble before you and one another. Help us to follow Jesus by finding greatness through servanthood. Amen.*

Day 281 — Reflection

October 7

Henrietta Mears, a great Christian educator of the last generation, used to say of the Old and New Testaments: *"The New is in the Old concealed; The Old is in the New revealed."* Originally attributed to Saint Augustine, it is a simple but effective way to frame the story of the Bible. It is one story, and its greatest achievement is to reveal Jesus to us.

We can't fully appreciate what Jesus said and did if we don't understand that his coming is a fulfillment of the Old Testament story. Let's review. As we have noted many times, the story begins by God revealing himself to Abraham, and then promising that Abraham would be the father of a great nation, with its own land. One day, a descendent of this nation will bless all nations on earth by making things right in the world: *"All the families on earth will be blessed through you"* (Genesis 12:3).

Now, Abraham came from a pagan tradition where it was believed that particular gods had power over certain geographical locations. It was surprising for Abraham to hear that God was going to give him a piece of land that was already occupied by other people with their own gods—the land of Canaan.

But God revealed to Abraham and his descendants that there were no other gods. The gods of the nations are lifeless, manmade idols. But the Lord God who has made himself known, is the Creator of the heavens and earth. He created everything for his own pleasure, and therefore he is its Judge. In the case of Canaan, the nations are warned well ahead of time that their religious and civil practices are evil, and that they will be destroyed if they do not change.

They do not change. Therefore, God warns that the land itself will *"vomit them out."*

God gives this land to Israel, where the twelve tribes can grow into a settled nation. But first they need to get there, for the tribes are slaves in Egypt. So God calls Moses to go to Pharaoh with an epic and preposterous demand: *"Let my people go."* Astonishingly, in the end Pharaoh lets them go, and they escape through the Red Sea.

During their long journey to occupation of Canaan, God reveals himself to the people as holy, meaning he is like no other. In his character, he is utterly righteous, yet thankfully, utterly loving as well. He cannot tolerate sin, so in order to have fellowship with him, the people needed to be holy themselves, at least symbolically, if not in fact.

So he gave the people his commandments through Moses. They outlined how the people should worship God and live in community with each other. The commandments were part of a Covenant agreement whereby God would bless his people, but they needed to remain faithful to them. This promise is known as the Old Covenant, or as we call it, the Old Testament.

Of course, the people couldn't keep the commandments consistently. Therefore, God also gave Israel a Priesthood to oversee sacrifices given by the people as offerings for their sins, before God, at least provisionally.

The system of sacrifice drilled into Israel's consciousness the meaning of substitution and atonement, a covering for sin. An innocent animal was offered, representing the guilty Israelite. The priest would then kill the animal, signifying that the guilt of the offender had been transferred to the innocent animal, which then bore the penalty.

All of this prepared Israel and the world for the coming of Christ, whom John the Baptist called the *"Lamb of God who takes away the sins of the world."*

Later, when Israel had kings, God promised that a king like King David would one day rule his people forever.

Later still, when Israel came under God's severe judgment because of her idolatry, immorality and lack of social justice, God allowed the people to be conquered and exiled. During these bleak years God spoke, through the prophets, about a Messiah who would come to forgive and restore Israel to the Covenant—but this time a renewed Covenant.

Here we discovered that the One who fulfills the promise of God to bless the world, who is the Lamb of God, and the Messiah and King, is Jesus.

Only Jesus is much more. He is also the Suffering Servant of Isaiah, the Heavenly Son of Man of Daniel, and most importantly, the incarnate Son of God—Immanuel, God with us.

In short, the Old Testament is about promise, while the New Testament is about fulfillment. In light of this, the saying rings true: *The New is in the Old concealed; the Old is in the New revealed.*

Prayer: Lord, thank you for the amazing gift of your Word, which tells us the story of Creation, Fall, Redemption and New Creation. Thank you for revealing who you are, what you are doing in the world, and what it means for us. Most importantly, we thank you for Jesus. When we follow him, we learn how to be human as you intended in the beginning. Amen.

October 8

> Key Text: "And the Good News about the Kingdom will be
> preached throughout the whole world, so that all nations will
> hear it; and then the end will come." (Matthew 24:14)

Readers of the New Testament have often asked the question, when will the end of the world come, which Jesus speaks of? We are not told specifically. Most speculation is misguided and fanciful, but chapter 24 gives us some clues about Jesus' thinking.

While walking with his disciples near the Temple in Jerusalem, Jesus comments that the Temple buildings will be completely demolished. This statement confuses and alarms the disciples. They ask him two anxious questions in response: When will this happen? What will be the sign of his return and the end of the world?

Jesus' answer is complex. He uses what we called in the Old Testament, prophetic foreshortening. Foreshortening is a method by which an artist relates the foreground of a picture with the background. Both the near and far are in sight. In prophetic foreshortening, the relationship is not space, but time. Jesus moves back and forth between the *near question* of the Temple's destruction, which happened in AD 70 by Emperor Titus, and the *far question* about the end of the world, in the indeterminate future.

To the far question, Jesus speaks with apocalyptic imagery to say, in effect, keep watch because you don't know what day your Lord is coming. This warning is valid for each generation of the Church.

There is, however, a general principle about when the end with come. Jesus says, *"And the Good News about the Kingdom will be preached throughout the whole world, so that all nations will hear it; and then the end will come"* (Matthew 24:14). So we learn that the return of Jesus at the end of the present world is connected with the work of the Church to take the Good News to the nations.

Next, in chapter 25, Jesus tells a story about being ready for the return of the Lord. He says the Kingdom of Heaven will be like ten bridesmaids, who in accordance with first-century Jewish wedding tradition, take their lamps to meet the bridegroom. But half of them are foolish. They don't bring enough oil for their lamps. So when the bridegroom arrives, they aren't ready. They run to buy oil and miss the wedding.

Another parable is about how we invest the years of our lives as we wait for the Lord to return. Jesus says that a wealthy man goes on a long trip, entrusting his wealth to his servants to invest on his behalf. He gives differing amounts to each servant, according to their ability.

When he returns, he calls them to give an account of how they used his money. Two have invested well and earned interest for their master. One, however, is lazy and has buried the money in the ground, essentially wasting the opportunity. He is judged harshly for his laziness. This is a parable about final judgment. The Lord will judge people and nations at the end of history concerning how they have lived and treated others. This story assumes that the presence or absence of love for God manifests itself in love for others. Those who truly love God demonstrate it by showing concern and compassion for others. Or to say it in reverse, those who love others show that they love God.

Those who don't show concern and compassion for others, reveal that they have no love for God either. These are serious matters, because heaven and hell are at stake.

Focus: The most important concern of every Christian ought not to be figuring out when Jesus is going to return, but rather being committed to showing love and compassion to others on earth until Jesus returns. Since Jesus links his return, generally, to the mission of the Church, his challenge, in Matthew 6:33 to *"seek the Kingdom of God above all else, and live righteously..."* takes on a sense of priority.

Prayer: Lord, we give ourselves to be your faithful servants while on earth, for as many years as you give us. For though we do not know when you will return at the end of history, we do know that our personal histories will end relatively soon. May we invest our lives well for your glory. Amen.

Day 283   Matthew 26–28

October 9

Key Text: Then the angel spoke to the women. "Don't be afraid!" he said. "I know you are looking for Jesus, who was crucified. He isn't here! He is risen from the dead, just as he said would happen." (Matthew 28:5–6)

Matthew finishes his story about Jesus by recounting the events of Jesus' Passion—his betrayal, trials, torture, crucifixion, and resurrection from the dead. Here is the dramatic center of the story of the whole Bible. From the moment Adam and Eve rebelled against God in Genesis 3, everything has been leading to this moment. God did not abandon his creation to sin and death, but immediately initiated his loving plan to reconcile the world to himself.

In Jesus' Passion we see the astonishing picture of Almighty God humbling himself through Jesus, to take our judgment and bear our punishment for sin. This means that he must experience death as one of us—as a human being. But the agony and sorrow of Jesus' unjust death is not the end. Forgiveness of sin clears the way for a new future because Jesus is raised from the dead by the power of God!

Sin is forgiven; death is overcome. Now our future is not nothing, but everything—following Jesus with resurrection bodies like his into a New Creation where we shall live forever.

What this means for our life *now* will be addressed in the rest of the New Testament.

Here, then, is Matthew's account of Jesus' Passion. Jesus knows that his time has come. The religious leaders are plotting to take his life, and Judas has negotiated a fee with them to betray him. Jesus gathers the twelve for a Passover meal to prepare them for what is coming. He says, *"The Son of Man must die, as the Scriptures declared long ago. But how terrible it will be for the one who betrays him. It would be far better for that man if he had never been born!"* (Matthew 26:24).

Jesus then takes the elements of the Passover meal—the bread and the wine—and explains how these ancient symbols of God's covenant love for his people would now point to a New Covenant established by his death. His body will be broken and his blood will be shed for them.

Judas betrays him to the religious leaders, just as Jesus predicted. The thugs they employ find Jesus and the disciples praying in the Garden of Gethsemane. They arrest him after Judas betrays him with a kiss. One of his disciples takes up a sword, but Jesus stops him. He rejects the way of revolution.

Jesus is quickly taken to the home of Caiaphas the high priest, where the religious leaders are gathered. A phony trial with false witnesses ends when Jesus testifies to being the Messiah and the Son of God. He is found guilty of blasphemy.

Events now move quickly. Jesus is mocked and tortured. His disciples go into hiding, with Peter denying three times that he knows Jesus. The religious leaders demand that the Roman governor Pilate condemn Jesus to crucifixion, which he reluctantly does when the mobs are stirred up and yelling, *"Crucify him!"*

Jesus is flogged and given a crown of thorns. When the soldiers tire of mocking him, they lead him away to be crucified. While hanging on the cross, and being verbally assaulted by the crowds, Jesus cries out, *"My God, my God, why have you abandoned me?"* (Matthew 27:46).

Then Jesus dies. An earthquake tears the curtain in the Temple and opens graves in the cemetery. The Roman guards take special precautions with Jesus' tomb, lest someone try to steal his body and claim that he rose from the dead.

The next day, the women disciples go to the tomb and find it empty. An angel explains: *"'Don't be afraid!' he said. 'I know you are looking for Jesus, who was crucified. He isn't here! He is risen from the dead, just as he said would happen'"* (Matthew 28:5–6).

After a few days, Jesus appears to his amazed disciples and gives them a Great Commission: *"Go and make disciples of all the nations, baptizing them in the name of the Father and the Son and the Holy Spirit. Teach these new disciples to obey all the commands I have given you. And be sure of this: I am with you always, even to the end of the age"* (Matthew 28:19–20).

Focus: C.S. Lewis once remarked that the uniqueness of Christianity is grace. The Gospel is Good News of a gracious God who gives us eternal life through his crucified and resurrected Son. All who receive his grace by faith belong to him and have the gift of eternal life.

Prayer: Lord, our hearts are moved again by the story of such love. We can hardly believe that it's true. May we be faithful witnesses to the Good News with those we know in our lives. Amen.

October 10

> Key Text: John announced: "Someone is coming soon who is
> greater than I am—so much greater that I'm not even worthy
> to stoop down like a slave and untie the straps of his sandals. I
> baptize you with water, but he will baptize you with the Holy
> Spirit!" (Mark 1:7–8)

Most scholars believe that Mark was the first gospel to be written. If
so, Mark invented the form of literature that we call a "gospel." It appears that Matthew and Luke borrowed from Mark's gospel in writing
their own.

Mark was not one of the twelve apostles. The evidence suggests that
Peter was his mentor and the source of the stories that only an insider
would know. Mark apparently writes his gospel to make Christianity ac-
cessible to Gentiles, since so much about the Jewish roots of Jesus and
the references to the Old Testament prophecies and events are omit-
ted—references that Gentiles might not be familiar with.

His style is fast paced, focusing not so much on Jesus' teaching but on
his powerful actions—something that a Roman Gentile could relate to!

Chapter 1 begins not with the birth of Jesus, but with the launch of his
public ministry. John the Baptist is calling Jewish people to repent and
prepare themselves through the ritual cleansing of baptism, because
God is up to something new and they need to be ready.

Then, John announces what it is—Jesus, God's Son, has arrived, and
he is going to change everything from the inside out by the power of the
Holy Spirit. *"I baptize you with water, but he will baptize you with the Holy
Spirit!"* (Mark 1:8).

After his baptism, Jesus retreats to the wilderness to face his primary spiritual opposition. Satan tries to talk Jesus out of his mission by
tempting him with an alternative kingdom, based on celebrity, wealth
and power. All Jesus must do is worship him! A bold temptation, revealing Satan's fall from grace and opposition to God.

Jesus resists the temptation and chooses instead service and self-sacrifice, the way to God's Kingdom. His message: *"'The time promised by
God has come at last!' he announced. 'The Kingdom of God is near! Repent*

of your sins and believe the Good News!'" (Mark 1:15).

After calling the Galilean fishermen Simon (Peter), Andrew, James and John to follow him, Jesus begins to teach the crowds. They are amazed at his teaching because he teaches with personal authority. The authority of his word is dramatically demonstrated by his casting out demons and healing the sick. He even touches and heals a leper out of compassion. So the crowds grow.

Back at home in Capernaum, Jesus heals a man and forgives his sins. This creates an angry response from the religious leaders who are already nervous about Jesus' popularity. So Jesus heals and forgives another man in their very presence, to demonstrate his authority. This only creates greater tension, for now they label him a blasphemer. But the people are amazed and begin praising God!

A further offense by Jesus, in the eyes of the religious leaders, is his association with those considered to be disreputable sinners, notably tax collectors. One particular tax collector, named Matthew, will eventually become one of his twelve apostles. When asked why he associates with such "scum," Jesus shrewdly observes, *"Healthy people don't need a doctor—sick people do. I have come to call not those who think they are righteous, but those who know they are sinners"* (Mark 2:17).

Clearly something new is happening within Judaism if Jesus is the Son of God, with power to forgive sins and welcome outsiders into the Kingdom. As Jesus explains it, his ministry is like *"new wine,"* and *"new wine calls for new wineskins."* Things are going to look different from now on. God is doing something new! Meanwhile, the Jewish Pharisees go away and meet with the supporters of Herod to plot how to kill Jesus.

Events move quickly in Mark's gospel. Jesus personally chooses twelve men to be his apostles. He immediately gives them his power to preach the Good News and cast out demons.

His family thinks he is out of his mind, and the religious leaders think he is possessed by Satan. But the truth is, the Kingdom of God has come with power through the words and works of Jesus! Nothing will be the same.

Focus: The Gospel comes with power to change people and disrupt the existing power structures of this world. Expect opposition, even violent opposition, as the demonic proxies of this world scream out: *"Why are you interfering with us, Jesus of Nazareth?"*

Day 285   Mark 4–7

October 11

> Key Text: "For everything that is hidden will eventually be brought into the open, and every secret will be brought to light." (Mark 4:22)

Mark does not focus on Jesus' teaching as much as Matthew, but chapter 4 includes a representative sample. Jesus ordinarily teaches the crowds through everyday stories, called parables, which describe the nature and function of the Kingdom of God.

As we noted in Matthew, the Kingdom of God is presently the reign and rule of God in human hearts. One day, God will reign over his whole creation once again. In the meantime, Jesus' parables about the Kingdom speak to those who are spiritually seeking and want to know more.

Chapter 4 begins with the parable of the farmer who casts seed on various kinds of soil, with varying results. Only the seed that lands on fertile soil takes root and grows. By this, Jesus teaches his disciples not to be surprised that when the Kingdom of God is proclaimed, there will be varying responses, negative and positive.

The Kingdom is like a light shining in the darkness. It exposes all of our secrets, but not everyone welcomes the exposure! Those who listen carefully to Jesus' teaching will understand and their faith will grow.

At the end of history, the *"harvest time,"* God will judge what people have done with the message of the Kingdom. In the parable of the mustard seed we are reassured that the Kingdom will grow large, even though there are so few disciples now.

Chapter 5 contains three wonderful healing stories. They demonstrate the power of God over things which afflict human life. The first story is of an exorcism of a possessed man who is so wild and dangerous that he is put into chains, which he often breaks. He wanders among burial caves during the night, howling and cutting himself with sharp stones. Jesus mercifully casts out the many demons inside him into a herd of pigs, which runs down a steep hillside and drowns in a lake.

The second healing is of a desperate woman who pushes her way through a crowd to touch Jesus, and the third is the raising of Jairus' daughter from the dead. Jairus is a leader of a local synagogue, showing that not all the religious leaders are hostile to Jesus.

Miracles like these demonstrate that the Kingdom of God has come with power in the ministry of Jesus, even power over death itself!

Chapter 6 recalls how people from Jesus' hometown of Nazareth have a hard time believing in him, because they watched him grow up! Here we learn that Jesus is a carpenter, has four brothers (James, Joseph, Judas and Simon), and has sisters also, still living in Nazareth.

Because there is so much unbelief in Nazareth, Jesus travels on to other villages, now giving his disciples authority to call people to repent of their sin and turn to God. Mark reports that they also *"cast out many demons and healed many sick people, anointing them with olive oil"* (Mark 6:13).

Chapter 6 also reports the death of John the Baptist by Herod Antipas, as well as the feeding of the 5,000 and the calming of a storm by Jesus.

Chapter 7 describes some of Jesus' conflict with the religious leaders about Jewish law. Jesus accuses them of being more concerned about the letter of the law than the intent of the law. Except, of course, when they want to avoid a particular law—then they find devious ways around it. Moral behavior is a matter of the heart, not rigid rule-keeping for its own sake.

Chapter 7 ends with Jesus' praise for a Gentile woman who demonstrates more wisdom and faith than the Jewish religious leaders!

Focus: God wants to reign as king in his world once again. In Jesus, his kingly power has begun. By believing in him, we become part of God's Kingdom family, sharing in an unbelievable inheritance of a coming New World.

Prayer: Father, what a wonderful reality that your coming Kingdom has already begun in our hearts through faith in Jesus. We thank you for the joy of your presence in our lives, and the privilege of answered prayer. May we continue to experience more and more of your amazing love, which is beyond comprehension. Amen.

October 12

> Key Text: "For even the Son of Man came not to be served but to serve others and to give his life as a ransom for many." (Mark 10:45)

Chapter 8 begins with a second miraculous feeding of a large crowd, possibly Gentiles. As before, bread and fish are multiplied, everyone has their fill, and leftovers are collected. Jesus is more than able to feed his people, body and soul.

The religious leaders, however, demand that Jesus show them another miracle to prove his authority. Jesus says no. He doesn't perform miracles to prove anything. He heals and provides for needy people out of compassion, and to make clear that God's Kingdom has arrived in Jesus who is, as John's gospel reports, *"the bread of life."*

But even his disciples are slow to understand the meaning of Jesus' feeding miracles. They are preoccupied with their physical hunger, and they want Jesus to make more bread for them. He asks, *"Why are you arguing about having no bread? Don't you know or understand even yet? Are your hearts too hard to take it in?"* (Mark 8:17).

Later, Jesus flat out asks his disciples who they think he is. Peter responds for the group, saying, *"You are the Messiah."* Peter has his identity right, but misunderstands his mission as Messiah. Jesus tells them that he must suffer and then be killed, but three days later will rise from the dead.

This is too much for Peter, who rebukes Jesus for talking like this. So Jesus tells Peter that his well-meaning concern is really an idea Satan has put into his head to keep him from doing what he must do. God's plan is for the Messiah to die and rise from the dead. Those who follow him must be willing to die in a different sort of way—die to selfishness. *"If any of you wants to be my follower,"* Jesus says, *"you must turn from your selfish ways, take up your cross, and follow me. If you try to hang on to your life, you will lose it. But if you give up your life for my sake and for the sake of the Good News, you will save it"* (Mark 8:34–35).

Chapter 9 says that Jesus then takes Peter, James and John with him to a high mountain to be alone. It is time for them to see another side of

Jesus so that they can better understand his identity and mission. Right before their eyes, his appearance is transformed and his clothes become dazzling white. Then Moses and the prophet Elijah appear, representing the Old Testament Law and prophets. The disciples sense the presence of God and then hear him speak! He affirms Jesus as his Son and directs the disciples to heed his teaching. This event, known as the Transfiguration, dramatically reveals that Jesus is what the Old Testament Law and prophets were pointing to.

A lengthy story follows about the exorcism of an evil spirit from a boy. The frightening details of its abuse of the boy and then its fierce struggle to resist Jesus, illustrate the severity of spiritual warfare and our need of Jesus' power to resist the demonic.

Several vignettes about ministry follow: Jesus describes leadership as servanthood, not power grabbing. He warns us not to judge the ministries of others, but instead ruthlessly judge ourselves, lest we undermine ministry by our sin.

Chapter 10 presents a series of challenges to Jesus. The Pharisees try to entrap him with a question about divorce. The disciples try to keep children from getting in the way when Jesus teaches. And a rich young man wants to know how to inherit eternal life without it impacting his lifestyle too much. In his responses, Jesus highlights the integrity of marriage, the importance of children, and the power of wealth to keep us from God.

He tells his disciples that the Kingdom of God must reorder our priorities and redirect our passions. The Kingdom life is the way of the cross, meaning the way of servanthood and death to selfishness: *"For even the Son of Man came not to be served but to serve others and to give his life as a ransom for many"* (Mark 10:45).

Focus: The Christian life is not merely a philosophy to admire, nor a respectable service club to join. It is following Jesus into battle. The struggle is not just against the demonic in the world, but also—and perhaps primarily—the selfishness within our hearts.

Prayer: Father, we confess that our first concern is usually, "What's in it for me? What will it cost?" But when we see the life of your Son, we are humbled. Give us the strength, courage and faith it will take to serve you in this chaotic world of spiritual danger and powerful temptations. Amen.

October 13

> Key Text: "Give to Caesar what belongs to Caesar, and give to
> God what belongs to God." (Mark 12:17)

About forty percent of Mark's gospel is devoted to the final eight days of Jesus' life. This shows that he wants us to understand the importance of Jesus' death on the cross for our salvation.

As we have seen, the religious leaders of Israel feel threatened by Jesus and believe him to be a false prophet and dangerous man. So they have been quietly plotting his death. Jesus is aware of their plans, but even more aware of God's plan, so he begins his final days with a Messianic act. He rides a young donkey into Jerusalem, which the crowds understand to mean that he is coming as their king. The Old Testament prophets predicted that the Messiah would do this when he came.

The crowds are electric. People spread their garments and palm branches on the road. They loudly praise God by quoting ancient psalms that speak of their coming Messianic King: *"Praise God! Blessings on the one who comes in the name of the Lord! Blessings on the coming Kingdom of our ancestor David! Praise God in highest heaven!"* (Mark 11:9–10).

While in Jerusalem, Jesus acts like a prophet. He enters the Temple, which has become corrupted by unjust financial practices, turning the Father's House into a marketplace. He is angered by what he sees, and begins to knock over the tables of the money changers and the sellers of doves to the poor. His Father's House is meant to be a place of prayer.

Jesus encourages his disciples to pray with faith, but says that doing so requires a clean heart. They should first forgive those they have a grudge against before they pray. Then their Father in heaven will forgive their sins, which may be far greater.

The religious leaders confront Jesus over his actions at the Temple, demanding to know by what authority he does these things. He refuses to answer, and instead tells a parable about the owner of a vineyard who leases his land to tenant farmers while he is away. When he sends his servants to collect his share of the crops, the farmers beat—or even kill—them. Finally, the owner sends his son, and they kill him. The religious leaders want to arrest Jesus right then, because they realize that he is telling this story about them. But Jesus is still too popular with the crowds.

They try again and again to trick him with difficult questions about politics, about the resurrection of the dead, and then about his opinion of the most important commandment. His answers amaze them, frustrate them, and finally expose their hateful hearts. The greatest commandment, Jesus says, is to love God with all your heart, soul, mind and strength. And then, to love your neighbor as yourself.

Jesus warns the people about the teachers of religious law. They like to look good, and they love attention and special honor. They shamelessly cheat widows out of their property and then pretend to be pious by making long prayers in public. Because of this, they will be more severely punished.

By contrast, Jesus points to a poor widow—a nobody without power or wealth. She puts two small coins in the offering at the Temple. Jesus says that she gave more than the rich rulers because she gave all that she had to live on, trusting God for her next meal.

Chapter 13 is devoted to Jesus' teaching about the Day of Judgment. He speaks first of a near judgment that is coming when Jerusalem will be destroyed by Titus in AD 70. The horror of that event portends the final days of the whole world, when *"everyone will see the Son of Man coming on the clouds with great power and glory. And he will send out his angels to gather his chosen ones from all over the world—from the farthest ends of the earth and heaven"* (Mark 13:26–27).

Jesus' message to his disciples, and to all of us, is to live purposefully and pay attention, for we don't know when that time will come.

Focus: The surprise of the New Testament is that, before the Messiah returns at the end of history as our Judge, he comes first as a Suffering Servant to offer his life for our sins. For those who receive his forgiveness, the Last Judgment has already occurred.

Prayer: Lord, we are grateful beyond words for your grace and mercy toward us. We are glad to have the assurance of salvation now. Help your Church to stay alert and focused on its mission until you return again at the end of history. Amen.

Day 288   Reflection

October 14

The idea that God is revealed as a king with a kingdom should not be surprising. Of all the people who had ever lived on earth, most had lived under a king or king-like ruler, so this is a metaphor that they could easily understand.

Typically, a king has all power, and owns everything. A benevolent king is a blessing to the people of the community because he provides for the safety and well-being of his subjects.

Of course, the Bible also says that God is like a shepherd who watches over his sheep, a father who provides for his children, and a husband who loves his wife, each of which expresses an aspect of God's nature. So the central metaphor of God as King should be understood not as a power-obsessed dictator, but as a generous king who administers the absolute power of a monarch as a righteous and benevolent ruler.

When God delivered the tribes of Israel from slavery in Egypt and constituted them as a nation, Israel became a theocracy. God was their king who promised to love, protect and bless them as his special people. Through the Mosaic Covenant, the people promised to worship and follow God alone.

In time, Israel lost faith in God's ability to protect them as king, and began to insist on having an earthly king like the nations around them. God accommodated their unbelief and fear by adjusting his mode of operation. He would rule Israel through her anointed kings. But this didn't work out so well, because in time Israel's kings behaved like the pagan kings around them, and eventually worshiped the pagan gods as well.

There were some exceptions. One notable exception was King David, who was a man after God's heart. David was far from a perfect human, but he trusted God and didn't worship idols. When Israel forgot God as its king, its national life deteriorated to the point where it was conquered and exiled by its enemies. But there was hope. God promised to send a new king, from the family line of David, who would be faithful to him and rule over his people forever.

This Messianic King would lead Israel in a second Exodus from her enemies and reestablish her in the Promised Land. But 400 years had passed since God last spoke through a prophet. Had God changed his mind?

Suddenly, John the Baptist began to preach, telling the Jews to prepare for the return of their king. The Gospels tell us that this king was Jesus, only his rule was not what Israel expected. The people expected a political and military deliverer, but Jesus came as a Suffering Servant like the prophet Isaiah had prophesied.

A new Exodus was coming, but it would not be deliverance from the power of Rome. It would be deliverance from the power of sin.

After Jesus was crucified and raised from the dead, the Gospels tell us that he ascended to heaven to sit at the right hand of God the Father. This is a picture of the throne room of a king. Once again God is ruling the earth as King, only now he is doing so through his crucified and risen Son.

Through the preaching of the Good News, the world is called to make Jesus its king, and enter his Kingdom. All who do so are adopted as children of the King, sit at his table, and become heirs of all his riches.

At the end of history, the King will return a second time to judge the nations. He will banish sin and death, and all who refuse his grace. His adopted children, of all nations, will then be ushered into a Kingdom that will never end, and he will dwell among them as their loving and benevolent king forever!

This is a wonderful hope, but it is just a metaphor; the reality will be far more wonderful than we can imagine. The apostle Paul tells the Christians at Corinth that this plan had been in God's mind from the beginning, and that he made it for our ultimate glory. Sadly, *"the rulers of this world have not understood it; if they had, they would not have crucified our glorious Lord. That is what the Scriptures mean when they say, 'No eye has seen, no ear has heard, and no mind has imagined what God has prepared for those who love him'"* (1 Corinthians 2:7–9).

> *Prayer: Lord, may we as your adopted children faithfully serve you as our king. May we be found faithful to grow your Kingdom on earth until you return again, for then your Kingdom will fully come and your will be perfectly done on earth, as it is in heaven! Amen.*

October 15

> Key Text: "Abba, Father," he cried out, "everything is possible for you. Please take this cup of suffering away from me. Yet I want your will to be done, not mine." (Mark 14:36)

The final chapters of Mark complete the account of Jesus' Passion.

Jesus knows that the religious leaders are looking for an opportunity to capture and kill him. Meanwhile, a gesture of great devotion by a woman who pours expensive perfume on his head, represents for Jesus the anointing of his body for burial ahead of time.

It has become clear that Jesus is not going to lead Israel into a revolution, so a deeply disappointed disciple, Judas Iscariot, betrays him to the religious leaders. Perhaps Judas thinks that if he forces Jesus' hand, he will rise up and lead the people. But Judas will be bitterly disappointed.

The evening that Jesus is betrayed by Judas, he shares the Passover meal with his disciples. During the meal, the disciples are stunned as Jesus applies the elements of the Passover meal to himself. Jesus takes the Passover bread, breaks it, and says: *"Take it, for this is my body."* Later he takes the cup of wine and gives thanks to God for it. He gives it to the disciples, and they all drink from it. Then he says to them, *"This is my blood, which confirms the covenant between God and his people. It is poured out as a sacrifice for many."* Little do they know that Jesus is soon going to be the fulfillment of the Passover, not only for them, but for the whole world.

Then, mysteriously, Jesus says he will not drink wine again until the day he drinks it new in the Kingdom of God. This makes the Passover meal, which we now celebrate as "The Lord's Supper," an eschatological meal. It is a celebration and a declaration of where history is now heading because of Jesus' death and resurrection. Victory is ahead! Christ is returning, and through him God will once again reign as King over his creation. Sin and death are put on notice and will be eliminated in the Last Judgment. In their place is eternal life in a New Creation!

In the meantime, there is suffering ahead for Jesus, but suffering that leads to glory. In Gethsemane, we see his humanity recoil from the anticipation of crucifixion. But we also see his deity as the Son, obeying the will of the Father: *"Yet I want your will to be done, not mine"* (Mark 14:36).

When later betrayed by Judas' kiss, Jesus is arrested. He is taken to the high priest's home where the religious leaders are gathered. He is subjected to the humiliation of false witnesses. When the witnesses can't keep their stories straight, the high priest impatiently stands up and demands to know, *"Are you the Messiah, the Son of the Blessed One?"* Jesus responds, *"I AM. And you will see the Son of Man seated in the place of power at God's right hand and coming on the clouds of heaven"* (Mark 14:61–62).

Guilty!

Events move quickly now. Jesus is roughed up and sent to Pilate. Meanwhile, Peter denies three times that he knows Jesus. Pilate is uncomfortable with the situation, but succumbs to the pressure of the crowds, who demand, *"Crucify him!"* The soldiers take over now. Jesus is struck, spit upon, mocked, and impaled with a crown of thorns. He is nailed to a cross and suffers one of most horrific of all deaths, crying out, *"My God, my God, why have you abandoned me?"*

Mark reports that when Jesus dies, the curtain in the sanctuary of the Temple is torn in two, from top to bottom. The symbolism of this tear means that the privilege of being the people of God is now open to Jews and Gentiles alike. Sure enough, Mark notes that a Roman soldier, seeing how Jesus died, exclaims, *"This man truly was the Son of God!"* (Mark 15:39).

This happens on a Friday—Good Friday, as we know it. Three days later, the women go to the tomb to anoint the body of Jesus and find it empty, with the stone rolled away. An angel at the tomb tells them, *"He isn't here! He is risen from the dead!"*

Two endings of Mark appear in the textual history of the Gospel. The longer ending includes post-resurrection appearances of Jesus to the disciples, during which he teaches and commissions them to *"go into all the world and preach the Good News to everyone."* After the Lord is taken up into heaven, the disciples obey.

Focus: Isaac Watts captured the wonder of the cross perfectly in his famous hymn: *"See from his head, his hands, his feet, / Sorrow and love flow mingled down! / Did e'er such love and sorrow meet, / Or thorns compose so rich a crown?"*

Prayer: *Lord, it is impossible to comprehend what Jesus went through on the cross—not just his physical suffering, but the spiritual horror of bearing human*

Day 290   Luke 1–2

October 16

> Key Text: …the angel reassured them. "Don't be afraid!" he said.
> "I bring you good news that will bring great joy to all people."
> (Luke 2:10)

The third gospel is written by Luke, a medical doctor and meticulous
historian of the story of Jesus, to a friend named Theophilus. The book of
Acts is a continuation of his gospel, beginning with events immediately
after Jesus' resurrection when the Church is born on the Day of Pentecost.

The opening verses of Luke give us a peek into how the Gospels came
into being: *"Many people have set out to write accounts about the events
that have been fulfilled among us. They used the eyewitness reports circu-
lating among us from the early disciples. Having carefully investigated everything from the beginning, I also have decided to write a careful account
for you, most honorable Theophilus, so you can be certain of the truth of
everything you were taught"* (Luke 1:1–4).

Luke's story begins with the angel Gabriel visiting two women who
are related. One is old and barren; the other young, single and a virgin.
The old woman, Elizabeth, is told that she will have a son who is to be
named John. Her son *"will be a man with the spirit and power of Elijah.
He will prepare the people for the coming of the Lord."* The virgin, named
Mary, is told that the Holy Spirit will come upon her and create life with-
in her. *"The baby to be born will be holy, and he will be called the Son of
God."*

When these two women visit later, and share their incredible stories
with one another, it becomes apparent that God is up to something. Mary
cries out in praise for the honor shown to her by God, and for the expectation that God is acting in behalf of his people Israel, remembering to
be merciful.

When John is born, his father Zechariah is filled with the Holy Spirit
and prophesies about the significance of his son. He will be the prophet,
John the Baptist, who will *"prepare the way for the Lord."* God's tender

mercy toward Israel is arriving like morning light from heaven, breaking upon them.

About that time the Roman emperor, Augustus, decrees that a census should be taken throughout the Roman Empire. All must return to their ancestral towns. Among the pilgrim travelers are Joseph and a very pregnant Mary, his fiancée. They are traveling to Bethlehem, King David's ancient home, because Joseph is a descendant of David. They find no lodging available and so they create space in a barn among animals. There, Jesus is born and makes his first bed in a manger—a feeding trough.

Quite a humble beginning for a king!

Meanwhile, an angel announces to shepherds nearby that something extraordinary has just happened. A Savior has been born, and it is *"good news that will bring great joy to all people."*

Suddenly a whole battalion of angels joins the first angel, praising God and saying, *"Glory to God in the highest heaven, and peace on earth to those with whom God is pleased."* So the shepherds go quickly to Bethlehem and find the child whom the angels declared to be the Savior. They rejoice and begin to spread the word about what has happened.

Luke adds other testimonies to the identity of the child when Jesus is later brought to the Temple to be presented to the Lord. A man named Simeon praises God that the child *"is a light to reveal God to the nations, and he is the glory of your people Israel!"* And a prophet, Anna, adds her praise and testimony as well, talking about the child to everyone who had been waiting expectantly for God to rescue Jerusalem.

Luke briefly touches upon Jesus' early years where it becomes apparent that he is strong and filled with wisdom, and God's favor is on him. Is this the Messiah at last?

Focus: It is notable that the story of Christianity begins in obscurity and humility, not with great fanfare and tribute by the powerful of the earth. Christianity thrives when it continues its mission with compassion and servanthood, resisting the temptation of earthly power.

Prayer: Lord, help us not to be selfish or try to impress others. May we instead have the same attitude of Jesus, who, though he was God, did not think of equality with God as something to cling to, but instead gave up his divine privileges in order to serve us through his death and resurrection. May people see Jesus in us as we serve. Amen.

Day 291   Luke 3–6

> Key Text: As the sun went down that evening, people throughout the village brought sick family members to Jesus. No matter what their diseases were, the touch of his hand healed every one. (Luke 4:40)

Today's chapters are loaded with details about Jesus' ministry and teaching, beginning with his baptism by John. John the Baptist warns the people about their need to repent and prepare themselves for God's judgment: *"Prove by the way you live that you have repented of your sins and turned to God. Don't just say to each other, 'We're safe, for we are descendants of Abraham'"* (Luke 3:8).

When Jesus presents himself for baptism by John, it is not because he is sinful himself. He is baptized to fully identify with sinful people, because that is why he has come. Luke notes that when Jesus is baptized, the Holy Spirit descends upon him like a dove, and the voice of God from heaven commends Jesus as his *"dearly loved Son."* In time, the Church will see the events of Jesus' baptism as a manifestation of the triune God—Jesus, the Son, is commended by God the Father, who sends his Holy Spirit.

Chapter 3 is a lengthy genealogy establishing Jesus' credentials as Messiah and more. Luke's genealogy, however, moves backwards, beginning with Jesus as the son of Joseph, and going back through the prophets to his ancestor, King David. From David, the narrative goes back to Abraham, and from Abraham back to Adam. It is important for Luke's Jewish readers to know that Jesus meets the requirements for being the Messiah.

In chapter 4, Jesus is tempted by the devil, who tries to persuade him to forgo his mission of dying on the cross for sins. Luke indicates several times that even demons are very clear about who Jesus is and what he has come to do. But Satan fails to tempt Jesus. He returns to Galilee to teach and heal, full of the Holy Spirit's power.

The people there are amazed at his teaching because he speaks with authority, especially when he interprets the Hebrew Messianic prophesies to be fulfilled in himself.

In addition to his teaching, the people are amazed at his power. Jesus moves from town to town, teaching in the synagogues, healing disease and casting out demons. These are acts of compassion, but also manifestations of Kingdom power. They anticipate the great reversal which is to come in the New Creation, where there will be no more sin, death, or powers of evil.

In chapter 5, Jesus calls the first four disciples to follow him, all of whom are fishermen. When Jesus performs a fishing miracle and loads their boats with fish, he tells his amazed disciples, *"From now on you'll be fishing for people!"* (Luke 5:10). Later, in chapter 6, Jesus will call together the remainder of his twelve disciples. But beginning with these four disciples, he starts to teach about the Kingdom of God.

Luke now includes several representative stories related to Jesus' teaching and healings, which we find in the other Gospels. Luke also notes that Jesus goes out of his way to associate with people whom the Jewish religious leaders shun, like lepers and tax collectors.

Jesus challenges the leaders' authority by contradicting their interpretation of the Law of Moses. This, of course, makes them furious and reveals them to be more concerned about their own power than the Kingdom of God.

In contrast to their hypocrisy, Jesus teaches his disciples about acts of radical obedience, such as loving their enemies, not judging others, and being generous to the poor. Being a true child of Abraham, Jesus explains, is not a matter of racial heritage, but an attitude of the heart that is revealed in good deeds.

He concludes by saying that establishing our lives upon his teaching is like building a house on solid rock. It will stand firm against anything that comes, because it is well built.

Focus: Jesus' conflict with Israel's religious leaders reveals that outward religiosity alone is meaningless to God. What he looks for is our heart attitude. To love and trust God from the heart is what it means to be a child of Abraham.

Prayer: Lord, give us eyes to see the needy around us. Give us compassion to share in their sorrow and need through generous hands and hearts. Keep us from the sin of becoming religious pretenders who justify ourselves while we judge others. Amen.

October 18

> Key Text: A crowd soon gathered around Jesus, and they saw
> the man who had been freed from the demons. He was sitting
> at Jesus' feet, fully clothed and perfectly sane, and they were all
> afraid. (Luke 8:35)

Luke now takes us on what we might call a travelogue of compassion. In a series of events, occurring in different towns, Jesus reveals the character of God. For example, he shows compassion to a Roman soldier by healing his highly valued slave. The soldier demonstrates a purity of faith not seen in Israel as a whole, says Jesus.

In another village, Jesus performs a stunning miracle. While observing the funeral procession of a widow's only son, his heart *"overflowed with compassion."* He walks up to the coffin and touches it—a violation of Jewish law—and quietly tells the young man to get up. And he does! Great fear sweeps through the crowd and they praise God that he has shown compassion to his people that day.

Later, Jesus finds out that John the Baptist, who is in prison because of Herod Antipas, is having doubts about whether he is the Messiah. Perhaps John has heard negative reports and rumors. Jesus takes time to reassure him by telling his messengers to report what they have seen: *"The blind see, the lame walk, the lepers are cured, the deaf hear, the dead are raised to life, and the Good News is being preached to the poor"* (Luke 7:22). John would recognize this as a Messianic fulfillment of Isaiah 35:5–6.

Later, while Jesus is having dinner with a Pharisee, a grateful woman who is a prostitute hears that Jesus is there and comes uninvited to anoint him with expensive perfume. The Pharisee seethes with disdain that Jesus would allow an immoral woman to touch him. Sensing his judgment, Jesus tells him a parable that conveys the message that a person who is forgiven little, shows only little love. But though her sins are many, this woman has shown great love. Jesus forgives her and tells her to go in peace.

In chapter 8, Luke follows Jesus on a ministry tour of the nearby towns. Luke notes that in addition to his twelve disciples, several women who had been cured of evil spirits and diseases accompany him. Jesus' treatment of women and children is a distinctive feature of his ministry. On this tour he tells the parable of the soils, explaining that there will be different responses to the Gospel when it is shared. Only upon *"fertile soil"* will the seed of the Gospel take root and grow.

The rest of chapter 8 contains the dramatic story of a man delivered from many demons. The demons, who have long tormented this poor man, recognize Jesus and seem to be aware that his ministry is an omen of their future destruction. He casts them out into a herd of pigs, which are unclean animals to the Jews, and the herd plunges down a steep hillside into a lake and drown. Meanwhile, we find the man sitting at Jesus' feet, fully clothed and perfectly sane!

After this, while on the way to the home of Jairus, who is a leader of the synagogue, Jesus heals a woman who pushes through the crowd to touch him. She has suffered for twelve years with constant bleeding. Jesus tells her to go in peace because her faith has made her well. He then continues to the home of Jairus, whose daughter has died. Amidst the weeping and wailing of sorrow, Jesus raises her from the dead!

In chapter 9, Jesus calls his twelve disciples together and makes them his apostles, meaning "sent ones." He sends them out with his power and authority to cast out demons, heal diseases, and tell everyone about the Kingdom of God. They experience his power in their ministry, but they still lack a mature understanding of the mission. So Jesus demonstrates the world's need for spiritual food by performing a miracle of feeding 5,000 people with only five loaves of bread and two fish. It also demonstrates what he can do with the little that we offer him.

But there are deeper lessons of faith ahead. Jesus continues to prepare them for the fact that he is going to die, and that they must die spiritually if they want follow him: *"If you try to hang on to your life, you will lose it. But if you give up your life for my sake, you will save it"* (Luke 9:24).

Focus: Jesus' ministry is the beginning of a new future for the present world. In the coming world—the New Creation—we will finally be free from all that holds us back from our calling and potential as humans. No more sickness and death! No more demonic activity! No more impulse to sin! It is the Church's privilege to announce this Good News to all people!

Prayer: Lord, we are moved by the compassion of Jesus to human need. Help us to do likewise by laying aside our indifference or our judgment of others. Help us to

Day 293   Luke 10–12

October 19

> Key Text: "I have come to set the world on fire, and I wish it were already burning!" (Luke 12:49)

Jesus now expands his ministry team from the twelve apostles to seventy-two other disciples. He warns that he is sending them out as lambs among wolves, and they should take precautions to cause no offense beyond the offense of the Gospel itself. They should minister to towns that welcome them, and leave the towns that don't.

He then gives them his power and authority for their task: *"Anyone who accepts your message is also accepting me. And anyone who rejects you is rejecting me. And anyone who rejects me is rejecting God, who sent me"* (Luke 10:16).

When the seventy-two return with a great report, Jesus is filled with joy. He tells them that he saw Satan fall from heaven like lightening! The spiritual battle has begun, and the Kingdom is winning! These early ministry tours by the first disciples are prototypes of the Church in its mission after Pentecost.

The ethics of the Kingdom are guided by the two great commandments—to love God and to love one's neighbor. Jesus tells the parable of the Good Samaritan to illustrate that loving one's neighbor includes everyone, even those we despise, like the Jews despised Samaritans.

The priority of the Kingdom is illustrated by Jesus' visit with Martha and her sister, Mary. Mary sits at Jesus' feet to learn from him while Martha is distracted by preparing dinner—and even annoyed because Mary isn't helping! Jesus tells Martha that Mary has made the right choice in determining that the Kingdom should be our first priority.

Chapter 11 begins with instructions about prayer. The Lord gives his disciples what we call the Lord's Prayer, which is essentially a Kingdom prayer, asking God to come soon and do on earth what he's doing in heaven. As his Kingdom people, his disciples are to ask for the physical and spiritual resources they need for life and service. And when they pray, they should persevere and not give up. Keep on asking, seeking and knocking.

Meanwhile, people are accusing Jesus of casting out demons with the power of Satan. Jesus explains how illogical this is. Why would Satan work against himself? Jesus' ministry of exorcism is tied to the message of the Kingdom of God. We need to be cleansed of evil, but then filled with the Spirit of God. The Kingdom changes us from the inside out with humility and holiness. We must avoid the outward pride and concern for honor that marks the Pharisees.

Chapter 11 ends with Jesus' confronting the Pharisees over their hypocrisy and spiritual abuse of the people: *"What sorrow awaits you experts in religious law! For you remove the key to knowledge from the people. You don't enter the Kingdom yourselves, and you prevent others from entering"* (Luke 11:52).

In chapter 12, Jesus warns the people to beware of the Pharisees' hypocrisy, and instead live lives of integrity and transparency. The time is coming when everything will be revealed, including the dark secrets of the heart. So, live courageously...don't be afraid of death...and trust God to be with you always, no matter what happens.

And then he tells them a story to warn them about pursuing wealth instead of God. Those who do will lose it all when they die, including eternal life. But God will provide for all who make his Kingdom their number one priority now. Such a faithful servant of God will be richly rewarded.

Finally, Jesus warns his disciples that not everyone will accept the Gospel. The Gospel comes as light in a dark world. Some welcome the light and others don't want to be exposed. The division of belief and unbelief, therefore, divides even families in a fallen world. Indeed, the Gospel sets the world aflame with the fire of judgment: *"I have come to set the world on fire, and I wish it were already burning!"* (Luke 12:49). But after judgment—and Jesus will take our judgment on the cross—comes the warmth of salvation.

Focus: The Gospel is not benign; it is a burning fire. As the apostle Paul puts it, it is the fragrance of salvation to some, but the stench of death to others. Therefore, don't be surprised when the world fiercely rejects Jesus and tries to put out the fire.

Prayer: Lord, prepare us for the mission of sharing the Good News with the world. Protect us from the enemy, and reveal your glory so that all may see that Jesus is Lord. Amen.

October 20

> Key Text: "There is more joy in heaven over one lost sinner who
> repents and returns to God than over ninety-nine others who are
> righteous and haven't strayed away!" (Luke 15:7)

Chapter 13 begins with warnings about the need for humility and repentance. Jesus refers to two reports of tragedy—a mass murder in the Temple ordered by Pilate, the Roman Governor, and the collapse of a tower which killed eighteen people. It was believed that events like these happened because the victims were sinners and deserved it.

Jesus challenges this harsh and unwarranted judgment, warning the people that those who think they are righteous but judge others will die in their sins if they do not repent. They are like fig trees which bear no fruit and are cut down by the gardener.

Luke then tells a story of Jesus healing on the Sabbath, which, as we have seen, causes the religious leaders to react with indignation. Jesus calls them hypocrites because they condemn others while breaking their own rules. They too are like fig trees that bear no fruit.

The lack of faith in Jesus by Israel's leaders caused some to ask whether only a few will be saved. Jesus responds with the parable of the mustard seed, saying that the tiniest seed of the Gospel will grow into a great tree. Furthermore, some who are included in the Kingdom may come as a surprise. Those who think they are righteous but do evil will be excluded. Others—people from all over the world—who are considered evil by the religious leaders, will be included. Jesus says, *"And note this: Some who seem least important now will be the greatest then, and some who are the greatest now will be the least important then"* (Luke 13:30).

Chapter 14 continues Jesus' conflict with the religious leaders who claim that healing on the Sabbath violates the commandment against working on the Sabbath. They refuse to acknowledge that they too work on the Sabbath if it suits them. They use the Law to get away with violating the Law.

Jesus also points out how the leaders always insist on sitting in the place of honor at public events. Of this he says, *"Those who exalt themselves will be humbled, and those who humble themselves will be exalt-*

ed." These are examples of how the Kingdom of God is different from the kingdom of proud and self-righteous men in this world.

If the powerful wish to enter the Kingdom, they must show compassion and respect for *"the poor, the crippled, the lame, and the blind,"* and not just associate with their rich friends. Specifically, if the leaders of Israel don't want to follow Jesus and enter the Kingdom, others will be invited to take their place.

Each person should count the cost before saying they want to follow Jesus, because his Kingdom must become their first priority. If you are not willing to identify with the needy and help bear their burdens—even if it makes your life more difficult—then you cannot be Jesus' disciple. Jesus tells his followers to think very carefully about what they really want: *"So you cannot become my disciple without giving up everything you own"* (Luke 14:33).

Chapter 15 notes that Jesus' appeal among the tax collectors and other notorious sinners creates alarm among the religious leaders. Holy men were not supposed to defile themselves by associating with "sinners." So they come to listen closely to Jesus' teaching.

He tells several parables that are meant to convict the religious leaders about God's love for the very people they despise. In one, he compares a shepherd finding a lost sheep to the joy in heaven over one lost sinner who repents and returns to God. He also compares the distress of a woman who loses one of her silver coins and searches frantically until she finds it, to those sinners who earnestly seek the Kingdom. Jesus claims that the angels party in heaven when even one sinner repents!

To conclude, Luke tells the epic story of the Prodigal Son. A younger son demands his inheritance. He embarrasses his father and then leaves home to ruin his life by wild living. When bottomed out, he returns home, expecting to be punished at best, and shunned at worst. To his amazement, the father runs to meet his son as he approaches in the distance, for he has been looking for him and longing for him to come home all along. The father represents God, while the young man represents the sinners and outsiders whom Jesus hangs around with.

When the younger son returns with humility and sorrow, the waiting father receives him with joy, and then throws a party. The righteous older brother protests. He has been a good son, thus representing Israel, but is angry that his father shows mercy to the younger son.

His father says to him, *"Look, dear son, you have always stayed by me, and everything I have is yours. We had to celebrate this happy day. For your brother was dead and has come back to life! He was lost, but now he is found!"* (Luke 15:31–32).

> **Focus:** The Gospel is hard for self-righteous people to accept because it forces them to embrace the fact that God forgives those who don't deserve it. In their pride, they feel that this is not just. Such people, though outwardly good, are far from the Kingdom because they cannot see their own sin to repent of it.

> **Prayer:** *Lord, grant us the gift to see ourselves as you see us, so that we may take ownership of our sin and thereby come to recognize how totally unworthy we are to receive your grace. And, having seen our own unworthiness, may we be more tolerant of other sinners around us. Amen.*

Day 295   Reflection

October 21

The Lord's Prayer is so named because it was given to us by Jesus in response to a request by his disciples to teach them to pray. As we have noted, it is a prayer about the Kingdom of God. It gives us some interesting insight into our present mission as well as our future hope as Christians. The prayer is mentioned in Matthew 6:9–13, and a shorter version appears in Luke 11:2–4.

One of the surprises of the Lord's Prayer is the intimacy implied by addressing God as *"our Father."* Jesus regularly referred to his *"Father,"* but of course in a unique way as the Son of God. Yet permission for ordinary people to approach God in a familiar way is quite extraordinary. Some would translate the Aramaic word "Abba" by the child's expression, "Daddy."

While the idea of the Kingdom of God sounds regal and institutional, it should be thought of foremost as a family relationship. After all, in the New Testament, we are called God's adopted children and heirs to his eternal riches. When we pray *"Our Father,"* we are praying to the One who cares about us as much as, or more than, our earthly fathers.

Our Father exists in a realm or dimension called heaven. Heaven is not exactly "up there," but rather is all around us. It is invisible and noncorporeal, but just as real as the material realm in which we exist. So when we pray to *"Our Father in heaven"* (Matthew 6:9), we are praying to One who is spiritually present, active and available. The present separation of heaven and earth has come about as a result of the Fall, but the prayer we are taught looks forward to their reconciliation.

The first request of the prayer is that God's name be honored on earth. The second request makes this even clearer: *"May your Kingdom come soon"* and *"your will be done on earth, as it is in heaven."* Here we get a clue about our present mission and our future hope as Christians. Our present mission is to embody and live out God's love for the world. Our future hope is to experience the fullness of God's presence in our lives and throughout the whole creation.

Who can imagine what life will be like when death and evil are gone, and heaven and earth are reunited under God's loving and wise rule? On one hand, the terrible things about our present world will no longer plague our existence. On the other, life will be transformed in ways unimaginable to us now. Eternal life opens up an unhindered, never-ending existence of discovering the wonders of God's love, imagination and generosity toward us. We will never run out of new things to learn, new experiences to have, new places to discover, and new reasons to celebrate and give thanks!

The Lord's Prayer teaches us that God's Kingdom is not just a future realm; it is also a present reality. It is not yet fully realized, but it is experienced now in part. Think of it as a down payment. Already, we have received forgiveness of sin and the gift of the Holy Spirit. Already we experience God's loving presence in worship and prayer.

Each day we pray for what we need during our mortal life of serving God. We need daily bread, forgiveness of sin, and deliverance from the temptations of the evil one. These simple requests cover our physical, social and spiritual needs. Even the humble act of asking for these things brings glory to God, because he is a loving Father who willingly gives us all we need.

So to sum everything up, in the Lord's Prayer we ask our Heavenly Father to grow his Kingdom on earth until Jesus returns at the end of history and raises us from the dead. Then we will live in the fully realized New Creation where heaven and earth are reunited and the whole creation worships the Lord, saying, *"Thine is the kingdom and power and glory forever, amen!"*

Day 296   Luke 16–18

October 22

> Key Text: "I tell you the truth, anyone who doesn't receive the Kingdom of God like a child will never enter it." (Luke 18:17)

In these chapters, Jesus teaches his disciples extensively about the Kingdom of God and what it means to live the Kingdom life here and now. In one parable, for example, Jesus teaches them to use their minds just as shrewdly in the service of God's Kingdom as they do in their personal business. And they must know which is more important, because no one can serve God and their own self-interest at the same time.

The religious leaders, who serve their own self-interests, scoff at Jesus because he exposes their hypocrisy. They like to appear righteous in public, but their hearts are focused on themselves and God knows it! They need to "*do*" the Law, not just teach it, because the Law and the Ten Commandments outline our responsibilities to God and our neighbor. The commandments can be summarized in a single word—love. Love God and love your neighbor, and you will fulfill the intent of the commandments.

To illustrate, Jesus tells a story about a rich man who considers himself righteous, and a poor, homeless man who lies nearby hoping for compassion and help. The poor man receives nothing but scorn from the rich man, because the rich man probably assumes that his poverty is evidence of his unworthiness. In a similar vein, the rich man's wealth must be evidence that God is pleased with him.

When they die, the rich man loses everything and lands in Sheol, the very warm place of the dead. Meanwhile, the poor man gains heaven. With roles reversed, the rich man begs for mercy, but it is too late. Jesus observes, sadly, that those who refuse to obey God on earth are refused by God when they complain and demand mercy later. Today is the day to show mercy to the needy!

In chapter 17, Jesus distinguishes between a sinner who is weak but repentant, and a person who preys on the weaknesses of others by tempting them to sin. The former deserves forgiveness and understanding; the latter deserves a millstone around his neck and a quick toss into the sea!

Next, a question is asked about how to increase one's faith. Jesus explains that we increase faith by using what little faith we have. Even the tiniest amount of faith, honestly exercised, will get a response from God, encouraging us to trust him even more.

Sometimes the insiders to faith are shown up by the behavior of the outsiders. This is demonstrated one day when Jesus enters a village and is confronted with ten lepers standing at a distance, crying out for mercy. Considered unclean by Jewish law, they are isolated from others and shunned. Jesus does not avert his eyes, but looks straight at them with compassion. He heals them all, and tells them to show themselves to the priests so that they may be reintegrated into the community. Only one of the ten comes back to thank Jesus, and Luke notes that this man is a Samaritan—an outsider who is looked down upon even by his fellow lepers.

The rest of chapter 17 is a conversation about when the Messiah will come with his Kingdom. Jesus says the Kingdom is already here in his person and ministry, and not to look anywhere else. His coming death and resurrection will be a flashing sign that the last days are upon us. The time of Jesus' second coming, in judgment and salvation, is unknown. However, it will be a cosmic event, suddenly occurring in the midst of our business-as-usual world. Best not to wait too long, but to follow the Messiah now.

In Chapter 18, Jesus tells a parable encouraging us to persevere in prayer, and another urging us to forsake pride and self-righteousness. He warns, *"For those who exalt themselves will be humbled, and those who humble themselves will be exalted"* (Luke 18:14). We should receive the Kingdom of God with the sincere and simple faith of a child. Jesus acknowledges to his disciples that it is hard for the rich to enter the Kingdom of God, but that those who forsake riches for the sake of the Kingdom will be richly rewarded. Jesus himself is our example. He mentions again that he will be tortured and killed, but will rise from the grave on the third day.

Focus: Following Jesus is serious business. It is not playing Church, but committing oneself wholeheartedly to sharing Jesus' life and ministry. This puts us at odds with the world and practically guarantees that we will share Christ's suffering in some measure. Only the serious need to apply. But fear not, there is glory ahead!

Prayer: Lord, help us with our fear of not being accepted by the world because of our loyalty to you. You have warned us not to fear even those who can kill our body, because they cannot touch our soul. Grant us courage to share our faith, our wealth and our compassion freely so that you may be honored and others may come to believe. Amen.

Day 297   Luke 19–21

October 23

> Key Text: "Keep alert at all times. And pray that you might be strong enough to escape these coming horrors and stand before the Son of Man." (Luke 21:36)

Before Luke presents Jesus' "triumphal entry" into Jerusalem on a colt, he includes some teaching by which Jesus reshapes the popular expectations of the Kingdom of God.

First, he shows that the invitation to be part of God's Kingdom is given to sinners and not just to those who think they are righteous. The story of Zacchaeus the tax collector illustrates that the net of the Kingdom is cast wide.

Tax collectors were hated by the Jews and considered to be extortionists and traitors to their countrymen. Many became rich by collecting taxes for the Romans and then keeping extra for themselves.

Jesus invites himself to be a guest at Zacchaeus the tax collector's home, while the people grumble in disapproval. But soon, Zacchaeus embraces the Good News of the Kingdom for himself and demonstrates his new faith by action: *"I will give half my wealth to the poor, Lord, and if I have cheated people on their taxes, I will give them back four times as much!"* (Luke 19:8). To which Jesus declares that salvation has come to his home because this man has shown himself to be a true son of Abraham. *"For the Son of Man came to seek and save those who are lost."*

Next, Jesus teaches the crowds through a parable that the Kingdom of God will not occur in the time or manner that they expect. This parable illustrates that there will be an interim time between the Messiah's first coming as a Suffering Servant and his second coming at the end of history as Savior and Judge. During that time, the followers of the Messiah must be faithfully at work using the gifts he has given.

Luke now reshapes the common understanding of the Kingdom by telling the story of Jesus' coming to Jerusalem on a colt, a Messianic event prophesied long ago. The people cheer, though they misunderstand his intentions. The religious leaders feel threatened and plot to kill him because they do not believe in him.

In chapter 20, the leaders demand to know by what authority Jesus does what he is doing. He won't tell them because it's a trick question. Instead, he tells a parable that implicates them as they plan to kill him.

They continue trying to trap him with trick questions, such as what obligation they have to Caesar, and about the nature of resurrection life, but he outwits them every time. Jesus then turns to the crowds and warns them to be careful about these religious leaders. He accuses the leaders of acting unjustly toward the poor because they are only concerned about themselves.

In chapter 21, Jesus points to a poor widow as a better example of spiritual maturity. While the rich conspicuously drop their gifts in the collection box, a poor widow comes by and quietly drops in two small coins. Jesus notes that she has given more than all the rest. They have given from their surplus, while she has given everything she has.

The chapter concludes with Jesus' solemn, and somewhat complex, warning to the present generation of Jews. Their leaders reject the way of Jesus, who brings a spiritual Kingdom, and instead seek an earthly, political kingdom through revolt against Rome. He warns that within their lifetime, Jerusalem will be besieged and the Temple destroyed. And so it is, in AD 70, when Titus, the future Roman emperor, attacks.

Before this catastrophe occurs, there will be a period of persecution against the first generation of Christians. Jesus encourages them to stay alert, be strong in faith, and be ready to bear witness when they are dragged into synagogues and prisons.

These terrible events for the first-century believers are a picture of how life will be for believers in this world throughout history until Jesus returns in final judgment. For quieter times along the way, Jesus says, *"Watch out! Don't let your hearts be dulled by carousing and drunkenness, and by the worries of this life."* And for those times when the persecution really gets intense: *"Pray that you might be strong enough to escape these coming horrors and stand before the Son of Man."* In general:

"Keep alert at all times."

Focus: The way of Jesus always challenges the way of the world. Powerful men and nations continue to pursue Utopian visions through power, conflict and revolution, with disastrous results. Meanwhile the Kingdom of God slowly and persistently grows in the hearts of men and women around the world. Nothing stops it. It moves toward the Great Day when the story of fallen earth is finished at the return of Jesus, and the story of the New Creation begins and continues forever.

Prayer: Lord, wake us from our spiritual sleep and help us to stay alert during our tour of duty on earth. May we be faithful to bear witness to Jesus in good times and bad, so that many will be ready and waiting when your Son comes again! Amen.

Day 298   Luke 22–24

October 24

> **Key Text: And Jesus replied, "I assure you, today you will be with me in paradise." (Luke 23:43)**

Luke concludes his gospel with its most important revelation, the death and resurrection of Jesus.

Significantly, the Passover Festival is approaching. This is the feast that celebrates God's passing over the Israelite families when the plague of death swept through Egypt, and resulted in Israel's deliverance from slavery in Egypt.

But with Jesus, a greater deliverance is coming—deliverance from slavery to sin. And not just for Israel, but for the whole world. Meanwhile, Luke says that *"Satan entered into Judas Iscariot"* to betray Jesus to the religious leaders of Israel.

Jesus has prepared to eat the Passover meal with his disciples. There he prepares them for the meaning of his death. Taking the Passover bread, he says, *"This is my body, which is given for you. Do this to remember me."* After supper he takes *another cup of wine and says, "This cup is the new covenant between God and his people—an agreement confirmed with my blood, which is poured out as a sacrifice for you"* (Luke 22:19–20).

His disciples are confused and upset. To make matters worse, Jesus says that one of them will betray him. This shocking announcement prompts denials and an argument among them later about who is the most important to Jesus. But Jesus reminds them that his Kingdom is not like that. In his Kingdom, the most important one is the one who serves.

From there, Jesus walks to the Mount of Olives to pray. In time, Judas arrives with a crowd and betrays him with a kiss. After Jesus is arrested and falsely tried at the high priest's home, Peter, when questioned, denies three times that he knows Jesus. Jesus is beaten by the guards, and the next day taken before the whole high council of the Jews. There he enrages the leaders by saying, *"But from now on the Son of Man will be seated in the place of power at God's right hand"* (Luke 22:69).

Jesus is quickly taken to Pilate, then to Herod Antipas, and back to Pilate again, where he is sentenced to death by crucifixion. The crowd shouts their approval: *"Crucify him! Crucify him!"*

While hanging on the cross between two thieves, Jesus is asked by one thief for mercy: *"'Jesus, remember me when you come into your Kingdom.' And Jesus replied, 'I assure you, today you will be with me in paradise'"* (Luke 23:42–43).

After Jesus dies, the Roman officer overseeing the execution worships God, saying, *"Surely this man was innocent."* Jesus' body is taken by Joseph of Arimathea, a member of the Jewish High Council, and graciously laid in a tomb he owns.

On Sunday morning, when the women come to anoint Jesus' body with spices, they find that the stone to his tomb has been rolled away and his body missing. Suddenly, two angels tell the women that Jesus is risen from the dead as he predicted. The women return to tell the eleven disciples what has happened, but it sounds like nonsense and most of them don't believe it.

But Peter, who had denied Jesus, goes back to the tomb to look for himself, and wonders.

That same day, two of Jesus' followers are walking to the village of Emmaus and talking about everything that had happened with Jesus. As they walk along, the resurrected Jesus suddenly appears and begins walking with them. But God keeps them from recognizing him. They tell him that they had hoped that Jesus was the Messiah, but their leaders turned him over to be condemned and crucified. Yet, some women from their group had told them that his body was missing from the tomb, and some angels had told the women that Jesus is alive.

Then Jesus opens their eyes to recognize him! He explains that the

Scriptures had predicted all of this: *"Then Jesus took them through the writings of Moses and all the prophets, explaining from all the Scriptures the things concerning himself"* (Luke 24:27).

The two return to Jerusalem and share their experience with the other disciples. As they do, Jesus appears among them, reassuring them that it is he, and not a ghost. He then persuades them from the Scriptures that he had to suffer, die and rise so that all who believe in him may have forgiveness and new life. God's great Promise to Abraham is being fulfilled!

He then impresses upon them that, as eyewitnesses, they have an important mission ahead—to bring this Good News to the nations. For now, they should stay in Jerusalem and wait for the Holy Spirit to come upon them.

With that, he blesses his disciples and is taken up into heaven. They return to Jerusalem filled with great joy and anticipation of what is coming next!

Focus: The death and resurrection of Jesus was in the mind of God from the very beginning, and even when God spoke to Abraham. The great joy sung by the angels at his birth, and now filling the hearts of the disciples after his death and resurrection, is the same joy that was in God's heart when he first decided to make us human beings in the image of his Son, so that we might share his life and eternal future.

Prayer: Lord, we never tire of hearing the story of the Gospel. It is almost too good to be true that you would pay such a price in order to have fellowship with people who could freely love you. Thank you! Thank you! Thank you! Amen.

Day 299 — John 1–2

October 25

Key Text: So the Word became human and made his home among us. He was full of unfailing love and faithfulness. And we have seen his glory, the glory of the Father's one and only Son. (John 1:14)

The Gospel of John is different in structure and emphasis from the other Gospels. It contains long sections of teaching, plus a number of events that are unique to John. Together, they paint a rich theological portrait of Christ. Notably, Jesus is the fulfillment of all the Messianic hopes of the

Jewish people.

John's purpose in writing, therefore, is evangelistic: *"But these are written so that you may continue to believe that Jesus is the Messiah, the Son of God, and that by believing in him you will have life by the power of his name"* (John 20:31).

In a clear reference to the opening words of Genesis, John begins his gospel, *"In the beginning...."* He identifies Jesus as the Word of God who existed in the beginning before the creation. He was with God and was God. This is a clear statement of Jesus' divinity and equality with God.

Furthermore, God created the physical universe through him, giving life and bringing light to everyone. And now, the same Word which created the universe and gave it life, has come into the universe to give it new life: *"The Word became human and made his home among us"* (John 1:14).

Importantly, this Word, who is Jesus, the Son of God, has come to reveal God to us. We might say that Jesus puts a face on God. If you want to know what God is like, study the words and deeds of Jesus.

John the Baptist, meanwhile, has been called by God to present Jesus to Israel as their Messiah. Significantly, he identifies Jesus as the *"Lamb of God who takes away the sin of the world!"* As such, Jesus becomes the final, sufficient and universal sacrifice for human sin, fulfilling the provisional role of the Old Testament Temple priesthood and sacrifices.

At Jesus' baptism, the Holy Spirit descends from heaven upon him, like a dove. Jesus in turn will be the one who baptizes others with the Holy Spirit. John's baptism was for repentance and openness to God. Jesus' baptism is his presence with us, and later, through the gift of the Holy Spirit at Pentecost, his continuing presence in us.

Jesus next calls his first four disciples to follow him: Andrew, Peter, Philip and Nathaniel. He tells them that they will see great things—notably, that he is the one who reconnects heaven and earth, because he comes from the Father in heaven.

Jesus takes his disciples, in chapter 2, to a wedding in the city of Cana. Here he performs his first *"miraculous sign."* John regards Jesus' miracles as pointers (signs) to a greater spiritual reality. Jesus' first sign is to turn barrels of water into good wine, in order to spare the bridegroom a terrible social embarrassment when his wine runs out. The sign of new wine means that God is doing a new thing for his people through Jesus. The vineyard was frequently a metaphor in the Old Testament for Israel as God's possession.

After the wedding, Jesus and his disciples go to Jerusalem for the Passover celebration. When Jesus visits the Temple, he becomes angry at how the Temple has been permitted to become a place of business—corrupt business at that—instead of a house of prayer. To show God's displeasure, he makes a whip and chases the money changers and merchants, along with their sheep and cattle, out of the Temple. He shouts at them: *"Stop turning my Father's house into a marketplace!"* (John 2:16).

When confronted by Jewish leaders about his action at the Temple, Jesus cryptically responds, *"Destroy this temple, and in three days I will raise it up."* The leaders take him to mean the Temple building, but he is referring to his own body. The disciples will remember this saying after his resurrection.

> **Focus:** One of the unique claims of Christianity is that Jesus is God embodied. He is therefore the clearest revelation of who God is and what he is like. Angels appear at times as messengers of God, but only Jesus reveals God to us. At the same time, he reveals what it means to be human. So Jesus not only comes to reveal God to us; he comes as the first of a new humanity destined to share life with the Father in the New Creation forever, as God intended in the beginning.

> **Prayer:** *Lord, we rejoice in your Son who has been connected with the life of the universe from the very beginning. To think that he was willing to join us in our humanity so that we could share life together, now and forever, is amazing and wonderful. May we always keep Jesus before us, behind us, beneath us and above us. Amen.*

Day 300 — John 3–5

October 26

> Key Text: "For God loved the world so much that he gave his one and only Son, so that everyone who believes in him will not perish but have eternal life." (John 3:16)

Encounters with four people—an insider, a heretic, an outsider, and a lost soul—powerfully express the new life Jesus has come to bring.

His first encounter is with a religious leader named Nicodemus, the quintessential insider. He is curious about Jesus, but comes to him in the anonymity of night. Nicodemus probes Jesus, but Jesus punctures

Nicodemus. He says straight out, *"I tell you the truth, unless you are born again, you cannot see the Kingdom of God"* (John 3:3).

Jesus explains to this leader and theologian something he ought to have sensed already—that spiritual life comes from the Spirit of God through the words of Jesus. The Spirit uses Jesus' words to give us spiritual life so that we may experience the renewing presence of God. Jesus calls this being "born again." God desires this for the whole world, so he has sent his Son, Jesus, on a rescue mission. All who are lost in sin may cling to him as a lifesaver, and be rescued from spiritual death and final judgment.

Sadly, not all want to be rescued. Jesus is like a light shining in the darkness, but some love the darkness more than the light and refuse to go near it for fear that their sins will be exposed.

Those who love the light find the darkness dwellers puzzling, but John the Baptist explains, *"No one can receive anything unless God gives it from heaven."* Jesus is *"from heaven,"* but those whose hearts are closed to heaven, because they are captive to earthly desires, neither want nor understand spiritual truth.

Jesus' second encounter is with a woman in Samaria. Samaritans were considered outsiders and heretics by the Jews. Yet Jesus goes out of his way to speak with a Samaritan—and not only a Samaritan, but a woman—and an immoral woman at that! Shocking for the day.

He knows her story: five divorces and presently living with a man to whom she is not married. Jesus perceives that she is spiritually thirsty and offers her *"living water."* Drink this water, he tells her, and you will never be thirsty again. He is speaking of the new life he has come to bring.

The woman runs back to her village and tells everyone what has happened: *"Come and see a man who told me everything I ever did! Could he possibly be the Messiah?"* (John 4:29). The witness of this notorious but well-known woman ignites curiosity, and the whole town comes to hear Jesus' message. Many more believe and confess, *"Now we know that he is indeed the Savior of the world."*

Jesus' third encounter is with a Gentile government official with a critically ill child. The man humbles himself, begging Jesus to heal his son. Jesus tells him to go back home because his son will live. The man believes what Jesus says and starts home. With great joy he discovers that his son is well: *"And he and his entire household believed in Jesus"* (John 4:53).

Jesus' fourth encounter is with a paralyzed man beside the pool of Bethesda—a pool that allegedly had healing power for the first person to get in whenever an angel stirred the water. This false hope has held the man captive for years, sitting by the pool. But Jesus has compassion and heals the man immediately. The healing is reported to the Jewish leaders, who become upset because Jesus has healed the man on the Sabbath, an act that supposedly violates the Sabbath commandment forbidding work.

When confronted by the Jewish leaders, Jesus makes amazing claims. He claims to be equal with God, doing God's work. This includes giving life to anyone he wants. Those who do not honor the Son also do not honor the Father who sent him. Even more, *"those who listen to my message and believe in God who sent me have eternal life"* (John 5:24).

Jesus explains that the Old Testament witness about the Messiah, plus the miracles he performs, demonstrate that he is the Messiah and Son of God. Their refusal to believe him can only mean that they don't have the Father's love within them, and therefore don't recognize the Son.

Focus: Jesus' life-changing encounters with a variety of people show that God loves the whole world. But resistance to him also shows that some people will choose darkness over light. In some cases, the darkness will ferociously seek to put out the light. In this way, the light of the Gospel divides people, even as it unites those who embrace it.

Prayer: Lord, help us see the world the way you see it, so that we may reach out in love to people different from us. Protect your Church in those places in the world where the name of Jesus is fiercely resisted and his followers persecuted. Amen.

Day 301   John 6–8

October 27

Key Text: **"You are truly my disciples if you remain faithful to my teachings. And you will know the truth, and the truth will set you free."** (John 8:31–32)

As a teacher, Jesus shares his message about eternal life using a variety of metaphors. In previous chapters he has said that the new life he gives is like being born again. It is also like water being transformed into wine, and like living water that continually satisfies.

Now, in chapters 6 through 8, Jesus shares three more metaphors. The first is bread. Jesus is the bread of life, and whoever comes to him will never be hungry again. This teaching follows the miracle of feeding a crowd of over 5,000 people with only five barley loaves and two fish. Many in the crowd miss the metaphor—they follow Jesus in hopes of getting more bread. But Jesus says that they need to feed on him—to eat his flesh and drink his blood. This strange saying confuses them further: *"Then the people began arguing with each other about what he meant. 'How can this man give us his flesh to eat?' they asked"* (John 6:52). At this point, many of Jesus' disciples desert him.

After Jesus' resurrection the people would understand that the reference to his flesh and blood was a cryptic way of speaking about his atoning death for them. By faith in him (i.e., eating his flesh and drinking his blood), they would receive forgiveness of sin and new life—eternal life.

In chapter 7, Jesus defends his teaching to the divided crowd. He claims to come from God in heaven, and consequently his teaching is from God. Those who are earnestly seeking to do the will of God will recognize that Jesus comes from God—they will see the family resemblance, so to speak, and receive his teaching as spiritual refreshment. To them, Jesus reveals himself as a flowing river. This is the second metaphor: Jesus is the river from whom people may drink.

This river is the Holy Spirit, which will be poured out for spiritual refreshment to all who believe in Jesus. The metaphor is given at the Jewish Festival of Shelters, where for seven days a priest ceremonially pours water on the altar at the Temple in Jerusalem—a ceremony that anticipates the prophesy that God will one day pour out his Spirit on earth. By saying that he is the source of that river, Jesus claims to be the fulfillment of the Promise. Again, some believe, but some leave and others want to stone him.

In chapter 8, using a third metaphor, Jesus claims to be the Light of the world. He says, *"If you follow me, you won't have to walk in darkness, because you will have the light that leads to life"* (John 8:12). As light, Jesus is the truth that will set us free from spiritual, moral and intellectual darkness.

Some protest that they don't need to be set free, for they have never been slaves to anyone. After all, they are descendants of Abraham! But Jesus explains that though they are physical descendants of Abraham, they are not necessarily spiritual children of Abraham. The evidence points against it: *"Yes, I realize that you are descendants of Abraham. And yet some of you are trying to kill me because there's no room in your hearts for my message"* (John 8:37).

They don't understand Jesus, and continue to forcefully declare that Abraham is their father. But Jesus does not back down, insisting again that they are planning to kill him and that Abraham would never do such a thing. He presses, *"If God were your Father, you would love me, because I have come to you from God."*

Jesus then says to them that they can't understand him because they do evil. God does not put evil or violent thoughts in human minds. The shocking truth is that the devil is their father when they follow his murderous impulses: *"He was a murderer from the beginning. He has always hated the truth, because there is no truth in him. When he lies, it is consistent with his character; for he is a liar and the father of lies"* (John 8:43–44).

As if to prove him right, the people counter by calling Jesus a Samaritan devil! They further denounce him for presuming to be greater than Abraham. But Jesus doesn't back down: *"Your father Abraham rejoiced as he looked forward to my coming. He saw it and was glad. ... I tell you the truth, before Abraham was even born, I AM!"* (John 8:56, 58).

At that point, the people pick up rocks to stone him.

Focus: Jesus is spiritual food in a world of spiritual hunger, and a flooding river of living water in a world of spiritual thirst. He is a shining light of reality and truth in the darkness of a lost and confused world. In sum, he is the fulfillment of God's ancient Promise to Abraham to bless the whole earth with salvation.

Prayer: *Lord, we thank and praise you for sending your Son to give us life and hope. Who would have guessed that you would assume our humanity and live as one of us so that we might know your heart in ways that we can understand. Be our spiritual food and drink so that we can live forever. Amen.*

Day 302　　Reflection

October 28

It becomes apparent when reading the Gospels that the Jesus we meet therein is no "gentle Jesus, meek and mild." Nor is he a translucent mystic, such as medieval paintings portray him to be. There is no halo.

His humanity is robust. He is a compelling human, showing compassion, courage and righteous indignation, and above all, an absolute commitment to a mission that has been planned since the beginning of the world. Paul writes, *"Even before he made the world, God loved us and chose us in Christ to be holy and without fault in his eyes. God decided in advance to adopt us into his own family by bringing us to himself through Jesus Christ"* (Ephesians 1:4–5).

The moment he is conceived by the Holy Spirit, demonic powers are put on alert that their rule over planet earth is coming to an end. They launch a preemptive strike through a paranoid King Herod, who, having heard the Magi speak of a newborn King of the Jews, orders the slaughter of all boys in and around Bethlehem who are two years old and under. The next attack, thirty years later, was subtle, clever, and face to face. Before launching his public ministry, Jesus is led by the Spirit into the wilderness to be tempted there by the devil. It is a temptation he needs to face. The devil seeks to redirect Jesus' mission: Instead of a crucified Savior, why not be a populist hero? So the devil offers Jesus great wealth and power, suggesting that he use these gifts to dazzle people like a celebrity, or promise them bread forever like a politician. Why not wealth and power instead of self-sacrifice?

All that would be required of Jesus would be to kneel down and worship him.

Instead, Jesus silences the devil with Scripture and finally chases him away when he declares, *"For the Scriptures say, 'You must worship the Lord your God and serve only him'"* (Matthew 4:10). It was as if Jesus, representing all humanity, redid the original temptation of Adam in the garden, but obeyed God instead. It was as if Jesus was also representing Israel as a nation being tempted to worship the gods of the nations around them—only Jesus said no.

When Jesus begins his public ministry of proclaiming the Kingdom of God, it is the death knell for the demonic realm and all its earthly proxies. Jesus casts out demons with a simple command, and they beg for mercy because they know who he is and what is coming for them.

Tragically, even the religious leaders of Israel rise up to oppose Jesus and then begin plotting to kill him. But Jesus exposes their plots and attributes these to the fact that they don't love God—for if they did love God and sought to do his will, they would recognize that Jesus was indeed the Son of God. Know the Father, know the Son.

They, of course, are outraged, claiming that Jesus is deranged or even demon possessed. The irony of this charge is apparent, and Jesus confronts them with their hypocrisy. They want to kill him because that is what the one whose dictates they are following does—he is a murderer and liar. They are biologically children of Abraham, but the spiritual children of the devil.

Tragically, Jesus' own disciples unwittingly become agents of Satan. First there is Peter, who keeps trying to forbid Jesus from going to Jerusalem to be crucified. Jesus must say to Peter, *"Get away from me, Satan."* Then, there is Judas. His disillusionment with Jesus, who refuses to lead the people in armed rebellion against Rome, creates an openness to satanic suggestion. The devil enters into Judas, causing him to betray Jesus to the religious leaders.

In the face of temptation and resistance, within and without, Jesus moves purposefully and courageously toward the completion of his mission. He overcomes his own human aversion to suffering while praying in the Garden of Gethsemane. He observes the scattering of all his disciples. He submits to a wrongful arrest and phony trial, and then to brutish political leaders who think they are in control. He bears torture, mockery and then death on a Roman cross, one of the most horrific instruments of death ever invented. But the worst and loneliest moment comes as he is dying and bearing the sins of the world on his shoulders: *"My God, my God, why have you abandoned me?"*

Gentle Jesus, meek and mild? I don't think so.

Prayer: Lord, we cannot comprehend what Jesus went through on our behalf. Nevertheless, we stand amazed and grateful. How comforting to know that Jesus understands what it means to be tempted, rejected, persecuted and killed. This means that he is wonderfully able to empathize and help us when we pray. How comforting to know also that his power overcomes all the powers of hell, and keeps us safe until we arrive in your presence. Amen.

October 29

> Key Text: "I don't know whether he is a sinner," the man replied. "But I know this: I was blind, and now I can see!" (John 9:25)

In chapter 9, John brings the thinking and motives of the Jewish leaders into focus, as they continue to plot against Jesus. The chapter revolves around the healing of a blind man on the Sabbath. When Jesus sees the man, he tells his disciples that the man's blindness is an occasion for the power of God to be revealed.

After Jesus gives the man his sight, there is considerable amazement and confusion among the man's neighbors, friends and family. Is it really him? The formerly blind man is taken to the Pharisees who also question him, and then debate about Jesus. We discover that the Pharisees themselves are divided: *"Some of the Pharisees said, 'This man Jesus is not from God, for he is working on the Sabbath.' Others said, 'But how could an ordinary sinner do such miraculous signs?' So there was deep division of opinion among them"* (John 9:16).

We also discover that the Pharisees feel threatened by Jesus, and expel from the synagogue anyone who says that Jesus is the Messiah. They continue to interrogate the healed man, but become angry when he won't disavow Jesus.

Later, when Jesus reconnects with the man, he explains his mission: *"I entered this world to render judgment—to give sight to the blind and to show those who think they see that they are blind"* (John 9:39).

In chapter 10, Jesus reveals himself as the *"Good Shepherd,"* who willingly sacrifices his life for the sheep. He hints that Gentiles also will be part of his flock by saying, *"I have other sheep, too, that are not in this* [Jewish] *sheepfold."* Later, he tells some skeptics who keep asking if he is the Messiah, that they don't believe him because they are not his sheep. His true sheep—those who recognize that he is from God and believe in him—follow him. He gives them eternal life and they will never perish, nor can they be snatched away. The Father has given them to him, and *"the Father and I are one."*

This claim to be equal with God stuns the people and they pick up stones to kill him. He challenges them to drop the stones and pay attention to his miraculous works to see whether they are the works of God or not. They could find themselves opposing the very God they claim to know and worship!

Then, in chapter 11, John recounts the most memorable of Jesus' miraculous works. Jesus is told that his friend Lazarus is critically ill. Lazarus is the brother of two women who follow him, Mary and Martha. When Jesus reaches Bethany, Lazarus has already died and mourners have begun to arrive. The sisters are deeply disappointed that he didn't make it in time, because they believe he would have healed their brother.

However, Jesus comforts them with this amazing claim: *"I am the resurrection and the life. Anyone who believes in me will live, even after dying. Everyone who lives in me and believes in me will never ever die."* He then demonstrates the power of God to raise the dead by going into the tomb and shouting: *"Lazarus, come out!"* And he did! And John reports that from that time on, the Jewish leaders began to plot Jesus' death.

In chapter 12, Jesus returns to Bethany and visits with Lazarus and his sisters. After dinner, in an act of devotion, Mary anoints Jesus' feet with some expensive perfume and wipes them with her hair. Judas protests that the perfume was worth a year's wages. It was extravagant! The perfume should have been sold and the money given to the poor. But John comments: *"Not that he cared for the poor—he was a thief, and since he was in charge of the disciples' money, he often stole some for himself"* (John 12:6).

Jesus tells Judas to back off, saying that Mary's gesture was in fact *"preparation for my burial."* Then Jesus heads for Jerusalem, and enters the city during the Passover feast on a young donkey, a messianic gesture that all the Gospels note.

John includes the detail that some Greeks who had come to the Passover asked to see Jesus, a signal of the *"other sheep"* who will come into the sheepfold of the great shepherd! Jesus knows that *"'the time for judging this world has come, when Satan, the ruler of this world, will be cast out. And when I am lifted up from the earth, I will draw everyone to myself.' He said this to indicate how he was going to die"* (John 12:31–33).

Focus: The Gospels illustrate what we may call the mystery of unbelief. Some people will not believe in Jesus no matter what the evidence. There are probably many secondary reasons, but the root is pride—an unwillingness to humble themselves and bend a knee before God, their maker, in gratefulness and worship. This is the greatest irony of human life—the created ones refuse to acknowledge their Creator. This denial demonstrates how malignant sin can become in the lives of those who nurture it instead of repenting of it.

Prayer: Lord, give us humility and faith. Keep us from the proud stubbornness which refuses to recognize our sin and continues to resist your grace. May we teach our children the virtue of humility by our own example in the home. Amen.

Day 304 — John 13–17

October 30

Key Text: "I pray that they will all be one, just as you and I are one—as you are in me, Father, and I am in you. And may they be in us so that the world will believe that you sent me." (John 17:21)

John introduces the Last Supper with a brilliant summary of its meaning: *"Before the Passover celebration, Jesus knew that his hour had come to leave this world and return to his Father. He had loved his disciples during his ministry on earth, and now he loved them to the very end"* (John 13:1).

John describes how Jesus takes a towel, like a household slave, and washes the disciples' feet. This is a stunning act, portraying Almighty God, in the person of Jesus, humbling himself to love and serve the human race. And, of course, it is a theological statement about the meaning of the cross.

Judas leaves to betray him, but Jesus later tells the remaining disciples that the cross will reveal both the Father's and his glory. It is for us that Jesus submits himself to this terrible moment, which he and the Father agreed upon from the beginning of the universe.

He tells his disciples, *"So now I am giving you a new commandment: Love each other. Just as I have loved you, you should love each other. Your love for one another will prove to the world that you are my disciples"* (John 13:34–35).

Chapters 14 through 16 tell of how Jesus prepares the disciples for his *"going away,"* but they don't yet understand and are upset. So he says to them: *"Don't let your hearts be troubled. Trust in God, and trust also in me. There is more than enough room in my Father's home. If this were not so, would I have told you that I am going to prepare a place for you? When everything is ready, I will come and get you, so that you will always be with me where I am. And you know the way to where I am going"* (John 14:1–4).

Thomas is confused and speaks for all of them, saying that they don't know the way. Jesus replies with one of the great insights of the Gospel: *"I am the way, the truth, and the life. No one can come to the Father except through me"* (John 14:6).

When he goes away, Jesus will give them the Holy Spirit, whom he calls an "Advocate." By means of the Spirit, Jesus will remain with them and in them, enabling them to love one another. The Spirit will also remind them of what Jesus taught and how to live it out in their mission. In all these ways, Jesus will give peace of mind to his disciples, equipping them for what is ahead.

In chapter 15, Jesus uses the metaphor of a grapevine to further explain his relationship to them. He is the vine; they are the branches. By staying connected to him by faith, and through the Spirit, they will grow spiritual fruit, especially the fruit of love. Loving one another fulfills his great commandment, keeps them united and gives them joy.

He warns them, however, that the world will hate them as it has hated him, because his life and teaching expose their sin.

Tough times are ahead for them, especially with his crucifixion, but the resurrection will bring them wonderful joy. The Holy Spirit will continue Jesus' work through them, convicting the world of its sin and of coming judgment. This judgment starts with the devil. Jesus says, *"...the ruler of this world has already been judged."*

They are also given the gift of prayer. When Jesus is resurrected and then returns to the Father in heaven, the disciples may ask the Father directly in prayer for everything they need: *"Ask, using my name, and you will receive; and you will have abundant joy"* (John 16:24).

In chapter 17, Jesus prays for his disciples. It is sometimes called Jesus' high priestly prayer, because he prays to the Father in behalf of the disciples regarding the challenges they will face in the world when he has ascended. He tells the Father that the disciples now believe that he sent him. For their mission, in his name, they will need protection and unity. He further asks that the truth of his Word will make them holy, meaning specially devoted to his service in the unbelieving world. He is sending them into the world to bear witness, and therefore they must show the unity of love so that the world will be convinced.

Jesus concludes his prayer with these words: *"O righteous Father, the world doesn't know you, but I do; and these disciples know you sent me. I have revealed you to them, and I will continue to do so. Then your love for me will be in them, and I will be in them"* (John 17:25–26).

> **Focus:** It is wonderfully reassuring to know that Jesus prays for us. We know that the Church in its mission will face the same resistance in the world that Jesus did, but he will remain present with us by means of his Holy Spirit. The Spirit will guide the Church of each generation into effective ministry.

> *Prayer: Lord, how we thank you for giving us the Holy Spirit to be with us and in us, during our life on earth. May your Church demonstrate the unity of love that will convince the unbelieving world that Jesus really is the Savior. Amen.*

Day 305   John 18–21

October 31

> **Key Text:** But these are written so that you may continue to believe that Jesus is the Messiah, the Son of God, and that by believing in him you will have life by the power of his name. (John 20:31)

As the time of Jesus' arrest draws near, he takes his disciples to the Mount of Olives. He is fully aware of what is going to happen, so when Judas the betrayer arrives with Roman soldiers and Temple guards to arrest him, he calmly submits.

He is taken to the home of Annas, the father-in-law of Caiaphas the high priest, for questioning. Annas then binds him and sends him to Caiaphas for a trial. During the trial Peter is standing around outside in the courtyard, warming his hands by a fire. He is recognized and called out as Jesus' disciple. But three times Peter denies that he is one of Jesus' disciples. A rooster crows and a chill runs down Peter's cowardly spine.

Caiaphas now sends Jesus to Pilate, the Roman governor. John mockingly notes that Jesus' false accusers don't go inside the Roman headquarters with him because doing so would ceremonially defile them.

Pilate is annoyed at being used by the Jewish leaders because their laws don't permit the Jews to execute someone. So he asks Jesus sarcastically, *"Are you the king of the Jews?"* Jesus doesn't deny it but says, *"My Kingdom is not an earthly kingdom"* (John 18:36). Jesus tells Pilate that he has come to testify to the truth: *"All who love the truth recognize that what I say is true."* Pilate asks, *"What is truth?"* and then leaves it to the crowd to decide whether or not to crucify him.

Pilate presents Jesus to the crowd and they call for his death. But he is uneasy, for he believes Jesus is innocent. He pressures Jesus to give him a reason to let him go. But Jesus, fully in command, says, *"You would have no power over me at all unless it were given to you from above. So the one who handed me over to you has the greater sin"* (John 19:11). In the end, Pilate turns Jesus over to be crucified.

Jesus is nailed to the cross between two criminals, and Pilate posts a sign over him that reads, *"Jesus of Nazareth, the King of the Jews."* The sign is written in Hebrew, Latin and Greek so that many people can read it—an ironic act which, in retrospect, becomes an announcement that people of all nations and languages would indeed call him Messiah and King.

While hanging on the cross, Jesus knows that his mission is now complete. He asks for a sponge to moisten his lips so that he can say for all to hear: *"It is finished!"* Then he bows his head and releases his spirit.

After Jesus is confirmed to be dead, Joseph of Arimathea, a respected member of the Jewish High Council, asks for his body and places it in a new tomb. Joseph is a secret disciple of Jesus. Nicodemus, the man who had come to Jesus at night, goes with Joseph to buy seventy-five pounds of perfumed ointment for burial, a generous expression of love and respect.

Early on Sunday morning, Mary Magdalene goes to the tomb and finds the stone rolled away. She runs back to tell Peter and John, the writer of this gospel. They hurry to the tomb and find it empty. They leave believing in Jesus' resurrection, but Mary remains outside the tomb weeping.

When she finally dares to look in the tomb, she sees two angels at the place where Jesus has been laid. They say, *"Dear woman, why are you crying?"* When she explains, a man warmly and joyfully calls to her, *"Mary!"* It is Jesus.

Mary runs back to tell the others. Later that evening the resurrected Jesus appears among them, showing them the wounds in his hands and side. They are filled with joy! In this moment of faith, Jesus anticipates the Day of Pentecost by giving them his Spirit, and grants them authority to forgive sins as they declare the Good News to others.

Thomas, who arrives later, needs to be convinced, and Jesus accommodates his doubt by letting him touch the scars in his hands and side. *"'My Lord and my God!' Thomas exclaimed. Then Jesus told him, 'You believe be-*

cause you have seen me. Blessed are those who believe without seeing me'" (John 20:28–29).

Jesus appears to the disciples two more times after this. On the final occasion, he has breakfast with the twelve and then asks Peter three times if he loves him. Peter is concerned at first that Jesus doubts his love, but then realizes that he has been given an opportunity to publicly express his love three times, one for each time he had previously denied his Lord.

The gospel ends with these intriguing words: *"Jesus also did many other things. If they were all written down, I suppose the whole world could not contain the books that would be written"* (John 21:25).

Focus: From the beginning, Jesus' life was moving towards the cross. In that epic moment, he bore the sins of the world. Then through the resurrection, he overcame death, the final enemy. This Good News is meant to be shared with everyone, everywhere, in each generation. For all those who receive his forgiveness of sins as a free gift, death is no longer the last word. When our old bodies die, the Old Story will end, and when our new bodies are resurrected, the New Story will begin.

Prayer: *Lord, how can we ever fully appreciate what you have done for us through Jesus? Such love! May it wash through us, cleanse us, renew us and energize us for the task you have given, until the wonderful day of your return, and the resurrection of the dead. Amen.*

Day 306   Acts 1–4

November 1

Key Text: "But you will receive power when the Holy Spirit comes upon you. And you will be my witnesses, telling people about me everywhere—in Jerusalem, throughout Judea, in Samaria, and to the ends of the earth." (Acts 1:8)

Luke, the gospel writer, continues his account about Jesus, after his resurrection. In the book of Acts, we learn of the beginning and growth of the early Church and its mission of announcing the resurrection of Jesus, especially among the Gentiles.

In Acts, we learn that the resurrected Jesus appears to his apostles a number of times, teaching them about the Kingdom of God. Before he departs to be with the Father (which we call his ascension), he tells his disciples to wait in Jerusalem for the gift of the Holy Spirit. The Spirit will come upon them, and remain in them, empowering them to bear witness to him everywhere in the world, beginning in Jerusalem.

While waiting, the now eleven disciples choose Matthias to replace Judas Iscariot, who had hung himself. At last, during the Jewish Feast of Pentecost, Jesus' promise is fulfilled. The Holy Spirit comes upon the disciples in a dramatic fashion, giving them the ability to speak in the native languages of all the people who were present for the Feast of Pentecost from all over the region. They speak of the wonderful things God has done through Jesus. This is the fulfillment of the prophecy of Joel *(Joel 2:28–29)* and the first act of the Gospel being taken to the nations of world.

Peter steps forward and speaks to the crowd with the first-ever evangelistic sermon about Jesus, calling everyone to repent of their sins, turn to God and be baptized in the name of Jesus Christ.

Luke reports that about 3,000 people believe Peter's message and are baptized. They begin meeting together corporately and in small groups, *"devot[ing] themselves to the apostles' teaching, and to fellowship, and to sharing in meals (including the Lord's Supper), and to prayer"* (Acts 2:42). The Church grows like wildfire!

The apostles begin teaching and healing the sick, just like Jesus had done. One man is healed in Jesus' name and begins *"walking, leaping and praising God."* When a crowd grows in response to the healing, Peter begins to teach them, saying that all these things had been predicted by the prophets. They must now repent and believe in order to become part of God's amazing future, because the resurrected, glorified Jesus will return at the end of history.

In chapter 4, Luke mentions that the preaching of Peter and John has agitated the Jewish leaders, including the Sadducees who didn't believe in the resurrection. This is the Jewish leaders' worst nightmare. Those who had Jesus put to death now demand to know how his followers have healed a crippled man. Peter, filled with the Holy Spirit, addresses the leaders with a boldness he hadn't had before. He declares that the crippled man was healed in the powerful name of the resurrected Jesus of Nazareth! He is the Messiah; there is salvation in no one else!

The leaders don't know what to do with Peter and John, so they warn them not to speak to anyone in Jesus' name again. Peter and John refuse.

They are then threatened, but are released out of fear of starting a riot, because everyone is praising God about the healing of this man.

When they are freed, Peter and John join the other believers and tell them what has happened. Together they praise God in prayer, asking him to give them great boldness in preaching the Gospel: *"Stretch out your hand with healing power; may miraculous signs and wonders be done through the name of your holy servant Jesus"* (Acts 4:30).

Luke summarizes these exciting events by saying that the believers are united in mind and heart. They take care of one another by sharing their resources. The apostles continue to testify about the resurrected Jesus, and God's blessing is upon them.

> **Focus:** The pouring out of the Holy Spirit on the Day of Pentecost gave birth to the Church. The Spirit within the believers created a new community given to worship, fellowship, instruction, prayer and mission—a mission that continues to this day. The message of a crucified and risen Savior, who offers forgiveness and eternal life, continues to powerfully speak to men and women all over the world.

> *Prayer: Lord, we are grateful to be called your people, the Church. We are your body, making you visible on earth and going with your authority to call everyone, everywhere to believe and belong. Give us success in our mission, O Lord, for we have come to believe that the local church is the hope of the world. Amen!*

Day 307   Acts 5–7

November 2

> Key Text: But Peter and the apostles replied, "We must obey God rather than any human authority." (Acts 5:29)

As the early Church continues in its mission and grows in numbers, it immediately faces challenges within and without. Chapter 5 tells the chilling story of a couple, Ananias and Sapphira, who lie to Peter about a financial gift they have given for the needs of the Church. They want the praise of the people, but they also want their money, so they withhold some while saying that they have given it all. Peter confronts them, calling their deceit a lie against the Holy Spirit and an offense against the community of faith and its witness.

It is a deadly serious matter. Both Ananias and his wife drop dead when confronted with their lie. Luke writes, *"Great fear gripped the en-*

tire church and everyone else who heard what had happened" (Acts 5:11). If the Church now takes the place of the Old Testament Temple as the presence of God in the world, we can expect God's judgment against it just as certainly as he judged Israel when they willfully sinned against him.

Meanwhile, the apostles perform many miraculous signs and wonders, attracting large crowds of people just as Jesus had. And, like Jesus, they attract the anger of the religious leaders. The leaders had thought that all this madness was over with the death of Jesus, but now they wonder where it will all end. So they arrest the apostles and put them in the public jail.

But the next day when they are to be brought to trial, it is discovered that the apostles are gone. An angel of the Lord had come at night and set them free. They are found at the Temple teaching the people about Jesus. They are arrested again, flogged and told not to preach about him. But they refuse. Luke notes, *"And every day, in the Temple and from house to house, they continued to teach and preach this message: 'Jesus is the Messiah'"* (Acts 5:42).

As the Church grows, so do the problems within. Chapter 6 says that there were complaints that a certain segment of the congregation was being discriminated against in the daily distribution of food. But God gives the apostles wisdom for a solution. They form a ministry that today we call the deaconate, to make sure that the needs of all are looked after.

One of the deacons, a man named Stephen, has unusual faith and gifts of the Holy Spirit. Like the apostles, Stephen performs amazing miracles and signs among the people. He also debates about Jesus with learned Jews, none of whom can stand against his wisdom. So, out of jealousy, these religious leaders persuade some men to lie about Stephen and have him arrested.

In chapter 7, Stephen is brought before the Jewish high council to be interrogated. Instead of being afraid, Stephen manifests a sense of joyful peace, almost like an angel. The high priest confronts him with a false accusation about speaking against Moses and the Temple.

Stephen's reply is magnificent. He gives an overview of the Old Testament story of Israel, beginning with God's calling of Abraham. He continues through the patriarchs to the story of Moses and Israel's Exodus from slavery in Egypt. Then, through the wilderness wandering, the occupation of Canaan, David's kingship, and finally the building of the Temple. During this whole story, Stephen notes that the people complained, rebelled and disobeyed God's commandments. Whenever God sent his prophets to warn them, they persecuted and even killed them.

Then, Stephen shoots a Holy Spirit arrow at the religious leaders' hearts: *"You stubborn people! You are heathen at heart and deaf to the truth. Must you forever resist the Holy Spirit? That's what your ancestors did, and so do you!"* (Acts 7:51).

The Jewish leaders are furious and shake their fists at him in rage. Even as they do so, Stephen has a vision of the glory of God. He sees Jesus standing in the place of honor at God's right hand. When he tells the Jews what he is seeing, they put their hands over their ears and begin shouting. They rush at him, drag him out of the city and stone him to death.

Luke adds that a man named Saul of Tarsus is present, watching with approval.

Focus: Whenever the Church faithfully continues the ministry of Jesus, it must expect to be attacked from within and without. Ministry is spiritual warfare, as Paul will later write. But we use spiritual weapons, not earthly weapons, to knock down the strongholds of false human reasoning and excessive pride that keep people from knowing God.

Prayer: Lord, give your Church the wisdom and fortitude we need to stay focused when our mission is resisted and attacked. Help us not to be afraid, but to be prepared, remembering your promise that even the gates of hell will not prevail against your Kingdom. Amen.

Day 308   Acts 8–9

November 3

Key Text: "The church then had peace throughout Judea, Galilee, and Samaria, and it became stronger as the believers lived in the fear of the Lord. And with the encouragement of the Holy Spirit, it also grew in numbers." (Acts 9:31)

The martyrdom of Stephen, in chapter 7, sets off a wave of persecution toward the Church in Jerusalem. Many believers are scattered throughout the regions of Judea and Samaria, although the apostles stay in Jerusalem. The devoted Pharisee, Saul of Tarsus, aggressively joins in the persecution of believers, *"going everywhere to destroy the church. He went from house to house, dragging out both men and women to throw them into prison"* (Acts 8:3).

However, the persecution has an unintended effect. Like water poured on a grease fire, persecution doesn't put out the fire. Instead, the scattered believers *"preached the Good News about Jesus wherever they went."* Ironically, persecution facilitates the prophesy of Jesus in Acts 1:8, that the disciples will receive power from the Holy Spirit and be his witnesses everywhere—in Jerusalem, throughout Judea, in Samaria, and to the ends of the earth.

Chapter 8 follows the ministry of Philip, who escapes to Samaria. Through him, many men and women are baptized as believers in Jesus, including a well-known magician named Simon. After this, Philip is directed by an angel of the Lord to go down the desert road that runs from Jerusalem to Gaza. There he meets the treasurer of Ethiopia, a eunuch of great authority under its queen.

The Ethiopian is reading aloud from the book of Isaiah. Philip hears him and asks if he understands what he is reading. The man says no, and Philip explains that the passage is about Jesus: *"He was led like a sheep to the slaughter. And as a lamb is silent before the shearers, he did not open his mouth. He was humiliated and received no justice"* (Acts 8:32–33). Beginning with this Scripture, Philip tells him the Good News about Jesus. The Ethiopian believes and is baptized.

Chapter 9 notes: *"Meanwhile, Saul was uttering threats with every breath and was eager to kill the Lord's followers"* (Acts 9:1). Saul does this ignorantly, thinking that he is honoring the Lord by stopping this blasphemous cult. He soon learns otherwise. While on the road towards Damascus to arrest more followers of Jesus, he is suddenly stopped in his tracks by a blinding light! He falls on the ground and hears a voice say to him, *"Saul! Saul! Why are you persecuting me?"* It is Jesus.

Saul's companions hear the sound of someone's voice, but see no one. They are speechless. Saul is blinded by the light, so his companions take him to Damascus. For three days, he does not eat or drink. Meanwhile, the Lord speaks to a believer in Damascus named Ananias, directing him to a particular home to ask for Saul of Tarsus. Ananias resists because he has heard terrible things regarding Saul and what this man has done to believers. But the Lord says, *"Go, for Saul is my chosen instrument to take my message to the Gentiles and to kings, as well as to the people of Israel. And I will show him how much he must suffer for my name's sake"* (Acts 9:15–16).

Ananias obeys, finding Saul and praying for him that he may regain his sight and be filled with the Holy Spirit. God heals Saul and he is baptized. Immediately, he begins preaching about Jesus in the synagogues, saying, *"He is indeed the Son of God!"* People are amazed, of course, and wary. Who can explain such a turnaround? Saul's preaching becomes more and more powerful. The Jews in Damascus can't refute his proof that Jesus is the Messiah. Having lost the debate, they try to kill him! But believers whisk him away to his hometown of Tarsus.

Luke reports that after this, there is a period of peace throughout Judea, Galilee and Samaria. The Church continues to grow everywhere, and the Holy Spirit works with great power through the apostles—especially Peter, who raises a woman named Dorcas from the dead.

Focus: The conversion of Saul (later renamed Paul) was a significant event in Church history. Paul has been called a genius on the order of Aristotle, uniquely equipped to take the Gospel to the Gentile world. He shaped Christian theology by making Jesus the lens through which we understand the Old Testament, and also the present ministry of the Church in the world. The New Testament contains many of his teaching letters to churches.

Prayer: Lord, there is no one outside the scope of your amazing grace. How appropriate that you would choose a sworn enemy of Christianity to be converted and become the great apostle to the Gentile world. Surely, then, you are able to soften the hearts of the most hardened unbelievers that we know! Amen.

Day 309   Acts 10–12

November 4

> Key Text: "We can see that God has also given the Gentiles the privilege of repenting of their sins and receiving eternal life."
> (Acts 11:38)

The attitude of the early Church towards the Gentile world takes a great leap forward with the experience of the apostle Peter and a Roman army officer named Cornelius.

Chapter 10 tells how Cornelius, a "God-fearing" Gentile, is visited by an angel who tells him that his faith and piety have been noticed by God. He instructs Cornelius to summon Simon Peter, who lives in Joppa near the seashore.

Meanwhile, Peter is praying in the middle of the day and suddenly falls into a trance. He sees the sky open, and something like a large sheet descends, filled with all sorts of animals that are unclean according to Jewish law. Peter is told to kill and eat them, but refuses. A voice says, *"Do not call something unclean if God has made it clean."* But the vision is not just about Jewish laws regarding unclean animals. Many Jews considered the Gentiles unclean and refused to associate with them.

As Peter ponders the meaning of what he has seen and heard, Cornelius' messengers arrive. They ask Peter to meet with Cornelius so that he can hear the message about how to be saved. Against Jewish law, Peter enters the house of the Gentile Cornelius and they each share their stories.

Peter realizes that change is coming regarding the Gentiles because of Jesus. He says to Cornelius, *"I see very clearly that God shows no favoritism. In every nation he accepts those who fear him and do what is right. This is the message of Good News for the people of Israel—there is peace with God through Jesus Christ, who is Lord of all"* (Acts 10:34–36).

As Peter shares more with Cornelius about things that have happened concerning Jesus, the Holy Spirit falls upon all who are listening to the message. The Jewish believers who have accompanied Peter are amazed that the gifts of the Holy Spirit have been poured out on the Gentiles too—for they heard them speaking in tongues and praising God. So Cornelius and his household are baptized as believers.

Something significant has occurred. God has made clear to Peter that Gentiles do not have to first become Jews in order to become Christians. This will open the floodgates of ministry to the Gentiles.

Peter returns to Jerusalem and reports to the other apostles and believers there everything that has happened. When they hear this, they stop objecting and begin praising God. They say, *"We can see that God has also given the Gentiles the privilege of repenting of their sins and receiving eternal life"* (Acts 11:18).

So the believers who had been scattered because of the persecution in Jerusalem earlier begin sharing the Gospel with the Gentiles as well, and a large number believe and turn to the Lord.

In response, the Jerusalem church strategically sends Barnabas, a man who is strong in faith and the Spirit, to the important Gentile city of Antioch. He is encouraged by what he experiences, and goes to Tarsus to find Saul and bring him back with him to Antioch. They have great success in ministry together among the Gentiles. Luke notes that it is at Antioch that the believers are first called "Christians"—"Christ's ones."

But trouble is brewing for the Jewish Christians back in Jerusalem. King Herod Agrippa begins persecuting believers. Herod kills the apostle James, John's brother, and then has Peter arrested. The church prays fervently for Peter, and he is delivered from prison by an angel. At first he thinks it is a dream, but then he comes to his senses and realizes that it is actually happening! He returns to where the others are praying and presents himself. They can't believe their eyes either!

Herod Agrippa, however, is punished by God for his arrogance, and dies. *"Meanwhile, the word of God continued to spread, and there were many new believers"* (Acts 12:24).

> **Focus:** Peter's vision and subsequent visit with Cornelius opens the eyes of the Jewish Christians to realize that God's Kingdom is progressing in new ways they had not anticipated. The old wineskins of Judaism can no longer contain the new wine of the Gospel as it grows among the Gentiles. The Gospel is indeed for the whole world!

> *Prayer: Lord, forgive us for our lack of vision, and for our fear of change, as you do new things in the world through the power of the Holy Spirit. May we have the faith and courage to pray for new leaders for the next generation of your Church. Amen.*

Day 310   Acts 13–15

November 5

> Key Text: "God knows people's hearts, and he confirmed that he accepts Gentiles by giving them the Holy Spirit, just as he did to us. He made no distinction between us and them, for he cleansed their hearts through faith." (Acts 15:8–9)

The center of early Christianity is shifting from Jerusalem to the Gentile city of Antioch. The church in Antioch is blessed with gifted prophets and teachers, and will soon be the place where Phase Three of the early rapid expansion of Christianity is launched. The Holy Spirit indicates to the church that Barnabas and Saul are to be set apart for a mission to other Gentile cities.

Their strategy is to visit synagogues in the Greek and Roman cities and teach about Jesus to the residing Jews and the *"God-fearing Gentiles."* These are Gentiles who had been drawn to the moral and intellectual vision of Judaism, but didn't desire to become cultural Jews. They are, however, drawn to Christianity now that they don't have to become cultural Jews.

While in Antioch of Pisidia, for example, Saul (now called Paul) and Barnabas stand before the members of the synagogue and deliver their message. It begins with a synopsis of the Old Testament stories and ends with the coming of Jesus as God's appointed Savior. Paul then recalls how Jesus was rejected and condemned by his own people and turned over to Rome for crucifixion. However, Paul declares: *"God raised him from the dead! And over a period of many days he appeared to those who had gone with him from Galilee to Jerusalem. They are now his witnesses to the people of Israel. ... Brothers, listen! We are here to proclaim that through this man Jesus there is forgiveness for your sins. Everyone who believes in him is declared right with God—something the law of Moses could never do"* (Acts 13:30–31, 38–39).

Because of their powerful preaching and miracles, many Jews and devout Gentile converts begin to follow Jesus. But, some unbelieving Jews stir up trouble and incite mobs against Paul and Barnabas when they arrive in their cities. As a result, the people in the towns have divided opinions about the apostles and their message. For example, when they preach and heal in the town of Lystra, the locals think they are gods and begin to worship them. But then some Jews arrive from Antioch and Iconium to argue against Paul and his message, and win the crowds to their side. They stone Paul and drag him out of town, thinking he was dead.

When preaching to Gentiles who have no knowledge of the Old Testament, Paul and Barnabas adapt their message. They urge the people to turn from idols and false gods to the living God who made heaven and earth, the sea, and everything in them. In the past, they explain, God permitted all the nations to go their own ways, but he never left them without evidence of himself and his goodness. For instance, God gives them rain and good crops for food and joyful hearts.

Instead of presenting Jesus as the fulfillment of the Old Testament (which only the Jews would understand), they present him as the Son of the one and only Creator who graciously gives them life and providential care.

When Paul and Barnabas return to Antioch from their missionary journey, they report everything that has happened. However, the success of their ministry among the Gentiles still causes uncertainty among Jewish Christians, so Paul and Barnabas go to Jerusalem to meet with the leaders there. After much debate, the practices of Paul and Barnabas among the Gentiles are adopted as policy by all, with a few considerations to the sensitivities of the Jews.

The Jewish-Christian leaders agree that God accepts the Gentiles also and gives them the Holy Spirit by faith. So it seems that they need not adopt Jewish practices as well, such as circumcision, dietary restrictions and other practices regarding ceremonial cleanliness, which were part of the Law of Moses.

There is great joy among believers, Jew and Gentile alike. The mission of the Church to the whole world has begun!

> **Focus:** In Antioch, it became clear that God had expanded his call and promises to the Jews to now include the whole world. This should not have been a surprise. From the beginning, God said to Abraham that his intention was to bring salvation and blessing to all the nations of the world. Therefore, being a true Child of Abraham now is no longer about having a specific national or ethnic identity, but applies to anyone who has faith in Jesus.

> **Prayer:** *Lord, how amazing is your plan, from eternity past, to reconcile the world to yourself. How generous you are to include Gentiles as well as Jews in the Kingdom of God. May we be equally generous and gracious with one another. Amen.*

Day 311   Acts 16–18

November 6

> Key Text: "God overlooked people's ignorance about these things in earlier times, but now he commands everyone everywhere to repent of their sins and turn to him." (Acts 17:30)

Paul now begins his second missionary journey. He and Barnabas have gone in different directions, so Silas joins Paul. They take a young disciple, Timothy, with them as well. As they start out, the Holy Spirit twice changes their itinerary. It is unclear why, until Paul has a vision of a man from Macedonia in northern Greece. The man pleads with Paul to come and help them there, so they depart.

On the way, they stop at Philippi for several days, and there a prominent merchant named Lydia believes the Gospel and is baptized. Also, a young demon-possessed girl who is a fortune-teller follows Paul and the others. The demon in her continually interrupts them by shouting out, so Paul casts the demon out in the name of Jesus. Good for the girl—but not for her master, who earns money from her fortune-telling. He grabs the team, causing a scene. A mob forms and the city officials order Paul and Silas to be stripped, beaten with rods and thrown into the prison's dungeon in stocks.

Around midnight, Paul and Silas are praying and singing hymns, while the other prisoners listen. Suddenly, there is an earthquake. The prison doors fly open and the chains of every prisoner are broken. The jailer awakens to see the doors open and assumes they have all escaped. But they have remained. Paul calls out to the jailer as he prepares to commit suicide for failing in his job. The jailer is deeply moved by what has happened. He cares for them and washes their wounds. He asks about their teaching and decides to believe and be baptized, along with his whole household.

The city officials are distressed by what has happened. They let Paul and Silas go, but pressure them to leave secretly. But Paul shrewdly announces that he is a Roman citizen and has been wrongly treated. The officials are forced to apologize and allow them to leave freely and publicly, not like escaped criminals.

Next, Paul and the others go to Thessalonica and, as was his custom, Paul goes to teach about Jesus at the synagogue. Many believe, but once again Jewish believers form a mob and persuade the city officials to chase them out of town. They find a much better reception in the city of Berea. The Bereans *"listened eagerly to Paul's message. They searched the Scriptures day after day to see if Paul and Silas were teaching the truth. As a result, many Jews believed, as did many of the prominent Greek women and men"* (Acts 17:11–12). Here we are reminded that those who love God's Word in the Old Testament, will recognize Jesus as God's Son.

But an organized pattern of resistance is developing, and some Jews from Thessalonica come to Berea to stir up trouble against Paul. He and the others are escorted to the coast and forced to leave, traveling from there to Athens. While in Athens, Paul is deeply troubled by the blatant idolatry. He debates with some Epicurean and Stoic philosophers, who are curious about his message but offended by the claim that Jesus rose from the dead. He is taken to the high council of the city to speak further about the Gospel.

His conversation is a brilliant example of apologetics, which means explaining and defending the Gospel in a gracious and effective manner. He uses their own Greek writers as a point of reference. Paul explains, *"For in [God] we live and move and exist. As some of your own poets have said, 'We are his offspring.' And since this is true, we shouldn't think of God as an idol designed by craftsmen from gold or silver or stone. God overlooked people's ignorance about these things in earlier times, but now he commands everyone everywhere to repent of their sins and turn to him"* (Acts 17:28–30).

Paul leaves Athens for Corinth and stays there for some time. A Jewish couple, Aquila and Priscilla, prove to be great supporters of his ministry. As in all the cities, many believe and others oppose the Gospel. The Lord encourages Paul in a vision not to be afraid nor silent, for he is with him and no harm will come to him. Eventually, Paul says good-bye to the believers there and heads for Ephesus, Antioch, Galatia and Phrygia.

Meanwhile, a Jewish believer named Apollos, who has an extraordinary intellect and speaking skills, comes to Ephesus. He has an incomplete understanding of the Gospel, so Aquila and Priscilla explain it more accurately to him. Apollos is then sent to Achaia, where he has great success sharing the Gospel with powerful arguments in public debate.

So the Gospel continues to spread throughout the Greco-Roman region, and God adds gifted believers to the mission team, providing them with all that they need for the work of ministry.

Focus: These chapters illustrate the persuasiveness of the Gospel in the marketplace of ideas, whether debating with Jews, Greeks or Romans. Not all believe, of course, but many do in each major culture. Its message is compelling and self-authenticating. That is why, 2,000 years later, people around the world are still believing and confessing that Jesus is the resurrected Lord.

Prayer: Lord, your Word is a lamp unto our feet and a light unto our path. It speaks to what we know to be true from our human experience, and to our deep desire to know you, the living God. Empower your Word as it is proclaimed to every tongue, tribe, and nation on earth. Amen.

Day 312   Reflection

November 7

The book of Acts is an important historical and theological document for outlining how the Gospel mission to the Gentile world came about. Although the focus of the Old Testament story was on one race—the Jewish people with their unique calling from God—it was always understood that Israel was to be a "light to the Gentiles" regarding the one true God.

The fulfillment of this calling awaited the coming of Jesus. As we have seen, the story of Jesus arises out of the Old Testament and cannot be understood outside of it. Jesus and his twelve disciples were Jewish, of course, but from the beginning, Jesus' ministry reached out beyond Israel to Samaria and the Gentile nations.

In John, chapter 4, for example, we read of Jesus offering eternal life to a woman of Samaria, and then healing a Roman official's son, leading to the conversion of his whole household. These and other contacts with Gentiles show that Jesus knew that he came to save the whole world.

Consequently, the book of Acts begins with the resurrected Jesus directing his disciples to wait for the Holy Spirit to be given, and then tell people everywhere about him—in Jerusalem, throughout Judea, in Samaria, and to the ends of the earth. Ironically, it was the martyrdom of Stephen by the Jews in Acts 7 that scattered the believers everywhere. Wherever they went, they preached the Good News about Jesus!

In Acts 8, as we have noted, Philip is directed by the Holy Spirit to speak to the treasurer of Ethiopia, a eunuch of great authority. He was returning to Ethiopia in his carriage and reading aloud from the book of the prophet Isaiah. He had a seeking heart after the Hebrew God, but needed someone to teach him.

So Philip taught him, beginning with Isaiah, and explained the Good News about Jesus. The eunuch asked Philip to baptize him immediately! Here we learn that people everywhere have seeking hearts and are drawn to the story of the Bible.

In Acts 10, Peter is given a vision from God which suggested that God was doing something different among the Gentiles than he had done

594

with the Jews. Peter was directed to a Roman officer named Cornelius, who also was drawn to the God of the Hebrews. He had many questions. As Peter explained the Gospel to him, the Holy Spirit fell upon him just as he had upon the Jews at Pentecost. So Peter baptized Cornelius, with the understanding that God was not requiring that Gentiles first become Jews and follow Jewish traditions before they could become Christians.

This was a significant development, because the Romans culturally found many of the Jewish traditions, such as circumcision, offensive. Here we learn that the Gospel is not contained within any one culture, but is able to be experienced and expressed in many cultural forms.

In Acts 16, Paul has a vision from God about a man from Macedonia, in northern Greece. In the vision, the man is pleading with him to come to Macedonia and help them. Upon arriving, Paul meets a woman named Lydia who is a wealthy merchant. As she listens to what Paul is saying, the Lord opens her heart. She accepts the Good News and is baptized, together with other members of her household. Here we learn that God reveals himself to all, regardless of race, gender or social status. Lydia becomes a great help to Paul in his ministry there.

Lastly, in chapter 17, Paul goes to Athens and speaks in the public square to all who happen to be there. He interacts with the Epicurean and Stoic philosophers, and later with men of the city council of Athens. He uses references from their own writers and poets to build a bridge of understanding. He then very effectively shares the Gospel within those parameters. Some laughed at him, especially when he taught about the resurrection of Jesus, but others believed. Here we learn that God has prepared even the pagan world to hear the Gospel by means of their own intellectual searching. By carefully and respectfully listening to their thoughts, we can connect with unbelievers to share the Gospel effectively, because it resonates with the deepest longings of the human heart in a way that nothing else does.

Today, we rejoice that the Gospel has taken root all over the world, encompassing one- third of the earth's population. Millions of Bibles are sold each year, making it the annual bestseller by far around the world.

Prayer: Lord, you have made us for yourself. Consequently, our hearts respond when your Word is proclaimed and taught. It is like a homing beacon that we recognize and want to follow. Thank you for reaching out to us by your Word and

Spirit so that we may know you and find eternal life in your gracious gift of for-giveness. Amen.

Day 313   Acts 19–20

November 8

> Key Text: "But my life is worth nothing to me unless I use it for finishing the work assigned me by the Lord Jesus—the work of telling others the Good News about the wonderful grace of God." (Acts 20:24)

As the message about Jesus is taken to Jewish and Gentile communities around the Roman Empire, the apostles come across groups of believers who do not have complete or accurate information. One group of Jewish believers in Ephesus tells the apostle Paul that they have been baptized by John the Baptist, but have not received the Holy Spirit.

Paul explains that John had preached about Jesus, who later rose from the dead, and that they need to be baptized in his name. *"As soon as they heard this, they were baptized in the name of the Lord Jesus. Then when Paul laid his hands on them, the Holy Spirit came on them, and they spoke in other tongues and prophesied"* (Acts 19:5–6). Being baptized in Jesus' name declares that Jesus is the one who forgives and restores the world through his death and resurrection.

Paul stays in Ephesus for two years, initially teaching in the syna-gogue, which was his practice. But he experiences so much resistance from local Jews that he leaves the synagogue and begins holding daily discussions in a public lecture hall. During this time, people throughout the province of Asia—both Jews and Greeks—hear the Word of the Lord. Luke notes, *"Many who became believers confessed their sinful practices. A number of them who had been practicing sorcery brought their incantation books and burned them at a public bonfire. The value of the books was sev-eral million dollars. So the message about the Lord spread widely and had a powerful effect"* (Acts 19:18–20).

Paul is compelled to leave for Macedonia, but serious trouble is erupt-ing behind in Ephesus. Demetrius, a silversmith who has a large busi-ness manufacturing silver shrines for the Greek goddess Artemis, is up-set. His business has seriously declined because of Paul's teaching that handmade gods aren't really gods at all. Demetrius stirs up trouble in the city to the point where Paul's associates, Gaius and Aristarchus, are dragged into the town amphitheater. Inside, the crowds shout praises to Artemis for over two hours, but they are finally calmed down by the mayor, whose intervention avoids a major riot and probable martyrdom for Paul's friends.

As Paul travels towards Macedonia, he encourages believers in all the towns he passes through. At one point he gets wind of a plot to kill him and alters his route. While in Troas, a tragic but somewhat comedic event happens. Luke writes that Paul was preaching to a group in the third story of a home. It was late, but he went on and on until midnight. A young man named Eutychus can take it no longer. He falls sound asleep, then falls out of the third-story window and is killed! But God gives Paul the power to restore Eutychus to life. Eutychus, however, remains the patron saint of all who fall asleep during very long sermons!

Paul's journey now turns back toward Jerusalem. As he passes near Ephesus, where he had lived and taught for two years, he calls for the elders of the church there to meet with him. He recalls the joys and challenges of his time with them, emphasizing that he never shrank back from telling the truth, even in the face of danger.

Then he gets very serious: *"And now I am bound by the Spirit to go to Jerusalem. I don't know what awaits me, except that the Holy Spirit tells me in city after city that jail and suffering lie ahead. But my life is worth nothing to me unless I use it for finishing the work assigned me by the Lord Jesus—the work of telling others the Good News about the wonderful grace of God"* (Acts 20:22–24).

Finally, he exhorts them to faithfully do their duties as elders of the church: *"So guard yourselves and God's people. Feed and shepherd God's flock—his church, purchased with his own blood—over which the Holy Spirit has appointed you as elders. I know that false teachers, like vicious wolves, will come in among you after I leave, not sparing the flock"* (Acts 20:28–29).

Paul then prays with his coworkers in ministry, with tears all around. They say good-bye with sadness because of Paul's certainty that they will never see each other again.

Focus: Paul's testimony regarding his ministry illustrates that the Christian life involves following Jesus in his joys, sorrows and sufferings. However, this life is but the preseason of our existence. What is ahead in the New Creation is so awesome that it is worth whatever price we pay today to love and serve God, and to tell others the Good News about his wonderful grace.

Prayer: Lord, thank you for the example of great men and women of faith whose lives inspire us to stay the course and bear the burdens of ministry. May we be faithful stewards of the life you have given us. Amen.

Day 314   Acts 21–23

November 9

> Key Text: That night the Lord appeared to Paul and said, "Be encouraged, Paul. Just as you have been a witness to me here in Jerusalem, you must preach the Good News in Rome as well." (Acts 23:11)

Having said farewell to the Ephesian elders, Paul now continues his journey to Jerusalem, believing that the Holy Spirit has nudged him there. Along the way, Paul stops and meets with believers in various cities who prophesy through the Holy Spirit that he should not go to Jerusalem. Agabus, a prophet from Judea, also urges Paul not to go on. Even though there is agreement over what the Holy Spirit is saying, there is danger ahead and there is disagreement about what it means. Should Paul go to Jerusalem?

Paul is moved by their concern, but is also certain that the dangers ahead do not mean that he should change course. He says to his friends, *"Why all this weeping? You are breaking my heart! I am ready not only to be jailed at Jerusalem but even to die for the sake of the Lord Jesus"* (Acts 21:13). When it becomes clear that Paul will not be dissuaded, his friends give up and say, *"The Lord's will be done."*

Upon arriving in Jerusalem, Paul goes immediately to meet with the Jewish Christian leaders. He gives a detailed account of the things God has accomplished among the Gentiles through his ministry. They rejoice with Paul, but warn him that Jewish believers in Jerusalem have been told by agitators that he has been speaking against Moses. Paul decides, out of respect for the Jewish Christians, to show in public that he personally observes the Jewish laws, although he knows that this is not required in order to be a Christian.

But there is too much misinformation, and emotions are volatile. A mob quickly forms, threatening to kill Paul. Word reaches the commander of the Roman regiment, who immediately calls out his soldiers to arrest Paul, sparing him a worse beating. After talking with the crowd and then Paul, the commander allows Paul to address the crowd.

Paul quiets the crowd as he shares his life story, up to the appearance of Jesus on the road to Damascus. But as soon as he mentions that God has called him to offer eternal life to the Gentiles as well as the Jews, the crowd erupts again. So Paul is taken away, but when threatened with a lashing, he claims his Roman citizenship status again. As a citizen, Paul cannot be punished without a trial. So the soldiers quickly back off.

The commander decides to have Paul stand before the Jewish High Council the next day to defend himself. So Paul tells his story once again. However, he notices that among the group are Sadducees who do not believe in resurrection. So Paul cleverly says, *"Brothers, I am a Pharisee, as were my ancestors! And I am on trial because my hope is in the resurrection of the dead!"* (Acts 23:6).

This quickly divides the council—the Pharisees against the Sadducees. The argument back and forth gets so violent that the Roman commander orders his soldiers to rescue Paul and take him back to the fortress. That night the Lord appears to Paul and says, *"Be encouraged, Paul. Just as you have been a witness to me here in Jerusalem, you must preach the Good News in Rome as well"* (Acts 23:11).

Some Jews hatch a plot to kill Paul but are found out. Paul is safely escorted by a large company of troops to Caesarea, where he will be interviewed by the Roman governor, Felix.

Focus: Caught in the midst of political pressures and misguided religious fervor, Paul is directed by the Holy Spirit on his journey. He avoids or outwits his enemies so that he may fulfill God's calling on his life to take the Gospel to the Gentiles— and especially to the great Gentile city of Rome. By his story we are encouraged to believe that the Kingdom of God will overcome the kingdom of this world.

Prayer: Lord, it seems that the problems of this world are too complex and its powers too overwhelming. And yet we see, over and over again, that you are able to overcome earthly powers and demonic forces to grow your Kingdom. Help us not to be afraid, but to desire more than anything that your will be done, on earth as in heaven. Amen.

Day 315   Acts 24–26

November 10

> **Key Text:** "I teach nothing except what the prophets and Moses said would happen—that the Messiah would suffer and be the first to rise from the dead, and in this way announce God's light to Jews and Gentiles alike." (Acts 26:22–23)

Paul is being held in Caesarea by Governor Felix until Ananias, the high priest, arrives from Jerusalem to present charges against him for preaching the Gospel.

The trial begins with accusations that Paul is a troublemaker, the ringleader of a cult known as the "Nazarenes," and a desecrater of the Temple. Paul responds by saying, *"I worship the God of our ancestors, and I firmly believe the Jewish law and everything written in the prophets. I have the same hope in God that these men have, that he will raise both the righteous and the unrighteous"* (Acts 24:14–15). Where he differs from the Jews—and this they cannot tolerate—is his belief in the resurrection of Jesus.

Felix wants to please the Jews, and therefore is nervous about a trial. Paul's preaching makes him anxious, especially when he speaks about the coming Day of Judgment. Felix hopes that Paul will bribe him, but of course that doesn't happen. His cowardly decision, then, is to leave Paul in prison for two years until the governor's successor, Festus, arrives.

Later, when Festus takes control, the religious leaders in Jerusalem begin to lobby him to return Paul to Jerusalem for trial. Luke notes that they were planning to ambush and kill him on the way. But Festus refuses and the new trial is held in Caesarea again.

The Jews up the ante, bringing many serious charges against Paul. Festus weakens and decides to please the Jews by moving the trial to Jerusalem after all. But Paul resists: *"If I have done something worthy of death, I don't refuse to die. But if I am innocent, no one has a right to turn me over to these men to kill me. I appeal to Caesar!"* (Acts 25:11).

Festus confers with King Agrippa. He is concerned about sending Paul to Caesar without a clear charge and hopes that Agrippa will examine him. So Agrippa meets with Paul, who respectfully shares his story, saying: *"Now I am on trial because of my hope in the fulfillment of God's prom-*

ise made to our ancestors. In fact, that is why the twelve tribes of Israel zealously worship God night and day, and they share the same hope I have. ... Why does it seem incredible to any of you that God can raise the dead?" (Acts 26:6–8).

Paul explains that God has sent him to the Gentiles *"to open their eyes, so they may turn from darkness to light and from the power of Satan to God. Then they will receive forgiveness for their sins and be given a place among God's people, who are set apart by faith..."* (Acts 26:18).

He insists that his teaching is entirely consistent with what the prophets and Moses said would happen—that the Messiah would suffer and be the first to rise from the dead, and in this way announce God's light to Jews and Gentiles alike.

Paul's energetic and persuasive account makes Festus anxious, because he is more worried about placating the Jews than discerning the truth about their charges against Paul. So he suddenly shouts out in the middle of Paul's explanation to Agrippa: *"Paul, you are insane. Too much study has made you crazy!"* (Acts 26:24). Apparently, Paul discerns that Agrippa is sympathetic to his story. He presses for Agrippa's agreement to blunt Festus' outburst: *"King Agrippa, do you believe the prophets? I know you do—"*

Agrippa is taken aback, perhaps embarrassed about his sympathy towards Paul. So he interrupts Paul: *"Do you think you can persuade me to become a Christian so quickly?"* After they all talk it over, they agree that Paul hasn't done anything deserving of death or imprisonment. And Agrippa even says to Festus, *"He could have been set free if he hadn't appealed to Caesar."*

Focus: You may notice a similar pattern between Jesus and Paul. Both are falsely accused, taken from one trial to another, beaten and threatened with death because of the Gospel. Though Paul appeals to his Roman citizenship and demands his right to appear before Caesar for a fair trial, he does so not to escape suffering for his faith, but for the unique opportunity to share the Gospel with the leaders of Jerusalem and Rome. His willingness to face suffering and death for doing so, is a response to Jesus' call for disciples to *"deny themselves, and take up their cross and follow him."*

Prayer: *Lord, you have said that we should be prepared to share the reason for the hope we have in Christ. Help us to be as bold as Paul when opportunities arise.*

Day 316 — Acts 27–28

November 11

> Key Text: "I asked you to come here today so we could get acquainted and so I could explain to you that I am bound with this chain because I believe that the hope of Israel—the Messiah— has already come." (Acts 28:20)

After King Agrippa concedes that Paul has done nothing to deserve death or imprisonment, Governor Festus sends Paul and his companions to Rome by sea, since Paul has appealed to Caesar. The journey is difficult because of threatening weather, so they lose a lot of time. There is a difference of opinion about continuing on, with Paul recommending that they go to port at Fair Havens and spend the winter. But the sailors want to find a more enjoyable harbor for the winter, so they continue.

As they pass near Crete, a typhoon hits. The sailors take steps to avoid shipwreck, including throwing the cargo and then the ship's gear overboard. The men become afraid for their lives, but Paul comforts them by saying, *"Last night an angel of the God to whom I belong and whom I serve stood beside me, and he said, 'Don't be afraid, Paul, for you will surely stand trial before Caesar! What's more, God in his goodness has granted safety to everyone sailing with you'"* (Acts 27:23–24).

After fourteen days of the storm, the sailors sense that land is near. But there are dangerous shoals, so Paul urges the captain to keep everyone on board and not try to land in lifeboats. The captain agrees and Paul steps forward to encourage and calm the men. They eat together before lightening the boat by throwing the remaining wheat overboard.

The next morning, they attempt to run the ship aground on the shore. They lower the rudders, cut the anchors and raise the foresail, but hit a shoal and run the ship aground too soon. The bow is stuck and the stern is repeatedly smashed by the force of the waves and begins to break apart.

We learn now that there were other prisoners on board the boat besides Paul. The soldiers want to kill them so they don't swim ashore and escape, but the commanding officer wants to spare Paul and forbids it.

Everyone makes it to shore, as God has promised Paul, whether swimming or holding on to debris. Soon they learn that they have landed on the island of Malta.

Paul proves to be a further blessing to the sailors while on Malta. He heals a number of people from the island. Out of gratefulness, the people shower the sailors with supplies and send them off on another ship. Finally, they land at Rome. Paul is greeted by the believers there who have heard he is coming, and he is given his own private lodging, though he is guarded by a soldier.

Paul soon calls together the local Jewish leaders and tells them about his arrest and the accusations of the Jewish leaders in Jerusalem. He explains, *"I asked you come here today so we could get acquainted and so I could explain to you that I am bound with this chain because I believe that the hope of Israel—the Messiah—has already come"* (Acts 28:20).

They respond that they have not received any specific complaints about Paul, but know that this movement he talks about is denounced everywhere. So a meeting is scheduled, and a large number of people come to Paul's lodging to listen to him. There he explains and testifies about the Kingdom of God and tries to persuade them about Jesus from the Scriptures. Using the Law of Moses and the books of the prophets, he speaks to them from morning until evening.

As has happened everywhere, some believe and others do not. They argue among themselves about the things Paul has taught them, so he finally says to them: *"The Holy Spirit was right when he said to your ancestors through Isaiah the prophet, 'Go and say to this people: When you hear what I say, you will not understand. When you see what I do, you will not comprehend. For the hearts of these people are hardened, and their ears cannot hear, and they have closed their eyes ... and they cannot turn to me and let me heal them'"* (Acts 28:25–27).

Finally, he tells them that this salvation from God has also been offered to the Gentiles, and that unlike them, the Gentiles will accept it. The book of Acts ends by noting that Paul lives in Rome at his own expense, and for the next two years welcomes all who come to him. He boldly proclaims the Kingdom of God, teaching about the Lord Jesus Christ, and no one tries to stop him.

Focus: We see the hand of God protecting Paul at every turn in this amazing shipwreck story. Even though he is endangered at sea and placed under house arrest

603

in Rome, he takes the opportunity to boldly preach the Gospel to whomever will listen. We will find, as did Paul, that when we proclaim the Gospel, some believe and others don't. It is not our responsibility to "save" anyone. That is God's business. Our responsibility is to tell about Jesus, in the power of the Spirit, and leave the results up to God.

Prayer: Lord, grant us your protection and blessing as we take the initiative to tell others about Jesus. We know that not all will believe, and some will become hostile. Nevertheless, we want to be faithful and then be amazed at what you will do! Amen.

Day 317   Romans 1–3

November 12

> Key Text: For everyone has sinned; we all fall short of God's glorious standard. Yet God, with undeserved kindness, declares that we are righteous. He did this through Christ Jesus when he freed us from the penalty for our sins. (Romans 3:23–24)

The book of Romans is one of the great books of the Bible. Its teaching has changed the course of human history, especially the shaping of Western Civilization. It is a tightly argued case for the Gospel, declaring that we are justified before God by grace alone, through faith, and not by human merit.

Paul begins his letter by establishing that the whole world is guilty before God—good guys and bad guys alike. Because of the Fall *(Genesis 3),* sin is the default position of every human being, meaning that we all fall short of God's glorious intent for human life. And what is that glorious intent? The early Christian leader Irenaeus (AD 130–202) responded: *"Man fully alive is the glory of God."*

As it stands now, all humans outside of God's grace are barely alive. We exist, but we do not flourish as God intended.

In this understanding, the doctrine of sin establishes human life as tragic. It also explains God's wrath. God hates what sin has done to us, and he is angry when we live it out. We are made in his image; therefore, our sin is first of all an offense against his nature. It disrupts what God wants most—a relationship with us. Think of God's anger, for example, as the anger of a parent who sees the child they love ruining their life with drugs.

In Romans 1, Paul directs his attention to the pagan world, which suppresses the truth about God by their wickedness: *"They know the truth about God because he has made it obvious to them. For ever since the world was created, people have seen the earth and sky. Through everything God made, they can clearly see his invisible qualities—his eternal power and divine nature. So they have no excuse for not knowing God"* (Romans 1:19–20).

Think of it as failing the study of God 101.

Their refusal to worship God, as he is generally known through reason and intuition, produces dark and confused thinking. They lose track of God and their humanity, worshiping idols and giving themselves over to sexual depravity in a downward spiral of antisocial behavior.

To keep society from total destruction, God ordains that they will suffer the natural consequences of their behavior, which he lists in detail. Like an addict, some will only cry out to God for forgiveness and help when they hit rock bottom.

In chapter 2, Paul continues his indictment of human sinfulness, but now he turns to the Roman moralists and the Jews, both of whom would have agreed with Paul in his remarks about paganism. And yet, they too are indicted. Why? Because knowing what is right and good, and even agreeing with it, does not make them right with God if they don't actually *do* what is right and good. If anything, such people are in a worse position because they cannot claim ignorance, like the pagans.

This is especially true of the Jews who have had every advantage of special knowledge about God through the history of their ancestors, the Law of Moses, and the writings of the prophets. They think they are a guide to the spiritually blind, but they themselves walk in darkness. They do the very things they know and teach others not to do. Paul's conclusion is: *"For everyone has sinned; we all fall short of God's glorious standard"* (Romans 3:23).

The rest of Romans is an exposition of what God has done through Jesus, and what it means for our lives: *"But now God has shown us a way to be made right with him without keeping the requirements of the law, as was promised in the writings of Moses and the prophets long ago. We are made right with God by placing our faith in Jesus Christ. And this is true for everyone who believes, no matter who we are"* (Romans 3:21–22).

In short, we cannot become righteous in God's sight through our own best efforts, because they always fall short. But out of love for us, God *declares* us to be righteous on the basis of Jesus, who paid the debt of our sin by offering his life as a substitute for ours. When by faith we accept this gracious gift of forgiveness, and follow Jesus with the help of the Holy Spirit, we have eternal life!

Focus: Many have noted that before we are able to understand and gratefully accept the "Good News" of the Gospel, we must first understand and humbly accept the "Bad News" about ourselves as sinners. This is perhaps the most difficult step because we are so prone to defend and excuse ourselves. It is undeniable that some people are better than other people in this fallen world. And while it is better to do good than evil, this is not the point. The point is, when we compare ourselves to the standard of what God created us to be, we all fall short. Pride is the greatest obstacle to the Gospel.

Prayer: *Lord, grant us the humility to accept the truth about ourselves, and then accept the gift of your grace and mercy. It almost seems too good to be true. In this world where we are so used to being deceived and disappointed by others, it is amazing that we can absolutely trust what Jesus has done for us through his death and resurrection! We praise your holy name! Amen.*

Day 318   Romans 4–5

November 13

> Key Text: So just as sin ruled over all people and brought them to death, now God's wonderful grace rules instead, giving us right standing with God and resulting in eternal life through Jesus Christ our Lord. (Romans 5:21)

Paul has established the fact that all human beings are under God's judgment because of sin. The word "sin" literally means "to miss the mark." In this case, the "mark" is that which God intended human beings to become when he created us. Because of sin, we miss the mark and therefore are not now fully human, or fully alive. Most of us sense it. We sense that things are not right. We long to be more than we are—to be perfect. At the very least, we know we are not the people we want to be.

In order for God to make things right in our lives, we must first understand the truth about ourselves. To this end, he gave us the Ten Commandments, which define what a "fully alive" human being looks like in relationship to God and one another. When we try and fail to keep his commandments, or when we willfully rebel against them, we are made aware of the fact that we miss the mark—we are sinners. Our sin, rooted in weakness and sustained by pride, undermines us, keeping us from being "fully alive." This is the Bad News we need to know.

The Good News is that we *can* be made right with God. This doesn't come about by human wisdom or goodness, nor by any natural process. It only comes about by God's gracious decision to bear the guilt of our sin and take its judgment upon himself through Jesus' death on the cross. So, we are made right with God by grace through faith alone!

Paul now explains, especially to his Jewish readers, that this is not new teaching, but has always been the case, beginning with Abraham in the book of Genesis.

In chapter 4, Paul shows how Abraham, the father of the Jews, discovered that favor with God came not from his good deeds, but from his faith. Genesis 15:6 says, *"Abraham believed the Lord, and the Lord counted him as righteous because of his faith."* This righteousness—think of righteousness as a "right relationship"—came long before the Law of Moses or even the Jewish mark of circumcision. Paul says that *"circumcision was a sign that Abraham already had faith and that God had already accepted him and declared him to be righteous—even before he was circumcised."*

This means—and it is an important theme of Paul's—that Abraham is the spiritual father of all who have faith, not just circumcised Jews. The Promise of God is offered to Jews and Gentiles alike! This theological insight underlies Paul's ministry to the Gentile world: *"So the promise is received by faith. It is given as a free gift. And we are all certain to receive it, whether or not we live according to the law of Moses, if we have faith like Abraham's"* (Romans 4:16).

In chapter 5, Paul rejoices about the Good News. It brings us *"peace with God,"* and a standing of *"undeserved privilege"* where we *"confidently and joyfully look forward to sharing God's glory"* (Romans 5:1–2). Knowing this, we can become joyful people no matter what. No present problem or trial can take away our present privilege and future glory.

Something amazing happens in us when we embrace this. The Holy Spirit opens our mind and heart, and we become aware of God's love for us. It fills us with joy. For the first time, we feel spiritually alive.

Paul explores this idea by making a theological comparison between Adam (as the old humanity) and Christ (as the new humanity). It is a complex analysis, but in short, he says that each introduced something into the human experience by their respective actions. Adam introduced sin and death by his rebellion against God. But Christ introduced a restored relationship with God, and new life by his obedience to God. In each case, the representative action of the one affects the lives of all. Adam's sin brought condemnation, but Christ's obedience brings righteousness.

The Good News is that, in the end, grace wins! As people sinned more and more, God's grace became more abundant: *"So just as sin ruled over all people and brought them to death, now God's wonderful grace rules instead, giving us right standing with God and resulting in eternal life through Jesus Christ our Lord"* (Romans 5:21).

Focus: When we connect our lives to Christ through repentance and faith, we not only receive forgiveness of sin, but also enter into a new life with a new future. That future has been initiated by Jesus' resurrection. As a resurrected human, Jesus is the prototype of a new humanity. We too shall share in his resurrection and in the New Creation. It will be eternal life, "fully alive."

Prayer: *Lord, we rejoice that your grace is greater than all our sin. We are so grateful that your love moved you to give us what we do not deserve, in order that we may be reconciled to you. We joyfully affirm that we are children of Abraham by faith! Amen.*

Day 319   Reflection

November 14

Romans 5:1 says that those who have faith in Jesus are made right with God and consequently have *"peace with God."* What can be more amazing than this?

Those who have followed the story of the Bible from the beginning will know that the coming of Jesus is the big event that God has been moving towards all along since the Fall of Adam and Eve in Genesis chapter 3! Specifically, Jesus is the fulfillment of God's ancient Promise to Abraham to bring the blessings of salvation to the whole fallen world through a descendent.

According to Romans 5:2, Jesus brings us to a place of *"undeserved privilege where we now stand"* because of our faith in him. Even more, *"we confidently and joyfully look forward to sharing God's glory."*

But what is this present privilege and future glory?

The idea of *"standing"* comes from the Old Testament Temple, where certain privileged people got to stand in the holy presence of God. Paul is saying that because of Jesus, all believers now receive the privilege of standing in the presence of God, like one is standing in the presence of a great king.

In his presence we are surrounded by a love, joy and peace like we have never experienced. We realize that this is what we were made for; this is what it means to be fully human in the image of God.

Even now, in this present life, we sense that our new life in Jesus is the beginning of something amazing—something massively and unimaginably beautiful and powerful. Paul describes it as sharing God's glory.

"Glory" is one of those words that is hard to get a handle on, because it points to realities beyond our present experience. God's glory is his very being and nature. Like him, it is without limit. When God shows himself to us, he reveals his glory.

All that God does is shaped and scented by the greatness of who he is. For humans made in his image and likeness, to know God's glory is to experience a fullness of joy that will never run out or grow stale.

What will it be like?

We can't say exactly. 1 Corinthians 2:9 says, *"No eye has seen, no ear has heard, and no mind has imagined what God has prepared for those who love him."* Even if we were to take the happiest moment of our lives, or the greatest vision for this world we can imagine, and multiply it a hundredfold, we still wouldn't come close. In our present mortal condition, we are not equipped to say what sharing God's glory will be like—not any more than a mosquito could explain the beauty of Mozart.

Since God's full glory would blow us away, he lets it leak out with greatly reduced wattage so that we might have some light but not be blinded. Beginning in the Old Testament with Abraham, God gradually and progressively makes himself known throughout the Bible, like a dimmer switch on a light. The light becomes brightest—at least as bright as we can now manage—with the coming of Jesus.

Hebrews 1:3 says that Jesus is God's clearest, brightest revelation of himself to us: *"The Son radiates God's own glory and expresses the very character of God, and he sustains everything by the mighty power of his command."*

So, to see Jesus is to see the glory of God in a manner we can access. Through him, we learn that the infinite, eternal God is a God who loves us and gives himself for us. So that we might share his glory.

Now that is amazing!

> **Prayer:** *Lord, our imagination fails us when we try to understand what it means to share your glory. Yet we have already begun to experience something of your glorious life through faith in Jesus. We sense your presence...feel your joy...and are filled with hope about what life will be in your presence when we become fully alive! Remind us of our future glory when we go through the present hard times! Amen.*

Day 320   Romans 6–8

November 15

> Key Text: So you also should consider yourselves to be dead to the power of sin and alive to God through Christ Jesus.
> (Romans 6:11)

God's abundant grace raises a question among skeptics. If God forgives our sins without any co-pay from us, why not just go ahead and sin? In other words, doesn't grace encourage us to sin because we know that God will forgive us anyway?

For Paul, this misunderstanding of grace is abhorrent. Faith in Christ, as evidenced in baptism, means that we are identified with Christ in his death and resurrection. His death, in our place, means that our sins are forgiven. His resurrection to new life means that we too have a new life. Therefore, in God's eyes, sin and death no longer determine our future life; therefore, they should not dictate our present life. We are free from sin—not to carelessly return to it, but to live in obedience with God.

To return to sin after being set free from it, would be like a death row inmate, pardoned at the last moment by the governor, choosing to use his freedom to return to a life of crime. Impossible? No. Inconceivable? Yes.

Since we now belong to God by faith, our whole selves—body, soul and spirit—should be given to the service of God. Paul writes, *"Do not let sin control the way you live; do not give in to sinful desires. Do not let any part of your body become an instrument of evil to serve sin. Instead, give yourselves completely to God, for you were dead, but now you have new life. So use your whole body as an instrument to do what is right for the glory of God"* (Romans 6:12–13).

But how can we obey God now when we couldn't (and didn't) obey him before? Earlier, in chapter 3, Paul explained that the Ten Commandments, which show us the goal to aspire to, could never make us right with God because we couldn't perfectly keep them. In the end, all they could do was point out what we already knew—that we have a nature bent towards sin. So if rules don't work, what does work?

In chapter 7, Paul explains that what works is the Holy Spirit in us. God's Spirit in us is a new power that resets the default settings of our sinful nature. We serve God now not by trying and failing to keep his commandments, but by allowing his Spirit to redirect our desires and empower us to do his will.

This is something that is more easily experienced than explained. It is like being in love. Love motivates us to do what we would never have desired to do before because of our selfishness and weakness.

Paul uses his own experience as exhibit A. He recalls, as a young Jewish boy, taking on the demands of the Law at the age of accountability. He discovered to his great dismay that knowing the demands of the Law—to not covet, for example—did not help him keep it. In fact, it created an irresistible desire to disobey! It was distressing to discover that he was a lawbreaker, because as a Jew he wanted to do what was right and not do what was wrong. But he found himself failing in both cases.

His conclusion: *"I love God's law with all my heart. But there is another power within me that is at war with my mind. This power makes me a slave to the sin that is still within me. Oh, what a miserable person I am! Who will free me from this life that is dominated by sin and death? Thank God! The answer is in Jesus Christ our Lord"* (Romans 7:22–25).

So the nature of the Christian life is not merely trying harder to be a better person than we were before. Rather, it is continually receiving fresh grace from God by our faith, and yielding to the influence of the Holy Spirit within us. The Holy Spirit gives us the desire and the ability to obey God's commands.

In addition, the Spirit makes us aware that we are God's children and that we have a great expectation of future glory as resurrected people. Even though we experience suffering in this present life, it is nothing compared to the glory that God will reveal in us later.

So the Gospel gives us great hope and assurance. Paul writes, *"And I am convinced that nothing can ever separate us from God's love. Neither death nor life, neither angels nor demons, neither our fears for today nor our worries about tomorrow—not even the powers of hell can separate us from God's love"* (Romans 8:38).

> **Focus:** These difficult chapters are nonetheless some of the most encouraging and enlightening chapters of the whole Bible. By studying them diligently, we will understand how sinful people are made right with God. Knowing this will set us free from condemnation and fear to live with joy and hope as the Holy Spirit energizes us. And we can be assured, even in our sufferings, that God causes everything to work together for the good of those who love him and are called according to his good purpose for them.

> **Prayer:** *Lord, there is so much here to praise you for! We praise you for setting us free from the penalty and the power of sin, and giving us a new life with new desires instead. Most of all, thank you that the same Spirit who raised Jesus from the dead lives in us and will raise us as well. Amen!*

Day 321   Romans 9–11

November 16

> Key Text: Some of the people of Israel have hard hearts, but this will last only until the full number of Gentiles comes to Christ. And so all Israel will be saved. (Romans 11:25-26)

Paul's argument thus far is that all—Jews and Gentiles alike—are saved by grace alone, through faith alone, and not by religious or moral merit. But this raises a question for those Jews who reject God's grace through Jesus. What will become of them? Has God rejected his Old Testament people?

Paul's heart is filled with *"bitter sorrow and unending grief"* over the unbelief of his people, Israel. He says that he would be willing to be cursed himself (i.e., go to hell) if doing so would save them! After all, Israel was chosen by God and given the blessings of his wonderful promises, his powerful presence, his Covenant and Law.

Given that many Jews in Paul's day rejected the Messiah, did God fail to fulfill his promises to Israel? Paul says emphatically that God has not failed. The truth is, as we saw so frequently in the Old Testament, not all who were physically Jewish were truly God's people. He did not force his people to believe, and many didn't. While he showed great patience with those who left him for idolatry, in the end they were judged by being exiled from the land.

Nevertheless, there was always a *"faithful remnant"* among the Israelites, and it was true in the time of Jesus as well. Paul was an example. The disciples, too, and of course Jesus himself, were quintessential faithful Jews. So while God judged the nation as a whole, there were individuals to whom he showed his mercy. This is his prerogative. As God said to Moses: *"I will show mercy to anyone I choose, and I will show compassion to anyone I choose"* (Romans 9:15).

Ironically, Israel's stumbling over Jesus as the Messiah resulted in a redirection of missionary work to the Gentile world where many believed! As the prophet Joel had written hundreds of years before: *"Everyone who calls on the name of the Lord will be saved."* And indeed, Paul offers hope that Israel too will one day turn from her unbelief and accept the Gospel of grace through faith in Jesus.

In that day—when the full number of Gentiles have been grafted into Israel, and when Israel returns to her God—then *"all Israel will be saved"* (Romans 11:26). Depending on how Paul is using the term "Israel" here (whether he means ethnic Jews or spiritual Israel, including Gentiles), he probably isn't claiming that every single ethnic Jew will be saved, but only that all true children of Abraham—Jew and Gentile alike—will be saved.

Paul's bitter sorrow over ethnic Israel's unbelief is lessened by his expectation that many Jews will eventually find their way home to Jesus. In his passionate and complex narrative, Paul makes clear that God is not done with Israel. He also restates his view that being a child of Abraham is not just a racial identity, but a theological identity. There are ethnic Jews who don't believe and therefore are not the True Israel. The True Israel is being populated with ethnic and spiritual Jews—those who are Jewish by birth but followers of Jesus by faith, and those who are Gentiles by birth but children of Abraham by faith.

All those whom God has chosen, Jews and Gentiles alike, will become part of the people of God.

Are you confused? Don't feel bad. Paul's reflection on the status of his countrymen has been difficult for many to figure out!

But the thought of these things causes Paul to cry out with a doxology: *"Oh, how great are God's riches and wisdom and knowledge! How impossible it is for us to understand his decisions and his ways! For who can know the Lord's thoughts? Who knows enough to give him advice? And who has given him so much that he needs to pay it back? For everything comes from him and exists by his power and is intended for his glory. All glory to him forever! Amen"* (Romans 11:33–36).

Focus: We conclude that Paul expects that his people Israel will be restored, but in a way that was unexpected in the Old Testament. The New Israel is composed of the fullness of Jews and Gentiles alike. But this broadening of the definition of Israel does not mean that God has forgotten his Old Testament people. As always, he reaches out to them with special affection.

Prayer: *Lord, we wish to have the same kind of sorrow for our unsaved friends as Paul had for his countrymen, the Jews. We pray for all people—Jews and Gentiles alike—that they would come to see Jesus as Messiah and receive eternal life in his name. Amen.*

Day 322   Romans 12–16

November 17

Key Text: **We must not just please ourselves. We should help others do what is right and build them up in the Lord. For even Christ didn't live to please himself.** (Romans 15:1-3)

The book of Romans concludes with Paul moving from theology to application. He urges us to respond to all that God has done for us through Christ, by offering our bodies—our whole selves—to him as a living sacrifice. This is a powerful image, drawn from the Old Testament Temple worship. It calls for a radical break from the ways of the world so that God can transform us into new people who do his will instead of conforming to the culture.

This involves a humble assessment of ourselves, realizing that we need other believers in order to become the person God wants us to be. We must love others sincerely, hate what is wrong, and hold tightly to what is good. Using the spiritual gifts God has given us, we must live in harmony with one another and serve the Lord together. We are better together.

By refusing to retaliate when mistreated, we live honorable lives and leave judgment to God. In this way we conquer evil by doing good.

With respect to the government, Christians must understand that all authority comes from God, and those in positions of authority have been placed there by God. Therefore, we should respect governing authorities even if we don't like them. Paul is speaking to those who live under the absolute power of a monarch, and is telling them not be anarchists.

The legitimate authority of any governing authority is to ensure peace by enforcing the rule of law. In a free democracy, of course, elected leaders are accountable to the citizens and should be respected unless there is a legal or moral reason not to.

As citizens, Christians should pay taxes, behave properly, and live in community by loving their neighbors, because doing this fulfills the requirements of God's Law.

With respect to fellow believers who have different scruples about particular secondary matters, we should follow the way of love. Don't argue about debatable matters. Instead, be convinced of your own position and respect those who believe differently. Don't look down on them or pressure them to violate their conscience. The Kingdom of God is about living a life of goodness and peace and joy in the Holy Spirit. Aim for harmony.

Chapter 15 elaborates on the subject of unity and love: *"We must not just please ourselves. We should help others do what is right and build them up in the Lord"* (Romans 15:1–2). What pleases God is for followers of Jesus to join together, as Jews and Gentiles with one voice, giving praise and glory to God, the Father of our Lord Jesus Christ.

As a symbol of unity, Paul plans to go to Jerusalem with a financial gift for poor believers living there, from the Gentile believers in Macedonia. The Macedonians are glad to offer this because they feel they owe a real debt to the Jews. *"Since the Gentiles received the spiritual blessings of the Good News from the believers in Jerusalem, they feel the least they can do in return is to help them financially"* (Romans 15:27).

Paul concludes his letter in chapter 16 with extended greetings to friends and coworkers in Rome. Then, after warning his readers against people who cause divisions and upset the people's faith by false teaching, he leaves them with a strong doxology: *"Now all glory to God, who is able to make you strong, just as my Good News says. This message about Je-*

sus Christ has revealed his plan for you Gentiles, a plan kept secret from the beginning of time. But now as the prophets foretold and as the eternal God has commanded, this message is made known to all Gentiles everywhere, so that they too might believe and obey him. All glory to the only wise God, through Jesus Christ, forever. Amen" (Romans 16:25–27).

> **Focus:** Theology becomes active and transformative when it is lived out in practice by loving one another. Love is stronger than evil and overcomes it. Love also overcomes racial, religious and cultural differences. A Christian community made up of Jews and Gentiles is a powerful witness that the Kingdom of God is among us.

> **Prayer:** Lord, teach us to resist the pressure of secular culture so that we may become a counterculture for the common good. We offer our whole selves to you as an act of worship, so that by our transformed lives we may make Jesus visible and believable. Amen.

Day 323   1 Corinthians 1–6

November 18

> **Key Text:** For the Kingdom of God is not just a lot of talk; it is living by God's power. (1 Corinthians 4:20)

The city of Corinth was known for its immorality and paganism, but Paul managed to plant a church there during his second missionary journey *(Acts 18)*. However, the church is seriously dysfunctional, so Paul writes to urge them to live in harmony and in holiness. Reading this letter is like listening to one end of a phone call. Paul is responding to a number of issues and questions from the congregation.

There are divisions in the church over personalities. The people of Corinth are drawn to celebrities with charisma. This means that the great oratory of Apollos has made him a favorite over the deep teaching of the apostles. For Corinthians, there is a preference for rhetorical skill. Style triumphs over substance.

Paul warns the people against the clever and entertaining rhetoric which was common among the Greeks. The power of the Gospel is not human charisma, but the work of the Holy Spirit opening our eyes to the proclaimed word. Those who resist the Spirit judge the Gospel's message to be foolishness. Paul explains, "So when we preach that Christ was cru-

cified, the Jews are offended and the Gentiles say that it's all nonsense" (1 Corinthians 1:23).

But those who listen with an open mind and heart discover that the "*foolish*" plan of God is wiser than the wisdom of the world, and God's "*weakness*" is stronger than the world's strength.

Ordinary people can know God's thoughts, even as the great and the gifted completely miss out. The Holy Spirit gives them understanding. Great faith with humility always trumps great intellect with pride.

In chapter 3, Paul remembers from his visit with the Corinthian believers, that he couldn't talk with them as mature believers at that time. They thought and acted more like unbelievers than followers of Jesus! He urges them now to move beyond their immaturity and competitiveness to become mature in their faith. Otherwise, their lives will not survive the judgment of Christ when he returns. They may escape hell, but their contribution to the Kingdom of God will be nil.

In chapter 4, Paul points to himself as an example of a once proud man, humbled by the Gospel. Where once he feverously sought the approval of others, now he is concerned only with being faithful to Jesus. He urges the congregation not to pit one leader against the other, as if one has to be "for" Paul or Apollos. Apollos may be a popular favorite because his rhetorical skills and physical presence resonate with the Corinthians' love of powerful celebrities and worldly success, but what does this have to do with the Gospel?

Paul then gets very personal about the way he conducts his life as an apostle. He admits that he and the other apostles look like fools next to the gifted and overly confident Corinthians, but this is the way of humility: *"Instead, I sometimes think God has put us apostles on display, like prisoners of war at the end of a victor's parade, condemned to die. We have become a spectacle to the entire world—to people and angels alike"* (1 Corinthians 4:9).

This is certainly not "feel good, look good" Christianity: *"Even now we go hungry and thirsty, and we don't have enough clothes to keep warm. We are often beaten and have no home. We work wearily with our own hands to earn our living. We bless those who curse us. We are patient with those who abuse us. We appeal gently when evil things are said about us. Yet we are treated like the world's garbage, like everybody's trash..."* (1 Corinthians 4:11–13).

[The bottom line is this: *"The Kingdom of God is not just a lot of talk—it is living by God's power."*]

In chapter 5, Paul addresses a shocking case of unrepentant immorality within the congregation. A man is living in sin with his stepmother, a perverse act that even pagans don't do. The matter has been tolerated by the leaders, perhaps because their success in ministry has made them overly concerned with being liked, and unwilling to deal forcefully with issues of sin.

Paul insists that they call a meeting of the church and force the man out. They should, shockingly, hand him over to Satan for whatever consequences may follow. Perhaps the grip of his sinful nature will be broken and he can return to fellowship. But for now, his presence is a scandal and a misrepresentation of Christ's Church.

In chapter 6, Paul addresses other matters of sin, such as believers taking one another to court because they cannot resolve their differences, and also the visiting of temple prostitutes as they did when they were pagans. These and other willful sins are inconsistent with the Kingdom of God and must be stopped. Our freedom in Christ is not freedom to sin, but freedom to obey God. Our bodies are not our own, but are now the Temple of the Holy Spirit who lives in us, and should not be used for sin. We must honor God with our bodies.

> **Focus:** The Christian life is a life of holiness, meaning that we belong to God. Our total selves—body and soul—are now set apart for his service. Therefore, we must live a different life and resist the impulses of our sinful nature. We must, instead, obey the Holy Spirit.
>
> **Prayer:** *Lord, we confess our sins and commit ourselves as your Church to faithfully representing your will and purpose in our individual and corporate lives. We offer our bodies as living sacrifices. Amen.*

Day 324   1 Corinthians 7–10

November 19

> Key Text: So whether you eat or drink, or whatever you do, do it all for the glory of God. (1 Corinthians 10:31)

Paul has established the principle that Christian freedom means freedom to do what is right, not freedom to indulge our sinful nature. He now continues by answering a series of questions that have been asked by the Corinthian congregation, giving his best advice about what is right.

There is evidence in chapter 7 of a social crisis which somewhat colors the advice that Paul is going to give. Historians say there was a growing famine at this time that disrupted everyone's present circumstances and future plans. In addition, Paul seems to have in the back of his mind the conviction that the Lord is going to return soon, even within his lifetime. In either case, there is a sense of urgency and caution in his responses to their questions about life decisions.

In chapter 7, the questions pertain to marriage and celibacy. The common wisdom of the day, influenced by Stoic philosophy, was that celibacy was a higher virtue which enabled spiritual growth. Along with it was a bias against the physical realm, and therefore against sex. But Paul reflects the Hebrew virtue of the goodness of the physical life with its senses. He is also practical. So his answers to questions about marriage and remarriage, and sex, celibacy and temptation are shaped by both the goodness of marriage and the crises of the moment. Notably, he expresses equality in sex: *"The husband should fulfill his wife's sexual needs, and the wife should fulfill her husband's needs. The wife gives authority over her body to her husband, and the husband gives authority over his body to his wife"* (1 Corinthians 7:3–4).

Further advice is given to those who are widowed and single, engaged to be married, or are married to an unbeliever. Paul always leans toward the goodness of marriage, but with common sense. Given the present crisis, each should do what they are able to, as long as it honors God. Those who are married to unbelievers should remain married unless their spouse abandons them because of their faith. Those who can, should consider postponing marriage.

It is the same for all situations that people find themselves in: *"Each of you, dear brothers and sisters, should remain as you were when God first called you"* (1 Corinthians 7:24). In other words, do what you can to be free from the concerns of this life in order to serve the Lord. His advice is timely for all those in every generation who find themselves living in times of crises.

In chapter 8, Paul addresses the specific matter of whether a Christian should purchase and eat meat that has been offered to idols at the pagan temples. Theologically aware Christians will know that there is one God only, and therefore gods of idolatry are not deity. But not all understand this yet. So, Christians should do what love dictates. Don't tempt someone to violate their conscience about this. It is better to abstain for their well-being.

In chapter 9, Paul expresses his view that missionaries and ministers deserve financial support for their work of teaching and preaching the Gospel. He points out that this was how the nation of Israel functioned with its priests and Temple workers. It is right to be financially supported, but Paul himself has never used this right. So as not to offend anyone, he has always supported himself. This has enabled him to be as free as possible for the sake of ministry to both Jews and Gentiles. He says, *"Yes, I try to find common ground with everyone, doing everything I can to save some"* (1 Corinthians 9:22).

In chapter 10, Paul reminds the Corinthians of Israel's constant testing of God by her idolatry, and warns them not to do the same. Instead, obey God and work towards unity and love in the congregation. Use freedom for the sake of others: *"So whether you eat or drink, or whatever you do, do it all for the glory of God"* (1 Corinthians 10:31).

> **Focus:** The Christian life is founded upon and shaped by the grace of God and the prompting of the Holy Spirit. The Ten Commandments provide us with moral boundaries, but it is not possible to create a rule for every circumstance in life. The Holy Spirit will guide us with loving wisdom to make good decisions that honor God, respect the needs and feelings of others, and preserve unity in the Church.

> **Prayer:** *Lord, we thank you for the freedom from guilt and shame that we have through Christ. Show us how to use our freedom to best serve you and others. Amen.*

Day 325   1 Corinthians 11–14

November 20

> Key Text: So, my dear brothers and sisters, be eager to prophesy, and don't forbid speaking in tongues. But be sure that everything is done properly and in order. (1 Corinthians 14:39–40)

Paul now turns to a number of specific problems related to the public worship service at Corinth. The first concern is about head coverings for women—a sign of marriage, like a wedding ring today. Apparently, some married women are worshiping with "uncovered heads," sending the cultural message (intended or not) of sexual looseness. This provocative behavior would have shamed their husbands.

Many of the men and women believers at Corinth came from a background of paganism, and therefore need instruction in Christian ethics and sensibilities. The paganism that they had previously practiced was notable for its gender bending and unhinged sexual immorality. So it appears that certain practices at Corinth, such as women not having a head covering—which only prostitutes would do in public—have created controversy. It is possible that the women mean to express their "*freedom*" in Christ, but they are doing so in ways that are culturally divisive. Paul again calls for personal behavior to be guided by love and unity and concern for others.

What is in view here is the Jewish and Christian understanding of the meaning of gender, as well as the relationship between men and women. In particular, the head covering symbolized that the married woman had a "*head*," her husband. This has been widely misunderstood. In Christian understanding of marriage, *head* does not imply power or superiority. It identifies the husband as uniquely responsible before God to love and protect his wife.

Jesus taught that in the Kingdom of God, things are turned upside down: The first are last; the greatest is least of all. In this way, power is redefined as love and servanthood. So Jesus himself is the example of what this means for husbands. Paul writes in Ephesians 5: "*For husbands, this means love your wives, just as Christ loved the church. He gave up his life for her...*" (Ephesians 5:25).

Since worship expresses new life and the coming New Creation, worshipers should reflect their new identities as sons and daughters of Christ—not their old identities as fallen humans in a fallen society who act out in rebellion against God.

Paul next addresses divisions occurring during the Lord's Supper. The worship event which should express the love and unity of the body of Christ has instead become an occasion for selfish behavior. Paul explains how they should administer the Lord's Supper, and adds a warning about the seriousness of the matter: "*So anyone who eats this bread or drinks this cup of the Lord unworthily is guilty of sinning against the body and blood of the Lord*" (1 Corinthians 11:27).

In chapters 12 through 14, Paul turns his attention to the misuse of spiritual gifts in worship. Spiritual gifts are God-given abilities to serve others. In a lengthy explanation, Paul shows that the Holy Spirit gives spiritual gifts to all believers to be used for the building up of the Church in its faith and ministry. There is a wide diversity of gifts—some of which Paul lists here—but they are all given by the same Spirit: *"It is the one and only Spirit who distributes all these gifts. He alone decides which gift each person should have"* (1 Corinthians 12:11).

The Corinthians, as noted, come from pagan worship experiences where they had been led astray and swept along by frenzied, demonic behavior. Therefore, they tend to be attracted to the more exotic gifts of the Spirit such as speaking in tongues. Paul explains to them that while the gift of tongues is given by God to some for their personal edification in prayer, speaking in tongues in public does not edify the congregation in worship, because the words cannot be understood, unless interpreted.

Paul insists that all the gifts of the Spirit be honored, not just the supernatural gifts. The Church needs helpers, teachers and administrators in its ministry, as well as those who heal and perform miracles. No one gift is most important, and no one person is sufficient in themselves— or deficient. Using the analogy of the human body, Paul writes that the "foot" can't say that it is not needed because it's not a "hand," nor can the "ear" say *"I am not part of the body because I am not an eye."* If the whole body were an eye, how would you hear?!

The great chapter 13 makes clear that spiritual gifts must be guided by love. Therefore, love is more important than particular spiritual gifts. Love builds the character of the congregation and grows it up in faith. Gifts like prophecy and tongues are temporary, but love lasts forever!

So love must be the highest goal of any congregation, and the use of gifts must be directed by love. Those who speak in tongues (unknown languages) should ordinarily use their gift for personal edification. In public worship services, tongues are not edifying without interpretation. The other gifts of the Spirit—especially prophecy, or preaching— are what strengthen the church as a whole.

In summary, the gifts are good, and should be welcomed as God gives them, but the Church should be sensitive to the purpose of public worship and the needs of the congregation, especially for teaching. Paul concludes chapter 14 by saying, *"So, my dear brothers and sisters, be eager to prophesy, and don't forbid speaking in tongues. But be sure that everything is done properly and in order"* (1 Corinthians 14:39–40).

> **Focus:** The purpose of the worship service is not to assert ourselves and our needs, regardless of what others think. The purpose of worship is to focus on the Lord who draws us together in community by his Holy Spirit. The local church is built up in unity and faith as each believer uses their own spiritual gifts for the glory of God and for sake of others, whether in worship or throughout the week.

> **Prayer:** *Lord, may the gifts you have given each one of us be expressed in unified worship and service so that you will be glorified. Forgive us for the times we abuse our gifts by asserting ourselves for attention, or to control others. May your Church everywhere experience greater and greater unity, so that the unbelieving world may see Jesus in us. Amen.*

Day 326   Reflection

November 21

The eyebrow-raising problems of the Corinthian congregation illustrate the theology of the book of Romans, which says that Christians are sinners who live in a broken world, but are nevertheless loved and redeemed by God, and destined for a glorious future.

As Christians, we live in the tension between the "already" and the "not yet" of the Kingdom of God. This means that we "already" have been declared righteous by God because of our faith in Jesus as Savior. We already experience his loving and joyful presence in our lives through the Holy Spirit. We also experience the gifts of worship, prayer, fellowship and spiritual gift-empowered ministry. But we do not experience these things in fullness or perfection. Not yet.

According to Paul, we should think of the Spirit in our lives as a down payment and foretaste of what is to come, and there is much more. The truth is that the "not yet" part is by far the best part! It includes the return of Jesus, the final judgment, the destruction of Satan, the resurrection from the dead, and the dawn of the New Creation. However, we should give thanks for what we have "already" received from God, because it sustains us in the present struggle of this mortal life and creates a sense of expectation of what is yet to come.

Romans, chapter 8, is a clear exposition of this tension we experience between the "already" and "not yet." After reminding us that we have already received God's forgiveness, and the gift of his Spirit, Paul adds that we are God's children and therefore heirs of God's glory. We will share in all the awesome things God is going to do in eternity. This puts our present life into perspective: *"Yet what we suffer now is nothing compared to the glory he will reveal to us later"* (Romans 8:18).

Paul explains that the whole creation, including nature, has been damaged by sin and death. Suffering is universal. It is the default condition of living as fallen people in a fallen world. But because of Jesus, it is not meaningless suffering. It is like the pains of childbirth. Giving birth is painful, but the end result is new life: *"And we believers also groan [with suffering], even though we have the Holy Spirit within us as a foretaste of future glory, for we long for our bodies to be released from sin and suffering. We, too, wait with eager hope for the day when God will give us our full rights as his adopted children, including the new bodies he has promised us"* (Romans 8:23).

This means that we should not expect our lives as Christians to be free of pain. There will always be a measure of dissatisfaction in this life. We will always struggle with temptation when our desires are inflamed. Our present bodies are weak, prone to sickness, and will one day die. So we are not presently able to experience the fullness of life that is yet to come. For that, we will need resurrection bodies, like Jesus' resurrection body, suited to living in the New Heavens and New Earth.

But dissatisfaction with this life doesn't mean that we have no joy or hope. Quite the opposite. Jesus' resurrection gives us assurance that we too will be resurrected and enabled to live the amazing life of the New Creation. With hope for the future, we can be patient with the imperfections, disappointments, losses and sorrows of the present. Paul says that the Holy Spirit helps us in our weakness, praying on our behalf to the Father when we are too weak, discouraged or depressed to pray for ourselves.

Our hope is fortified by the fact that God knows us, loves us, and is totally on our side. Consequently, *"we know that God causes everything to work together for the good of those who love God and are called according to his purpose for them"* (Romans 8:28).

When we inhabit the New Creation in our resurrection bodies, we will at last achieve the glory for which we were created. We will share the glory of God as custodians of his universe, with a life that is more real and full of possibilities than anything we can now imagine. The suffering of our mortal life will hardly be remembered in comparison to the glory we will experience.

> **Prayer:** *Lord, we struggle with the brokenness of our present lives. Sometimes we are tempted to think that this is all there is, and therefore we should live for now to maximize personal pleasure—just in case! But Lord, when we think about Jesus' crucifixion and consider the persuasive evidence for his resurrection, we are once again filled with joy and hope from the Holy Spirit. Grant us the grace we need to patiently endure the troubles of the day, while praising you for the glory that is to come. Amen.*

Day 327 1 Corinthians 15–16

November 22

> Key Text: So, my dear brothers and sisters, be strong and immovable. Always work enthusiastically for the Lord, for you know that nothing you do for the Lord is ever useless.
> (1 Corinthians 15:58)

Chapter 15 begins with Paul's synopsis of the Gospel, which he insists is consistent with the Old Testament Scriptures. The simple Gospel which saves us is this: Christ died for our sins, was buried and then raised from the dead after three days. This was all witnessed by his twelve disciples. In addition, five hundred of his followers saw him after he was resurrected, and then, last of all, the apostle Paul himself.

Paul now addresses the importance and nature of resurrection life. Apparently there are some new converts who are doubting the possibility of their own resurrection because they cannot imagine how it could come about. Perhaps Jesus' resurrection, which they can hardly deny, was a one-off event, and simply can't be explained.

In response, Paul reminds them that the resurrection of Christ has been verified by many witnesses who are still alive and can be asked about it. If Christ rose, then it is certainly something God can do, and therefore something he can do for them.

Logically, if there is no resurrection of the dead, then faith in Christ is useless because he cannot have risen either. If not, then all who believe

625

in Christ are lost and their faith is useless: *"And if our hope in Christ is only for this life, we are more to be pitied than anyone in the world. But in fact, Christ has been raised from the dead. He is the first of a great harvest of all who have died"* (1 Corinthians 15:19–20).

So if resurrection from the dead is possible because it happened to Jesus' earthly body, what is resurrection life like? What will our bodies be like? Paul offers some metaphors from nature to assist our thinking. First, he says that resurrection is like a seed planted in the ground. Our mortal bodies will die, but in the sense that a seed dies when planted in the ground. When planted, the seed dies in order that it may grow into something new and far more glorious than bare seed. God gives each seed a new and unique body, so to speak.

Nature demonstrates that God is able to make different, glorious kinds of things. We see glorious beauty and diversity and strength in plants as well as all living creatures, whether birds, animals, fish or human beings—the greatest of all. We see it also in the heavens where the sun, moon and stars are different in glory from one another.

We need to think of our resurrection bodies as being gloriously different from our earthly bodies: *"Our earthly bodies are planted in the ground when we die, but they will be raised to live forever. Our bodies are buried in brokenness, but they will be raised in glory. They are buried in weakness, but they will be raised in strength. They are buried as natural* [mortal] *human bodies, but they will be raised as spiritual* [immortal] *bodies"* (1 Corinthians 15:42–44).

Resurrection is necessary because our present bodies are subject to sin and death, and therefore are not suited for life in the New Creation. Our new life will require glorious, immortal bodies—transformed bodies. The resurrection of our bodies will be the final victory of God over sin and death, preparing us for our unimaginable and everlasting existence in a New Heavens and New Earth.

It is important to note that our future resurrection life does not mean that our present mortal life doesn't matter. Quite the contrary. All that is done in this life for the glory of God will carry over. Therefore, Paul urges us to take our present life seriously: *"So, my dear brothers and sisters, be strong and immovable. Always work enthusiastically for the Lord, for you know that nothing you do for the Lord is ever useless"* (1 Corinthians 15:58).

Paul concludes his letter in chapter 16 by encouraging the Corinthians to continue with one particular work of ministry for the Lord—raising money to give as a gift to poor believers in Jerusalem because of a famine there. He encourages them to do it intentionally and transparently. It will be a powerful witness to the nature of the Church for the Gentile Christians to acknowledge and support their Jewish Christian brothers and sisters.

He concludes his teaching in this chapter by saying, *"Be on guard. Stand firm in the faith. Be courageous. Be strong. And do everything with love"* (1 Corinthians 16:13).

Focus: Belief in the afterlife as bodily existence in a transformed heavens and earth does not diminish our present life. Indeed, it affirms it and suggests that there is continuity as well as discontinuity. What we have created now by faith and obedience, out of love for God, will continue. This belief motivates us to serve others in the world, as well as to create beauty, goodness, truth and justice, because these things will be part of the New Creation.

Prayer: Lord, how good it is to know when we say goodbye to our deceased loved ones that their existence continues in your presence immediately, and then at your return, will blossom into resurrection life. What a great hope we have! We thank you for reassuring us of these things by raising Jesus from the dead! Amen.

Day 328   2 Corinthians 1–5

November 23

> Key Text: This means that anyone who belongs to Christ has become a new person. The old life is gone; a new life has begun! (2 Corinthians 5:17)

Paul's second letter to the Corinthians is prompted by trouble brewing in the congregation in response to his first letter. A troublemaker is slandering Paul to the congregation with accusations of disloyalty, wrong motives, pride, amateurism, weakness, dishonesty and even mental instability!

This letter is a defense of his ministry and motives.

Paul begins in chapter 1 by grounding his defense in the larger context of God's purpose for all our troubles—especially those which come in ministry. He writes, *"God is our merciful Father and the source of all com-*

fort. He comforts us in all our troubles so that we can comfort others. When they are troubled, we will be able to give them the same comfort God has given us" (2 Corinthians 1:3–4).

Paul's accuser apparently believes that Paul's sufferings in ministry are an indication of God's disfavor and of his own inadequacies. Therefore, he cannot be trusted. Paul believes quite the opposite. Suffering always accompanies Gospel ministry because we are called to participate in Christ's sufferings. We will get the same response that Jesus got from the unbelieving world when we declare the Gospel. Authentic ministry is marked by patient endurance, utter reliance on Christ, constant prayer, a clear conscience, and transparency of message and motives.

In chapter 2, Paul graciously calls for the congregation—which has disciplined the immoral troublemaker mentioned in the first letter—to forgive and restore him, lest Satan create a division in the church.

Those who are mature understand human nature and therefore accept the fact that troubles will come when the Gospel is declared. But the Gospel has its own offense. Paul says that the truth about Christ is like a sweet perfume to those who are truly seeking God, and they are drawn to it. But for those who resist God, Christ is the dreadful smell of death and gloom, and they resist it.

In chapters 3 through 5, Paul outlines the defense of his ministry and motives. He begins by insisting that the Corinthians themselves, by the witness of their changed lives through faith in Christ, are evidence that Paul seeks to honor Christ and not himself. His ministry is shaped by the New Covenant which was established by Jesus' death and resurrection. It is therefore grounded in grace and energized by the Holy Spirit, not by more Old Covenant law.

The Old Covenant of Moses had a purpose—to convict us of sin and show our need for redemption. But with the coming of Christ, this purpose has been fulfilled. Now, the life of the believer is directed by the Holy Spirit within, and not by conformity to the Law without.

It is the Holy Spirit who opens our eyes to see the glory of God in Christ, and then prompts us to become more and more like Christ. So Paul's ministry is all about the Gospel—who Jesus is and what he has done for us. It is not about pursuing popularity or power. His message is truth, not trickery. His methods are transparent, not manipulative.

628

What keeps people from seeing Christ is the maneuvering of Satan, not a lack of charisma in Paul: *"We now have this light shining in our hearts, but we ourselves are like fragile clay jars containing this great treasure. This makes it clear that our great power is from God, not from ourselves"* (2 Corinthians 4:7).

Yes, we get exhausted from the stresses of life and ministry, but the glory of resurrection life will vastly outweigh any present suffering. In one sense, the future has already begun for us because we are new people through the presence of the Holy Spirit in us. We commit ourselves to the mission of sharing the message of reconciliation as long as we live.

> **Focus:** Christian life and ministry cannot be evaluated through the lens of worldly success. In the many ways that the world measures success, we may seem to be failures. Our ultimate goal is not personal success, fame or power. It is to be servants of Jesus. If necessary, we will suffer for his name's sake. A life given in the service of God produces for us a future glory that is beyond comparison.

> *Prayer: Lord, make us an instrument of your peace and reconciliation. Though we are weak and ordinary, like clay pots, we are honored to bear the treasure of the Gospel in our lives and testimonies. May people see Jesus in us. Amen.*

Day 329   2 Corinthians 6–9

November 24

> Key Text: You know the generous grace of our Lord Jesus Christ. Though he was rich, yet for your sakes he became poor, so that by his poverty he could make you rich. (2 Corinthians 8:9)

Paul has just explained that anyone who belongs to Christ has become a new person. The old life is gone; a new life has begun. He continues now in chapter 6 to urge the Corinthians to live out their new life. Paul has set an example for them by his faithful ministry in the face of verbal opposition and physical suffering. His life has been an open book of integrity. The Corinthians must live this way also, and not like unbelievers. As *"new people"* in Christ, they cannot continue in their old way of thinking and behaving.

Chapter 7 continues this challenge by calling for the people to forsake sin and seek holiness of life out of respect for God. Paul refers to an unknown *"painful letter"* sent earlier, which was quite blunt and caused

629

them sorrow. Some think his blunt talk is repeated in what he writes in 6:14–7:1. It caused them sorrow, but then led them to repent and change their ways: *"For the kind of sorrow God wants us to experience leads us away from sin and results in salvation"* (2 Corinthians 7:10).

Along with his challenge, Paul brings words of encouragement to the church. He congratulates them for the spiritual growth that he sees and, in chapters 8 and 9, he presents a specific opportunity to demonstrate that Christ has united Jews and Gentiles by the Gospel. There has been a famine in Jerusalem that has brought great hardship among the poor in the Jewish Christian community. He challenges the Corinthian Gentile believers to follow the example of the Macedonian Gentiles who collected a generous offering for the poor—even though they themselves were poor. They did so eagerly of their own free will.

Paul wants the Corinthians, who excel in so many areas of ministry, to excel also in the grace of giving. To do so is to be like Christ: *"You know the generous grace of our Lord Jesus Christ. Though he was rich, yet for your sakes he became poor, so that by his poverty he could make you rich"* (2 Corinthians 8:9).

He further explains his challenge to give by stipulating that they each should give in proportion to what they have. His principle in giving is not equal gifts, but equal sacrifice. In this way, everyone—rich and poor alike—can participate equally. Sacrifice will mean different things for different people. But all should give willingly and not under compulsion or guilt.

Paul wants them to know that he is taking pains to organize the receipt and delivery of their gifts in such a way as to be entirely transparent and beyond reproach. We see again how important integrity in ministry is to Paul.

As they each decide in their hearts what to give, they should offer it as a cheerful act of worship. Paul is certain that in response to their generosity and sacrifice, God will provide all that they need and more: *"Yes, you will be enriched in every way so that you can always be generous"* (2 Corinthians 9:11).

Many good things will come from their generosity, which is prompted by the love of God and the needs of others. First, it will demonstrate that the Corinthians have not only believed the Gospel, but are also living it out. This will encourage others to live out their faith. Second, those who receive the blessing of the offering in Jerusalem will joyfully express their thanks to God in worship. The sufferings of the poor will be lightened, and their hearts made glad by the fact that Gentile believers they have never met have sacrificed for their sake. And last, the Gentile generosity to the Jews will demonstrate to the skeptical watching world that the Gospel does indeed bring people together.

> **Focus:** The Gospel gains visibility and credibility when it is lived out in generosity for the sake of others. God wants to use each of us as a conduit of generosity to the needy world that he loves. When we make our time, talent and resources available for serving others, God always replenishes us. The end result—the best result imaginable—is that recipients of God's generosity through us begin themselves to worship God and become conduits of further generosity.
>
> **Prayer:** *Lord, we are so grateful for those you sent to be generous with us—with love, assistance, compassion and the Gospel. Through them, we came to know who you are, so that we too could praise and thank you. We want to be your eyes, ears, mouth, legs and hands in the world. We desire to be a blessing to others in your name. We offer ourselves to you; please use us! Amen.*

Day 330 2 Corinthians 10–13

November 25

> Key Text: That's why I take pleasure in my weaknesses, and in the insults, hardships, persecutions, and troubles that I suffer for Christ. For when I am weak, then I am strong.
> (2 Corinthians 12:10)

Paul finishes his second letter to the Corinthian believers by preparing them for his third visit. He hopes that his strong exhortations, coupled with humble self-disclosure, will persuade them to take him seriously and cease listening to those who tear him down with false testimonies.

They think that Paul should be more aggressive, assertive and combative in service of the Gospel.

Paul admits that their mission may involve conflict with the world. But this conflict is not centered in people, but in ideas and false reasoning that keep people from knowing God. Interestingly, Paul said earlier that Satan is behind this. So, our ministry is not of bullying, but of persuasion, supported by strong reasoning, to teach people to obey Christ. The authority of the Gospel is not an authority to tear down, but to build up.

A false understanding of the Gospel, and subsequently of Gospel ministry, underlies the complaints of Paul's detractors at Corinth. They regard Paul as weak in person, ethically challenged, and a terrible speaker. They shamelessly commend themselves as "super apostles" for their insights and forcefulness, but Paul thinks that these things don't count for much: *"The important thing is for the Lord to commend them."*

But the Lord cannot commend them, because their faith has become corrupted by some who *"preach a different Jesus"* and who are motivated by a different kind of spirit, about a *"different kind of gospel,"* than what Paul taught them. In short, like Eve they have been deceived by the cunning ways of the serpent, Satan. *"They are deceitful workers who disguise themselves as apostles of Christ. But I am not surprised! Even Satan disguises himself as an angel of light."* And so do his servants!

By contrast to their hunger for power and recognition, Paul points out that he purposefully has never asked them for financial support, though he believes that it is proper to do so. He doesn't boast, manipulate or bully. If he *did* boast, he could point out that his racial and religious pedigree was far superior to theirs, not to mention his unbelievable history of suffering and persecution. Paul is poking a pin in their "We Are Awesome" balloon and choosing instead to *"boast about the things that show how weak I am."*

They have boasted about visions and revelations, but Paul has had them too, being *"caught up to paradise"* and hearing things so astounding that they could not be expressed in words. But again, he chooses to *"boast"* in his weakness. He mentions in particular his *"thorn in the flesh"* (a disease perhaps, or possibly migraines, epilepsy or bad vision), which hobbles and humbles him. Indeed, he takes pleasure in his weaknesses and in the insults, hardships, persecutions and troubles which he suffers for Christ: *"For when I am weak, then I am strong"* (2 Corinthians 12:10).

So as Paul prepares to visit them again, he pours out his pastoral heart of concern that they not get stuck or misled, but continue to grow. He expresses sorrow because many have not given up their old pagan sins of *"impurity, sexual immorality, and eagerness for lustful pleasure."* He hopes that he has established the fact that Christ speaks through him, and that they ought to listen to him and not to false teachers.

Before he arrives, he wants the people to examine themselves to see if their faith is genuine. He comes with the authority God has given him, not to tear them down, but to strengthen and encourage them. Something any real spiritual leader would want to do!

> **Focus:** Paul's exemplary life is enhanced by his surprising transparency. We learn from him the power of humility and fortitude in the midst of many painful trials. The mission of the Church to confront the strongholds of human reasoning and the false arguments that keep people from knowing God, is strengthened when unbelievers not only hear convincing arguments, but also see transformed lives.

> **Prayer:** *Lord, grant us the steadfast courage and perseverance that we see in Paul's life, even in the face of incredible suffering. We fear that we could never face terrible suffering without denying our faith. Yet we know, dear Lord, that you give us whatever we need to face whatever challenges that you allow in our lives. Amen!*

Day 331 — Galatians

November 26

> Key Text: Jesus gave his life for our sins, just as God our Father planned, in order to rescue us from this evil world in which we live. All glory to God forever and ever! Amen. (Galatians 1:4–5)

Paul's missionary journeys throughout the Roman Empire were devoted to evangelism, teaching, church planting, and mentoring leaders for the new congregations. He planted seeds of faith and nurtured the flower of new life.

What greatly facilitated Paul's mission to the Gentiles was the theological decision by the early Church leaders in Jerusalem that a Gentile did not have to become a Jew in order to become a Christian. Most of the Jewish Christian leaders accepted this fact because God had made it clear by giving the Holy Spirit to the Gentiles.

Nevertheless, a vocal minority, who were called *"Judaizers"* or "legalists," rejected this decision, and took it upon themselves to follow after Paul and contradict his teaching when he was away. Not surprisingly, this caused a crisis in the congregation at Galatia. At stake was not just the unity of the congregation, but also the very meaning of the Gospel itself.

Paul is very upset when he hears that the new believers are backing away from the Gospel message of grace: *"I am shocked that you are turn-*

ing away so soon from God, who called you to himself through the loving mercy of Christ. You are following a different way that pretends to be the Good News but is not the Good News at all. You are being fooled by those who deliberately twist the truth concerning Christ" (Galatians 1:6–7).

By "turning away," he means that they are doubting the fact that Jesus' death was sufficient to forgive their sins. The Judaizers are insisting that a person has to keep the Law of Moses to be saved. Paul pronounces the strongest possible condemnation of those who are leading the new believers back into bondage to the Law, and away from the only means of salvation. This is followed up with a new defense of his message and ministry among them.

He begins with his own testimony of faith. Paul was an educated and devoted Jew, violently persecuting Christians because he did not understand who Jesus was. After his life-changing encounter with the resurrected Jesus, he went away to Arabia to think, pray and study. Gradually he understood how Jesus fulfilled the Law for us, so that we might be saved by grace. In time, the Jewish Christian leaders agreed with Paul that *"a person is made right with God by faith in Jesus Christ, not by obeying the law"* (Galatians 2:16).

But the Judaizers undermine Paul by insisting that Jesus is not enough. A believer must also keep the Jewish Law to be saved. Paul reminds the Galatians that it is faith, and not good works, that makes us right with God. This has been true from the beginning with Abraham—the father of the Jews.

Jewish Law was added later, and it had an important but provisional role in the story of redemption. It was like a babysitter. The purpose of the Law and commandments was to make us aware of God's character and will, and of our inability to live up to it. In other words, the Law made us aware that we are sinners, so that we could understand our need for grace. The Gospel message is that grace has been given to us through Jesus' death and resurrection. Therefore, the true children of Abraham are those who live by faith, whether Jew or Gentile, slave or free, male or female *(Galatians 3:28–29)*.

Christ has set us free from the condemnation of the Law. To return to the Law, as the Judaizers are insisting upon, is to deny our sinfulness and consequently our need for Christ. Therefore, by its very nature, to return to the Law is to fall from grace. We must understand that our only hope is to live by the Holy Spirit, who empowers us to express our faith through works of love.

The Judaizers have argued that grace encourages sin. If God forgives sin so easily, why obey at all? Paul forcefully argues that the "freedom" we have from the grace we have received, is freedom to do what is right, not permission to satisfy our sinful nature. The Holy Spirit in us produces the fruit of Christ-like character: *"love, joy, peace, patience, kindness, goodness, faithfulness, gentleness, and self-control"* (Galatians 5:22–23).

And by the way, Paul adds, these virtues fulfill the Law.

Paul concludes his letter, in chapter 6, with an exhortation for the Galatians to help each other grow in faith, because what really counts is that we have become new people by virtue of our faith in Christ.

> **Focus:** It seems reasonable to us that our relationship with God should be based on merit—on our working hard to earn it. But the Law reveals that we all fall short. The Law can show us what is right, but it can't help us *do* what is right. We need grace, and God gives it by Jesus' death on the cross. We also need power to change. God gives that also, by his Holy Spirit working in our life. This is the dynamic of the Christian life.

> **Prayer:** *Lord, thank you for your gracious forgiveness of our sins, and for the gift of the Holy Spirit, which gives us the desire and ability to do your will. Keep us from guilt and condemnation on the one hand, and from the temptation to misuse our freedom on the other. We are free only when we worship and serve you—and to that end, we yield our lives to you! Amen.*

Day 332   Ephesians

November 27

> Key Text: I pray that from his glorious, unlimited resources he will empower you with inner strength through his Spirit. (Ephesians 3:16)

Paul begins his letter to the church at Ephesus with a doxology—heartfelt praise to God for his amazing plan to *"bring everything together under the authority of Christ—everything in heaven and on earth"* (Ephesians 1:10).

The fact that the world, and human life, are presently disordered because of sin and death, masks the fact that God has always had some-

635

thing much better in mind for us. Paul reveals that we have been in God's mind from the beginning. His plan for us to share life with him was settled before he made the world: *"Even before he made the world, God loved us and chose us in Christ to be holy and without fault in his eyes"* (Ephesians 1:4). To this end, it pleased him to create a physical universe as our home where we would exist as embodied beings, and he would fellowship with us.

So with great delight he created us, loved us and forgave us when we sinned. He did this so that we could be in relationship with him. He was determined to do everything necessary to maintain this relationship, including the self-sacrifice of Jesus. By his life offered in our place, there is forgiveness and freedom from the judgment of sin. After his resurrection from the dead, Jesus' Spirit was given to each believer so that he could always be with each of us, anywhere.

This means that all who belong to Jesus by faith have his Spirit and are already receiving spiritual blessings of all kinds, even in this present broken world. And one day everything in heaven and earth will be healed, united and blessed under Jesus' benevolent rule.

Following this magnificent doxology, Paul tells the Ephesians that he has been praying for them since he first heard of their strong faith in Jesus. Broadly speaking, he has been praying for two things: First, that God would give them spiritual wisdom and insight to grow in their knowledge of God and what is ahead for them. Second, that they would understand that the resurrected Jesus now reigns from heaven with authority over all powers on earth, for the sake of the Church. He wants them to have hope and courage in their service of Christ, especially in the face of persecution.

In chapter 2, Paul explains to the Ephesians how God's great plan was revealed in the world, especially the surprise that the Gentiles as well as the Jews were included! It begins with what we all once were—spiritually dead in our rebellion against God, following our commander, the devil, who urged us on in disobedience.

But then Christ came and set us free from slavery to sin and death. We embraced this Good News by faith when we realized that we could not attain salvation by our own efforts: *"God saved you by his grace when you believed. And you can't take credit for this; it is a gift from God. Salvation is not a reward for the good things we have done, so none of us can boast*

Good News of the Gospel!

about it" (Ephesians 2:8–9). We are saved from our sins so that we can become fully human in the image of God, as he originally intended. We are his masterpiece!

This Good News comes about through the story of Israel, but it is for the whole world. Talk about inclusiveness!

Christ has brought us all together, making peace and creating *"one new people from the two groups"* (Ephesians 2:15). Together, we are a New Humanity, God's holy family, sharing the same spiritual inheritance and promise of blessings. This is what it means to be the "Church." It is God's purpose to create his Church as a work of art, because it is here that peace with God and with one's neighbor is on display, not only for inhabitants of earth, but also for *"the unseen rulers and authorities in the heavenly places. This was his eternal plan, which he carried out through Christ Jesus our Lord"* (Ephesians 3:10–11).

Having explained this, Paul once again prays for the Ephesians. He asks God to empower them with inner strength through his Spirit. *"Then Christ will make his home in your hearts as you trust in him. Your roots will grow down into God's love and keep you strong"* (Ephesians 3:17).

Paul now concludes his letter in chapters 4 through 6 with a series of encouragements to lead a life worthy of the reality that he has just explained. He focuses on the need for unity, humility and patience with each other. The Ephesians must use their spiritual gifts to mature each other, meaning that they must hold each other accountable so that they no longer live as the Gentile pagans do. Instead, they are to imitate God by following the example of Christ.

Furthermore, they must understand the seriousness of faith. Honoring God by following Jesus puts us in conflict with the devil and all fallen spiritual powers in the unseen world. These powers oppose God and his Kingdom by actively seeking to keep people from faith. Failing that, they seek to keep believers distracted, discouraged, divided, prayerless and afraid.

Paul uses the armor of a Roman soldier to illustrate the defensive and offensive resources we have for our battle, not the least of which are the Word of God and prayer.

Focus: The Christian faith is not just a system of morality; it is an entire worldview which encompasses eternity. It reveals a sovereign God firmly in control of time and space, bringing about his eternal purposes. Most remarkably, it says that we humans are at the center of what God is doing and will do in the creation for eternity. As we try to wrap our minds around this, it should lead all of us to doxology!

Prayer: Lord, the deeper we think about who you are and what you have done— especially for us—we find ourselves without words. We can only rejoice, praising and thanking you for honoring us with the gift of your image, and for including us in your glorious future. We praise your holy name! Amen.

Day 333   Reflection

November 28

After the resurrected Jesus appeared to Paul on the road to Damascus, and he subsequently became a follower, the apostle Paul explains in Galatians 1:17 that he did not consult with anyone about what this meant for him as a Jew, but went immediately to Arabia.

There, he wrestled with God. As one writer expresses it, *"This God, to Saul's horror and amazement, had now revealed his son, and had done so in order that he, Saul [his birth name], an ultra-orthodox Jew, might tell the pagan nations that Israel's God loved them just as much as he loved Israel."* (N.T. Wright)

After Paul rethought the Old Testament story of Israel in light of Jesus, it became clear that Jesus was indeed the fulfillment of Abraham's ancient Promise to bless the whole world with salvation. He was Israel's eternal King from the family of David. He was the promised Messiah. He was the Suffering Servant predicted by Isaiah. He was also the *"light to the Gentiles,"* a role given to Israel. God indeed loved the whole world!

So Paul's theology became Christ-centered, instead of Law-centered, and cosmic in scope. The depth of his thinking reveals him to be a genius, yet he has been humbled by the Gospel. His once prideful, angry and ambitious religiosity has been reshaped by the one he now worships and follows as his Lord. He now considers it an honor to suffer for the one who suffered for his sins on the cross.

Like John, Paul regards Christ as cosmic. The Christ who humbled himself to embrace our humanity, and to give his life for us, is the same eternal Son who was present in the beginning with the Father. Together, they decided to create a physical universe populated by humans made in their image and able to have fellowship with their Creator! Paul writes in Ephesians 1:5 that it pleased God to decide in advance to adopt the human race as his family, through Christ. He wants to share his life with us for eternity!

God's eternal plan has a grand conclusion—to bring everything together under the authority and rule of Christ—everything in heaven and on earth. This was in keeping with the Old Testament's vision of a *"New Heavens and New Earth."* It means that the broken and divided creation, both the visible and invisible parts, will be forgiven, healed and united. Evil will be judged and banished; death will be overcome by our resurrection.

Amazingly, you and I are at the heart of God's great plan. When his plan is complete, we will become fully human in the image of God, as he intended from the beginning.

Paul believes that resurrection life for believers in a New Heavens and Earth, is both a future hope and a present reality. It was initiated by Jesus' victory over sin and death, and is subsequently experienced through the gift of the Holy Spirit in us. The Spirit awakens spiritual life and calls us together into a new community of faith called the "Church."

Paul understands the Church to be *"the body of Christ,"* his continuing presence on earth through the lives of believers in whom his Spirit dwells. His Spirit gives spiritual gifts to every believer, moving us to worship, discipleship, fellowship and mission, until Jesus comes again at the end of history.

Paul comes to realize that God chose to make all this known gradually, over the generations. Each chapter of the story, like a dimmer switch, added more light. The Old Testament story of Israel was always leading to Jesus. And now, Jesus takes us the rest of the way.

There is a lot more going on in heaven and earth than we realize! Human history is "His-story." It is stirring up things in the spirit realm also: *"For we are not fighting against flesh-and-blood enemies, but against evil rulers and authorities of the unseen world, against mighty powers in this dark world, and against evil spirits in the heavenly places."* What is their interest in what is happening on earth? What will be the role of resurrected human beings in the New Heavens and New Earth? Even a great mind like Paul's has its limits!

"Oh, how great are God's riches and wisdom and knowledge! How impossible it is for us to understand his decisions and his ways! For who can know the Lord's thoughts? Who knows enough to give him advice? And who has given him so much that he needs to pay it back? For everything comes from him and exists by his power and is intended for his glory. All glory to him forever! Amen" (Romans 11:33–36).

> **Prayer:** *Lord, we thank you for your chosen servants, like Paul, whom you gifted to make the glory of Christ and the wonders of our salvation clear to us. As we marvel at what you have done already, we look forward with joy to all the wonders yet to come. All glory to you forever! Amen.*

Day 334 — Philippians

November 29

> Key Text: Always be full of joy in the Lord. I say it again—rejoice! Let everyone see that you are considerate in all you do. Remember, the Lord is coming soon. (Philippians 4:4–5)

Paul writes the book of Philippians while in prison, probably in Rome. He writes to a congregation that he clearly loves. Unlike the Corinthians, they have been a joy to him. In fact, the theme of joy in Christ permeates this letter, even though Paul does not know whether or not he will be executed for his faith while in prison.

Throughout the letter, Paul urges the Philippians to live out their faith so that their salvation can be seen by others. He helpfully explains that the willingness and ability to do this comes from God: *"Work hard to show the results of your salvation, obeying God with deep reverence and fear. For God is working in you, giving you the desire and the power to do what pleases him"* (Philippians 2:12–13).

He begins his letter with thanksgiving for their partnership in the Gospel. He doesn't want them to worry about him. In fact, his imprisonment has served to spread the Gospel among the Roman palace guard. What will give him joy in his imprisonment is their growth in faith: *"May you always be filled with the fruit of your salvation—the righteous character produced in your life by Jesus Christ—for this will bring much glory and praise to God"* (Philippians 1:11).

As for Paul himself, he accepts the fact of his imprisonment and wants to be bold for Christ, whether he lives or dies. Either way he wins—*"to be with Christ ... would be far better for me."* He expects to live, however, and he reminds the Philippians that they too may have the privilege of suffering for Christ, like him.

In chapter 2, Paul urges the congregation to love one another and work together with one mind and purpose. To do so will require the same kind of humility demonstrated by Christ. To illustrate, he writes one of the most beautiful statements on the incarnation of Christ to be found in the New Testament: *"Though he was God, he did not think of equality with God as something to cling to. Instead, he gave up his divine privileges; he took the humble position of a slave and was born as a human being. When he appeared in human form, he humbled himself in obedience to God and died a criminal's death on a cross"* (Philippians 2:6–8).

After sharing some plans for further communication through his messengers Timothy and Epaphroditus, Paul shares some personal concerns. He warns them against the "Judaizers" who have hounded him on his journeys and who deny the Gospel, saying that they must keep the Mosaic Laws, especially circumcision, in order to be saved. Paul insists, however, that the mark which God wants to see is not on the physical body, but on the heart and given by the Holy Spirit—faith in Jesus.

He then shares his own story, beginning with his impeccable résumé as a Jew. He jealously obeyed the Law. As a Pharisee, he harshly persecuted the Church. But those things which he once took pride in, he now regards as worthless compared to *"the infinite value of knowing Christ Jesus my Lord."* For Christ, he has discarded everything—his position, his power, and his pride of accomplishment. Now his greatest ambition is to know Christ and experience the mighty power of his resurrection. He wants to suffer with him, sharing in his death, so that he too will experience the resurrection from the dead.

Paul is realistic about the process: *"I don't mean to say that I have already achieved these things or that I have already reached perfection. But I press on to possess that perfection for which Christ Jesus first possessed me. No, dear brothers and sisters, I have not achieved it, but I focus on this one thing: Forgetting the past and looking forward to what lies ahead, I press on to reach the end of the race and receive the heavenly prize for which God, through Christ Jesus, is calling us"* (Philippians 3:12–14).

As he sits in prison, an old man with a battered body from all his sufferings for Christ, he finds joy in resurrection hope: *"And we are eagerly waiting for [Jesus] to return as our Savior. He will take our weak mortal bodies and change them into glorious bodies like his own, using the same power with which he will bring everything under his control"* (Philippians 3:20–21).

He concludes his letter with an ode to joy. He tells the Philippians to *"always be full of joy in the Lord."* They shouldn't worry about anything, but let the Lord know what they need through prayer. By this, they will experience God's peace in their minds and hearts—a peace beyond understanding, that defies circumstances. *faith in action*

Finally, he urges the church not to worry about him. He has learned how to be content with whatever he has, whether plenty or almost nothing, with a full stomach or empty.

> **Focus:** The book of Philippians is loved because of its Christ-centered joy. Joy is the emotion of hope produced by the Holy Spirit in us. Unlike happiness, it is not dependent on circumstances. To "always be full of the joy of the Lord" is therefore a way of life, grounded on the certainty of God's love and on the hope of sharing a glorious future with him.

> **Prayer:** *Lord, grant us the grace to be content in any circumstance, and to feel your joy even in the midst of suffering. We sense something of our glorious future already, by the Holy Spirit in our heart. We long to experience it fully when you return as our Savior. Amen.*

Day 335 — Colossians

November 30

> **Key Text: For God in all his fullness was pleased to live in Christ, and through him God reconciled everything to himself. He made peace with everything in heaven and on earth by means of Christ's blood on the cross. (Colossians 1:19–20)**

Colossians is one of four letters Paul writes to churches from prison. He has never visited the city of Colossae, but he has heard good things about the believers' faith. They are demonstrating what Paul believes is the strongest indicator of genuine faith—love for one another.

He begins his letter by telling them that they are part of a growing movement of God: *"This same Good News that came to you is going out all over the world. It is bearing fruit everywhere by changing lives, just as it changed your lives from the day you first heard and understood the truth about God's wonderful grace"* (Colossians 1:6).

Paul's prayerful concern is for the congregation to mature and produce the good fruit of holy living. This comes about by a process of learning God's Word. By yielding our will to the teaching of the Bible and the leading of the Holy Spirit, we are empowered to put a stop to the *"sinful, earthly things lurking within you."* Therefore, *"put on your new nature* [like new clothes], *and be renewed as you learn to know your Creator and become like him."*

Paul believes that theological understanding precedes spiritual growth, so he shares, in chapter 1, a magnificent theology of Christ. Its form suggests that it is a liturgical or catechetical resource of the early Church.

It begins by declaring Christ to be *"the visible image of the invisible God. He existed before anything was created and is supreme over all creation, for through him God created everything in the heavenly realms and on earth. ... Everything was created through him and for him ... and he holds all creation together"* (Colossians 1:15–17).

Here the deity of Christ is confessed. Skeptics of Christianity claim that Christ's deity was an invention of the Church later, to maintain power over the unlearned masses. But more honest historians accept this confession as the belief of the early Church. It declares that Jesus has a unique and intimate relationship to the physical universe, as its Creator. Thus, his fingerprints are all over the universe, with its mindboggling unity, diversity, complexity, beauty and power. It comes *from* him, exists *for* him, and is sustained *by* him.

Not only is Christ the head of the creation; he is also the head of the Church, his body. For all these reasons, he is worthy of our worship and obedience. Most amazing of all, this same Christ lives in us by his Spirit!

The Colossians must take care to keep Christ clearly before them—letting their roots go down into him and letting their lives be built upon him, while ignoring all high-sounding nonsense that comes from human thinking, which denies Christ. Greek philosophers, for example, considered the material world to be evil. But Christians consider the world to be good, not only because God created it, but also because he was willing to enter it as a human: *"For in Christ lives all the fullness of God in a human body"* (Colossians 2:9).

Paul warns the Colossians, as he has the other churches, to beware of the false teaching that Christ is not enough—that circumcision and keeping Jewish rules and laws are also required for salvation. He says, *"These rules may seem wise because they require strong devotion, pious self-denial, and severe bodily discipline. But they provide no help in conquering a person's evil desires"* (Colossians 2:23). The good news is, Christ is all that matters!

Since Christ is our life and he reigns in heaven, Paul tells the Colossians to set their sights on the realities of heaven, where Christ sits in the place of honor at God's right hand.

To speak of heaven here may be confusing, if we think of heaven as some faraway place "up there" and away from here. But heaven is a dimension of reality that is nearby and all around, though invisible. It is God's space—where he exists and rules, and where his will is done. Remember, Jesus taught us to address God as *"our Father in heaven"* (Matthew 6:9). We are to pray that his Kingdom will come and his will be done on earth *as in heaven.*

Setting our sights on the realities of heaven does not mean speculating about heaven, but focusing our priorities to doing God's will now, during our earthly lives. By keeping the focus of our lives on doing God's will, we keep our heads in reality and our hearts in future hope. This is our motivation for holiness—to live a different life that is focused on pleasing God and sharing the Gospel by our words and deeds.

To this end he says, *"Live wisely among those who are not believers, and make the most of every opportunity. Let your conversation be gracious and attractive so that you will have the right response for everyone"* (Colossians 4:5–6).

Focus: After reading Paul's magnificent poem to Christ in chapter 1, it is hard to argue that Christ is not enough. In fact, Christ is all there is—he is preeminent in all things relating to our lives in this universe. The fact that he created all things and holds all creation together, suggests that the material world, and we ourselves, are a manifestation of the joyful, loving and creative imagination of God—just like we read in Genesis 1 and 2!

Prayer: *Lord, once again we are overwhelmed by the magnificent mystery of who you are and all that you do and have done for us. By your purpose, we have existence; by your grace, we have forgiveness; by your power, we have new life and*

Day 336   1 Thessalonians

December 1   Believed to be the earliest letter

Key Text: For God chose to save us through our Lord Jesus Christ, not to pour out his anger on us. Christ died for us so that, whether we are dead or alive when he returns, we can live with him forever. (1 Thessalonians 5:9–10)

The church at Thessalonica was planted by the apostle Paul on his second missionary journey, with good results *(see Acts 17)*. The people turned away from idols to serve the living and true God!

Paul begins his letter by commending them for their faith, loving deeds and enduring hope because of the Lord Jesus Christ. They have followed Paul's example of faithful ministry and severe suffering for the Gospel. Their example has encouraged other believers in Greece, Macedonia and Achaia.

In chapter 2, Paul recalls his ministry among them. He came to Thessalonica after a period of opposition and suffering. In fact, he points to his suffering as proof against critics who claim that his purpose in ministry is to trick people and make money off them.

As was his practice, Paul had financially supported himself to remove all doubt as to his motives. He set an example of hard work among those he taught about Jesus. He writes, *"Night and day we toiled to earn a living so that we would not be a burden to any of you as we preached God's Good News to you. You yourselves are our witnesses—and so is God—that we were devout and honest and faultless toward all of you believers"* (1 Thessalonians 2:9–10).

Paul's integrity, and his self-support, showed that he loved the people. Therefore, they were able to receive what he preached and taught as the *"very word of God."* Paul's great reward for his ministry was not financial gain, but the spiritual life and ministry of the Thessalonians. They were his pride and joy and reward.

As we have seen with several of the churches, the Thessalonians have been confused by the same false teachers and troublemakers who have sought to undermine the Gospel of grace. Paul was deeply concerned about how they were holding up, so he sent Timothy to check on them. And now Timothy has reported that they are remained strong in faith and love. He prays that their love for one another and for all people will grow and overflow, making their hearts strong, blameless and holy.

In chapter 4, Paul reminds them that God's will is for them to be holy, especially regarding sexual sin. They must live with self-control and not in lustful passion like the pagans who don't know God and his ways. Sexual self-control (i.e., honoring God with our bodies) is a mark of Christian maturity, as is living a quiet life of personal responsibility so that people who are not Christians will respect the way we live. Effective ministry begins with a foundation of integrity and trust.

Paul now turns to a question the Thessalonians have raised about the status of believers who have died before Christ returns. He assures them that both the living and the dead will be resurrected on that day. When Jesus *"will come down from heaven with a commanding shout, with the voice of the archangel, and with the trumpet call of God,"* we shall rise up to meet him and accompany him back to earth. Paul draws upon the well-known spectacle of the citizens of a Roman colony going out to meet the emperor when he paid them a visit, and then accompanying him back to the city.

The time of Jesus' return is not revealed, except to say that it will come unexpectedly, *"like a thief in the night."* So Christians aren't *"in the dark"* about the fact of his return. We don't know when, but we do know that it is certain, and that all believers, dead or alive at the time, will be resurrected.

Since we know the day is coming, each generation of Christians must live their lives with clearheaded faith and disciplined holiness, honoring God.

Paul ends his letter with a long list of ways to live this out in their common life: Honor those who are your leaders. Live peacefully with each other. Warn the lazy and encourage the timid. Take tender care of those who are weak. Be patient with everyone. Don't pay back evil for evil, but always try to do good to each other and to all people. *"Always be joyful. Never stop praying. Be thankful in all circumstances, for this is God's will for you who belong to Christ Jesus"* (1 Thessalonians 5:16–18).

Focus: The hope of Christ's return, and our resurrection, is a motivation not to ignore the world and its needs, but to live disciplined lives of holiness and service so that others may be persuaded to believe the Gospel. Since our future will be here, in a renewed heavens and earth, what we do now matters, and all that is done for the glory of God carries over.

Prayer: Lord, how wonderful it is to think that our future is resurrection life with you, and not simply "nothingness." The glory of your return for your long-suffering and eagerly waiting Church will be a sight to behold! May the anticipation of that great day motivate us to be good stewards of our lives and of this earth today. Amen.

Day 337   2 Thessalonians

December 2

> Key Text: But the Lord is faithful; he will strengthen you and guard you from the evil one. (2 Thessalonians 3:3)

Paul's second letter to the Thessalonians begins with thankfulness to God for their flourishing faith and growing love for one another. This has been the case despite persecution and hardship.

Their example has become known to congregations in other cities, for having *"turned away from idols to serve the living and true God."* They have shared Christ's suffering and thereby shown themselves worthy of the Kingdom of God. God has promised justice for them and for all believers who suffer for his name's sake.

When Jesus appears from heaven, *"with his mighty angels, in flaming fire,"* he will bring judgment on those who don't know God and on those who refuse God's grace through Jesus. God's judgment is always preceded by his grace. Everyone will be given the opportunity to repent and believe.

But some will refuse God's grace. Their pride will get in the way. They will demand the freedom to believe what they want. But this will not prove to be the freedom that the rebels expect. Paul warns, *"They will be punished with eternal destruction, forever separated from the Lord and from his glorious power"* (2 Thessalonians 1:9).

These are serious matters and are due careful consideration.

Those who suffer for the sake of the Gospel will be honored with the Lord when he returns. To this end, Paul prays that God will enable the Thessalonians to live a life worthy of his call by accomplishing all the good things

Take heart ministry

their faith prompts them to do: *"Then the name of our Lord Jesus will be honored because of the way you live, and you will be honored along with him. This is all made possible because of the grace of our God and Lord, Jesus Christ"* (2 Thessalonians 1:12).

With the return of the Lord in mind, Paul clarifies some matters about that event, in chapter 2. It is a bit complex, but consistent with the Old Testament prophets who viewed history with "prophetic foreshortening." As we've noted, they would see in a particular crisis a harbinger of the final crisis at the end of history when Jesus returns. Thus, they would call the present crisis "the day of the Lord," which is a reference to the end of history. The prophet Joel, for example, described a plague of locusts in Israel as "the day of the Lord" *(Joel 2:1–2)*.

Presently, the Thessalonian congregation has been shaken by false teaching from those who claim to have received a special revelation that "the day of the Lord" has already taken place. Paul would have been aware of troubling events in Jerusalem. The terrible Roman Emperor Caligula, who was convinced of his own divinity and angry at the Jews, ordered a huge statue of himself to be set up in the Jewish Temple. This terrible crisis was eventually averted when Caligula was murdered.

Later, however, in AD 70, the Romans destroyed the Temple and the Jews faced a catastrophe. So Paul, thinking like a prophet, sees in this near crisis the future coming of the Lord in judgment upon the whole earth. As upsetting as these present events are, Paul encourages the Thessalonians not to panic and not to listen to the false teachers. The Lord is in control and he knows what he is doing: *"With all these things in mind, dear brothers and sisters, stand firm and keep a strong grip on the teaching we passed on to you both in person and by letter"* (2 Thessalonians 2:15).

Paul concludes his brief letter, in chapter 3, with a request for prayer that the Gospel will spread rapidly and be honored wherever it goes. Also, that he and his associates will be rescued from evil people who seek to silence them. Finally, he blesses them: *"May the Lord lead your hearts into a full understanding and expression of the love of God and the patient endurance that comes from Christ"* (2 Thessalonians 3:5).

Focus: Of all people, Christians ought not to live in fear of current events, nor be led astray by conspiracy theories. This is not to say that fearful events and conspiracies don't happen, but that we ought not to be focused on them as if the Lord

personally challenging as I wrestle w/ anxiety

648

were not in control of history. The doctrine of the return of Christ, followed by the Last Judgment, gives us hope that life's injustice and evil will be made right, and we will at last rejoice.

Prayer: Lord, we thank you for the hope of Jesus' second coming, when everything in life will be sorted out, and victory of God over sin and death will be final. Help us not to live in fear, but to courageously face life as it comes, sustained by faith and hope. Amen.

Day 338   1 Timothy 1–3

December 3

> Key Text: For there is only one God and one Mediator who can reconcile God and humanity—the man Christ Jesus. He gave his life to purchase freedom for everyone. (1 Timothy 2:5–6)

At the beginning of Paul's second missionary journey, he looked for a disciple he could mentor who could accompany him. He found his disciple in the person of Timothy from Lystra. The child of a Jewish mother and Gentile father, Timothy was a young man highly regarded by the Christian community there.

Paul must have had confidence in Timothy's knowledge of the faith, for he left him in Ephesus *"to stop those whose teaching is contrary to the truth."* Apparently, would-be *"teachers of the law of Moses"* have been stirring up and wasting the time of the Ephesian believers over meaningless speculations. By their diversions, they are leaving believers confused and distracted from what Paul considers to be his most important teaching: *"The purpose of my instruction is that all believers would be filled with love that comes from a pure heart, a clear conscience, and genuine faith"* (1 Timothy 1:5).

A particular area of concern is the misleading teaching about the function of the Law of Moses. Paul reminds Timothy that the Law was given to convict sinners of their sin and reveal the need for redemption. It was not a means toward a prideful righteousness.

Paul illustrates by his own testimony how God showed him his sinful pride, and then by his grace filled him with the faith and love that come from Christ Jesus. Paul's story is simple, but powerful: *"This is a trustworthy saying, and everyone should accept it: 'Christ Jesus came into the world to save sinners'—and I am the worst of them all"* (1 Timothy 1:15).

In chapter 2, Paul gives Timothy some wise pastoral guidance about his role in the congregation. Timothy should first faithfully pray for the people, and for those in secular authority to do their job so that the Christians may live in peace, quietly serving God. Peace in the community facilitates evangelism, and God *"wants everyone to be saved and to understand the truth"* about Christ who gave his life to purchase freedom for everyone!

Paul now counsels Timothy about a particularly delicate issue in the congregation concerning men and women. In a culture—not unlike our own—where sexual stereotypes abound, and divisive reactions to them have produced their own dysfunctional relationships, Paul is mentoring Timothy about how Christ recalibrates the meaning of gender in worship and mission.

Unfortunately, his teaching in chapter 2, verses 8 through 15, has caused many to think of Paul as being hostile to women. One writer explains their thinking: To them, *"the whole passage seems to be saying that women are second-class citizens. They aren't even allowed to dress prettily. They are the daughters of Eve, and she was the original troublemaker. The best thing for them to do is get on and have children, to behave themselves and keep quiet."* (N.T. Wright)

To fairly interpret Paul, we need historical context. The paganism that these believers were converted from featured the goddess Artemis, whom the Romans called Diana. The most prominent and influential shrine in Ephesus was dedicated to her. As she was a female deity, the priests were all women. They ran the show and kept the men in their place. It was a mirror image of the dysfunction of patriarchy.

Paul argues here, and elsewhere, that the Gospel gives equal status to men and women. Both are gifted, called to ministry and participation in worship. Not surprisingly, there were adjustments of thinking and behavior to be made among those schooled by Artemis. The women are encouraged to reject the pagan stereotypes of women as objects of lust, or of being second class citizens, which was part of cultural patriarchy.

Unlike Eve, who was misled by the serpent because she was unaware, women are encouraged to become knowledgeable and wise by learning the Scripture and submitting themselves to God. They are not to be bossy or seductive in order to control others, as was the habit in Artemis worship.

650

In this way, Paul hopes that men and women alike can develop the spiritual gifts God has given them for the sake of the church. Furthermore, women must not repudiate their calling from God to bear children, thinking that pain in childbirth *(Genesis 3:16)* is a sign of God's displeasure with women and a directive to be subservient to men.

Childbirth is a high calling upon which the growth of human culture and economy depends, fulfilling the creation mandate *(Genesis 1:28)*.

Finally, in chapter 3, Paul counsels Timothy on choosing elders and deacons to lead and serve the church. The requirements are mostly about character. They must not be people who are new believers. They must live lives above legitimate criticism and have a good reputation among people outside the church.

By choosing leaders based on character, we demonstrate that in the church, leadership is about wisdom and service, not power.

Focus: We learn from Paul's mentoring of Timothy that leadership in the church requires maturity and wisdom. There are always dysfunctions in the church because of our fallen nature and cultural pressure. Change is difficult, and conflict inevitable. Leaders are to lead by example and instruction, aligning congregational belief and behavior with the new life demonstrated by Christ—notably here, the transforming view that men and women are equal before Christ—in their calling and service.

Prayer: Lord, we pray that you would continue to raise up gifted and wise leaders to guide your Church, so that both men and women may fulfill their callings as Christians and as individuals. Amen.

Day 339 1 Timothy 4–6

December 4

Key Text: Don't let anyone think less of you because you are young. Be an example to all believers in what you say, in the way you live, in your love, your faith, and your purity.
(1 Timothy 4:12)

Paul continues his mentoring of the young pastor Timothy in chapters 4 through 6. He urges him to be an example to all the believers in what he says and how he lives. This is followed by a strong reminder to preach and teach the true faith, focusing on *"reading the Scriptures to the church, encouraging the believers, and teaching them."*

He must confront those in the congregation who want to be teachers and leaders for the wrong reasons. Some want to make people dependent on them, or to enrich themselves. These, Paul warns, have dead consciences. Some will even prove to be false teachers whose imaginations and motives have been influenced by the demonic.

One crisis Timothy is already facing in the congregation is false teaching about the Christian's relationship to the material world and to human desire. Some are saying, for example, that marriage is wrong, as is eating certain foods, etc. The first thing Timothy must understand is this: *"Since everything God created is good, we should not reject any of it but receive it with thanks"* (1 Timothy 4:4).

And so, for example, a believer may gratefully drink wine as part of God's good creation. It is false to insist that wine is inherently evil. It is also false, on the other hand, to insist that drunkenness is no big deal. Neither extreme honors God's creation. Christianity believes in the goodness of the creation. Paul warns Timothy that misusing the good things God has given us is a barrier to spiritual growth.

Next, in chapter 5, Paul goes over Timothy's pastoral responsibilities to the various age groups of both genders in the congregation. He elaborates on the special situation of caring for widows. In short, family members of widows have first responsibility for their financial support, but those without family should be helped by the congregation. Widows who receive assistance must be at least 60 and of good reputation. They must not abuse the help they receive. Younger widows are encouraged to remarry. We see that there must be compassion, common sense and accountability in the congregation.

Paul then explains to Timothy that elders like him who work hard at preaching and teaching, should be respected and get paid well. Though Paul himself always refused financial assistance as an evangelist, he insists that local pastor/elders who shepherd a congregation should be supported so that they can devote all their time and attention to their calling.

Also, since leaders are always subject to criticism, the congregation must be careful not to listen to an accusation against an elder unless it is confirmed by two or three witnesses.

Paul concludes, in chapter 6, by again urging Timothy to preach what Paul has taught him with confidence. Though his teachings may be contradicted by some, they are *"wholesome teachings of the Lord Jesus Christ. These teachings promote a godly life."* Some contradict good teaching in order to get a following, hoping to become wealthy off of people's support, but *"true godliness with contentment is itself great wealth."*

Longing to be rich is a trap that ruins lives. The love of money is the root of all kinds of evil, causing people to wander away from the faith to their eventual sorrow. Paul knows that Timothy is not this kind of man, and so he encourages him to continue pursuing righteousness and a godly life, along with faith, love, perseverance and gentleness—all qualities needed in a pastor.

Those who are rich in this world must be warned not to be proud or to trust in their money: *"Their trust should be in God, who richly gives us all we need for our enjoyment"* (1 Timothy 6:17). They must generously use their money to do good works in behalf of those in need. By doing this, they will be storing up their treasure as a good foundation for the future, so that they may experience true life.

Focus: Effective congregations have pastors and leaders who are guided by sound teaching and who live disciplined lives. Such congregations are strong in good works, and generous to the needy among them and out in the community.

Prayer: Lord, may we all—and especially our leaders—be devoted to studying the Scriptures, so that by them we may order our lives and beliefs, for the sake of our own salvation and the salvation of those who hear us. Amen.

Day 340   2 Timothy

December 5

> Key Text: All Scripture is inspired by God and is useful to teach us what is true and to make us realize what is wrong in our lives.
> (2 Timothy 3:16)

Paul's second letter to Timothy is meant to encourage him to stand strong, while preaching and teaching the Gospel without fear.

Paul recalls, in chapter 1, how he had laid hands on Timothy and prayed about his gift and calling. Now he encourages him to *"fan into flames"* the spiritual gift God gave him: *"For God has not given us a spirit of fear and timidity, but of power, love, and self-discipline"* (2 Timothy 1:7). This is an exhortation a young pastor needs in order to grow in confidence as a leader.

Perhaps Timothy is being discounted by others because Paul, his mentor, is in jail. Who can trust a prisoner? Paul counsels Timothy not to be ashamed of him nor of the Gospel, as others have been. Suffering goes with the Gospel. Paul notes that the same God who saved us by the death and resurrection of his Son, *"chose me to be a preacher, an apostle, and a teacher of this Good News."* Paul is not ashamed of his imprisonment because of the Gospel, and neither should Timothy be ashamed.

The remainder of Paul's second letter is given to the subject of faithfully preaching the Gospel. He urges Timothy to *"hold on to the pattern of wholesome teaching"* that he has received, carefully guarding the truth that has now been entrusted to him as the second generation of witness. The Holy Spirit will empower him to do so. Timothy, in turn, must now *"teach these truths to other trustworthy people who will be able to pass them on to others"* (2 Timothy 2:2). In this way, the Gospel is preserved for the Church.

The particular issue that has created opposition and suffering for Paul, and now presumably for Timothy, is the issue of the resurrection. This seems to be a particular offense to Jews and Gentiles alike. But Paul stresses: *"Always remember that Jesus Christ, a descendant of King David, was raised from the dead. This is the Good News I preach. And because I preach this Good News, I am suffering and have been chained like a criminal. But the word of God cannot be chained"* (2 Timothy 2:8–9).

Along with faithful preaching and teaching, Timothy must guard his personal life. He must lead by example. This means avoiding foolish talk and arguments, like the idea some are teaching that the resurrection of the dead has already occurred. He must also *"run away"* from anything that encourages youthful lust, and instead pursue righteous living, faithfulness, love and peace.

This will be a challenge, Paul says, because people in these last days are preoccupied with themselves and their money. Nothing is sacred to them. They don't love God or others. They are self-absorbed, cruel, reckless, uncaring about truth, and focused only on seeking pleasure. To resist this way of life and speak out against it, means that Timothy will suffer persecution.

In these last days, false teachers will flourish, deceiving themselves and others, but Timothy must remain faithful to the things he has been taught. The Scriptures give wisdom and understanding that enable us to live the new life that comes from trusting Christ. They have this power because they are God's words: *"All Scripture is inspired by God and is useful to teach us what is true and to make us realize what is wrong in our lives. It corrects us when we are wrong and teaches us to do what is right. God uses it to prepare and equip his people to do every good work"* (2 Timothy 3:16–17).

The accounts of what Jesus said and did were written down and preserved by eyewitnesses. Their testimonies were the source material for the Gospels, and the other New Testament books. In time, through a rigorous process, the New Testament books were accepted by the Church as inspired of God, and a faithful testimony to Jesus. In this recognition lay their authority.

authority of Scripture

It is helpful to think of the Scriptures as both divine and human, just as Jesus is both divine and human. In this sense, they are the Word of God in the words of man. The idea of "inspiration" comes from the recognition that the Spirit of God spoke to the minds and hearts of God's chosen writers. Their respective personalities and insights shaped the character of their writing, leaving us a diversity of literary forms and styles through which Jesus is revealed to us. The reader of inspired Scripture is guided by the Holy Spirit to confirm that this is God speaking. Thus, the Scriptures have a self-authenticating nature.

What the Church has learned over the ages is that the Holy Spirit guides us into all truth. We believe that the Bible is God's Word to us; that its primary function is to make Jesus known as God's Son; that it is truthful in what it claims to affirm; and that the Word and Spirit always speak in harmony. God's Spirit will never tell us to do what is contrary to his Word.

Paul concludes with a final exhortation to Timothy—*"keep a clear mind in every situation."* Don't be afraid of suffering for the Lord. Work at telling others the Good News, and fully carry out the ministry God has given you. In other words: "Do what I have done!"

Paul senses that his life is nearly up, and so he leaves Timothy with this inspiring testimony: *"As for me, my life has already been poured out like an offering to God. The time of my death is near. I have fought the good fight, I have finished the race, and I have remained faithful. And now the prize awaits me—the crown of righteousness, which the Lord, the righteous*

Judge, will give me on the day of his return. And the prize is not just for me but for all who eagerly look forward to his appearing" (2 Timothy 4:6–8).

Focus: The Christian life and ministry are grounded in the authority of the Scriptures. When faithfully preached and taught, they have the unique authority to speak to us as the very words of God, and thereby transform us.

Prayer: Lord, give us ears to hear and respond to your Word so that we may know you, worship you, and live lives that are pleasing to you. Amen.

Day 341   Titus

December 6

Key Text: He gave his life to free us from every kind of sin, to cleanse us, and to make us his very own people, totally committed to doing good deeds. (Titus 2:14)

The book of Titus is a letter to another young pastor that Paul has mentored. Paul calls him his *"true son in the faith,"* an expression that reveals the affection Paul feels for those he has trained for ministry. Titus has been left by Paul on the island of Crete to organize believers and appoint elders in each town.

Chapter 1 indicates that Titus faces the same troublemakers we have heard about in the other churches Paul has established. They are false teachers who insist on circumcision for salvation. They deceive the believers by *"useless talk"* and manipulate them for financial gain.

Apparently, Titus is dealing with people of bad reputation. There is a saying, perhaps well deserved: *"The people of Crete are all liars, cruel animals, and lazy gluttons."* (Now you know where the pejorative label "Cretans" comes from!)

Therefore, the elders that Titus appoints must have *"strong belief in the trustworthy message he was taught,"* as well as live blameless lives. This will set them apart from the troublemakers who are *"corrupt and unbelieving."*

Paul continues in chapter 2 with instructions for Titus about priorities in ministry. He must focus on training the new believers in holy living so that their doctrine and their lives match up. Paul's particular areas of concern are with the former life of converted pagans. Pagan religion and morality were notorious—far from the teaching of the Ten Command-

656

ments! So there were deeply rooted patterns of thought and behavior that had to be overcome. On the other hand, many pagans were so tired of the immorality of their culture and religion, that they were drawn to the moral vision of Judaism, and now Christianity.

As always, Paul emphasizes the importance of both personal moral discipline and doing good works of every kind in the community. This is important for Christian witness because it makes the *"teaching about God our Savior attractive in every way."* For this behavior to take root in the congregation, Paul insists that the leaders set the example.

Having established the importance of Christian behavior, Paul now reviews the core of Christian teaching in two key sections of his letter. The first is Titus 2:11–14: *"The grace of God has been revealed, bringing salvation to all people. And we are instructed to turn from godless living and sinful pleasures. We should live in this evil world with wisdom, righteousness, and devotion to God, while we look forward with hope to that wonderful day when the glory of our great God and Savior, Jesus Christ, will be revealed. He gave his life to free us from every kind of sin, to cleanse us, and make us his very own people, totally committed to doing good deeds."*

In the second section, Titus 3:4–8, he essentially repeats the above, but adds the following: *"He generously poured out the Spirit upon us through Jesus Christ our Savior."* Teaching about the Spirit is important because it is by the Spirit's working in us that we can change our old patterns of thought and behavior to become new people.

It is obvious in Paul's writings that he is not just concerned about right doctrine. He insists that right doctrine must lead to right living. Christianity is not just a belief system; it is a way of life. Truth lived out is far more beneficial than truth merely asserted. For this reason, Paul again reminds Titus to confront and not ignore the harmful quarreling in the church over doctrine and life. It not only harms the believers—it also makes witness to the watching world nearly impossible.

Focus: The Word of God, rightly understood and faithfully practiced, brings about unity and love within the diversity of the congregation. It is important for leaders to set the example for both, living a devout and disciplined life.

Prayer: Lord, forgive us for being more concerned about right doctrine than right living. We ask for both, so that what we say and do are pleasing to you and attractive to the watching world. We are so grateful that you have called us to a relationship, and not just a religion. Amen.

Day 342   Reflection

We have gotten through most of the Bible now. Of all its wonderful themes, none is more important than this: The God of the Bible is a God who speaks. More specifically, he is a God who wishes to be known by us.

The first clue about this is given in Genesis chapter 1. It declares that God created everything that exists by "speaking" it into existence, and then noted to himself that it was just as he wanted: *"Then God said, 'Let there be light,' and there was light. And God saw that the light was good"* (Genesis 1:3–4).

We might dare to ask, who was God talking to when he spoke these words? Clearly it wasn't us, because we didn't yet exist. Later in the creation story there is a hint: *"Then God said, 'Let us make human beings in our image, to be like us.'"*

It appears that God was speaking to himself! This is more than a "me, myself, and I" enigma—a clever way of speaking about "me." Here we get a strong hint that God is an "us," or as we would later understand it, God is a Trinity. He is one God, in three distinct persons—Father, Son and Holy Spirit. So what is it like to be God? It is to exist eternally in community within himself! That's a mouthful, and a mystery. But it is also a wonderful revelation.

It means that God is not an isolated unit, but a loving unity of persons, who speak, listen, love, fellowship and rejoice together—always! This strongly suggests that God did not create out of loneliness or need, but out of the pleasure it gave him to share his life. It is not strange, therefore, that God would speak the universe into being, and make creatures in his image who could know him and *speak back*!

Throughout the Bible, we see God making himself known and calling people into relationship with him. And we see humans responding to his invitation through worship, prayer, meditation, song, and the arts. This is possible for us because God has always spoken contextually, in ways that we can understand. Martin Luther famously wrote that God "lisps" to us, speaking in a childlike way.

We've learned that God speaks in a general way through his creation:

✱*"The heavens proclaim the glory of God. The skies display his craftsmanship. Day after day they continue to speak; night after night they make him known"* (Psalm 19:1-2). We intuitively hear his voice in the things he has made.

We've learned further, in Romans chapter 2, that God also speaks through human conscience, giving us an intuitive sense of right and wrong so that we may do his will. In these ways, all people everywhere have been able to sense enough of God's self-revelation to discern his *"eternal power and divine nature,"* so as to give him worship and thanksgiving *(Romans 1:20).* Think of it as God 101.

We also learn that God speaks to particular people in a special way, for the common good. He chose Israel, for example, to be his Covenant people. He revealed himself to them so that they could reveal him to the other nations around them. His special revelation included his mighty power, as demonstrated in delivering Israel from slavery in Egypt and the parting of the Red Sea. It also included the gift of his Law and commandments, by which the people learned the wisdom of a right relationship with God and their neighbor. With the Law as a guide, the Hebrew writers probed deeply into the nature of suffering (Job), existential happiness (Ecclesiastes), wisdom for life (Proverbs), and the nature of worship (Psalms).

And whenever Israel rebelled against God—which was often—he would give prophets a "word" for the people, warning them, encouraging them and comforting them. Finally, when the time was right, God spoke his clearest word of all. The New Testament book of Hebrews says, *"Long ago God spoke many times and in many ways to our ancestors through the prophets. And now in these final days, he has spoken to us through his Son"* (Hebrews 1:1-2).

✱There is a reason why the Gospel of John calls Jesus the *"Word"* of God. He is God's self-revelation. By his words and deeds, he reveals God to us, and draws us into the life and loving fellowship that he enjoys as the triune God.

To this end, God's chosen spokesmen carefully recorded, explained, and preserved all that Jesus said and did, for the continuing guidance and edification of the Church. 2 Timothy 3:16 describes those Scriptures as *"inspired by God."* The word "inspired" literally means "breathed out" by God. In this divine aspiration lies the authority of the Scriptures.

So the speech of God that created the universe, became the word of God spoken to human beings, then the Word incarnated among human beings, and then written and proclaimed in the world through the Gospel. These are the words which point us to salvation!

Prayer: Lord, how amazing it is to hear your voice in the things you have made, and in our conscience, and most clearly through your inspired Scriptures. Give us ears to hear carefully and eyes to see clearly so that we may enter into the Divine Conversation which you have initiated. Amen.

Day 343   Philemon

December 8

> Key Text: And I am praying that you will put into action the generosity that comes from your faith as you understand and experience all the good things we have in Christ. (Philemon 1:6)

While Paul is in prison in Rome, he meets a runaway slave named Onesimus. We don't know how they met, but Paul shares the Gospel with Onesimus and he becomes a believer. Out of gratefulness to Paul, he begins to care for him in prison.

It turns out that Onesimus has run away from his master, Philemon—a crime that is punishable by death. Paul urges Onesimus to stop running and return to Philemon with a note he has written appealing for leniency. That note is the letter to Philemon.

It may seem odd that a personal letter of only twenty-five verses would be included in the canon of Scripture, but its contents are a powerful expression of the meaning of the Gospel and its implications for transforming society.

Paul begins his brief letter by praising Philemon because he has heard of his faith in Jesus and love for all of God's people. He then boldly asks Philemon to love a new member of "God's people"—Onesimus, his runaway slave. Would he be generous to Onesimus, just as God in Christ has been generous to him?

This is more than a sentimental request; it is a subversive suggestion! Slavery was taken for granted as an integral part of the economic system of the ancient world. Though it's true that many slaves were well-treated by their masters and became like family members, they were still considered inferior as human beings, without freedom or rights. Therefore, for a slave to run away was a capital offense against the whole system.

Paul is not given enough credit for his courage here in asking Philemon to defy Law and convention in order to live out the Gospel. He could have demanded it as an apostle, but instead he appeals to Philemon's character and conscience: *"I appeal to you to show kindness to my child, Onesimus. I became his father in the faith while here in prison. Onesimus hasn't been of much use to you in the past, but now he is very useful to both of us"* (Philemon 1:10–11). The name, Onesimus, means "useful," so Paul is making a play on words here. Onesimus has lived up to his name.

Paul is very careful in how he asks this extraordinary favor of Philemon. After praising him as a man of faith, he chooses not to play the "apostle card," but instead gives Philemon the opportunity to do the right thing on his own and without pressure.

Paul frames his request within the meaning of the Gospel itself: *"It seems you lost Onesimus for a little while so that you could have him back forever. He is no longer like a slave to you. He is more than a slave, for he is a beloved brother, especially to me. Now he will mean much more to you, both as a man and as a brother in the Lord"* (Philemon 1:15–16).

By these words, Paul plants a seed in the cultural soil of every generation to come, about the possibility of a society without divisions, united by Christ. As Paul wrote to the Galatians: *"There is no longer Jew or Gentile, slave or free, male and female. For you are all one in Christ Jesus"* (Galatians 3:28).

Paul's vision is not utopian, based on a faulty premise of human goodness, rationality and progress. It is a vision based on the death and resurrection of Jesus, who came to create a new humanity. One of the ways this new humanity *"in Christ"* manifests itself is by confronting and breaking down the sinful patterns of individuals and institutions that enforced racism, sexism, and religious bigotry.

Of course, monumental societal change doesn't occur overnight. However, as we noted, the seed was planted by this brief but powerful little letter to Philemon. Notably, it would be a text cited by William Wilberforce in finally persuading the British Parliament to outlaw slave trafficking, and by Dr. Martin Luther King Jr. in bringing about racial equality in America, as well as by Nelson Mandela in South Africa to end racial apartheid.

In the end, the apostle Paul does more than persuade Philemon to do what is right. He offers to help him to do what is right: *"So if you consider me your partner, welcome [Onesimus] as you would welcome me. If he has wronged you in any way or owes you anything, charge it to me. I, Paul, write this with my own hand: I will repay it"* (Philemon 1:17–19).

> **Focus:** The Gospel is the only power that can begin to heal and unite a diverse and conflicted world.

> **Prayer:** *Lord, thank you for Paul's example in persuading Philemon to live out the implications of the Gospel in a revolutionary way. Give us a vision for our own time of a just society, united by the grace and love that come from the Gospel. And most importantly, help us practice what we preach! Amen.*

Day 344   Hebrews 1–2

December 9

> Key Text: The Son radiates God's own glory and expresses the very character of God, and he sustains everything by the mighty power of his command. (Hebrews 1:3)

As the title implies, the book of Hebrews is written to a community of Jewish believers. The author is unknown, but there are many suggestions, including the missionary associates of Paul—Barnabas or Apollos.

The recipients of this letter seem to be in danger of drifting away from the faith because of continued hostility towards Christians from unbelievers. The writer challenges them to persevere in faith with a strong argument about the uniqueness and supremacy of Christ.

He begins, in chapter 1, by declaring that Jesus is God's clearest revelation of himself to us. His credentials, the writer notes, are impeccable: *"God promised everything to the Son as an inheritance, and through the Son he created the universe. The Son radiates God's own glory and expresses the very character of God, and he sustains everything by the mighty power of his command. When he had cleansed us from our sins, he sat down in the place of honor at the right hand of the majestic God in heaven"* (Hebrews 1:2–3). This is deep and impressive theology, worthy of earnest study and reflection.

An issue in the congregation is the relative status of Jesus and the angels. The readers hold to the popular Jewish belief that angels were involved in the giving of God's Law to Moses. If Jesus is the bringer of a new and final revelation from God, is he greater than the angels?

The writer insists that *"the Son is far greater than the angels."* The angels are created beings and servants of God who watch over believers, but Jesus is the Son who rules with God over everything. He is the Creator, sustainer and King, whose glory reflects the power and holiness of God the Father.

So getting Jesus right is critical. The readers are urged, in chapter 2, to keep the Gospel of grace clearly in mind, lest they drift away from it.

The mention of angels being present when Moses gave the Law and commandments to the people of Israel, raises the question of the purpose of the Law. As we have noted several times, the Law cannot save anyone from their sins because no one keeps it. In fact, the function of the Law is to remind us that we are sinners. It is Jesus who saves us from sin by his death on the cross for us. Our faith in him, makes us right with God. To drift away from grace is to lose sight of our salvation!

Furthermore, it is the incarnate Jesus and not angels in heaven who will *"control the future world"*—the coming New Heavens and New Earth. This vision of the future may be hard to imagine while looking at Jesus hanging on a cross in weakness and dying a sinner's death. But it is in his humiliation and servanthood that Jesus' glory is revealed. He has become our elder brother—the first of a new humanity with a glorious future.

It was necessary that Jesus do this. The writer explains, *"For only as a human being could he die, and only by dying could he break the power of the devil, who had the power of death. Only in this way could he set free all who have lived their lives as slaves to the fear of dying"* (Hebrews 2:14–15). As glorious as angels may be, human beings are greater. We occupy a unique status in God's creation. It was not for the sake of angels that Jesus came, but for our sake. He became like us so that he could represent us before God, just like the Old Testament high priest. As our High Priest, he is presenting before the Father the sacrifice of his own life for our sins.

This means that when we suffer as humans, and our faith is tested, we can turn to Jesus, our High Priest, for help. We can trust him because he too has suffered and been tested.

Focus: The uniqueness of Christianity is Christ himself, the Son of God, Creator and sustainer of the universe who rules as king in resurrection power. Yet he gave himself as a humble servant to rescue us from the peril of our sin. By his grace, we are saved. By his love, we are restored. By his power, we shall share in his glory!

Prayer: Lord, we are amazed and humbled that you would enter our humanity and absorb the judgment of our sin, in order to share eternal life with us. We strain to imagine what that will be like! Help us to remain faithful to Jesus now, as his brothers and sisters. Amen.

Day 345   Hebrews 3–4

December 10

> Key Text: For all who have entered into God's rest have rested from their labors, just as God did after creating the world. So let us do our best to enter that rest. (Hebrews 4:10–11)

The writer of Hebrews continues with the challenge for his readers to remain faithful to Christ, our great High Priest. Just as Christ is greater than the angels who accompanied the giving of God's Law to Moses, he is also greater than Moses. Therefore, as followers of Christ, they must keep their courage and remain confident of their hope in Christ, not the Law. There is no other way to forgiveness of sins.

But we have a tendency to drift from faith in Christ, like a sailboat pushed by the wind or pulled by the tides. Israel's history serves as a warning. The Israelites continually hardened their hearts and rebelled against God in the wilderness, and consequently received God's judgment. We too must be careful that our hearts *"are not evil and unbelieving, turning [us] away from the living God"* (Hebrews 3:12).

Those who are faithful to the end, trusting God just as firmly as when they first believed, will share in all that belongs to Christ—including the glory of eternal life. But we can't take this for granted. Israel experienced God's judgment and was not permitted to enter the Promised Land when she repudiated his grace. It is possible for us also to drift so far away from grace that we may fail to enter.

For Israel, the Promised Land meant something greater than having property; it represented being home with God. The writer of Hebrews describes it, not as entering the Promised Land, but as entering God's rest. Consequently, when Israel failed to trust God, *"they were not able to*

664

enter his rest" (Hebrews 3:19).

The idea of *"rest"* is explored more deeply in chapter 4. The writer says that this *"rest"* is something God has prepared for us as he did for Israel. In fact, it has been ready since God first made the world. You'll remember from Genesis chapter 2, that on the seventh day God finished his work of creation and then *"rested"* from all his work. *"And God blessed the seventh day and declared it holy, because it was the day when he rested from all his work of creation"* (Genesis 2:3).

God's rest is not a reference to divine fatigue; it indicates the divine purpose of creation, which is for God to live among us and enjoy life together.

As we have noted, divine *rest* was associated with temple-building in the ancient world, so the writer of Genesis is saying that God desires to "dwell" with his people in the "temple" of the whole earth so that we may enjoy all the blessings of his presence. Earth is not meant to be a container unit to warehouse humans, but a paradise for divine-human fellowship.

So there is a lot at stake in our faith in Jesus. We must be very careful not to drift from that faith: *"So let us do our best to enter that rest. But if we disobey God, as the people of Israel did, we will fall"* (Hebrews 4:11).

His warning is an encouragement to read the Scriptures and learn from the successes and failures of those before us. When we read the Bible this way, it analyzes us: *"For the word of God is alive and powerful. It is sharper than the sharpest two-edged sword, cutting between soul and spirit, between joint and marrow. It exposes our innermost thoughts and desires. Nothing in all creation is hidden from God. Everything is naked and exposed before his eyes, and he is the one to whom we are accountable"* (Hebrews 4:12–13).

The writer of Hebrews urges us hold firmly to what we believe, and trust Jesus with our prayers because, as our High Priest, he understands our weaknesses and advocates for us before the Father. Before the Father's throne, *"we will receive his mercy, and we will find grace to help us when we need it most"* (Hebrews 4:16).

Focus: God's singular purpose in creating a physical universe with human beings in his image, is to dwell with us here and share in our lives. This vibrant, joyful understanding of life gives dignity and hope to humanity, as compared to the meaningless and ultimately futile existence envisioned by atheism.

Day 346   Hebrews 5–7

December 11

> Key Text: But because Jesus lives forever, his priesthood lasts forever. Therefore he is able, once and forever, to save those who come to God through him. He lives forever to intercede with God on their behalf. (Hebrews 7:24–25)

The writer of Hebrews continues his explanation of the greatness of Christ to Jewish Christians. He also warns them not to drift away from faith in Christ by going back to the Old Testament system of law, which cannot save them.

We've noted in our reading of the Bible that the Old Testament system of worship, with its ritual laws, priesthood, animal sacrifices and Tabernacle/Temple, was provisional until the coming of Christ. Now, Jesus fulfills and embodies what those institutions meant to God's people. To summarize:

The "ritual laws" were ceremonial and symbolic of the holiness God requires. Jesus fulfills and embodies that holiness. He himself is without sin. By faith in him, we are declared holy by God.

The "priesthood" was given to establish a line of communication between sinful people and a holy God. But the priests themselves were sinful—so Jesus, the holy one of God, has become our permanent connection by being our great High Priest.

The "animal sacrifices" represented the penalty for our sin and the need for atonement. As an offering, they symbolized the possibility of an innocent substitute bearing the sin of the guilty offerer: the lamb was slain instead of the offerer. These practices help us understand that Jesus is our substitute—he is the *"Lamb of God who takes away the sin of the world"* (John 1:29).

The Temple represented the presence of God among his people, though separated from them by a room called the Holy of Holies. Only the appointed high priest could enter this space, and only once a year—and only after completing the elaborate ceremonial cleansings. But the death of Jesus opened the way for all of us to come into the very presence of God. Indeed, our bodies have become his Temple and his presence on earth.

So then, having argued from this perspective about the greatness of Christ, the writer of Hebrews now turns in chapters 5 through 7 to a lengthy and complex explanation about the nature of Jesus as our High Priest. His line of reasoning is hard to follow, but it gets us to a very important conclusion.

Using a brief Old Testament reference, in the story of Abraham, to a mysterious priest and king named Melchizedek, the writer establishes the superiority of Christ as an eternal High Priest. After recalling the high priest's role of offering sacrifices for the sins of the people before God, the writer notes that this role can be fulfilled only by those called by God to do so. He references Psalm 110, a Messianic psalm, to establish that Christ was promised and chosen by God for this role long ago. The psalmist says of this promised High Priest, *"You are a priest forever in the order of Melchizedek"* (Psalm 110:4).

Melchizedek is a mysterious person. The writer notes that we know nothing of his origin and, oddly enough, he disappears without trace. He has no predecessors and no successors. Melchizedek, therefore, foreshadows the unique and never-ending priesthood of Christ.

More important than this foreshadowing, however, are the death, resurrection and ascension of Jesus. His ascension establishes him as our divine and everlasting High Priest in heaven. His suffering as a human means that he is a compassionate and sympathetic Lord whom we can confidently approach with our prayers.

This teaching is definitely beyond basic doctrine. The writer of Hebrews is concerned that believers are still eating theological "baby food" and are not able to eat solid food. This concerns him because it makes them vulnerable to being misled by those who reject God's grace. The danger is that there is no other way to be right with God. If you drift away from grace, claiming that Jesus is not enough, there is no way back.

Therefore, understanding Jesus as our High Priest is critical. The writer sums it up by saying: *"But because Jesus lives forever, his priesthood lasts forever. Therefore he is able, once and forever, to save those who come to God through him. He lives forever to intercede with God on their behalf"* (Hebrews 7:24–25).

Focus: The doctrine of Jesus as our High Priest is rich with application. It means that we need not fear judgment for sin anymore—Jesus is both the offerer of the sacrifice before God, and the sacrifice itself. Furthermore, he will forever be our advocate before the Father when we pray. In his humanity he knows us intimately and sympathetically. He will ensure that we always receive from the Father what we need for a full and meaningful life.

Prayer: *Father, we praise you for Jesus, our High Priest, who gives us access to you and who always has our best interests in mind. We can hardly believe that, by his sacrifice, our sins are forgiven and our relationship with you is forever established. Amen!*

Day 347   Hebrews 8–10

December 12

> Key Text: Patient endurance is what you need now, so that you will continue to do God's will. Then you will receive all that he has promised. (Hebrews 10:36)

Hebrews 8 through 10 continues with the writer's concern that the Jewish believers are growing weary or apathetic because of ridicule and persecution. He encourages them to continue to place their trust in Christ alone for their salvation. There is no need for Jewish believers to return to the Old Covenant when it has been fulfilled by the New Covenant in Jesus' blood. Indeed, to do so risks falling from grace, when there is no other way to salvation outside of grace.

These three chapters finish up the lengthy theological and historical explanation of the superiority of Christ as our High Priest, and also the superiority of the New Covenant that Christ initiated with his death on the cross.

His explanation is shaped by the needs of the Jewish believers, and therefore may seem complex and repetitive to us, but the conclusion he draws is important. Christ has accomplished what God began with Abraham and continued with Moses. We cannot fully appreciate the grace and mercy we have received from Christ without placing it in the context of the Old Testament story.

Once again—there is no need for an Old Covenant priesthood and Temple with sacrifices anymore. Christ has fulfilled all these roles, institutions, ceremonies and laws. They were provisionally given to explain to God's people their need of forgiveness and to be a means by which they could receive it: *"For that old system deals only with food and drink and various cleansing ceremonies—physical regulations that were in effect only until a better system could be established"* (Hebrews 9:10).

The writer concludes in chapter 9 with a nice summary: *"But now, once for all time, [Christ] has appeared at the end of the age to remove sin by his own death as a sacrifice. And just as each person is destined to die once and after that comes judgment, so also Christ was offered once for all time as a sacrifice to take away the sins of many people. He will come again, not to deal with our sins, but to bring salvation to all who are eagerly waiting for him"* (Hebrews 9:26–28).

After making his argument sufficiently clear, the writer turns, in chapter 10, to a couple of specific applications regarding persevering in faith in Jesus. First, *"Let us hold tightly without wavering to the hope we affirm, for God can be trusted to keep his promise."* Right doctrine is important for right living, especially when it involves the person and work of Jesus. Almost all unorthodox sects and heretical groups begin with a faulty view of Christ.

Next, the writer says: *"Let us think of ways to motivate one another to acts of love and good works."* Correct doctrine doesn't automatically produce right living. We need to encourage one another to pursue it, especially to overcome selfishness and indifference so that we may love others by doing good works.

Finally, he says: *"And let us not neglect our meeting together, as some people do, but encourage one another, especially now that the day of his return is drawing near."*

Staying connected to Christ is not just a warm sentiment; it is a spiritual life preserver. As we said earlier, if we deliberately reject God's grace through Christ, there is no other way to salvation: *"There is only the terrible expectation of God's judgment and the raging fire that will consume his enemies"* (Hebrews 10: 27).

We must be careful to take our faith seriously: *"It is a terrible thing to fall into the hands of the living God."*

> **Focus:** In all its diversity and complexity, the main subject of the Bible is Christ—who he is and what he has done for us. Everything else either leads up to his coming or moves forward with him towards the conclusion of our salvation—resurrection life in a New Heavens and Earth.

Day 348   Hebrews 11–13

December 13

> Key Text: And it is impossible to please God without faith. Anyone who wants to come to him must believe that God exists and that he rewards those who sincerely seek him. (Hebrews 11:6)

The letter to the Hebrews concludes with a strong appeal to faith and perseverance. The writer defines faith as a way of knowing about things which we cannot access by empirical observation, such as the creation of the universe by God.

There are many things that are true and supported by reason, evidence and experience, but cannot be absolutely "proven." In fact, the most important things in life, such as the existence of God, cannot be proven in this way.

So faith is a gift of God which enables us to know reality outside of the visible, material realm—notably that God exists and rewards those who sincerely seek him. We experience this gift as an intuition of certainty. Faith gives us confidence and hope to persevere in following God, even when it seems impossible or when our lives are in peril.

Chapter 11 is a list of great men and women of faith from the Old Testament who have so lived. We could call it, "Faith's Hall of Fame." Beginning with the faith demonstrated by Abel, Enoch and Noah, the writer then turns to Israel's father, Abraham, and the nation that arose from his descendants, pointing out that these people believed God for what they had not yet received: *"All these people died still believing what God had promised them. They did not receive what was promised, but they saw it all from a distance and welcomed it"* (Hebrews 11:13).

Faith gave them insight. They discerned that the present world in its brokenness was only a temporary home. As people of faith who were *"looking for a better place, a heavenly homeland,"* they considered themselves to be *"foreigners and nomads here on earth."*

Their stories are given to inspire and instruct us.

670

In one example, Moses left the land of Egypt by faith, not fearing Pharaoh's anger: *"He kept right on going because he kept his eyes on the one who is invisible"* (Hebrews 11:27). As time went on, others were tortured for their faith because they refused to turn from God. *"They placed their hope in a better life after the resurrection."*

The writer honors these heroes of the faith by saying, *"They were too good for this world."* They are remembered as men and women of faith, even though none of them received all that God had promised. That is where we come in. What they only saw by faith, we have witnessed in the coming of Jesus.

We who now believe in Christ follow a great heritage of faith. Chapter 12 encourages us to draw strength and encouragement from their example. The writer imagines them to be spectators in the stands of the present race we the readers are running. They are cheering us on, urging us to lay aside every impediment to faith and *"run with endurance the race God has set before us. We do this by keeping our eyes on Jesus, the champion who initiates and perfects our faith"* (Hebrews 12:1–2).

Jesus is our inspiring example in this race: *"Because of the joy awaiting him, he endured the cross, disregarding its shame. Now he is seated in the place of honor beside God's throne."* When we consider what he faced on our behalf, we cannot help but be motivated to finish the race.

And God is for us, cheering us on. Even when we experience his discipline for our disobedience, it is for our good, that we might grow to maturity. So we must individually, and together, do everything necessary to live a holy life.

This is a serious matter with important consequences, especially for those who drift away from Christ. The world will one day be shaken by God's judgment so that only unshakable things, like faith, will remain: *"Since we are receiving a Kingdom that is unshakable, let us be thankful and please God by worshiping him with holy fear and awe. For our God is a devouring fire"* (Hebrews 12:28–29).

Chapter 13 finishes with a series of specific exhortations about living in love with one another, doing good, respecting spiritual leaders, and keeping Christ at the center of our lives: *"Jesus Christ is the same yesterday, today, and forever. So do not be attracted by strange, new ideas. Your strength comes from God's grace..."* (Hebrews 13:8–9).

Focus: Faith is a powerful way of knowing about the things we cannot see. The power of faith is not the act of believing, but the object of our belief—God the Father and our Lord Jesus Christ. By faith in him, we remain focused on what is true, and right, and good, and worthy of praise.

Prayer: *Lord, thank you for the testimonies of men and women throughout the generations who have inspired us by their faith and endurance out of love for you. May we also keep you first in our lives, willing to endure every hardship—just as Jesus did for us. Amen.*

Day 349   Reflection

December 14

The book of Hebrews is a strong encouragement to persevere in faith and not drift away from Christ. There are two ways a believer can "drift away." A believer can drift away from Christ as a *means* to salvation and seek another way. Or, a believer can drift away from *growing* in faith by failing to stay engaged in the disciplines that help us grow.

Since this letter is directed to Jewish Christians, the warning against drifting away from Christ is of primary concern. They are in danger of being persuaded to return to the Jewish legalism that could never save them in the first place. We have seen repeatedly in our reading of the Old and New Testaments, that moral or religious law cannot make us righteous. Our sinful nature constantly undermines our efforts to keep God's commandments, or even our personal resolutions.

Think of it this way: Sin has metastasized like cancer throughout the "body" of the human race. If you have cancer, getting most of it removed isn't good enough. It is the same with being justified before God by our good works. We may be mostly good, even better than others we know, but "mostly good" still falls short of God's standard if you are seeking to be justified by keeping the commandments.

Righteousness is a serious matter with God. For this reason, the book of Hebrews presents a strong argument for our need of Christ. He is the only way to be right with God. Chapter 1 declares that God created the universe through his Son, Jesus: *"The Son radiates God's own glory and expresses the very character of God, and he sustains everything by the mighty power of his command"* (Hebrews 1:3).

This same Son became human. Consequently, there is no greater human in the universe. Yet he humbled himself, offering his life for our sins so that we might be declared forgiven and righteous before God. There is no other name by which a sinner can be saved.

It is a dangerous thing to drift away from grace, back to a merit system of any kind, whether religious or philosophical. The writer of Hebrews poses a very serious question to those who are thinking this way: *"So what makes us think we can escape if we ignore this great salvation that was first announced by the Lord Jesus himself and then delivered to us by those who heard him speak?"* (Hebrews 2:3). If a person who has heard the Gospel of grace and experienced its power and goodness, then turns away from grace because of pride or rebellion, there is no way forward.

But willful unbelief is not the only way to drift away from Christ. We may also drift by failing to grow in faith. This kind of drifting occurs when we don't persevere in following Christ, especially in showing our love for him by caring for other believers. The writer of Hebrews says, *"Our great desire is that you will keep on loving others as long as life lasts, in order to make certain that what you hope for will come true. Then you will not become spiritually dull and indifferent. Instead, you will follow the example of those who are going to inherit God's promises because of their faith and endurance"* (Hebrews 6:11–12).

Indifference is a spiritual life killer. It is easy to fall into a pattern of life where Christ is displaced as the center of our desires, and only occasionally appears as merely one of the many things we "do." We are warned not to allow our hearts to become evil and effectively unbelieving, even though we may have the outer appearance of belief. We can go through the motions, keep the traditions and identify as Christians, while living like an unbeliever in our daily life.

The writer of Hebrews says, *"You must warn each other every day, while it is still 'today,' so that none of you will be deceived by sin and hardened against God. For if we are faithful to the end, trusting God just as firmly as when we first believed, we will share in all that belongs to Christ"* (Hebrews 3:13–14).

As Hebrews chapter 12 puts it, we are running a race to the finish line where joy awaits us. Christ has run before us and makes it possible for us to run. When we get our feet entangled in things of this world, or grow weary from the race, we need to get back on the track and endure to the finish line.

★And remember—fellow believers, who have died and are in God's presence, are cheering us on!

> *Prayer: Lord, make us aware of the spiritual danger of indifference and willful unbelief. Don't allow our hearts to be hardened towards you, but keep them tender and teachable so that we may continue to grow in faith. And may that faith express itself in loving relationships with others. Amen.*

Day 350   James

December 15

> Key Text: So you see, faith by itself isn't enough. Unless it produces good deeds, it is dead and useless. (James 2:17)

The book of James makes a strong argument that the faith which saves us is a faith that produces good deeds. Good deeds are not the root of our salvation, but they are the fruit. The fruit reveals spiritual life. We are saved by grace through faith *for* good works. A faith that produces no good works is really no faith at all.

James writes to a church under pressure from economic persecution and oppression because of their faith in Jesus. Suffering can break up community or it can fortify our faith together. James urges the readers not to fear suffering but consider it an opportunity for great joy. Why? Because when faith is tested, endurance grows, wisdom is gained, and maturity follows.

Mature Christians, faced with persecution, are energized by joy and hope because they experience the power of God in them, bringing about the Kingdom. God doesn't tempt anyone to do wrong, but he blesses those who patiently endure testing and temptation.

James bluntly confronts the angry tension that has developed within the congregation. He says, *"You must all be quick to listen, slow to speak, and slow to get angry. Human anger does not produce the righteousness God desires. So get rid of all the filth and evil in your lives, and humbly accept the word God has planted in your hearts, for it has the power to save your souls"* (James 1:19–21).

In addition to anger, favoritism is a problem among the people. James calls out the discrimination that dishonors the poor and weak. Faith in

Jesus means that we keep the commandments of God which show us how to love our neighbor as ourselves. God will judge believers on how we live.

The issue is not ignorance of God's will, but acting on what we know: *"But don't just listen to God's word. You must do what it says. Otherwise you are fooling yourselves"* (James 1:22). It does no good to say we have faith if we don't show it by our actions. Such faith isn't enough. Unless it produces good deeds, it is dead and useless. One may make a right confession of faith—such as affirming that there is one God—but that in itself is no virtue. Even the demons believe that there is one God *(James 2:19)!*

Abraham is our example. He was shown to be right with God by his actions. He left his family and country and moved toward the land God had promised him. He passed the supreme test of faith by being willing to sacrifice his own son in response to God's command. God, of course, staid Abraham's hand, and then provided the ram for the sacrifice. This pointed forward to the time when he would give his Son as a sacrifice for the sins of the world.

In chapters 3 through 5, James speaks to the issue of controlling our tongues, which can be instruments of blessing or destruction. Loose tongues always bring disorder and evil of every kind. Those who are peacemakers, however, will plant seeds of peace and reap a harvest of righteousness.

Looking deeper, James notes that the disorder that arises from anger comes from our evil desires. He says to the congregation, *"You want what you don't have, so you scheme and kill to get it. You are jealous of what others have, but you can't get it, so you fight and wage war to take it away from them. Yet you don't have what you want because you don't ask God for it"* (James 4:2). *Rely on Him for all your needs*

The solution is to humble ourselves before God, and then resist the temptations of the devil. When we do, God will lift us up.

James concludes his letter by pointing to one of the greatest temptations we face—the love of wealth, especially ill-gotten gain. In the congregation some of the wealthy are treating their workers unjustly. He warns them: *"Hear the cries of the field workers whom you have cheated of their pay. The cries of those who harvest your fields have reached the ears of the Lord of Heaven's Armies"* (James 5:4).

Instead of living selfishly, for immediate gratification, believers are urged to take God seriously and wait patiently for his return, because he is coming as Judge! With that day in mind, they should pray for each other, not prey upon each other. *"The earnest prayer of a righteous person has great power and produces wonderful results"* (James 5:16).

Focus: The attitude that we can freely sin because God freely forgives is a grave misunderstanding of grace. We receive God's grace by faith so that we can give ourselves to obeying God without feeling condemned by our sin. Authentic faith is measurable; it is a faith that manifests itself in good deeds of love.

Prayer: Lord, we thank you for the grace that gives us what we don't deserve, so that by faith we might find forgiveness and new life. Help us by your Spirit to demonstrate our faith through acts of love, so that we make you visible in the world. Amen.

Day 351   1 Peter

December 16

> Key Text: So if you are suffering in a manner that pleases God, keep on doing what is right, and trust your lives to the God who created you, for he will never fail you. (1 Peter 4:19)

The letter of First Peter is written to congregations composed of Jewish and Gentile believers in six provinces of the Roman Empire. They are undergoing persecution because of their faith. It is not likely state-sanctioned persecution yet, but rather local harassment from people they know. The believers no longer participate with them in the obligatory pagan activities, expected of everyone in the community.

Peter addresses the believers as *"God's chosen people who are living as foreigners"* in the world, meaning that belonging to Christ has changed their identity, their behavior, and their true home. They now have a *"priceless inheritance"* that is kept in heaven for them, which they will receive when Jesus returns. Peter encourages them, therefore, not to be troubled by their present trials: *"So be truly glad. There is wonderful joy ahead, even though you have to endure many trials for a little while. These trials will show that your faith is genuine. It is being tested as fire tests and purifies gold..."* (1 Peter 1:6–7).

The salvation that is their inheritance is something wonderful. It has been spoken of, and wondered about, by the Old Testament prophets.

And the angels are eagerly watching it come about in the world. This great inheritance of eternal life should motivate the people to *"think clearly and exercise self-control."* Their lives belong to God now, and they are set apart for his service, which is what the word *"holy"* means.

They must remember that God paid a ransom to save them from the empty lives they once lived. If they live as God's obedient children, they won't slip back into those old pagan ways of living to satisfy their selfish desires.

A holy life is characterized by love, and maintained by resisting the evil behavior of their old life. Christians must live up to the fact that they are now God's presence on earth—God's spiritual temple. They serve as priests, offering the sacrifice of praise and obedience.

Such a life bears witness to their unbelieving neighbors. Christians must not be seen as troublemakers, but as peacemakers. This will be reflected in the relationships between Christian slaves and their masters, of wives to husbands and husbands to wives, and between fellow believers in the congregation.

Showing love, sympathy and forgiveness in the congregation will create peace and give the opportunity to witness. When people ask about the reason for their Christian hope, they must be prepared to explain it, but in a gentle and respectful way. If they are suffering, let it not be for doing wrong, but for doing good. In so doing, they follow the way of Christ who *"suffered for our sins once for all time"* (1 Peter 3:18).

Those who are willing to give it up for Christ have given up *"the evil things that godless people enjoy—their immorality and lust, their feasting and drunkenness and wild parties, and their terrible worship of idols"* (1 Peter 4:3).

Peter explains that they should expect their former friends to be surprised and offended that the believers no longer *"plunge into the flood of wild and destructives things they do. So they will slander you."* But he encourages them not to be dismayed by persecution, because *"the end of the world is coming soon. Therefore, be earnest and disciplined in your prayers. Most important of all, continue to show deep love for each other, for love covers a multitude of sins"* (1 Peter 4:7–8).

We don't know when the Lord is going to return. The Bible often says, *"soon."* I take it to mean, sooner than it was before. Besides, we each have our own personal eschatology, because we're going to see Jesus when we die.

In summary—our life as *"foreigners"* in this world should be devoted to serving God through the spiritual gifts he has given us, so that glory will be given to God through Jesus Christ. If suffering comes, don't be surprised; instead, be glad. Regard these trials as partnership with Christ in his sufferings. Those who suffer with him will also share with him in his glory when he is revealed to all the world.

Peter ends his letter, in chapter 5, with specific instructions for the elders of the churches. They should willingly and humbly lead the congregation by example. Their motivation to be leaders must not be selfish gain, or pride of position, or the need to control people.

Everyone must stay alert in these things because our voracious enemy, the devil, *"prowls around like a roaring lion, looking for someone to devour. Stand firm against him, and be strong in your faith"* (1 Peter 5:8–9).

Focus: As spiritually reborn believers, we have a new identity, a new future hope, and a new ministry in this broken world. We should consider ourselves as outsiders in this world. We shouldn't be surprised when we are persecuted, nor should we retaliate, but consider it a privilege to be partners with Christ in his sufferings. Others will become followers of Jesus also, when they hear our testimonies given in a gentle and respectful way.

Prayer: *Lord, give leaders the strength to live exemplary lives before their congregations, and give courage to all of us to live honorable lives before the watching world so that our neighbors may see Jesus in us. Amen.*

Day 352   2 Peter

December 17

Key Text: But we are looking forward to the new heavens and new earth he has promised, a world filled with God's righteousness. (2 Peter 3:13)

Peter's second letter to Christians who live in five Roman provinces, is focused again on troubles within the congregations. He warns them against listening to those who teach false doctrines and thereby lure them into shameful immorality. Instead, they must commit themselves to a holy life: *"By his divine power, God has given us everything we need for living a godly life"* (2 Peter 1:3).

678

A godly life is possible because, by their faith, they share God's divine nature and power. The promises of God will be fulfilled in them when they make every effort to live by them. Faith will grow and manifest itself in moral excellence, knowledge, self-control, endurance, and love for everyone.

The willingness to make this effort is evidence of genuine faith. Peter says, *"So, dear brothers and sisters, work hard to prove that you really are among those God has called and chosen. Do these things, and you will never fall away"* (2 Peter 1:10).

By carefully studying the writings of the prophets, the believers can protect themselves from false teachings. Just as there were false teachers in Israel, there will be false teachers in the Church, who cleverly teach destructive heresies about Christ and lead their listeners into shameful immorality. The false teachers of which Peter writes may have been saying that if God freely forgives all our sin, then we might as well go ahead and sin all the more.

But false teachers who lead others into immorality will bring destruction upon themselves, Peter says, as well as upon those who listen to them. God demonstrated throughout Israel's history that he will judge the wicked who lead others astray. Even angels weren't spared, nor the ancient world. Noah's contemporaries, and later the citizens of Sodom and Gomorrah, were judged. So it will be with the false teachers in the churches.

Peter denounces these false and immoral teachers with the fury of an Old Testament prophet in chapter 2: *"They love to indulge in evil pleasures in broad daylight. They are a disgrace and a stain among you. They delight in deception even as they eat with you in your fellowship meals"* (2 Peter 2:13).

He continues by pointing out that they lure unstable people into sin. Consequently, they live under God's curse. They are doomed to blackest darkness. *"It would be better if they had never known the way to righteousness than to know it and then reject the command they were given to live a holy life"* (2 Peter 2:21).

Peter has learned that false teachers are lying to the congregations about Jesus' return, saying that it wasn't going to happen: *"What happened to the promise that Jesus is coming again? From before the times of our ancestors, everything has remained the same since the world was first created"* (2 Peter 3:4).

Peter assures his readers that Jesus is indeed coming again to judge the world. But he has his own timetable. A day is like a thousand years to him. He isn't slow in keeping his promise to return, but instead is being gracious and patient, giving everyone as much time as possible to repent.

Nevertheless, the day will come. It will come by surprise—like a thief in the night. And it will be a cosmic event. The heavens and earth will be lighted up with the purifying fire of judgment, and every scrap of sin will melt away in the flames.

In their place will come *"the new heavens and new earth he has promised, a world filled with God's righteousness. And so, dear friends, while you are waiting for these things to happen, make every effort to be found living peaceful lives that are pure and blameless in his sight"* (2 Peter 3:13–14).

Focus: The Christian community must always be vigilant to maintain the truth about Jesus doctrinally and the life of Jesus morally. When these slip away, the Church can expect the judgment of God, because there is a lot at stake. False teaching and immoral living hurt the witness of the Gospel in the world.

__Prayer:__ Lord, keep us from the skepticism and moral laziness that tempt us to slip away from the Gospel and remake Jesus into an agent of our own agendas. We ask for more and more grace, so that we may continue to grow in knowledge and wisdom for your glory. Amen.

Day 353   1 John

December 18

> Key Text: This is real love—not that we loved God, but that he loved us and sent his Son as a sacrifice to take away our sins. (1 John 4:10)

The letter of First John is sermon-like in its structure. Its themes are introduced and recur in concentric circles of thought throughout the letter. Each time something further is added or explained.

The apostle John writes for two reasons. The first is to explain how to experience Christian fellowship. The second is to warn early Christians of a nascent heresy among them, which will grow over time into full-blown Gnosticism, which was a heresy that plagued the Church for centuries.

John begins his letter with a declaration of faith in Christ, whom he calls the "Word of life." Echoing the opening of his gospel, John affirms that the Word existed from the beginning, but has now become flesh and blood: *"We saw him with our own eyes and touched him with our own hands. He is the Word of life. This one who is life itself was revealed to us, and we have seen him"* (1 John 1:1–2). A common faith in the incarnate Jesus is the basis of fellowship with God and one another.

Drawing again from themes in his gospel, John says that God is Light and there is no darkness in him. To have fellowship with him, and with one another, we cannot continue to live in spiritual darkness. We must live in the Light morally and spiritually because that is where God exists. Jesus came among us as the Light so that we could be freed from darkness.

Living in the Light, however, does not mean that we have achieved perfection. That is not possible while we exist in a fallen world, with dying bodies and a sinful nature. So if we claim that we have no sin, as some were doing, we are only fooling ourselves and calling God a liar: *"But if we confess our sins to him, he is faithful and just to forgive us our sins and to cleanse us from all wickedness"* (1 John 1:9).

In chapter 2, John expands upon the topic of Christian sin. There is occasional sin, done out of weakness, but then confessed and resisted thereafter. God knows we are weak, so the blood of Jesus continues to cover our sins as we keep on trying to obey his commandments—especially the commandment to love one another—and keep on confessing and leaning upon his strength and mercy, when we fail.

But there is another kind of sinning that is dangerous: willful, habitual sinning by those who think that sin does not matter, not even sin against one's fellow believers. John warns, *"If anyone claims, 'I am living in the light,' but hates a fellow believer, that person is still living in darkness"* (1 John 2:9).

It may seem strange for a believer to claim to be "in the light" while they hate their fellow Christians. Where would this notion come from?

There was an idea brewing at the time which said that the physical world was intrinsically evil. The way to salvation was escaping the world through secret knowledge known only by initiates. This secret knowledge "enlightened" them, and therefore they thought that they "walked in the light."

By this secret knowledge, they hoped to escape the material "prison" of the body at some point and rise spiritually and mystically to God. In repudiating the physical world, these people also minimized the importance of worshiping God morally with our bodies. Some thought they could indulge their physical lusts without consequences, since the body was evil anyway. It just didn't matter.

So the logic of this idea—later called Gnosticism (gnosis means "knowledge" in Greek)—meant that God, being good, would have nothing to do with "evil matter," and therefore would never have become a man! So Gnosticism denied Jesus' humanity. John writes, in 1 John 4:1–3, that false prophets can be recognized by their denial that Jesus came in a real body. Such a person has the spirit of an antichrist.

By contrast to this heresy, John affirms the goodness of the material world, though it is presently fallen. He also acknowledges the reality and importance of Jesus' flesh-and-blood body. Jesus himself told us that we use our bodies to love and serve God, and one another.

Chapters 3 through 5 beautifully articulate the source, meaning, expression and priority of love. In short, these chapters say that God is love, and this is demonstrated most vividly in the cross of Christ. Love, therefore, is the moral center of our lives as embodied people. Its priority is established by God's love for us: *This is real love—not that we loved God, but that he loved us and sent his Son as a sacrifice to take away our sins. Dear friends, since God loved us that much, we surely ought to love each other"* (1 John 4:10–11).

Loving one another is the heart of God's commandments, and it is our obligation to God. But how do we love God whom we cannot see? By loving one another whom we *can* see! Love is God's victory over sin and it becomes ours as well: *For every child of God defeats this evil world, and we achieve this victory through our faith."*

Focus: More than any religion or philosophy, Judeo-Christianity affirms the goodness of creation and the physical nature of men and women. As embodied people, now joined by the embodied Son of God, we serve the Lord through the moral vision of love as defined by the commandments of God. This is life as God intended. It is the basis of human fellowship. Not surprisingly, then, our hope is for eternal life with resurrected bodies in a New Heavens and Earth.

Prayer: Lord, we praise you for your wonderful creation, conceived by love and brought into fullness by an act of ultimate sacrifice through Jesus. We worship you by offering our bodies to you as living sacrifices. Amen.

Day 354   2 John

December 19

> **Key Text:** Anyone who wanders away from this teaching has no relationship with God. But anyone who remains in the teaching of Christ has a relationship with both the Father and the Son. (2 John 1:9)

The second letter of John, and his third letter, are the briefest books of the New Testament, with only thirteen and fifteen verses, respectively.

In his second letter, John writes to *"the chosen lady and to her children."* Most think this is a cryptic reference to the Church (chosen lady) and its congregation (her children).

John's reason for writing is to warn the "lady" about false teachers, and in particular about allowing them to come to the home meetings (Bible studies?). The false teaching is only briefly described here, but is clearly the emerging Gnosticism that John addresses more fully in his first letter.

John's pastoral concern and theological purpose is to protect the loving fellowship of this congregation. As he indicates in his first letter *(1 John 1:1–4)*, spiritual fellowship is made possible by the fact of Christ's incarnation, atoning death and victorious resurrection on our behalf.

Therefore, John speaks of loving the woman and her children *"in the truth,"* meaning the truth of the Gospel. The Gospel has brought them together in fellowship with God and one another, enabling them to love one another graciously, beyond human kinship.

John understands the "truth" of the Gospel to be more than an idea or abstraction. Truth is relationship—a relationship with God through Christ, and thereby with all others who hold to the same "truth." John says that this truth *"lives in us and will be with us forever"* (2 John 1:2). Therefore, the truth of the Gospel is not secret heavenly knowledge, as Gnosticism claimed, but a practical way of living in our bodies, on this earth, in relationship to God. So the Gospel does not inspire us to *abandon* ordinary life in the physical world, but to infuse it with God's loving

683

presence, which enriches our daily life by his grace, mercy and peace.

John reminds his readers that these gifts are not just to be savored for themselves—they are to be shared. Christians are called to *"love one another,"* a commandment from God which goes back to the beginning.

Such love is not mere sentiment. It means *"doing what God has commanded"* and caring for the well-being of one another just as earnestly as we care for our own well-being.

John wants to remind us that such fellowship, and the love which creates it, is grounded in the truth of who God is, and what he has done for us in Jesus his Son. That is why doctrine is important. It describes and bears witness to reality. There really is a God of grace and mercy who does loves us and wants to be in relationship with us. And his Son, Jesus Christ, really did become human to live among us and give his life for us so that we could be made new—body, soul and spirit.

False teachers threaten Christian faith by denying *"that Jesus Christ came in a real body."* This denial is based not on historical facts about Jesus, but on a pagan presupposition that whatever god there is would have nothing to do with the physical world. In their thinking, all matter is evil. Salvation is found only by escaping our bodies and this world. To them, the idea that God the Son would be become *"flesh and blood"* was inconceivable and offensive.

John knows that denying the deity of Jesus is dangerous. It is just as dangerous as denying the law of gravity. One may imagine that God would never become flesh and blood, just as he may imagine that he could leap off a skyscraper and land softly. But in both cases, the result will be death.

Anyone who denies that Jesus Christ came in a real body is a deceiver and an antichrist, John declares. The false teachers may believe it to be an enlightened idea, but it is a lie from hell.

Why is John so agitated about this? Because if Jesus did not become a flesh-and-blood human, then he could not have offered his life as a substitute for ours, meaning that we are still in our sin and under God's judgment.

It would also mean that there is no resurrection from the dead, nor a New Heavens and Earth to inhabit for eternal life. At best, all that would survive this mortal life would be a disembodied, ghostlike, half-life existence, with no personal identity, no memories, no ongoing relations with friends and loved ones, and above all, no hope. In other words—hell.

In light of this, John urgently warns the lady: *"If anyone comes to your meeting and does not teach the truth about Christ, don't invite that person into your home or give any kind of encouragement. Anyone who encourages such people becomes a partner in their evil work"* (2 John 1:10–11).

Focus: The Christian life is based upon and made possible by the bodily life and ministry of Christ. His atoning death reconciles us to God. His physical resurrection is a victory over physical death and guarantees our own resurrection. His teaching and example show us a new way to be human in a broken world. The gift of his Spirit in us, enables us to experience fellowship together, motivates us to love one another, and energizes us to serve him—in our bodies, and in the physical world! In short, doctrine matters.

Prayer: Lord, help us resist the temptation to dismiss the world because of its sin. We praise you for coming into the world through Jesus. We know that you are going to restore the whole creation when you come at the end of history. In the meantime, help us to keep our eyes focused on Jesus, so that we may experience your presence in our lives and become people who love one another. Amen.

Day 355   3 John

December 20

> Key Text: Follow only what is good. Remember that those who do good prove that they are God's children, and those who do evil prove that they do not know God. (3 John 1:11)

John addresses his third letter to a man named Gaius, *"my dear friend, whom I love in the truth."* The phrase, *"love in the truth,"* is also used at the beginning of his second letter in referring to *"the chosen lady and her children."* John, like the apostle Paul, believes that Christians everywhere are united by their common faith and possession of the Holy Spirit. In this sense, *"whom I love in the truth"* is equivalent to "whom I love in the Gospel," as a fellow believer. Believers are a spiritual family and are called to love one another.

As we have noted, John believes that such love only comes from God. It is not the love we instinctively feel as humans, whether erotic desire, love of family, or even friendship. John employs the Greek word, *"agape,"* to describe God's love. God's agape love is unconditional, sacrificial, and concerned above all for the well-being of others. It was supremely demonstrated by the death of Christ for us.

As John wrote in his first letter, God's agape love for us comes with responsibility: *"Dear friends, since God loved us that much, we surely ought to love each other"* (1 John 4:11). Therefore, if people claim to love God, but hate their Christian brothers or sisters, they are liars *(1 John 4:20)*.

Agape love, working in the believer, breaks down the walls that keep us from loving those who are not like us—and even those we do not like personally.

John rejoices in his third letter that his reader is learning to love others in this way. In particular, he has demonstrated Christian hospitality. John has heard from some traveling teachers of the Gospel that they were offered hospitality and financial support while visiting the reader. They enjoyed worship, instruction, and mutual edification around the Gospel. John encourages his reader to continue supporting such ministers through love and hospitality, even if the teachers are from outside the congregation. Christian work must be financed by Christian people.

Unfortunately, this principle of ministry is being opposed by an influential man in the congregation named Diotrephes. John says of him that he *"loves to be the leader."* Translated, this means he wants to be in control. Consequently, Diotrephes does not want to have anything to do with the apostles or any other outside traveling teachers. He refuses to welcome them and is telling others not to help them either. If they do, Diotrephes puts them out of the church, so he must be a person of influence.

John urges Gaius not to let this bad example influence him. He says, *"Follow only what is good. Remember that those who do good prove that they are God's children, and those who do evil prove that they do not know God"* (3 John 1:11).

Diotrephes is only concerned about his position among the people, and does not want this threatened by any outsiders. This is hardly an expression of agape love. It is pride, and the abuse of power masquerading as leadership. Congregations need to carefully discern the motives of those they choose as their leaders.

Focus: Hospitality is an expression of agape love because it is willing to generously share what one has with others in need. For the Christian, hospitality is a response to the amazing generosity of God's love—a debt we can never repay. By loving the people in our lives, we love the invisible God.

Prayer: Lord, keep us from being selfish or afraid about sharing our resources with the needy or deserving. Remind us that everything we have comes from you, and that you can easily replenish what we give to others so that we can continue to give. Teach us the joy of being an agent of your love and generosity on earth. Amen.

Day 356   Reflection

December 21

John's first letter contains a verse often quoted by believers in a liturgy of confession: *"But if we confess our sins to him, he is faithful and just to forgive us our sins and to cleanse us from all wickedness"* (1 John 1:9).

It is often pointed out that the Greek verb translated *"confess"* is in the present, active tense, designating an ongoing action. Therefore, John means to say that if we continue to confess our sins, God continues to forgive our sins and cleanse us from all wickedness.

We may ask why we need to continue to confess our sins if, as the New Testament teaches, we are already forgiven by the blood of Jesus. It also teaches that we are already the children of God, saints, citizens of heaven, justified by faith, holy, and in possession of eternal life.

These declarations are examples of what we have become by God's gracious decree. Some describe it as God's legal ruling on our behalf. These wonderful things are true about us because God has decided, through Christ, to declare them so. This is a wonderful, and humbling, reality.

However, just because these things are *legally* so, does not mean that they are fully realized in our experience yet. A simple illustration is marriage. Newlyweds are legally married before the State and spiritually married before God. The husband and wife pledge to love each other to the end. Yet to experience the full meaning of marriage takes a lifetime. The vows taken on their wedding day must be reaffirmed each successive day, "until death they do part." Vows must be lived *into*.

As Christians, we are already "forgiven" by God's grace. Therefore, in God's mind, the Last Judgment regarding heaven and hell has already taken place for us. Our baptism symbolizes and testifies that our old, sinful self has died with Christ, and a new self has been resurrected with

Christ. Importantly, we know that if we were to die tonight, we would be with God.

However, in our experience we still sin. We are saints who sin. That is why John writes of our continuing need to confess and be forgiven. We must think of our salvation as having three tenses: we *were* saved, we are *being* saved, and we *shall be* saved.

The first tense is "justification." When we first believed by confessing our sins and asking Jesus to be Lord of our life, we were saved. The second tense is "sanctification." During our present, mortal life, we continue to grow in faith and in our knowledge of Jesus Christ—we are being saved. The third tense is "consummation." In the resurrection from the dead, we shall finally realize what God has done for us and be fully saved.

We find all three tenses addressed in the New Testament in various places, but Philippians 1:6 contains all three: *"And I am certain that God, who began the good work within you, will continue his work until it is finally finished on the day when Christ Jesus returns."*

A healthy Christian life keeps these three tenses in balance. The fact that God *has* saved us, once and for all, is a source of comfort and security. The knowledge that God is continuing to work in us now, and expects us to keep working out our salvation, is a source of challenge. And the hope that our salvation will be perfected when Jesus returns and raises the dead, is a source of wonder and expectation. Then we will begin to experience life as God intended!

As Jesus explains in John 10:10, he came in order to give us a rich and satisfying life—now and forever.

Prayer: Lord, your Word helps us make sense of the Christian life. Thank you for the assurance we have in Christ that our sins are forgiven. Thank you for the Holy Spirit working in us, leading us to desire and do your will. Thank you for the hope we have of resurrection life in a New Heavens and Earth, when we will be able to fully experience the joys of our salvation. You are a great God and Savior! Amen.

Day 357   Jude

December 22

> Key Text: Now all glory to God, who is able to keep you from falling away and will bring you with great joy into his glorious presence without a single fault. (Jude 1:24)

Jude, the writer of this brief letter, is probably the younger son of Mary and Joseph, and therefore the brother of Jesus, and of James who wrote the book of James. Interestingly, he identifies himself in verse 1 as a brother of James, but *"a slave of Jesus Christ."* (None of the interesting questions about what it was like to grow up with Jesus are addressed in the New Testament! It's probably just as well).

Jude explains to his readers that he had hoped to write a theological letter about the salvation they share, but that he has since heard news from them which causes him alarm. So this letter is written instead to warn them about false teachers.

It is interesting to note how quickly false teachings about Jesus began to circulate among the early churches, whether it was Jewish legalism and the teaching that Christians needed to keep the Law of Moses to be saved, or nascent Gnosticism, which stated that Jesus could not have been truly human because the material world is evil.

Of course, this is something that Jesus warned his disciples to expect. He said that false teachers who come among the congregations *"disguised as harmless sheep but* [who] *are really vicious wolves"* can be identified by their moral character: *"Yes, just as you can identify a tree by its fruit, so you can identify people by their actions"* (Matthew 7:15–20).

So Jude echoes Jesus when he writes that the congregation must defend the apostolic teaching that God has entrusted to them, by watching out for ungodly people who worm their way into people's trust, but then mislead them. In this case, the false teachers are *"saying that God's marvelous grace allows us to live immoral lives"* (Jude 1:4).

This is a dangerous teaching for many reasons, but most importantly it completely misrepresents the Gospel. God is not an indulgent old-man-upstairs whose only concern is that people have a good time. He cannot just look away when we live immoral lives.

God's plan from the beginning, as Paul expresses it in Ephesians 1:4, has been to make us holy through Christ, so that we can become like him in his humanity. To use God's grace as an excuse to sin, instead of as a means to become like Jesus, is not only false teaching—it is an invitation for God's judgment. Jude writes: *"The condemnation of such people was recorded long ago, for they have denied our only Master and Lord, Jesus Christ"* (Jude 1:4).

Several examples from the Old Testament are then given to show how willful disobedience has always brought God's judgment.

Writing of the false teachers, he says that they live immoral lives, defy authority, and scoff at supernatural beings—meaning that they mock the spiritual realm, and act like unthinking animals, following their sinful desires, because they don't have God's Spirit in them.

Jude continues now with a fiery denunciation, saying that false teachers follow in the footsteps of well-known Old Testament sinners such as Cain, who killed his brother, Balaam, who deceived people for money, and Korah, who led Israel in rebellion against God.

These people, Jude says, are bad news and should not be included in fellowship meals. They are like dangerous reefs that can shipwreck you; like shameless shepherds who care only for themselves; like clouds blowing over the land but giving no rain; like trees in autumn that bear no fruit; like wild waves of the sea, churning up the foam of their shameful deeds; like wandering stars, doomed forever to blackest darkness.

But God's judgment is coming. It comes provisionally in this life through consequences, or when God acts decisively to stop sin. But it comes in finality at the Last Judgment when all sin will be judged and forever stopped.

We must understand that in the Last Days (our days—the days between the first and second coming of Jesus), there will be *"scoffers whose purpose in life is to satisfy their ungodly desires"* (Jude 1:18). Christians will be their targets, but we must not lose heart. We must build each other up in faith and in sound doctrine, always praying in the power of the Holy Spirit. If any find their faith wavering because of these false teachers, the congregation must show them mercy, but hold them accountable for sin.

Jude ends with a doxology, which alone makes this little letter worth reading: *"Now all glory to God, who is able to keep you from falling away and will bring you with great joy into his glorious presence without a single fault. All glory to him who alone is God, our Savior through Jesus Christ our Lord. All glory, majesty, power, and authority are his before all time, and in the present, and beyond all time! Amen."*

Focus: False teaching is akin to slandering God and to leading people astray. Therefore, it is confronted with the strongest of denunciations. Discipleship in the Church needs to be focused on sound doctrine and knowledge of the Bible. Despite what some may claim, the Spirit of God will never lead us to think or act contrary to the Word of God.

Prayer: Lord, keep your people safe from those who would mislead by false doctrine and clever manipulation. Grant us teachers to help us with the discipline of studying the Bible, so that we may protect ourselves from lies and fortify ourselves with the truth, and live in a manner that honors you. Amen.

Day 358   Revelation 1–3

December 23

> Key Text: "Look! I stand at the door and knock. If you hear my voice and open the door, I will come in, and we will share a meal together as friends." (Revelation 3:20)

The last book of the Bible is attributed to John (possibly not the apostle) while exiled as a prisoner on the island of Patmos during the reign of the Roman Emperor Domitian, who ruled from AD 81–96.

Revelation was written as a pastoral and prophetic letter to encourage suffering believers not to be afraid in the midst of the chaos of persecution. Instead, they are urged to keep the resurrected Christ in view: *"I, John, am your brother and your partner in suffering and in God's Kingdom and in the patient endurance to which Jesus calls us. I was exiled to the island of Patmos for preaching the word of God and for my testimony about Jesus"* (Revelation 1:9).

Stylistically, Revelation is full of the themes, striking images, symbolism and cryptic language which is characteristic of apocalyptic literature. Most agree that it is the most perplexing and difficult to interpret of all the books of the Bible. And yet it holds a unique fascination for readers. It presents a hopeful vision of the course of human history in light of the victory of Christ and his enthronement in heaven.

The Church Fathers rightly placed Revelation as the last book of the Christian canon, because it brings the Bible's story to its God-intended conclusion. While Genesis narrates the beginning of humanity's rebellion against God in the Garden of Eden, Revelation narrates God's eventual triumph over sin, death and the devil.

In doing so, it presents a distinctly Christian view of history, asserting that Christ's resurrection and enthronement in heaven have initiated a new phase of human history. This phase, known as the Last Days, initi-

691

ates the "end" of the present order to make way for a new beginning—a new Genesis.

At Christ's second coming, the old creation will give way to the New Creation, where heaven and earth are joined forever under the gracious rule of Christ, and where all the sorrows of sin and death are gone.

Chapter 1 begins with this purpose: *"This is a revelation from Jesus Christ, which God gave him to show his servants the events that must soon take place. He sent an angel to present this revelation to his servant John."*

It is written to *"the seven churches in the province of Asia."* The introduction gives us a clue that Revelation's first concern is about events which were happening to Christians at that time.

Chapter 1 also tips us off that the focus of John's message is about Christ: *"He is the faithful witness to these things, the first to rise from the dead, and the ruler of all the kings of the world. ... All glory and power to him forever and ever! Amen"* (Revelation 1:5–6). This same Jesus is coming again and everyone will see him, even those who pierced him.

John writes to the seven churches about what he received from Jesus in a dream. He sees Jesus in his glory, and falls at his feet, overwhelmed. Jesus reassures him: *"Don't be afraid! I am the First and the Last. I am the living one. I died, but look—I am alive forever and ever! And I hold the keys of death and the grave"* (Revelation 1:17–18).

John is instructed to write down what he sees—both the things happening then and the things that will happen later—and send his account to the seven churches, along with a special message for each one.

Chapters 2 and 3 contain John's messages for the churches—first Ephesus, then Smyrna, Pergamum, Thyatira, Sardis, Philadelphia, and Laodicea.

Each church receives commendation and correction from Jesus. For example, the believers at Ephesus are commended for their hard work and patient endurance, and for not tolerating false teachers. But then Jesus says to them: *"But I have this complaint against you. You don't love me or each other as you did at first! Look how far you have fallen! Turn back to me and do the works you did at first"* (Revelation 2:4–5).

The message to each church reflects their present situation, but the commendations and corrections are applicable to the Church Universal as well. The message of Jesus to the church at Laodicea is particularly memorable: *"Look! I stand at the door and knock. If you hear my voice and open the door, I will come in, and we will share a meal together as friends"* (Revelation 3:20).

> **Focus:** N.T. Wright explains that the book of Revelation offers one of the clearest and sharpest visions of God's ultimate purpose for the whole creation, and of the way in which the powerful forces of evil—at work in a thousand ways, but not least in idolatrous and tyrannous political systems—can be and are being overthrown through the victory of Jesus the Messiah.

> **Prayer:** *Lord, give us courage to remain faithful to you not only in hard times, but especially in good times. It seems, Lord, that we are in greater spiritual danger in good times, because then we are tempted to think that we don't need you. Thank you for the ongoing invitation to share a meal together as friends! Amen.*

Day 359   Revelation 4–5

December 24

Key Text: "Holy, holy, holy is the Lord God, the Almighty—
the one who always was, who is, and who is still to
come." (Revelation 4:8)

The revelation that gives this book its title begins in chapter 4: *"Then as I looked, I saw a door standing open in heaven, and the same voice I had heard before spoke to me like a trumpet blast. The voice said, 'Come up here, and I will show you what must happen after this.' And instantly I was in the Spirit, and I saw a throne in heaven and someone sitting on it"* (Revelation 4:1–2).

Heaven is God's sphere of reality—God's place. We tend to think of heaven as "up" in the stars, and far away. In truth, God's realm is everywhere, intersecting with the physical realm where we exist, though it is invisible to us.

In John's vision, there is a door standing open in heaven. Think of it as appearing right in front of him, in his room—a portal to a different room where God's elevated throne exists. John is invited by God to come up to his throne and receive information about what must happen soon. It is like going behind the curtain of human history to see how it works, and what is going to happen.

The throne room is an audiovisual wonder! God's countenance is brilliant and colorful, shining like gemstones: *"And the glow of an emerald circled his throne like a rainbow."* Surrounding him on thrones are twenty-four elders representing the twelve tribes of Israel and the twelve disciples of Christ, who consult with the Lord. It represents the unity of witness by the Old and New Testaments to God's sovereign plan, and also the shared rule of believers with God over the world.

First-century readers would also have noted that the picture of God in his throne room, surrounded by senior consultants, was a counterpoint to the Roman emperor with his consultants who conspired to worldly power and glory. However, the pretentious earthly powers of this fallen world are only a parody of the true Ruler over heaven and earth, and one day they will succumb to his rule. This is a comforting vision for those who are presently being persecuted by those earthly powers.

The vision of God's throne room also includes seven torches in front of the throne. These represent the sevenfold Spirit of God, meaning the fullness of God's Spirit. Surrounding the throne are four strange living creatures with faces representing man and animals, with six wings each. Day and night, John reports, they keep on worshiping: *"Holy, holy, holy is the Lord God, the Almighty—the one who always was, who is, and who is still to come."* Whenever they do this, the twenty-four elders fall down and worship, laying their crowns before the throne and saying, *"You are worthy, O Lord our God, to receive glory and honor and power. For you created all things, and they exist because you created what you pleased"* (Revelation 4:11).

Perhaps this shows that all creation worships God in its appointed ways—even animals. But only human beings are given the ability to know God and understand his ways.

The final detail—a mysterious one—is the shiny sea of glass in front of the throne, sparkling like crystal. It seems benign, but in Revelation 13:1, a great, threatening beast rises up out of the sea. So the picture here is a statement that even though God is on his throne, evil and danger still threaten the present world. God allows it for now, but it will be overcome.

The focus changes in chapter 5, to a scroll that is in the right hand of the one sitting on the throne. The scroll has seven seals protecting God's secret plan to rescue and restore the whole creation. The question is asked—the key question of the book of Revelation, and indeed the whole Bible: *"Who is worthy to break the seals on this scroll"* and fulfill God's plan? Adam and Eve failed. So did Israel. John notes that *"no one in heaven or on earth or under the earth was able to open the scroll and read it."*

John is shaken by this and weeps bitterly. But one of the twenty-four elders speaks out: *"Stop weeping! Look, the Lion of the tribe of Judah, the heir to David's throne, has won the victory. He is worthy to open the scroll and its seven seals"* (Revelation 5:5).

Then John sees a lamb that looks as if it had been slaughtered. The lamb steps forward and takes the scroll, causing an explosion of praise and song in heaven: *"You are worthy to take the scroll and break its seals and open it. For you were slaughtered, and your blood has ransomed people for God from every tribe and language and people and nation. And you have caused them to become a Kingdom of priests for our God. And they will reign on the earth"* (Revelation 5:9–10).

This pronouncement is followed by *"the voices of thousands and millions of angels around the throne and of the living beings and the elders,"* singing in a mighty chorus: *"Worthy is the Lamb who was slaughtered—to receive power and riches and wisdom and strength and honor and glory and blessing!"*

> **Focus:** The vision in chapters 4 and 5 is as powerful a revelation of the glory of heaven and of God's saving plan as human words can express. You may recognize the text used in two wonderful choruses of Handel's *Messiah*. Such a vision of the victory of God through Christ can sustain the people of God during the troubles of this life.
>
> **Prayer:** *Lord, give us the imagination to see the glory of God at work behind the curtain of human history. We praise you for the Lamb who has ransomed people from every tribe, language, people and nation to belong to you, and to reign with you in the New Creation. Amen!*

Day 360   Revelation 6–7

December 25

> Key Text: After this I saw a vast crowd, too great to count, from every nation and tribe and people and language, standing in front of the throne and before the Lamb. (Revelation 7:9)

John's revelation continues as Jesus, the Lamb of God and the victorious Lord of history, breaks the first of seven seals on the scroll. Breaking the seals is equivalent to revealing foreordained history. The scroll outlines the coming of divine judgment and salvation—the *"great and terrible day of the Lord"* of which the Old Testament prophets spoke. Six seals are broken in chapters 6 and 7, and the seventh in chapter 8.

It is important to remember here that the great victory of God through Christ has been witnessed to in chapter 5. Now that victory will be carried out within human history.

Upon the breaking of each of the first four seals, one of the four living creatures around the throne in heaven says, *"Come!"* In response, four riders appear on four horses of different colors, symbolizing four judgments.

The first is a white horse whose rider carries a bow and wears a crown. He rides out to fight and win many battles. This probably represents the conquering kings—now nation states with modern weapons of war—wreaking havoc on earth. The Lord allows them to do their worst. As Jesus had predicted, *"nation will go to war against nation,"* and *"sin will be rampant everywhere"* before the end comes. (See Matthew 24:4–14.)

The second is a red horse whose rider has a mighty sword and disrupts peace on earth with war and slaughter, like the world wars and terrorism of our own time.

The third is a black horse with its rider holding a pair of scales in his hand, representing the economic injustice that lies at the root of so much conflict.

The fourth is a pale horse whose rider is named *"Death,"* and whose companion is *"the Grave."* These two are given authority over a quarter of the earth to kill with the sword and famine and disease. These represent the threat of tyrants and anarchists who bring premature death to so many innocent people.

All together, the four horses of the Apocalypse represent the evils which humans inflict upon one another. The terrors of a fallen world in rebellion against God are not whitewashed, but acknowledged. God allows human sinfulness to fully reveal itself before he comes in judgment and salvation. Thus, human sinfulness will bear witness to the rightness of God's judgment against us.

The fifth broken seal reveals *"the souls of all who had been martyred for the word of God and for being faithful in their testimony"* (Revelation 6:9). These would include Christians fed to lions in the Roman amphitheater, as well as those killed today by ISIS. They are given white robes. Though they long for peace on earth, they are asked to be patient because the trouble on earth is not over yet.

The terrifying sixth seal is a picture of cataclysmic events on earth, felt by everyone. It is a symbolic, but frightening picture of the created order coming apart: *"The sun became as dark as black cloth, and the moon became as red as blood. Then the stars of the sky fell to the earth like green figs falling from a tree shaken by a strong wind. The sky was rolled up like a scroll, and all of the mountains and islands were moved from their places"* (Revelation 6:12–14).

All the people on earth hide in caves and rocks, for they rightly sense these earth-shattering events to be *"the wrath of the Lamb."* They are the tremors of coming judgment. Yet the wonderful paradox here is that the Lamb, whose wrath these events portend, is the same Lamb who is self-giving love. The divine wrath against sin has already been absorbed in Christ himself on the cross. All who cling to him by faith will escape his judgment and receive his salvation. So while God's wrath will be *revealed*, it will also be *removed* by Christ, so that all will finally understand the enormity of what God has done for us.

Chapter 7 now reminds us that though the earth will be blown around and shaken—and Christians will experience great suffering—they will be restored on the other side of resurrection, along with the whole creation.

The people of God are represented symbolically by the 144,000 *"sealed"* from all the tribes of Judah (12 x 12 x 1,000). Then they are represented literally by *"a vast crowd, too great to count, from every nation and tribe and people and language, standing in front of the throne and before the Lamb. ... And they were shouting with a great roar, 'Salvation comes from our God who sits on the throne and from the Lamb!'"* (Revelation 7: 9–10).

This is a breathtaking vision at the end of history of the success of the Church in its mission to the world. It is wildly successful, and culturally, racially, geographically and historically diverse! The great tribulation on earth is over in this vision: *"For the Lamb on the throne will be their Shepherd. He will lead them to springs of life-giving water. And God will wipe every tear from their eyes."*

Focus: Revelation employs the themes and imagery of the Old Testament prophets to tell its story of the victory of Christ over sin and death, and therefore the ultimate

Daniel

victory of the whole creation. It acknowledges the evil and injustice of human history, and the suffering of Christians who declare that God is King, but it brings a vision of great hope for the future.

Prayer: Lord, how grateful we are that Christ holds the key to human history in his hand. We praise him as the Lion who is also the Lamb—our Savior and Lord! Amen.

Day 361   Revelation 8–9

December 26

> Key Text: When the Lamb broke the seventh seal on the scroll, there was silence throughout heaven for about half an hour. I saw the seven angels who stand before God, and they were given seven trumpets. (Revelation 8:1–2)

In chapter 8, the seventh seal of the scroll is broken. The number seven, which is prominent in Revelation, was sacred in the ancient world, suggesting perfection, fullness and completion. The book of Revelation contains three visions of seven judgments, written to seven congregations. This structure represents the truth and certainty of God's work in history.

John reports, *"When the Lamb broke the seventh seal on the scroll, there was silence throughout heaven for about half an hour."* After this, the seven angels who stand before God's throne are given seven trumpets. Another angel appears with a great amount of incense to burn on a gold altar before the throne. The incense smoke ascends to God, together with all the prayers of his holy people.

Next, an angel takes fire from the altar and hurls it upon the earth, causing thunder, lightning, and a terrible earthquake. This is a prelude to the seven angels blowing mighty blasts from their seven trumpets. The trumpet blasts announce further judgments in addition to those which already have passed. Most believe these new judgments to be thematic, not chronological events. The judgments of God on earth reveal his determination to stop the evil that is destroying his creation, so that the whole creation may be renewed by his grace and mercy.

The first trumpet blast causes hail and fire mixed with blood to be thrown on earth. One-third of all trees and green grass is burned. The fraction one-third represents a significant, but not fatal, catastrophe from these judgments.

A second trumpet blast causes a mountain of fire, like a volcano, to be thrown into the sea. A third of the sea becomes blood, and a third of all living things in the sea and ships traveling on the sea are destroyed. Again, significant but not total destruction.

A third trumpet blast causes a great, burning star, whose name is Bitterness (or sometimes translated "Wormwood") to fall from the sky. It probably represents a destroying angel, and causes one-third of all drinkable water on earth to be poisoned.

A fourth trumpet blast causes darkness to come upon one-third of the sun, moon and stars, as well as one-third of the day and night. These horrors upon the earth are given voice by the screeching of an eagle flying through the air calling out, *"Terror, terror, terror to all who belong to this world because of what will happen when the last three angels blow their trumpets"* (Revelation 8:13).

Each trumpet blast seems to bring greater terror than the one before, and now as the eagle warns, it will get even worse. Accordingly, in chapter 9, the fifth trumpet blast releases another star, which is again probably an angel, falling to earth with a key. This key represents authority from God, and opens the *"bottomless pit"*—the mythological place of evil powers. It is a place of chaos and disorder from whence the forces of darkness wreak havoc upon the fallen earth. From its depths, smoke pours out as from a furnace, while the air turns dark from the smoke. This image is theological, not geographical. Some think the bottomless pit represents human institutions overcome by evil—whether social, political, economic or religious. They seem to unleash a bottomless supply of evil which destroys creation and creature alike, generation after generation.

The king of this realm is Abaddon, or in Greek, Apollyon—the destroyer, which is one of the biblical names for the devil. When this realm is unlocked by the angel with the key, a horrible plague of locusts is released from the pit, bringing great misery and suffering. A sixth trumpet blast then releases four angels of destruction, leading an army of 200,000 mounted troops and killing one-third of the people on earth.

The events described in the fifth and sixth trumpet judgments recall the plagues unleashed upon Egypt in the book of Exodus. You'll remember that during the last plague, the destroyer was released to kill all the firstborn sons of Egypt, but the Hebrew homes were *"passed over"* because of the blood they put on their doorposts in obedience to God. Now, in the sixth trumpet judgment, those who repent of their sins and turn to God are *passed over.*

Some who do not repent are nevertheless spared by chance from the destruction. One would think that they would surely repent then, but they do not. They continue in their dark and confused thinking, giving themselves over to idolatry, murder, witchcraft, sexual immorality and theft.

They are like the pagans described by Paul in Romans: *"Claiming to be wise, they instead became utter fools. And instead of worshiping the glorious, ever-living God, they worshiped idols made to look like mere people and birds and animals and reptiles"* (Romans 1:22–23).

Thus, we see how deeply rooted sin is in the human heart. It appears that repentance will not be universal, even with more grace and mercy offered.

Focus: The relentless terrors of Revelation are a little hard to take. Yet, in our day of instant communication, we are beset by disturbing images of all kinds of evils, misfortune and disaster from around the world. It doesn't make the images of Revelation less upsetting, but it does make them believable to a degree that premodern cultures have never experienced. And it makes the hopeful message of Revelation all the more precious: Jesus is the Lord of history and has triumphed over sin and death.

Prayer: *Lord, in our moments of fear, keep us from despair, for we know the outcome of the great struggle on earth between good and evil. You win, and it isn't even close. Give us courage to faithfully serve your purposes in our generation. Amen.*

Day 362   Revelation 10–13

December 27

> **Key Text:** "The world has now become the Kingdom of our Lord and of his Christ, and he will reign forever and ever."
> (Revelation 11:15)

We come to chapter 10, where there is another pause in the vision. This gives the readers a moment to reflect on the judgment and salvation of God, which have been revealed and will come to pass without delay after the seventh trumpet is sounded.

Before that blast, another glorious angel descends from heaven with a small, opened scroll in hand. The angel straddles the sea and the land—i.e., the whole earth—and gives a great shout like the roar of a lion.

John begins to write down what he hears, but is stopped by God, for it is to be kept secret. Instead, he is directed to take the opened scroll from the angel and eat it: *"It will be sweet as honey in your mouth, but it will turn sour in your stomach!"* (Revelation 10:9).

Having eaten the scroll, and indeed finding it both sweet and bitter, John is told to *"prophesy again about many peoples, nations, languages, and kings."* This indicates that things yet to come are to be brought about when God's word becomes John's words. But first they must become part of his life, as with any prophet or preacher. Thus, he is directed to *"eat the scroll."* The sweetness and bitterness of God's sovereign purpose will be manifested in the prophet's words. In this way God's word becomes reality and changes the world. We humans are his agents in doing so.

Chapter 11 is one of the most puzzling chapters of Revelation, and of the whole Bible, so we'll do the best we can to decipher it. John is told to go and measure the Temple of God and its worshipers, probably an action meant to protect the believing community from destruction. But they will still be vulnerable, because the *"outer courtyard"* is not to be measured and *"has been turned over to the nations."*

Two witnesses are now brought forth. They are prophets, perhaps like Moses, who stood up to Pharaoh, and Elijah, who stood up to the evil King Ahab. Some think that they symbolize the whole Church in its mission to the world, accompanied by Jesus' authority and speaking Gospel truth to power.

But this powerful ministry in the world agitates unbelievers, and the prophets face martyrdom: *"When they complete their testimony, the beast that comes up out of the bottomless pit will declare war against them, and he will conquer them and kill them"* (Revelation 11:7). This vivid image of the suffering and martyrdom of Christians in ministry has been borne out in human history, continuing to this very day.

✝ Jesus does not exempt his followers from suffering—they are partners with him in his suffering. *(See 1 Peter 4:12–14.)* This is the nature of ministry in a fallen world. But martyrdom is not a sign of defeat. It is a prophetic sign that God's enemies cannot tolerate his Word. They will seek to destroy his people, and stop their testimony. However, their martyrdom will be the means through which many will come to worship God.

This insight now gives way to the blowing of the seventh trumpet, a blast of triumph, made famous by Handel in his "Hallelujah Chorus": *"Then the seventh angel blew his trumpet, and there were loud voices shouting in heaven: 'The world has now become the Kingdom of our Lord and of his Christ, and he will reign forever and ever'"* (Revelation 11:15).

This triumphal shouting, in turn, causes the twenty-four elders in heaven, around God's throne, to fall on their faces and worship him. Their prayer declares that God has now assumed his great power to move in judgment and salvation, *"to destroy all who have caused destruction on the earth,"* and to reward his *"holy people."*

In chapter 12, the scene gets cosmic. A woman—probably representing Israel—gives birth to the king who will rule all nations, Christ the Lord. Confronting him right away is a large red dragon with seven heads, each with crowns and ten horns. This is the ancient serpent, the devil.

A war in heaven is engaged between the angels, led by Michael, and the devil, with his fellow fallen angels, the demons. The devil loses, and he and his fallen angels are forced out of heaven and thrown down to earth. From the heavens, a shout of victory is heard—the Lord is King! The blood of the Lamb has defeated the devil. Enraged, the devil declares war against Christians and takes his stand on the shore beside the sea.

Chapter 13 opens with a beast rising out of the sea. It has seven heads and ten horns with crowns on them. The original readers would have recognized the beast as the devil embodied in the evils of the Roman Empire. Other beasts like Rome have risen over the millennia. John writes, *"This means that God's holy people must endure persecution patiently and remain faithful"* (Revelation 13:10).

A second beast arises out of the earth. Its purpose is to serve the first beast. His role seems to be to force people into worshiping the Roman emperor, under the threat of death. He commands that everyone receive a mark enabling them to buy or sell. It is the mark of the beast, branding people as worshipers of the emperor. The number of the beast is 666, a cryptogram spelling out the name, NERO CAESAR.

Focus: The great conflict at the center of human history is the kingdom of this world versus the Kingdom of God. Spiritual warfare is behind all conflicts on earth.

fueling the fire and causing great suffering upon God's people. But as hopeless as it sometimes seems, the fact is that the battle has already been won by Christ's death and resurrection. The present struggle will come to an end, and the Lord will reign forever and ever!

Prayer: Lord, grant us patient endurance so that we may remain faithful to you during our time of testing. We rejoice that the victory has already been won and the future is bright with hope! Amen.

Day 363 — Reflection

December 28

As we near the end of our year-long journey through the Bible, let's take a moment to revisit the four great themes that have driven its story—Creation, Fall, Redemption and New Creation.

The book of Genesis begins the story by announcing that the physical universe was spoken into existence by the powerful Word of God, the one and only Creator. In response to the universal human question—"Where did we come from and why are we here?"—the Bible declares that we are the product, not of random chance and impersonal forces, but of the infinite power and loving purpose of a personal God who wishes to be known by us.

His loving purpose is best understood to be his desire to share with us the eternal life he has always experienced. He wishes to fill the earth with human life that enjoys his blessing, sings his praise, and serves with him as administrators of the universe!

To this end, he created human beings in his image and likeness. He created them as sexual, gendered beings so that the growth of human life and culture on earth would be centered in the loving embrace of marriage and family, and echo the love and unity of his own triune nature. He placed them in his garden to live as embodied beings and care for his creation.

It was Paradise, but it soon became Paradise Lost. What began with Creator and creature in unity and fellowship, quickly dissolved into their expulsion from Paradise and the eternal life it had promised.

This tragedy came about when humans broke covenant with God by believing the intoxicating lie of the serpent, that they could be as God, determining good and evil for themselves. They coveted God's power and rejected his authority by willfully eating the forbidden fruit. But it turned out to be bitter fruit.

Choosing to live without God had an immediate effect, but not what they expected. Sin and death entered the creation. Men and women began living for themselves, using others to get what they wanted and resorting to violence to settle their conflicts. Instead of living in joyful fellowship with their Creator, and in loving community with one another, they lived in spiritual alienation and personal despair.

Human wickedness got so bad, so quickly, that God was sorry he had ever made the human race. It broke his heart. But God determined, out of his love for them, that he would not let humanity go. He would allow humans to do their worst to him, but resolved to overcome it all and be their king again.

His resolve to redeem us was revealed along the way, but was formally implemented through Abraham. Abraham's offspring would eventually become the nation of Israel, through whom God would rescue lost humanity and renew the whole earth.

All of this happens in only twelve chapters of Genesis!

The rest of the Bible is the long, unfolding story, which we have explored, about how God would bring about his rescue plan, beginning with Israel, a people he calls out from the world to belong to him. Israel's story, as we have seen, is a great struggle—Jacob wrestling with God. There are moments of great faith, and many others of hardhearted rebellion. Their struggles with faith, and its mixed results, is the story of the world.

By the end of the Old Testament, it seems as if God's plan has failed because his people have failed to embrace it as a nation. But this struggle prepares us for the coming of the "One True Israelite" who does God's will, Jesus of Nazareth, God's own Son. His coming is like a retelling of Israel's story, but with a different outcome—with a New Creation, a new Exodus, and a new Promised Land offered to all nations, not just Israel. It is a Promised Land (a Promised Universe, really) where God reigns as King through Jesus.

The book of Revelation brings this great story to its conclusion. In its own striking way, through an apocalyptic lens and imagery, it presents Christ as the Lord of human history. It pulls back the curtain a bit to re-

704

veal the invisible heavenly realm which exists all around us.

There we see Jesus as the Lamb of God, our Savior, enthroned with the Father, having defeated the great serpent, the devil. He is guiding the course of history, protecting his Church, and preparing to return at just the right time for final judgment and salvation.

We will see in the next few days, as Revelation concludes, that God is going to restore the entire fallen creation, along with us. Heaven and earth will be reunited. God will live among us through Jesus, and he will wipe away every tear from our eyes. There will be no more death or sorrow or crying or pain. There begins the life that is truly Life—eternal life with God our Maker!

Coming to the end of the story, we see why it is the greatest story ever told. No other story tells of such a great and gracious God. No other story gives such dignity and hope to human beings, nor envisions a world united in joyous diversity by Christ the King. No other story excites the imagination like this one, causing us to wonder about what is possible when human beings spend eternity discovering and celebrating and living out the infinite possibilities of the infinite mind of God!

Prayer: Lord, we rejoice again in the Gospel! How great are your riches and wisdom and knowledge! How impossible it is for us to understand your loving decisions and gracious ways! Everything comes from you, is sustained by your power, and is intended for your glory. All glory to you! Amen.

Day 364   Revelation 14–16

December 29

Key Text: "Blessed are those who die in the Lord from now on. Yes, says the Spirit, they are blessed indeed, for they will rest from their hard work; for their good deeds follow them!" (Revelation 14:13)

Chapter 14 contains seven short segments. The first describes another vision of the 144,000 faithful believers who were first mentioned in chapter 7:4–10. These believers have the Father's name written on their heads. There is thunderous praise from harpists and choirs, celebrating their redemption before God's throne.

The second through seventh visions introduce judgment on earth. An angel flies through the sky announcing the Gospel to every nation, tribe, language and people, calling everyone to fear and glorify God because the time of judgment is near.

Another angel follows, shouting, *"Babylon is fallen—that great city is fallen—because she made all the nations of the world drink the wine of her passionate immorality"* (Revelation 14:8). He also warns that anyone who worships the beast or accepts his mark will face God's anger. Believers must endure persecution patiently, obeying his commands and maintaining their faith in Jesus.

A voice from heaven cries out, blessing those who die in the Lord, for they will rest from their hard work, and their good deeds will follow them. Then Jesus, the Son of Man, appears with a kingly crown and a sickle of judgment in his hands. He "harvests" the entire world. Two angels follow, assisting with this work of judgment.

Chapters 15 and 16 introduce seven more angels, who hold the seven last plagues which bring God's wrath to completion. This vision begins with victorious Christians who have resisted worshiping the beast and his statue. The writer John may be alluding to one of the Roman emperors of the early Christian era. There are also several references to the Exodus here. The believers stand near a sea, *"singing the song of Moses, the servant of God, and the song of the Lamb."* The lyrics celebrate the greatness of God's word and deeds. They declare that all nations will eventually glorify him and worship before him.

After this, the seven angels with the seven plagues come away from the Lord's presence in the heavenly Temple. They are handed bowls filled with wrath. Chapter 16 begins with a mighty voice from the Temple saying to these angels, *"Go your ways and pour out on the earth the seven bowls containing God's wrath."* As the angels leave the Temple, one by one, they each pour out their bowl of wrath upon the earth.

The first angel pours out his bowl on the earth, causing horrible, malignant sores to break out on everyone who has the mark of the beast. Again, we are reminded by these sores of the Exodus story when God afflicted the Egyptians with boils. The second angel pours out his bowl on the sea, so that it becomes like a bloody corpse, and everything in the sea dies.

The third angel pours out his bowl on the rivers and springs, and they become blood. Finally an angel praises God for his judgments: *"Since they shed the blood of your holy people and your prophets, you have given them blood to drink. It is their just reward"* (Revelation 16:6).

The fourth angel pours out his bowl of wrath on the sun, and it scorches everyone with its fire. There is angry blowback to God's judgment, but *"they did not repent of their sins and turn to God and give him glory."*

The fifth angel pours out his bowl on the throne of the beast, and its kingdom is plunged into darkness. The beast's subjects grind their teeth in anguish and curse God, but again they do not repent of their evil deeds and turn to God.

The sixth angel pours out his bowl on the Euphrates River, causing it to dry up. So the kings from the east march their armies toward the west. Three evil spirits that look like frogs leap from the mouths of the dragon, the beast and the false prophet—the unholy trinity. The demonic spirits have power to work miracles and deceive the rulers of the world who want to retain their power. They gather for battle at Armageddon against the Lord on judgment day.

The Lord announces that he will come unexpectedly, like a thief. Those who keep watch and are ready will be blessed! As the seventh angel pours out his bowl of wrath into the air above the earth, a mighty shout from the throne is heard, saying, *"It is finished!"* We are reminded, of course, of Jesus calling from the cross, signifying the fulfillment of his mission to destroy sin, death and the devil.

There is thunder and lightning. And a great earthquake strikes—the worst in history—causing the city of Babylon, which is another name for Rome, to split into three sections, while the cities of many nations collapse into rubble. The Roman nation is made to drink the cup of God's wrath to the dregs. The people curse God as hailstones weighing 75 pounds fall from the sky on them.

Focus: The challenge for Christians in times of persecution is to endure it patiently, while continuing to obey God's commands and maintain their faith. The "mark of the beast" represents the various ways believers may conform in order to get along and avoid persecution. But to suffer for the Gospel is to share in Christ sufferings, meaning that we shall also share in his glory.

Prayer: *Lord, these terrifying visions of judgment are being lived out today in concrete events of our fallen history. Give us eyes to see clearly. Give us also the strength to stand strong in faith until the day we shall rest in your presence. Amen.*

December 30

> Key Text: "Babylon is fallen—that great city is
> fallen!" (Revelation 18:2)

The book of Revelation vividly tells the big story of the present suffering and the future hope of our fallen world. Though frightening in its imagery, it brings incredibly good news: Christ is the Lord of history and he is coming soon to restore it and reign as our king.

In a sense, his coming will signal the end of human history, if we define human history as beginning at the Fall, when we humans sought to make a life for ourselves apart from God.

Looking at fallen human history from our perspective, it appears normal. This is the way life has always been. The powerful conquer and rule, while the rest endure as best they can. Each individual, group and nation views themselves as righteous and others as evil. Things would be better if they were in control. The struggle continues and history stumbles along.

But the view from God's throne is quite different. The world is lost. Nature and human nature are devastated, similar to coastal cities after a tsunami. Even the spiritual realm is divided by chaos and war because of the fall of Satan. From top to bottom, the whole creation has fallen far from the glory of God.

Almost from the moment human beings abandoned God, they went to war with one another. Countless little would-be gods have sought to replace the one true God. But as soon as a nation, like Babylon or Rome, has gained supremacy, it begins to oppress and not bless. Nations rise and fall, only to be replaced by other nations which are just as evil. The world needs to be cleansed by the justice of God before it can be restored.

In chapter 17, the cleansing judgment continues after the vision of the seven bowls. One of the seven angels shows to John the judgment that is coming upon Rome, which is variously called "Babylon" and the "great prostitute," because it has repressed the people of God and corrupted the whole earth.

The "great prostitute" is seen seated on a terrible, blood-red, devilish beast, covered with obscenities—the claims of the Roman emperors to be divine. She is drunk with cruelty against Christians. The seven heads of the beast, and what follows, represent the political power struggles and alliances after the death of Nero. Even with Nero gone, things do not get better for the Christians who are still targeted.

However, John hears a hopeful word: *"Together they will go to war against the Lamb* [Jesus and his Church], *but the Lamb will defeat them because he is Lord of all lords and King of all kings. And his called and chosen and faithful ones will be with him"* (Revelation 17:14). This prophecy was borne out in Church history. It was said of the Christians that they eventually overcame the Roman Empire because they "out-thought, out-lived and out-died the pagans."

In chapter 18, another angel, bright with splendor, announces the great news of what is coming: *"Babylon is fallen—that great city is fallen! She has become a home for demons."* This language is reminiscent of, and summarizes, the Old Testament prophecies against all the rebellious nations of the world. All who are politically and economically aligned with evil practices are likewise doomed. In only a moment, all her wealth is gone. Her glory is diminished and her fate is secured: *"Just like this, the great city Babylon will be thrown down with violence and will never be found again"* (Revelation 18:21).

Then, a thunderous voice from heaven is heard: *"Praise the Lord! Salvation and glory and power belong to our God. His judgments are true and just. He has punished the great prostitute who corrupted the earth with her immorality. He has avenged the murder of his servants"* (Revelation 19:1–2).

The roar of the vast crowd in heaven continues with praise for Almighty God and rejoicing for the Church, his bride: *"For the time has come for the wedding feast of the Lamb, and his bride has prepared herself."* Here begins God's great blessing upon his people. At last, they will celebrate with him and experience fullness of joy.

Next, John sees heaven open, and standing there is a white horse with a rider named *"Faithful and True, for he judges fairly and wages a righteous war."* It is a vision of the glory of Christ's return. His eyes are like flames of fire, and his head is crowned with many crowns. His robe is dipped in blood, and his title is *"the Word of God."* This title echoes the Gospel of John 1:1–14, where Jesus is also called *"the Word."*

The armies of heaven, dressed in pure white linen, follow him on white horses. The Word of the Gospel, like a sharp sword, is proclaimed to the nations—a Word of both judgment and salvation.

Another angel appears to summon vultures, to eat the flesh of the armies of the corrupt and rebellious nations which are about to be defeated. The battle begins, and the beast and his false prophet, who deceived the nations, are captured and thrown alive into the fiery lake of burning sulfur. Meanwhile, the vultures gorge themselves.

Focus: As we have noted along the way, the Christian understanding of human history is eschatological, meaning that it is moving towards God's predetermined end—the "eschaton." The disturbing images of Revelation are well-suited to describe the view of history from heaven. It is not nearly as benign as we imagine it to be from our perspective, especially when we see ourselves as the "good guys." Sin has metastasized throughout human life and culture. The demonic grows like a tumor. And yet the end is not despair, because Jesus is victor over sin and death. Humanity will be restored to begin a new history, that is truly His-story.

Prayer: Lord, we shake in our boots, yet rejoice with all the voice we have, as we consider the end of things, which is really the beginning. We are so grateful that you are at work in history. Praise the Lord! For the Lord our God, the Almighty, reigns! Amen.

Day 366   Revelation 20–22

December 31

> Key Text: He who is the faithful witness to all these things says, "Yes, I am coming soon!" Amen! Come, Lord Jesus! (Revelation 22:20)

We come at last to the final chapters of God's story, yet it is not truly the end. It is the beginning of a glorious future for the whole creation, and in particular the long-suffering people of God.

In chapter 20, an angel comes down from heaven with the key to the bottomless pit and a heavy chain in his hand: *"He seized the dragon—that old serpent, who is the devil, Satan—and bound him in chains for a thousand years."*

It is an undramatic end to the ultimate enemy who had inspired the rebellion against God in the heavens, and then seduced humans to join the rebellion on earth. There is no epic struggle here. God has always been in control, and now the time has come. The angel merely seizes the devil and binds him for a thousand years. This vision follows the vision of chapter 19, where the beast and false prophet are thrown into the fiery lake of burning sulfur.

The big question in this chapter is the meaning of the thousand-year reign of Christ on earth *(Revelation 20:4)*, along with the thousand-year binding of Satan so that he has no influence on earthly affairs. As we have noted, Revelation is not chronological, but theological and thematic. What does this thousand-year, or millennial, period represent? Since most numbers in Revelation are symbolic, we assume this is the case here.

There are three main views, but a plausible interpretation, consistent with the rest of Scripture, is to see the millennium as a symbolic reference to the time of the Church between Jesus' first and second coming at the end of history. In other words, our present time.

We remember that the Gospels speak of Satan being defeated by Christ's death on the cross. The Church's mission since Pentecost has been to declare the victory of Christ to the nations. When the Gospel is proclaimed, people from every nation have their eyes opened and respond in faith. In this sense, Satan is bound. He can't stop the saving power of the Good News. But he can deceive and torment. When John says that Satan is released for a short time at the end of the thousand years to once again deceive the nations, he seems be referring to a time of intense spiritual warfare against God's people, leading up to Christ's second coming at the end of history.

But this final blaze of spiritual warfare quickly burns out: *"Then the devil, who had deceived them* [the nations], *was thrown into the fiery lake of burning sulfur, joining the beast and the false prophet. There they will be tormented day and night forever and ever"* (Revelation 20:10). Following this is the great white throne judgment, from which no one can run or hide. The living and dead all stand before God to be judged according to their deeds.

Now comes the great moment toward which the whole story of the Bible has been moving—the reuniting of heaven and earth. Chapter 21 describes the descent of heaven to embrace earth. Fallen history has ended; redeemed history is being consummated. John sees *"a new heaven and a new earth, for the old heaven and the old earth had disappeared."*

God's home, like a new Jerusalem, is now among his people, and they are loved by him as a groom loves a bride.

"I heard a loud shout from the throne, saying, 'Look, God's home is now among his people! He will live with them, and they will be his people. God himself will be with them. He will wipe every tear from their eyes, and there will be no more death or sorrow or crying or pain. All these things are gone forever" (Revelation 21:3–4).

A lengthy, symbolic description of the idealized City of Jerusalem follows, revealing it to be a perfect cube, made of precious stones and having streets paved with pure gold. There is no temple in this Jerusalem because "the Lord God Almighty and the Lamb are its temple." It is illuminated by the glory of God, and believers from all nations walk in its light. Nothing evil will be allowed to enter.

Chapter 22 begins with a striking image of a river "with the water of life, clear as crystal, flowing from the throne of God and of the Lamb." Echoing Eden, a tree of life grows on each side of the river. The curse of Eden is gone. Everlasting life has returned. There is no night or darkness because the Lord God shines on his people.

Though these images are symbolic, they are achingly wonderful and point us to reality: "Then the angel said to me, 'Everything you have heard and seen is trustworthy and true.'"

Having shared with us the visions he has seen, John now falls down to worship. An angel tells him to not be silent, but to let the world know that the time is near! The Lord is "the Alpha and the Omega, the First and the Last, the Beginning and the End." Blessed are those who trust in the Lamb who was slain; they will eat from the tree of life.

Our journey through the Bible ends with a joyful invitation to a new beginning—Come! "Let anyone who is thirsty come. Let anyone who desires drink freely from the water of life" (Revelation 22:17).

And that, dear reader, is what the Good Book says!

Focus: There is a reason why the Bible is annually the best-selling book in the world, by far. It is indeed the greatest story ever told. There is nothing like it. It alone contains the words of life. We read it and then discover that it reads us. It describes life as we know it. It speaks to our minds and hearts in a self-authenticating way. Its great themes of Creation, Fall, Redemption and New Creation resonate with us. It calls us to faith. It moves us to great acts of goodness, beauty, truth, justice and compassion. Above all, it reveals how passionately our Creator desires to be in relationship with us—forever. Amen! Amen! Amen!

Prayer: *Lord, we are overwhelmed by your Word. It gives us life. It is a lamp unto our feet and a light unto our path. May we continue to experience the joys of those who delight in the Law of the Lord, and meditate upon it day and night. Amen!*

Love your enemies
— those who are offended by
your faith / testimony

Jesus — New covenant
God keeping His promise